Word Recognition:
- Sight
- Context
- Phonics
- Str. Analysis - (Syllabication)
- Dictionary Skills

Comprehension:
- Literal
- Inferential
- Evaluative
- Appreciative

Study Skills:

Diagnosis and Remediation
of the
Disabled Reader

DIAGNOSIS AND REMEDIATION
OF THE DISABLED READER

ELDON E. EKWALL
UNIVERSITY of TEXAS at EL PASO

ALLYN and BACON, Inc.
boston   london   sydney   toronto

Fourth printing . . . July, 1977

Library of Congress Cataloging in Publication Data

Ekwall, Eldon E
  Diagnosis and remediation of the disabled reader.

  Includes bibliographical references.
  1. Reading disability.   2. Reading—Remedial
teaching.   I. Title.
LB1050.5.E37   428'.4'2   75-40420

ISBN 0-205-05416-1

To
Cindy and Dwight

and to
Enrique Solis, Jr.

CONTENTS

PREFACE

This book is designed to be used by students who are taking their first course in diagnosis and/or remediation of reading disabilities. It was also written for practicing teachers who want to broaden their knowledge and skills in diagnostic and remedial techniques. I have assumed that anyone reading this material will have a basic knowledge of the teaching of reading as taught in a reading foundations course. However, because of the diversity of the subject matter and the manner in which foundation courses are often taught, I have in a number of places defined the terminology necessary to develop a general background for the discussion of major concepts.

This book begins with a chapter on the reasons for pupils' failure in reading. In this case I am operating under the premise that to be an effective diagnostician, as well as an effective remedial reading teacher, you must have a broad knowledge of causal factors in reading disabilities. A number of factors have a significant correlation with reading disabilities but do not appear to exhibit a direct causal relationship. I have discussed these as well, since there is still much to learn in this ever-changing subject and to ignore any factors relating to reading would, in effect, be educating for obsolescence.

Chapter 2 contains a discussion of some operational procedures of which I believe all reading specialists should become aware. Portions of Chapter 2 are expanded upon in later chapters; the added emphasis should serve to alert you to the importance of these topics.

Chapter 3 contains a framework for the examination of educational problems in reading diagnosis and remediation. Chapters 4–8 discuss diagnosis and remediation under the categories of educational, psychological, sociological, and physical factors. Chapter 9 is devoted to the diagnosis and treatment of severe learning disabilities. You will note that each of these chapters is broken down into Diagnosis and Remediation sections distinguished by the change in text typeface.

The remaining chapters deal with additional diagnostic and remedial techniques and administrative procedures with which the reading specialist should become familiar. Chapter 16 covers the interpretation of tests and research results in relation to reading. If you have not had a course in educational research or educational statistics, you may wish to read Chapter 16 first. Included at the end of the book are appendices containing material that you should find helpful in your day-to-day work with disabled readers.

As someone who has always taken pride in offering something concrete to be of practical use to teachers I trust you will find this book stimulating. This book is meant to be more than a tool for the training of technicians and I hope that many of the principles you learn from it will be applicable to reading diagnosis and remediation in a world of change.

E.E.E.

ACKNOWLEDGMENTS

I would like to thank a number of people who have in some way contributed to the completion of this book. First I would like to thank Irma Alcala and Blanca Enriquez who helped with the typing of the manuscript during its various stages of production. My appreciation is also extended to Judy Solis and Martha Alden who spent many hours in helping me document certain information. I would also like to thank Dr. Don Swink for his help in the preparation of the section on vision. My appreciation is also extended to Richard Allington, State University of New York at Albany, Lois Bader, Michigan State University, Maurice Kaufman, Northeastern University and Stanley L. Rosner of Temple University who all reviewed the manuscript throughout its production and contributed many scholarly suggestions. Julie Alden deserves a special thanks for the encouragement she provided through her kindness and for the many hours she spent in proofreading the initial manuscript. I would also like to thank the many fine graduate students who have taken my courses in clinical diagnosis and remedial reading, who along with my doctoral advisor, Dr. Ruth Strang, have helped me learn what I hope I have been able to communicate to the reader in this book. And finally, I would like to extend my very sincere appreciation to Jane Dahl of the Allyn and Bacon editoral staff who spent many long hours in editing the final manuscript.

E.E.E.

TO THE TEACHER

This is a textbook designed to be used in a first course in diagnosis and/or remediation of reading disabilities. It is designed for either advanced undergraduates or graduate students who have had at least one course in the foundations of reading instruction.

You will note that Chapters 4–9 contain a section on diagnosis (Part A) and a section on remediation (Part B). If your institution offers separate courses in diagnosis and remediation, this format should facilitate the assignment of readings to supplement classroom activities. On the other hand, if the courses are combined, the student should read Parts A and B of these chapters.

I have yet to find a textbook concerning diagnosis and/or remediation of reading difficulties that presents various topics in the order in which I wish to present them in my classes. In this text, I have presented the topics in an order in which I believe to be a logical sequence in relation to a student's learning needs. However, some professors may wish to cover certain topics in a somewhat different sequence. For example, some professors may wish to cover the administration and scoring of informal reading inventories before Chapter 11. This should present no problems.

Many students have expressed that books presenting a constant deluge of research and a long list of references to each research study are ineffective. I have tried to make this book scholarly enough to maintain the faith and respect of both the student and professor; also, I have tried to avoid listing many references to research readily available to anyone with access to a library. Yet, where issues are controversial or where the research is meager, I have tried to reference each study.

It is my hope that you will find the overall format stimulating and the material rewarding.

E.E.E.

1

REASONS FOR FAILURE IN READING

This chapter contains a discussion of the various factors that contribute to, or are related to, retardation in reading. At this point no attempt will be made to discuss diagnostic and remedial procedures for various causal factors. The purpose of this chapter is to give an overview of these factors, and the relative prevalence of each factor, so that appropriate diagnostic and remedial procedures can then be devised.

It is fascinating to see the pieces of a diagnostic puzzle begin to take shape through the process of interviewing, collecting background data, and testing. It is also extremely rewarding to see the progress of a disabled reader as the information derived from the diagnostic process is implemented in the teaching program. However, regardless of the thoroughness of the diagnostic process, you are likely to see little positive results unless it is followed by a remedial program based on the results of the original diagnosis. Likewise, a remedial program that is not based on the results of a thorough diagnosis is likely to fail. Since a child is constantly growing and changing, it is imperative that diagnosis and remediation be a continuous process.

Since reading diagnosis and remediation can seldom be separated for practical purposes, it becomes imperative that the reading specialist be well-trained in both areas. As a practicing or future reading specialist you must know what kinds of problems to look for and what to do about these problems when they are found to exist. Most of the diagnostic-remedial process for the reader deals with problems that could be classified under four major categories. These categories are illustrated in Figure 1–1.

In making a thorough diagnosis then, you must be concerned with all four areas. A study of the problems related to reading retardation should also make you more aware of various causal factors which are often different from those that appear obvious when a diagnosis is made. In many cases, even though remedial procedures are instituted for a particular student, they are of less value than they might have been if some precautions had been taken to alleviate conditions or factors that caused the reading disability in the first place. Perhaps it should be emphasized at this point that there are also many factors that seem to have a close relationship to reading disability but cannot be established as having direct causal relationships. Since this textbook is not directed solely for the training of reading "technicians," it seems important to stress more than the "how to" of test administration and the "how to" of certain remedial techniques. Testing methods and materials, as well as

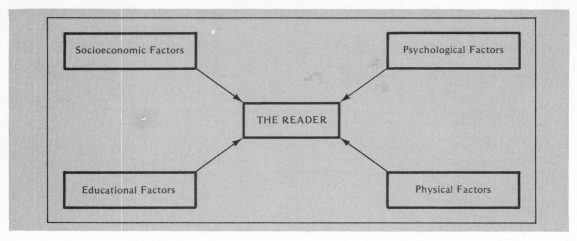

Figure 1–1. Factors that influence the reader.

teaching methods and materials, are constantly being updated and revised. To teach only those used at this time without examining other important aspects of reading would, in effect, be educating for obsolescence. There is still much to learn in the field of remedial reading and although many problems are ambiguous we cannot simply ignore them as being of little importance.

A monumental study done by Helen Robinson and described in her book entitled *Why Pupils Fail in Reading*[1] is perhaps the best known, and has contributed more to our knowledge about the reasons for pupil failure in reading than any other single study. In the remainder of this chapter the results of Robinson's study will be summarized and her findings will be compared with those of more recent studies. Keep in mind, however, that it is seldom possible to determine the exact percentage of retarded readers whose reading disability stems from a particular anomaly as Robinson did in her research. This is true because we know that reading retardation is often the result of multiple problems, or in many cases multiple problems are present which tend to mask the retarding effect of any one problem. Because of this problem many studies only report the percentage of retarded readers versus the percentage of normal readers who have exhibited certain anomalies. Other studies simply report whether there is a significant difference in the mean number of retarded readers versus the mean number of normal readers who exhibit certain anomalies. The term "disabled reader" has often been used to describe readers who are not reading well as measured by a combination of reading test scores compared to their potential as measured by intelligence tests. Or the term "disabled readers" may simply mean those students who are reading below the level of most students in their class. A more thorough definition of the term "disabled reader" and its implications for the remedial reading program is contained in Chapter 13, for either those students who have a serious discrepancy between their reading ability and their reading potential or those students who are not able to deal effectively with the read-

[1]Published by the University of Chicago Press, 1946.

ing materials used for instruction in their classrooms. In Robinson's study those students who were below nine years of age and who had a reading grade level 0.9 years below their mental age and chronological age were accepted for study. Those students who were nine years or older and had an average reading grade two years or more below both their mental and chronological ages were also accepted for further study.

In conducting her study Robinson planned three steps. The first step was to summarize the literature concerning pupil failure, and with the aid of various specialists an attempt was made to evaluate the information found in the literature. The second step in Robinson's study was to identify and evaluate the causal factors in a group of severely retarded readers. The third and final step in Robinson's study was to present significant conclusions concerning causal factors and to discuss various problems needing further study.

In conducting her study Robinson enlisted the aid of various specialists. Included in this group were the following: a social worker. a neurologist, a psychiatrist, three ophthalmologists, an otolaryngologist, an endocrinologist, a speech specialist, a reading specialist, and Professor Robinson, who acted as psychologist and reading specialist. Thirty severely retarded readers with Binet IQ's between 85 and 137 were examined by each of the various specialists. Following the examinations all specialists met to present their findings. An intensive remedial program was then begun with twenty-two of the original thirty cases. During the remedial program an attempt was made to determine the "potency" of each of the possible causes listed as anomalies in the original diagnosis of each pupil.

In the initial diagnosis a number of factors were found in Robinson's group of disabled readers. At the conclusion of the remedial program Robinson's group again met to discuss the various anomalies that were considered to be probable causes of pupils' failure. Some of these factors were later determined to have had little or no impairing effect on the reading ability of the group. This information is summarized in Table 1–I:

Table 1-I. Percentage of anomalies considered to be important versus probable causes in Helen Robinson's study

	Percentage of Anomalies Considered Important	Percentage of Anomalies Considered To Be Probable Causes
1. Visual Difficulty	63.6	50.0
2. Neurological Difficulty	22.7	18.1
3. Auditory Difficulty	13.6	9.1
4. Speech or Discrimination Difficulty	27.3	18.1
5. General Physical Difficulty	9.1	4.5
6. Endocrine Disturbance	22.7	9.1
7. Emotional Maladjustment	40.9	31.8
8. Social Problems	63.6	54.5
9. School Methods	22.7	18.1

As you will note the percent of agreement between anomalies considered important and those considered to be probable causes do not agree. This, of course, indicates that the group did not believe that certain anomalies, even though definitely present, were necessarily contributors.

Although the number of pupils examined in Robinson's study was relatively small it had a number of outstanding features, some of which have been lacking in more recent studies. For example, every pupil was thoroughly examined by specialists in every area considered important to reading success or failure. Robinson was then able to carry on a remedial program and follow the progress of each student. Where necessary, students were even removed from their home environments and placed in a special school to determine whether home environmental conditions were causal factors in the pupils' failure. The social worker was able to visit homes to get a first-hand look at students' environment. Additionally there were several specialists working in certain fields to check on any biases that any one tester might possess.

Reasons for pupils' failure are classified under the four major categories previously mentioned plus a fifth category that is a combination of all four. These categories will be discussed in the following order:

1. Physical factors
2. Psychological factors
3. Socioeconomic factors
4. Educational factors
5. Combinations of the four major categories listed above

PHYSICAL FACTORS

The Eyes and Seeing

Robinson's initial analysis indicated that 63.6 percent of the pupils had some sort of visual difficulty. However, in the final analysis the specialists concluded that sight difficulties were the cause of reading retardation in only 50 percent of the cases.

It is almost impossible to find any substantial amount of agreement among the researchers concerning exact percentages of disabled readers who exhibit seeing difficulties. It would appear, however, that Robinson's study is in general agreement with others who have studied seeing problems. For example, Howard Coleman (1968), examined eighty-seven children in grades one to six who had severe deficits in the reading and/or language arts areas. He reported that approximately 50 percent of these children had either sight or visual-perceptual dysfunctions. Of the 50 percent mentioned, Coleman reported that 19.5 percent of the group had refractive errors and 30 percent had visual-perceptual dysfunction. Many researchers also agree with the position taken by Thomas Eames (1962), who states,

> One child might be greatly handicapped by a visual defect while another might perceive adequately on the basis of very poor retinal images. Statistically, it has been

shown that defective visual acuity is not much more frequent among reading failures than among non-failures, although individual cases occur in which failure is definitely the result of impaired vision. Such cases are greatly benefitted by glasses if the poor vision is due to refractive error (eyes out of focus) but glasses are of no benefit when the visual deficiency is of amblyopic (insensitivity) nature. The mere existence of low acuity is to be regarded as a possible but not invariable cause of poor reading.

There is some disagreement among various researchers concerning the types of seeing problems responsible for reading retardation. Certain types of eye and seeing problems do, however, tend to appear to be more closely related to reading retardation than others. Chapter 8 contains a detailed discussion of these problems.

Auditory Difficulties

In discussing auditory difficulties it is necessary to make a distinction between auditory acuity and auditory discrimination. *Auditory acuity* refers to the ability to hear various frequencies at various intensities of loudness (measured in decibels). *Auditory discrimination* refers to the ability to hear major or slight differences in sounds.

It is somewhat difficult to interpret Robinson's percentages in these categories because difficulties in these areas were viewed somewhat differently than at the present time. One reason for this is that we now have better tests of auditory discrimination than were available to Robinson and her researchers. Robinson lumped speech and discrimination difficulties together. Each of these will be discussed separately.

AUDITORY ACUITY.   Robinson reports that inadequate auditory acuity was an anomaly considered to be a cause of reading difficulty in 9 percent of her reading disability cases. However, Robinson also states that her study reinforces the general opinion that insufficient auditory acuity is relatively unimportant as a cause of severe reading retardation. It would be difficult, however, to determine whether Robinson's 9 percent figure would be valid for disabled readers in general, since most researchers have tended to study auditory difficulties as a whole rather than isolate auditory acuity and study it as a separate factor.

Guy Bond and Miles Tinker (1967) report that various studies have shown that 3 to 20 percent of children tested have hearing deficiencies with a median of about 10 percent. They estimate that approximately 5 percent of the total population of school children have a serious hearing impairment. They also believe that many additional children have a slight hearing loss that may develop into a serious impairment if not treated early.

Studies tend to show that there are more cases of impaired auditory acuity among groups of retarded readers than among groups of average or good readers. However, even though the differences are sometimes statistically significant the fact that a child has impaired auditory acuity is not necessarily predictive that he will become a disabled reader.

It appears that hearing losses in the high frequency ranges are more likely to result in reading impairment than hearing losses in the middle or low frequency ranges. It also appears that boys tend to experience loss in the high ranges more often than girls. The fact that the percentage of women teachers in the primary grades is much higher than the percentage of men teachers also makes a loss of acuity in the high frequency range more detrimental since women's voices tend to range closer to the high frequencies.

In summary, it appears that although inadequate auditory acuity as a whole is seldom responsible for retardation in reading it may be an important factor in some isolated cases, especially if very severe and if not detected soon enough. There is general agreement that a test for auditory acuity should be included as a part of a general diagnosis of a disabled reader. Recommendations in respect to testing in this area follow the discussion of auditory discrimination.

AUDITORY DISCRIMINATION. Robinson combined the categories of speech, general auditory discrimination, and memory span for sounds into a category called "Speech or Discrimination Difficulty." She reported that these factors were contributing anomalies in 18 percent of her severely retarded readers. However, she believed that dyslalia (a speech impairment due to a defect in the speech organs) was responsible for 14 of the 18 percent and that only the remaining 4 percent were caused by inadequate auditory discrimination or inadequate memory span.

It should be emphasized at this point that inadequate memory span is seldom studied in conjunction with inadequate auditory discrimination, however, both are now considered to be important factors in the diagnosis of disabled readers. As mentioned previously, better instruments have also been developed for the purpose of measuring impairment in both of these areas.

It should also be emphasized that children's auditory discrimination skills improve considerably as they progress through the primary grades. Bertha Thompson (1963), conducted a longitudinal study of auditory discrimination in a group of 105 children. She concluded that, "Inaccurate discriminative ability is more characteristic of first grade entrants than accurate ability. The reverse is true at the end of the second grade." (p. 377) Thompson also reported that at the end of the second grade approximately 24 percent of the students had inaccurate auditory discrimination ability. Approximately half (12 percent) of this group were classified as poor readers. Thompson's view of the relationship between auditory discrimination and reading is representative of a number of researchers. She states, "This again points toward the importance of adequacy in auditory discrimination to success in primary reading. However, it definitely reveals that other factors are important in reading disability." (p. 377)

It would again be difficult to determine the percentage of the reading failures caused from difficulties with auditory discrimination since this is often just one of several or many causal factors likely to be contributors or at least to be present in cases of reading retardation. The evidence from various research studies do, however, indicate that auditory discrimination is a factor that should be tested in attempting to diagnose difficulties with reading. The author is inclined to believe that auditory discrimination testing should be a routine procedure in all classrooms and should always be done when testing disabled readers. Rather than routine testing of auditory acuity, it would surely be more rewarding to test auditory discrimination abilities. When a problem appears, further testing of auditory acuity would be needed to determine whether the problem is in the area of impaired physical functioning of the ear or whether the student has simply not developed the ability to discriminate between or among various phonemes.

As stated earlier, several tests of auditory memory have been developed since Robinson completed her study; these will be discussed in Chapter 8. Little is known concerning the relationship between auditory memory and reading. Various studies indicate that a larger percentage of disabled readers have impaired auditory memory span or ability to sequence than do good readers. The mystery that remains, however, is what to do about this problem since the training of auditory memory per se seldom seems to have any appreciable effect on children's reading ability.

SPEECH. Robinson reported that speech problems were considered to be probable causes of reading failure in 14 percent of her cases. This is in general agreement with a number of studies reported by Thomas Eames (1950), and Guy Bond and Miles Tinker (1967), although, the above mentioned authors stated that some studies showed that the number of students with speech defects was no higher among disabled readers than in a normal population.

There is some feeling that certain neurological dysfunctions contribute to inadequacy in speech as well as reading and therefore there is a tendency to view the reading disability as stemming from the speech problem when in reality both result from the neurological dysfunction. Some researchers also believe that emotional reactions caused from defective speech may, in turn, contribute to reading disability. Eames (1950) states that certain broad generalizations may be drawn concerning the relationships that exist between reading and speech. These are as follows:

1. Neurological lesions in the language centers or their interconnections may impair both speech and reading.
2. Failure or inadequacy of auditory association and discrimination may predispose to either speech or reading trouble.
3. Speech defects occur in a certain proportion of reading failures and vice versa.
4. Emotional reactions to speech difficulties may impair reading.
5. Oral reading is more difficult for a person with a speech defect. (p. 53)

Laterality, Mixed Dominance and Directional Confusion

Before beginning a discussion of the topics of laterality, mixed dominance and directional confusion, it would be helpful to first define these terms as they are commonly used. The definitions that follow are those of Alice Cohen and Gerald G. Glass (1968), as derived from Albert Harris (1958).

> *Lateral Dominance* refers to the preference or superiority of one side of the body over the other (hand, eye, foot) in performing motor tasks. Right lateral dominance would indicate preference for the right hand, eye, and foot.

Laterality is another term for lateral dominance.

Consistent Dominance refers to the preferential use of one hand, eye, or foot.

Mixed or Incomplete (hand, eye, or foot) Dominance exists when the individual does not show a consistent preference for one (eye, hand, or foot).

Mixed Dominance without specific reference to hand, eye, or foot includes both crossed dominance (see below) and mixed dominance.

Crossed Dominance exists when the dominant hand and dominant eye are on opposite sides.

Visual Motor Consistency occurs when the subject's dominant hand, eye, and foot are on the same side of the body.

Directional Confusion refers to knowledge of left and right. "Knowledge of Left and Right" is demonstrated by the subject in response to questions such as, "show me your right hand, left eye" etc. (This is distinguished from actual use of the dominant hand, eye, or foot in performance tasks.)[2] (p. 343)

Robinson did not attempt to determine what percentage, if any, of her retarded readers' problems resulted from mixed dominance or difficulties with laterality. She stated that tests for mixed dominance were given but that the specialists cooperating in her study did not know how to interpret their findings.

The research on the relationship of laterality, mixed dominance, and directional confusion to reading is voluminous. From all of this, however, there are still no clear-cut answers as to what we should test for and what we can do about these problems when they are found to exist. Some of the proponents of various approaches to the remediation of problems in this area have been very vociferous and consequently, in my opinion, have oversold the value of remedial materials and techniques in this area. Studies such as those of E. Shearer (1968), Steven Forness (1968), and R. J. Capobianco (1967), are in general agreement with the findings of Alice Cohen and Gerald G. Glass (1968) who studied 120 subjects in the first and fourth grades. Half of their sample were defined as "good" readers and half were defined as "poor" readers. Their statistical analysis revealed the following relationships as being significant:

1. *Knowledge of left and right and reading ability in the first grade.* Good readers were more likely to be "normal" and poor readers were more likely to be "hesitant" or "confused" in their knowledge of left and right.

2. *Hand dominance and reading ability in first grade.* Good readers were more likely to have a dominant hand and poor readers were more likely to have mixed-hand dominance.

3. *Knowledge of left and right between first and fourth grade children.* There were significantly more first grade children who were hesitant or confused in their knowledge of left and right than fourth grade children. There were significantly more fourth grade children who were normal in their knowledge of left and right than first graders.

4. *Knowledge of left and right and hand dominance.* Right handed children were more likely to have a knowledge of left and right. Left handed and mixed children were more likely to be hesitant or confused in their knowledge of left and right.

However, no significance was found between fourth graders' reading ability and knowledge of left and right. The same was true for hand dominance. The reader may

---

[2]Reprinted by permission of the authors and the International Reading Association.

be most concerned with the factor of *crossed dominance*. This factor is what most people are referring to when the area of laterality is discussed. No significant relationship was found between crossed dominance and reading ability in the total population studied.[3] (p. 345)

As stated earlier Robinson's researchers administered tests for lateral dominance, but did not feel that they knew how to interpret their findings. These researchers were simply being conservative in their beliefs. Very little more is known today regarding the accurate interpretation of findings such as those reported by Cohen and Glass. Until more is known regarding effective remedial procedures for these areas that will, in turn, improve children's reading ability, a diagnosis for laterality, mixed dominance, and directional confusion seems to be of dubious value.

Neurological Problems

Laterality, mixed dominance, and directional confusion could be quite properly, and often are, classified as neurological dysfunctions. They are separated here from the general heading of neurological problems for purposes of clarifying the discussion of these factors. General neurological problems also include an array of dysfunctions related to difficulties in reading. It is believed that neurological dysfunctions may stem from genetic mutations and that certain characteristics are also heritable. A further cause of neurological dysfunctions is brain injury.

Robinson and her researchers believed that neurological difficulties were an important anomaly in 22.7 percent of her retarded readers and they were considered as a probable cause in 18.1 percent of these cases. It would be difficult to determine whether these percentages would apply to retarded readers in general since the term "neurological difficulty" is interpreted so broadly. Furthermore, some authorities also feel that neurological difficulties can only be accurately diagnosed by a neurologist; therefore, the results of a number of studies of so-called neurologically impaired retarded readers may be contaminated by other factors. A further problem exists in that many children exhibit symptoms of neurological dysfunction and yet read perfectly well.

Children classified as dyslexic or alexic[4] are usually categorized under the general heading of neurological difficulties. Robinson believed, as have many others since, that children are often classified as alexic or dyslexic when in reality they do not exhibit the symptoms of the typically dyslexic or alexic child. This again complicates any attempt to determine the percentage of disabled readers who have neurological difficulties.

The fact does remain that a certain proportion of disabled readers do have neurological difficulties but that neurological difficulties probably account for a small percentage of the actual causes of reading disability. However, as Barbara

[3]Ibid.

[4]The term dyslexic refers to a condition of severe reading disability. Some authors have stated that it is related to neurological dysfunctions and others simply define the term as a condition in which a student is severely disabled in reading for no apparent reason. (For a more thorough discussion of this term, and severe reading disability, see Chapter 9.)

Bateman (1974), has stressed, the fact that a student is classified as having a minimal brain dysfunction (MBD) does not help in the diagnosis of his reading problem. If the student is an extremely disabled reader then ultimately he must be taught to read regardless of how we label his condition.

Other Physical Factors

Researchers who have studied other physical factors than those discussed previously have often concluded that glandular disturbances contribute to reading disability. Robinson and her researchers believed that endocrine disturbances were anomalies important in 40.9 percent of her reading disability cases. They did, however, conclude that endocrine disturbances were the actual causes in only 9.1 percent of her cases. This still, of course, represents a rather high figure and makes glandular disturbances an important factor in reading retardation. Robinson also stressed the point that when endocrine disturbances were present they not only retarded progress in learning but also tended to interfere with progress in other areas such as orthoptic treatment, social adjustment, and physical well-being. She stated that although this anomaly was less frequent in occurrence it did have a marked influence on certain cases.

Other researchers, such as Donald E. P. Smith (1958), and Lyman Cavanaugh (1948), have also concluded that glandular disturbances are an extremely important factor in contributing to reading disability. Cavanaugh studied 660 children and concluded that 18 percent had rather serious thyroid deficiencies that could contribute to retardation in learning. Smith believed that treatment for endocrine disturbances could, in some cases, yield promising to dramatic results.

Other physical factors often listed as either causal or concomitant are malnutrition, poor dentition, allergies, infected tonsils and/or adenoids, vitamin deficiencies, and susceptibility to colds. However, among these disorders Robinson found that only malnutrition could be considered a causal factor. She believed that, although various physical disorders are often present in cases of reading disability, they are seldom the actual cause of reading disability.

PSYCHOLOGICAL FACTORS ✓

A number of studies have been conducted to determine the relationship of various psychological factors to reading disability. Among the psychological factors often studied are various emotional problems, intelligence, and self-concept. It should be stressed that all of these factors are, no doubt, highly interrelated so that it becomes difficult, if not impossible, to completely separate them for isolated study.

Emotional Problems

In researching emotional problems the question that most often arises is whether reading disability is caused by emotional problems or whether reading disability results in emotional problems. It appears that each tends to contribute to the other with reading disability causing emotional problems more often than emotional problems causing reading disability.

Robinson reported that 40.9 percent of her retarded readers had a significant degree of emotional maladjustment, but she believed that it was an anomaly that caused reading retardation in only 31.8 percent of her cases. Robinson's reported percentages in this category probably vary more from those reported in other studies than do her percentages for any of the other categories. For example, Nila B. Smith (1955) reported that 90 percent of 200 cases of reading disability that she studied were emotionally disturbed. Smith also reported the results of studies by Paul Witty (1950) and Arthur Gates (1941). These researchers reported the percentage of emotionally disturbed among retarded readers to be 52 percent and 75 percent respectively. Smith also reported on a study of seventy-eight cases of extreme reading disability, conducted by Grace Fernald (1943). Fernald found that only four cases (5 percent) of the total group had a history of emotional instability before they entered school. Fernald believed that the remainder of her cases with emotional problems were caused by the difficulties which they encountered in reading. On the other hand, Gates reported that 75 percent of the retarded readers studied by him showed personality maladjustment; Gates believed that in about 25 percent of these (or about 19 percent of the total group of disabled readers) the emotional maladjustment was a contributing cause of reading disability. Albert Harris (1970) also reports that of several hundred cases of reading disability seen in the Queens College Educational Clinic during a fifteen year period, close to 100 percent showed some kind of maladjustment. Harris reports that emotional maladjustment was a causal factor in about 50 percent of the cases in this group.

It is evident that there is wide disagreement not only about what percent of disabled readers we might expect to have emotional problems, but there is also wide disagreement as to the contribution of emotional maladjustment as a causal factor in reading retardation. The important point, however, is that when the retarded reader comes to the educational diagnostician or the remedial reading teacher he is quite likely to exhibit some sort of emotional maladjustment. For this reason proper diagnosis and remediation for emotional problems must be considered as a necessity in a remedial reading program.

Intelligence

A number of research studies have been done to determine the relationship between reading achievement and intelligence. Albert Harris (1963) indicates that the correlation between reading and individual verbal intelligence tests, such as the Stanford-Binet, tends to be in the neighborhood of .60 to .70. However, as children enter the middle grades and begin to take group intelligence tests that are more verbally oriented the correlation may range from .70 to .85. On the nonverbal or nonlanguage tests, however, the correlations range much lower—between .20 to .40. The question that reading specialists must ask then is whether IQ is really a valid predictor of reading ability.

Louise Ames and Richard Walker (1964) did a study to determine whether fifth grade reading achievement could be predicted from WISC IQ scores administered at the kindergarten level. In their conclusions Ames and Walker stated that they believed that the usefulness of their reported findings did not lie in their employment for predicting fifth grade reading scores. Rather they offered the suggestion that individual subject characteristics other than either general intelligence or specific reading skills contributed to individual differences in reading at the above-average level as well as below average.

George and Evelyn Spache (1969) expressed a similar viewpoint; they stated:

> . . . research studies of school beginners show that intelligence test results are not highly predictive of early reading success. If pupils are arranged in the order of their reading test scores after a period of training, the order just does not neatly parallel a ranking based on mental age or intelligence quotient. Only the extreme cases, the very superior and the mentally retarded pupils, tend to agree in their ranks in reading and intelligence. The degree of reading success for most pupils is determined not by their exact level or rank in intelligence but by other more influential factors.

 It seems evident then that we should not place a great deal of faith in IQ scores as predictors of potential reading ability. However, as Spache and Spache point out, the IQ is a fairly good predictor of reading ability for children with extremely high IQs or for children who are mentally retarded. Most researchers agree that children with very low IQs are at a considerable disadvantage in learning to read; therefore, a low IQ is often an important hindering factor. For this reason it is often helpful to administer an individual intelligence test as part of the normal diagnostic procedure with a disabled reader. An important point to remember, however, is that many children with low IQs become good readers and many children with medium and high IQs become disabled readers. Therefore, the IQ should only be considered in conjunction with other factors.

Some estimates have been made regarding the percentage of disabled readers whose problem stemmed from having a low IQ. The author believes, however, that any percentage figure based on IQ alone is misleading because of the interaction of low IQ with a multitude of other factors such as home environment and teaching methods.

Self-Concept

The self-concept and its close relationship with teacher expectation is a psychological factor that should not be overlooked in the diagnosis of a disabled reader. Studies such as those of William Padelford (1969), and Maxine Cohn and Donald Kornelly (1970) have shown that a significant positive relationship does exist between reading achievement and self-concept. Padelford found that this relationship exists regardless of ethnic group, socioeconomic level, or sex. Cohn and Kornelly indicate that a program of remediation for a low self-concept can produce positive achievement in reading.

Little is known regarding the percentage of disabled readers whose problems are directly related to the possession of a low self-concept. However we do know the problem exists and as Frances Pryor (1975) states, "Changing a poor reader's self-concept by bolstering his feelings about himself is perhaps the first step toward improving the academic problem." For this reason this factor should not be overlooked in the initial diagnosis of the reader.

Robinson reported that maladjusted homes or poor inter-family relationships were found to be contributing causes in 54.5 percent of her cases studied. As she stated, this percentage was somewhat higher than those reported in other studies. Robinson believed that we often underestimate the importance of this factor. In her study a social worker was especially diligent in obtaining information from parents concerning difficulties and problems. Robinson apparently believed that, because information concerning inter-family relationships and other related factors are somewhat difficult to obtain, the percentages of these factors that appear as causal factors in reading retardation are often unrealistically low.

✓ Socioeconomic factors are usually so closely related that it would be impossible to list any specific percentage of reading disability cases resulting from any one isolated factor. Factors often studied, however, are presence of father in the home (or broken homes), ethnic background and its social relationships, economic level, dialect, presence of books or stimulating reading materials in the home, sibling relationships, and parent-sibling relationships.

Martin Deutsch (1967) studied family relationships including broken homes where the father was not present in the home. Deutsch stated that, ". . . intact homes are more crowded than broken ones, although the children from the intact homes do better in scholastic achievement. . . . Apparently, _who_ lives in the home is more important than _how many_." (p. 104)

✓Ethnic background and its social ramifications are also important influences on reading achievement. For example, the United States Commission on Civil Rights reported as follows:

> The Commission found, on the basis of information provided by school principals, that from 50 to 70 percent of Mexican American and black students in the fourth, eighth, and twelfth grades are reading below the level expected for the grade to which they are assigned. In contrast, only 25 to 34 percent of all Anglo youngsters in these grades are reading below grade level. This approaches a two to one ratio of below average reading achievement for students of minority groups. (p. 24)

This is, of course, only one example of the numerous cases that are known to exist. Economic level is also, in many cases, tied to ethnic background and even where it is not, many studies have shown that the overall reading level of children from poor communities is often far below that of children from more affluent communities.

The problem of dialect and its relationship to reading retardation has received considerable attention in recent years. Researchers and writers such as S. Alan Cohen and Thelma Cooper (1972) have stressed, however, that dialectical differences of the urban disadvantaged reader are not a hindering factor in learning to read. Studies by Richard Rystrom (1968) and W. Labov (1969) have tended to confirm Cohen and Cooper's beliefs.

Studies dealing with the relationship of reading ability and such factors as the number of books found in the home or between reading ability and the amount of time children's parents spend reading are of little value in furnishing us with information concerning the contribution of these factors to reading achievement. The problem, of course, lies in the fact that the number of books found in a home, or the amount of time that parents spend reading is so often related to a host of other factors. Among these factors are education, occupation, and economic level of the parents. Perhaps about all we can say with any certainty is that there appears to be a group of other socioeconomic factors that interact to influence reading ability.

Social relationships between siblings and/or between parents and siblings is another social factor that appears to be worthy of consideration in a thorough diagnosis. However, definite information on the percentage of reading disability cases caused by inter-family relationships is sadly lacking due to the complexities involved in their identification.

✓ EDUCATIONAL FACTORS

Robinson mentioned a number of school factors or conditions which she and others believed often influenced or were conducive to reading failure. Among these factors were teachers' personalities, methods of teaching reading, school policy on promotions, materials available, and class size. In her final analysis Robinson believed that school methods were a probable contributing causal factor in 18.1 percent of the cases she studied. She admitted, however, that there are so many factors involved in assessing educational factors that any definite conclusion is nearly impossible.

It is my opinion that Robinson's figure in this case is not representative of the total percentage of reading failures caused by educational factors. If one views educational factors contributing to reading disability as strictly those that are so bad that many children within any classroom fail to learn, then perhaps Robinson's figure would be representative of the situation that exists in general. However, another viewpoint is that the teacher is at fault if she fails to provide adequate auditory instruction for children predisposed to that method of learning or if she fails to provide adequate visual and/or kinesthetic experiences for children who are visual and/or kinesthetic learners. One might also criticize a teacher who does not adequately diagnose each child's strongest learning modality and then provide individual experiences in accordance with that diagnosis. If one takes this point of view then he might be in agreement with John Manning[5] who expressed the viewpoint that more than 90 percent of our reading failures could or should be blamed on poor teaching. Since only approximately 2 percent of our students experience learning disabilities so severe as to require the services of a specialist, it seems logical that near perfect teaching would result in a failure rate of no more than this 2 percent.

S. Jay Samuels (1970) expresses the opinion that instruction in reading is quite likely to be less than adequate. He states,

> It is this author's contention that the assumption of adequate instruction is probably false in numerous instances because at the present time a complete analysis of the skills which must be mastered in the process of learning to read has not been made. Without a complete analysis of each of the subskills and concepts which must be mastered in the process of learning to read, it is difficult to understand how any instruction can be considered adequate. In the absence of a complete analysis of skills necessary for reading, there is danger that the teacher may omit teaching important skills because she does not realize they are essential; or falsely assuming that certain skills have already been mastered, she may not teach them; or she may teach nonessential skills believing they are important. (p. 267)

[5] From a speech given by John Manning at the University of Kansas, Summer, 1969.

As one can see, the problems in assessing educational factors as a cause of reading failures are so complex that any stated percentage is, at best, an educated guess. The fact remains, however, that educational factors should not be overlooked in the diagnostic procedure.

PHYSICAL, PSYCHOLOGICAL, SOCIOECONOMIC AND EDUCATIONAL FACTOR COMBINATIONS

During the past two decades a number of combinational factors have been reported as having a moderate to high degree of relationship to reading. Robinson mentioned a number of these factors in her study, but did not study most of them in detail because of their unwieldy nature and/or because not enough was known about them at the time to study their exact contribution as causal factors to reading retardation. Although we now know somewhat more about some of these factors only a meager amount of information is available regarding the exact role that these factors play in reading retardation. Therefore, in the discussion that follows some of these factors will be discussed, but no attempt will be made to designate any specific percentage of disabled readers who possess these problems nor will any attempt be made to designate the percentage of disabled readers whose problems originated from these factors.

The Relationship of Intelligence to Organic and Functional Etiological Factors

Stanley Krippner (1968) studied the etiological factors in reading disability of the academically talented in comparison to that of pupils of average and slow-learning ability. Organic disorders referred to disorders in the central nervous system or in the endocrine system, whereas functional disorders were those arising from social, emotional, educational, or cultural handicaps. Krippner reported that the academically talented group demonstrated significantly less organic etiology as a major factor and significantly more functional etiology as a major factor than either the average or slow-learning group.

Krippner reported that many of the pupils seen in his reading center did not improve even under intensive remediation. He states,

> Tutoring in reading is a process of sinking shafts into sand if the basic physiological foundations for learning do not exist. Satisfactory auditory discrimination must be present before a child can memorize whole words. A child must know the difference between his right and his left hand before he can master the difference between such words as "was" and "saw."

> Once the bases of perception and symbol-making have been established, the academically talented child who is a poor reader shares many of the same remedial needs as other children with neurological inadequacies. He needs to improve his visual discrimination of letters and to improve his ability to blend phonemes into words. (pp. 277–278)

Krippner also states that, "The customary skills of abstract thinking and concep-
tualization which most academically talented children possess cannot be relied on if
emotional disturbance, brain injury, or disturbed neurological organization is present." (p. 278) Krippner also stresses the fact that because a child has relatively high
intelligence does not mean that he will overcome his reading problem automatically. Furthermore, children of varying intelligence levels demonstrate different
modes of learning.

The Relationship of Visual-Motor Perception to Reading Disability

A number of studies have dealt with the relationship between visual-motor perception and its relationship to reading disability. Typical of the results of many of these
studies is one conducted by Ernest Schellenberg (1962), who studied thirty-six
matched pairs of disabled and adequate third grade readers. Schellenberg used the
Marianne Frostig Developmental Test of Visual Perception, the E. Koppitz scoring method of the Bender Visual-Motor Gestalt, and the deviation measurements of
the Bender Gestalt to measure visual-motor perception. He also used the Silent
Reading Diagnostic Tests of the Developmental Reading Tests to measure word
perception. Schellenberg found that the Silent Reading Diagnostic Tests significantly differentiated the retarded and adequate readers. However, the distribution scores on the Developmental Test of Visual Perception failed to differentiate
retarded and adequate readers. Also the Bender figures drawn for the Bender
Visual-Motor Gestalt Test did not differentiate retarded from adequate readers.
This test did, however, show differences between matched pairs of girls when the
Bender figures were measured to the nearest one-sixteenth of an inch. Schellenberg
concluded that tests such as the Silent Reading Diagnostic Test have greater usefulness at the third grade level than nonverbal perception tests.

Although certain items of the visual-motor perception tests relate to reading
disabilities they appear to be of dubious value in the actual diagnosis of disabled
readers. It would probably be more profitable to simply determine whether a child
recognizes words and to examine the kinds of errors made when words are miscalled. Remediation would then be directed at specific letter reversals and similar
obvious problems rather than requiring the disabled reader to spend a great deal of
time in non-word perceptual training. Non-word perceptual training seems to be of
little or no value in reading. Studies usually indicate that children receiving this
type of training consequently perform better on perceptual tests, but fail to reach a
higher level of reading achievement.

The Relationship Among Socioeconomic Level, Visual and Auditory Discrimination, and Modality Shifting

Several recent studies have indicated that socioeconomic status does have an effect
upon visual and auditory discrimination. These researchers believe that the noisy

conditions prevalent in large families, often from low economic levels, impairs children's ability to discriminate between auditory and visual stimuli. It is further believed that many of these same children have difficulty in shifting from one modality to another and back again.

A study by Phyllis A. Katz and Martin Deutsch (1963) indicated that, although it is somewhat difficult for most children to shift from one modality to another, disabled readers experience significantly more difficulty in modality shifting than normal readers. They also found that IQ was *not* related to modality shifting ability nor was IQ considered to be related to perceptual behavior. They suggested that non-intellective factors, which are not usually included in assessments of children's ability, may be playing a very important role in reading performance.

The Relationship Between Teacher Expectation and Self-Concept

A number of researchers and writers during the past decade have placed a growing emphasis on the relationship between teacher expectation and student performance growing from students' self-concepts. Among those who have studied these relationships are James M. Palardy (1968), Dale L. Carter (1970), and Robert Rosenthal and Lenore Jacobson (1966). Palardy studied the effects of teacher attitudes on the achievement of first grade boys and girls. He found that when first grade teachers reported that they believed that boys are far less successful in learning to read than girls then the boys in these teachers' classes did achieve significantly less than boys in classes where teachers believed that boys are just as successful as girls.

Carter studied the effect of teacher expectations on the self-esteem and academic performance of seventh grade students. He found that teacher expectations are in part determined by cumulative records and that these expectations significantly affect students' level of confidence and scholastic potential.

In a series of extensive studies Rosenthal obtained similar results and also found that teacher expectations even affect childrens' measured IQs.

Results such as these leave little doubt that students' self-concepts and attitudes are often adversely affected by teacher expectations and that teacher expectation can be a major factor in reading disabilities.

Syntactic Competence and Problem Readers

Recent research indicates that there is a relationship between syntactic competence and reading ability. Bruce Denner (1970) studied Head Start pre-schoolers as well as older problem readers. He found that problem readers tend to read sentences much the same as the pre-school Head Start children. That is, they tended to not read sentences, but rather see sentences as a series of individual words. He felt that the problem readers, therefore, see sentences as a conglomerate of individual word meanings rather than as a unified contextualized conception. On the other hand, Denner found that normal readers seemed to appreciate that words derive their meaning from the sentence context. In discussing his results Denner states,

> This would lead one to conclude that Head Start children begin the first grade with an atomistic, mechanistic conception of reading that stresses the relationship of individual graphic forms to the context of perception and action. And problem readers, even as late as the fifth grade still fail to subordinate the perceptual-motor meaning of the separate words to the larger linguistic reality of the sentence. (pp. 886–887)

Reading Disability Is Usually a Result of Multiple Factors

I have attempted to list the various factors shown by research to be responsible for reading disabilities among school-age children. It should be stressed, however, that seldom is any child's reading disability a result of any single factor. The cases studied in detail by Robinson and her group showed that nearly every student's reading disability was considered to be a result of multiple factors rather than any one single factor. In a discussion of learning disabilities, Jules Abrams states,

> There is no one single etiology for all learning disabilities. Rather, learning problems can be caused by any number of a multiplicity of factors, all of which may be highly interrelated. Unfortunately, all too often the child who is experiencing learning disorders is approached with a unitary orientation so that extremely important aspects of his unique learning problem may very well be ignored. The tendency of each professional discipline to view the entire problem "through its own window of specialization" often obscures vital factors which may contribute to, or at least exacerbate, the basic difficulty. It is just as invalid to conceive of one cure, one panacea, applied randomly to all types of learning disorders. (p. 299)

Margaret Early also cautions us to be aware of multiple factors in reading diagnosis as well as in future research. She states,

> Causes of reading disability are multiple. All research points to this conclusion, either directly as in Robinson's study, or indirectly by the very inconclusiveness of studies related to single factors. Future research should be concerned with broad studies, centered in schools rather than clinics involving both retarded and able readers, to determine the interactions among causative factors. Of the physical, emotional, mental, environmental, social, and educational factors that may affect reading ability, what combinations produce results?

> Three implications for the classroom teacher, in addition to those already mentioned are as follows:

> 1. Insight into the causes of reading failure requires study of all phases of the learner: his health, home and family, personality, experience background and learning abilities, including detailed evaluation of the complex of skills that constitute reading. Adequate study of many of these facets is beyond the teacher, or reading clinician, or psychologist. Each of these persons

needs to know when to make referrals when his diagnostic tools prove inadequate.

2. Since causation is multiple, remediation must also use many approaches. A single method of attack may be detrimental as well as useless.

3. As research in causation is tentative, so is diagnosis of individual cases. As hunches are confirmed or rejected by new insights, plans for treatment must also be changed. Diagnosis of the complex process of reading is continuous. (pp. 61–62)

SUMMARY

A student's ability or inability to read is affected by a number of factors. These factors might be classified as socioeconomic, psychological, educational, and physical. A monumental study was done by Helen Robinson a number of years ago. In her study Robinson employed the services of a number of specialists in fields that relate to reading disabilities. Robinson and her group attempted to determine the kind and number of problems that each of her cases possessed. Through subsequent study they then attempted to determine which problems were causal factors in each student's reading retardation. The various causal factors listed by Robinson, as well as the percentage of students who have reading disabilities caused by these factors are generally in agreement with more recent studies.

There are, of course, many causes of reading disabilities and many of these cannot be completely isolated since they often appear in conjunction with other factors that are believed to contribute to problems in reading. For example, because of the nature of a student's environment he is likely to possess combinations of physical, psychological, socioeconomic, and educational problems, all of which contribute to his reading disability.

A number of research studies have also shown that certain problems such as those of a visual-perceptual nature may also be related to, if not direct causal factors of, reading disability. Many studies, however, have also shown that remediation of this type of problem has little, or no, direct effect on a student's ability to read.

Other more recent studies have shown that problems other than those studied by Robinson may also affect students' ability to read. For example, there appears to be a relationship between socioeconomic level, visual and auditory discrimination, and modality shifting. There is also believed to be a relationship between syntactic competence and reading disability. To date, however, little concrete research has been done that will help the remedial reading teacher diagnose and remediate these problems even when they are known to exist.

One of the most important points to be learned from Robinson's and subsequent studies is that students' reading disabilities are not usually the result of any single factor. The remedial reading teacher should be especially careful to keep this in mind in both diagnostic and remedial work.

Chapter 1:   REFERENCES

Abrams, Jules C. "Learning Disabilities—A Complex Phenomenon," *The Reading Teacher*. Vol. 23, (January, 1970), 299–303.

Ames, Louise B., and Walker, Richard N. "Prediction of Later Reading Ability From Kindergarten Rorschach and IQ Scores," *Journal of Educational Psychology*. Vol. 55, (December, 1964), 309–313.

Bateman, Barbara. "Educational Implications of Minimal Brain Dysfunction," *The Reading Teacher*. Vol. 27, (April, 1974), 662–668.

Bond, Guy L., and Tinker, Miles A. *Reading Difficulties: Their Diagnosis and Correction*. 2d ed., New York: Appleton-Century-Crofts, 1967.

Capobianco, R. J. "Ocular-Manual Laterality and Reading Achievement in Children with Special Learning Disabilities," *American Educational Research Journal*. Vol. 4, (March, 1967), 133–138.

Carter, Dale L. "The Effect of Teacher Expectations on the Self-Esteem and Academic Performance of Seventh Grade Students," Doctoral dissertation, University of Tennessee, 1970.

Cavanaugh, Lyman. "Reading Behavior with Regard for Endocrine Imbalances," Thirteenth Yearbook of the Claremont College Reading Conference, Claremont, California, 1948, 95–102.

Cohen, Alice, and Glass, Gerald G. "Lateral Dominance and Reading Ability," *The Reading Teacher*. Vol. 21, (January, 1968), 343–348.

Cohen, S. Alan, and Cooper, Thelma. "Seven Fallacies: Reading Retardation and the Urban Disadvantaged Beginning Reader," *The Reading Teacher*. Vol. 26, (October, 1972), 38–45.

Cohn, Maxine, and Kornelly, Donald. "For Better Reading—A More Positive Self-Image," *The Elementary School Journal*. Vol. 70, (January, 1970), 199–201.

Coleman, Howard M. "Visual Perception and Reading Dysfunction," *Journal of Learning Disabilities*, Vol. I, (February, 1968), 116–123.

Denner, Bruce. "Representational and Syntactic Competence of Problem Readers," *Child Development*. Vol. 41, (September, 1970), 881–887.

Deutsch, Martin, et al. *The Disadvantaged Child*. New York: Basic Books, Inc., 1967.

Eames, Thomas H. "The Relationship of Reading and Speech Difficulties," *Journal of Educational Psychology*. Vol. XLI, (January, 1950), 51–55.

Eames, Thomas H. "Physical Factors in Reading," *The Reading Teacher*. Vol. 15, (May, 1962), 427–432.

Early, Margaret J. *Reading Disabilities: Selections on Identification and Treatment*. Edited by Harold Newman. Indianapolis: The Odyssey Press, 1969.

Fernald, Grace M. *Remedial Techniques in Basic School Subjects*. New York: McGraw-Hill, 1943.

Forness, Steven R. "Lateral Dominance in Retarded Readers with Signs of Brain Dysfunction," Doctoral dissertation, University of California, Los Angeles, 1968.

Gates, Arthur J. "The Role of Personality Maladjustment and Remedial Reading," *Journal of Generic Psychology*, Vol. 59, (1941), 77–83.

Harris, Albert J. *Harris Tests of Lateral Dominance—Manual of Directions*. 3d ed., New York: Psychological Corporation, 1958.

Harris, Albert J. *Readings on Reading Instruction*. Edited by Albert J. Harris. New York: David McKay, 1963.

Harris, Albert J. *How to Increase Reading Ability*. 5th ed., New York: David McKay, 1970.

Katz, Phyllis A., and Deutsch, Martin. "The Relation of Auditory-Visual Shifting to Reading Achievement," *Perceptual Motor Skills*. Vol. 17, 1963, 327–332.

Krippner, Stanley. "Etiological Factors in Reading Disability of the Academically Talented in Comparison to Pupils of Average and Slow Learning Ability," *The Journal of Educational Research*. Vol. 61, (February, 1968), 275–279.

Labov, W. "The Logic of Non-Standard Dialectic," *Ed. J. Alatis*. School of Languages and Linguistics Monograph Series, 1969.

Padelford, William B. "The Influence of Socioeconomic Level, Sex, and Ethnic Background Upon the Relationship Between Reading Achievement and Self-Concept," Doctoral dissertation, University of California, Los Angeles, 1969.

Palardy, James M. "The Effect of Teachers' Beliefs on the Achievement in Reading of First-Grade Boys," Doctoral dissertation, Ohio State University, 1968.

Pryor, Frances. "Poor Reading—Lack of Self Esteem?" *The Reading Teacher*. Vol. 28, (January, 1975), 358–359.

Rosenthal, Robert, and Jacobson, Lenore. "Teachers' Expectancies: Determinants of Pupils' IQ Gains," *Psychological Reports*. Vol. 19, (August, 1966), 115–118.

Rystrom, Richard. "Effects of Standard Dialect Training on Negro First Graders Being Taught to Read," *Report Project No. 81–053*. U.S. Dept. of HEW, 1968.

Samuels, S. Jay. "Research-Reading Disability," *The Reading Teacher*, Vol. 24, (December, 1970), 267+.

Schellenberg, Ernest D. "A Study of the Relationship Between Visual Motor Perception and Reading Disabilities of Third Grade Pupils," Doctoral dissertation, University of Southern California, 1962.

Shearer, E. "Physical Skills and Reading Backwardness," *Educational Research*. Vol. X, (June, 1968), 197–206.

Smith, Donald E. P. "A New Theory of Physiological Basis of Reading Disability," *Reading for Effective Living*. Conference Proceedings of the International Reading Association. Newark, Delaware: International Reading Association, 3 (1958), 119–121.

Spache, George D., and Spache, Evelyn B. *Reading In The Elementary School*, 3d ed., Boston: Allyn and Bacon, Inc., 1973.

Thompson, Bertha B. "A Longitudinal Study of Auditory Discrimination," *The Journal of Educational Research*. Vol. 56, (March, 1963), 376–378.

United States Commission on Civil Rights. *The Unfinished Education*. October, 1971.

Witty, Paul A. "Reading Success and Emotional Adjustment," *Elementary English*, Vol. 27, (May, 1950), 281–296.

2

SOME IMPORTANT OPERATIONAL PROCEDURES

The experienced diagnostician and teacher have usually discovered that there are certain operational procedures which, if applied, tend to make their jobs easier and the results of their labor more successful. These are sometimes discovered while working with children over a period of years, and sometimes they are learned through the professional literature and by taking courses in reading diagnosis and remediation. The first part of this chapter contains a discussion of some important operational procedures for the diagnostician. This is followed by a list of important operational procedures for the teacher. The chapter then concludes with a discussion of some common reasons for failure in the diagnostic-remedial process.

IMPORTANT OPERATIONAL PROCEDURES FOR THE DIAGNOSTICIAN

The Amount of Diagnosis Before Remediation Is Begun

One of the operational procedures facing personnel in the field of reading is whether it is better to do a great deal of diagnosis before remediation is begun or whether it is better to do only enough diagnosis to initiate remediation and then continue the diagnosis while teaching.

Proponents of a system of doing a great deal of diagnosis before beginning remedial procedures often argue that their method of operation is better because more information is available for planning a program of remediation. They also state that time may not be wasted in doing unnecessary remediation, and that a thorough initial diagnosis provides a basis for measuring progress. They also believe that children with similar difficulties can be located and grouped for more efficient instruction.

Those who oppose doing a great deal of initial diagnosis before beginning remediation argue that children tend to become discouraged if too much initial testing is done. They also believe that diagnosis continued during remediation deals with the problem as the child sees it, and that when the diagnosis is continuous the remedial program is likely to be flexible.

I would suggest that the best method of operation lies somewhere between the two extremes with the observation of certain precautions. Some of these precautions are explained in the following.

Make Sure Test Information Is Accurately Communicated

If the person doing the diagnostic work also carries out the remedial procedures, there is seldom cause for concern; however, a plan that seems to be gaining popularity in many larger school systems is to employ a number of full-time diagnosticians. These people spend their entire day doing diagnostic work. After each child is diagnosed they then write prescriptive procedures in accordance with their diagnosis. Where this type of procedure is in operation, the normal problems are often compounded because of the difficulty in accurately relaying diagnostic information to the person charged with carrying out the remedial procedures.

Anyone who has read psychological testing reports or reports from educational diagnosticians would probably agree that frequently these reports leave you wondering what has really been prescribed as treatment. Because of this problem of communication, many people feel that the person who will eventually do the remediation should also do the diagnostic testing. A typical example of what happens in the communication of test results is illustrated by the following excerpt from a test report: "Dwight exhibits problems with lateral dominance and would probably benefit from procedures to correct this problem."

A group of experienced remedial reading teachers were asked to explain what they would do with this information. Following are some of the answers:

Teacher 1.   "I would have him practice pacing his reading with his hand, using a left to right motion."

Teacher 2.   "I would start him on the Frostig program."

Teacher 3.   "Research shows that there is no relationship between lateral dominance and reading so I would ignore it."

At this point no attempt will be made to evaluate the teachers responses, but it is evident that each teacher interpreted the information differently. Such is often the case when one teacher attempts to interpret what another has written.

Another problem with test reports is that they often use such statements as, "Dwight has difficulty with the initial consonant blends." This statement is too vague to be of any real significance. For example, one might then ask the following questions: Does he have difficulty with all blends? Does he not know the phonemes represented by various graphemes? Or does he lack the ability to blend various initial consonant blends with word families or phonograms? In this case the person doing the remediation would still have to do further diagnosis before meaningful teaching could begin. On the other hand, if the person who did the testing also did the remedial procedures with the same child, then there would be no communication problem.

Gather Enough Initial Diagnostic Information to Begin a Program of Remediation, But Make Sure the Program Remains Flexible

A major problem that sometimes occurs is that the program of remediation becomes set or inflexible and is not changed according to the changing needs of the child. For example, a child who is slightly nervous or who is reading at his frustration reading level is likely to make a number of substitutions for basic sight words. A child who does make substitutions for some basic sight words may in fact really know these sight words when the words are tested in isolation. The problem would then be to determine why the substitutions were made. However, if the original diagnosis indicated that the child should have instruction on the basic sight words, then that child is very likely to have to sit through a great deal of instruction that is not really needed. This situation occurs more often when the original diagnosis is done by someone other than the person doing the remediation. It is also more likely to occur when one child is placed with other pupils who indicate similar weaknesses.

Do Not Do Unnecessary Testing But Gather Enough Information to Serve as a Data Base for Measuring Improvement

In determining initial versus ending performance in a remedial program, consider such factors as (1) progression in reading grade placement, (2) various phoneme-grapheme relationships learned, and (3) number of basic sight words learned. It would, of course, be very difficult to accurately determine whether the child had actually learned from day-to-day if there was no accurately determined base or beginning point.

Attempting to measure progress without some base point is somewhat like the situation of parents who are told how much their child has grown. This growth is often very difficult for the parents to notice since they are in daily contact with the child. The visiting relative, however, who has not seen the child for a year is very much aware of the child's growth. The parents may also get out last year's blanket sleeper as cold weather approaches and find that it is now too small for the child. The size of the child when it did fit the sleeper versus a year later when it was tried on, is analogous to a beginning and ending measurement of the reading skills. That is, we become much more aware of growth from a beginning to ending period than we do when we are exposed to a child's daily growth in reading skills.

Since many remedial reading programs are supported by some sort of federal funding, accountability becomes extremely important. Often the very existence of remedial reading programs is dependent on the demonstration of success with the pupils with whom you are working. When such a situation occurs, no choice remains but to attempt to show improvement in students from the beginning to the end of the program.

It should be emphasized, however, that certain precautions should be observed in doing the initial testing. A very common and often deserved criticism of remedial reading programs is that a great deal of testing is done and then little time is left for remediation. One school system, with which I am familiar, tests children who are candidates for the remedial reading program for about one-fourth of the school year before any remedial work is done. These children often become even more discouraged about their reading than they were in a normal classroom situation. This is, of course, true by the nature of the testing itself. In order to find a child's IQ or frustration reading level, the child must be taken up to a level of questioning or reading that is extremely difficult for him. This, of course, often results in discouragement, feelings of inadequacy, and consequently a loss of rapport between the child and the tester.

If the person who has done the initial testing with the child is also the same person who will later be doing remedial work with the child, it is often difficult to re-establish the good rapport that may have been lost during the testing periods. For this reason alone it would seem that only a minimal amount of initial testing would be desirable.

A highly skilled tester can usually administer a test in such a manner that almost any child will appear to enjoy the test. Some children are also delighted to be excused from the classroom to participate in a testing program. When such is the case, it is less damaging to the self-confidence of the child than when he is forced to participate. The tester should, however, remember that most children soon tire of any activity in which they are not entirely successful and in a test situation complete success for the child is nearly always lacking.

Do Not Be Overly Concerned About the Repetition Involved in the Teaching of a Few Skills Already Known by the Child

It is quite natural for a remedial reading teacher to begin remedial work with some help being given in the comprehension skills even though she may know that the child's diagnosed problem is in word attack skills. Some teachers would logically argue that this time would be wasted since it does not focus on the exact needs of the child. If the time in which the child is to be tutored by the remedial reading teacher is severely limited, this argument would be somewhat valid.

A number of research studies such as those of Joseph Lillich (1968) and Keith Dolan (1964) have shown, however, that the guidance and counseling aspects or establishing of rapport with a disabled reader is just as important as teaching reading skills per se. It would then appear that some time in working with a skill in which the child was somewhat more adept may, in fact, not be harmful but that the benefits from the improved relationship between the disabled reader and the teacher may far outweigh the fact that there is some repetition of materials. Furthermore, it seems doubtful that any class can claim efficiency to such a degree that there is never repetition of known facts even if repetition *was* completely undesirable.

Lillich
Dolan

Diagnosis for a Disabled Reader Should Involve More Than an Appraisal of Educational Factors

A teacher who has a student who has developed a minor problem with some phase of the reading skills, such as learning certain initial consonant sounds, may only be interested in locating and correcting that particular problem. The student may have failed to learn certain initial consonant sounds because he missed a day or two of school, he may have not been listening closely when those consonant sounds were initially taught, or he may have simply required more time and drill to learn them. When a student only misses an occasional concept, the teacher is not usually concerned with factors other than the educational problem itself. In the case of a somewhat severely disabled reader, however, a diagnosis should involve more than an appraisal of educational factors.

Imp.

One of the major reasons that school personnel are faced with as many seriously disabled readers as they are is that teachers often fail to locate and correct incipient reading problems while they are still in an easily correctable stage. However, the reasons for failure to learn are often more complicated than those mentioned previously, i.e., absence from school or failure to listen closely on one occasion. When failure to learn stems from other causes, often more serious, even a teacher who is well trained in locating and correcting incipient reading problems may find certain students who do not learn. When this is the case, a much more thorough diagnosis involving more than educational factors is necessary.

When a child fails to learn in a normal educational setting, somewhat more complicated causes of the learning disability such as physical, psychological, or socio-educational factors may be responsible. Each of these factors, of course, can be broken down into a number of sub-factors or sub-categories which may contribute to, or in some cases, result from, a reading disability. The essential point for the reading diagnostician to remember is that what often appears as a problem may be only a symptom of a more difficult and involved problem.

Make the Diagnosis as Efficiently as Possible

A diagnosis should be as thorough as necessary, but should not extend beyond what is required. The problem of the reading diagnostician, of course, is to determine just what is, and is not, necessary. Although this is often somewhat difficult, there are some very definite guidelines that the experienced diagnostician will soon learn to follow.

One of the most common problems leading to inefficient diagnosis is that the diagnostician falls into the habit of giving the same diagnostic tests to each student regardless of his apparent problem or problems. This can often lead to inefficiency as well as inadequate diagnosis. In some cases, certain phases of commonly-used diagnostic procedures can easily be omitted. When this is the case, a great deal of time can be saved. For example, you may note that a child who is in the fifth or sixth grade reads orally very poorly. For a child such as this, a somewhat logical approach would be to diagnose a number of questionable areas such as initial, ending, and medial consonants sounds, consonant clusters, vowel, vowel team and special letter combination sounds, vowel rules, and syllabication principles. However, if the student can read the Nonsense Words Section of the Botel Reading Inventory,[1] you can automatically eliminate testing in each of the above mentioned areas because a child weak in these areas would not be able to read long nonsense words. There are

[1]Botel, Morton. *Botel Reading Inventory.* Chicago: Follett, 1966.

also other areas where certain commonly administered tests may be omitted for certain children, such as visual screening tests for a child who has recently been examined by an optometrist or an ophthalmologist or IQ tests for a child who definitely demonstrates an ability to learn.

Just as it is easy to fall into the habit of using tests that are not needed, it is also easy to omit tests or further checks that may be indicated in some instances. The reading diagnostician should continually examine his methods of diagnosis by asking such questions as: Am I giving this test only because I am in the habit of doing so? Are there more efficient methods of locating problems than I am now using? Is the information I seek already available in the child's cumulative records? Will the cause of the child's disability also affect future attempts at remediation?

Test in a Situation That Is Analogous to Actual Reading

A serious problem with group diagnostic tests is that they often do not measure reading skills in a situation that is analogous to actual reading. This is also a criticism of some individually administered tests. My research has indicated that many types of tests do not measure what they purport to measure.[2] It appears that only in some areas such as comprehension and vocabulary can the reading diagnostician feel fairly sure that he is really measuring what the test purports to measure when group tests are used. The implications are also quite clear that if you really want to measure certain reading skills, you must use an individually administered test.

Typical examples of the type of group tests that often give misleading information are tests for basic sight words and tests for beginning consonant sounds. I once taught an evening reading class to a group of elementary and secondary teachers in the school district in which these teachers were employed. After discussing ways of testing for knowledge of the basic sight words, one ninth grade teacher of a group of extremely poor readers asked me to administer a group basic sight word test in his class. In taking this test the student is required to underline or circle one of a choice of four words that is the same as a word pronounced aloud by the person administering the test. There were approximately thirty students in the class who took the test. Each student was tested on 220 words or, in other words, had to underline or circle 220 words from a choice of 880 words. This meant that 220×30 or 6600 choices were made. When these tests were corrected, only six errors were found. Certainly this many mistakes would be expected on the basis of clerical errors alone.

Next, several consultants sat down individually with students and asked each of them to simply pronounce each of the 220 basic sight words on the test. This time many students missed from twenty-five to fifty words each. The results in this case are quite typical of those obtained when you try to test in a situation that is not analogous to actual reading. It is, of course, much easier to pick one word pronounced by a tester from a choice of four than to see the same word and then pro-

[2]Ekwall, Eldon E. "An Analysis of Children's Test Scores When Tested With Individually Administered Diagnostic Tests and When Tested With Group Administered Diagnostic Tests," *Final Research Report.* University of Texas at El Paso, University Research Institute, 1973.

nounce it. The latter case is, however, what you must do when you read orally. As you can see, what we wanted to know was which students did not know which words. Administration of the test to a group simply did not give us this information.

As in the case just illustrated, most group tests require students to choose one of several answers as a correct choice. This is simply not what a student does when he reads and, therefore, in most cases does not tell us what we want to know.

Group phonics tests also present problems typical of the problem encountered in the basic sight word test. For example, in testing initial consonant sounds a test may call for a student to circle one of four letters that represents the same sound as the beginning sound of a word pronounced by the teacher. Here again, it is easier to circle one of four letters (for example *d, p, b, c*) that represents the beginning sound in the word "dog" than it is to see a "d" and pronounce the "d" phoneme which is what a student must do when he reads a new word beginning with "d."

Authors of tests often claim that since the kinds of group tests mentioned above have a high correlation with individual tests they are therefore a valid instrument for diagnosis. You must keep in mind, however, that a high correlation between two tests only means that those students who scored high on the group test also scored high on the individual test. This would usually happen whenever two highly related skills are tested and the results of two groups scores are correlated. Keep in mind, however, that what the reading diagnostician wants to know in testing for phoneme knowledge, for example, is which phonemes each student does not know and not which students rank highest and lowest.

This is not meant to imply that all group tests are bad or that all individual tests are good. A number of individual tests also contain subtests designed to measure certain skills that in reality do not require the student to use the same skills in taking the test as he would in actual reading. Chapters 4–6 deal with the testing of various educational factors in reading. Problems encountered in test construction and administration are covered in considerable depth in those chapters. The essential point for the reading diagnostician to keep in mind from the foregoing discussion is that testing should be done in a situation that is analogous to actual reading.

Major Decisions Concerning the Welfare of a Child Should Be Based on Known Facts

Most of us who have worked in the public schools have at some time heard about or witnessed a case of a child suddenly "taking hold" or "blooming" after having been a poor student. Even the best of teachers, psychologists, or diagnosticians are unable, in many cases, to predict whether this sort of thing will happen to a child. The important point to remember, however, is to leave the door open to the possibility of such an occurrence.

Any major decisions for prolonged remedial work which will remove a child from his normal learning environment should be based on the opinions of several people and the results of several tests. A psychologist, for example, who examines a child for as long as several hours may develop some excellent insights about a child, yet this same person may lack a great deal of information that has been available to the child's classroom teacher, the principal, or the child's parents. I once heard an elementary principal say, "When the school psychologist works with one of our children for several hours and then writes his report, it often tells us that now *he* knows as much about the child as we did when the psychologist started testing." This statement should not be taken to discredit the work of the school psychologist, but it does illustrate the previous point that no individual can hope to gain enough information about a student in an hour or two to make decisions which will often affect his entire life.

School personnel who are involved with making decisions concerning intensive remedial work or assignment to special classes should develop procedures for placement of students. A diagnostic-referral procedure, such as that outlined in Figure 2–1 (page 30), will enable school personnel to place children according to the best information that can be derived from all sources.

Become Aware of the Strong Points and Limitations of Group Standardized, Individual Standardized, and Informal Measuring Instruments

The reading diagnostician should make every effort to become familiar with as many tests as possible. This is not to say that any one person will or should continually change the tests that he commonly uses in diagnosis; however, he should continually search for newer and better tests and methods of testing. The process of examining new tests and test procedures is certain to be excellent in-service training in itself. For example, the authors of tests are not likely to stress the weaknesses inherent in their own material; however, they are likely to explain why certain techniques or procedures they use are better than others. This explanation in itself will often enable the diagnostician to better evaluate his own tests and testing procedures.

The strong points of various group and individual tests and testing techniques are discussed in considerable detail in later chapters. There are, however, some inherent weaknesses and strong points in certain types of testing that are of such importance to personnel concerned with reading that they should receive special emphasis at this point.

GROUP STANDARDIZED TESTS.   Group standardized tests are perhaps more misused than any other type of tests on the market today. Some of this misuse can be attributed to the users of the tests, but certainly some of the blame also lies with the authors who have a tendency to overstate the test's value for some purposes.

The most flagrant misuse of group standardized tests is, no doubt, in using them to make final decisions about individual students. Although the publishers of group achievement tests often claim that their tests have considerable individual diagnostic value, it is doubtful that this claim can be substantiated in most cases. For any individual, group test scores are often so unreliable that it would be difficult to place any real confidence in their results. The author recently administered a nationally-used reading achievement test designed for grades four through six to a

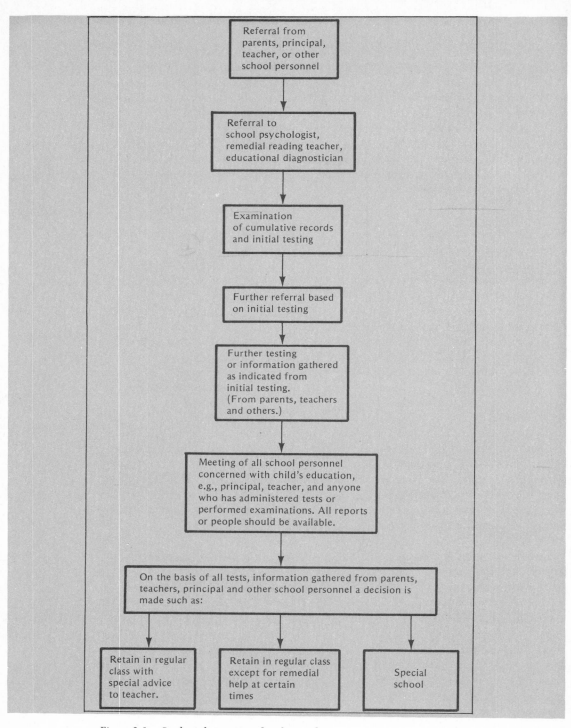

Figure 2.1. Student diagnostic referral procedure.

class of college students. The students, however, were not given the questions but were instructed to mark the answer sheets at random. One of the subtests on this test purports to measure childrens' reading vocabulary in science. The class of college students scored from a low grade level of 2.5 to a high grade level of 6.5 on this subtest. Remember, of course, that this was a situation similar to one in which none of the students could read at all! The grade placement of the students on the entire test ranged from 2.9 to 4.3 which also makes it evident that individual students' total reading scores varied too much to place any credence in them for individual grade placement. The users of these tests should also keep in mind that if the total reading scores are used for grade placement, they are not being analyzed as a group test but are making individual decisions for each member of the group.

Another inherent weakness of group tests is that they cannot test many of the reading skills in a situation that is analogous to actual reading. This point was discussed in more detail earlier in this chapter. Reading skills such as vocabulary and comprehension are, however, more amenable to testing with group tests.

Some of the strong points of group standardized tests are that they are useful for measuring overall class achievement during a specified period of time. If one examines the subtests rather carefully, they can also be useful in determining whether overall areas, such as the study skills are receiving adequate attention in the curriculum. Another important point in favor of using group tests is that they are less time consuming to administer. Group standardized tests also allow school personnel to compare the achievement of their students with that of the nation as a whole or the norm group on which the test was originally standardized.

INDIVIDUAL STANDARDIZED TESTS.   Individual standardized tests are less misused than group standarized tests for several reasons. To begin with, the people who find a need to use individual standardized tests, such as the Durrell Analysis of Reading Difficulty,[3] are usually more experienced in test administration and are therefore better informed about the strong points and limitations of various tests. Individual standardized tests are also more difficult to administer than group standardized tests. For this reason they are likely to be given only when needed in contrast to group tests which are often given simply because it is "test time."

Individual standardized tests can be given in a situation that is analogous to actual reading and thus have a tremendous advantage over group standardized tests. For example, you can simply ask a child to read orally while you mark the kinds of mistakes he makes, or he can be asked to simply pronounce basic sight words. Individual standardized tests also have the advantage of being standardized which will enable you to compare a child's reading abilities with other children of the same age and/or grade level. A further advantage of individual standardized tests is that the tester can easily omit certain subtests which may not be relevant to a certain student.

Perhaps the greatest disadvantage of individual standardized tests is that they are time consuming to administer. In many cases they are somewhat difficult for a classroom teacher to administer and, therefore, do or should require some special training. This could, however, be interpreted as a blessing in disguise.

[3]Durrell, Donald D. *Durrell Analysis of Reading Difficulty.* New York: Harcourt, Brace & World, 1955.

INFORMAL MEASURING INSTRUMENTS. Informal measuring instruments such as word lists, informal reading inventories, and cloze passages are also valuable diagnostic tools. One of the most important advantages of this type of instrument is that they are readily adaptable to the materials within the classroom. By using the standard criteria for the informal reading inventory or cloze procedure, the teacher can rather quickly and easily determine whether a certain student can read a certain book at his "instructional" or "free" reading level. The teacher can also use these procedures to determine whether a new textbook is written at a proper reading level for the students. The use of word lists from a book commonly used in the school will also enable teachers to make a rapid check on a student's ability to deal with the vocabulary load in that book.

Informal measuring instruments have several rather serious disadvantages. They must be used by someone who can understand and use the standard criteria for their application or they are no better than simply listening to a child read and then guessing at his grade level. Although the procedure for using them is rather simple, they are still somewhat difficult to construct. For example, it is a tremendous task to find questions which measure more than simple recall of facts for use in an informal reading inventory. It is also difficult and time consuming to construct and check cloze passages to use for measuring a student's ability to read a certain book. Other specific advantages and disadvantages of using informal reading inventories are discussed in detail in Chapter 11.

IMPORTANT OPERATIONAL
PROCEDURES FOR THE TEACHER

As experience is gained in working with disabled readers, the reading teacher is likely to find that some techniques work especially well with some students and yet seem somewhat less successful with others. One of the characteristics of a successful teacher is that she can quickly determine whether a certain teaching procedure is producing the desired results with a particular student. When a certain teaching procedure does not produce the desired results, the experienced teacher will alter her approach. Certain teaching procedures have, however, proven to be consistently successful with almost all students regardless of such factors as their specific reading problems, age, grade, sex, and mode of learning. It is imperative that the remedial reading teacher becomes aware of these teaching procedures and makes every effort to implement them. Some of these important procedures are as follows:

1. Select a remedial reading program that is highly individualized.
2. Start at the child's level.
3. Start with the child's strongest area.
4. Provide an opportunity for success for the child.
5. Make the disabled reader aware of his progress.
6. Make the learning process meaningful to the child.
7. Use materials appropriate to the needs of the child.
8. Continue the diagnosis while you teach.

9. Be alert to pick up any clues given by the child.
10. Capitalize on the motivation that the child may already possess.
11. Make use of the teaching method with which the child is most successful.
12. Maintain a relaxed attitude.
13. Do not be too authoritative.
14. Have confidence in the child's ability to learn.
15. Direct the child toward self-instruction.
16. Begin each period with a summary of what you intend to do and why you intend to do it and end each period with a summary of what you did and why you did it.
17. Provide for a follow-up program.

Select a Remedial Reading Program That Is Highly Individualized

Terms such as "a well-balanced program" or "a well-rounded program" sound good and are appropriate for a developmental reading program, but they do not describe the type of reading program that is desirable in remedial reading. In most cases the remedial reading program must be highly individualized and directed toward correcting certain individual reading deficiencies rather than giving a child a well-rounded program.

Many children in remedial reading classes are simply retarded a year or more in almost all of their reading skills; however, a large percentage of children are retarded a year or more only in certain areas of reading. For those students who are lacking only in certain reading skills it would prove inefficient to provide a remedial program that covered all reading skills. These children can be brought up to reading grade level much more rapidly by receiving an intensive instructional program only in the skills in which they are deficient. One might think of a child's progression in developmental reading as the steps or rungs on a ladder or as a continuum of skills with each step representing the accomplishment of a certain skill such as learning the initial consonant sounds, the initial consonant blends, or the short vowel sounds. Whenever a child fails to learn one of these important skills, a step is omitted from the ladder or continuum of skills. The task of the corrective or remedial reading teacher is to fill in these omitted steps or rungs in the ladder or continuum of reading skills rather than to build a whole new ladder. For this reason the remedial reading teacher must be very specific in her diagnosis and then specific in the remediation provided for noted weaknesses in order to provide for efficient use of both teacher and student time.

Start at the Child's Level

The educational cliché "Start where the child is" has special relevance for the remedial reading teacher who may get a child who is advanced in some areas and extremely retarded in others. As mentioned previously, a thorough diagnosis is a prerequisite for beginning the remedial program. The diagnosis must not only include the area or areas in which the child is deficient, but for the sake of efficiency should report the level of each skill in which the child is deficient. For example, it is not enough to say that John is a fourth grader who is deficient in comprehension skills, but the diagnostic report should also state the level at which he does comprehend. Likewise, a student who is having difficulty with consonant blends should be reported as deficient in his knowledge of the "bl," "fl," "pl," etc. blends and not simply as "having trouble with consonant blends." In both cases the teacher will be able to begin at the child's level of achievement if the diagnostic report is precise. An important point of which both the remedial teacher and classroom teacher must be cognizant is that the disabled reader must not merely begin to make normal progress, but that he must progress at a faster than normal rate that will enable him to catch up with children of a normal age-grade level.

Start with the Child's Strongest Area

Most readers, whether disabled or not, have at least one area in which they are strong or in which they are somewhat more competent than others. The strength may be in a certain area of reading itself, e.g., knowledge of initial consonant blends, or it may be in an area such as mathematics. Because of the extreme importance of establishing proper rapport with a disabled reader, it often works well to begin remedial work by focusing on the strong area. This will allow the disabled reader to experience initial success and thus create an atmosphere in which the child feels he can enjoy working on his reading problem. To continue work in an area in which the disabled reader is already competent would, of course, be inefficient in terms of both student and teacher time; however, the value to be gained from improving the initial attitude of the child will usually outweigh the fact that certain material in the beginning stages is repetitious.

Provide an Opportunity for Success for the Child

Most teachers realize the importance of providing lessons in which children can experience considerable success. This concept has usually been stressed in various methods courses and in psychology courses as well. In remedial reading, however, providing an opportunity for success for the child is even more crucial and deserves special emphasis. The reason for this special emphasis is that the child who ultimately comes to the remedial reading teacher has already experienced a series of failures which led to his disability. In spite of good teaching or at least a proper attitude on the part of the disabled reader's classroom reading teacher, the disabled reader is almost certain to have experienced less success than most children in the classroom.

Since the disabled reader has usually experienced considerable failures, his overall attitude toward learning will often need to be reoriented. This reorientation may be changed somewhat by "educational engineering" in which the teacher consistently arranges for situations to occur in which the child is able to succeed; such as in winning a word game or in doing a series of easy exercises in which the child gets 100 percent correct. Some children, however, may need more than normal success to change their attitude. The teacher may find, for example, that the reorientation process will require not only constant success, but counseling as well. A typical counseling procedure is described in Chapter 7.

Make the Disabled Reader Aware of His Progress

The disabled reader needs to be aware of his progress. To simply say, "You're doing better" is often not sufficient to convince the child that you are actually helping him. Just as a child's physical growth is not clearly noticeable to him, neither is his growth in reading. If you really wanted a child to "believe" that he was growing, you might be likely to mark a line on the wall when he was measured, and label it "John's height on February 20, 19___." A year later you could measure John and mark another line to show his year's growth. Most children would accept such evidence as proof that they were growing.

The remedial reading teacher can, and should, use measurements which are just as concrete as the line on the wall. One excellent method of demonstrating a child's progress is to code all of the errors that a child makes in reading material at, and slightly above, his grade level. These coded errors can then be tallied as shown in Figure 2–2.

After the child has improved in his reading, he can read the same material while the various types of errors are again coded by his teacher. The child can then be shown the reduction in each type of error from the first to the second readings. A tape recording of the first and second readings is also an excellent way to demonstrate improvement to a child. A tape recording in conjunction with a coded series of reading passages is, of course, still better.

Children who make a number of errors on the basic sight words can be given cards with known words on them. Each time a child learns a new word he can be given a new card. In this way a child can easily watch his basic sight-word vocabulary grow. The teacher can also elect to take the card from the child when he has mastered the word. In this way the child sees his pile of cards gradually disappear until his basic sight word "troubles" are gone.

In phonics the teacher can simply check or circle phonic elements not known. This checklist can then be shown to the child. As the various phonic elements are learned, the check marks or circles can be erased by the student.

By seeing active growth in his own reading skills, the child is much more likely to be motivated. And the child who is aware of his progress is more likely to take an active interest in increasing his rate of progression.

Make the Learning Process Meaningful to the Child

A college student was working with a disabled reader on a phonics problem. The disabled reader was in the fourth grade, but was reading on a first grade level. After learning several initial consonant blends and several phonograms, the child was given an opportunity to form some new words by blending the initial consonant

TYPES OF ERRORS
(Indicate number of each type)

First Trial		Second Trial	Percent of Increase (+) or Decrease (−)
6	Omissions	2	66 2/3
2	Insertions	0	100
14	Partial mispronunciations	7	50
0	Gross mispronunciations	0	—
2	Substitutions	0	100
8	Repetitions	2	75
3	Inversions	0	100
0	Aid	0	—
6	Self-corrected errors	0	100

CHARACTERISTICS OF THE READER
(Indicate with check mark)

First Trial		Second Trial
✓	Poor word-analysis skills	0
✓	Head movement	0
✓	Finger pointing	0
✓	Disregard for punctuation	0
✓	Loss of place	0
✓	Overuse of phonics	0
✓	Does not read in natural voice tones	0
✓	Poor enunciation	0
✓	Word-by-word reading	0
✓	Poor phrasing	0
✓	Lack of expression	0
✓	Pauses	0

Student _James Wilson_ Teacher _Ann Updike_
Date _9/23_ School _Lincoln Elementary_

blends with the phonograms. After forming several new words, the child exclaimed, "Hey, this helps you figure out new words!" Perhaps one would be critical of the college student for not explaining why the blends and phonograms were being taught, but one must certainly be critical of the child's former teachers who had allowed the child to progress to the fourth grade without really ever knowing why he should learn his phonics lessons. It is evident that this child simply perceived phonics as a subject or an activity completely different and unrelated to reading.

Children, until they reach the junior high level or beyond, will seldom question why they are being taught various concepts and subject matter. However, the fact that they do not question why it is being taught does not mean that they believe in the necessity of learning it; in fact the attitude that children often demonstrate makes it a certainty that they do not.

Most children, just as adults, when told that they must learn the basic sight words because they account for over half of the words that they will ever need to read can understand the importance of thoroughly learning them. Children also understand, if told, that they must do comprehension exercises to help them understand what they are reading so that they can get more out of their science and social studies books. Likewise children need to be shown how learning the various word-attack skills helps them unlock new words.

Use Materials Appropriate to the Needs of the Child

The reading program in many classrooms is dictated by the kinds of materials found within each classroom. This sort of situation is not desirable even in a developmental reading program, but it is completely intolerable in remedial reading. Excellent reading materials are no better than poor materials if they are not appropriate to the needs of the learner. Many remedial reading programs have failed because an untrained teacher simply gave the disabled reader "more of the same."

The remedial reading teacher must remember that her students are, for the most part, retarded only in certain areas and that the weak areas must receive special attention. For example, a readily available book designed to improve a child's comprehension skills is of little value to a child who is experiencing problems with word-attack skills.

Teachers and administrators should be extra cautious when buying materials to be used in remedial reading. Some materials attempt to do too many things to be really worthwhile in any one area of difficulty. For example, materials that attempt to enrich vocabulary, improve comprehension, and improve word-attack skills in each lesson are likely to be of questionable value in remedial reading since a child is more likely to need an intensive saturation in one area rather than a well-rounded program of teaching each of these three skills. Educational research has also shown that many of the devices designed to speed up reading are of questionable value in developmental reading and may very well be detrimental to a disabled reader. In most cases there is simply no valid reason for using them. Materials appropriate for the remedial reading classroom should contain lessons which are designed to remedy specific reading difficulties. Chapter 15 contains considerable information on the selection and evaluation of materials for remedial and/or corrective reading.

Continue the Diagnosis While You Teach

A student who is being tested will often fail to perfom as well as he does in the somewhat more relaxed day-to-day reading situation. If this happens, there is, of course, the danger that the student will fail certain items, while being tested, that he actually knew. The student would then be channeled into remedial work which was unnecessary. For example, after testing a child, you may discover that he may have missed a number of phonic elements and a number of basic sight words. He may also have missed a number of comprehension questions. You are quite likely to find that later in a normal classroom atmosphere he will know some of the phonic elements and basic sight words and may improve a great deal on his comprehension.

Improvement in the area of phonics and basic sight words is often accounted for simply on the basis of stress during the testing situation or the difference in performance criteria between testing and actually reading. In the area of comprehension a child is likely to show improvement simply because he knows more about subject matter in general than he demonstrated on a particular passage or on a set of passages on a test. The prevalence of such cases emphasizes the need for continual diagnosis during the remediation period.

Be Alert to Pick Up any Clues Given by the Child

Regardless of how thoroughly a disabled reader may be tested, in the beginning you will find many opportunities to expand upon the initial diagnosis while you work with him. It is most important that you develop an alertness to significant clues that children may give concerning their reading disability. Some clues may lead you to change your initial diagnosis while others will allow you to expand upon or confirm the original diagnosis. Following are some clues that were dropped by children who were being taught by university students:

Casey: "Sometimes Mom makes me study in the evening for five minutes and sometimes she makes me study for three or four hours. It just depends on what kind of a mood she's in."

Casey's mother was divorced and was working full time in the daytime and dated quite often at night. Casey did his homework if his mother supervised it; however, she often simply ignored him and did not really concern herself with whether it was done or not. Sometimes she would tell him that he had to read for three hours for punishment. Most importantly, Casey did not know what to expect and had developed some poor work habits as a result of his mother's erratic behavior. Since reading was used as punishment, he had come to view reading as something to be done only when you are bad.

Counseling sessions with Casey's mother helped her to see the need to be more consistent. She also was made aware of the negative feelings that Casey was developing toward reading because it was used as punishment.

Jeffrey: "Sometimes I can see a word and sometimes I can't."

Jeffrey's eyes had been tested by the school nurse earlier in the year. She had reported that Jeffrey had normal vision. This clue, however, led the teacher to refer Jeffrey, through his parents, to an eye doctor who discovered that he was farsighted (had poor nearpoint vision). Glasses were prescribed and his vision and reading both improved.

Tim: "Dad doesn't read and he gets along fine."

Tim's father was a truck driver who spent a great deal of time away from home. Tim had indicated that he would like to be like his dad and he had never seen him sit down and read. During an ensuing conference with both Tim's mother and father, the teacher found that both of Tim's parents read a great deal. Tim was later brought into the conference. Tim's father explained that his job depended on the ability to read. For example, he had to read road maps and road signs and a considerable amount of paperwork connected with his work, such as delivery instructions and Interstate Commerce Commission regulations. Tim's father also told Tim that when he stayed in motels at night he often read a book each night. This conference proved well worthwhile and improved Tim's attitude toward reading.

Clues such as those listed above often lead the teacher to examine certain aspects of a child's reading problem which might otherwise go unnoticed. The remedial reading teacher who is alert to such clues will often be able to add considerable worthwhile information to the original diagnosis.

Capitalize on the Motivation That the Child May Already Possess

Most children have at least one thing that seems to interest them somewhat more than others. If the remedial reading teacher is able to determine that area of interest, she can often capitalize on it in reading. For example, Kurt came to the reading center after being referred by his classroom teacher. After his teacher at the reading center had talked with him at length, she found that he had seldom, if ever, read at home or for that matter he had seldom read anything that his teachers had not required him to read. After several work sessions with Kurt, the teacher at the reading center discovered that he was very interested in airplanes. His father was an Air Force pilot and had taught him to identify a great many commercial, as well as Air Force planes. The teacher asked Kurt if he would be interested in reading if he could find some books about airplanes. He said that he thought he might. For several succeeding sessions Kurt and his teacher searched the library for books about airplanes and flying in general. Kurt found eleven books that he expressed an interest in reading. By the end of the semester Kurt had read eight of the eleven books and had asked several times if his teacher knew where he could find some more books on the subject.

Other teachers have been successful in getting students interested in reading about various occupations in which the students were extremely interested. Still others have motivated students to read by showing them how and why reading is a necessary part of occupations in which the student someday hoped to work. Teachers are often successful in motivating students in an area in which they previously had no interest. However, this extrinsic interest is often much more difficult to generate than intrinsic interests or motivation that the student may already possess.

Make Use of the Teaching Method with Which the Child Is Most Successful

Most children who succeed in school are either inclined toward learning by the methods used by their classroom teacher or they successfully adapt themselves to a method or methods that their teacher uses a great deal of the time. The disabled reader in many cases, however, either cannot learn well by conventional methods because of some impairment, or because the teacher may use several methods, he does not get enough instruction in a particular one in which he learns most readily.

The remedial reading teacher must make a concentrated effort to determine the method by which a child is most successful. Methods commonly used by the classroom teacher are the visual method, the phonic or auditory method, and the combination method. The kinesthetic method, although quite successful with certain students, is less often used. Perhaps to some extent this is as it should be since the kinesthetic method is less efficient when used with students who do not really need it.

One way of learning more about the method with which a child is successful in learning new words is the Learning Methods Test.[4] The Learning Methods Test enables the teacher to teach ten words to a child by each of the visual, phonic or auditory, combination, and kinesthetic methods. The method that is considered best for the child is the one from which he knows the most words on a delayed recall test. Methods of determining children's strongest mode of learning will be discussed further in Chapter 10.

Maintain a Relaxed Attitude

Children often come to remedial reading possessing feelings of hostility. Many of these children have failed for a number of years and can see no reason why the special class in reading should be any different. As adults, we often forget how it feels to experience constant failure. For example, can you imagine what kind of an attitude you might have toward a college statistics course if you were in it for the third time after either having failed it or after receiving the lowest grades in the class the first two times. Certainly you would not bounce exuberantly into the class asking, "When do we get started?"

When a child comes to remedial reading possessing a negative or hostile attitude, it becomes very easy for this same attitude to be transferred to the teacher working with the child. The remedial reading teacher must, however, learn to not take such an attitude too seriously. You must maintain a relaxed attitude and teach the child that you will accept his mistakes and that he need have no fear of correction from you. Once the child sees that there is no reason to possess a hostile attitude, the hostility will usually disappear.

One young man that I worked with almost always came to remedial reading with a negative attitude. In fact, in all honesty, it was very difficult for me to maintain a pleasant attitude toward the child. During the course of the year the child's reading improved considerably, but the child's overall attitude remained pretty much the same. At the end of several years, I happened to revisit the school and met this same boy walking back to his classroom from an outside recess period. The boy exclaimed, "Say, you're the guy who helped me learn how to read. You know that sure helped me!" This, coming from what was probably the most hostile student I

[4]Mills, Robert E. *Learning Methods Test.* Fort Lauderdale, Florida: The Mills School, 1970.

ever taught, is an excellent example of a child whose only defense against failure and all things connected with it was a hostile attitude.

Do Not Be Too Authoritative

As mentioned previously, the remedial reading teacher must maintain a relaxed attitude. Maintaining such an attitude should also preclude becoming too authoritarian in the remedial reading classroom. This is not to say that the teacher should not be firm in demanding certain standards of work and behavior, but merely that the remedial reading teacher's job should not be that of disciplinarian or authoritarian in the eyes of the child. Studies such as those of Sarah D. Muller and Charles H. Madsen, Jr. (1970), James Garder and Grace Ranson (1968), and Richard Cheatham (1968) would indicate that the counseling aspects of teaching remedial reading are just as important as the teaching of reading per se. The teacher who is too authoritative would, of course, soon become an ineffective counselor.

[handwritten margin note: Muller Madsen Garder Ranson]

The teacher must strive to maintain a climate in the remedial reading classroom where the child can express his fears and resentments. For example, a child should be able to say, "I hate to try to sound out new words." without hearing a sermon on why he must try harder. The remedial reading teacher will have ample opportunity to show the child why sounding out new words is a necessary part of reading.

Have Confidence in the Child's Ability to Learn

Not only must the remedial reading teacher have confidence in the child's ability to learn, but she must also transfer this belief to the child so that he too will have confidence in his own learning ability. A study by J. Michael Palardy (1969) demonstrated that what the teacher believes regarding students' abilities can significantly affect final student achievement. Palardy also indicates that teachers can either positively or negatively influence students' self-concepts which in turn influence achievement. Several other studies have, however, shown that teachers' attitudes need not necessarily be changed by teachers' beliefs.

The remedial reading teacher must be cognizant of this type of research and constantly strive to maintain a positive attitude toward each student's ability to learn. Perhaps the best way to develop this attitude is through careful record-keeping as described under the section entitled, "Make the Disabled Reader Aware of His Progress." Such procedures will allow both teacher and student to see the student's week-by-week progress and thus give both of them the needed confidence in the child's ability to learn.

Direct the Child Toward Self-Instruction

Although the specific instruction that a child may receive in a remedial reading classroom is almost always certain to be of considerable benefit to him, the amount that a child learns on his own is often of equal or greater importance. This is, no doubt, true of almost any class that a student attends regardless of the subject matter involved. The learning that takes place within the classroom is, of course, of greater importance in the beginning, but it only serves as a stepping stone to the broadening of one's knowledge. One might say that the classroom learning points the student in the right direction from which he then proceeds to expand and broaden his knowledge. This is especially true in remedial reading. Often the amount of time available for special tutoring sessions is severely limited due to the lack of an adequate teaching staff. Because of these factors, the remedial reading teacher must direct the child toward self-instruction.

Self-instruction may take many different forms depending on the age-grade level of the student, the nature of his reading disability, and a host of other factors. For example, a teacher may diagnose a child as having a very limited sight vocabulary and as a result spend many hours teaching him words that he should have learned during his progression through the grades. Such effort, however, can be quite futile if the child does not begin to read on his own so that he is continually exposed to the new words he has learned during the remedial sessions. Our work at the University of Texas at El Paso has shown that even the brightest child needs many exposures to a word before it becomes a sight word for him.

In the area of comprehension and study skills children can be taught to improve themselves by teaching them study techniques such as SQ3R (see Chapter 6) to be used in reading their science and social studies lessons. They can also be taught the use of full and half signals such as "in the first place," "secondly," and "and then," which will enable their comprehension to improve while reading on their own.

Begin Each Period with a Summary of What You Intend to Do and Why You Intend to Do It and End Each Period with a Summary of What You Did and Why You Did It

As parents, most of us have at some time or another asked our children what they learned at school today. An all too common answer to this question is "Oh nothing." As teachers most of us also realize that the "Oh nothing." statement is probably incorrect. What you must remember, however, is that the "Oh nothing." represents the child's perception of what he learned. For the purpose of stimulating or motivating a child to want to learn you must be cognizant of how *he* feels about it. A child may, in reality, be learning a great deal, but if *he* does not really believe that learning is taking place, chances are he will take little active interest in what is being taught.

In order to avoid the "Oh nothing" response the child should be briefed on what he is going to learn and why he needs to learn it and then at the end of the remedial session the teacher should review what has been learned and why it was learned. If you follow this procedure you will find an overall improvement in the children's attitude toward learning and, in addition, you are likely to improve your public relations program with the parents of the children you teach.

Provide for a Follow-up Program

Remedial reading programs in which the disabled readers have been kept for a considerable length of time have tended to be more successful than those that have only brought children in for short periods of time. This is especially true where some sort of follow-up program was not instituted for children who were terminated from short-term remedial reading programs.

Bruce Balow (1965) reported on a study of three groups of disabled readers some of whom were, and some of whom were not, given assistance during a follow-up period. He states,

Balow

> Continuing growth seems to depend upon continued attention to the problem. While the second and third groups received additional remedial assistance throughout the follow-up period, few of the pupils in Sample I had any further special help. Sample I pupils did not lose the reading skill they had acquired during the time in the clinic, but neither did they continue to develop on their own. Quite in contrast is the continuing progress of the second and third groups. Given far less intensive, but nonetheless supportive, help over the follow-up period, these pupils continued to develop in reading at a pace more rapid than that preceding intensive tutoring. Rate of growth over the follow-up period was approximately 75 percent of normal growth. (p. 585)

Balow indicates that, unfortunate as it may seem, short-term intensive programs have not been successful, although children are helped somewhat during the course of instruction. He believes that reading disability should probably be considered a relatively chronic illness needing long-term treatment.

Similar results were reported by Theodore A. Buerger (1968), who also did a follow-up study of remedial reading instruction. In his conclusions Buerger stated, "What is needed after a rather intensive remedial period is provision for supportive reading assistance during the follow-up period." (p. 333)

Buerger

E. Shearer (1967), studying the long-term effects of remedial reading instruction, also concluded that children do make gains in remedial reading and that these gains can be preserved if follow-up remedial help is given.

Shearer

The activities of the follow-up program in most cases will closely parallel the period of more intensive remediation. Some teachers prefer to cut the time allotted to each remedial session while others prefer to keep the length of remedial sessions the same but have the child come to class less often.

REASONS FOR FAILURE IN THE DIAGNOSTIC-REMEDIAL PROCESS

Certain factors, if allowed to interfere, can seriously impede the diagnostic-remedial process. The educational diagnostician and/or remedial teacher should constantly examine their own diagnostic-remedial procedures to insure that certain influencing factors are not adversely affecting either their diagnostic or remedial procedures. Some common reasons for failure in the diagnostic-remedial process are as follows:

1. Too much time is spent on the diagnosis so that no time is left for remediation.
2. Sometimes the data are inadequate.
3. Some single causes of reading disability are overemphasized.
4. Sometimes the diagnosis is done by one person and turned over to another.
5. Some diagnosticians come up with the same factors time-after-time.
6. We sometimes diagnose and work on factors that do not help children's reading.
7. Previous bias may exert an undue influence.

Too Much Time Is Spent on the Diagnosis So That No Time Is Left for Remediation

The problem of spending so much time on diagnosis so that little or no time is left for remediation is more prevalent than many people working in remedial reading realize. In some schools the initial testing system for admitting a child to remedial reading and then the initial diagnosis once he enters the remedial reading program may take up nearly one-half of the first semester of school. Even though the child himself may not be directly involved in testing every day, the admittance procedure often becomes so involved that the child loses out on valuable remedial time. School personnel who deal with disabled readers should attempt to simplify procedures for initial diagnosis as much as possible in order to avoid unnecessary testing. For some children certain tests which are given as routine procedure for all students may be omitted. For example, routine hearing tests could probably be omitted for children whose problem is in an area such as reading comprehension. Likewise, individual intelligence tests may often be omitted if the child is to be admitted to the remedial reading program regardless of the outcome of the test. Chances are the type of instruction given the child will not be influenced by his IQ even if it were extremely high or extremely low. In most cases a good remedial reading teacher would simply use those methods or procedures that proved successful with the child.

Another problem in this area is that people involved in reading simply become curious about certain children's abilities and administer tests to satisfy their own curiosity. The remedial reading teacher should be able to justify the administration of all tests given a child on the basis that the test results will ultimately help the child. Curiosity is healthy and much good research and practical knowledge stems from it. However, unless some justifiable research is involved, the point should again be stressed that children should not be subjected to unnecessary testing. The remedial reading teacher should also remember that a great deal of useful information, such as how the child learns, his success in learning certain concepts, and his stated reasons for failure, will be uncovered in working with the child on a day-to-day basis.

Sometimes the Data Are Inadequate

Although the diagnostic-remedial process can easily be hampered by the collection of too much unnecessary data, it can just as easily be hampered when the data collected are inadequate. Some children are simply referred to the remedial reading teacher who then immediately begins work on specific problems. Operating in this fashion can often be inefficient and wasteful of the teacher's, as well as the child's, time.

Data are often readily available that could help the remedial reading teacher plan a more effective program. For example, many children are not successful in learning phonics through the application of a great many rules, therefore, some of these children come to remedial reading with a deficiency in phonics knowledge. In some cases children may even come to the remedial reading teacher in the fourth grade with a deficiency in phonics knowledge after having completed three years of intensive "rule type" phonics. If the remedial reading teacher is not aware of a child's inability to learn phonics through this type of approach, the child may continue to be exposed to more of the same. On the other hand, a short interview with the child's former teachers, or in some cases, a check of the child's cumulative folder would make this information readily available to the remedial reading teacher and thus avoid duplication of the same type of efforts. Another example of data that may be readily available is information on the child's physical condition which could adversely affect the child's reading. A short interview with the child's parents can often provide information which will be helpful in planning the remedial program.

Some Single Causes of Reading Disability Are Overemphasized

Unfortunately some diagnosticians and remedial reading teachers become extremely interested in some particular aspect of reading and consequently have a tendency to overemphasize that aspect in their diagnoses and remedial work. This may happen as the result of the reading of a journal article on the subject, a report for a class, a speech at a professional meeting, etc. No professional person would deny the value of any of the above activities; however, you should guard against becoming so involved in diagnosis in any specific area that other important deficiencies are overlooked.

Other areas that often receive undue emphasis are the learning of vowel rules, syllable principles, and accent generalizations. The remedial reading teacher should remember that the learning of any of these is merely a means to an end; that end being the ability to properly attack and pronounce an unfamiliar word. If a child can already pronounce words on or above his grade level, or if he can readily pronounce difficult nonsense words, there is little reason to learn the vowel rules, syllable principles, or accent generalizations as word attack skills.

The diagnostician and remedial reading teacher may do well to constantly ask themselves such questions as: Do I consistently find myself teaching the same thing regardless of the original diagnosis? Do my diagnoses indicate that I constantly prescribe the same remediation? Do I use only one or two tests with which I am familiar that may tend to give me the same results each time? Do other diagnosticians concur with my findings and recommendations? Would the total number of disabled readers I have diagnosed show approximately the same percentage of reading problems in each category as reputable studies have indicated are the causes of reading disability?

Sometimes the Diagnosis Is Determined by
One Person and the Remedial Work Is Done
by Another Person

When a diagnosis is done by one person and turned over to another for remediation, communication problems often arise. Communication concerning reading deficiencies is sometimes difficult because of semantic differences in reading terminology. Helen Robinson (1970) states, "Examples of differences in terms and labels may be found by comparing articles dealing with reading in almost any publication. In learning to read, a child may be expected to identify words, discriminate words, recognize words, or perceive words."(p. 78) Unless the reading diagnostician has the ability to accurately communicate his findings to the person who will be carrying out the remedial procedures, the child is quite likely to receive inadequate or unnecessary help.

Most of the problems encountered in the area of communication between the diagnostician and teacher are a result of a lack of preciseness. For example, a part of one diagnostician's report read as follows:

"This child should be provided with help in word attack skills." Such a statement is of little value to a teacher since there are so many word attack skills. Even if the statement was narrowed to any one word attack skill such as phonics, the diagnostician should still be exact in describing what the child needs. For example, a report that reads as follows will provide much more direction for immediate remedial help:

"This child should be provided with help in learning the initial consonant blends, 'bl,' 'pl,' 'fl,' and 'pr.' He should then be given help in learning to blend them with various phonograms."

Another problem encountered when the diagnosis is done by one person and then turned over to another is that children who are exposed to a strange person in a testing situation often fail to perform up to their normal standards. When this happens, the person doing the remedial work will, of course, find discrepancies in the original diagnosis which will, in turn, lead to an inefficient diagnostic-remedial procedure.

Some Diagnosticians Come Up with the Same
Factors Time After Time

Most educational diagnosticians tend to rely on certain tests with which they have become familiar through continued use. The use of the same test or tests time-after-time can be beneficial in that the tester becomes more efficient in the diagnostic process. Efficiency in administration of tests is of little value, however, if the diagnostician fails to diagnose certain important causal factors and continually comes up with the same recommendations for remediation time-after-time.

Unfortunately, in reading psychologists' and educational diagnosticians' reports, I often find that nearly all reports even on different students diagnosed by one person contain the same recommendations. The reports on various students diagnosed by another person may contain different types of recommendations but again often contain the same recommendations for all students. All personnel dealing with the diagnosis of disabled readers should continually evaluate their findings and recommendations to determine whether they are generally in line with educational studies showing various causal factors and the percent of time we might expect each to occur.

We Sometimes Diagnose and Work on Factors
That Do Not Help Children's Reading

In most cases there is little value in diagnosing factors for which we either do not expect to provide remediation or for which remediation has not proven effective in the past. For example, Donald Hammill, Libby Goodman, and J. Lee Wiederholt (1974) summarized the research in the areas of eye-motor coordination and visual perception. They concluded that readers with visual perception problems, such as eye-motor coordination, discrimination of figure-ground, and position in space, were not helped by training in these areas per se. Therefore, unless these tests can be justified strictly for research purposes there seems to be little, if any, value in their routine administration in the public schools.

A child who has difficulty in discriminating a "b" from a "d" may, for example, also score low on Frostig's *Developmental Test of Visual Perception*[5] subtest "Position in Space." However, simply having the child read or write the letters of the alphabet will quickly enable the diagnostician to determine whether the child is making letter reversals. If he is, it seems more logical to work on the "b" and "d" problem directly, rather than to do the types of exercises recommended by Frostig when children obtain a poor score on the "Position in Space" subtest. In doing the type of remediation recommended by Frostig one only hopes that the remediation will transfer to the "b" and "d" reversal problem.

The remedial reading teacher and/or educational diagnostician should continually examine their diagnostic procedures to determine whether unnecessary testing is being done in terms of what is being provided in the remedial program. Care should also be taken to provide adequate diagnosis for any suspected areas of difficulty for which remediation has proven effective.

Previous Bias May Exert an Undue Influence

Few, if any, of us would deny that we are somewhat biased on matters such as politics, religion, and certain beliefs concerning education. We must, however, continually examine our own beliefs and practices to determine whether they are exerting an unhealthy influence in diagnosing and treating reading disabilities. It is all too easy, for example, to simply ignore research that indicates that our beliefs may be wrong and look for research that tends to confirm any bias that we may possess.

Reading personnel should constantly guard against developing attitudes

[5]Frostig, Marianne. *Developmental Test of Visual Perception.* Palo Alto: Consulting Psychologists Press, 1966.

which are likely to be detrimental to their diagnostic or remedial procedures. While serving as a reading consultant in the public schools, the author encountered a reading teacher with very little formal training in the teaching of reading. The procedures that the teacher was using were far from being in line with procedures that have proven their worth in the past. Still this teacher insisted that his ideas and methods were successful. A subsequent check of the standardized test scores of this teacher's classes during the four previous years indicated that his pupils class average had dropped about ten percentile points each year during the time he had taught them. There was certainly no doubt that his own personal bias concerning methodology was adversely affecting his pupils.

Experimentation should be encouraged and when certain procedures prove successful they should be adopted. On the other hand, when test results or experience proves that procedures are detrimental to the welfare of students, those procedures should be revised.

SUMMARY

Through a combination of research and experience remedial reading teachers have found that certain procedures can make their remedial reading programs more effective It is important to know which operational procedures have been successful and which have lacked success in the diagnostic process. Some of these have been discussed in this chapter. It is also important to know which procedures have been successful in the remedial process. These have also been discussed in this chapter. Quite often remedial reading programs have failed to achieve the kind of results that have been expected from students. The information presented in this chapter should help remedial reading teachers avoid the same mistakes.

Chapter 2: REFERENCES

Balow, Bruce. "The Long Term Effect of Remedial Reading Instruction," *The Reading Teacher*. Vol. 18, (April, 1965), 581–586.

Buerger, A. Theodore. "A Follow-up of Remedial Reading Instruction," *The Reading Teacher*. Vol. 21, (January, 1968), 329–334.

Cheatham, Richard Beauregard. "A Study of the Effects of Group Counseling on the Self-Concept and on the Reading Efficiency of Low-achieving Readers in a Public Intermediate School," Doctoral dissertation, The American University, 1968.

Dolen, Keith G. "Effects of Individual Counseling on Selected Test Scores for Delayed Readers," *Personnel and Guidance Journal*. Vol. 42, (May, 1964), 914–919.

Gardner, James, and Ransom, Grayce. "Academic Reorientation: A Counseling Approach to Remedial Readers," *The Reading Teacher*. Vol. 21, (March, 1968), 529–536.

Hammell, Donald; Goodman, Libby; and Wiederholt, J. Lee. "Visual-Motor Processes: Can We Train Them?" *The Reading Teacher*. Vol. 27, (February, 1974), 469–478.

Lillich, Joseph M. "Comparison of Achievement in Special Reading Classes Using Guidance, Skill-Content and Combination Approaches," Paper Presented at International Reading Association Conference, Boston, Massachusetts, (April, 1968), 1–11.

Muller, Sarah D., and Madsen, Charles H., Jr. "Group Desensitization for 'Anxious' Children with Reading Problems," *Psychology in the Schools*. Vol. 7, (April, 1970), 184–189.

Palardy, J. Michael. "For Johnny's Reading Sake," *The Reading Teacher*. Vol. 22, (May, 1969), 720–721.

Robinson, Helen. "Significant Unsolved Problems in Reading," *The Reading Teacher*. Vol. 14, (November, 1970), 77–82.

Shearer, E. "The Long-Term Effects of Remedial Education," *Educational Research*. Vol. 9, (June, 1967), 219–222.

A FRAMEWORK FOR THE DIAGNOSIS AND TEACHING OF EDUCATIONAL FACTORS

The first purpose of this chapter is to develop a framework for the diagnosis and remediation of educational factors in reading. The second purpose is to illustrate a scope and sequence of the commonly taught reading skills to enable the teacher to determine which reading skills a child should have mastered at various stages in his progression through the grades. This is then followed by a discussion which is intended to clarify the usage of materials for diagnosis, teaching, or reinforcement.

Many definitions for the act of reading have been proposed over the years. Many of these are very similar to the following: Reading is the act of interpreting, by the reader, what was written by the author. This definition, although somewhat useful for theoretical purposes in discussing the act of reading, is not concrete enough to be meaningful for the remedial teacher in the diagnosis and remediation of educational factors. For the purpose of diagnosis and remediation of educational factors you might want to think of reading as a process of recognizing words and of understanding words and ideas.

I often hear beginning teachers make such statements as, "I have a student in my class who is a good oral reader, but he can't seem to understand what he reads." Still others will say, "One of my students can really understand what he reads, but he just can't seem to say all of the words." When hearing this type of statement I am reminded of the story of the man who was raised in a Spanish speaking community. He spoke both Spanish and English but only learned to read and write English. During the process of learning to read he never seemed to have learned to "sound out" words, or as we would say in reading, he didn't learn sound-symbol correspondence. During his college years he began to date a young lady from Mexico City. One Christmas vacation when the young lady went home she sent the young man a letter written in Spanish. Since the young man had only learned to speak Spanish he could not read the letter. He solved the problem, however, by getting one of his friends to help him. His friend could not speak Spanish, but he could pronounce the words since Spanish is a phonemic language and his friend had a good knowledge of sound-symbol relationships. The essential point here was that neither one of the young men could "read" the letter. One of them could pronounce the words and one of them could understand the words and ideas, but it took both of them to "read" the letter.

Reading, then, as stated previously, is a process of recognizing words and understanding words and ideas. What the beginning teachers mentioned earlier meant was that certain students in their classes were either poor in their knowledge of sight words or word attack or they were poor in their comprehension of words and ideas. A lack of knowledge in either area would make a student a poor reader.

The scope of the reading skills as discussed thus far would be illustrated as follows:

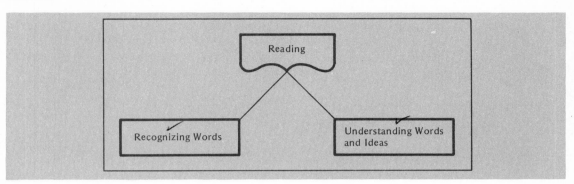

Figure 3–1.   Two basic categories of reading skills.

"Recognizing words" is usually broken down into two subdivisions (See Figure 3–1). These two subdivisions are "sight words" and "word attack skills." Here then are two situations for a reader who must recognize words. He will either have come in contact with a word enough times so that it is instantly recognized or, if it is not instantly recognized, he must apply one or more of the word attack skills in order to determine how to recognize and thus say or think that word.

If the word is one that the reader has come in contact with a number of times before, and it is recognized instantly, it is considered a sight word. The number of sight words in any one reader's storehouse of words will, of course, vary with such factors as the amount of previous reading the student has done, his grade level, and intelligence. For example, the word "and" will become a known sight word for most readers shortly after they begin to read because of its high utility in the English language. On the other hand, the word "sextant" would not become a sight word for most readers until much later in their life.

The term *sight vocabulary* is often used by authors and reading specialists to refer to the total stock of words that are recognized by a student by sight. In this case they would not be concerned with whether the student knew the meaning of the word, but only whether he could recognize it and say it instantly. For example, a word might be in a student's "recognition" vocabulary, but it may not be in his "meaning" vocabulary, or it may be in his "meaning" vocabulary and still not be in his "recognition" vocabulary. Still other authors reserve the word "vocabulary" strictly for "word-meaning." When the term "vocabulary building" is used, most authors are referring to the building of a word-meaning vocabulary at which time the word may or may not also be learned as a sight word. In this book the term "sight vocabulary" means the same as "sight words," i.e., simple word recognition. The term "vocabulary" used by itself indicates "meaning vocabulary."

Under the "sight word" category are two sub-categories. These are "basic sight words" and "other sight words." The term "basic sight word" usually refers to a certain list of *high utility words* (words that appear most often in print) compiled by writers and researchers in the field of reading. Examples of some of these are the Dolch List (1955), pp. 373–374; the Fry List (1972), pp. 58–63; the Harris-Jacobson List (1973), pp. 392–395; and the Ekwall List (1975, see Chapter 4). The term "basic sight word" is also used to simply indicate that a certain word is one of high utility which should be known as a sight word and should, therefore, not require the application of word analysis or word attack skills.

Listed under "sight words" is another category called "other sight words." This category includes all words known instantly or known without the use of word attack skills. The number of "other sight words" would, of course, vary from reader to reader and would vary within any one reader as he continues to come in contact with new words time after time. For example a word such as "establish" might require the application of word attack skills for quite a number of times in which a student encounters it, but it would eventually become a sight word. It would then be classified here as one of the "other sight words." That is, it would be known instantly by the student, but it would not be of such high utility that it would appear on someone's list as a "basic sight word."

The scope of the reading skills as explained this far would now be illustrated as follows:

As stated earlier, the other sub-category of "recognizing words" is "word

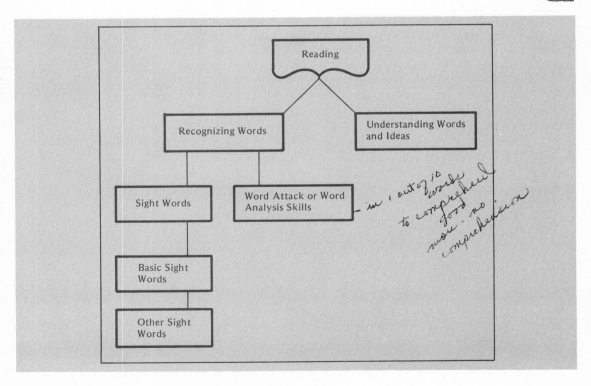

Figure 3–2. A partial breakdown of the skill of recognizing words.

attack skills" or "word analysis skills." When a reader does not have instant recognition of a word, then he must apply one or more of these word attack skills. The subcategories of "word attack skills" are usually referred to as "configuration clues," "context clues," "phonics," "structural analysis," "dictionary skills," and parts of the "study skills." Configuration clues refers to the hints a student receives by the overall shape or configuration of a word. The configuration of a word is influenced by such factors as length (elephant versus bed), use of capital and lower case letters (BED versus bed), use of extenders and descenders ("l," "b," versus "p," "j"), and use of double letters (look versus have). Context clues refers to the clues a student receives from a word by the way it is used in the context of a sentence. (The old car rattled as the farmer drove down the country _____ [road].) Another kind of context clue that is often useful to beginning readers is the picture context clue. It tells the reader what the word might be, based on a picture illustrating the reading passage. Phonics usually refers to the sound-symbol relationships between the small, usually non-meaning-bearing, parts of words. This would include learning the sounds represented by consonants, consonant blends, consonant digraphs, vowels, vowel teams, and special letter combinations. Phonics also includes the knowledge of phonetic generalizations, e.g., rules governing vowel sounds. Syllabication principles are also often considered as a phonics skill, although, they are sometimes listed under the category of structural analysis. Structural analysis is similar to phonics; however, the term as commonly used refers to larger parts of words that bear meaning, such as root words, suffixes, prefixes, word endings, apostrophe "s" to show possession, contractions, and compound words. The dictionary skills of course, apply to a number of abilities such as alphabetizing of letters and words, locating a specific word, using guide words, and interpreting preferred spellings. Some of the study skills are also helpful in word analysis such as the ability to find a word in an encyclopedia and/or dictionary. With the addition of the sub-categories of "word attack" or "word analysis" skills the scope of the reading skills would now be illustrated as in Figure 3–3.

Note the use of the broken line from the end of the listing of "word attack skills" to "study skills." The broken line indicates that only a part of the study skills would be considered as a subcategory of "word attack skills" and that the relationship would not be so direct as in the case of the other five sub-categories. The ability to use the encyclopedia would contribute to, or could be considered, a word attack skill, but many of the other study skills would not necessarily be related to the ability to attack words.

The problem of deriving sub-categories to illustrate the skills required for understanding words and ideas, or what is usually referred to as comprehension, is much more complicated and less clear-cut than the area of word attack or word analysis skills. Research to date has generally shown that we are not able to accurately differentiate more than about two or three broad factors. According to George and Evelyn Spache (1973) these factors might be referred to as a knowledge of word meanings, the ability to see relationships among ideas, and the ability to use reasoning processes.

Most commonly used measures of reading achievement only attempt to measure two broad categories of comprehension—vocabulary and reading comprehension. It would appear, then, that one would be justified in categorizing the

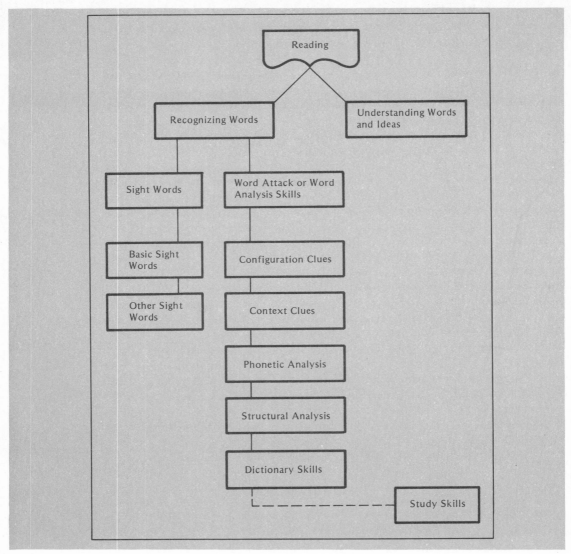

Figure 3–3. A breakdown of the skill of recognizing words.

subskills of comprehension as "vocabulary *important* development" and "other comprehension skills."

 Thomas Barrett (1967) suggests that the cognitive dimension for comprehension *usually get this far* categories might be classified as: "(a) literal meaning, (b) inference, (c) evaluation, and (d) appreciation." (p. 21) Literal meaning, as defined by Barrett, would be concerned with ideas and information explicitly stated in a reading selection. The first of these, in terms of pupil behavior would be "recognition" and the second of these would be "recall." Inference, as Barrett states, occurs when the student,

" . . . uses the ideas and information explicitly stated in the selection, his intuition, and his personal experience as a basis for conjectures and hypotheses." (p. 22)

In explaining his concept of evaluation Barrett states, "Purposes for reading and teachers' questions, in this instance, require responses by the student which indicate that he has arrived at a judgment by comparing ideas presented in the selection with external criteria provided by the teacher, other authorities or written sources, or with internal criteria provided by the reader's experiences, knowledge, or values. In essence, evaluation deals with judgments and focuses on qualities or correctness, worthwhileness, or appropriateness, feasibility, and validity." (p. 22)

Barrett's last category of appreciation would involve all of the other mentioned levels of thought, but would go beyond them. Barrett states, "Appreciation, as used here, calls for the student to be emotionally and aesthetically sensitive to the written work and to have a reaction to its psychological and artistic elements. For example, when a student verbalizes his feelings about part or all of a reading selection in terms of excitement, fear, dislike, or boredom, he is functioning at the appreciational level." (p. 23)

It should be kept in mind that Barrett's taxonomy of skills for comprehension are only suggested and could not necessarily be defended in terms of factoral analysis studies dealing with concretely measured categories. They do, however, add meaning to our goals for viewing and teaching these skills.

Using Barrett's categories under the category of "other comprehension skills" would then appear as in Figure 3–4.

In addition to the subskills of comprehension mentioned by Barrett a number of authors have listed other categories such as the ability to see "main ideas," "important details," "the author's purpose," "develop mental images," "see a sequence of ideas" or to see the "author's organization."

Note the broken line from "comprehension" to "study skills." This again indicates that the study skills have a relationship to, or contribute to, reading comprehension. This relationship is, however, less direct than the relationship between comprehension and the other sub-categories previously mentioned.

Perhaps this breakdown of the comprehension skills is not justified on the basis of research. I believe, however, that it is helpful to examine, in at least this much detail, what we have commonly believed to be some of the other subskills of comprehension. This list of subskills is probably incomplete, but there is little doubt that these subskills do account for a large part of the reasoning and relationship factors mentioned by Spache and Spache.

The relationships that are shown to exist in Figure 3–4 no doubt grossly oversimplify the reading act. For example, we know that the purpose and/or state of mind that a student might possess previous to reading a passage can greatly affect his comprehension. These might be considered as psychological factors and this should be shown in the comprehension part of Figure 3–4. There are, however, so many factors of this nature that it would be virtually impossible to illustrate them in a diagram. Furthermore, at the present time, we do not know how to measure many of these complex factors that are known to exist. Figure 3–4 then represents those relationships that are generally known to exist, and the educational factors in reading that, to some extent, can be measured.

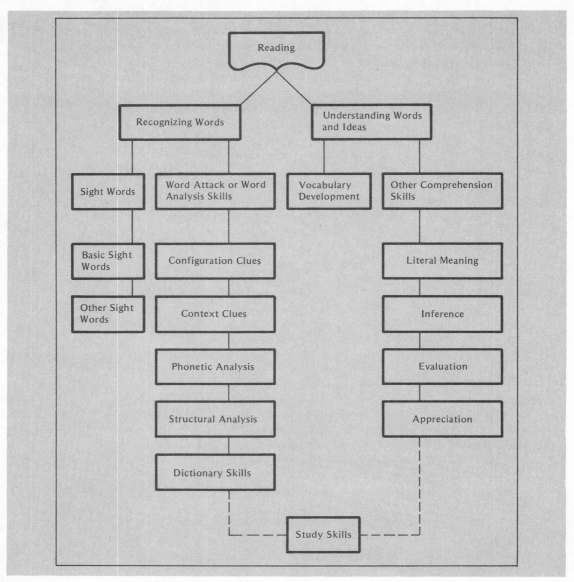

Figure 3–4. Scope of the reading skills.

Competencies That Students Should Achieve in Their Progression Through the Grades

If you were to wait until a secondary student was seriously retarded in reading, there would be no need to be concerned about which of the various skills should be tested. That is to say, you could simply assume that the student should have mastered all of the commonly tested reading skills and, therefore, it would be appropriate to test any or all of the reading skills. On the other hand, with a younger and less retarded reader you must be more familiar with the scope and sequence of the reading skills in order to avoid testing beyond the point at which that student should have normally progressed. It is imperative, then, that the reading diagnostician be familiar with the scope and sequence of reading skills. In this section reference will again be made to the skills and subskills presented in Figure 3–4. This time, however, we will be more concerned with a further breakdown of these skills and the points at which each of the various skills should have been mastered by a student with normal achievement.

It is also imperative that the classroom teacher become familiar with the scope and sequence of the reading skills in order to locate students with incipient reading problems. For example, a teacher who does not know when her students should have mastered the basic sight words is not likely to notice a student with a mild disability in this area until somewhat later when the problem becomes obvious. At that time the problem will, of course, be more difficult to correct and the student will not only be more retarded in his reading ability, but may also have developed concurrent psychological problems resulting from his difficulty with reading. In order to determine the point at which each of the reading skills should be mastered, five sets of basal readers[1] were analyzed. As one might expect, the points at which the authors of the various series of basal readers chose to introduce each of the skills varied to some extent. For the diagnostician, however, these minor disagreements as to time of introduction of the reading skills are not extremely important. What the diagnostician must be concerned with is the latest point at which all authors agree the skills should have been taught. This is the point at which the diagnostician can test for any particular skill and safely assume the student has been taught that skill.

An important point for the diagnostician to keep in mind is that some of the reading skills should definitely be mastered and others will be extended and refined ad infinitum. For example, the basic sight words (Dolch's List) should definitely be known by average students by the middle of their third year in school. On the other hand, a student's knowledge of other sight words will continue to expand throughout his lifetime. Likewise, there is no point at which one can assume the comprehension skills are completely mastered. The ability to make inferences from a paragraph, for example, probably continues to improve as our vocabulary and background of experiences continue to expand. Skills that are extended and refined rather than completely mastered should then be learned by the student and should also be tested; however, we should keep in mind that a student who continues to learn will also continue to improve in his ability to use these skills. In the breakdown of the reading skills that follows you will note the use of single and cross-hatched lines which appear under various grade levels (see key). The level at which either of these appears is opposite the listing of that skill or subskill and indicates the general point at which you could assume that the skill had been taught and likewise the point at which you could logically assume the student should have mastered (in some cases) or should have a knowledge of the use of that skill. In interpreting the chart you should keep in mind that the designation of grade level serves only as a general guideline. Also, in using the scope and sequence chart several precautions need to be observed. First, you should not consider any one skill that appears on the chart to

[1]Publishers whose books were analyzed were as follows: Allyn and Bacon, Inc., American Book Co., Ginn and Co., Houghton Mifflin Co., and The Macmillan Co.

necessarily be a prerequisite to a child learning to read. For example, knowledge of vowel rules is only necessary if a child cannot correctly pronounce various short and long vowel sounds. The learning of vowel rules is only a means to an end. If the child can pronounce various vowel sounds and combinations of vowels and vowel controlling letters then there is no need for the child to master that skill. Many very good adult readers can pronounce almost any word or syllable; however, it would be very difficult for many of these same adults to give the vowel sounds in isolation. It should again be emphasized that the following chart does not attempt to point to a specific time when a skill should be taught. The points of time illustrated represent the stage when all of the basal reader programs examined agree that the skill should be known.

A final, but very important, consideration is that there are often considerably different levels of development of a certain skill. For example, a child may be able to recognize and circle one of four phonemes that is the same as the initial sound heard in a word pronounced by a tester. However, he may not be able to pronounce the same phoneme in a strange word that he encounters in his reading. This would, of course, be the level of competency that would be necessary in actual reading. This point will be emphasized again in later chapters as methods of testing for various competencies are discussed.

SUMMARY

In order to begin doing diagnosis work in the field of reading the remedial reading teacher must have a thorough knowledge of the scope and sequence of the reading skills. The teacher must not only understand what needs to be diagnosed in terms of educational problems, but must also know when to expect each student to have mastered each of the reading skills.

In doing diagnostic work it should be kept in mind that we have identified certain skills which are definitely necessary for a student to learn to read. On the other hand there are some areas in which skills have been identified as being helpful to some readers in learning to read, but these same skills are often not known by some very excellent readers. In other words some of the reading skills are only a means to an end, and if the student has already reached the end there is little or no use in diagnosing the skills which supposedly lead to that end.

Classification of Diagnostic, Teaching, and Reinforcement Activities

The diagnostician and remedial reading teacher should keep in mind that there is a distinct difference between diagnosis, teaching, and reinforcement activities. For example, when a student does a page in a workbook in which he is required to use concepts taught in a previous lesson we would not necessarily expect him to "learn" anything new. We would, however, expect to "reinforce" these previously taught

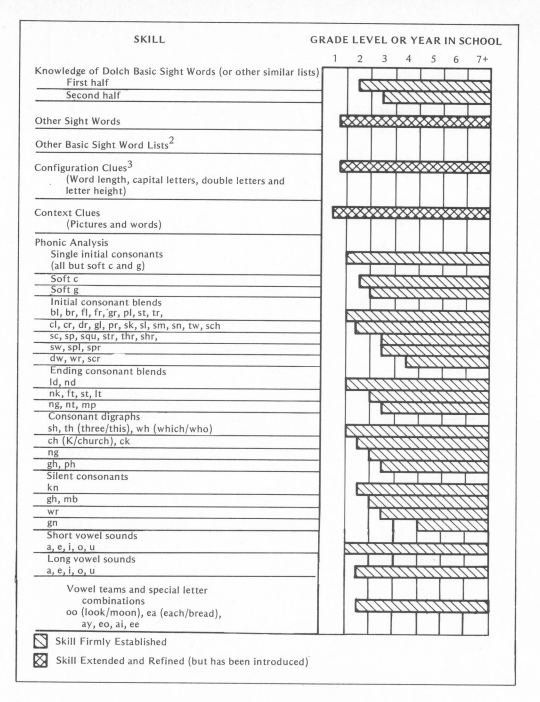

SKILL	GRADE LEVEL OR YEAR IN SCHOOL
	1 2 3 4 5 6 7+

Knowledge of Dolch Basic Sight Words (or other similar lists)
   First half
   Second half

Other Sight Words

Other Basic Sight Word Lists[2]

Configuration Clues[3]
   (Word length, capital letters, double letters and letter height)

Context Clues
   (Pictures and words)

Phonic Analysis
   Single initial consonants
   (all but soft c and g)
   Soft c
   Soft g
   Initial consonant blends
   bl, br, fl, fr, gr, pl, st, tr,
   cl, cr, dr, gl, pr, sk, sl, sm, sn, tw, sch
   sc, sp, squ, str, thr, shr,
   sw, spl, spr
   dw, wr, scr
   Ending consonant blends
   ld, nd
   nk, ft, st, lt
   ng, nt, mp
   Consonant digraphs
   sh, th (three/this), wh (which/who)
   ch (K/church), ck
   ng
   gh, ph
   Silent consonants
   kn
   gh, mb
   wr
   gn
   Short vowel sounds
   a, e, i, o, u
   Long vowel sounds
   a, e, i, o, u

   Vowel teams and special letter combinations
   oo (look/moon), ea (each/bread),
   ay, eo, ai, ee

◩ Skill Firmly Established

⊠ Skill Extended and Refined (but has been introduced)

[2]*See the graded list of basic sight words compiled by the author which appears in Chapter 4.*

[3]*The use of configuration clues is taught in grade one, but older students continue to use and improve in this skill as their knowledge of structural analysis increases.*

SKILL	GRADE LEVEL OR YEAR IN SCHOOL
	1 2 3 4 5 6 7+
oa (oats, ow (o/cow), ir, ur, or, ar, aw, ou (trout), oi, oy, al, er, au, ew	▨ (grades 3–7+)
Rules for y sound	▨ (grades 3–7+)
Vowel rules for open and closed syllables	▨ (grades 3–7+)
Syllable principles (1, 2, and 3) 1. When two like consonants stand between two vowels the word is usually divided between the consonants.	▨ (grades 3–6)
2. When two unlike consonants stand between two vowels the word is usually divided between the consonants (unless the consonants are digraphs or blends).	
3. When a word ends in a consonant and "le" the consonant usually begins the last syllable.	
Syllable Principles (4, 5, and 6) 4. Compound words are usually divided between word parts and between syllables within these parts.	
5. Prefixes and suffixes are usually separate syllables.	
6. Do not divide between the letters in consonant digraphs and consonant blends.	
Structural Analysis Word endings ed, ing, 's, d	▨ (grades 2–5)
er, es	▨ (grades 2–6)
est	▨ (grades 3–6)
Word families all, at, et, em, etc.	▨ (grades 1–7+)
Word roots	▨ (grades 1–7+)
Contractions let's, didn't, it's, won't, that's, can't, wasn't, isn't, hadn't	▨ (grades 3–6)
don't, I.ll, we'll, I.ve, he'll, hasn't, haven't, aren't, I'm, he's we're, you're, what's, there's, she's, wouldn't, she'll, here's	▨ (grades 4–6)
ain't, couldn't, they're, they'd	▨ (grades 4–6)
you'll, she'd, weren't, I'd, you've, you'd, we'd, anybody'd, there'll, we've, who'll, he'd, who'd, doesn't, where's, they've, they'll	▨ (grades 4–6)
Possessives	▨ (grades 3–6)
Accent Rules[4] 1. In two-syllable words, the first syllable is usually accented.	▨ (grades 5–6)
2. In inflected or derived forms the primary accent usually falls on or within the root word.	▨ (grades 6–7+)
3. If two vowels are together in the last syllable of a word, it may be a clue to an accented final syllable.	▨ (grades 6–7+)

[4]*At present no definitive research is available as to which accent generalizations are of high enough utility to make them worthwhile to teach. The four listed here are believed to be quite consistent and also of high utility.*

60

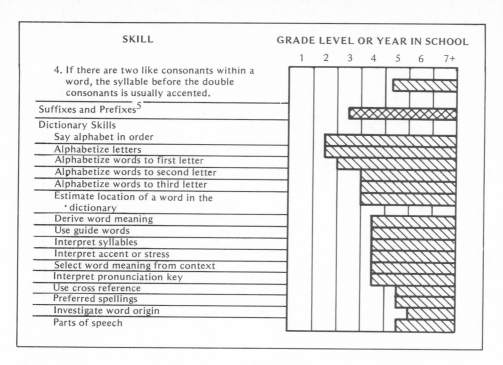

SKILL	GRADE LEVEL OR YEAR IN SCHOOL
	1 2 3 4 5 6 7+
4. If there are two like consonants within a word, the syllable before the double consonants is usually accented.	
Suffixes and Prefixes[5]	
Dictionary Skills	
Say alphabet in order	
Alphabetize letters	
Alphabetize words to first letter	
Alphabetize words to second letter	
Alphabetize words to third letter	
Estimate location of a word in the dictionary	
Derive word meaning	
Use guide words	
Interpret syllables	
Interpret accent or stress	
Select word meaning from context	
Interpret pronunciation key	
Use cross reference	
Preferred spellings	
Investigate word origin	
Parts of speech	

[5]*The prefixes "a" and "un" should be known by the middle of the third year in school. From that point on, the student should continue to extend and refine his knowledge of prefixes. This extension and refinement would continue throughout his elementary and high school years. The suffixes "er" and "ly" should be known by the middle of the second year of school. From that point on the student should continue to extend and refine his knowledge of suffixes. This extension and refinement would continue throughout his elementary and high school years. (The author suggests that "known" in this case only means that the student recognizes the prefix and/or suffix, but that he not be required to know its meaning.)*

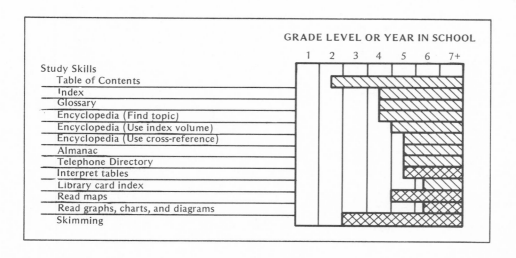

	GRADE LEVEL OR YEAR IN SCHOOL
	1 2 3 4 5 6 7+
Study Skills	
Table of Contents	
Index	
Glossary	
Encyclopedia (Find topic)	
Encyclopedia (Use index volume)	
Encyclopedia (Use cross-reference)	
Almanac	
Telephone Directory	
Interpret tables	
Library card index	
Read maps	
Read graphs, charts, and diagrams	
Skimming	

Examples

1. Basic sight word lists

Provides the teacher with diagnostic information on the basic sight word knowledge of the student. The *student learns little or nothing unless he is told each word as he misses it.*

2. Cloze technique for assessing student's level of reading comprehension (see Chapter 11)

If used only for finding a percentage score of right and wrong answers to determine grade placement, little or no teaching is done. If the exercises are discussed after the student has completed them, some teaching and possibly some reinforcement takes place.

3. Informal reading inventories

Provides the teacher with an overall grade placement and considerable information on specific weaknesses. Little teaching is accomplished other than when aid is given when a word is unknown.

Teaching Materials

1. Material held in the hands of students and explained by the teacher

This is a typical teaching situation. If it is material that is being reviewed, then it may teach *and* reinforce. Unless the teacher provides for some type of feedback, little or no diagnostic information will be derived.

2. Worksheets used in conjunction with a tape recorder

If the directions on the audiotape provide for instruction on how to do the worksheets, and then give the student the answers and provide him with an opportunity to correct any that are wrong, this would teach and reinforce. If provisions are made for the teacher to see which answers were missed, some diagnosis may also take place.

Reinforcement Materials

1. Worksheets

Most worksheets only provide for reinforcement of concepts that have already been learned but which need to be mastered more thoroughly.

2. Reading games

Many games *do not* teach since they require that nothing new be learned in order to play the game, e.g., recalling and using previously learned material. Games in which one pupil competes with another may teach, for example, if one pupil creates words from initial consonants or consonant blends and phonograms or uses words in sentences in which the other pupil learns the meaning from context.

concepts so that the student would become thoroughly familiar with their use and thus be less likely to forget them. On the other hand, a page in a programmed textbook would be likely to teach, as well as reinforce, various concepts. Most testing is done so that the teacher can learn more about the student, but testing, as such, has no immediate benefit to the student unless he is provided with answers to the questions upon which he is being tested.

The double-column listing illustrates the three categories (Testing or diagnosis, teaching, and reinforcement or practice) and some activities that might be associated with each. As you examine the various suggestions in the following chapters for remediation of various reading skills, keep these three categories in mind. That is, do not expect a straight practice exercise to teach or do not expect a teaching exercise to test, although examination of student performance on reinforcement or practice materials will provide some diagnostic information.

In using the diagnostic, teaching, and reinforcement materials that appear in this text as well as in other textbooks and commercially or teacher-made materials you should then consider your overall instructional purpose and use the appropriate materials to accomplish this purpose.

Chapter 3:   REFERENCES

Barrett, Thomas C., ed. *The Evaluation of Children's Reading Achievement. Perspectives in Reading No. 8.* Newark, Delaware: International Reading Association, 1967.

Dolch, Edward W. *Methods in Reading.* Champaign, Illinois: The Garrard Publishing Co., 1955.

Ekwall, Eldon E. *Corrective Reading System.* Glenview, Illinois: Psychotechnics, Inc., 1975.

Fry, Edward. *Reading Instruction for Classroom and Clinic.* New York: McGraw-Hill, 1972.

Harris, Albert J., and Jacobson, Milton D. "Basic Vocabulary for Beginning Reading," *The Reading Teacher.* 26, (January, 1973), 392–395.

Spache, George D., and Spache, Evelyn B. *Reading in the Elementary School.* 2d ed. Boston: Allyn and Bacon, Inc., 1973.

4

DIAGNOSIS AND REMEDIATION OF EDUCATIONAL FACTORS: *letter knowledge and sight words*

One purpose of this chapter is to examine the need for, and methods of, testing for letter knowledge and knowledge of sight words and basic sight words. A second purpose is to examine some of the pros and cons of each method. A third purpose of Chapter 4 is to discuss some ways of teaching letter knowledge, sight words, and basic sight words.

PART A.   *diagnosis*

✓   ALPHABET KNOWLEDGE

A number of research studies have shown that letter knowledge is not necessarily a prerequisite for learning to read. On the other hand numerous studies have also shown that children who begin their schooling with a knowledge of the ABC's are more likely to become better readers than children who lack this knowledge. For some time this was taken to mean that letter knowledge was helpful or necessary in learning to read. Most authorities now agree, however, that knowledge of the ABC's, for entering school-age children, is simply indicative of a host of factors that are often conducive to learning to read. Among these factors are a natural potential for learning to read, educational level of parents, and good reading environment at home.

It should be stressed, however, that children who reach the middle or upper elementary grades without a thorough knowledge of the alphabet are quite likely to be disabled readers. It should also be stressed that, although children *can* learn to read without being able to identify the name of each letter, it becomes a difficult task in most classrooms simply because of communication problems. Furthermore, children who cannot distinguish a *b* from a *d* or a *q* from a *p* are likely to encounter a great deal of difficulty in learning to read. For these reasons a check on children's knowledge of the alphabet should be included as a regular part of the diagnostic procedure.

Beginning teachers and inexperienced diagnosticians are likely to take it for granted that children in the middle and upper grade levels possess a thorough knowledge of the alphabet. Testing at this level soon reveals, however, that a rather large percent of disabled readers still experience difficulty in this area. Since the diagnosis for alphabet knowledge is so quick and simple, it should be included as one of the beginning procedures.

One procedure that is relatively easy is to put the letters of the alphabet on two cards approximately 5 in. × 8 in. Put the lower case alphabet on one card and the upper case alphabet on the other. On one side of the card you may wish to type the letters with a primary typewriter or print them by hand. On side two of the card you can then reproduce what is on side one plus any directions you may wish to look at while the child looks at side one. It is also better to put the letters in random order since some children will have learned the alphabet song or will have simply learned the alphabet in order which would, in turn, make it appear as though they know letters that, in reality, they do not know.

Another procedure that you may wish to use instead of or in addition to that described above is to ask the child to write the alphabet. After he finishes you may wish to ask him to write any omitted letters or any he appeared to have difficulty with while writing them.

Flash cards with one letter on each card also work well for testing alphabet knowledge. Some disabled readers prefer to work with flash cards since they tend to have an aversion to a typical reading type situation in which the letters are printed on a line. In either case, it will be necessary to note letters with which the student has difficulty. In using flash cards you may simply put all the troublesome cards on one pile and the known cards on another. After the testing is completed you can then take note of letters that need remediation. If the 5 in. × 8 in. card system is used you may wish to have a record sheet with the letters in the same sequence as they are in on the card so that they can be marked as they are missed.

Some children will have a great deal of difficulty with many, or nearly all, letters. When this is the case, you should then proceed to the next easier task in alphabet knowledge. This involves having the child identify letters as you call them. The 5 in. × 8 in. card will work well for this, or you may wish to arrange flash cards so the child can see at least five to ten of them at a time. A few extremely disabled readers will not even be able to accomplish this task. When this is the case, you may wish to determine whether the child is able to match letters, which is a task still easier than identifying them when their names are called.

The subtest of the *Durrell Analysis of Reading Difficulty*[1] (The Naming Letters—Identifying Letters Named—Matching Letters subtest) contains materials for doing the testing outlined above. If this test is available for your use you may simply wish to use it instead of constructing your own testing materials. The *Sipay Word Analysis Test*[2] and the *Corrective Reading System*[3] also contain tests for alphabet knowledge.

[1]Durrell, Donald D. *Durrell Analysis of Reading Difficulty.* New York: Harcourt, Brace & World, Inc., 1955.

[2]Sipay, Edward R. *Sipay Word Analysis Tests.* Cambridge, Massachusetts: Educators Publishing Service, Inc., 1974.

[3]Ekwall, Eldon E. *Corrective Reading System.* Glenview, Illinois: Psychotechnics, Inc., 1975.

Sometimes the words *sight vocabulary* are used to refer to overall sight word knowledge. And, although the term sight vocabulary is a proper one, in this case it should be stressed that this discussion will be concerned only with instant recognition of words and not with meaning vocabulary. The difference between "sight words" and "basic sight words" was discussed in Chapter 3. However, it should again be stressed that the terms are not being used interchangeably. *Sight words* refer to all words any one reader can recognize instantly, while *basic sight words* refer to a designated list of sight words, usually of high utility, that appear on someone's list. Any word if read enough times can become a sight word, and thus each of us possesses a different sight vocabulary depending upon such factors as our occupation, reading interests, and ability to remember. However, anyone reading above middle third grade level would have the same basic sight word vocabulary since we would instantly recognize all of the commonly designated high utility words.

Because of the difference in meaning of the terms *sight word vocabulary* and *basic sight word vocabulary*, techniques for diagnosis of each will be discussed separately. In testing for sight word knowledge we usually use a sampling of words referred to as a *graded sight word list* while in testing for basic sight word knowledge we usually test the entire population of words on a designated list. The following discussion explains the need for, and methods of testing for, knowledge of basic sight words.

A number of researchers and writers have studied the utility of various words. Although these studies are seldom in exact agreement because of the differences in the materials they choose to study, they are in general agreement concerning the percent of total running words that are accounted for by certain numbers of words. Table 4-I shows a general summary of the results of these studies.[4] In interpreting these figures you should keep in mind that the percent of total running words for each specific number of words is likely to be slightly higher for beginning reading materials and slightly lower for adult reading materials.

Words such as *I*, *the*, and, *and* make up the highest utility words and appear so often in reading matter that it is imperative that children know these as sight words. As Table 4-I also shows, even in learning only approximately 200 words a child is likely to have mastered considerably more than one-half of the words he is likely to encounter in his reading. As you will also note, the percentage of utility begins to drop off rather rapidly after a child has learned the 500 words most used in his reading. For this reason most basic sight word lists contain from two hundred to five hundred words.

[4]Stone, Clarence R. "Vocabularies of Twenty Preprimers," *Elementary School Journal*. Vol. 41, (February, 1941), 423–429.

Stone, Clarence R. "Most Important 150 Words for Beginning Reading," *Educational Method*. Vol. 18, (January, 1939), 192–195.

Hockett, J. A. "Comparative Analysis of the Vocabularies of Twenty-Nine Second Readers," *Journal of Educational Research*. Vol. 31, (May, 1938), 665–671.

Curtis, H. M. "Wide Reading for Beginners," *Journal of Educational Research*. Vol. 32, (December, 1938) 255–262.

Table 4-I. The percent of total running words in reading materials accounted for by various numbers of words

Number of Words	Percent of Total Running Words
3	8 — 12
10	20 — 25
100	60 — 65
200	66 — 70
500	75 — 80
1000	83 — 85
1500	87 — 88
2000	89 — 90
3000	91 — 92
5000	92.5 — 93.5

The importance of learning to read and spell high utility words was emphasized by Richard Madden (1945) in a study of low and high utility words. Madden pointed out that in spelling there is very little value in attempting to teach students to spell words of lower utility until they have completely mastered all of the words of high utility. To illustrate this futility Madden states that a child in grade five with only five percent misspellings in a random sample of the first 500 words in frequency will make more errors in writing than if he misspells all 600 words in the commonly designated list for grade five. The same concept is, of course, true for reading.

In a more recent study of the high frequency words in popular juvenile trade books, William Durr (1973) found that ten words were of such high frequency, in the eighty books studied, that a young reader could expect to meet one of the ten words in nearly every four words read. Durr further stated that the 188 high frequency words he listed, although making up only six percent of all the different words found, would make up nearly 70 percent of the running words in print in the eighty library books he studied.

Studies such as those mentioned above illustrate the importance of learning certain "core" or "basic" sight words instantly so that no word analysis skills are required when a student encounters them in print. Furthermore, many of these high utility words are not phonetically regular and do not lend themselves to phonic word attack. Glen Gagon (1966) quotes Arthur Heilman as saying that approximately 35 percent of the usual primary reading vocabulary is phonetically regular. I have analyzed my own basic sight word list and find it to be from 30 to 77 percent phonetically regular depending on the number of phonic rules applied.

A discussion of "how" to test for knowledge of basic sight words may at first appear so elementary that it would seem that almost anyone could, and would, be likely to find this an easy task. During the past several years, however, I have researched several different methods and found the results obtained differ considerably depending on the method employed. There has also been considerable controversy over whether basic sight words should be tested in or out of context.

Many people assume that children know more basic sight words, which are often referred to as *service words*, when they are used in context than when they are not used in context. However, there seems to be little evidence that the context setting of most service words is such that it is of great value in helping the student with word identification. H. Alan Robinson (1963), in a study of techniques of word identification, found that only about one-seventh of one percent of the words he studied were identified by students through context clues alone. Even when context, configuration, and phonic and structural elements in initial and final positions were all used together, students only scored 3.93 correct out of twenty-two possible responses.

I have also heard reading specialists say it is not "fair" to the child to test a word out of context. First of all, we might say, "What is fair?" Even if the context were a valuable aid in word identification some of the time, we would not want a child to get a word right in one situation and not know the same word at another time when it was not used in as meaningful a context. What seems unfair to the child then, is to test him on a word in meaningful context and later find that he does not really know the word when it is not in a meaningful context. If testing words in isolation is more difficult, then we should test them that way since we are more likely to discover words that may later prove difficult for the child. Again, remember that basic sight words appear so often that children cannot afford to miss or be unsure of any of them. In reality, testing a word in a meaningful context may be depriving them of the opportunity to learn it. This should not be construed to mean, however, that I am necessarily suggesting that basic sight words be "taught" in isolation.

One of the points stressed in Chapter 2 was that you should always try to test in a situation that is analagous to actually reading. This principle is extremely important in the case of basic sight words. A common mistake that is often made by beginning reading teachers is thinking that they can use a group test to assess children's knowledge of basic sight words. A group test often used for this purpose is the Dolch Basic Sight Word Test.[5] In using it the teacher gives each student a sheet of paper that has numbers down the left hand column of the page. Opposite each number are four words. The teacher calls out one of the four words, and each child is expected to underline or circle the word that is the same as the one called by the teacher. One of the problems with this type of test is that even if a child did not know any of the words he would be likely to get one-fourth of them right by simply guessing. A second problem with this type of test is that it is not analagous to actually reading; i.e., underlining a word when you hear it is much easier than seeing a word and saying it. The author's research has shown that many children who get almost every word right on this type of test will miss from twenty-five to fifty words when they are required to take a test in which they are to look at words and say them. Because of these problems it seems logical to conclude that any attempt to assess children's basic sight word knowledge with a group test is of little value.

The problem then becomes one of how to best test the child in a one-to-one situation. This, of course, is not difficult, but even here there are some important considerations. One can simply give a child a list of words and ask him to read them while you mark his right and wrong responses on a similar list. We have found,

[5]Dolch, Edward W. *Basic Sight Word Test*. Champaign, Illinois: Garrard Press, 1942.

however, in trying this method with children in our University Reading Center, that disabled readers often get tense when confronted with a long list of words and will, in turn, make more errors than if the words are presented one at a time on flash cards. A further problem with this method is that it is difficult to control the length of exposure that the child has to each word. What happens, in reality, is that this often becomes a "word analysis" test where the child has time to apply various word attack skills to each word. This can be prevented to some extent by using a card and sliding it over each word after the child has been exposed to the word for about one second. This, however, is difficult to judge and some children resent having you cover the word if it is difficult for them.

Perhaps the most practical method for most teachers and/or diagnosticians is to put the words on flash cards and simply give the student about a one-second exposure to each word. The teacher can also make this more of a game situation. All of the words that the child gets right can be put in one pile, or given to the child and all of those gotten wrong can be put in another pile or kept by the teacher. After the testing is completed the child can be asked to compile a list of the words missed so that a permanent record may be kept. If you choose to use this method you may also wish to color code the cards according to levels, e.g., green for all pre-primer words, or pink for all primer words.

In using flash cards it is also convenient for the teacher to have a record sheet on which to mark right and wrong responses as the child looks at each card. The cards may be kept in the same order as they appear on the record sheet by punching a hole in one end of each card and putting the cards on a ring.

In the author's experience the best method for testing children's basic sight knowledge is with a filmstrip and tachistoscopic testing device. The basic sight word list that appears at the end of Part A of this chapter is available for use on the Tachomatic 500®.[6] In using this device you simply insert the filmstrip in the Tachomatic 500® and set the machine on a speed of about 57½ which flashes a word on the screen every 1½ seconds. This gives an actual exposure time of slightly under one second. Scoring sheets are also available from the same company which, of course, have the words printed on them in the same order in which they appear on the filmstrip.

The advantages of using this method are that it enables you to test a child on all of the basic sight words in a period of only about seven minutes. It also leaves both hands free for scoring and controls the length of time each word is exposed to the child. A further advantage of using this method is that the words are being advanced by the machine. The child is not tempted to say, "Wait, let me see that one again," or "Let me have a longer look at the words." Thus, the teacher does not lose rapport with the child. The only disadvantage to this system is the cost of the original equipment. However, the Tachomatic 500® was designed as a training device and if it is already available in your school, it would only be necessary to obtain the filmstrip and record forms.

You should find the basic sight word list that follows helpful in your own diagnostic work. It is a part of the *Corrective Reading System* that is designed to test children and correct various skills before they cause children to become seriously

[6]Manufactured by Psychotechnics, Inc., Glenview, Illinois.

V=knows word   O = make word card   ___ =on card

PRE-PRIMER

a	do	here	look	put	two
and	down	him	make	run	water
are	eat	his	my	said	we
away	for	house	no	the	what
be	get	I	not	then	where
big	go	in	of	this	who
but	good	it	oh	three	will
can	has	know	one	to	you
come	have	like	play	too	your
did	her	little			

PRIMER

about	came	help	on	some	up
after	could	how	other	something	us
all	day	is	over	stop	very
am	find	jump	ran	take	want
an	fly	let	red	that	was
around	from	man	ride	them	way
as	funny	may	sat	there	went
back	give	me	saw	they	when
blue	green	mother	see	time	would
by	had	now	she	tree	yes
call	he	old	so		

FIRST READER

again	buy	girl	Mrs.	rabbit	think
any	children	got	much	read	thought
ask	cold	happy	must	shall	took
at	color	high	name	side	under
ate	cry	if	never	sleep	walk
ball	dog	into	new	soon	well
been	door	just	night	stand	were
before	far	laugh	or	tell	white
began	fast	light	out	than	why
better	father	long	party	thank	with
black	five	more	please	their	work
boy	four	morning	pretty	these	yellow
brown	fun	Mr.	pull		

READER 2

always	end	grow	live	place	ten
another	enough	hand	made	right	thing
because	even	hard	many	round	those
best	every	head	men	say	together
book	eye	hold	near	school	told
both	fall	home	next	should	until
box	first	hot	once	show	wait
bring	found	hurt	only	sit	warm
carry	friend	keep	open	six	which
clean	full	kind	out	start	while
cut	gave	last	own	still	wish
does	going	left	pick	sure	year
each					

Handwritten notes (right side):

Not on this list but on my cards: (Harris)

cat -PP	fish	boat
zoo	duck	birthday
TV	dress	bike
sound	daddy	cage
sun	cow	catch
stopped	can't	coat
money	car	dark
miss	cake	didn't
kitten	bear	drop
it's	bed	farm
ice	bee	fat
I'll	bus	feet
hop	airplane	fight
hill	along	fire
hen	animal	food
hat	build	goat
grass	bird	#gone
fox	behind	good-by
	barn	#guess
	bark	game
	balloon	hair
	bag	hear
	baby	hello
		horse
		hurry

READER 2

dear	present	today
done	seem	try
drink	seven	turn
most	sing	use
off	small	wash
people	such	write

READER 3

also	its
don't	king
draw	leave
eight	myself
goes	upon
grand	

disabled readers. This list, incidently, contains all of the Dolch words, the first 200 words of the Fry List, and words found common to eight sets of basal readers.

Sight Words in General

Graded sight word lists are usually used to assess children's knowledge of sight words in general or reading level in relation to word knowledge. In doing this it is also possible, in many cases, to make a close estimation of a child's overall reading level. A number of graded sight word lists are available; however, one that I have found to be extremely useful is the San Diego Quick Assessment List.[7] A description of the list, directions for its use, and the list itself follow:

PP	PRIMER	1	2
see	you	road	our
play	come	live	please
me	not	thank	myself
at	with	when	town
run	jump	bigger	early
go	help	how	send
and	is	always	wide
look	work	night	believe
can	are	spring	quietly
here	this	today	carefully

3	4	5	6
city	decided	scanty	bridge
middle	served	business	commercial
moment	amazed	develop	abolish
frightened	silent	considered	trucker
exclaimed	wrecked	discussed	apparatus
several	improved	behaved	elementary
lonely	certainly	splendid	comment
drew	entered	acquainted	necessity
since	realized	escaped	gallery
straight	interrupted	grim	relativity

7	8	9	10	11
amber	capacious	conscientious	zany	galore
dominion	limitation	isolation	jerkin	rotunda
sundry	pretext	molecule	nausea	capitalism
capillary	intrigue	ritual	gratuitous	prevaricate
impetuous	delusion	momentous	linear	risible
blight	immaculate	vulnerable	inept	exonerate
wrest	ascent	kinship	legality	superannuate
enumerate	acrid	conservatism	aspen	luxuriate
daunted	binocular	jaunty	amnesty	piebald
condescend	embankment	inventive	barometer	crunch

[7]La Pray, Margaret, and Ross, Ramon. "The Graded Word List: Quick Guage of Reading Ability," *Journal of Reading.* Vol. 12 (January, 1969), 305–307. (Reprinted with permission of the authors and the International Reading Association.)

ADMINISTRATION

1. Type out each list of ten words on index card.
2. Begin with a card that is at least two years below the student's grade level assignment.
3. Ask the student to read the words aloud to you. If he misreads any on the list, drop to easier lists until he makes no errors. This indicates the base level.
4. Write down all incorrect responses, or use diacritical marks on your copy of the test. For example, *lonely* might be read and recorded as lovely. *Apparatus* might be recorded as *a per' a tus*.
5. Encourage the student to read words he does not know so that you can identify the techniques he uses for word identification.
6. Have the student read from increasingly difficult lists until he misses at least three words.

ANALYSIS

1. The list in which a student misses no more than one of the ten words is the level at which he can read independently. Two errors indicate his instructional level. Three or more errors identify the level at which reading material will be too difficult for him.
2. An analysis of a student's errors is useful. Among those which occur with greatest frequency are the following:

Error	*Example*
reversal	*ton* for *not*
consonant	*now* for *how*
consonant clusters	*state* for *straight*
short vowel	*cane* for *can*
long vowel	*wid* for *wide*
prefix	*inproved* for *improved*
suffix	*improve* for *improved*
miscellaneous	(accent, omission of

3. As with other reading tasks, teacher observation of student behavior is essential. Such things as posture, facial expression, and voice quality may signal restlessness, lack of assurance, or frustration while reading.

Other sources of graded word lists are the *Botel Reading Inventory*,[8] the *Diagnostic Reading Scales*,[9] and the *Wide Range Achievement Test*.[10] The results of the *Wide Range Achievement Test* tend to be spuriously high in many cases. Perhaps part of this problem lies in the fact that the norms are becoming outdated.

[8]Botel, Morton. *Botel Reading Inventory*. Chicago: Follett, 1966.

[9]Spache, George. *Diagnostic Reading Scales*. 2d ed. Monterey, California: California Test Bureau, 1972.

[10]Jastak, J. F., and Jastak, S. R. *The Wide Range Achievement Test*. Wilmington, Delaware: Guidance Associates, 1965.

We know that, as a rule, children at any given grade level read better than they did ten years ago and children ten years ago read better than children read twenty years ago, etc. Thus, tests with outdated norms tend to place children at a higher reading level than they actually belong today.

Graded word lists may also be constructed from basal readers or from social studies and science books. These can be helpful in assessing children's sight word knowledge in materials in which they are likely to be placed. When constructing your own graded word lists you should expect children to know approximately ninety-five percent of the words at their instructional level.

In using graded sight word lists you should keep their limitations in mind. For example, remember that you are only sampling a few words at each level as an overall estimate of a child's ability to pronounce words at that level. A child who is very good at word attack skills may tend to correctly pronounce quite a few words that are not in his sight vocabulary. You should, however, be able to determine whether this is happening, to some extent, based on the time and ease with which he responds to each word. You should also keep in mind that many children are disabled in reading because of their inability to comprehend what they read. For this type of child the graded word list is quite likely to be inaccurate in terms of placement level.

PART B. *remediation*

In this part of the chapter no differentiation will be made between techniques for teaching basic sight words from techniques for teaching sight words in general. Likewise, there is no separate section devoted exclusively to teaching letter knowledge. The techniques for teaching basic sight words also apply to teaching sight words in general. Many of the general techniques and principles that apply to the teaching of sight words are also useful in teaching the alphabet. It should also be emphasized that the techniques for teaching sight words as a remedial procedure differ very little from those used in teaching sight words in a developmental program. Quite often, in fact, the same techniques and materials are used. For that reason many of the suggested procedures and materials will be the same as those commonly used in many developmental programs. There are, however, a few specialized procedures for children who exhibit severe difficulties in learning. These procedures will also be discussed in this part of Chapter 4.

Most teachers present new words in many ways and children are exposed to a variety of situations in which they can learn these new words. Some teachers, of course, tend to lean heavily on specific techniques utilizing one mode of teaching considerably more than others. Luckily most children seem to be able to adapt their learning to the teaching method with which they come in contact. However, as a remedial teacher you should be aware of the fact that certain children seem to be predisposed to a specific mode of learning. For example, a student who receives a great deal of oral instruction may not readily learn basic sight words if he is predisposed to learning from a sight approach. Likewise, a child who learns readily from a kinesthetic approach may not learn his basic sight words if he has generally been taught by sight alone. For this reason it is often necessary for the remedial reading teacher to determine which mode of learning is appropriate for a specific child. Techniques for the diagnosis of specific learning modes are discussed in detail in Chapter 10. Keep in mind that specific techniques discussed in this chapter will be more appropriate for some children than for others.

One of the first problems often encountered is how to group remedial students for instruction on basic sight words. One very effective solution is to buy a number of different colored 3 in. × 5 in. (or smaller) cards. Designate a color to each of the levels on the basic sight word list shown earlier in this chapter, e.g., green for pre-primer, pink for primer. As the words are tested write each word missed on a separate card, color coded according to level. Children are then given these cards, which they file in junior sized shoe boxes by color. When you are ready to teach a certain word from the pre-primer list, for example, you simply write the word on the chalkboard or overhead projector transparency and tell children to look through their pink cards to see if they have the word. If they do, then this is their "ticket" to admission to the group to work on that specific word. After you are convinced that a child knows the word you may keep his card and he will no longer be included in a group formed to learn that word.

SOME BASIC PRINCIPLES AND TECHNIQUES

In teaching any sight word, one of the most basic things to remember is that for any normal child without problems in reading, a word is not likely to become a sight word until the child has encountered the word many times. The studies on how many times it takes a child to learn a word well enough so that it is instantly known have tended to disagree. However, we do know that before most words are instantly recognized a student must encounter them a number of times (probably a minimum of around twenty for most words). The number of exposures would, of course, depend on such factors as the potential of the child for word learning tasks, the meaning or relevance of the word for a child, the configuration of the word, and the context in which it is used. The important point, however, is that in teaching any word you must arrange for the child to come into contact with the word many times before he can be expected to recognize it instantly.

There are many ways to teach a new word to a student or to a group of students; however, a method somewhat similar to the following will often prove successful:

1. Write a sentence on the chalkboard in which the new word to be introduced is used in a meaningful context. Underline the word.
2. Let students read the sentence and attempt to say the new word using context clues along with other word attack skills. If you are introducing a new story that students

are to read, it is especially important that they are not told each new word in advance as this deprives them of the opportunity to apply word attack skills themselves.

3. Discuss the meaning of the word or how it is often used in talking and writing. Try to tie it to something in their background of experiences. If possible attempt to illustrate the word with a picture or some concrete object.

4. Write the word as students watch. Ask them to look for certain configuration clues such as double letters, extenders, and descenders. Also ask them to look for any well-known phonograms or word families, e.g., "ill," "ant," "ake," but do not call attention to little words in big or longer words.

5. Ask students to write the word themselves and to be sure and *say* the word while they write it. Research done by the Socony-Vacuum Oil Co. showed that we tend to remember about 90 percent of what we say as we do a thing, 70 percent of what we say as we talk, 50 percent of what we see and hear, and only 10 to 20 percent of what we simply read or hear.

6. Have students make up and write sentences in which the word is used in context. Have them read these sentences to each other and discuss them as they are read.

THE USE OF THE LANGUAGE-EXPERIENCE APPROACH

Some severely disabled readers will know hardly any words at all. In this case it is somewhat difficult to even follow a procedure as simple as that explained above. When this occurs, the methods used in the language-experience approach are often quite successful. Furthermore, the language-experience approach, in its latter stages, can also be used with great success with average or better readers. In using the language-experience approach with a group of disabled readers a method similar to the following may be used:

1. Discuss some event of great interest. After discussing the event, ask students if they would like to write a story about it.

2. As students dictate the story write it on chart paper using the following methods:
   a. Use manuscript or cursive writing—whichever is common to the age-grade level of the group with whom you are working.
   b. Use a heavy writing instrument such as a felt tip pen.
   c. Use the language of the students and do not attempt to alter it.
   d. Make sure students see the words as they are being written.
   e. Try to adhere to the one important event and follow a sequence of events.
   f. Use one-line sentences for severely disabled readers and gradually increase sentence length as improvement is noted.
   g. In beginning each new sentence emphasize the fact that you start on the left and proceed to the right.
   h. Emphasize the return sweep from the end of one sentence to the beginning of the next.

3. After the story has been completed, reread it as a choral exercise. Either you or a child may point to each word as it is read. It is important that the word being read is the same one being pointed to.

4. Have individual children take turns rereading the story sentence by sentence.

5. Duplicate the story on a large piece of tagboard and have students cut it into sentence strips. These can then be put in a pocket chart to form the original story. Go back to the original chart when necessary. Also let students rearrange the sentences to form a different order of events in the story.

6. After students have read the story over many times, you may wish to cut the tagboard sentences up into words and let students form the original sentences and new sentences.

7. As more stories are dictated and read and students build a larger sight vocabulary you may wish to duplicate stories on ditto paper and give each individual student a copy to be cut up into sentences and/or words for building varying story order and new sentences.

8. As students reading ability grows you should begin to let each student write and illustrate his own stories. These can be bound into booklets with attractive covers on them indicating the "author" of each book. Students should then begin to read each other's books.

9. A great deal of emphasis should always be placed on rereading materials that were written earlier, as children require a great many exposures to each word before they become sight words. After sight vocabularies begin to grow considerably, students can begin to read library or trade books.

When using the language experience approach with an individual student you may wish to use a process somewhat similar to the following:

1. As with a group, find some event of interest to the student and ask him if he would like to record the event on paper.

2. As the student dictates the events you should write them on a piece of paper with him seated so he can observe the words being written. The same methods listed in a.–h. for a group should be observed, except the writing may be done on 8½" × 11" paper with a pencil or felt tip pen.

3. After the story has been completed you may wish to type it on a pica or primary size typewriter as appropriate to the grade level of the student. (For third grade and above use regular pica type.)

4. Have the student reread the story with either you or he (if done properly) pointing to each word as it is read. Depending on the ability of the student at this stage, he may reread it sentence by sentence in varying order.

5. Let the student illustrate the story if he wishes. Finally, he should place it in a booklet to be kept and reviewed each time you meet.

6. You may wish to duplicate the typewritten copies of these stories so that students can cut them up and rearrange the sentences, and later the words within each sentence.

7. Bind groups of experience stories into booklets with illustrated covers and encourage all students to exchange and read each other's booklets.

8. Gradually encourage the student to branch out into the reading of trade books.[11]

The language-experience approach is especially appropriate for disabled readers because it is immediately meaningful to them—being written about events in their

[11]For a more detailed explanation of this approach see the following sources: Hall, Mary Anne. *Teaching Reading as a Language Experience*. Columbus, Ohio: Charles E. Merrill, 1970; Lee, Dorris M., and Allen, R. V. *Learning to Read Through Experience*. 2d ed., New York: Appleton-Century-Crofts, 1963; Stauffer, Russell G. *The Language Experience Approach to the Teaching of Reading*. New York: Harper & Row, 1970.

own life and using their own speaking vocabulary. Another advantage is that it develops a feeling of security and success and keeps pace with their development. It also gives meaning to their reading because students learn to associate printed stories with their own experiences from having seen their own experiences transferred into print.

Although the language experience approach offers a number of advantages for beginning or disabled readers there are also some disadvantages of which the teacher should be aware. For example, there is no step-by-step teacher's manual, and an inexperienced or untrained teacher is likely to fail to present a complete program. That is, she may fail to use certain high utility words enough times simply because students in the area where she teaches seldom use them. Or, she may fail to diagnose specific problems with various word analysis skills. There may also be difficulty in transferring from material written by students to that written by adult authors. Most of the problems encountered in using the language experience approach can, however, be overcome if the teacher is well trained and aware of the problems that she is likely to encounter in using this approach.

As stated, earlier words should usually be taught in context; however, a tachistoscopic presentation of words and phrases is also helpful for some students. Tachistoscopic presentations of words a student often confuses can be helpful in improving his ability to note details of configuration useful for identification. For example, for the student who confuses words such as ''that'' and ''them'' or ''what'' and ''when,'' a few sessions with a tachistoscopic presentation of these words mixed in with other more familiar combinations can be extremely helpful.

The use of the tachistoscope and controlled reading devices tended to fall into disrepute during the 1960s because a number of studies showed that tachistoscopic presentations of gradually widening spans of numbers and phrases did not contribute appreciably to reading speed. Furthermore, studies indicated that hand pacing in a book was equal to, or in some cases, more effective than controlled reading devices. This kind of research information should not, however, be interpreted as meaning that the tachistoscope has no value whatever in a reading program. The same is true for controlled reading devices. Although often expensive, they can serve as excellent motivating devices and are useful in helping children overcome problems with habitual repetitions.

A tachistoscopic presentation of phrases can also be of considerable value in helping children learn sight words. When using either words or phrases, a good technique to use is to let several children work together and yell out the words and phrases as they appear on the screen or the window of a hand-held tachistoscope. Although this is a noisy technique it is one in which most children love to participate. As with any other reading activity most of the words (95 percent or more) should be previously known by the students.

I have contrasted various factors (p. 78) which I believe have tended to separate studies that reported successful results from the use of the tachistoscope from those who have reported less success.

It should be stressed that the factors shown above only represent a general trend toward the more versus less successful use of the tachistoscope. It should, however, be useful in establishing guidelines for the use of the tachistoscope in your own remedial program.

SUCCESSFUL	LESS SUCCESSFUL
Elementary school students (grades 1–6).	*Older students of high school or college level.*
1. Used for giving multiple exposures of words or phrases or to get children to attend to the configuration of words.	1. Used to attempt to widen vision span and thus increase reading speed.
2. Students had follow-up activity writing words or words and phrases after each lesson.	2. No written follow-up.
3. Children yelled out or read words and phrases aloud.	3. Reading usually done silently.
4. Tachistoscope used by someone who believed in its effectiveness. (This factor would, of course, tend to make any device or material often appear to be superior because one would be dealing with the Hawthorne Effect.)	4. Tachistoscope used as just another device.

Several studies have provided some important information on how students learn words and/or letters which is important in using the tachistoscope and other learning devices. For example, Joanna Williams, Ellen Blumberg, and David Williams (1970) studied cues used in visual word recognition. They concluded, as did several previous researchers, that the overall shape of a word, or word "configuration," may not be as important for beginning readers in word recognition as is simple knowledge of first and last letters. They found that beginning readers used initial letters as an important clue in word recognition and that ending letters also provided an important clue. They did, however, state that older or adult readers tended to use a different method of word recognition strategy which would perhaps depend more on overall configuration. These authors' research indicates that, for younger readers, it may be highly important to discuss beginning and ending letter differences in words that are unknown, or in words with similar configurations that are often confused.

Richard Allington (1973) studied the use of color cues to focus attention in discrimination, visual memory, and paired-associate tasks. He found that discrimination, visual memory, and paired-associate tasks were all improved on letter-like figures when maximum color was added and then taken away. The results of his study also indicated that the vanishing color was superior to a method in which no color was added at all or to a method in which maximum color was added and remained. Allington's study may indicate that it would be helpful to some students to learn letters and/or words if they were first presented with a strong color cue in order to focus their attention. It may also be helpful to add color cues to words that have similar configurations such as "though" and "through," "county" and "country," and "when" and "what" in order to help students distinguish between these words when they are confused.

A study done by Joanna Williams (1969) also indicates that some methods of teaching letters or letter discrimination are apparently more effective than others. She concluded that too much time is often spent in copying and tracing. She suggested that more time be devoted to discrimination training that involves comparison of letters with their transformations. It should be stressed, however, that Williams' recommendations were based on children's initial problems in kindergarten or first grade and may not necessarily apply to older students.

Another study by Ernest Adams (1970) indicated that when words were introduced via a tape recording (referred to as response familiarization) before they were introduced visually, they were learned more easily. Adams also found that words of high meaningfulness were easier to learn than words of low meaningfulness. This evidently means that words should always be in a student's listening-speaking vocabulary before they are introduced in their printed form. Most reading specialists are aware of this, but perhaps often fail to take it into consideration when teaching. However, in Adams study even basic sight words (which were probably already in students' speaking-listening vocabulary) were learned more easily when students were familiarized with words by hearing them before seeing them.

WRITTEN EXERCISES AND GAMES

There are many different types of written exercises that are helpful in teaching sight words. However, in using any type of written exercise with disabled readers it should be kept in mind that certain students are likely to experience a great deal of failure if they are simply left to do these types of exercises on their own. When using written exercises with disabled readers it is helpful to have a teacher's aide or a student tutor work closely with the student to help him with difficult words and to provide for immediate feedback and correction. It is also helpful to tape record written exercises so that the student can listen to the material if he cannot read all of the words. The tape recorder can also provide immediate feedback to the student by providing the answers after each question.

EXAMPLES OF WRITTEN EXERCISES AND GAMES

There are many different types of written exercises that are helpful in teaching sight words. Some examples of these are as follows:

1. Have students fill in the blanks in sentences from a choice of sight words that are often confused as in the following example:
   a. Jim _____ he could run faster than Ann.
      (though, thought, through)
2. Have students write sentences, using as many sight words as they can from a list of about ten sight words in the same sentence. Have students underline all sight words used.
   (See example below)

   (Sample list)

go	him
not	am
she	will
with	when
from	after

   a. When I *go after him, she will not* be *with* me.

3. Make students aware of context and teach them to read up to the word and slightly beyond and then attempt to get the word from a combination of context and beginning and/or ending phonemes. This is a good way to give practice on words that present a great deal of difficulty.
   a. Fred liked his new t _ _ _ _ _ r very much. (teacher)
   b. Amy found a b _ _ _ _ r way to do the job. (better)

4. Have students draw pictures of scenes that represent certain words such as "wash," "throw," and "run." Be sure to "label" each scene.

5. Give students lists of words and several different colored crayons or pencils. Give them directions as follows:
   a. Use your yellow pencil to circle all of the things that are alive.
   b. Use your red pencil to circle all of the words that show action.
   c. Use your blue pencil to circle all of the words that could be used to describe something.

(Sample list)

cow	throw
the	did
when	go
dog	run
pretty	man
ugly	brown

This is a good scanning exercise to be done in x number of seconds (depending, of course, on the age of the students and the length of the list.)

6. Give students envelopes containing about ten words on cards. Place a pocket chart in the front of the room and then give directions such as the following:
   a. Place any cards in the pocket chart that tell (a) what we eat, (b) where we go in the morning, (c) what you like to do, etc.

(Sample list)

home	food
table	work
chair	apple
room	have
school	pie

These are but a few examples of the many types of exercises that can be devised for the remediation of difficulties with sight words. Games are also beneficial in teaching sight words. They have the added benefit of presenting the reading task in a new dimension in which the child has not experienced failure. Some examples of games for teaching sight words follow:

HEAD CHAIR GAME

Line up chairs and designate the chair on one end as the "head chair." Students then occupy the chairs. The teacher then flashes words to the student in the head chair. The student in the head chair continues to occupy that chair until a word is missed. When he misses a word he goes to the end of the line and everyone moves up one chair. The idea, of course, is to see who can stay in the head chair.

BOW

Flash cards to students giving each a turn. If a student does not know a word he must bow and remain in that position until he can beat another child in saying a new word. If he says it before the student whose turn it was to say the word, then the student who first bowed stands up and the second student bows. Students who do not have to bow win the game.

SIGHT WORD BEE

Use the same rules as you would for a spelling bee, but instead of spelling words have students say words as they are flashed.

SIGHT WORD HUNT

Two or more students are blindfolded while other students hide sight word cards around the room. When the signal is given the blindfolded students remove the blindfolds and begin to hunt the sight word cards. After the "hunt" is completed students must say all of the words on the cards they have found in order to keep them. The one who has the most cards after saying the words is the winner.

WHAT WORD

Fill the pocket chart with sight words. Let children take turns trying to answer questions such as: "What word tells a number?" "What word is a color?" "What word begins with the 'p' sound?" etc. Either the teacher or students can make up the questions.

These are only a sample of the many types of games that are effective for teaching sight words. Many commonly played games can be adapted to be played using sight words, for example, Bingo, rummy, checkers, etc. Appendix D also contains a listing of commercial programs, games, and other materials useful in teaching sight words and basic sight words.

THE USE OF THE TAPE RECORDER

One of the best aides a teacher can have for teaching sight words is the tape recorder. Although Chapter 15 deals with the topic of using the tape recorder in reading, I would also like to illustrate several of its many uses in teaching sight words in this chapter. One of the values of the tape recorder, of course, is that it never gets bored or tired with simple tasks. It is also a great motivator for children, and can provide for homework activities to extend the lessons carried on in the regular classroom. Following are some specific ways in which the tape recorder can be used in teaching sight words:

1. Write words a student has missed in sentences and give him the list of sentences. The tape recorder script to accompany his list would be as follows:
"Read sentence number one. *Pause.* Now let's check to see if you got it right. It says, 'John and Bill were going to go fishing.' Read it once more to be sure you have it right. *Pause.* Now read sentence number two . . . ."

2. Give the student a list of sight words with each word numbered. The tape recorded script to accompany his list would be as follows:
"I will say number one and then wait two seconds and then say the word by number one. You are to try to say the word before I say it. Be sure to listen each

time to see if you got it right. Number one *(two-second pause)* 'at,' number two *(two-second pause)* 'go,' number three . . . .''

3. Make up a group of eight sight words—one on each card. Number the cards on the back from one through eight. The tape recorded script to accompany the cards would be as follows:
"Lay the cards out in front of you in two rows. Place four cards in each row. Turn the tape recorder off until you have done this. *Four-second pause.* As the words are called pick up the word and place it on a pile in front of you. Place the second card over the first card, the third card over the second and so on. Here are the words: 'go' (five), 'do' (five), 'of' (four), 'from' (four), 'went' (three), 'want' (three), 'had' (three), 'have' (three). Now turn the pile of cards over and check to see if they are numbered from one to eight with one on top and eight on the bottom. If they are not in that order, change them so that they are in that order. Turn the tape recorder off until you have done this. *Four-second pause.* If they were all in the right order you knew all of the words and you may rewind the tape and put the tape and the cards away. If they were not in the right order then turn the cards over and pick each one up and say it after me. Ready 'go,' 'do,' 'of,' 'from,' 'went,' 'want,' 'had,' 'have.' Now rewind the tape and begin again."

This exercise is completely self-correcting with the number system, and, as you will note, students who miss words are given a chance to learn the word by

Figure 4–1. The Language Master® card reader/recorder.[12]

[12]Reproduced by permission of the Bell & Howell, Audio Visual Products Division, 7100 McCormick Road, Chicago, Illinois 60645. (The "Language Master" is a registered trademark of the Bell & Howell Co.)

hearing and saying it, and they are automatically channeled back into the same exercise again and again until they learn all of the words. The numbers after the words the first time through represent the number of seconds you should pause before giving the next word. Keep in mind that the student needs slightly longer on the first words than on the last because he has more words in front of him to discriminate among. The words must be called in the same order as they are numbered on the back. Also note the four-second pause after the instructions to turn the tape recorder off. In recording the directions you should not stop the recorder but simply pause for four seconds. This is just about the right amount of time for the student to respond to the directions when he hears it and *does* have to shut it off.

Again, these are but a few of the many ways in which the tape recorder can be used in teaching basic sight words. Trial and experience will bring to mind many more ideas.

Another type of instrument that is useful in teaching letters, sight words, or phrases is the electronic card reader such as the Language Master® shown on page 82. The Language Master is a device used for recording and playback of a strip of audio tape attached to the bottom of a card. These cards are available in various sizes. They are available in either blank or prepared form. The device contains a built-in microphone and a "Student-Instructor" switch. When the switch is set on "Student" mode, the student can pronounce a word written on a card while pressing the record button. This will record his voice on the tape. He can then insert the card again and listen to the word as he pronounced it. If he is using a prepared card he can then set the selector switch to "Instructor" mode and again insert the card. This time a voice will pronounce the word written on the card so that the student can compare, and correct if necessary, his answer in accordance with the one pronounced by the instructor.

Since blank cards are available, this and similar instruments allow the teacher to record on cards those words, letters, phonemes, phrases, etc. missed by a particular student. This, of course, allows the student to work alone and correct his own errors, thus making the program highly individualized. Prepared cards also come in many forms from which the teacher can select and assign those needed by a certain student.

CHILDREN WITH ESPECIALLY DIFFICULT LEARNING PROBLEMS

Children who do not learn by normal sight or auditory approaches are sometimes quite successful when taught by use of a kinesthetic approach. The kinesthetic approach is described in detail by Grace Fernald (1943); however, since the publication of the text by Fernald a number of variations of her original method have been used. In teaching words using the kinesthetic approach the procedure is usually somewhat like that described on page 84.[13]

[13]For a thorough explanation of the "Fernald Technique" that is similar to this see Chapter 9, p. 232.

1. The child should be shown a word and the word should be pronounced for him. The word may be written on the chalkboard, on a large sheet of paper, or on a flashcard approximately 3" high by 9" wide. Wherever it is written, the letters should usually be about two inches high. A very broad felt tip marking pen works well for writing on tagboard flashcards. It may be written either in manuscript or cursive writing. The one chosen is usually that with which the child is most familiar or the one he is presently using in school.

2. The child should be asked to trace the word while saying it. He is to say each part of the word as he traces that part; however, he is directed not to sound it out letter by letter. It is also important that his finger or fingers contact the surface of the paper or tagboard at all times while it is being traced. Some teachers have children use only their index finger. I would suggest, however, that you have the child use his middle and index finger at the same time as though they, both together, were one large pencil or piece of chalk. The child should continue this tracing until both you and he are relatively sure he knows the word.

3. The child should then be asked to write the word himself while looking at the original copy. When the child writes it, it should also be written in letters that are about two inches high. He should also be directed to say each word part as it is being written.

4. In the final step of this procedure the child should be told to write the word again, but this time from memory. He should also be told to say the word again as he writes it.

In using the kinesthetic approach some teachers prefer to have the child write the words in sand or in salt sprinkled in a container such as a shoebox lid. Another approach that works well is to lay paper over a piece of window screen and then write the words with a crayon. This has the advantage of leaving a series of raised areas on the paper that the child can actually feel when he traces it with his fingers.

For children who have a great deal of difficulty with some words or letters you may wish to cut letters or words out of sandpaper so that they are easily felt. The same effect can also be achieved by using felt material or by forming letters or words with white glue and then sprinkling them with salt or sand. When dry, these have a texture that can easily be felt.

The kinesthetic approach has an advantage over other forms of instruction in that it combines the sense of touch (tactile) and kinesthesia (muscle and/or body movement perception) with the normal auditory and visual modes of learning. The disadvantage, on the other hand, of using this approach is that it is time consuming. Studies have not shown the kinesthetic approach to be superior to other modes of learning for groups of children as a whole. Its superiority is evident only for those children who are not successful with a normal auditory and/or visual approach to learning.

SUMMARY

Although it is possible to learn to read without complete letter knowledge, most teachers would agree that letter knowledge is an important part of learning to read. However, reading teachers often feel that any student above the first grade level will automatically know the alphabet. Such is often not the case even for older students, and a part of the diagnostic procedure should include testing for letter knowledge.

An extremely important part of the diagnostic procedure is the testing of sight word knowledge, including basic sight words. Students can never expect to become fluent readers until they have mastered the basic sight words or the high utility words that appear so often in print. Basic sight words should be tested using some means of tachistoscopic presentation (which might be something as simple as flash cards) so that you can be assured that students have "instant" recognition of these words. Sight word knowledge, in general, is usually done by using a graded list of words which samples representative sight words at each grade level.

For those students who are extremely disabled in their knowledge of the alphabet or sight words it may be necessary to diagnose their strongest mode of learning. For example, some students who are predisposed to learning from an auditory approach will not do well in attempting to learn from a visual approach. Information on modality testing is presented in Chapter 10.

Some general and specific techniques for teaching letter knowledge and sight words have been presented. Among these are the language experience approach, the Fernald Technique, and methods of using the tape recorder as a teaching device.

Chapter 4: REFERENCES

Adams, Ernest L. "Influence of Meaningfulness and Familiarization Training on Basic Sight Vocabulary Learning With First-Graders," Doctoral dissertation, Michigan State University, 1970.

Allington, Richard L. "An Evaluation of the Use of Color Cues to Focus Attention in Discrimination and Paired-Associate Learning," Doctoral dissertation, Michigan State University, 1973.

Durr, William K. "Computer Study of High Frequency Words in Popular Trade Juveniles," *The Reading Teacher*. Vol. 27, (October, 1973), 37–42.

Fernald, Grace. *Remedial Techniques in Basic School Subjects*. New York: McGraw-Hill, 1943.

Gagon, Glen, "Modern Research and Word Perception," *Education*. Vol. 86, (April, 1966), 464–472.

Madden, Richard. *Language Arts Notes-Number 11*. New York: World Book Co., 1959.

Robinson, H. Alan. "A Study of the Techniques of Word Identification," *The Reading Teacher*. Vol. 16, (January, 1969), 238–242.

Williams, Joanna P. "Training Kindergarten Children to Discriminate Letter-Like Forms," *American Educational Research Journal*. Vol. 6, (November, 1969), 501–514.

Williams, Joanna P.; Blumberg, Ellen L.; and Williams, David V. "Cues Used In Visual Word Recognition," *Journal of Educational Psychology*. Vol. 61, (August, 1970), 310–315.

5

DIAGNOSIS AND REMEDIATION OF EDUCATIONAL FACTORS: *word analysis skills*

The first part of this chapter contains a discussion and examples of the problems involved in various types of testing for word analysis skills. This is followed by a description of some of the more commonly used commercial tests and surveys along with a discussion of their strengths and weaknesses. A method of constructing your own phonics survey is then described along with the rationale for use of the Ekwall Phonics Knowledge Survey which appears in Appendix A. The remainder of the chapter deals with specific methods of diagnosing and remediating reading difficulties in other word analysis skills.

PART A.   *diagnosis*

PHONICS AND STRUCTURAL ANALYSIS

Before making a decision about which test to use in the area of phonics and structural analysis, you must decide how you are going to use the information obtained. For example, if you plan to group a number of children who are simply labeled "weak" in overall phonics knowledge, chances are a *group* diagnostic test would suffice for your needs. On the other hand, if you intend to teach to students' specific weaknesses, for example, lack of knowledge of the initial consonant sounds "p," "f," and "g," and consonant blends "fl," "gr," and "pl," you will need to administer an *individual* diagnostic test.

Many educators have been under the impression that they can accurately diagnose an individual's specific weaknesses with a group diagnostic test. Research in our reading center has shown that this is not so.[1] Once again, you should keep the testing principle stated earlier in mind, i.e., test in a situation that is analogous to actually reading. In other words, the test should require that the student perform the task being tested in the same manner as the student will be required to do when he reads. When a student takes a group diagnostic test, it is impossible by the nature of the test for him to respond to the answers, in most cases, in a way that is analogous

[1]Ekwall, Eldon E. "An Analysis of Children's Test Scores When Tested with Individually Administered Diagnostic Tests and When Tested with Group Administered Diagnostic Tests," Final Research Report, University Research Institute, University of Texas at El Paso, 1973.

to actually reading. For example, in taking a group diagnostic test the student is usually given directions somewhat similar to the following:

> "Write the beginning sound you hear in the following words: Number one, *need*, number two, *teach*, etc."

The student in this case is to write an "n" in blank number one and a "t" in blank number two. A second set of directions for group testing for knowledge of the "n" and "t" sounds might be as follows:

> "On your papers are four letters. Circle the beginning sound you hear in the following words. The first word is *need*. The second word is *teach*, etc."

In this case the students' answer sheets would be similar to the following:

1. p f n d
2. g t h r

At first glance, both tests may appear to be valid; however, upon examining them more closely you will realize that hearing the words "need" and "teach" and writing "n" and "t" in a blank or hearing "need" and "teach" and circling their beginning sounds from a choice of four letters is simply not the same skill as is required for seeing the "n" and "t" graphemes and responding with the "n" and "t" phonemes. Extensive research in our reading center has shown that the item-by-item agreement on items missed on various group and individual type tests is extremely low and that group diagnostic tests do not diagnose accurately enough for prescriptive teaching. Since remedial reading is usually a process of filling in the gaps in a student's reading skills then prescriptive teaching is a necessity. And, in most cases remedial reading teachers will need to give individual diagonostic tests in order to accurately diagnose and remediate specific problems students are experiencing in phonics and structural analysis. In all fairness to the authors and publishers of group diagnostic tests it should also be stated that much of our teaching of phonics and structural analysis is done by simply grouping those children with the lowest overall scores and teaching them practically everything covered on the test. In a situation where a teacher is dealing with a large number of children in a group, this approach, although somewhat inefficient in terms of the students' time, is quite efficient in terms of the teacher's time. And, if this type of teaching is to be done, a group diagnostic test will serve the purpose; that is, it will generally pinpoint those students who are extremely poor in word attack skills from those who are at a medium or higher level.

Although it would seem that testing phonics knowledge is an easy task this is not necessarily the case. For example, listed below are some commonly used methods of assessing children's phonics knowledge and what I believe to be the shortcomings of each method.

Method 1.   Children are shown letters, e.g., "a," "b," "c," and told to give the sounds of these letters. First of all, although perhaps a minor point, the letters do not "have" sounds, they represent sounds and we should ask the child to tell us the sounds that these letters stand for. One of the major problems with this method, however, is in determining whether a certain sound given is correct. In playing tape recordings of children taking this type of test in my classes I find that the agreement among the scorers is so low that this method, although appearing somewhat valid, cannot in reality be at all valid since it is not even reliable. That is, the scorers do not agree on which answers are right and which are wrong. This type of test then lacks interscorer reliability. The main problem among the scorers is that they do not "hear" the same thing. For example, they cannot agree on whether they hear "er" or "ruh" for the "r" sound. Another problem with this method is that some children who know their sounds in the context of a word do not know the sounds in isolation. Testing sounds in isolation would yield irrelevant information in such cases.

Method 2. Children are given a piece of paper on which four letters, blends, etc. appear by each number. They are told to circle or underline the letter, blend, etc. that begins or ends or has the same middle sound as a word pronounced by the tester. The problem with this type of test, as stated earlier, is that hearing a word and circling a sound heard in it is not the same as actual reading. Furthermore, if there are four possible choices on each question, the student has a one-fourth chance of guessing the correct answer. There is a fairly high correlation between being able to do this and actually attacking a new word and thus those children who are good at this task will probably be good at attacking words and vice versa; however, this type of test, as shown by our research, is simply not accurate enough for prescriptive teaching purposes.

Method 3. Children are given a sheet of paper with a blank by each number. They are then instructed to write down the beginning sound, beginning blend, vowel sounds, etc. heard in a word pronounced by the tester. This method has the same weaknesses as those described in Method 2. That is, it is not analagous to actual word attack in reading.

Method 4. Children are shown nonsense words which contain the initial consonants, blends, vowels, etc. to be tested. For example in testing for knowledge of the "p" sound a child may be given the nonsense word "pide." For some children this presents major problems. In order to pronounce the nonsense word "pide" they would have to know the following:

    a. The long and/or short vowel sound for "i"
    b. The "d" sound
    c. The vowel rule stating that when we have a vowel-consonant-final "e" the first vowel is usually long and the "e" is silent.

As you can see all of the knowledge listed in a, b, and c are equal to, or more difficult than, simple knowledge of the "p" sound. Therefore, if the child does not respond, you would not really know if it was because he did not know the "p" sound or if, in reality, he had no knowledge of one of, two of, or all three areas listed in a, b, and c above. It should also be kept in mind that vowel sounds and/or vowel rules are usually taught somewhat later than initial consonant sounds. Therefore, many children having difficulty with initial consonant sounds are likely to experience even more problems with vowel sounds and/or vowel rules.

Method 5. Children are given a list of real words each beginning with a specific initial consonant, blend, etc. to be tested. The problem here, of course, is that if the words are already in the child's sight vocabulary, it is not a test of phonic word attack skills at all. And, if the words are not in the child's sight vocabulary, the same problems encountered in using nonsense words are also encountered here.

Some Commercially Published Tests and Surveys: Their Strengths and Weaknesses

In this section a number of tests are described in detail along with their strengths and weaknesses. The purpose of the somewhat lengthy descriptions is to make the user aware of the common shortcomings of some of our most popular reading diagnostic tests. The information gained in this section should also help you in critically analyzing other reading tests that are now on the market or in analyzing those that are likely to appear in the future.

The *Botel Reading Inventory* [2] contains a "Phonics Mastery Test" with eight subtests most of which may be given as group or individual tests. It consists of the following subtests: Knowledge of Consonant Sounds, Consonant Blends, Consonant Digraphs, Rhyming Words, Long and Short Vowel Sounds, Number of Syllables, Accented Syllable, and Nonsense Words. The Nonsense Words subtest is the only test that must be administered individually.

In giving the Consonant Sounds, Consonant Blends, Consonant Digraphs, Long and Short Vowels, and Other Vowel Sounds subtests the examiner says a word, which is usually difficult enough that it would not be in the student's sight vocabulary, and the student is to write the respective consonant, blend, etc. being tested. In giving this type of test it should be noted that hearing a word and writing a sound heard (encoding) is not the same skill as that required for reading (as explained in Method 3) in which the student must look at a letter(s) (grapheme) and give the sound for the letter(s) (phoneme). The research done in our reading center (mentioned initially in Chap. 5) indicates that there is a reasonably high correlation between these two skills, but a low percentage of agreement on which specific items are not known. Therefore, these tests seem more appropriate as a prerequisite for spelling skills (encoding) rather than for reading (decoding). It will, however, locate those students who are generally good in phonics versus those who are generally poor in phonics.

The "Rhyming Words" subtest is easy to administer; however, I have never been sure what to do with the results of such a test. In giving the "Number of Syllables" subtest the examiner reads a series of words and the student circles a number that corresponds to the number of syllables heard in the word. Before giving a test of this nature the purpose of teaching syllabication should be examined. Syllabication is taught as an aid to break words into syllables so the reader will know which sounds to apply to various vowels, depending on their position in the syllable. A test of the nature of this one, however, seems to be of little value. The "Accented Syllable" subtest also seems to suffer from the same problem. In giving that subtest the examiner is to read words and the student is to circle a number that corresponds to the number (first = 1, second = 2, etc.) of the accented syllable. What the student must know about accent is which syllable *he* must accent when he

[2]Botel, Morton. *Botel Reading Inventory*. Chicago: Follett, 1966.

says a word. Therefore, this subtest appears to be of dubious value.

The "Nonsense Words" subtest is probably the most useful of the various subtests. It contains a number of difficult words such as "ringtrape" and "concealter." It is quite logical to assume that a student that can pronounce these words has an adequate knowledge of single consonant sounds, vowel sounds, consonant digraphs, consonant blends, vowel rules, syllable principles, and to some extent accent generalizations. This test is, therefore, very useful as a quick screening device, i.e., if a student can pass this subtest, the above mentioned skills would not need to be tested, thus saving a considerable amount of time in the diagnosis of certain students.

The *Corrective Reading System*[3] is a complete testing, record keeping system for students, or monitoring system for students' reading skills (except comprehension) from grades one through grade six. It is designed for the teacher who wishes to do exact prescriptive teaching on the basis of test results. It contains subtests for upper and lower case letter identification, basic sight word knowledge, phoneme knowledge of approximately eighty graphemes of high utility (consonants, vowels, digraphs, blends, diphthongs, "r" controlled vowels, silent consonants, sounds of "y," etc.), word endings, vowel rules, syllabication principles, accent generalizations, contractions, suffixes, prefixes, and dictionary skills.

In devising this testing system the author attempted to test each skill in a situation that was analogous to what the student would actually do in applying each skill in reading. Since the *Corrective Reading System* is a system of pupil testing and monitoring for students in grades one through grade six one would not expect to give the entire battery of tests to any one student at one time. However, any subtest can be given to a student at any point when he should have mastered the skill being tested. The point in a student's progression through the grades when he should have mastered each skill is given in the *Teacher's Manual to Accompany Corrective Reading System.*

The phonics testing system is similar to that described following the description of various commercially published tests in this section. It is also similar to the phonics knowledge survey shown in Appendix A. Knowledge of vowel rules is tested by having the student pronounce nonsense words such as "rud" and "flo" ("rud"—a single vowel in a closed syllable is usually short and "flo"—a single vowel at the end of a word [not syllable] is usually long). It was the author's belief that if a student could pronounce these words, he did not need to be able to recite the rules, since the rules are only a means to an end and not an end in themselves.

Syllable principles are tested by showing the student words such as "alpil" and "illoc" and asking him to show the examiner where the word would be divided. This again, approximates what a student must do in applying this skill in actually reading. However, if he can apply it then he does not need to be able to recite the rule.

Because of the length of the test each subtest will not be analyzed in this section. However, the directions for each subtest and the rationale for using each method of testing is given in the *Teacher's Manual to Accompany Corrective Reading System.*

---

[3]Ekwall, Eldon E. *Corrective Reading System.* Glenview, Illinois: Psychotechnics, Inc., 1975.

The *Diagnostic Reading Scales*[4] (DRS) contain a series of eight phonics tests to provide an analysis of a student's phonic knowledge and word-attack methods. Spache does not contend that his DRS measures all of the phonic skills a student may need to know as he progresses through the elementary school. He states, "Each test samples a phonic skill to enable the teacher or clinician to identify possible areas of weakness which will be thoroughly explored subsequently." (p. 11) (Apparently the areas of weakness will be explored by the remedial reading teacher.)

The eight subtests of the DRS are as follows:

Test 1.   Consonant Sounds: In this subtest the student is to give the letter sounds in isolation. The author states that the examiner is to accept a pronunciation such as "bu" for "b." This type of test presents the sort of problems mentioned in Method 1.

Test 2.   Vowel Sounds: In this subtest the student is to take nonsense words such as "gat," and "nit" and give the pronunciation of the word as though the vowel had the long sound and then as though it had the short sound. This test presents the problems mentioned in Method 4, i.e., if the student does not respond, it may be because he does not know the consonants rather than the vowels. Furthermore, it is not natural for an older student to give the long vowel sound in a nonsense word like "gat" because single vowels in closed syllables and/or words usually have the short sound. A student who innately knows this will simply be hesitant to give the long vowel sound.

Test 3.   Consonant Blends and Digraphs: This subtest is administered the same as Test 1 for single consonants.

Test 4.   Common Syllables or Phonograms: In this subtest the student is to say the sounds of common syllables and/or phonograms such as, "ail," "op," and "tion."

Test 5.   Blending: In this subtest the student is to take common elements of words and blend them into whole words. Some examples are "se-ter," "con-ell," and "cl-ide." This test, no doubt, does test the ability to blend, however, it should be stressed that the student would need to know the elements thoroughly in order to test his ability to blend.

Test 6.   Letter Sounds: I   this subtest the examiner gives the letter sounds and the student is to identify the letter that each sound stands for. The student may respond either orally or in written form. Spache states, "In this fashion it is possible to determine his ability to connect the auditory and written images, as well as the auditory and vocal." (p. 21)

Test 7.   Initial Consonant Substitution: In this subtest the student is given (orally a number of words such as "ball" and then asked what the word would be if the "b" were taken away and replaced with an "f." This is an important skill to be mastered in order to make phonic word-attack functional.

Test 8.   Auditory Discrimination: In this subtest the student is given a number of word pairs such as "bin-pin," "four-four," and "robe-rove" and asked to determine whether the words are the same or different. Pass-fail norms are given for second, third, and fourth-grade readers. This again measures an important skill which must be mastered before a student can become proficient in phonic word-attack.

[4]Spache, George D. *Diagnostic Reading Scales*. Monterey, California: CTB/McGraw-Hill, 1973. (Revised Edition)

Most diagnosticians will find the phonics tests of the DRS to be a useful instrument in the initial screening of various phonic skills. The test for vowel sounds seems to be the only one of which I would offer serious criticism. It should be remembered that (as the author states) the DRS only presents a general picture of weak and strong areas and more testing would need to follow in order to do prescriptive teaching of phonics skills.

The *Durrell Analysis of Reading Difficulty*[5] contains a series of tests designed to measure various aspects of a student's reading. It contains subtests, some of which are normed, ranging from non-reader to sixth-grade reading level. Several of the subtests measure various aspects of word-attack skills such as the subtests entitled: Word Recognition and Word Analysis, Visual Memory of Word Forms, Auditory Analysis of Word Elements, Learning Sounds in Words, Learning to Hear Sounds in Words, and Sounds of Letters.

The *Durrell Analysis of Reading Difficulty* does not contain enough depth in phonics testing to do prescriptive teaching. For example, in the "Sounds of Letters" subtest only sixteen consonant blends and digraphs are tested. This testing is done in isolation and, therefore, suffers from the problems mentioned in Method 1. It is, however, important for students to be able to remember letter forms and to hear sounds in words as a prerequisite to learning the various word analysis skills. Perhaps the real value of the *Durrell Analysis of Reading Difficulty* is in the training it can provide the diagnostician in terms of what to observe in students' reading abilities. Once this has been learned, however, many diagnosticians and teachers will find that the time required for the administration of the various subtests is too time consuming for the diagnostic information that they provide.

The *Gates-McKillop Reading Diagnostic Tests*[6] contains a series of seventeen subtests for measuring individual reading performance. There are two forms—Form 1 and Form 2. The subtests dealing with word analysis are as follows: Recognizing and Blending Common Word Parts, Giving Letter Sounds, Naming Capital Letters, Naming Lower-Case Letters, Nonsense Words, Initial Letters, Final Letters, Vowels, Auditory Blending, Syllabication, and Auditory Discrimination.

The "Recognizing and Blending Common Word Parts" subtest tests the student's ability to pronounce nonsense words such as "spack" and "smew." If he cannot pronounce the word, he is then shown each part separately, e.g., "sp" and "ack." After pronouncing each part, he attempts to blend the parts into a whole word. This subtest is a good measure of a student's ability to blend and will give a gross measure of his knowledge of blends, digraphs, diphthongs, and phonograms or word families.

The "Giving Letter Sounds" subtest, as the name implies, is a test for the letter sounds of the consonants. Each sound is tested in isolation. All letters are presented and the results should be thorough enough for prescriptive teaching. However, since the sounds are tested in isolation it suffers from the problems mentioned in Method 1.

[5]Durrell, Donald M. *Durrell Analysis of Reading Difficulty*. New York: Harcourt Brace Jovanovich, Inc., 1955.
[6]Gates, Arthur I., and McKillop, Anne S. *Gates-McKillop Reading Diagnostic Tests*. New York: Teachers College Press, 1962.

The "Nonsense Words" subtest tests the student's ability to identify a nonsense word from a choice of four nonsense words when that word is read by the examiner. There is, no doubt, a fairly high correlation between the ability to perform well on this test and phonic word-attack, but its use for diagnostic teaching would be questionable, i.e., regardless of how well or how poorly a student performed on this subtest more information would be needed to plan a teaching strategy. The testing principle that a test should not be given if it will not influence the way a student is taught might very well apply in this case.

The "Initial Letters" and "Final Letters" subtests are similar to the "Nonsense Words" subtests except that in these subtests the examiner reads a word and the student is to circle a letter, from a choice of five, that stands for the sound at the beginning or end of the word. The problems inherent in testing using Method 2 are encountered in this type of subtest, i.e., if a student achieves well on this skill, it still does not mean that it will insure success when he has to look at a letter (grapheme) and give its sound (phoneme).

In giving the "Vowels" subtest the examiner reads a list of nonsense words such as "vum" and "kino." As this is done the student is shown the letters *a, e, i, o,* and *u*. He is to point to the one he "hears" in the nonsense word. This subtest again suffers from the problems inherent in testing using Method 2, i.e., the fact that a student can perform well on this task does not insure that he will be able to look at a word and pronounce the vowel in that word correctly, which is what the student must do when he reads.

In giving the syllabication subtest the student is shown a group of nonsense words such as "inmo" and "nilow" and told to pronounce them. The Gates-McKillop *Teacher's Manual* states, "The purpose of this test is to determine whether the child can blend the syllables, not whether he can identify and sound the component syllables." (p. 11) This test might, more properly, be named "Blending"; however, it requires a knowledge of phoneme-grapheme correspondence *and* blending. In my opinion it might, more properly, be used as a quick screening device to determine which students possess adequate phonic and structural analysis skills, to eliminate further testing, such as is done with the "Nonsense Words" subtest of the *Botel Reading Inventory*.

The "Auditory Discrimination" subtest is administered by having the student sit with his back to the examiner while the examiner reads a number of pairs of words. The student is to say whether the words are the same or different. No norms are given for this subtest and only fourteen pairs of words are used which is not enough to test all of the phonemes with which a student is likely to encounter difficulty. In my opinion this subtest would only serve as a very rough screening device. The examiner might well skip this subtest and use a more thorough auditory discrimination test such as the Wepman.

The *Phonics Knowledge Survey*[7] is designed to test a number of phonic word-attack skills. It contains fifteen subtests designed to test knowledge of letter names, letter sounds, vowel sounds, vowel rules, soft and hard "c" and "g" sounds and rules, sounds and rules for "y," consonant blends, consonant digraphs,

---

[7]Durkin, Dolores, and Meshover, Leonard. *Phonics Knowledge Survey.* New York: Teachers College Press, 1964.

diphthongs, "r" controlled vowels, sounds of "qu," "oo," "x," and silent consonants, and some syllabication principles. Both consonant and vowel sounds are tested in isolation and thus this part of the test presents those problems explained in Method 1. Vowel rules are tested in the context of nonsense words. This seems feasible since students should not be required to know or recite the rules if they can apply them in attacking a strange word. (It is only when they cannot apply the rules and sounds that they need to learn the sounds and rules.) This same method is applied to knowledge of the soft and hard sounds of "c" and "g" which again seems logical. Knowledge of the sounds and rules for "y" are tested in the same manner in words such as "yad," "bly," "adsy," and "fyth." Consonant blends and digraphs, diphthongs, "r" controlled vowels, and the sounds of "qu," "oo," "x," and silent consonants are all tested in isolation. This again presents some problems as mentioned in Method 1. This is even more pronounced in testing silent consonants which are extremely difficult, even for good readers, when shown in isolation. The test for syllable rules appears to be effective since it also requires the student to divide nonsense words into syllables. The division of words into syllables is done to help the student in knowing which vowels appear in open and closed syllables, therefore, this test requires that the student perform a task he would have to do in actually reading, yet it does not require him to recite rules which is not necessary if he can innately apply them.

The *Sipay Word Analysis Tests* (SWAT)[8] are a series of seventeen subtests, administered individually, to test students' knowledge of word analysis skills. The subtests are as follows: Survey Test, Letter Names (Lower-case and Upper-case), Symbol-Sound Association: Single Letters (Sounds and Words), Substitution: Single Letters (Initial Consonants, Final Consonants, and Medial Vowels), Consonant-Vowel-Consonant Trigrams, Initial Consonant Blends and Digraphs (Blends, Digraphs and Triple Clusters), Final Consonant Blends and Digraphs (Blends and Digraphs), Vowel Combinations (Most Common and Consistent Vowel Digraphs, Most Common and Consistent Diphthongs, More Common Vowel Combinations that Usually Represent One of Two Sounds, Less Common Vowel Combinations That May Represent One of Two Sounds), Open Syllable Generalization, Final Silent "e" Generalization, Vowel Versatility, Vowels + "r" (Single Vowel + "r," Two Vowels + "r," Single Vowel + "r" + Silent "e"), Silent Consonants, Vowel Sounds of "y," Visual Analysis (Monosyllablic Words, Root Words and Affixes, Syllabication), Visual Blending (Component Elements into Syllables, Syllables into Words), and Contractions.

Each of the SWAT subtests has four components: a "Mini-Manual," a set of test cards (approximately 57 mm × 90 mm), an Answer Sheet, and an Individual Report Form. The Mini-Manuals provide general information on the subtest, what skills are measured, how to administer and score it, how to analyze and interpret the results, and suggestions for follow-up testing. The Test Cards are used to present the stimuli to the student. The Answer Sheets are used for recording the student's responses and to allow the examiner to make a more detailed analysis of the learner's performance. The Individual Report Forms are used by the examiner to summarize and report his findings.

[8]Sipay, Edward R. *Sipay Word Analysis Tests.* Cambridge, Massachusetts: Educators Publishing Service, Inc., 1974.

Because of the length of this test each subtest will not be analyzed in this section. However, it should be noted that the author of this test recognized that word-attack skills generally cannot be tested in a group situation and took considerable care to construct a test that will allow the student to perform on each subtest in a situation such as he would be likely to encounter in actually reading. He also did considerable research in order to find which graphemes were of high enough utility to make them worthwhile testing. This test should yield results that are accurate enough for exact prescriptive teaching.

One feature of the test that some teachers may find undesirable is that they are required to handle a great many cards while administering the various subtests. However, this is also an advantage since it takes the test materials out of the traditional setting and puts them into a context that a student is more likely to perceive as a game or fun type of activity.

The *Stanford Diagnostic Reading Test*[9] is a group diagnostic test in two levels. Level I is for use from the latter part of the second grade to the middle of grade four. Level II is for use in the latter part of grade four to the middle of grade eight. Both levels of the test contain the following subtests: Reading Comprehension, Vocabulary, Syllabication, Blending, and Sound Discrimination. Level I also contains subtests for Auditory Discrimination and Beginning and Ending Sounds. Level II contains a subtest for Rate of Reading.

In Level I the "Auditory Discrimination" subtest tests students' ability to listen to two words pronounced by the teacher and determine whether sounds in each pair are the same in the beginning, in the middle, or at the end. This is an important readiness skill for phonics and could be useful as a gross measure of that skill. The "Syllabication" subtests of both Level I and Level II require the student to locate the syllable break in words as they look at the words. This is, of course, much more like what one does in actually reading than the syllabication subtests used by some test authors. The "Beginning and Ending Sounds" subtest in Level I requires the student to look at a picture and then indicate, from four choices, which sound is either at the beginning or end of a word that stands for the name of the picture. This subtest would not be likely to give information that would be accurate enough for diagnostic teaching, but would only give a gross measure of a student's knowledge of phoneme-grapheme correspondence.

In the blending section of both tests the student is required to match parts of words so that they blend together to form a word. An example of a correctly marked word (sand) follows:

1. ⊗ s	⊗ a	◯ mb
◯ e	◯ e	⊗ nd

This test does require a knowledge of phoneme-grapheme correspondence and would require a blending process analogous to actually reading. However, if the

[9]Karlsen, Bjorn; Madden, Richard; and Gardner, Eric F. *Stanford Diagnostic Test.* New York: Harcourt Brace Jovanovich, Inc., 1966.

student did not know all of the sounds it would not be likely to test his ability to blend.

In the "Sound Discrimination" subtests of both tests the student is required to read a word that has a sound underlined. He then reads three words to the right of this word and is to determine which word contains a sound like the one that is underlined. This requires that the student be able to read all of the words. In cases where he did not know the words it would, of course, not measure his knowledge of the sounds.

In summary, the authors have done a good job of devising subtests that, for the most part, test in a situation that would be analogous to actual reading. However, the test only provides a gross measure of some word-attack skills and would not provide sufficient information for diagnostic teaching as one would need to do in remedial reading.

The *Woodcock Reading Mastery Tests*[10] are a series of five tests designed for individual administration. They are for use from kindergarten to grade twelve. One of the five tests is designed to test word-attack. Two alternate forms of the battery are available. The author of this test states,

> This battery of tests is particularly useful for clinical or research purposes and in any situation for which precise measures of reading achievement are desired. Raw scores can be converted to traditional normative scores including grade scores, age scores, percentile ranks and standard scores. Primary interpretative emphasis, however, is directed toward using the specially designed Mastery Scale which predicts the individual's relative success with reading tasks at different levels of difficulty. Separate norms are available for boys and girls in addition to total group norms. An innovative feature is the provision of SES (socioeconomic status) adjusted norms based on communities having SES characteristics similar to the local community. (Page 1, *Teacher's Manual.*)
>
> The Word Attack Skill Test contains 50 items which measure the subject's ability to identify nonsense words through application of phonic and structural analysis skills. Items are arranged in order of difficulty. At the lower end of the test the nonsense words are simple consonant-vowel or consonant-vowel-consonant combinations such as "dee" and "lat." Multisyllable words such as "ipdan" and "depnonlel" are presented at the upper end of the test. Represented within the set of nonsense words are most consonant and vowel sounds, common prefixes and suffixes, and frequently appearing irregular spellings of vowels and consonants ("ph" for "f" and "igh" for long "i"). (Page 3, *Teacher's Manual.*)

This test has the advantage of being rather easy to administer and is contained in an easel type notebook that is functional. The student who is able to read all of the nonsense words would, no doubt, have adequate word-attack skills. However, as described earlier in Method 4, the use of nonsense words presents a number of problems. If the student does not respond, the tester does not really know whether the student does not know the initial consonant, the medial vowel, the ending consonant, etc. or whether the student does not know how to blend.

For this reason the only "precise measurement" that can be obtained is whether the student does or does not possess adequate word-attack skills. This test would not be

[10]Woodcock, Richard W. *Woodcock Reading Mastery Tests.* Circle Pines, Minnesota: American Guidance Service, Inc., 1974.

adequate for prescriptive teaching of specific phonemes. It also seems that overall adequacy of gross word-attack could be more easily measured by using a smaller number of words such as those used in the Botel Reading Inventory, or of greater difficulty such as those near the end of Woodcock's test.

Constructing Your Own Test or Using the Ekwall Phonics Knowledge Survey

Before choosing or constructing a test for phoneme-grapheme relationships you should first examine the research on which graphemes are of high enough utility or which represent a specific sound or phoneme to a degree that makes them worthwhile testing and teaching. For example, Lou Burmeister (1968), in examining the 17,310 words from a study by P. R. Hanna and others (1966), found that the vowel pair "ie" appeared 156 times. In those 156 words the "ie" grapheme represented six different phonemes as heard in the following words (p. 448):

WORD	FREQUENCY	PERCENT
thief	56	35.9
Lassie	30	19.2
die	26	16.7
patient	23	14.7
cashier	17	10.9
friend	4	2.6

The "ie" sound heard in the word "thief" accounted for 35.9 percent of the total words, the "ie" sound heard in "Lassie" accounted for 19.2 percent of the total words, etc. As you can see, however, it would not be practical for a teacher to try to teach students all six of the "ie" variations. For this reason decisions need to be made concerning which graphemes are of high enough utility to make them worthwhile teaching, based on such factors as the percent of time that vowel combinations represent certain phonemes, frequency of appearance in children's literature, etc. Oswald and Ekwall[11] have developed a list of phonic elements that are recommended to be tested and taught to children in grades one through three and to older disabled readers. These are the graphemes tested in the Ekwall Phonics Knowledge Survey shown in Appendix A. In that survey you will note that some graphemes represent two phonemes. Where it is recommended that both be taught it is because both sounds are approximately equal in utility.

There is a way of testing for the various phonic elements that establishes a situation that is nearly analogous to actual reading and which does not possess the innate disadvantages of the methods used in many commercial tests. An example of this type of test along with complete directions for its administration is shown in Appendix A. The procedure for constructing such a test, and the rationale for its use, is as follows:

[11]Ekwall, Eldon E., and Oswald, Lowell D. *Rx Reading Program*. Glenview, Illinois: Psychotechnics, Inc., 1971.

1. Choose about four small stimulus words that are usually known by children in their early reading. The words should contain only one syllable and should begin with a vowel. The author suggests the following four words:

> at
> in
> all
> ate

Print these words on four cards to be used as flash cards or print them all on one larger card or at the top of the stimulus sheet that the student will see.

2. Place each initial consonant, consonant blend, or consonant digraph before one of these small words to form a nonsense word. The element to be tested and the stimulus word should precede the nonsense word on the same line as follows:

> 1. m ate mate
> 2. t ate tate
> 3. p ate pate
> 4. s all sall
> 5. pl in plin
> 6. ch all chall
> 7. qu at quat

The use of at least four stimulus words will enable you to form nonsense words with any combination of initial consonants, blends, and digraphs.

3. In constructing the test be sure to place about eight to twelve of the easier consonants first, e.g., the following: p, n, s, t, r, m, b, and d. These are later used in nonsense words to test for vowel knowledge.

4. Combine each vowel, vowel team (vowel digraphs and diphthongs), and special letter combinations ("r," "l," and "w" controlled vowels, etc.) with one or two of the easier consonants listed above to form a nonsense word as shown below:

> 1. a bam
> 2. i mip
> 3. o tope
> 4. a mape
> 5. oi poi

Be careful to construct long-vowel and short-vowel nonsense words that do not violate common vowel rules. For example, put short vowels between two consonants to conform to the cvc pattern in which we expect the vowel to be short. Put the long vowels in a pattern of cv final "e" or cv[12] in which we would expect the vowel to be long.

The procedure for administering the test using this method is as follows:

1. Make sure that all children to be tested know the four stimulus words so they can say them without any hesitation. Before administering the test always show the student these words and ask him to pronounce them. If he does not know one or more of them, teach them to him and have him come back at a later date when he has learned them thoroughly.

2. Have the student respond to each line by saying the *name* of the letter or letters (not the letter(s) sound), the small stimulus word, and then the nonsense word. It is important that he say all three exactly as outlined here.

---

[12]Although there are some exceptions to the rule that vowels are usually long in the cv pattern in "words" (it is not a good rule when dealing with syllables) many more words do have the long vowel sound in this pattern, e.g., go, me, he, and she. A few exceptions are "do" and "the" when "the" is pronounced with a schwa sound at the end.

3. In the vowel section the student should respond by saying the name of the vowel and then the nonsense word. Before administering the vowel section you should, of course, make sure that the student knows the initial consonant letter sounds chosen to combine with the vowels, vowel teams, and special letter combinations. If the student does not respond, you can feel assured that it is because of a lack of knowledge of the vowel sound rather than a lack of knowledge of the rest of the word.

Administering a test of this nature is not at all difficult and the results will be gratifying. You will also find this type of test to be highly reliable. Some of the reasons for, and advantages of, using this type of test are as follows:

1. It places the testing in a situation that is analogous to actual reading. That is, the student has to react as he would in reading or "decode" words rather than "encode" as one does in spelling. Also sounds are not tested in isolation when this method is used.

2. Although nonsense words are used you can feel assured that the student will know all of the word but the element being tested. This way if he fails to respond properly you can be reasonably sure it is because he does not know the element being tested and not some other part of the word. In a few instances students will fail to respond because they do not know how to blend. If you find that a student does not respond then you can easily check to see if blending is a problem by having him give the sounds in isolation. If he can give them in isolation, you can assume that blending is a problem. If he cannot do that you can assume that he does not know the letter sounds.

3. He is not being tested on words that may already be in his sight vocabulary, therefore, if he responds correctly, you are assured that he does know the element being tested.

4. When the student responds it is not at all difficult to determine whether the response is correct or incorrect. I have often demonstrated this with fifty or more teachers when testing a child and have gotten 100 percent agreement on all answers. When testing sounds in isolation one seldom gets 100 percent agreement from fifty teachers on any answer. It should be stressed that you should not attempt to test students until all of the stimulus words are known.

A complete diagnosis for a disabled reader's knowledge of phonics skills usually includes testing for weaknesses in consonants, consonant blends and digraphs, vowel sounds, vowel rules, and syllabication. Thorough testing in this area can easily consume from one-half hour to one hour's time. And, after all of this time the diagnostician may find that the disabled reader is really not weak in phonics knowledge at all.

For students who have adequate phonic word attack skills the diagnostician can save a great deal of time by simply administering a group of long nonsense words such as those in the *Botel Reading Inventory*. These are words such as "chummertracing," and "craminstate." If the student is able to pronounce these words, there is really no need to test in the areas of phonics mentioned above. You should keep in mind that the learning of vowel rules, syllable principles, etc., is simply a means to an end. If the student is able to attack new words then there is really no need for him to be able to "tell" you the vowel rules, or syllable principles, or for that matter, there is no need for him to be able to give vowel or consonant sounds in isolation. For example, many students in beginning reading methods courses can pronounce almost any word, but they have long since forgotten, or never knew, how they learned to do so. For this reason, I would recommend that students above the third grade level (where most of these skills should have been learned) be given Botel's list of nonsense words prior to beginning the diagnostic procedure to determine whether they possess a knowledge of the various phonic word attack skills. If, however, after attempting one or two of these words, it becomes obvious that the student cannot pronounce them, they should put the list aside and further diagnosis would be necessary to discover the phonic skills in which the student is weak.

Vowel Rules, Syllabication Principles, and Accent Generalizations[13]

Research during the past decade has shown that some of the vowel rules and syllabication principles formerly taught are, in reality, of very little value. As a result most textbooks are beginning to reflect this change. Although some research has been done on word accent there is still very little definitive information to guide us in selecting worthwhile generalizations for teaching.

In testing for knowledge in these areas you should again remember to devise or use a test that is analogous to what the student does when he is actually reading. For example, in testing for knowledge of various vowel rules you should ask the student to respond to a nonsense word such as "rup" rather than have him recite the rule. (A single vowel in a closed syllable usually has the short sound.) Many students are able to recite rules that they are unable to apply, and conversely, many students seem to have learned or developed a "sixth sense" for the application of rules that they cannot recite. What the teacher should remember in testing, once again, is that various rules and generalizations are a means to an end. And, if a student can already apply the rule or generalization, he has achieved that end and there is little or no value in discussing or teaching the means to that end.

Vowel Rules

In the discussion of vowel rules that follows the most useful rules will be listed and then a method or methods of testing for knowledge of the rule will be presented.

1. In *words* containing a single vowel letter that appears at the end of the word, the vowel letter usually has the long vowel sound. (Note that this rule refers to words and not just syllables. There is a similar rule for single vowel letters at the end of syllables—(see number two, (p. 101).

   Testing: Write several nonsense words with this pattern (such as those that follow) and say to the student, "If these were real words, how would you say them?"

   sho
   bri
   na

   Note that it is assumed the student will know the "sh," "br," and "n"

[13]The terms *rule*, *principle*, and *generalization* are often used interchangeably in referring to the study of vowels, syllabication, and accent.

sounds as well as short and long vowel sounds. If he does not, it would not normally be appropriate to test for vowel rule knowledge anyway.

2. In syllables containing a single vowel letter that appears at the end of the syllable, the vowel letter may have either the long or short vowel sound. Try the long sound first. (Note that this is the same rule as in number one (p. 100). Here, however, the reference is to all syllables rather than syllables that are words.)

   Testing: Use the same test as in number one above. When teaching this rule be sure to stress that the student should be flexible, i.e., try the short vowel sound if the long one does not form a word that is in the student's speaking-listening vocabulary.

3. A single vowel in a syllable usually has the short vowel sound if it is not the last letter or is not followed by "r," "w," or "l."

   Testing: Write several nonsense words with this pattern (such as those that follow) and say to the student, "If these were real words, how would you say them?"

   > pid
   > pud
   > lat

4. Vowels followed by "r" usually have a sound that is neither long nor short.

   Testing: The directions for this would be the same as in number three. Use nonsense words such as the following:

   > bur ⎫
   > ber ⎬   All rhyme with fur
   > bir ⎭
   > bor   (bore)
   > dar   (rhymes with star)

5. A "y" at the beginning of a word has the "y" consonant sound, "y" at the end of a single syllable word, when preceded by a consonant, usually has the long "i" sound, and "y" at the end of a multi-syllable word, when preceded by a consonant, usually has the long "e" sound. (Some people hear it as short "i".)

   Testing: The directions for this would be the same as in number three. Use nonsense words such as the following:

   > cly
   > fory
   > mippy
   > yint
   > yand

6. In words ending with vowel-consonant-silent "e" the "e" is silent and the first vowel may be either long or short. Try the long sound first.

   Testing: The directions for this would be the same as in number three. Use nonsense words such as the following:

   > tete
   > papt
   > mide

In teaching this rule you should also stress that the student should be flexible, i.e., try the short vowel sound if the long one does not form a word in his speaking-listening vocabulary. It has been demonstrated that students who are taught to be flexible in attacking words when applying rules such as this become more adept at using their work-attack skills than those who are not taught this flexibility.

7. When "ai," "ay," "ea," "ee," and "oa" are found together the first vowel is usually long and the second is usually silent.

Testing: This would normally be tested under vowels, vowel teams, and special letter combinations section of the test described earlier in the chapter and shown in Appendix A. The directions would again be the same as in number three. Use nonsense words such at the following:

> dea
> dee
> boap

8. The vowel pair "ow" may have either the sound heard in cow or the sound heard in crow.

  Testing: This would also normally be tested under the vowels, vowel teams, and special letter combinations section of the test described earlier in the chapter; otherwise, show the student a nonsense word such as "fow" and say, "If this were a real word how would you say it?" If the student says it so it rhymes with "cow" then say, "Yes, and how else could we say it?" He should then pronounce it so it then rhymes with "crow" if he knows both common pronunciations. If not, then you would need to teach whichever one he did not give you.

9. When "au," aw," "ou," "oi," and "oy" are found together they usually blend to form a diphthong.

  Testing: This would also normally be tested under the vowels, vowel teams, and special letter combinations section of the test described in Appendix A. If not, handle the testing the same as described in number three.

10. The "oo" sound is either long as in "moon" or short as in "book."

  Testing: This is the same situation and can be handled the same as "ow" described in number eight above.

11. If "a" is the only vowel in a syllable and is followed by "l" or "w", then the "a" will usually be neither long nor short.

  Testing: This is the same situation and can be handled the same as the "r" control rule listed in number four above.

Syllabication Principles

As mentioned previously, the syllabication principles should be tested in a situation analogous to actual reading. Many teachers, as well as the authors of commercial tests, devise syllabication tests in which the teacher pronounces a word and the student is to tell how many syllables he hears in the word. This, of course, is not what the student has to do when he reads. Another type of test that is quite often given to students is one in which the student is told to pronounce the words on his sheet and then tell how many syllables he hears. The problem with this type of test is that if the student were able to pronounce the word, he would not need to know the syllable principles at all!

A good way to test for knowledge of syllable principles is to simply give the student some nonsense words, or long words that are not likely to be in his sight vocabulary and ask him to draw lines separating the syllables. When doing this you must be careful to use words that could be divided only according to the rule you are testing and not in several places according to other rules. Below is a list of some of the most commonly taught and generally accepted syllable principles as well as words you can use to test students' knowledge of these principles.

1. When two consonants stand between two vowels the word is usually divided between the consonants, e.g., dag-ger and cir-cus.

   > botnap
   > daggal

   In some of the newer materials words are divided after the double consonant, e.g., dagg/er. It should be remembered that in reading we are usually teaching syllabication as a means of word-attack. Therefore, you should also accept a division after double consonants as correct even though the dictionary would not show the division in that way.

2. When one consonant stands between two vowels, try dividing first so that the consonant goes with the second vowel, e.g., pa-per and mo-tor. Students should be taught that flexibility is required in using this rule, e.g., if this does not place the vowel in a pattern to give a word in his speaking-listening vocabulary then he should divide it so that the consonant goes with the first vowel as in "riv-er" and "lev-er."

   > lador
   > mafel

3. When a word ends in a consonant and "le," the consonant usually begins the last syllable, e.g., ta-ble and hum-ble.

   > nable
   > frable

   (The "le" sound is usually heard as "ul.")

4. Compound words are usually divided between word parts and between syllables in these parts, e.g., hen-house and po-lice-man.

   > cowperson
   > dogthrower

5. Do not divide between the letters in consonant blends and consonant digraphs. In syllabication treat them as though they were a single letter, e.g., hy-dro as in principle number two, treating "dr" as a single letter.

   > pacher
   > pasher

Accent Generalizations

Accent generalizations are of less importance for a disabled reader than either the learning of vowel rules or syllabication principles. This is partially true because a student that properly attacks a new word that is in his speaking-listening vocabulary, but not in his sight vocabulary, is likely to get the right accent without any knowledge of accent generalizations. Although we have been given some guidance as to which accent generalizations to teach by a study done by Carol Winkley (1966), we are still lacking information concerning the utility of various accent generalizations. For these reasons the testing of a disabled reader's knowledge of accent generalizations is probably not worthwhile.

Contractions

Another area of structural analysis that often causes problems for children is the learning of contractions. The method of testing them should be very similar to that of basic sight words, i.e., simply give the student a list of them and ask him to first read the contractions and then tell what two words each contraction stands for. In scoring each contraction keep in mind that it is important that a student know each contraction since they appear so often in print. Although it is less important, the student should also know what two words each contraction stands for. Following is a list of contractions, taken from five commonly used sets of basal readers, that may be used for testing purposes. Although many of the following contractions do not appear on basic sight word lists at least one of the two words from which these contractions were derived does appear on these lists. Because writing styles vary a great deal it would be difficult to find an "average" utility value for these words. However, it is known that contractions do cause some students considerable difficulty and for those students who experience these difficulties remedial exercises with contractions improve their reading. Note that following each contraction is a grade level designation. This designation represents the point at which you might expect that most students should know that contraction. Remember, however, that the grade level designations are only guidelines.

WORD	GRADE LEVEL	WORD	GRADE LEVEL
let's	2.9	wouldn't	3.5
didn't	2.9	she'll	3.5
it's	2.9	here's	3.5
won't	2.9	ain't	3.9
that's	2.9	couldn't	3.9
can't	2.9	they're	3.9
wasn't	2.9	they'd	3.9
isn't	2.9	you'll	4.5
hadn't	2.9	she'd	4.5
don't	3.5	weren't	4.5
I'll	3.5	I'd	4.5
we'll	3.5	you've	4.5
I've	3.5	you'd	4.5
he'll	3.5	we'd	4.5
hasn't	3.5	anybody'd	4.5
haven't	3.5	there'll	4.5
aren't	3.5	we've	4.5
I'm	3.5	who'll	4.5
he's	3.5	he'd	4.5
we're	3.5	who'd	4.5
you're	3.5	doesn't	4.5
what's	3.5	where's	4.5
there's	3.5	they've	4.5
she's	3.5	they'll	4.5

Affixes

Suffix and prefix knowledge is also an area of structural analysis that sometimes receives attention in diagnosis. Based on studies such as those of Russell Stauffer (1969, pp. 348–351), I would suggest that the diagnostician not concern himself with disabled readers' knowledge of the *meaning* of any suffixes and only about eleven prefixes. Stauffer found only fifteen prefixes that tended to be of rather high utility and have generally the same meaning each time they are used. In a further analysis of Stauffer's fifteen words I found that only eleven of these tend to be used in conjunction with root words that would be meaningful for children in grades one through six. Teaching disabled readers to recognize the more common prefixes and suffixes by sight, however, is often helpful in improving their word analysis skills.

The eleven prefixes that tend to be worthwhile teaching (for meaning) along with their meanings are as follows:

Prefix	Examples of Prefix in Common Words	Meaning of Prefix	Point at Which Prefix Should Be Known
1. re	repay, remake	back or again	6.5
2. un	unhappy, unmade	not	6.5
3. en	enliven, entomb	in, to make, put into	6.5
4. ex	export, expel	out, forth, from	6.5
5. de	debar, deform	from, away, from, off	6.5
6. com	combine, compose	with, together	6.5
7. in	inboard, include	input, into	6.5
8. in	incapable, inactive	not	6.5
9. pre	preschool, prejudge	before, prior to	6.5
10. sub	submarine, subsoil	under	6.5
11. dis	disconnect, dismiss	apart, away from	6.5

As can be seen the point at which the authors of most basal reader series agree that these prefixes should be known would not be until the middle of sixth grade. For this reason, unless you were dealing with an older disabled reader, reading at or near this level, there would be little need to test or teach the meanings of even these most consistent prefix meanings.

CONTEXT CLUES

Research such as that done by Alan Robinson (1963) on context clues indicates that a student would be able to attack an unfamiliar word with the use of context clues alone only a small percent of the time. However, when a student uses context clues it is usually in conjunction with phonics or structural analysis. For example, a student may often read up to an unfamiliar word, sound the first letter and then, using the clues gained from both, say the word. (He saw the man who was coming h _ _ _ _ [home].) Or, the student may read up to a word and pronounce the first syllable. (When the dis _ _ _ _ _ _ was determined they stopped the measurement [distance].) The use of context clues is one of the most important word attack skills a student can possess.

Beginning teachers often make the mistake of thinking that children will automatically learn to use context clues without any instruction in their use. Many children do seem to use both picture clues as well as written context clues almost innately; however, some children, especially those who become disabled readers, need specific instruction in this important skill.

For teaching purposes context clues are often categorized according to type such as "Summary Clues," "Experience Clues," and "Synonym or Definition Clues" as explained by Ruth Strang, et. al. (1967). However, for testing purposes this is not necessary.

Strang — categorized context clues.

In constructing exercises for testing you should obtain several short paragraphs written at varying grade levels, e.g., first, third, and fifth grade. Be sure not to employ materials commonly used such as well-known graded reading inventories, as many children will have already been given these reading passages or they are quite likely to encounter them later. Type or print the passage on one side of a 5 in. × 8 in. card and leave out several words. Passages written for first or second graders should be typed with primary type or printed in letters of at least an equivalent size or larger. Words chosen to be omitted should be those for which few or no substitutions could be made in the context in which they are used. They should also be words that could easily be derived from the context if the student is able to use context clues. Where words are omitted you should substitute X's or dashes for each letter in the word. This also gives the student a clue as to word length, which again is analogous to the clues he would have in actually reading. On the back of the card you may wish to include the directions you will give the student along with the reading passage and answers to be supplied in each of the blanks.

The front of the card might appear as follows:

> Fred had a pet cat.
>
> Its name xxx Jiffy.
>
> Jiffy liked xx run xxx play.
>
> Jiffy xxx not like Fred's dog.
>
> And, Fred's dog xxx not xxxx Jiffy.

The back of the card would then appear as follows:

> Read this story. Some of the words have been left out. When a word was left out some x's were put in its place. As you read the story try to say the words that you think belong in the story where the x's are.
>
> Fred had a pet dog.
>
> Its name was Jiffy.
>
> Jiffy liked to run and play.
>
> Jiffy did not like Fred's dog.
>
> And, Fred's dog did not like Jiffy.

The testing of context clues in this manner should not be confused with the "cloze" technique which is a method of testing students' comprehension—explained in Chapter 6. In using the standard "cloze" procedure every fifth word is omitted and a standard sized line is left for each omitted word on which the student is to write the word he thinks was omitted. In using the procedure described above there are no standards in terms of number of words to be omitted or percent of right and wrong answers. Your judgment of the students' ability to supply oral answers in the reading passages used for context clues will be based on your opinion of how well the student does in relation to other average readers of the same grade level.

If students are unable to use context clues when they read they should be tested on their ability to use them orally. For example, you may wish to simply read a sentence leaving out a word and then ask the student what word might be used where the blank appeared in oral context. Students who are able to do considerably better on oral context clues than on written context clues may be lacking so severely in word recognition skills that they are unable to concentrate their efforts on the use of context clues. On the other hand, those students who do no better in oral exercises using context clues than they did in written exercises are usually simply unaware of the value and use of context clues and need to be taught how to make use of this important word attack skill.

CONFIGURATION CLUES

Many authorities believe it is helpful for beginning and/or disabled readers to receive instruction in the use of configuration clues. I would simply suggest that in your day-to-day teaching procedures you note whether the student is confusing words of similar configuration and whether he seems to be aware of differences in words with extenders and descenders, capital and lower case letters, and words with double letters.

Where it is apparent the student is not fully aware of these differences remediation as described in Part B of this chapter (under the heading Configuration Clues) would be appropriate.

DICTIONARY SKILLS

Although few would argue the importance of a thorough knowledge of the use of the dictionary for students from the middle elementary grades through their adult lives the lack of knowledge of dictionary skills is not a serious problem for disabled readers. Most of the basic word analysis skills are, or should be, achieved by the time most students begin to work with the dictionary. Furthermore, only a very small percent of our total meaning vocabulary is achieved through the use of the dictionary. Therefore, for seriously disabled readers it is not recommended that a test for knowledge of dictionary skills even be included in the initial diagnosis. For older, less disabled readers, however, you may wish to take inventory of their ability to use the dictionary.

PART B.   *remediation*

The whole word approach or sight approach to the learning of words is rapid at first but as a student begins to encounter many new words he usually finds that he must use some method of word analysis or word attack. In most cases a student attacks new words by using a combination of several methods such as phonics, structural analysis, configuration, and context clues. Many readers become disabled because they have not developed one or more of these word attack skills. Before beginning work on the remediation of a student's word attack skills you should first determine whether he is lacking in only one area of word attack skills or whether he needs to "start from scratch" and learn how to use all of the skills mentioned above.

There are several ways of teaching the various word attack skills. For example, some commercial programs present a great many rules for long and short vowel sounds, vowel combinations, syllabication, etc. Students are taught these rules and are expected to memorize the rules as well as their application. Other programs present lists of graphemes for which the students are to learn their phoneme equivalent either in isolation or when blended with a familiar phonogram. In this type of program few rules are taught. An attempt is simply made to get the student to the automatic response level. Before beginning a specific program of remediation you should also attempt to discover what type of word attack program each student has had. If, for example, a student has been through a rule-oriented phonics program and failed to learn, it may be more productive if he is instructed in techniques that do not require the learning and application of a great many rules. On the other hand, a student who has been taught using a program in which few, if any, rules are taught can often benefit by learning certain worthwhile rules and/or principles.

Most students are unable to describe the type of program they have been through and are also unaware of the publisher of the materials from which they have been taught. However, if they are asked whether they ever had a book in which there were stories about Tag and Dot and Jim, or Baby Sally or Dick and Jane they can usually tell you with little hesitation. For this reason I would suggest that a part of your diagnostic kit contain a list of characters from the most common basal readers and supplementary readers or phonics programs used in your state. This can easily be compiled by looking through the various materials commonly used in your state or from areas from which you receive transfer students. You will, of course, need to be somewhat familiar with the type of word attack program presented in each series.

In teaching word attack skills in remedial reading you should consider that students who are deficient in their ability to attack new words may have gotten that way because they were not able to learn by the method used by their regular classroom teacher. An eclectic approach to word analysis skills may have been used, and a student predisposed to learning through any one approach may not have gotten enough instruction in that one approach. On the other hand, his classroom teacher may have used a rule-oriented program, as mentioned previously, from which some students experience success, yet, from which some are doomed to almost certain failure if not exposed to other methods.

In beginning a program of word attack skills with a new student you should first attempt to discover whether he is immediately successful with whatever approach you choose in the beginning. If you then discover that he is still not successful, be prepared to switch to another approach. You should also examine your own methods of teaching from time-to-time to insure that you are not wedded to any one approach. The use of any one approach which seems best to you may often be beneficial in teaching developmental reading. However, being a "one approach" teacher in remedial reading is highly undesirable.

PHONICS AND STRUCTURAL ANALYSIS

Many of the activities that follow appear to be simple testing situations if they are not followed up with correctional procedures when a student fails to respond correctly. Remedial reading, if done properly is, of course, a highly individualized procedure. When the student responds incorrectly on either written or oral exercises he should be corrected immediately so as not to reinforce a wrong response. These correctional procedures can either be carried out by the teacher while the student works or it can be done by a teacher's aide, or by an older student who is familiar with the material and who can, in turn, immediately correct any wrong answers.

PHONIC ELEMENTS

The term *phonic elements* is often used to define various letter combinations and the sounds they represent. I have chosen to use the term rather than phoneme for sounds and grapheme for its written equivalent in this case because some letter combinations (phonic elements) consist of more than one phoneme and consequently more than one grapheme.

There are, of course, many methods that can be used in teaching the various elements. One typical procedure is as follows:

1. Developing awareness of hearing the sound:
    1.1. Say, "Listen to these words. Each of them begins with the 'bl' sound. Circle the 'bl' on each word on your paper as you hear the sound. Blow—blue—blunder, etc."
2. Developing awareness of seeing the sound:
    2.1. Tell the student to circle all of the words in a passage that begin with "bl."
3. Providing practice in saying words with the "bl" sound:
    3.1. Pronounce each word and have students pronounce it after you.
       blow
       blue

blunder
bleed
blast

4. Providing practice in blending the "bl" sound with common word families or phonograms:

    4.1. Teach or use several phonograms with which students are already familiar such as "ock" and "ush". Put the "bl" in one column, the phonogram in a second column, and the two combined in a third column as follows:

bl	ock	block
bl	ack	black
bl	ur	blur
bl	under	blunder

Instruct the student to say "bl" (the two letters and not the sound) and then the phonogram (this time sound represented by the letters in the phonogram) and then the word formed by the two.

    4.2. Another similar exercise that works well and gives practice in blending is to place the letters and words as follows:

bl	<u>f</u>lock	(block)
bl	<u>l</u>ack	(black)
bl	<u>f</u>ur	(blur)
bl	<u>th</u>under	(blunder)

Instruct the student to say "bl," then the middle word, and then take off the underlined letters from the middle column word and replace it or them with "bl" and say the new word that is formed. If students cannot do this mentally, have them write the complete word shown in column three above.

5. Asking the student to make a list of some words that begin with "bl." If this is too difficult for the student, provide him with a list of some phonograms from which some "bl" words can be formed. Ask the student to say each word as he writes it.

6. Providing practice in reading "bl" words. Either present a paragraph or story that has a number of "bl" words in it or write a paragraph using the "bl" blend in a number of words.

One important factor to remember in teaching any phonic element is that you should not expect to teach it and then assume the student has full recall and use of it from then on. To begin with, remember that you are likely to have received the student because he did not learn at a normal rate or through whatever methods his classroom teacher used initially. Furthermore, we know that it takes many exposures to a word before it becomes a known sight word. It is unlikely that a student can learn a certain phonic element without some initial teaching and then repeated exposures to that element in various types of written and/or oral exercises.

When teaching a group of students to listen for, and become aware of, sounds in words you can increase participation by giving everyone three cards on which are printed the numbers 1, 2, and 3 and/or the words beginning, middle, and end on the reverse side of the card. As you say words have each student respond by holding up the appropriate card. For example, in teaching a lesson on the "h" sound you might say, "I am going to say some words, some of which have the "h" sound in them. If you hear it at the beginning of the word, hold up your number one card. If you hear it in the middle of the word, hold up your number two card and if you hear it at the end of the word, hold up your number three card. Some words may have more than one "h" sound in them. If you hear the "h" sound at the beginning and middle then hold up both your number one and two cards." etc. This type of exercise will quickly enable you to evaluate which students are learning to recognize the "h" sound and which are not. When we only call on one student there is often a tendency to overlook other students who do not respond.

Some other types of exercises for teaching phonic elements are as follows:

1. Omit letters from a word used in context and give several choices to be filled in. This usually encourages the student to try several sounds in order to arrive at the correct answer.

   1.1. Cindy and Dwight like to go ___ishing.
       (g, f, b, h)

   1.2. Sam forgot his ___ooks at school.
       (d, p, b, q)

   1.3. Paul did a goo___ job of washing the car.
       (d, p, b, g)

2. Give each student an envelope with several cards in it. On the front and back of each card print one letter. For example, each student might have five cards each of which has one of the following letters: c, f, g, h, and d. As you say words have students hold up the card that has a letter representing the sound they hear at the beginning, middle, and end of various words. Do this same type of exercise having students hold up various vowel letters and vowel pairs that they hear in words.

3. Have students write and read their own and other students alliterative-type stories. For example, a junior high student's paragraph illustrating the use of "f" read as follows:

   > Once in a fir forest there were four fast fireflies. The four fireflies like to fly forward and backward. Once on the fourth of February the four fireflies flew fast forward and then fast backward into a flaming fire. Now there are not four fireflies in the fir forest.

4. Have students scan the newspaper and circle or underline learned phonic elements. Discuss the words found.

5. Start a "thing box" in which you simply put many miscellaneous articles such as a ball, book, bike (toy), toothbrush, tank, dress (doll), and drum. Have boxes labeled "b," "d," "t," etc. As students pick up each article, they say the name of the article and listen for the initial sound and then sort the items into their respective boxes. This type of exercise can be made self-corrective by using a label-maker to put the correct beginning letter on the bottom of each item.

6. The same type of exercise described in number five above can be done using a file folder in which an envelope is glued or taped to one inside fold. This en-

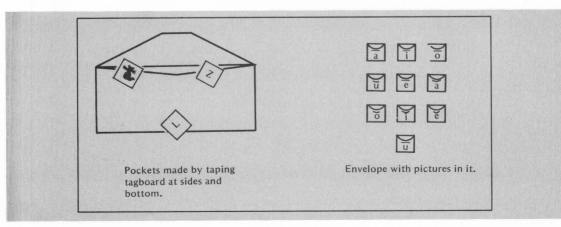

Pockets made by taping tagboard at sides and bottom.

Envelope with pictures in it.

velope can contain many pictures representing various initial consonants, blends, digraphs, vowels, etc. On the other side of the inside fold make pockets by cutting out pieces of tagboard and taping them on the sides and bottom. Students then take pictures out of the envelope and sort them into the proper pockets. This exercise can also be made self-correcting by writing the correct letter (grapheme) on the back of the pictures. A file folder done in this manner to teach vowel sounds is illustrated below.

7. Put an "X" in front of each word in the list on the right that has the same beginning sound as the thing shown in the picture on the left.

_____ dog
_____ from
_____ fright
_____ glow
_____ free

8. Say the words below and listen for the long or short vowel sound in each word. Write long in the blank after the word if you hear the long vowel sound in the word and short if you hear the short vowel sound in the word.

bid _____   he _____
make _____   lake _____
up _____   three _____

Another similar exercise calls for the student to say each word and mark the long and short vowels over each vowel letter using the breve ( ) and macron ( ).

9. Say each of the following words to yourself and listen for the vowel sound. Then write the words from the top list under the word that has the same vowel sound.

Spain   came   mood
freight   Mike   piece
ate   each   trial
me   ran   Sue
blue   meat   sleigh

too   line   tree   lake   cat
_____   _____   _____   _____   _____
_____   _____   _____   _____   _____
_____   _____   _____   _____   _____

10. Find the vowel sound that is heard in each blank by looking at the key word preceding each sentence. Then find the correct word from the list that has that vowel sound in it. (Help the student with the stimulus words to the left of the numbers if he does not know them before he begins the exercise.)

let—hop—lid—lake—lad—like

(Ed)   1. Father _____ me go with him.
(cat)   2. The small _____ went with his father.
(cake) 3. We went to the _____ to go fishing.
(it)   4. Mother put the _____ on the pot.
(kite) 5. I _____ to go fishing.
(top)   6. Can you _____ over the fence?

There are many ways in which the tape recorder can be used in teaching the various phonic elements. Several of these are illustrated below.

11. Tape record a number of words from which the student is to listen to determine whether he hears the long or short vowel sound. For example, in doing this exercise the student would hear the following: "First number your paper from one to twenty. Turn the tape recorder off until you have done this (*pause*). Now you will hear some words called. As you hear each word write 'long' or 'short' after the number of that word. Here are the words: number one—dog, number two—lake, number three—rod," etc. In doing this type of exercise you may wish to have the student simply mark each blank after the numbers with a breve (˅) or macron (—). (Do this only if the student has already learned diacritical marking.) A more advanced exercise using the same type of script is to have the student write the word "long" or "short" and the vowel sound he hears in each word. This type of exercise can also be done with initial consonants, consonant digraphs, etc.

One major advantage of the tape recorder is that it can act as a self-correcting device for various types of exercises. This is illustrated below:

12. Each student is given a sheet of paper prepared as follows:
    1. d f g t   f r b n
    2. t c v w   p l s n
    3. etc.

    The tape recorder script would be as follows: "On your paper are numbers and after each number are four letters, a space, and then four more letters. Now you will hear some words called. You are to circle the letter you hear at the beginning of each word from the first group of four letters and the letter you hear at the end of the word from the second set of letters by each number. Here are the words. Be sure to listen carefully. Number one—din, Number two—camps." etc. "Now we will check your work. The first word was *din*. You should have circled the *d* from the first group of letters and the *n* from the second group of letters. Circle these two letters now if you did not get them right the first time. The second word was camps. You should have circled the *c* from the first group of letters and the *s* from the second group of letters. Circle the two letters now if you did not get them right the first time. The third word was. . . ."

When using the tape recorder keep in mind that almost any type of material that you could check as a class exercise can be checked by the tape recorder.
Although it takes a little more time to record these exercises in the beginning it will certainly save much time in the long run.

BLENDING

Many students learn the various consonant and vowel sounds in isolation or are able to give the sounds in isolation but are unable to blend various sounds together to form words. The inexperienced teacher who tests sounds in isolation may be led to believe some students have no problem with sounds when, in reality, their inability to blend known sounds may be as disabling as not knowing the sounds at all. If the testing procedure, as described in Part A of this chapter, is followed, however, students' ability to blend will be tested along with their knowledge of grapheme–phoneme relationships. Those students who show weaknesses in blending should be assigned exercises such as the following:

1. After students have learned to hear beginning, middle, and ending sounds they can begin blending using the technique called *double substitution*. In using this technique you should start by using an oral presentation, e.g.:

   1.1. What word begins like "down" and ends like "hog"? (dog)

   1.2. What word begins like "dig" and ends like "log?" (dog)

   1.3. What word has two letters that begin like "white" and end like "hen?" (when)

   After considerable practice using an oral presentation you may wish to give students word lists and directions as follows:
   Using the beginning sound from the word in the first column and the ending sound from the word in the second column write a new word in the blank in the third column. Say the word as you write it.

   Initial Consonants
1. can	2. bar	3. _____ (car)
1. name	2. go	3. _____ (no)
1. to	2. lake	3. _____ (take)
etc.		

   Initial Consonant Blends
1. from	2. crank	3. _____ (Frank)
1. stair	2. land	3. _____ (stand)
1. plum	2. clay	3. _____ (play)
etc.		

   Initial Consonant Digraphs
1. champ	2. blew	3. _____ (chew)
1. wheel	2. gale	3. _____ (whale)
1. thin	2. sing	3. _____ (thing)
etc.		

2. Put several initial consonants, blends, or digraphs on the chalkboard in a column. To the right of these put several familiar phonograms (see example below).

ch	op
sl	ap

   Tell students that you will quickly point to a beginning consonant or blend on the left and then to one of the phonograms on the right. They are to say the word formed by the combination of the two. This exercise works well with three to four students. You should use your hand and sweep across from the initial sound to the phonogram very rapidly. Do not hesitate to use combinations that form nonsense words.

3. Read the questions below. Letters are missing from the beginning of each word. Write the missing letters in the blank using one of the sets from the row at the top to answer the question.

   br   cr   dr   fr   gr   pr   tr   bl   cl   fl   pl   thr
1. What do you do when you are thirsty?		_____ink
2. What do you do when you get bigger?		_____ow
3. What does a baseball pitcher do?		_____ow
4. What does a rooster do?		_____ow
5. What does the wind do?		_____ow
6. What do you do at recess time?		_____ay

RULES FOR HARD AND SOFT "C" AND "G"

Most reading specialists agree that students are more likely to learn and remember rules, generalizations, and/or principles governing sounds when they have been learned inductively or by the discovery technique. The rule, as generally stated, governing the hard and soft sounds of "c" and "g" is as follows: When "c" or "g" is followed by "e," "i," or "y" they usually retain their soft sounds. If they are followed by any other letter, they usually retain their hard sounds. In teaching this rule or generalization to a student or to a group of students the procedure would be as follows: (Only "c" is illustrated, however, "g" would be done in the same manner.)

1. Discuss the fact that the letter "c" stands for more than one sound.

2. Discuss the fact that rules can usually be applied which help us to remember which sound to use in various situations.

3. Suggest that a list be mde to examine a number of "c" words to see if students can make up their own rule.

4. Have students think of a number of "c" words while you list them on the chalkboard. Examples might be as follows:

can	came	cry
cent	cycle	cog
cigar	century	color
cancer	cut	certain
come	curve	cavity
cell	city	circus

5. Have students reread all the words to determine how many different sounds the "c" represents. (In this exercise the answer should be two—the "k" sound as in "cut"" and the "s" sound as in "cell."

6. Group all words under the following two headings:

k-sound	s-sound
can	cent
cancer	cigar
come	cell
came	cycle
cut	century
curve	city
cry	certain
cog	circus
color	cancer
cavity	
circus	

7. At this point after some discussion students will usually come up with the correct generalization. Do not rush them. Also, if necessary, find more words to make sure that all parts of the rule are covered.

8. Provide practice in applying the rule by giving students a list of "c" words and letting them mark a "k" or "s" over, or after, each "c" to indicate the correct sound according to the rule, e.g.,

ˢcent	*or*	cent <u>s</u>
ᴷcame		came <u>k</u>

etc.

The rules governing the various "y" sounds may be taught the same way. This same technique also works well with most other generalizations of fairly high utility.

"R" CONTROL RULE

The "r" control rule can easily be taught using a technique similar to that described above concerning the rules for hard and soft "c" and "g." A typical procedure would be as follows:

1. Discuss the fact that when "r" follows a vowel it usually "controls" or modifies the sound of the vowel.

2. Again, discuss the fact that rules can usually be made to help remember various "r-controlled" vowel sounds.

3. List a number of words in which "r" follows a vowel, e.g.:

fir	brother	cur	bird
fur	corn	torn	Ford
far	scorn	morning	herd
jar	happier	mar	

4. Categorize the different sounds

"ar" as in "car"	"or" as in "corn"	"er" as in "herd"
far	scorn	fir
jar	torn	fur
mar	morning	brother
	Ford	happier
		cur
		bird

5. Let students make up a generalization, e.g., "ir," "ur," and "er" usually have the sound heard in "herd". "Ar" usually has the sound heard in "car". And, "or" usually has the sound heard in "corn".

6. Give students a chance to practice using their newly gained knowledge, e.g., give exercises such as the following:

   6.1. Write the correct vowel plus "r" in the blanks below.
   I ate breakfast this m__ __ning.
   Many animals are covered with f__ __.
   Father came home in a new c__ __.
   etc.

VOWEL RULES, SYLLABICATION PRINCIPLES, AND ACCENT GENERALIZATIONS

As stated earlier, learning various vowel rules and syllabication principles can be of considerable benefit to a disabled reader. However, the commonly taught accent generalizations are of less utility. First of all there is insufficient research regarding which accent generalizations are of high enough utility to make them worthwhile teaching. Secondly, we need to consider *why* we teach accent generalizations.

When a student encounters a word that is in his speaking–listening vocabulary, but not in his sight vocabulary, he will have to apply one or more word analysis skills to determine that word. For example, a student may not know the word "cabin" in the sentence, "The Smiths went to their cabin in the mountains." After applying the necessary word analysis skills he would be left with accenting the word as cab-íń or cab́-in. With the help of the use of context clues he would be quite likely to accent it properly if "cabin" was in his speaking–listening vocabulary since he only has two choices to begin with. It is only when words are not in a student's speaking–listening vocabulary that accent really becomes useful. Since most disabled readers' reading levels are likely to be one or more years behind their speaking–listening vocabularies they have less need for learning accent generalizations than a normal reader. It is only when their reading level approaches a normal level that this need becomes more apparent.

In teaching beginning readers, certain vowel rules are taught before the syllabication principles. Where we are dealing, for the most part, with single syllable words this works quite well. However, in remedial reading, we also need to be cognizant of *why* we teach syllabication principles. We teach syllabication principles so that we know what positions various vowels have in words thus enabling us to give them the proper sound. For example, looking at "cabin" again, we see at least four possible ways which it could be pronounced if it were not divided into syllables. The pronunciations are as follows:

$$c\ \bar{a}\ b\ \breve{i}\ n$$
$$c\ \breve{a}\ b\ \breve{i}\ n$$
$$c\ \bar{a}\ b\ \bar{i}\ n$$
$$c\ \breve{a}\ b\ \bar{i}\ n$$

By dividing the word before the "b" (ca-bin) we see that the "i" is a single vowel in a closed syllable, therefore, it would probably have the short sound. This then leaves the student with only the decision of whether to try the long or short sound for the "a." This, of course, has automatically cut the number of possibilities by 50 percent. If the word "cabin" appeared in context and was in the student's speaking–listening vocabulary, he would be likely to get the right pronounciation of the word regardless of which "a" sound he tries first. On the other hand if he divided it so that the break came after the "b" (cab-in) then he would be quite likely to get the proper pronunciation on the first try.

The student who first begins to learn the various rules, principles, and/or generalizations discussed here may become somewhat discouraged. First of all, they may say (teachers included) that they see very little improvement in children's ability to apply phonic generalizations as they progress through the grades in elementary school. Research such as that of Margaret Hislop and Ethel King (1973), however, has shown that children do improve considerably in their ability to apply phonic generalizations as they receive more instruction from grade-to-grade. Secondly, students tend to become discouraged because of the rather laborious process of first thinking through the various principles for syllabication of a word and then applying the correct vowel sounds according to the position of the vowels within each syllable. Most older students quickly understand the analogy of this type of learning to that of riding a bicycle or of learning to drive a car. For example, in learning to drive a car we, at first, had to consciously think of every movement we made such as turning on the ignition, depressing the gas pedal, etc., but after only a short period of time all of these conscious motions became automatic. So it is with learning vowel rules and syllable principles. After only a short period of time the application of the rules and principles becomes an automatic process for many students.

A third problem that teachers and students encounter is the many exceptions to the stated rules. Teachers can alleviate this problem somewhat in the beginning by using words that do follow the rules. However, students will discover that there are many exceptions and they should be taught to be flexible to their approach to word attack. For example, the vowel rule, "when a vowel comes at the end of a syllable it is usually long", should be taught as, "when a vowel comes at the end of a syllable, try the long sound first." Even when exceptions appear students usually accept this fact quite well if we simply explain to them that we have derived the rules and generalizations to fit our complex language. Had we been able to design a language to fit a set of existing rules it would have been different.

The initial procedure for the introduction to either the vowel rules or the syllable principles can be done somewhat the same as the procedure explained for teaching the hard and soft "c" and "g" sounds, i.e., by use of the discovery technique. In introducing either the vowel rules or syllable principles, however, you may wish to introduce a word list, prepared prior to the lesson, from which your students can then derive various rules and/or generalizations. This word list should contain only words that are not exceptions to the rule or principle being taught. In the initial introduction use words that are already familiar to most students.

After the various vowel rules and syllable principles have been introduced provide students with the opportunity to practice the application of the material they have learned. Just as we would not expect most students to learn a new word well enough for it to become a sight word after one or two exposures, we should not expect students to learn the application of a particular vowel rule or syllable principle from only applying it one or two times.

WORD ENDINGS

Many disabled readers miscall the common word endings or varient endings "s," "ed," and "ing," even though they know them when given in isolation. In this case the student should be provided with the opportunity to focus on variant endings until he develops the habit of looking at and pronouncing each one carefully. A good way to provide this opportunity is to have the student do multiple choice exercises such as the following:

1. Each of the sentences below has a word left out. Pick the correct word from the choices below each sentence and write it in the blank.
   1.1. The boys were _____ ball.
      played   playing   plays
   1.2. The dogs _____ in the yard.
      plays   playing   played

1.3. Harry _____ to play baseball.
      liking   liked   likes

2. Each sentence below has a word with the ending left off. Fill in each blank with the right word-ending.

2.1. The girls were walk _____ home.

2.2. We walk _____ home yesterday.

2.3. Tim said that he walk _____ home from school every day.

WORD FAMILIES OR PHONOGRAMS

The teaching of word families or phonograms to disabled readers is often very beneficial. The practice of "looking for little words in big words" has usually been discouraged because the pronunciation of the little word often changes when it becomes a part of a longer word. Phonograms, however, tend to have fairly consistent pronunciations from one word to another. Phonograms are also extremely useful in teaching blending of initial consonants, blends, and digraphs.

One technique you may want to use in teaching word families is to simply call students' attention to the fact that there are certain clusters of letters that tend to have similar sounds from one word to another. Students can compile lists of the common phonograms and these can be used in exercises such as the following:

1. See how many words you can make by combining the list of initial consonants or consonant clusters on the left and the word families on the right.

br	ell
b	ank
sh	all
cr	anch
c	eak

2. Have students make, or you can make, a flash card for each phonogram with which they have difficulty. Pair students for study using exercises as described in number one and two above. Also have students test each other on their own and other students' phonogram lists or groups of flash cards.

CONTRACTIONS

Contractions often present difficulties for normal as well as disabled readers. Although a lack of knowledge of contractions alone will not cause a student to become a disabled reader it can be an important factor in his overall error pattern. One of the major reasons that students encounter difficulties with contractions is that their oral language is often less formal than what is found on the printed page. Therefore, students find a discrepancy between what might seem natural to say and what they actually read. Many contracted forms that are apparent in students' oral language are seldom seen in print and, therefore, are simply not seen often enough to be thoroughly learned.

The teaching of contractions then becomes a matter, for most teachers, of providing for multiple exposures to each contraction and insuring that each trial is practiced right and not wrong. Since contractions are common in our oral language, the tape recorder can be used as an excellent teaching device. Some examples follow:

1. Give students sheets of paper, with numbers, in which two to four contractions appear to the right of each number, e.g.,

    1.1. they've   they're   they'd

    1.2. wouldn't   would've

    Tape record sentences and have students circle the contraction they hear in the sentences, e.g., in numbers one and two above the sentences would be as follows:

    1.3. The boys said they'd rather not go.

    1.4. We would've gone if they would have asked us.

2. Do the same type of exercise as shown above only give students sentences in which the contracted word is blank. Students are to pick the correct contraction from a choice of several to make the sentence read correctly.

3. Give students numbered lists of contractions and have them write the two contracted words beside the contraction. Use a tape recorder to correct each answer immediately after it has been done. The students' papers would appear as follows:

    3.1. I've _____

    3.2. Haven't _____

    3.3. etc. _____

    The tape recorder script would be as follows: "Write the two words that stand for the contraction in the blank in number one. (Beep.) The contraction is *I've* and the two words it stands for are *I have*. Now do number two. (Beep.) The contraction is *haven't* and the two words it stands for are *have not*. Now do number three.", etc. (The "beep" is a signal to turn off the tape recorder.)

POSSESSIVES

Possessives usually present few problems for students; however, a few disabled readers tend to confuse them with contractions, i.e., when pronouncing words with possessive endings they attempt to contract the word in some manner. Disabled readers can usually correct this problem rather easily if they are simply told that whenever the apostrophe is followed by or comes after "s" it means that the word is simply pronounced as though the apostrophe were not there. A few practice sentences or phrases including contractions or possessives will be helpful in reinforcing student's learning, e.g.:

1. Jim's hat was lost.
2. I'd like to go.
3. Sam lost Frank's watch.
4. The boys found Frank's watch.
5. The boys said they'd like to go.

ROOT WORDS AND AFFIXES

The learning of root words, as with sight words, is simply a matter of providing for multiple exposure to words through varied reading and/or written excercises.

Students do, however, need to learn to identify commonly used affixes to facilitate the pronunciation of root words with attached suffixes and prefixes. As explained in the section on testing students' knowledge in this area, the remedial reading teacher should focus on pronounciation of affixes and not on meaning. Some commonly used exercises to help students in this area are as follows:

1. Have students underline all the affixes they can find in a newspaper article. Compile a list of the ones found. Discuss each affix and then compile a master list of all the different affixes found for a period of time.

2. Do the same thing as described in number one above, but furnish the students with lists of affixed words.

3. Give students one or more root words such as "do" and have a contest to see who can make the most variations of the word, e.g.,
   1. undo
   2. doing
   3. doer
   4. redo
   5. etc.

4. Have each student make flash cards for any affixes with which he has trouble. On the side of the flash card write the affix and several words illustrating its use. On the other side of the card write a sentence using the affix on a word in a sentence.

CONTEXT CLUES

Context clues are a very important word attack skill as well as an important means of vocabulary development. Although basal reader teacher's manuals tend to thoroughly teach the use of this skill today, many readers in the past were seldom given any instruction in the use of context clues. Even today, however, many disabled readers have failed to learn to use context as a word attack skill. Evidently teachers sometimes believe that the use of context is so obvious that students are likely to learn this skill with little or no instruction. This, of course, is simply not true. Many readers need a considerable amount of instruction and a great deal of practice in using this skill.

One of the first, and most important techniques for teaching context clues is to simply talk with students about their use. For example, many disabled readers do not have any idea that a word could often be attacked by the use of the context. Some students apparently figure it out for themselves, but the disabled reader often seems less adept at reaching these conclusions without some help.

Other types of ideas and exercises are listed below:

1. The tape recorder can be used to advantage in first making students aware of context clues in oral exercises. Note: Wait five seconds after reading each sentence. The script would be as follows: "I am going to read a short story. Once in a while I will leave out a word. Where a word is left out or omitted you will hear a beep sound. When you hear the beep try to fill in the word that belongs there before I give the answer. Here is the story.

   Once Jack and Jim were going to _____ fishing. (go) First they dug _____ worms. (some) Then they took. . . ." etc.

2. Give students sentences with words left blank. For every blank give the student several choices of words that might belong in the blanks, e.g.:

   2.1. Mary was _____ to visit her Uncle George.
       (they – going – did – being)

   2.2. Frank's dog did _____ like cats.
       (that – give – not – be)

3. Give students sentences such as those listed in number two above but give only the first letter of the missing word, e.g.:

   3.1. Mary was g _____ to visit her Uncle George.

   3.2. Frank's dog did n _____ like cats.

4. Give students sentences such as those listed in number two above but do not give any clues as to what word or words might be used in the blanks. After students have completed the blanks have each student read his sentence and hold a discussion about the appropriateness of the words chosen.

5. Use cloze passages where approximately every eighth to tenth word is omitted. Ask students to fill in the blanks. After students have completed the exercise, hold a discussion about what words were used in each blank. Research in the use of this technique has generally shown that this type of exercise has very little value without the discussion that follows, so do not omit that part. An example of a cloze passage follows:

   5.1. George was going to visit _____ Grandpa and Grandma. He _____ going to go on an airplane. His father _____ with him to buy his ticket. The clerk _____ the desk asked George _____ he wanted to . . . , etc.

CONFIGURATION CLUES

Although the use of configuration clues is an important skill in word analysis very little concrete information exists on effective ways of teaching students to become more aware of it. Most of the research tends to show that methods that have traditionally been used are of little value. For example, many textbooks on reading have suggested that lines be drawn around words printed in lower case to show contrasting shapes as in the words [what] and [when] . However, research by Gabrielle Marchbanks and Henry Levin (1965), as well as others, has shown that in actual practice this technique has very little value. The problem probably lies in the fact that so many words have exactly the same shape when outlined. If this technique has any value at all it would probably be for the student who constantly confuses two somewhat similar words. This technique might then be used to emphasize slight differences in the configuration of only those two words at a time.

We also know that words printed in lower case tend to be easier to read when the lower half of the word is masked. Thus, we would be led to believe that using the lower case alphabet in beginning reading would be more effective. However, even this argument does not tend to be supported by the research. In actuality it does not seem to make any difference in students' overall reading achievement when they are instructed in lower case, upper case, or as is normally done, by combining the two.

Occasionally, a student will have considerable difficulty with words such as "though," "through," and "thought." Where this is the case it seems somewhat effective to point out differences such as the "t" sound and the "t" letter at the end of "thought" and the "r" in "through." We also improve students' ability to note configuration in teaching word families—phonograms—such as "all" and "ate." Generally speaking, however, unless a student is confusing two similar words as "county" and "country" we could probably spend our time on more effective methods of word attack than dwelling on configuration clues.

DICTIONARY SKILLS

As stated earlier, in Part A, students do not become seriously disabled readers from a lack of knowledge of dictionary skills. This is not to belittle the importance of thoroughly learning the use of the dictionary. However, from the standpoint of economy of time the remedial reading teacher will probably spend most of his or her time in remediating problems that have a more immediate effect on most students' reading.

There are numerous filmstrips, workbooks, etc. which effectively cover the teaching of dictionary skills. Because of these factors, the author has not included discussion of the teaching of the dictionary skills. A list of sources for teaching the dictionary skills is shown in Appendix C.

SUMMARY

For the teacher who has no experience in the testing of word-attack skills the problem of assessing the students' knowledge in this area may seem quite simple. On the other hand the experienced diagnostician, who is familiar with an array of tests in this area, will know that there are many different ways of testing word-attack skills. Research has shown that although the correlations between any two of these tests may be rather high one is not likely to obtain item-by-item agreement on particular skills or phonemes when using one test as contrasted with another. If the remedial reading teacher is to do exact diagnostic teaching on the basis of test results, it will be necessary to examine the type of test to be used to make sure it tests students' word attack skills in a situation similar to what the student will do in actual reading (decoding) and not what he would do in encoding or spelling. Furthermore, in prescriptive teaching, as is necessary in remedial reading, the teacher should avoid the use of multiple choice tests which allow the student to get one-fourth to one-fifth of the answers correct by simply guessing. Most word-attack skills, and expecially a knowledge of phoneme-grapheme relationships is too critical to be omitted in the teaching process because they were guessed correctly on a test.

A number of tests containing subtests for word-attack skills have been discussed in this chapter. The beginning teacher, and even the experienced diagnostician would do well to familiarize themselves with a number of these tests. In many cases it will be better to use a combination of subtests from several different test batteries. You may also feel that in many cases testing materials can be constructed that will be as good as, and in many cases more appropriate, than some of the commercial materials that are presently being marketed.

A number of exercises and activities or games have been suggested for help in remediating students' difficulties in word-attack skills. In using many of these activities the teacher will find it necessary to supervise students work very closely so that wrong answers are not reinforced.

Chapter 5:   REFERENCES

Burmeister, Lou. "Vowel Pairs," *The Reading Teacher*. Vol. 21, (February, 1968), 445–542.

Gates, Arthur I., and McKillop, Anne S. *Gates-McKillop Reading Diagnostic Tests*. New York: Teachers College Press, 1962.

Hanna, P. R.; Hanna, Jean S.; Holdges, R. G.; and Rudorf, E. H., Jr. *Phoneme–Grapheme Correspondence as Cues to Spelling Improvement*. Washington, D.C.: Office of Education, United States Department of Health, Education, and Welfare, 1966.

Hislop, Margaret J., and King, Ethel M. "Application of Phonic Generalizations by Beginning Readers," *The Journal of Educational Research*. Vol. 56., (May–June, 1973), 405–412.

Marchbanks, Gabrielle, and Levin, Harry. "Cues by Which Children Recognize Words," *Journal of Educational Psychology*. Vol. 56, (April, 1965), 57–61.

Robinson, H. Alan. "A Study of the Techniques of Word Identification," *The Reading Teacher*. Vol. 16, (January, 1963), 238–242.

Stauffer, Russell G. *Teaching Reading as a Thinking Process*. New York: Harper & Row, 1969.

Strang, Ruth; McCullough, Constance M.; and Traxler, Arthur E. *The Improvement of Reading*. 4th. ed., New York: McGraw-Hill, 1967.

Winkley, Carol. "Which Accent Generalizations Are Worth Teaching," *The Reading Teacher*. Vol. 20, (December, 1966), 219–224.

DIAGNOSIS AND REMEDIATION OF EDUCATIONAL FACTORS: *comprehension, vocabulary development, and study skills*

One purpose of this chapter is to discuss methods of, as well as limitations of, diagnosing students' reading comprehension and vocabulary development. The first section on diagnosis contains a general description of commonly used methods of diagnosing general comprehension and vocabulary development. Following this general section specific suggestions are given for diagnosing difficulties with comprehension. Another purpose of this chapter is to identify methods of diagnosing those study skills which are likely to contribute to students' failure in school. The last purpose of Chapter Six is to discuss some practical methods for dealing with students who are disabled in these areas.

PART A.   *diagnosis*

THE NATURE OF COMPREHENSION

Over the years reading methods textbooks and basal reader teacher's manuals have often listed a host of different comprehension skills which students should supposedly master during their progression through the grades. Some examples of skills commonly listed are: the ability to note and grasp details, main ideas, the author's purpose, the ability to underline or note key words, the ability to make generalizations, and the ability to predict outcomes. As mentioned in Chapter 3, however, research in the area o. reading comprehension does not support the theory that these skills actually exist as separate entities. A statistical technique that is often used to attempt to locate or measure separate variables is factor analysis. If separate comprehension abilities actually exist, through the technique of factor analysis we should be able to identify each of these separate factors. Once located and identified we can then devise tests over each factor or skill and administer these subtests to groups of students. If, in reality, the factors are measurable entities, we would expect to obtain rather low correlations among these various factors or entities. That is, we would expect students to exhibit strengths in some factors, and weaknesses in others. For example, we know that musical ability and mathematical ability are not highly related. If tests were given to ten students measuring their abilities in each area, we would be quite likely to find that there was really very little relationship between the two or, in other words, some students who were extremely talented in music might do quite poorly in math and vice versa. This would produce a low correlation. We would, of course, obtain a high correlation if all of the students who were talented in music were also talented in mathematics and if all of the students who did poorly in music also did poorly in mathematics.

Research such as that done by Donald Spearritt (1972) has shown that we can identify a word or vocabulary factor as a separate entity from other comprehension skills but all other factors tend to correlate highly and thus fall into what one might quite practically describe as a big conglomeration termed "other comprehension skills" or simply "comprehension." Spearritt was able to locate three other comprehension skills in addition to word knowledge, through the process of factor analysis. He found, however, that these three factors correlated so highly that it was doubtful if they could, in reality, be considered as separate entities. Spache and Spache (1973, p. 550), state that some studies have indicated the presence of perhaps three factors that they classified as knowledge of word meanings, the ability to see relationships among ideas, and the ability to use reasoning processes. As you can see, it would still be very difficult to determine the difference between the latter of these two factors.

Perhaps Isidore Levine (1970) is nearly correct in his explanation of differences that exist in the ability of one person versus another to comprehend a reading passage. Levine contends that most people who comprehend well in a certain subject do so because of their wide reading and experience in that area and not because of their ability to "unravel paragraph complexities." Levine states, "We can conclude that the ability to select main ideas and supporting details in a paragraph is not a skill that can be developed and transferred from subject to subject. A grasp of the concepts and data in a body of knowledge is assured when one has perused thousands of paragraphs in that subject." (p. 675) The author agrees with Levine that major differences in comprehension probably can be accounted for by the experience factor. On the other hand, certain disabled readers who consistently have difficulty with reading comprehension, even though they comprehend well in an oral presentation, can usually benefit from specific instruction in comprehension skills. It should also be noted that Levine implies that knowledge of vocabulary will improve comprehension. For some students this is probably true but there is evidence to show that this would not necessarily be true for all students.

M. Wiener and W. Cromer (1967) have proposed a "difference" model and "disruption" model for students having difficulties in their reading. Unlike Levine, Wiener and Cromer contend that students who might be categorized in the "difference" model have reading difficulties because of a difference in the way material is written and the student's normal mode of responding. Students classified in the "disruption" model would be likely to possess emotional and psychological barriers which interfere with the reading process.

Cromer (1970) did a study to validate his theory of the difference model. He took two groups of junior college students who exhibited poor comprehension skills. One group was classified as "deficit" because of their low scores in vocabulary. The other students were in the "difference" model group. These students had normal scores on vocabulary. Reading materials were rewritten and organized differently to make phrasing and sentence patterns more apparent. These materials were then presented to both groups. When this was done the performance of students in the "difference" group was as high as that of good readers of a comparable grade level. However, the "deficit" students reading performance remained low. Cromer's experiment lends credence to his theory that students classified in his "difference" model might be helped by either having the materials changed to meet their needs or by instructing or changing the students mode of response in reading the materials.

From a testing standpoint, based on what we know about comprehension at this time, it does not seem justified to attempt to diagnose a student's comprehension abilities beyond word or vocabulary knowledge and another category of other comprehension in general.

METHODS OF DIAGNOSIS FOR GENERAL COMPREHENSION LEVEL

Traditionally used methods of diagnosing students' level of comprehension could be divided into five main categories. These categories would be group standardized tests, individual standardized tests, informal reading inventories, informal recall procedures, and the cloze procedure. The cloze procedure, however, as a somewhat standardized technique, is somewhat newer than either of the first four mentioned categories. A sixth method gaining popularity is that of the analysis of sentence meaning from its structure, sometimes referred to as "deep structure."

except I.Q. tests

most serious problem of group stand. tests

Group Standardized Achievement and Diagnostic Tests

The use of standardized tests is by far the most commonly used method for diagnosis in group situations. Although they have some major disadvantages they do have several advantages that have tended to make them popular. One advantage of group standardized tests is that they are quite efficient in terms of teacher time. They also have the advantage of being standardized so that you can compare the performance of a group of students with that of other students. It has been repeatedly mentioned in earlier chapters that one criteria for any reading test should be that it measures reading skills in a situation that is analogous to actually reading. Although it is nearly impossible to do this with tests of word attack or word recognition skills in a group situation, it does appear feasible to test reading comprehension with groups of students since this can be done in a situation nearly analogous to actually reading. Another often claimed advantage of group standardized tests is that they are usually written by "experts." On the other hand, a number of critics have pointed out that certain standardized tests, although well known and much used, contain many questions that tend to make them of dubious value.

Most group standardized tests do not attempt to classify various subskills of general reading comprehension beyond vocabulary knowledge and another category usually referred to as comprehension. This is somewhat confusing, however, since vocabulary knowledge itself is such an important factor in general reading comprehension. It is important to emphasize that when a test purports to measure vocabulary *and* comprehension, what they really mean is that they are attempting to measure vocabulary knowledge and *other* comprehension skills. Both of their categories collectively measure "general comprehension" or what has been referred to in the scope of the reading skills, shown in Chapter 3, as "Recognizing and Understanding Ideas."

As mentioned above, most group standardized tests do not attempt to categorize the subskills of vocabulary and comprehension. The *Stanford Diagnostic Reading Test*[1] (Level II) does, however, break reading comprehension down into two categories called "literal" and "inferential." The authors have provided norms for each of these two subcategories. However, because of the fill-in format of items it makes it difficult to believe that they can actually measure these categories accurately. A separate subtest is also provided for vocabulary. Within the category called *comprehension* most test authors have tried to devise questions that supposedly measure the student's ability to make inferences, remember important details, understand the author's purpose, see a sequence of events, etc. A careful reading of the questions on some of even the best known group standardized tests will often cause the well-trained reading specialist to become disenchanted. For example, in reading the passages and then reading the questions pertaining to these passages it soon becomes obvious that some generalizations the student is expected to make could not possibly be made from the information presented in the material itself. Success with a particular question of this nature may then depend entirely on the student's background of experiences. For more information on this and other problems with group standardized tests consult the article by Howard F. Livingston (1972) entitled, "What the Reading Test Doesn't Measure—Reading." In that article Livingston discusses, in much more detail, some of the problems encountered with group standardized tests.

As stated earlier, nearly all group standardized tests lump all of the various types of questions mentioned above into a broad category of "comprehension," from which you would only get a grade-level score.

One of the disadvantages of group standardized tests is that they will not allow the teacher to check on total recall in most cases since the student is usually able to look back over the material and find answers to the questions that he encounters at the end of the reading passage. However, the most serious problem encountered with group standardized tests, as far as disabled readers are concerned, is that students can often simply guess at all answers and yet make a somewhat respectable score. To illustrate this problem to students who are beginning their first course in reading, I have often given them the machine scorable answer sheet for the intermediate battery (Grades 4-5-6) of a nationally known

[1]Karlsen, Bjorn; Madden, Richard; and Gardner, Eric F. *Stanford Diagnostic Test—Level II.* New York: Harcourt, Brace & World, Inc., 1966.

reading test and instructed them to randomly mark their answers. In this case they do not even see the test questions. This would be similar to a situation in which every student was a complete nonreader. When all answers are marked the class is given the answers and their grade level scores are then computed. Invariably the class average is from 3.2 to 3.5 with individual subtest scores ranging as high as 6.5. It is not uncommon for individual subtest scores to range from 4.0 to 4.5. Upon seeing these kind of results we can see the futility of attempting to derive any meaningful grade level scores for extremely disabled readers. Perhaps a good rule to follow in interpreting individuals test scores on group standardized tests is to simply ignore any score at or below what could be achieved by chance.

In summary one might look at some ways in which group standardized tests might be useful and some ways in which they should not be used. Some ways in which they might be used are as follows:

1. To measure the achievement of a group from the beginning to the end of a remedial period. However, even then you must keep in mind that for those students who cannot read at all, or for those who are severely disabled, you are not likely to obtain an accurate beginning measurement and thus the full extent of student gains will not be shown.
2. To measure overall class or group weaknesses in certain areas, e.g., general vocabulary, study skills, or social science vocabulary, which should, in turn, point to specific areas for upgrading of the instructional program. This may, however, have little relevance for the remedial program.
3. To look at the specific types of questions that any one student or small group of students are missing.
4. To initiate a beginning point in the diagnosis of individuals.

Some ways in which group standardized tests should not be used are as follows:

1. For grade placement of disabled readers or in making any major decision concerning the welfare of a single student based on a grade placement score.
2. For judgment of the amount of gain in overall reading ability, for a single student, from the beginning to the end of an instructional period.

In summary, you should use a great deal of caution in interpreting the results of group standardized tests before making judgments concerning individual students unless you are simply examining the types of questions on which a student was, and was not, successful or unless the tests serve as a beginning point for a more thorough diagnosis.

Appendix B lists some commonly used group standardized reading tests, the grade levels for which they are appropriate, and the skills that each test purports to measure.

Individual Standardized Reading Tests

Individual standardized reading tests have been popular with reading specialists for many years. They have the disadvantage of being more time consuming to administer, but while administering the test the teacher has the distinct advantage of being able to observe various characteristics displayed by the reader. Individual standardized tests are also available for measuring oral as well as silent reading. This is also an advantage over group standardized tests which, of course, are limited to the measurement of students' *silent* reading ability.

The *Durrell Analysis of Reading Difficulty*[2] which is well known among reading specialists, contains a subtest for silent comprehension. This subtest is standardized although no information is given on the size and composition of norm group. In the silent reading passages the student is merely told to read the passage and to try to remember everything he can. The score sheet contains an exact reproduction of each passage, phrase-by-phrase or idea-by-idea. After the student has read the passage, he is simply told to tell all he can remember about the passage. The teacher then makes a check mark by each phrase or idea remembered through unaided recall. After the student has completed this, he is asked questions regarding portions that were omitted. The total of the aided and unaided recall is added and the total is then carried to the norm tables which give a grade-level placement for that particular raw score.

Durrell's method of measuring silent reading is rather unique but also has some disadvantages. First, it should be noted that this is not referred to as a test of silent reading comprehension. Durrell refers to it as a test of memories which is probably an honest representation of what it measures. For example, I have found a few children who seemed to possess eidetic imagery, who after having read a passage could recite it word-for-word. Yet when questioned about the meaning of certain aspects, it was evident they did not understand what they had read. On the other hand, older students and adults who tend to read for main ideas often cannot do well on this kind of task. These limitations should be kept in mind when using this subtest, but it does provide useful information on how much the student can remember. Joel Levin (1971) has shown that the ability to remember is enhanced if the student is adept at developing mental images. Since the ability to develop mental images apparently contributes to comprehension skill, this obviously makes this type of test useful in assessing that aspect of reading comprehension.

Another type of individual standardized reading test is the *Gilmore Oral Reading Test*[3] which, as its name implies, measures oral reading. It contains a subtest for oral reading comprehension and the norms provide for interpretation in terms of a grade level score, a stanine score, and a general rating for the actual grade level of the student being tested. The general rating for a student would be "poor," "below average," "average," "above average," or "superior." In administering this test the student is told to read carefully because he will be asked some questions about each story after he has finished reading it. There are five comprehension questions concerning each paragraph and the authors present some guidance in interpreting the answers to questions designed to test the student's ability to comprehend beyond simply the recall level.

This type of test can be very useful, especially for the beginning reading

[2]Durrell, Donald D. *Durrell Analysis of Reading Difficulty*. Rev. ed., New York: Harcourt, Brace & World, Inc., 1955.

[3]Gilmore, John V., and Gilmore, Eunice C. *Gilmore Oral Reading Test*. New York: Harcourt, Brace & World, Inc., 1968.

diagnostician, since it provides norms and gives other criteria by which to judge the adequacy of a student's reading. The norm group was also fairly large for a test of this nature. The authors report that the performance ratings for their scores were based on a distribution of scores of 4455 pupils from six school systems in various locations throughout the United States.

It should be stressed that certain individual diagnostic tests, although standardized for certain subtests, do not necessarily contain norms or standardized information for grading either silent or oral reading comprehension. For example, although Durrell presents comprehension norms for his silent reading subtest in the *Durrell Analysis of Reading Difficulty*, it should be noted that no norms are presented for the oral reading subtest. For that subtest norms are based on time only. The *Gray Oral Reading Test*[4] also provides questions to be asked of students after reading each passage. It should again be noted, however, that the norms for this test are based on time and number of oral errors and that comprehension was not considered in the norming.

Informal Reading Inventories ✓

Informal reading inventories have become quite popular as a measure of students comprehension abilities during the past twenty years and especially during the past decade. Part of the reason for this is that we now have many more well-qualified reading specialists than formerly. Another reason for the popularity of informal reading inventories is our mistrust of the results of group standardized test results which at one time were more-or-less the standard by which most pupils' reading was judged.

Informal reading inventories are usually constructed from materials from which students will be expected to use in the course of their normal instruction or they are written at specific grade levels using one of the better known readability formulas as the criteria for difficulty. Usually two reading passages are written or found for each grade level. The student then alternates from silent to oral reading at each grade level and is asked from about four to ten comprehension questions over each reading passage.

When constructing informal reading inventories (IRI's) teachers usually attempt to devise questions that cover main ideas, important details, vocabulary, and inferences. There is a more-or-less standard set of criteria for judging adequate performance on the comprehension section of IRI's, however, there is still some disagreement among authorities on the exact percentage necessary for placement at the *Free or Independent*, *Instructional*, and *Frustration* reading levels.

Informal reading inventories are often advantageous since they are usually constructed from the actual material from which a student is likely to be instructed. This puts him in a situation in which he is dealing with vocabulary, concepts and syntax that are truly illustrative of his instructional needs. On the other hand

[4]Gray, William S. Edited by Helen M. Robinson. *Gray Oral Reading Tests*. Rev. ed., Indianapolis: Bobbs-Merrill, 1967.

it is difficult to find passages that are representative of a book as a whole. And, it is also difficult to write good comprehension questions concerning the material once it is found. A further difficulty encountered by teachers and diagnosticians is the accurate interpretation of the adequacy of inferential-type questions. Any one teacher by herself may feel she is accurately interpreting a student's answers; however, when her rating is compared with that of several other people a rather large discrepancy is often found to exist.

In spite of their limitations informal reading inventories have become, and will probably continue to be, one of the most useful instruments that the reading diagnostician may possess. Chapter 11 is devoted to the construction and use of informal reading inventories and the cloze procedure. For this reason I will not discuss either of these methods of measuring reading comprehension in great detail in this chapter.

There are several rather well-known commercially published informal reading inventories and quite a number that are less well known. Among the better known are the *Classroom Reading Inventory*[5] and the *Standard Reading Inventory*.[6] The *Classroom Reading Inventory* is designed to enable a teacher to derive a grade placement through an analysis of a combination of comprehension and word recognition. However, it can readily be used as a measure of comprehension only, using the criteria given in the *Teacher's Manual*, which is in agreement with the most commonly used criteria for scoring informal reading inventories. The *Standard Reading Inventory* contains passages for diagnosis of both oral and silent reading comprehension. The *Standard Reading Inventory* (SRI) contains two forms. Each form consists of eleven stories for oral reading and eight stories for silent reading. The author of the SRI states that it measures vocabulary in context, vocabulary in isolation, recall after oral reading, and recall after silent reading.

Informal Recall Procedures

Although not often publicized by this term, *informal recall procedures* have largely been used as a measure of students' comprehension for as long as reading has been taught. This procedure may take the form of a teacher asking a student a number of questions from a teacher's manual or "off the top of the teacher's head" after the student has read a passage. Sometimes the teacher may simply ask the student to tell about what was read. One of the major disadvantages of this system is that there is no criteria by which to judge the adequacy of an answer. Teachers can often compare one student's answers against those of other students in the class, but even then, this is often misleading if the teacher has a low ability group, high ability group, or teaches in a community with an extremely low or high socioeconomic level which, in turn, usually influences overall achievement. Although this procedure has some advantages for the classroom teacher, it usually has limited usefulness for the reading diagnostician.

[5]Silvaroli, Nicholas J. *Classroom Reading Inventory*. 2d ed., Dubuque, Iowa: Wm. C. Brown, 1973.
[6]McCracken, Robert A. *Standard Reading Inventory*. Klamath, Oregon: Klamath Printing Co., 1966.

The Cloze Procedure ✓

The cloze procedure is a technique whereby every *nth* word is omitted from a reading passage and a blank is then left in place of each omitted word. The student is given the passage and told to fill in the blanks with proper words to fit the context of the sentences from which they were omitted. Many authorities in the field of reading believe this technique to be one of our better measures of reading comprehension. They contend that filling in the blanks requires a deeper comprehension of a reading passage than could generally be measured with oral or written questions or with multiple choice type questions. In fact, anyone who doubts the fact that a thorough comprehension of a reading passage is required in order to obtain a high score on a mutilated passage has but to try one for himself.

    A great deal of research has been done during the past decade in an attempt to develop a standardized procedure for building and scoring cloze passages. Much of this research concerned itself with developing specific percentages of correct responses that would be equivalent to a student's free or independent, instructional, and frustration reading levels. By comparing students scores on cloze passages with those of the same passages in multiple choice form (and in some cases administered as informal reading inventories) researchers such as John Bormuth (1967) and Earl Rankin and Joseph Culhane (1969) have developed what is now generally recognized as a standardized procedure for the percent of words to be omitted as well as the percent of correct responses corresponding to the three reading levels mentioned above. Most of the percentages have been developed on the basis of leaving out every fifth word and replacing each word with blanks of equal length. Based on the omission of one word in five the percentages of correct responses equivalent to the commonly recognized reading levels are as follows:

      57 percent plus   = Free or Independent Reading Level
      44 to 56 percent = Instructional Reading Level
      43 percent minus = Frustration Reading Level

    Cloze passages have the advantage of group type tests in that they can be administered to more than one student at a time. By using a plastic overlay to check the answers they are also quite easy to score and interpret. Chapter 11 deals with the construction, use, and scoring of cloze passages. (See Chapter 11 for details of the procedure.)

    At the time this book went to press there were no commercially available cloze tests to the best of my knowledge. However, a series that uses a cloze format, only with multiple choices, has been developed by Richard W. Burnett[7] and has been on the market for some time.

Sentence Structure or Deep Structure

While occasionally used as a single comprehension question in a test, very little formal research has been done on the use of the recovery of sentence structure as a

[7]Burnett, Richard W. *Burnett Reading Series Survey Tests*. Bensenville, Ill.: Scholastic Testing Service, Inc., 1966.

measure of students comprehension. Herbert Simons (1971), for example, believes that through linguistic theory and psycholinguistic research better comprehension tests may soon emerge. As Simons points out, Transformational Grammar is the theory of the inherent structure of our natural language. It includes a study of the way words are put together to form sentences, the meaning of which vary, according to the way in which they are strung together. Simons stresses the point that comprehension cannot take place without the recovery of the original underlying relationships in a reading passage.

Simons suggests several methods of using knowledge of sentence structure as a measure of comprehension. One of these methods would be to determine which two, of three, sentences is a paraphrase of another as in the following example:

"a. He painted the red house.
 b. He painted the house red.
 c. He painted the house that was red." (p. 359)

Another method suggested of recovering sentence structure suggested by Simons is the filling in of blanks to make sentences having the same meaning as follows:

"1.] For the girl to leave is what the boy would like.
     What the _____ would like is for the _____ to leave.
 2.] He painted the house that was red.
     He painted the _____ _____.
 3.] The girl asked the boy when to leave.
     The girl asked the boy when _____ should leave." (p. 359)

A third method suggested by Simons would be to simply have students paraphrase what was read. In order to do this, of course, one would have to have very objective scoring criteria. Simons suggestions seem to hold a great deal of promise for research in the area of construction of comprehension tests and could be adapted, to some extent, by reading specialists in their day-to-day diagnostic procedures.

DIAGNOSIS FOR VOCABULARY KNOWLEDGE

Some of the most commonly used methods of testing for vocabulary knowledge include the use of group standardized tests, the vocabulary section of individual standardized reading tests, the vocabulary section of individual intelligence tests, informal questioning, and informal reading inventories.

Group Standardized Tests

Group standardized tests have traditionally been popular as a measure of both group and individual vocabulary development. As in the case of general comprehension, group standardized tests are easy to administer, and are generally efficient in terms of teacher time. Most of the other advantages, as well as disadvantages, discussed in using group standardized tests as a measure of general comprehension also apply when using them as a measure of vocabulary development. However, most critics of group standardized tests have tended to be less critical in reviewing the vocabulary sections of these tests than in reviewing questions dealing with general comprehension. Perhaps this is simply because questions designed to measure vocabulary knowledge are inherently easier to construct.

Most group standardized tests report vocabulary development in terms of grade level placement. See Appendix B for a listing of a number of commonly used group standardized tests containing vocabulary subtests, publishers, and grade levels for which they are appropriate.

Some ways in which you may wish to use group standardized tests in vocabulary measurement are as follows:

1. To measure the overall vocabulary development of a group.
2. To compare a group's vocabulary development with their general comprehension development.
3. To find particular areas of weakness or strength such as mathematics or social studies vocabulary.
4. To establish a beginning point in examining the vocabulary of an individual, providing he scores above the level that could be achieved by chance.
5. To measure overall class achievement from the beginning to end of an instructional period providing that most of the group scores are high enough in the beginning to be above the level that could be achieved by chance.

Avoid using group standardized vocabulary tests for the following:

1. To determine grade placement of disabled readers or in making any major decision concerning the welfare of a student.
2. To judge the amount of gain in vocabulary development, for a single student, from the beginning to the end of an instructional period, especially where the initial score is low enough so that it could have been achieved by chance.

In using group standardized tests you should keep in mind that you are not only measuring students' knowledge of words but their ability to read the words being tested and, in most tests, a number of other words and synonyms. The fact that a student does not score highly on a group standardized test does not necessarily mean that he has a low listening or speaking vocabulary.

The Vocabulary Section of Individual Standardized Reading Tests

The vocabulary section of certain individual standardized tests such as the *Gates-McKillop Diagnostic Reading Tests*[8] are useful in diagnosing individual student's oral word knowledge. In this case, reading word knowledge is not measured, but rather students knowledge of word meaning when he hears words read to him. In

[8]Gates, Arthur I., and McKillop, Anne S. *Gates-McKillop Diagnostic Reading Tests.* New York: Teachers College Press, 1962.

administering the Oral Vocabulary subtest of the *Gates-McKillop Reading Diagnostic Tests* the tester reads a sentence such as "A head is a part of a . . ."and then reads "coat, saw, man, box." The student is to choose the correct answer from the four choices. The student's raw score is the number of correct choices minus one-third the number of incorrect responses (to compensate for guessing). By transferring this raw score to the norm tables a grade level score can then be obtained.

The Vocabulary Sections of Individual Intelligence Tests

The vocabulary sections of certain individual intelligence tests, such as the *Wechsler Intelligence Scale for Children*[9] (WISC), the *Wechsler Adult Intelligence Scale*[10] (WAIS), and the *Stanford-Binet Intelligence Scale*,[11] can also be useful in assessing children's oral vocabularies. The WISC and WAIS both contain a vocabulary subtest from which a raw score is obtained. This raw score can then be converted to a scaled score from which interpretations can be made in terms of IQ, percentile rating, grade equivalent, etc. (See Figure 16-1, Chapter 16.) The Stanford-Binet also contains a subtest for the measurement of oral vocabulary from which it is also possible to derive a mental age and thus a grade equivalent. The real value of tests of oral vocabulary, such as those obtained by using the Gates-McKillop or any of the three intelligence tests mentioned in this section, is to determine whether there is a discrepancy between a student's oral and reading vocabularies. When test results reveal a normal, or near normal, reading vocabulary for a student, very little would be gained by administering these tests. On the other hand, for the student who achieves a low reading vocabulary score the information obtained from an oral vocabulary test can be useful in determining whether the difficulty lies in a low oral or overall vocabulary.

Informal Questioning

The use of informal questioning can be a very valuable tool in determining whether a student is having difficulty with the vocabulary of a reading passage. You need only say, "What did the word _____ mean in this passage?" There is no need to prepare well thought out questions prior to the student's reading the passage as is almost necessary for assessing general comprehension. In informal questioning you also have the opportunity to delve further into questionable answers which, of course, enables you to place further confidence in the validity of your assessment. The major problem with informal questioning, as with any method of informal assessment, is that there are no standards with which you can compare the answers

[9]Wechsler, David. *Wechsler Intelligence Scale for Children*. New York: The Psychological Corp., 1949.
[10]Wechsler, David. *Wechsler Adult Intelligence Scale*. New York: The Psychological Corp., 1955.
[11]Terman, Lewis, and Merrill, Maud A. *Stanford-Binet Intelligence Scale*. Rev. ed., Boston: Houghton Mifflin, 1960.

you obtain, other than the answers given by other students. Where a teacher is working with very bright or very dull students this sometimes presents a problem.

Informal Reading Inventories

Informal reading inventories can also be used in assessing vocabulary knowledge and have the same advantages and disadvantages as informal questioning techniques. However, because informal reading inventories will have been prepared in advance they are more likely to contain a vocabulary more representative of a particular book or grade level.

A SUGGESTED SEQUENCE OF DIAGNOSIS FOR READING COMPREHENSION AND VOCABULARY DEVELOPMENT

Most diagnosticians would include an assessment for vocabulary knowledge as a part of a general diagnosis for general reading comprehension. The heading, "reading comprehension *and* vocabulary development," is used to note the fact that "vocabulary development" has been included as a part of this suggested sequence.

As a starting point for the diagnostician there are generally two situations— one in which a fairly recent (six months or less) group achievement or diagnostic test score is available and one in which no group scores are available. In a situation in which group achievement or diagnostic test scores are available for a student it can serve as a guideline for further diagnosis. Where these scores are available there will be several possibilities:

1. Average to high Vocabulary and average to high Comprehension
2. Average to high Vocabulary and low Comprehension
3. Low Vocabulary and low Comprehension
4. Low Vocabulary and average to high Comprehension

In situation one in which a student has an average to high score (in other words at grade level or above) in both vocabulary and comprehension you can feel fairly certain that overall comprehension (vocabulary and comprehension) is not a contributing factor in his reading retardation. As mentioned previously it is possible to score within approximately six months to one year of grade level on some tests by simply guessing; however, the chances of a student achieving a score up to his grade level, or above, on the entire battery are remote. In addition to this information you may wish to verify the group score using an informal reading inventory. This will also provide for a check on the student's comprehension while reading orally and will enable you to verify his group achievement test scores on vocabulary and comprehension. Although the informal reading inventory would not necessarily be a necessity, major decisions concerning the welfare of a student should not be made on the basis of one test score. Furthermore, the time spent in giving the informal reading inventory will not be wasted since valuable information can be obtained, while giving it, on problems the student may have in the area of word attack skills.

Situation two, in which a student achieves an average to high vocabulary score and low comprehension score on group achievement or diagnostic tests, is fairly common. Scores of this nature are common when students have problems with units larger than single words. The problem, of course, is to determine the level at which comprehension actually does break down. Since most group achievement or group diagnostic tests use reading passages of several paragraphs you can feel fairly sure the difficulty will be with units of two to three paragraphs or, quite likely, a paragraph or less. Since the group test score indicates a difficulty with silent reading you should also check to see if the student has the same problem when reading orally. Since an informal reading inventory will allow you to check on all of these things it can be used at this point. In giving the IRI note the level at which comprehension breaks down and then give the student individual sentences to read and ask him to paraphrase them for you. This can be done on both the oral and silent passages, i.e., have him read sentences from oral passages aloud and then paraphrase them and then have him read sentences from silent passages silently and paraphrase them also. If the student seems to comprehend sentence units but has difficulty with entire paragraphs, he is likely to need remediation in the understanding of larger units. While administering the IRI you can also ask informal questions on the vocabulary of the reading passages and verify the results of the vocabulary score obtained on the group test.

A student who does not understand sentence units will need further diagnosis. As the student reads orally, note whether he phrases properly or whether phrase units seem to have little meaning to him. Also note whether he is aware of punctuation marks or whether he ignores punctuation and thus fails to phrase properly.

Another factor that affects group achievement and group diagnostic test scores is the student's reading speed since these tests are timed. It may be necessary to check certain students' reading rates to see if they fall considerably below the norm for their grade levels. This can be done with the Oral Reading subtest of the Durrell Analysis of Reading Difficulty or it can be done by simply giving a student a timed reading test. The time can then be checked against that of normal readers. Albert Harris (1970) presents an excellent set of norms in his book entitled *How To Increase Reading Ability.*

For students with average to high vocabulary scores and low comprehension scores it is often helpful to administer a listening comprehension test. This will tell you, to some extent, whether the student's problem is in the mechanics of reading or whether he is having difficulty remembering facts and restructuring a sequence of events. The student who cannot do appreciably better in comprehending a passage read orally to him will need remediation concerned with restructuring events, remembering details by forming visual images, etc. On the other hand, the student who does well in listening comprehension, but poorly on reading comprehension will likely need help with the mechanics of reading. For example, some students do not comprehend well because they lack an adequate sight vocabulary. Consequently, while reading, so much effort is spent on word attack that overall comprehension suffers. For the listening comprehension test you may wish to use a test such as the Listening Comprehension subtest of the *Durrell Analysis of Reading Difficulty* or use IRI passages and apply the criteria as described in Chapter 11.

In situation three in which a student receives a low vocabulary and low comprehension score the possibilities of causation are increased over situation two. In this case you might first wish to determine whether the student's problem is actually one of comprehension or whether the comprehension score is symptomatic of a problem in word attack skills, i.e., a student cannot achieve a high comprehension score if he is not able to read the words in a reading passage. As a first step then you may wish to administer a word pronunciation test such as the *San Diego Quick Assessment* list described in Chapter 4, or the word pronunciation section of the *Wide Range Achievement Test* to determine his approximate grade level in terms of word pronunciation ability. If a serious problem is indicated here, very little can be done with overall comprehension until remediation is provided for his difficulty with word attack.

If the problem is not in the area of word attack you may then wish to determine whether the student has an adequate oral vocabulary. If the results of the *WISC* or *WAIS* (the *WISC* is for ages 5–15 and *WAIS* is for ages 16+) or *Stanford-Binet* are available these can be checked. If they are not available, you may wish to administer the Oral Vocabulary subtest of the *Gates-McKillop Reading Diagnostic Tests*.

If the student's problem is not in the area of word attack or oral vocabulary, you would proceed much the same as in situation two, i.e., administer an IRI and check for problems at the paragraph, sentence, and phrase level and check for his knowledge of the vocabulary used in each passage. Also check the possiblility that lack of speed was a factor contributing to poor performance on the group test. If you do not have an IRI available or do not feel proficient in their use, you may wish to administer an oral reading test such as the Oral Reading subtest of the *Gates-McKillop Reading Diagnostic Tests* or the *Gilmore Oral Reading Test* in conjunction with the Silent Reading subtest of the *Durrell Analysis of Reading Difficulty*. If you choose to use the Silent Reading subtest of the Durrell, however, I would recommend that it be supplemented with a few questions concerning vocabulary and interpretation that measure beyond the simple recall level.

As in situation two, it may prove helpful to administer a listening comprehension test for the same reasons as described there. In a case where a student has a low vocabulary and low comprehension score you may also wish to check the results of previously given individual IQ tests, or administer one yourself if you are qualified, to determine if the student is experiencing problems with both areas because of mental deficiency. As in any mental testing program, however, you should not let a slightly low IQ score influence your expectations for a student since there are many students with low IQ's who read perfectly well. It serves little purpose to administer an IQ test if the remedial procedures will remain the same regardless of the outcome.

Situation four in which a student scores low on the vocabulary section and average to high on the comprehension section of group achievement and diagnostic tests is somewhat less common than the first three situations. Your first step in this case might be to determine whether the student has a low oral vocabulary. This could be done, as described previously, by checking the subtest scores of the *WISC* or *WAIS* or *Stanford-Binet*, if available, or by administering the Oral Vocabulary subtest of the *Gates-McKillop Reading Diagnostic Tests*. If the student's oral vocabulary is low, chances are his reading vocabulary will not improve unless remediation is provided in that area first.

If the student's oral vocabulary is adequate, i.e., above the level of his reading vocabulary, you may wish to verify the results of the group vocabulary test using an IRI with informal questions concerning the vocabulary. If his reading vocabulary (in terms of meaning) is low, you will need to provide remediation in word meaning in a written format and provide for wide reading experiences.

In cases where there are no recent group achievement tests or group diagnostic tests to serve as a guideline for beginning diagnostic procedures the procedure would normally follow a somewhat standard pattern. A good beginning point would be to administer a word pronunciation test such as the *San Diego Quick Assessment* or the Word Pronunciation subtest of the *Wide Range Achievement Test*. If a student is considerably below grade level on this type of test then he is not likely to improve in his comprehension until he receives remediation for word analysis difficulties.

If the student is found to be somewhere near grade level on the word pronunciation test then the diagnosis should continue. At this point you may wish to use an informal reading inventory such as Silvaroli's *Classroom Reading Inventory* or Spache's *Diagnostic Reading Scales* or you may wish to use one constructed locally. If you do not choose to use an IRI you can use an oral reading test such as the *Gilmore Oral Reading Test* or the Oral Reading subtest of the *Gates-McKillop Diagnostic Reading Tests*. If you choose one of these oral reading tests, you should also give a silent reading test. As mentioned previously, the *Durrell Analysis of Reading Difficulty* contains a normed subtest for silent reading comprehension, but you should supplement it with vocabulary and inference type questions since the norms only provide for "memories" or literal recall.

In administering either an IRI or a combination of the other silent and oral tests be careful to note whether the student is having a great deal of trouble with vocabulary. If it is evident that the student is encountering vocabulary problems you would probably want to administer the Oral Vocabulary subtest of the *Gates-McKillop Reading Diagnostic Tests* or check his scores on the vocabulary subtest of the *WISC*, *WAIS*, or *Stanford-Binet* if they are available. If the student scores low on oral vocabulary, he will need remediation in that area before you can expect his reading vocabulary to improve to any great degree. However, the two can certainly be remediated, and probably should be remediated simultaneously. If the student's oral vocabulary is extemely low you may wish to check on previously administered IQ tests, or administer an individual IQ test, to determine whether the student has an extremely low IQ and thus reduced potential for learning. However, the vocabulary subtest itself is a good measure of reading potential and very little is gained, in many cases, by administering an entire IQ test. It serves little or no purpose to administer an IQ test if the course of the remediation stays the same regardless of the outcome of the test. If the student's oral vocabulary is considerably higher than his reading vocabulary, he would need work in building his understanding of written words which, as mentioned previously, should include broad reading experiences.

If the student's vocabulary proves adequate, the diagnosis should begin to focus on other comprehension problems. Check to see if he has difficulty only with passages longer than a paragraph or whether he experiences difficulty even at the paragraph level. If he experiences difficulty with paragraphs, check to see whether he can read and understand single sentences. As mentioned previously this should be done in both oral and silent reading by having the student paraphrase each sentence after it is read.

If the student cannot comprehend sentences adequately, check his phrasing as he reads orally to determine whether his comprehension of the phrase enables him to use the correct intonation, pitch, and stress. Also attempt to determine whether a lack of knowledge of punctuation is interfering with proper phrasing. Look for pauses before words that should be sight words. Students who have to expend a great deal of effort in analyzing words in a passage are not likely to comprehend well. If frequent pauses before many words are noted, the student will need to build up a larger sight vocabulary before his comprehension will improve to any great extent.

For the student who seems to possess an adequate reading vocabulary but inadequate comprehension, a listening comprehension test can be of considerable help in the diagnosis. Students who cannot comprehend well on either type of test will need help in skills such as structuring events and developing visual images. On the other hand students who do well on listening comprehension tests but poorly on reading comprehension usually have difficulty in areas such as sight word knowledge, word attack, and/or punctuation.

DIAGNOSIS OF STUDENTS' KNOWLEDGE OF STUDY SKILLS

There are a number of study skills that are of considerable importance to the student in developing a background for working in an academic setting. Any student who did not develop most of these skills would be somewhat handicapped in his ability to function in the elementary grades and would be even more handicapped in his ability to function in high school. However, the failure to develop adequate study skills is not likely to cause a student to become a disabled reader even though it may cause the same student to fail in an academic setting. The end result is, of course, the same. For this reason the diagnosis of an older student who is doing poorly in his school work should include an analysis of the student's study skills.

Diagnosis in the area of study skills is relatively easy since most of the skills involved can easily be tested using a group informal inventory. Some commonly listed study skills and methods of assessing students' ability to use these skills are as follows:

Skill	Method of Assessment
1. Using table of contents	Using students' textbooks ask questions such as, "What chapter contains

141

		a discussion of wild animals?" "On what page does Chapter 10 begin?"
2.	Using index	Using students' textbooks ask questions such as, "On what page would you find information on the topic of polar bears?"
3.	Using glossary	Using students' textbooks ask questions such as, "What does your book say the word 'armature' means?"
4.	Using encyclopedia	Ask questions such as, "On what page of what volume would you find information on the life of Abraham Lincoln?" "What other topics would you look under to find more informamation on Lincoln?"
5.	Using almanac	Ask questions such as, "What city has the largest population in the world?"
6.	Using telephone directory	Ask questions such as, "What is the telephone number for Amos Abrams?" "List the telephone numbers for three companies that sell firewood."
7.	Using library card index	Use questions such as, "How many cards have a listing for the book, *World War Two Airplanes*?" "What does the Author Card include?" "What does the Subject Card include?" "What does the Title Card include?" "What is the call number of the book, *Hitler*?"
8.	Learning to skim	Using a newspaper give timed exercises for finding such things as an article on atomic energy or auto accidents, or using students textbooks give timed exercises in finding a certain date, sentence, etc. in a specific chapter.
9-12.	Learning to read maps, graphs, tables, and diagrams	Use students' textbooks to derive questions. This will be more meaningful than questions commonly asked on standardized achievement tests.
13.	Learning to take notes	Play a short tape recording of a lecture or radio program on a subject in which the students are interested and ask them to take notes.
14.	Using time to good advantage	Use a time analysis sheet (see section on remediation of this skill, p. 157).

PART B. *remediation*

METHODS OF REMEDIATING GENERAL
COMPREHENSION DIFFICULTIES

There seems to be some question as to whether general comprehension is actually amenable to teaching. That is, some people believe that "teaching comprehension skills" per se does very little to increase the comprehension abilities of students. They would contend that given the ability to attack and thus "say" words properly a student's comprehension will depend almost entirely upon his background of experience with the subject he is "saying" words about. Others contend that unless a student has an average or higher IQ he will not be able to learn the higher level comprehension skills. Although it would be foolish to contend that background of experience is not of great importance you do not have to examine the research in reading too extensively to find that significant gains in comprehension have been achieved by students who have participated in certain programs designed to improve their comprehension. And, as Helen Caskey (1970) reports in a discussion of the research on the relationship between comprehension abilities and IQ ". . . it appears that if the pupil has skills adequate for dealing with the material at his level, a higher level of comprehension is dependent not so much upon intellectual ability as it is upon the kind of instructional assistance that is given him." (p. 651)

Assuming then that comprehension skills can be taught, the logical question is, "What kinds of programs and/or techniques are needed to successfully develop students' comprehension skills?" Leo Schell (1972) indicates that regardless of the type of program involved we cannot expect it to succeed unless it is carried out on a long-term basis. Schell suggests, for example, that ten minutes once a week for ten weeks will not accomplish it. He suggests that a reasonable minimal amount of time in which you could expect to see comprehension growth would be one in which the student received nothing less than three lessons per week for ten weeks. He further suggests that the student will continue to need periodic reinforcement of the instruction after the termination of the formal lessons.

There are a number of techniques that have proven their effectiveness; however, isolating any one or any small group of these as being better than others has not been successfully done. Furthermore, because of the complexity of the skills involved in comprehension and the array of instructional techniques and backgrounds of experience to which most students are likely to have been exposed, it seems improbable that any one method or small group of combined methods would be successful with all, or even most, students. In the material that follows, however, you will find a discussion and concrete illustrations of techniques which have proven their worth or which show promising possibilities for further development.

It is sometimes difficult to separate the process of diagnosis from remediation in reading since in some cases they appear to be one and the same. For example, the technique of questioning appears to be one of the best methods we have found for teaching comprehension. Although effective, this technique could be improved if teachers would ask more questions beyond the simple recall level. Frank Guzak (1967), for example, found that over half the questions asked by teachers he observed dealt with recall of facts. Other researchers have found that 10 percent, or less, of teachers' questions required students to use interpretative skills. Caskey suggests that we attempt to cure the "right answer syndrome," i.e., the idea that there is a correct answer that must exactly correspond with the material in the text. She suggests that we often condition pupils to respond with the "right answer" to the point that they are afraid to attempt to answer questions that call for them to speculate. Robert Willford (1968) reported that researchers with whom he worked had a great deal of success asking negative type questions. As an example he states,

Watch a five or six year old. You put a picture up and you say, "Okay, what can you do with a horse?" Out of a group of 10, five of them have had an experience. The others don't know what you can do with a horse. We turn it completely around and say, "What can't you do with a horse?" You ought to see the differences in responses we get. Every child can tell you what you *can't* do with a horse. "What can't you do?" "Well you can't take a horse to bed with you." Someone else might say, "You can too if you live in a barn." This kid never thought about this. So now we find, what can you do with a horse? You can take a horse to bed with you if you live in a barn. You can flip the thing over by using a negative question as a stimulus to get a variety of answers. Kids love to do this. You may get more conversation of a single picture than any single thing you can do. (p. 103)

One of the most important things to remember in beginning a program of remediation with a student is to use material that is familiar and extremely interesting to him. Most students have one or two hobbies or at least one or two subjects that tend to interest them. J. Harlan Shores (1968) points out that the most important factors in speed and comprehension are those factors that relate the reader to the material he is reading. Shores mentions, for example, the student's background of experience with the material, his interest in the field, his purpose for reading the material and his mental set for reading it. Shores also points out that students who are familiar with material in a certain field of interest are more likely to be familiar with the phraseology used by the author. Through interest inventories and interviews you can quite easily find the kind of things that are of interest to students at a particular time. Another technique for placing students in materials of interest to them is to simply display many books at their reading level and let them browse until they find something they want to read.

Teaching students to become aware of signal words can do a great deal to help them understand and follow a sequence of ideas or events. Some authors classify certain signal words as full signals and others as half signals. Words such as, "first," "second," "third," or "one," "two," and "three" are full signals; words such as "then," "after," "that," and "furthermore" are half signals. Note the use of full signals in the paragraph below:

First, I would like to recommend Mr. Edwards for this position. *Second,* I would like to elaborate on some of his accomplishments during his tenure in his former position. *Third,* I would like to discuss some of his fine qualities as a husband and father.

Note the use of half signals in the following paragraph:

> When hybrid corn first came on the market most farmers ignored it. *Then* they began to note the increased yields obtained by the farmers who used it. *After* that it was not long until nearly every farmer planted it. *Now* it would be almost impossible to find a farmer who plants anything but hybrid seed corn.

In reality, we often see a mixture of half and full signals in books such as those written in the social studies field. And, sometimes authors make points or lead us through a series of events or ideas without the use of any formal signals. They are, however, used consistently enough to make students aware of the value of recognizing them. In teaching students to become aware of signal words you can simply use the students' own textbooks as a source of material. In the initial stages you will need to read each unit paragraph-by-paragraph and count signals as you go.

For the student who has difficulty at the paragraph or sentence level a technique called "Structured Comprehension" described by Marvin Cohn (1969) works extremely well. In using this technique the author suggests choosing factual type material that is just difficult enough to be beyond the comprehension level of the students who will be reading it. Cohn suggests that students read the first sentence and then answer the question, "Do I know what this sentence means?" This forces each reader to be an active participant rather than a passive reader. If the reader does not understand all or part of the sentence he is to ask the teacher or one of his peers as many questions as are necessary to fully comprehend the meaning. After all student questions have been answered, the teacher then asks one or more questions about the sentence. The students are to write the answer to each question asked by the teacher. This, of course, again forces all students to actively participate. After all answers are written the question is then discussed and answers are checked. Cohn also points out that when answers are written the student cannot rationalize that a mental answer was right. The author stresses the point that in the beginning you should stress literal meaning more than relationships. He suggests asking for the antecedent of every pronoun, the meaning of figurative expressions, and any new or uncommon vocabulary words. After the teacher has begun to set a pattern for questioning, the students should begin to use the same type of question in their search for meaning. Cohn stresses the fact that the book should remain open during the entire process. After ten questions have been answered each student scores his own paper and compares it with those done previously.

A technique somewhat similar to structured comprehension is one called the "Request Procedure" as described by Anthony Manzo (1969). In using the request procedure the teacher begins by telling the student to ask the kind of questions pertaining to each sentence that he thinks the teacher might ask. He is also told that each question is to be answered as fully and as honestly as possible and that it is considered unfair for the teacher to pretend not to know the answer to try to draw out the student and it is also unfair for the student to say, "I don't know," since he should at least explain why he cannot answer the question.

The game begins by having the teacher and student both read the first sentence silently. The teacher then closes her book and asks as many questions concerning the content of the sentence as she feels will profit the understanding of the student. The teacher should attempt to be a model for good questions, i.e., using thought provoking questions that call for reasoning rather than strictly factual recall. After several sentences have been read, the teacher should ask questions that call for integration and evaluation of sentences read previously. Questioning is to continue until the teacher feels the student can answer the question, "What do you think will happen in the rest of the selection?" "Why?" Manzo recommends specific types of questions as follows:[12]

1. Questions for which there is an *immediate reference,* e.g., "What was the second word in the sentence?" or "What did John call his dog?"

2. Questions which relate to *common knowledge* and for which answers can be reasonably expected, e.g., "What kind of animal has been associated with the name Lassie?"

3. Questions for which the teacher does not expect a "correct" response, but for which he can provide *related information* e.g., "Do you happen to know how many varieties of dogs there are? . . . well I just happen to . . ."

4. Questions for which neither the teacher nor the selection is likely to supply a "right" answer but which are nonetheless worth pondering or discussing; "I wonder why some animals make better pets than do others?"

5. Questions of a *personalized type* which only the student can answers, e.g., "Would you like to have a pet?", "Why?", "How did the different members of your family react to your first pet?"

6. Questions which are answerable, but are not answered by the selection being analyzed; *further reference* is needed, e.g., "I wonder what is the average height and weight of a collie?"

7. Questions requiring *translation*. Translation questions frequently call upon students to change words, ideas, and pictures into a different symbolic form, e.g., translation from one level of abstraction to another, from one symbolic form to another, from one verbal form to another. "In a few words, how would you summarize what happened to Lassie?" "What is happening in this picture?" "What do you suppose the ex-convict meant by 'up at the big house'?" (p. 126)

One of the most effective aids to comprehension that has ever been devised is the SQ3R technique. It was first described by Francis Robinson (1941) and since that time a number of variations have been devised. None of the variations, however, seem to have proven any more successful than Robinson's original technique. SQ3R stands for, Survey-Question-Read-Recite and Review. This method is best adapted to material in which subject headings are used such as are commonly found in social studies and science books. In brief form, the technique a student would use in reading a chapter or unit would be as follows:

Survey: The student reads any introductory sentences that appear at the beginning of the chapter and then all boldface headings, captions under pictures, and questions at the end of the chapter. (Students who first use this technique should be timed to make sure they *only* survey. They have a tendency to

[12]Reprinted by permission of the author and the International Reading Association.

simply read the material as they have been doing, if they are not put under some time pressure. A period of two to three minutes is usually sufficient; however, time will depend on the age and proficiency of the readers and the length of the chapter.)

Question: Each heading is turned into a question. For example, the heading in a science book might read, "Iron is an important metal." This might then be changed to, "Why is iron an important metal?" (When students first begin to use this technique you should help them devise questions. One way to do this is to develop a list of common beginnings for questions such as, "When did," "Why are," "Why did," and "Why is.")

Read: Students then read down to the next boldface heading to find the answer to the question.

Recite: After reading down to the next boldface heading the student looks up from the book and attempts to answer the question. When students are first learning this technique this can be done orally as a class procedure. After they have had a chance to practice, they should recite silently to themselves. If a student cannot answer a question he should read the material under that boldface heading again.

Review: After the entire chapter has been read students go back and read only the questions derived from the boldface headings and see if they can answer them. If any questions cannot be answered, they would read the material under that question again.

Considerable thought about the nature of the material is required in order for the student to be able to change the boldface headings into questions. This technique also forces the student to actively seek answers to each question as he reads. Some students find this method to be extremely rewarding just as some find it to be rather burdensome. In teaching this method you should actually go through a number of chapters with students until they become adept at devising questions and following the other outlined procedures. You will find this technique to be generally suitable for students at the junior high school level and above.

The use of the cloze procedure as a teaching technique is becoming more useful as we uncover more and better ways to use it. Some past attempts to use this technique as a teaching procedure had ended in failure. Subsequent research on the cloze procedure has shown, however, that it cannot successfully be used as a teaching device in the same manner in which it is used as a testing device. For example, as a standard test procedure most teachers omit every fifth word. Therefore, there is no selection of specific types of words in the beginning stages. Passages in which every fifth word is deleted are extremely difficult for some students and, furthermore, the omission of certain words makes it almost impossible for the student to reconstruct the original passage. Also, as mentioned earlier, when used as a testing procedure, synonyms are not counted as corrected answers.

Several authors have suggested important modifications of the cloze technique. Among the most important modifications is the necessity of discussing why certain answers either are, or are not, correct. J. Wesley Schneyer (1965) made this important point a number of years ago when he stated that merely giving a student blanks fo fill in without a discussion of why certain words would and would not be correct is like a method of teaching comprehension in which a pupil reads a passage and then answers questions calling for knowledge of word meaning, main ideas, and conclusions. Schneyer emphasizes that a student, in checking which answers *are* correct and incorrect may never learn *why* they are correct or incorrect. Schneyer says, "The reasons for the appropriate responses must be verbalized." (p. 178)

Leo Schell (1972) and Robert Bortnick and Genevieve Lopardo (1973) have made specific suggestions for using the cloze procedure as a teaching technique. Some of these suggestions are as follows:

1. In the beginning stages use a multiple choice format rather than simply leaving blanks and forcing the reader to come up with answers on his own. As the student gains confidence and the ability to make correct choices you can then gradually switch to the standard format of simply deleting words altogether.

2. In the beginning delete only selected words such as nouns and verbs and do not be concerned about deleting every fifth or even every tenth word.

3. After students have been allowed time to read a paragraph silently, read it aloud, sentence-by-sentence. Students can then offer suggestions on what might fit in the blanks. Semantically- and syntactically-correct answers should be accepted but students should be asked to justify their answers. In doing this you may wish to compare the original passage with students' answers.

4. As students improve in their ability to read mutilated passages you should increase the difficulty of the material. This can be done by using material of a higher reading level to begin with and/or by omitting a larger percentage of the words.

The drawing of various sized rectangles to illustrate paragraphs showing the relationship between main ideas and important details is a technique that incorporates writing with reading. This is somewhat similar to having students underline key sentences and/or words but gives students a better overall

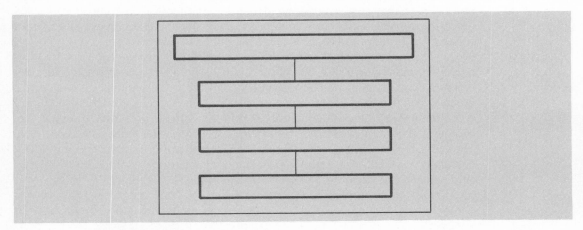

understanding of the relationships that exist among sentences. In using this technique, main idea sentences are represented by rectangles that are slightly larger than sentences that represent important details. For example, note the following paragraph and the corresponding illustration.

Meadowlarks are wonderful birds. They sing pretty songs. They are very beautiful. And, they destroy insects that would harm our gardens.

The large rectangle at the top (see illustration below) represents the main idea sentence, i.e., "Meadowlarks are wonderful birds" and each of the three supporting detail sentences are illustrated below it.

In using this system to teach paragraph structure you should start out by explaining that various sized rectangles represent main ideas and important details, and then have students write their own paragraphs to fit various structural patterns. Students seem to find it easier, in the beginning, to write paragraphs of their own to fit a specific pattern than to analyze the structure of someone else's paragraph. This also has the added advantage of helping students to improve their ability to write well-structured paragraphs, and for some to understand what defines a paragraph. In using this as a method of instruction I would suggest the following procedure:

1. Introduce the idea as explained above.
2. Draw a simple structural form and have students work in small groups to write a paragraph to fit the form.
3. Change the structure by putting the main idea at the end and then have students rewrite their paragraphs to fit the new form.
4. Illustrate different forms, e.g., where there is a main idea sentence at the beginning, then several important detail sentences and finally, a summary sentence.

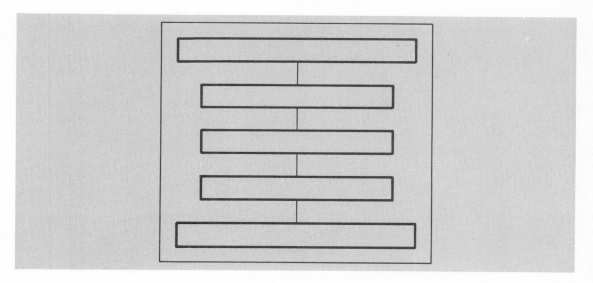

5. Provide students with well-written paragraphs that clearly show main idea and important detail sentences; have students illustrate them. Gradually increase the difficulty of the patterns.
6. In both writing their own and illustrating others' paragraphs be sure to discuss students' responses and allow them to justify what they write or draw. Be sure to accept reasonable alternatives. The important point is not necessarily that all students agree on how a paragraph form should be drawn, but it is important that students be able to justify their own illustrations.
7. As you work with differing forms have students illustrate each new form and place it on a chart showing various forms. Use different colors to differentiate the main idea rectangles from the important detail rectangles on the permanent models.

8. Students also enjoy naming different forms, e.g., one group of students named the one shown first "the natural," and the one with a larger rectangle at both the beginning and the end was called "the double natural."

In using this method of instruction you should remember that all paragraphs do not have a main idea sentence. It is very frustrating for students if they do not realize this in the early stages of looking for a structural pattern in paragraphs written by others. There are also paragraphs that have the main idea somewhere near the middle, and still others that have two main ideas with supporting detail sentences for only one of the two.

There is a growing body of research to indicate that certain types of phrase training can be helpful in a progam designed to improve students' comprehension. For example, Rollin Steiner, et al. (1971) compared a group of fifth-grade poor and good readers. Steiner stated that as contrasted with good readers, the poor readers failed to utilize syntactic and contextual cues in materials. He believed that poor readers tend to treat words as unrelated items in a series. Other researchers, such as John Downing (1969), have reported that children in their early stages of reading development encounter the same problems, i.e., they see little relationship between words and phrases in relationship to meaning.

Experimental studies in the past using the tachistoscope for training in reading skills have tended to indicate that at least some training is of very little value. It appears, however, that certain types of training can be especially helpful to the comprehension process. For example, Bruce Amble (1966) used a series of phrase training films to provide tachistoscopic-type practice in phrase reading with a group of fifth and sixth-grade students. Students using the phrase training filmstrips made significant gains in comprehension over a control group who did not use the phrase training films. Amble suggested several reasons why his students may have made more progress than students in other programs who have been instructed using a tachistoscopic technique. These reasons are as follows:

1. Students in Amble's group were at the elementary school level rather than at the high school or adult level as had often been the case where tachistoscopic training had not been successful.
2. Students were trained using meaningful phrases rather than abstract symbols or numbers or even letters.
3. Practice trials were inceased to over 5,000 rather than the average of around 1,000 in former studies.

The case for phrase training is also supported by Schell who quotes Carl Lefevre as saying that students must learn to master clause markers such as "if," "that," and "now." Lefevre said, "Reading clause markers quickly and accurately . . . is a first requirement of effective comprehension of meaning." (p. 423)

In phrase training students should also be taught the meaning of punctuation marks and how these influence the intonation, stress, and pitch of the reader. This can be illustrated by tape recording the oral reading of a student who phrases properly versus a student who does not read punctuation marks properly and thus fails to phrase correctly. Play the tape recording and then discuss why it is easier to derive meaning from material when the phrasing is accurate. Also construct exercises in which commas are omitted and show how the meaning of a phrase can often be influenced by the placement or omission of a comma.

Some students, especially those who are bilingual or who have meager language backgrounds, have difficulty with figures of speech. For these students it is often necessary to spend considerable time in discussing what is meant by commonly used figures of speech such as, "She was very upset," "She's sitting on top of the world," or "He's sitting on a gold mine." The problem, in the case of many students, is that they do not use these figures of speech in their conversations with their families at home and have often not had a chance to hear them often enough elsewhere to know what they mean. There are no fast or "sure cures" for this problem but you should note whether disabled readers come from bilingual or non-English speaking homes. For these students you will need to provide more opportunities for conversation time with their peers who do come from English speaking homes. In most cases the free interchange of conversation with other students in various school settings will do more to improve their language backgrounds than the remedial teacher has time for, or is trained to do. However, if you use a highlighting pen or some other method of marking figures of speech in materials commonly used for remediation, you will quickly and easily be able to locate them and prepare students for their meanings before they read them.

It was believed for some time that students who spoke with a dialect were often hampered in their comprehension of materials written in standard English. However, this problem has been studied much more thoroughly now and there is considerable evidence that shows that students who speak in a dialect different from standard English are not significantly hampered in their ability to comprehend. For this reason you should probably not be concerned about students who speak using a dialect unless it is indicative of a larger problem such as low socioeconomic level, meager background of experiences, or lack of vocabulary of the English language, any of which would be likely to have an adverse effect on comprehension.

Joel Levin (1971) and Peter Wolff and Joel Levin (1972) have demonstrated the importance of visual imagery in reading. In several studies they have shown that when students are told to develop a mental image of a scene or of word pairs they were able to remember details of the scene or the word pairs better than students who did not use this technique. They also stressed the fact that good readers seem to possess a greater innate ability to form mental images. Wolff and Levin also point out, however, that in line with the theories of Piaget, younger children (in the first grade or younger age-grade level equivalent) cannot generate mental images as well as older children without the aid of a picture or a concrete object. Research done prior to that of Levin and Wolff also demonstrated that children from low socioeconomic levels were not able to develop visual images as well as children from middle or upper socioeconomic levels.

There is also some evidence to indicate that those students who seem to be adept at developing mental images also tend to read more for pleasure, especially in the area of fiction. In order to enjoy certain fictional sequences one would, of course, have to develop some mental image of the scene. It should also be noted that if a student is able to develop a mental image of a sequence of events, it will later aid his recall. There is also evidence that some students tend to be "image thinkers." It is not known whether this trait is inherited or developed; however, most authorities believe it is amenable to training.

One of the easiest methods of developing mental imagery is through listening to short descriptions. For disabled readers listening exercises are especially helpful since the student can concentrate on developing a mental image rather than expending all of his energies on word attack skills. Read or play tape recorded short descriptive passages and then ask students to illustrate what they heard. In the beginning you may wish to have students close their eyes as they listen. After the illustrations have been completed ask students to compare them. At this time note important features that should have been completed and also any completely misleading details that are not justified based on the description. As students improve in illustrating scenes from descriptions they hear, have them read and illustrate short descriptive passages. Then discuss these using the original reading passages. Then discuss these using the original reading passage as a check on the accuracy of the illustrations.

The ability to follow directions is also an important comprehension skill. It is also one that is amenable to teaching as shown by Clarence Calder, Jr. and Suleiman Zalatimo (1970) who designed a program in which twenty-six, fourth-grade pupils participated for a period of thirty-six weeks. The twenty-six pupils received the same language arts program as a group of twenty-four pupils in a control group, but were requested to do work in "instructional booklets" that were designed to teach the skill of following directions as related to science, mathematics, art, social studies, and arts and crafts. Students in the experimental group did significantly better on a written test of following directions at the end of the experimental program.

Exercises for teaching the ability to follow directions are simple to devise and most students find them amusing and challenging to do. Some examples of exercises and materials that are helpful in developing this skill are as follows:

1. Have students write directions for getting from one place in the schoolroom to another. Then have a student (or students) read these written directions to see if they end up in the right place. For those who do not achieve success analyze what went wrong.

2. Have students read directions for drawing a certain design and then attempt to draw it, or draw it as they read. Show the correctly drawn design on the back of the direction sheet and analyze any obvious errors.

3. Have students work in pairs and assemble model cars and airplanes using the directions enclosed in the kits.

4. Have students practice following directions for paper folding. (There are several books written on the subject of origami that both illustrate and give written directions.)

Learning to place a sequence of events in the correct order is a skill that is important in reading social studies and science materials. Exercises for improving students' skills in this area can easily be devised by cutting short stories into paragraphs or by cutting paragraphs up into individual sentences. Exercises can also be made self-correcting by numbering the sentences or paragraphs on the back so that when the student has arranged all parts in what he thinks is a logical order he only has to turn them over to check the accuracy of his arrangement. Workbook exercises designed to give students practice in this skill have traditionally presented a story and then a series of events that the student is to place in a logical order by placing numbers by each event. The problem with this type of exercise is that after completing most of the work the student may find he has left out one or more events at or near the beginning. This, of course, necessitates erasing all the numbers. This can be avoided by cutting up the workbook pages into individual exercises and placing each one in an envelope. The events can then be arranged in sequential order and, if in doing the exercise the student discovers an event was omitted at the beginning, he only has to slide it into its proper place. When using this system each exercise can also be used many times.

When devising exercises for giving students practice in sequencing events properly you may want to begin by using only three or four short sentences for a paragraph as follows:

> They saw many animals.
> Soon Cindy was tired and wanted to go home.
> Cindy and her father went to the zoo.
> One of the animals was an elephant.

In the beginning stages of instruction discuss why a certain paragraph, such as the one illustrated above, could only be sequenced in one way. Also discuss any other logical sequences if they exist. After students become adept at sequencing sentences in paragraphs they can begin work on longer exercises as in sequencing paragraphs into stories. In devising exercises of this nature be sure to use stories or paragraphs that definitely show a sequence of events that can be properly sequenced through careful reasoning. Comic strips work well as beginning exercises since most of them contain clues to their logical sequence.

The use of pictures and/or cartoons are often helpful as a beginning point in helping students develop the higher level comprehension skills such as making interpretations and evaluations. Since the stimulus in a picture is continuously present, it is somewhat easier for students, in the beginning stages, to make evaluations than it is for them to make somewhat similar evaluations for written materials. As students look at a cartoon, for example, you can ask such questions as, "Why do you think the artist showed the president looking so mean?" "Does he usually look this way?" "Would you have shown him this way if you had been drawing the cartoon?" "What effect is this likely to have on the people who read it?" After students have begun to give answers that indicate they are beginning to understand interpretative and evaluative type questions, you can then switch to short reading passages and use questions that call for the same types of skills used in interpreting and evaluating the pictures.

Pictures also work well as a beginning point in teaching students to make inferences, e.g., in a picture of a high snow-capped mountain you might ask questions such as, "What do you think the weather is like at the top?" "Why?" "Do you think anyone lives at the top of this mountain?" "Why?" From working with pictures you can proceed to simple paragraphs such as the following:

Norma put on her bathing suit.

She sat down beside the pool.

The water was very still.

She soon moved under the umbrella.

Ask questions such as, "What kind of a day do you think it was?" "Why?" "Were there other people in the pool?" "How do you know?" One important point that should be stressed here is that the use of pictures to accompany written prose does not, in most cases, improve comprehension. In a review of the research S. Jay Samuels (1970) found that the use of pictures tended to interfere with the acquisition of a sight vocabulary when children are learning to read and that pictures did not facilitate comprehension. He did, however, find that pictures depicting multiethnic groups resulted in a positive change of students' attitude toward the ethnic groups that were depicted.

One of the most effective means of increasing students' comprehension is by getting them to do a great deal of free or recreational reading. Wide reading usually results in an increase in students' vocabularies as well as their general knowledge of their environment. Although some students will need instruction in certain aspects of comprehension such as following directions or seeing a sequence of events, there is no substitute for time spent in simply practicing the art of reading. Perhaps an analogy to sports is appropriate. No one ever made "all-American" by sitting on the bench listening to the coach tell how they should play. Likewise, no one ever became an expert reader by listening to the teacher tell them how they should read. Once the basics are mastered, the secret is to read, read, read.

There are many commercial materials designed to aid students in developing comprehension skills. Most of these, however, tend to be books or kits that provide reading materials at various levels of difficulty with accompanying questions. There is still a dearth of material actually designed to show the student "how" to comprehend. You will find a listing of programs for teaching comprehension, the level for which they are appropriate, and the publishers of the materials in Appendix C.

METHODS OF REMEDIATING VOCABULARY DEFICIENCIES

There are many ways of remediating vocabulary deficiencies, but there is no substitution for wide reading. Many students in remedial reading will be unable to read widely in the beginning stages, and others, if they could, would not. However, as you begin a program of remediation in vocabulary skills you should always attempt, as soon as possible, to encourage students to read as much as possible on their own. Since the meanings of many words can be learned through context through repeated exposure, it is not necessary to "teach" every new word. In reality, only a very small percentage of the total meaning vocabulary of adults is achieved through specific vocabulary instruction or through the use of the dictionary.

Another important point to remember in starting a program of vocabulary development is to try to break the habit of skipping unknown words, that many students will have developed. Not only disabled readers, but most of us have this habit to some extent. For example, most of us remember a number of times when we have learned a new word either from a discussion of its meaning or by looking it up in the dictionary. We then found that during the next few weeks we came across the word a number of times in our reading. Common sense, of course, tells us that the new word did not just happen to be read by us for the first few times during the weeks following our learning of it, but that it had probably appeared many times before when we merely did not notice it. The problem, of course, is that many people train themselves *not* to notice new words because it is much more convenient. You can help break this habit in disabled readers by simply talking about it and by calling their attention to new words. You can call their attention to new words by using games and contests. For example, you can give several disabled readers the same reading passage and see who can find the most words that other students will not know the meaning of. Or, you can have students read short passages and look up the meaning of any words they do not know. Then after reading the passage, let other students give the students who read the passage an oral quiz on the meanings of various words found in the passage. Another method of calling attention to new words is to have each student carry a pack of 3 in. × 5 in. cards with them. Each time they find a new vocabulary word they are to write the word on one of the cards. They should also write the original sentence in which it was found and then look it up in the dictionary and write its definition and new sentence using it in the same context as the original sentence. At the end of the week have each student discuss new words he has learned with several other students.

The important point to remember in doing activities such as those described above is that the number of new words learned is not so important as the fact that you are helping students break the habit of skipping unknown vocabulary words. And, the development of an awareness to word meaning is an important first step in vocabulary building.

A large part of our vocabulary is developed through both oral and written context. Although the exact meaning of a word often cannot be derived from the context, the sheer volume of words that we hear and read in context insures that many words will be repeated in context enough times so that word meanings gradually become known. Many students will realize that word meanings can, to some extent, be derived by noting their use in context. However, some students need specific instruction and reinforcement in the use of context clues as an aid to word meaning.

Kenneth Dulin (1970) states that students often expect words to have a specific meaning based on the way they occur in a sentence. As an example he uses the following excerpt from Lewis Carroll's *Jabberwocky,* "Twas brillig, and the slithy toves did gyre and gimble in the wabe." (p. 440) Using this material or normal narrative-type reading passages with words omitted, the teacher can help students become aware of what Dulin refers to here as "expectancy clues" by discussing various possibilities for replacement of words used by Carroll or possibilities for the meanings of words omitted in normal narrative-type reading passages.

Dulin, and Ruth Strang, et al. (1961) have listed a number of categories that may be used for classifying context clues for teaching purposes. For remedial purposes, however, you should focus on only the most obvious types and not become overly concerned with categorization. Both of these two sources, however, contain an excellent discussion of the subject and would be of considerable value to a teacher with little knowledge or experience in the teaching of context clues.

In the beginning stages of instruction in the use of context clues you should use sentences that contain obvious clues to word meaning, e.g., "It had been dry for some time, but now it is very *humid* ." Ask questions such as, "What do you think 'humid' means?" "How did you figure it out?" and "Are we often able to do this with other words?" After students have become somewhat adept at deriving the meaning of obvious context clues you should then use their own textbooks for instruction. The use of students' textbooks will give them a feeling of the immediacy of application of the skill. Find a certain paragraph that contains one or more new words and have students read silently and find these words. Then discuss the possible meanings of these words based on the way they were used and the position they occupy in the sentence. The teaching of the use of context clues should be a long-term effort, i.e., should continue on a somewhat regular basis for a long period of time. Even after the formal teaching has been completed, exercises should be designed from time-to-time to reinforce use of the skill.

The use of the dictionary should be taught to any student who is at a third to fourth-grade level equivalent, or above, and is not adept at its use. You should keep in mind, however, that only a rather small percent of our total vocabulary is developed through its use. Furthermore, it is usually only effective if used in conjunction with other techniques. For example, in a school where I worked as a reading consultant we once checked several classes who had just had an hour of work on word meaning with the dictionary. Immediately following the one-hour period students were checked to see what percent of the word meanings they had retained. These students were able to accurately recall the meanings of only about 20 percent of the words.

Some other specific types of exercises and activities for vocabulary development are as follows:

1. Make charts showing new words learned. Immediately below each word show how the new word was used in context the first time it was encountered. Review each chart regularly and have students use words on the chart in a sentence. Continue to review until words have been thoroughly learned.

2. When studying any new word, emphasize the meaning as well as the ability to recognize it. One of the best ways to determine whether students know words is to have them use it in a sentence different from the one in which it was originally encountered.

3. Set aside a specific time for word study. Words should also be studied whenever they appear, but setting aside a specific time for study will help make students more aware of new words when they appear.

4. Encourage students to try to think of synonyms and antonyms for new words as they are encountered. Work with crossword puzzles will help increase students' knowledge of synonyms.

5. Make certain that students know how to use the glossaries in each of their textbooks. Provide practice exercises in using the glossary and discuss word meanings as they are found.

6. Teach the meanings of the following prefixes and provide for practice in their use:

re	(back or again)
un	(not)
en	(in, to make, put into)
ex	(out, forth, from)
de	(from, away, from off)
com	(with, together)
dis	(apart, away from)
in	(into)
in	(not)
pre	(before, prior to)
sub	(under)

These are the only prefixes that tend to have fairly consistent meanings in conjunction with root words that most students, regardless of grade level, will be likely to know. There is always a temptation to go considerably beyond this list and to also attempt to teach the meanings of a number of suffixes. However, research on the utility of teaching affix meanings as a method of vocabulary development, especially for disabled readers, indicates that work beyond this list is likely to be of little value.

Commercial materials are available for vocabulary development alone, as well as for the development of vocabulary and general comprehension. Listings of these materials, the levels for which they are appropriate, and the publishers of these materials are included in Appendix C.

METHODS OF REMEDIATING DEFICIENCIES IN STUDY SKILLS

From the list of study skills previously discussed in this chapter, the author has found "inability to use time to good advantage" to be the most seriously disabling factor in contributing to students' academic failure. As a consultant at the high school level many students were referred as having a reading problem that contributed to failure in the subject taught by the teacher making the referral. A fairly large percentage of these students were, in reality, seriously disabled in reading. On the other hand, upon testing many of these students it was discovered that they often possessed the reading ability to deal with the reading matter in their textbooks but they simply never read. Upon interviewing these students their usual response as to why they did not read was that they did not have time. Most of them, of course, had a great deal of time, but the important point was that they perceived themselves as not having enough time. In order to determine how a student spent his time he was asked to fill in a form with listings for each half-hour time period throughout the day. As he went through a typical day he would fill in the blanks showing exactly what he did during each time period. The form had time periods shown up to midnight. After the student had gone through a typical day we would then go over it and discuss possible time periods when he could read and study. Such information is often shocking to the student. They often do not realize that such long periods of time are spent in "going home," "watching TV," etc. You will find this type of form especially useful with junior high and high school students.

Procedures for remediating difficulties with other study skills will not be presented since most of these procedures are intuitive for the average teacher. Furthermore, the level of teaching the other study skills, such as "skimming" and "map reading," depend to a large extent on the grade level and specific materials in which students are working. Commercial materials are also available for teaching the various study skills. Appendix C contains a listing of some of these materials, the companies that publish them, and the levels for which they are appropriate.

SUMMARY

A number of studies have been done during the past decade to help us understand more about the nature of reading comprehension. Although this research has helped somewhat, in reality we still know very little about the true nature of reading comprehension. This includes how to test it as well as how to teach it. Most researchers have not been successful in identifying various subskills if, in reality, they do exist. In most studies we have only been able to identify a vocabulary or word knowledge factor and one other broad factor simply labeled as "comprehension."

Although we are not able to identify subcategories of the comprehension skills we are still somewhat sure that with teacher observation we can identify such weaknesses as inability to obtain important details, inability to derive main ideas, and inability to make inferences. However, when we do this we are still not sure that we are actually observing any one specific skill. Joel Levin, and Peter Wolff and others, appear to have been successful in illustrating that students who have the ability to form mental images are able to learn better than those students who are not. This ability appears to be amenable to training. M. Wiener and W. Cromer have also been successful in identifying readers who are not able to read materials that are written in a "different" format from which they are used to responding. There also appears to be some hope of remediating students whose reading comprehension suffers because of this "difference" difficulty. This may be done by changing students' response patterns.

Although we have not been successful in identifying the subskills of comprehension, we do know that when students who have extremely poor comprehension are given intensive training in this area their reading comprehension does seem to improve. Therefore, although we are not able to identify various subskills we are still successful, in many cases, in improving students' reading comprehension. In this chapter a number of tests for reading comprehension have been reviewed and a number of suggestions have been given which seem to have proved their worth in teaching this complicated skill.

Chapter 6: *REFERENCES*

Amble, Bruce R. "Phrase Reading Training and Reading Achievement of School Children," *The Reading Teacher*. Vol. 20, (December, 1966), p. 210–215.

Bormuth, John R. "Comparable Cloze and Multiple-Choice Comprehension Test Scores," *Journal of Reading*. Vol. 10, (February, 1967), pp. 291–299.

Bortnick, Robert, and Lopardo, Genevieve S. "An Instructional Application of the Cloze Procedure," *Journal of Reading*. Vol. 16, (January, 1973), pp. 296–300.

Calder, Clarence R., Jr., and Zalatimo, Suleiman D. "Improving Children's Ability to Follow Directions," *The Reading Teacher*. Vol. 24, (December, 1970), pp. 227–231+ .

Caskey, Helen J. "Guidelines for Teaching Comprehension," *The Reading Teacher*. Vol. 23, (April, 1970), pp. 649–654.

Cohn, Marvin L. "Structured Comprehension," *The Reading Teacher*. Vol. 22, (February, 1969), pp. 440–444+ .

Cromer, Ward, "The Difference Model: A New Explanation For Some Reading Difficulties," *Journal of Educational Psychology*. Vol. 61, No. 6, Part 1 (December, 1970), 471–483.

Downing, John. "How Children Think About Reading," *The Reading Teacher*. Vol. 23, (December, 1969), pp. 217–230.

Dulin, Kenneth L. "Using Context Clues in Word Recognition and Comprehension," *The Reading Teacher*. Vol. 23, (February, 1970), pp. 440–445+ .

Guzak, Frank. "Teacher Questioning and Reading," *The Reading Teacher*. Vol. 21, (December, 1967), pp. 227–234.

Harris, Albert J. *How to Increase Reading Ability*. New York: David McKay, 1970.

Levin, Joel R. "Some Thoughts About Cognitive Strategies and Reading Comprehension," Report from the Project on Variables and Processes in Cognitive Learning—Verbal and Visual Components of Children's Learning, Wisconsin Research and Development Center for Cognitive Learning, University of Wisconsin, 1971.

Levin, Isidore. "The Fallacy of Reading Comprehension Skills," *Elementary English*. Vol. 47, (May, 1970), pp. 672–677.

Livingston, Howard F. "What the Reading Test Doesn't Test—Reading," *Journal of Reading*. Vol. 15, (March, 1972), pp. 402–410.

Manzo, Anthony V. "The Request Procedure," *Journal of Reading*. Vol. 13, (November, 1969), pp. 123–126+ .

Rankin, Earl F., and Culhane, Joseph W. "Comparable Cloze and Multiple-Choice Comprehension Test Scores," *Journal of Reading*. Vol. 13, (December, 1969), pp. 193–198.

Robinson, Francis P. *Effective Study*. New York: Harper & Row, 1941.

Samuels, S. Jay. "Effects of Pictures on Learning to Read, Comprehension and Attitudes," *Review of Educational Research*. Vol. 40, (June, 1970), pp. 397–407.

Schell, Leo M. "Promising Possibilities for Improving Comprehension," *Journal of Reading*. Vol. 15, (March, 1972), pp. 415–424.

Schneyer, J. Wesley. "Use of the Cloze Procedure for Improving Reading Comprehension," *The Reading Teacher*. Vol. 19, (December, 1965), pp. 174–179.

Shores, J. Harlan. "Dimensions of Reading Speed and Comprehension," *Elementary English*. Vol. 45, (January, 1968), pp. 23–28.

Simons, Herbert. "Reading Comprehension: The Need for a New Perspective," *Reading Research Quarterly*. Vol. 6, (Spring, 1971), pp. 338–362.

Spache, George D. and Spache, Evelyn. *Reading in the Elementary School*. 3d ed., Allyn and Bacon, Inc., 1973.

Spearritt, Donald. "Identification of Subskills of Reading Comprehension by Maximum Likelihood Factor Analysis," *Reading Research Quarterly*. Vol. VIII, (Fall, 1972), pp. 92–111.

Steiner, Rollin; Wiener, Morton; and Cromer, Ward. "Comprehension Training and Identification for Poor and Good Readers," *Journal of Educational Psychology*. Vol. 62, (December, 1971), pp. 506–513

Strang, Ruth; McCullough, Constance M.; and Traxler, Arthur E. *The Improvement of Reading*. New York: McGraw-Hill, 1961.

Wiener, Morton, and Cromer, Ward. "Reading and Reading Difficulty," *Harvard Educational Review*. Vol. 37, (Fall, 1967), 620–643.

Willford, Robert. "Comprehension: What Reading's All About," *Grade Teacher*. Vol. 85, (March, 1968), pp. 99–103.

Wolff, Peter, and Levin, Joewl R. "Role of Overt Activity In Children's Imagery Production," Report from the Project on Variables and Processes in Cognitive Learning in Program 1, Conditions and Processes of Learning, Wisconsin Research and Development Center for Cognitive Learning, University of Wisconsin, 1972.

DIAGNOSIS AND REMEDIATION OF PSYCHOLOGICAL AND SOCIOLOGICAL PROBLEMS

The first purpose of this chapter is to present information on the importance of, and nature of, diagnosis for psychological and sociological problems that the disabled reader may possess. A second purpose is to discuss some specific diagnostic procedures, and the last purpose is to present some techniques for dealing with problems in this area.

PART A.   diagnosis

AN OVERVIEW OF PSYCHOLOGICAL AND SOCIOLOGICAL PROBLEMS

The psychological and sociological problems with which we are concerned in reading are so often entwined that it is difficult to deal with one and not the other. For this reason, in this chapter, no attempt will be made to deal with the diagnosis and remediation of psychological and sociological difficulties as separate entities. However, it will be obvious at times that certain discussions will deal with one much more than the other.

Typical of the combinational situation mentioned above is the disabled reader who comes from a broken home in which the father is unemployed. Sociological studies have shown that the divorce rate is higher among lower income groups which is also more likely to cause more social-emotional problems among children from these families. Likewise, studies such as that done by Byron Callaway (1972) have shown that certain children who come from families in which the father does not work are not likely to read as well as children who have a working father. Callaway also found that children who come from homes where there is little or no reading material in the home do not read as well as children who come from homes where there is more reading material. From this kind of information we might conclude that the amount of reading material in a student's home directly affects his ability to read. This may be true to some extent; however, a more likely explanation is that the amount of reading material in the home is only indicative of a host of other factors. These other factors might include the parent's attitude toward reading and education, their economic level, educational level, and occupation, which are all combinations of psychological and sociological factors working together.

One of the major problems we face in diagnosing psychological problems is whether certain apparent emotional problems are the causes or effects of reading disabilities. As mentioned in Chapter 1, Arthur Gates (1941) believed that 75 percent of the students who came to remedial reading were likely to have a concomitant personality maladjustment. And he also estimated that one-fourth of these, or about 18.75 percent of the total group, would have developed a reading disability as a result of the personality maladjustment. On the other hand, Helen Robinson (1946) believed that emotional maladjustment was present in 40.9 percent of her disabled readers and that it was a contributing factor in 31.8 percent of the cases. Robinson also believed that social problems were present in 63.6 percent of her cases and that these social problems were a disabling factor in 54.5 percent of her cases. Exact agreement in this area is, of course, quite unlikely because of the nature of our measuring instruments. Stanley Krippner (1968) also studied various etiological factors in reading disability and stated, "Almost all children with reading disabilities have some degree of emotional disturbance, generally as a result of their academic frustration." (p. 277) Krippner also concluded, "Rarely is one etiological factor responsible for a reading problem . . . . Isolating the major factor was extremely subjective in many instances and the multifactor causation of reading disabilities became apparent to the clinicians involved in this study." (p. 277)

From the standpoint of remediation of psychosocial (combinations of emotional and social) problems it usually does not matter whether the psychosocial problem was a cause or result of a reading disability. You will simply need to recognize that it exists and that you will need to deal with it.

Studies such as those of D. Lawrence (1971) have shown that the counseling aspects of remedial reading are just as important as remediation of specific reading skills. Lawrence divided a group of disabled readers into four subgroups. One group received remedial reading only, a second group received remedial reading plus counseling, a third group received counseling only, and a fourth group served as a control group who received no treatment. At the end of a six-month period the group that had received only counseling had made significantly greater gains than any of the other groups except the one that had received both counseling and remedial reading. Lawrence also stated that the type of counseling received by the students in his program could have been done by any intelligent, sympathetic layman with only brief instruction in his techniques.

IDENTIFYING PSYCHOSOCIAL PROBLEMS

A number of techniques have been suggested for identifying students with psychosocial problems. It should be stressed, however, that most of these methods are somewhat unreliable. Furthermore, as Lawrence indicated in his study some of the students in his groups did not display any of the so-called typical signs of emotional disturbance and yet seemed to benefit from the counseling. In spite of their shortcomings, some of the methods you may wish to use are teacher observation, interviews, introspective and retrospective reports, projective techniques, personality inventories, and referrals to the school psychologist or counselor.

Teacher Observation

Although simple observation of a student in his day-to-day activities is a simple technique it can often be valuable. The advantage of teacher observation is that it is not a "one shot affair" as are some of our commonly used tests and inventories. Through the use of guided observation you have the opportunity to watch students in many situations that may cause stress. For example, you can observe his attitude relative to coming to the remedial class, his attitude towards his peer group, his work habits, his ability to concentrate for a sustained period of time, etc. Some of these same traits are difficult for the school psychologist to observe in a rather short period of time in which he would be likely to work with the student. The use of guided observation also has an advantage over the use of surveys or inventories for the same reason, i.e., you are not merely taking a sample of a student's feelings at any one particular period of time.

The use of teacher observation also has some distinct disadvantages. One of these is the bias of the teacher, i.e., we are often prone to see what we expect to see and ignore those characteristics that are not in keeping with our expectations. Another major problem with teacher observation is that some students who are apparently somewhat emotionally disturbed display no outward signs of this disturbance. Some psychologists also claim that to be effective an observer must be highly trained.

The characteristics most commonly listed as indicative of some degree of emotional disturbance are listed below:

1. Fails to sustain interest and effort
2. Does not work well with other students
3. Hostile toward adults
4. Withdrawal tendencies
5. Overly dependent
6. Low self-esteem
7. Cannot sit quietly
8. Fear of failure in group situations
9. Nervous
10. Refusal to oral read
11. Strong desire for attention from teacher
12. Prefers to play alone
13. Difficulty in separation of important from unimportant aspects of assignments
14. Prefers routine over new activities and assignments
15. Brags and continually seeks approval for accomplishments

16. Lack of initiative
17. Tendency to be compulsive in oral reading, i.e., skipping unknown words and miscalling words without analyzing them
18. Nail-biting

In using an observation checklist such as this it should be stressed that any conclusions or referrals for psychological help should be based on the observation of a cluster of these tendencies rather than on the observation of one or two. Yet it should be noted that most students, even though they do possess some degree of emotional disturbance, would not be likely to display all or even most of these symptoms.

Interviews

Interviews are advantageous because the skilled interviewer can often gain a great deal of information in a relatively short period of time. Another important advantage of the interview is that it will allow you to immediately delve further into any area that appears to have diagnostic significance. Certain answers a student may give either on written reports or in oral conversation often prove to be more than superficial when pursued by a skilled interviewer. For example, the interviewer can quickly gain a great deal of insight into a student's self-confidence by pursuing remarks such as "I don't think I can do that."

The use of open-ended questions in the interview can also give a great deal of insight as to how the student perceives his own reading ability. One important step in the remedial process is to get the student to accurately perceive and verbalize his reading problem. Through open-ended questions such as "What do you think about your reading?" you can quickly determine whether the student perceives himself as having a problem, and if so, if his perception is accurate. Chapter 12 is devoted exclusively to the development of the techniques of interviewing.

Introspective and Retrospective Reports

Ruth Strang (1969) lists several kinds of introspective and/or retrospective reporting methods that I have found to be especially effective with older students. One of these is the reading autobiography. The reading autobiography may be either oral or written and, as its name implies, is a biography of the student's life experiences in reading. As Strang indicates, the amount of information you are able to obtain will, to some extent, depend on the amount and types of questions asked. For example, when asking the student to write his reading autobiography you may want to provide a list of questions to be answered such as: Did you learn to read before starting school? Do you read materials other than those assigned at school? How many books have you read in your lifetime? Do other members of your family read a great deal? How do you feel about your reading? When did you first realize you had a reading problem? What were some things you especially liked about reading? What were some things you did not like about reading? The kinds of questions illustrated here are, of course, designed to encourage the student to discuss his feelings toward reading and reading related subjects. You may also wish to include more questions that assess other factors such as the kinds of material the student likes to read, and his use of the school and public library.

Some students will respond quite freely to a completely unstructured type of reading autobiography. In using the unstructured type of autobiography you can merely ask the student to write all he feels is important about his life as a reader, with no time limit or guiding questions.

Another technique suggested by Strang is the use of retrospective questioning following reading or reading related tasks. For example, immediately following a student's reading of a story you might ask questions such as, Did you like that story? How did you feel when you were reading it? If you wish to get information concerning *how* the student reads then you may wish to expand upon your questioning by asking such things as, What did you do when you came to a word you did not know? When you paused at the word "government" and then understood it, what did you do? How did you remember all of the details?

Another introspective-retrospective technique is the use of short student essays on reading tasks. Subjects for the essays may vary according to the area in which you feel you need more information. For example, if you feel the student does not work well with his peers you might ask for a short essay entitled, "Working With Groups At School" or for the student who continually disturbs others you might ask for a short essay entitled, "My Behavior At School." When using this technique you should be sure that the student does not perceive the writing of the essay as punishment. This can often be done by explaining to the student that by knowing more about how he writes you should know more about how to help him with his reading. Writing short essays also serves as a good catharsis for students who have strong feelings that they are hesitant to express orally.

Projective Techniques

Projective techniques have been used by psychologists and psychiatrists for years; however, most of the techniques used by them require rather extensive training and should not be attempted by someone who is not well-versed in their use. These techniques include the use of such instruments as the *House-Tree-Person Projective Technique*,[1] the *Draw-A-Person Quality Scale*,[2] the *Thematic Apperception Test*,[3] and the *Rorschach*.[4] There are, however, other projective techniques that can be used by someone with less training. One of these is the use of incomplete sentences. Although the interpretation of this type of instrument is somewhat difficult, it often uncovers obvious areas for further exploration. See page 166 for an example of this type

[1]Buck, John N., and Jolles, Issac. *House-Tree-Person Projective Technique.* Los Angeles: Western Psychological Service, 1955.

[2]Wagner, Mazie Earle, and Schubert, Herman J.P. *Draw-A-Person Quality Scale.* Los Angeles: Western Psychological Services, 1955.

[3]Murray, Henry A. *Thematic Apperception Test.* Los Angeles: Western Psychological Services, 1951.

[4]Rorschach, Hermann. *Rorschach Psychodiagnostic Plates.* Los Angeles: Western Psychological Services, 1960.

[5]Written by Eldon E. Ekwall and Everett E. Davis.

Date: February 19, 19_____   Grade: 6th   Name: Nancy_____   Age: 11 years

Directions: On each line below add words to make a good sentence. Each time tell what you think. There are no wrong answers, and no right answers. Write the first thing you think of. Work quickly.

1. When I read _my eyes get dizzy_

2. I don't like to read when _I'm having fun_

3. I wish I could _Live forever_

4. I seem to understand what I read best when _I won't to read_

5. When I read, my eyes _hurt._

6. I like to read when _I feel Like Reading_

7. School is ~~Okay~~ _Alright_

8. The most important thing to me _is Life._

9. I don't understand what I read when _I feel Sick_

10. My father _Is divorced from My Mom_

11. When I read words seem _mixed together_

12. My family _is Great!_

13. When I have to read _I ~~fell mad~~ feel mad_

14. I can't seem to _Get together with some people._

15. New words _seem Very different like a new word_

16. The easiest thing I read _is Baby Books_

17. My mother _Loves dogs._

18. When I read, my body _feels like a ~~Blo~~ block of ice_

19. Teachers seem to _get meaner & Nicer_

20. Reading classes always seem _terrible_

21. Other classes are always _great_

22. The hardest thing I read _is colledge work_

23. When I read, my mind _almost falls apart_

24. I would read more if _I liked reading_

25. Compared to reading, TV is _much Better_

26. I wish my parents _would go back together_

27. I am afraid _of gangsters_

of instrument and the results that were obtained by giving it to a sixth-grade student.

It does not take an expert to spot some obviously important information derived from this student. She is evidently upset about her parent's divorce (10, 26) and appears to be somewhat insecure (3, 8). It is also highly apparent that she has a negative attitude toward reading and her reading class (9, 13, 15, 18, 20, 23, 24, 25). There is also a suggestion of a physical problem with her eyes (1, 5, 11).

Another projective technique that often provides useful information for the remedial reading teacher is the use of wishes. In using this technique the student is simply asked, "If you had three wishes what would you wish for?" The three sets of examples shown below reveal the type of responses you might expect from this technique.

Student A:
1. I would wish my family would be happy.
2. I would wish I would get good grades at school.
3. I would wish we were still living in Louisiana.

Student B:
1. I would like to have a new ten-speed bicycle.
2. I would like to have lots of money.
3. My third wish would be that I could have all the wishes I wanted.

Student C:
1. I would wish my Mom didn't have to work so hard.
2. I would wish I could read better.
3. I would wish I was the smartest person in the whole world.

The wishes shown above are all verbatim responses of three disabled readers who visited our university reading center. Although responses such as these must be interpreted with some caution, they do help provide more information about these students. For example, because of the responses given by Student A, further questioning was done which revealed that his father and mother were in the process of getting a divorce and he was very anxious about the outcome in terms of where he would live, etc. He was also being berated by both parents for making poor grades in reading, social studies, and science. And, he had a desire to go back to the past when his family lived in Louisiana at which time life for him was understandably happier.

The responses of Student B are less revealing than for either of the other two students. His wishes did, however, reveal that the school situation, including his low grades and his inability to read were not uppermost in his mind. Students often have a desire to please adults by telling them what they perceive the adult wants to hear. This student, however, was not overly concerned with pleasing anyone other than himself. This student also had a very high IQ as shown from his school records. Later work with this student revealed that he did not really perceive himself as having a reading disability.

Student C was the only child in the family and was often left in the care of a maid because his mother and father both worked. He realized he was a very poor reader and had a strong desire to improve. His classroom teacher revealed that his peer group had sometimes poked fun at him for not being able to read well in class.

Although the three-wish technique often fails to reveal anything of significant value it is not time consuming and is usually perceived as an enjoyable experience by the student making the wishes. The responses you receive are not likely to be especially revealing by themselves; however, they often lead to further, more meaningful, diagnosis.

Another technique similar to the three wishes is to ask the student what he would do if he had a million dollars. This tends to solicit similar responses to those elicited by using the three-wishes technique. You may wish to try this in addition to the three wishes.

Other types of projective techniques are the use of student drawings and illustrated picture stories. I would suggest, however, that unless you have had extensive training in the interpretation of student drawings that you would be better off not to attempt to use this technique. First of all the natural artistic ability of students varies a great deal and secondly, minor recent events in the student's life may greatly influence his drawings. And thirdly, the interpretation of students' drawings often tells more about the interpreter than the student!

Personality Inventories

Through numerous research studies a number of personality variables have been shown to have a relationship to reading. Some of these variables and the reseachers who found them are as follows:

DAVID BELL (1970)—POOR READERS CHARACTERISTICS:

1. Negative attitude or lack of acquiescence to authority (important among Caucasians)
2. Passivity
3. Aggression
4. Excitability
5. Impulsivity

R. J. BRUNKAN AND F. SHEN (1966)—LOW RATE INEFFECTIVE READERS CHARACTERISTICS:

1. Preferred to follow rather than lead
2. Tendency to be passive
3. Need for constant reassurance

GLEN CHRONISTER (1964)—
SIGNIFICANT CORRELATIONS
BETWEEN READING
AND PERSONALITY FOR THE
FOLLOWING VARIABLES:

1. Self-reliance (in other words good readers were more self-reliant and poor readers less self-reliant)
2. Personal worth
3. Personal freedom
4. Feeling of belonging
5. Freedom from withdrawal tendencies
6. Freedom from nervous symptoms
7. Social standards
8. Social skills
9. Freedom from antisocial tendencies
10. Family relations
11. School relations
12. Community relations
13. Cooperation
14. Friendliness
15. Integrity
16. Leadership responsibility

Chronister also studied these relationships for boys and girls separately. All correlations between reading and these variables were statistically significant for the boys (p < .01) but only freedom from nervous symptoms was significant (p < .01) for the girls.

GEORGE SPACHE (1957)—
DISABLED READERS:

1. Showed more hostility and overt aggressiveness than normal readers
2. Showed less ability to accept blame than normal readers
3. Were poor in knowing how to handle conflict with adults
4. Exhibited a passive but defensive attitude or negativism toward authority figures

As you will note from these studies, several characteristics tend to appear with some regularity. On the other hand, some characteristics seem to be peculiar to each study, depending to some extent on the measuring instrument. Most researchers have been of the opinion that disabled readers as a whole possess personality characteristics somewhat different from those of normal readers. These same people, however, are quick to point out that within any group of disabled readers you are likely to find a great deal of variation in personality patterns.

The logical question for the educational diagnostician or remedial reading teacher to ask at this point might be, "Should I use personality inventories in the normal course of my diagnostic work with disabled readers?" As a rule I would suggest that your time could be better spent in other endeavors. Most group personality tests do not discriminate sufficiently between various levels of personality adjustment to allow one to accurately adjust the course of remediation to suit a particular individual. They would, however, in many cases allow you to distinguish between a student with serious personality problems from one who was relatively free of such problems. You should keep in mind, however, that the simple fact that a student is a disabled reader is quite likely to mean that he will have personality problems to some degree. And unless giving a personality test, or any other test, will alter the course of the remediation, there is nothing to be gained by giving the test.

On the other hand if you are highly trained in the interpretation of individual personality assessment techniques then their administration may prove worthwhile. For example, George Spache (1957) studied the personality characteristics of a group of disabled readers using the Rosenzweig Picture Frustration Test. This is a test designed to reveal information on personality characteristics such as aggressiveness or hostility, feelings of martyrdom, and self-blame. Spache found that within the group there were many individuals and small groups which presented their own peculiar patterns of adjustment. He stated, "It is highly desirable to identify and interpret these patterns in order to facilitate the matching of teacher personality with pupil personalities and the planning of the social climate of the tutoring situation." (p. 466).

Although I have not recommended the use of group personality inventories a list of some of those most commonly used, the grade levels for which they are appropriate, and the publishers appear in Appendix B.

Self-Concept

The self-concept is a personality factor and could have, quite logically, been discussed under the previous section. However, because of the extreme importance of the self-concept for students in remedial reading it will be discussed here in a separate section. The important effect of the self-concept has been illustrated in numerous research studies such as those of Mary Lamy (1963), and William Wattenberg and Clifford Clare (1964). Lamy found that the self-concept of kindergarten children correlated as highly with their success in beginning reading as their IQ scores. Wattenberg and Clare found that measures of self-concept and of ego-strength taken at the kindergarten level were predictive of reading achievement 2½ years later. Since self-concept evidently has a strong influence on academic success, it is important that every effort be made to locate those students who possess low self-concepts to try to improve them.

A well-trained counselor or the school psychologist should, in most cases, be able to diagnose a student's self-concept with some degree of accuracy. If you refer students to them you should make it a point to ask for a report on this aspect of the student's personality. However, there will be many students whom you will not be able to refer for a psychological evaluation. For these students you will need to make some sort of evaluation on your own. This can be done through observation and informal questioning and inventories. Although the psychologist has the advantage of formal training and more sophisticated instruments, the remedial reading teacher has the distinct advantage of being able to observe students over a longer period of time.

Students with low self-concepts are likely to give up easily and will often be inattentive. They may also be antagonistic and insecure and show signs of loneliness and indecision. Although they may at times present a braggadocio attitude, in the long run it will usually be apparent that this is simply a defensive mechanism.

One of the best ways of determining the type of self-concept a student may possess is to simply talk with him. During the conversation ask questions such as, Tell me about how you learn? and Why do you think you have had problems in learning how to read? Sometimes students are hesitant to say things that they will quite readily put in writing. You can take advantage of this by having students write short essays with titles such as, "What I think about myself" or "My ability to learn." The use of incomplete sentences as explained under the section on projective techniques can also be helpful in assessing self-concept. In using this technique include incomplete sentences such as, My ability to learn . . . , and Compared to other students . . . .

Referrals

In making referrals to the school counselor or school psychologist there are several factors or questions you should consider. Some of these are as follows:

1. Is the student making satisfactory progress in the tutoring situation?
2. Does the student exhibit a cluster of abnormal behavorial symptoms?
3. What is the student's attitude toward me and towards remedial reading?

The student who is progressing well and who is not antagonistic toward remedial reading is not likely to need psychological help even though he may appear to be slightly negative about certain aspects of school life or even though he may possess a poor self-concept. If you are somewhat familiar with some general counseling techniques and attempt to provide materials and activities that foster improvement in students' self-concepts you are quite likely to find a corresponding improvement in their attitudes. On the other hand, if after working with a student for several weeks, he does not appear to respond to your teaching then you should strongly consider referring the student for further evaluation and counseling. Lastly, if after several weeks the student's overall attitude toward either you or the remedial reading program does not appear to have improved, a referral would again be in order.

IQ and Reading

It has been a fairly regular practice over the years to include an IQ test as a part of the diagnostic procedures with disabled readers. To some extent this may have been justified, but in many cases it was probably wasted time and effort. As mentioned in Chapter 2, you should attempt to make the diagnosis as efficient as possible by eliminating any testing that will not ultimately affect the course of the remedial procedures. If this criterion were applied to the practice of IQ testing, there would be considerably fewer IQ tests given.

As a beginning point you should examine the reasons why IQ tests are often given. Probably the most often stated reason for their administration in reading is to determine whether a student has a greater potential for reading than his achievement indicates. Another often stated reason for giving an IQ test is that it allows us to see how the student functions while taking the test and to see how well he does on various subtests. The thought behind this line of reasoning is that the student can then be helped by receiving remediation in areas in which he shows weaknesses which, in turn, should help his reading.

In examining the validity of these reasons we will first look at the relationship of reading and IQ. As stated in Chapter 1, there is a statistically significant relationship between IQ and reading, as shown from correlational studies. It appears, however, that the reason we tend to get significant relationships between the two is because the very high IQ students usually tend to read well and the very low IQ students tend to do poorly in reading. If we were to eliminate the high and low IQ students from the studies (perhaps above 115 and below 85), it is doubtful if the remaining group's IQ scores would then correlate significantly with their reading achievement scores. Yet approximately 70 percent of the students we deal with would be likely to lie within the 85-115 IQ range. Furthermore, the innate abilities that are required for learning to read are evidently not completely the same innate abilities that are measured by IQ tests. This was illustrated in a study by Berj Harootunian (1966) who studied the relationship between reading achievement and various intelligence variables. Harootunian concluded, "The results suggest two conclusions: first, that several of the tests measure variables that are relevant in reading; second, that these variables are not being elicited by intelligence tests." (p. 391). Harootunian also stressed the fact that intelligence is composed of many factors and that we should not use a "single haphazardly composed score."

If the same innate abilities required for learning to read were measured by intelligence tests, it would certainly seem logical to use intelligence tests as a predictor of future reading ability. However, since studies such as those of Harootunian and others indicate that many of the abilities required for learning to read are not being measured by intelligence tests, it would appear that the argument that we should administer intelligence tests to measure students' reading potential loses a great deal of its validity.

The logical question at this point might be, how then, do we measure a student's reading potential? Perhaps a more logical approach is to simply teach the student a sample of whatever he needs to know about reading and see if he is able to learn and retain it. If he can do this, do we really care whether his IQ is 80 or 150? We might also consider whether the actual course of instruction would be changed had the student's IQ been 150 versus 80. The answer to this in most cases might be, *no*.

The second reason, as stated above, for giving IQ tests is to observe the way the student works and to observe and analyze his performance on various subtests. There is certainly something to be gained by the reading diagnostician in analyzing the way the student works and in analyzing his performance on various subtests. For example, it is helpful to know how well a student did on the subtest of vocabulary on the *Wechsler Adult Intelligence Scale* (WAIS), the *Wechsler Intelligence Scale for Children* (WISC) or the *Stanford-Binet Intelligence Scale* (S-B). This information can be especially beneficial in the diagnosis of comprehension difficulties as explained in Chapter 6. Scores achieved in the Information and Comprehension subtests of the WISC and WAIS can also provide information on the student's awareness of his environment and his ability to reason. We also gain information on how a student performs by watching him duplicate designs on the Block Designs subtest and by watching him assemble the puzzles of the Object Assembly subtests.

The question we must ultimately ask, however, is: Do we get enough worthwhile information to warrant giving the test? This, of course, must be answered by each diagnostician as he works with students in various testing situations. From personal experience, after administering over 500 WISC, WAIS, and S-B tests to children and adults, the author's opinion is that seldom, if ever, is enough information obtained about the way the student worked or about his subtest scores to have justified taking the time to give the test. If the same type of information could not be obtained in any other way, perhaps this would not have been so, but this is not the case. There are short vocabulary tests available that will give you an estimate of the student's word knowledge. And, might it not be better to observe the way the student works and reacts in a reading task than in an intelligence testing situation?

Psychological reports pertaining to students' performance often contain statements such as, "Juan seems to have difficulty integrating pieces into wholes," or "Frank has difficulty with eye-motor coordination." These kinds of statements may be quite true, but what do they tell us about how to teach Juan or Frank to read? Problems integrating pieces into wholes might show up in learning to sound words after learning phonemes, and problems with eye-motor coordination might show up in writing words. The problem we face, however, is that programs designed to teach part-to-whole integration and eye-motor coordination have not as a rule been successful in carrying over into reading instruction. What has generally been successful is a more direct attack on the problem, i.e., actual teaching of phonic blending or actual teaching of handwriting. Furthermore, problems with phonic blending can easily be located by giving a phonics test and problems in handwriting can easily be spotted by having the student write.

As the preceding information indicates we probably tend to administer intelligence tests in many cases where it is really not necessary. In spite of this there are times when information from intelligence tests can be beneficial. For example, if after having worked with a student for a short period of time he still does not learn, an intelligence test might be beneficial to help you determine whether the student is an unusually slow learner as indicated by an extremely low IQ. Also, if intelligence test scores are already available to you when you receive a student in remedial reading, the subtest scores can provide information on his vocabulary, his ability to reason, etc., which may eliminate the need for certain reading tests. (See Chapter 16 for methods of interpreting scores made on the WISC and WAIS.)

You may also find yourself in a school system where intelligence test scores are used as a partial basis for accepting or rejecting students in a remedial reading program. Although I believe there are better ways of doing this (See Chapter 14) it is a quite common practice; therefore, most remedial reading teachers should be familiar with the most commonly used intelligence tests.

One important point that should be stressed is that group intelligence tests that require reading (often referred to as verbal intelligence tests) are usually not suitable for use with disabled readers. For example, researchers such as Donald Neville (1961) have generally concluded that for children in the intermediate grades, a reading level of 4.0 is required for obtaining reasonably valid IQs on group tests that require any reading at all. Since many disabled readers do not read at, or even near, the 4.0 grade level, these tests would obviously not accurately measure these students' intelligence. There are other group intelligence tests that do not require reading but these tests have an extremely low correlation with reading ability, or in other words, do not measure reading potential to a degree that would make their administration worthwhile.

If intelligence tests are to be used as a measure of reading potential, obviously we must use individual type tests in order to achieve any degree of accuracy. The most commonly used tests of this kind are the *Wechsler Intelligence Scale for Children* (WISC), the *Wechsler Adult Intelligence Scale* (WAIS), and the *Stanford-Binet Intelligence Scale* (S-B). The *Slosson Intelligence Test* (SIT),[6] and the *Peabody Picture Vocabulary Test* (PPVT)[7] which take considerably less time to administer have also been used for this purpose. As a remedial teacher you are likely to find that many of the students referred for remediation have already been given an individual intelligence test, or as mentioned previously, there may be times when you would wish to request that one of these tests be given to a student with whom you have been working. In order to help you interpret the results of these tests a short description of each one follows.

(WISC) *Most useful when used in entirety*

The WISC is designed for students from ages five to fifteen and must be given by a skilled examiner who has had special training in the administration and interpretation of this test. It contains a Verbal Scale with six subtests and a Performance Scale that also consists of six subtests. In most cases, however, only ten or eleven of the twelve subtests are used. In reporting intelligence, scores are given for the Verbal Scale, the Performance Scale and a combined measure referred to as the Full Scale. The Verbal Scale is usually administered first and consists of the following subtests:

INFORMATION.   This subtest consists of thirty questions designed to measure subjects' general range of knowledge and information. It may be

[6]Slosson, Richard L. *Slosson Intelligence Test.* East Aurora, New York: Slosson Educational Publications, 1961.
[7]Dunn, Lloyd M. *Peabody Picture Vocabulary Test.* Minneapolis: American Guidance Service, Inc., 1959.

influenced to a small degree by culture and background; however, care was taken to include only questions that could normally be answered by anyone alert to their environment. One of the easier questions deals with the number of legs on a well-known animal and one of the more difficult questions deals with the use of a specific weather instrument.

COMPREHENSION.   This subtest consists of fourteen questions that Wechsler believes is a test of common sense that evaluates the subject's ability to use past information and to evaluate past experience. One of the easier questions deals with the student's knowledge of what to do when he has a certain type of injury and one of the more difficult questions deals with the ethics of keeping a promise.

ARITHMETIC.   This subtest of sixteen questions evaluates the subject's ability to solve arithmetical problems. All questions are to be answered orally and the subject is not allowed to use paper and pencil.

SIMILARITIES.   This subtest of sixteen questions measures the subject's ability to use logical reasoning processes to see similarities. One of the easier questions deals with the similarities between two types of fruit and one of the more difficult questions deals with the similarities between two numbers.

VOCABULARY.   This subtest containing forty words measures the student's knowledge of the meaning of words. This type of subtest, although influenced to some extent by formal education, has traditionally been one of the best predictors of academic potential.

DIGIT SPAN.   This is a measure of the subject's ability to recall a series of digits forward and backward. Wechsler does not maintain it is an especially good measure of intelligence at the higher levels, but he believes that the results of this subtest often have diagnostic value. All of these subtests are administered verbally and the subject has no visual stimulus and is, in no case, allowed to use paper and pencil.

The Performance Scale consists of the following subtests:

PICTURE COMPLETION.   This subtest consists of a series of twenty pictures each of which has something missing. The subject is required to indicate, either by pointing or with a verbal answer, which part is missing. Wechsler states this test measures the subject's perceptual and conceptual abilities and the ability of the individual to differentiate essential from nonessential details.

PICTURE ARRANGEMENT.   This subtest consists of seven different series of pictures. Each series is placed in front of the subject in mixed order. The subject must place them in an order so as to make a sensible story. Wechsler believes this subtest measures the subject's ability to comprehend and assess a total situation.

BLOCK DESIGN.   In this subtest the subject is given blocks with varying designs on them. He must arrange the blocks so as to match a pictured design shown by the examiner. Wechsler believes that this is a good test of overall intelligence and he also believes that the way the subject goes about the task has considerable diagnostic significance.

OBJECT ASSEMBLY.   This subtest consists of four form-boards which the subject is required to complete. Each is a timed exercise. Wechsler believes it measures the subject's ability to see whole-part relationships and tell something about the subject's thinking and working habits.

CODING (DIGIT SYMBOL).   In this subtest the subject is required to make associations between various symbols. This subtest gives some information about the subject's speed and accuracy of learning.

MAZES.   This subtest is seldom used unless one of the other subtests are spoiled in the administration of the test. It consists of a series of eight pictured mazes that the subject is to find his way through.

WAIS ✓

The WAIS is very similar to the WISC, but it is designed for subjects of ages sixteen and older and it does not include the Mazes subtest. Both tests tend to take from approximately forty-five minutes to two hours to administer, depending on the subject.

In scoring each subtest the examiner first determines the raw score. This raw score is transferred to a scaled score through the use of tables found in the manual. The scaled scores are easy to interpret since each has a mean of ten and a standard deviation of three. Knowing this it is also easy to find a percentile rating for each subtest using Figure 16-1, in Chapter 16. The scaled scores of each subtest are added and from these scores tables are provided for determining the subject's Verbal Scale, Performance Scale and Full Scale intelligence quotients.

A number of studies have shown that disabled readers tend to have higher Performance Scale than Verbal Scale IQs. However, the Verbal Scale tends to have a higher correlation with the ability to read.

Stanford-Binet ✓

The *Stanford-Binet Intelligence Scale* is designed to test subjects ranging from children of two years old through adults. Although it is an excellent all around intelligence test it has less diagnostic significance than the WISC and WAIS since most of the subtests are not scored separately. It is, however, possible to obtain a subtest score for the Vocabulary section which, in most cases, would be of greatest concern to the reading specialist. The scoring manual gives standards for passing the Vocabulary section at various age levels. This information, of course, serves as a guide in judging the age level of a subject's vocabulary. You will find this information in the manual at the beginning of the section on the scoring of the Vocabulary subtest.

SIT ✓

The *Slosson Intelligence Test* is a rather short test that takes from twenty to forty-five minutes to administer. Although a shorter time administration is listed in the manual, my experience has shown that the times that I have listed are more realistic. In devising this test the author adapted and used a number of items from the S-B. In most cases these were the items that are easy to administer. And, since many of the items are the same, the SIT naturally has a rather high validity when the S-B and/or WISC are used as the criterion for validity measurement. In spite of its brevity the research that has been reported on its use in reading diagnosis has been quite favorable. Furthermore, it is easy to administer and does not require extensive training. Although Slosson suggests that classroom teachers can easily learn to give it by reading the manual I feel it is wise, if possible, to practice giving it under the supervision of someone who is trained in the administration of the WISC, WAIS and/or S-B. In a study by Robert Armstrong and Robert Mooney (1971) designed to study the implications of the SIT for the reading specialists the authors concluded that it could be used by a test specialist or classroom teacher with as much confidence in the scores obtained as those of the S-B administered by a test specialist. It should be remembered that the SIT will only provide an overall intelligence quotient and that no subtest scores are reported in the scoring of the results.

PPVT

The *Peabody Picture Vocabulary Test*, as its name implies, consists of a series of plates (pictures) that the subject is to identify as they are shown to him. The time for its administration may run from fifteen to twenty minutes. It can be somewhat useful to the reading specialist to simply determine the range of the subject's vocabulary and experiences as reflected by his knowledge of pictures. Studies concerning its reliability and validity tend to vary a great deal depending on the type of students studied. My own research in its administration and through the examination of students records in a large district where both the A and B forms are routinely given indicate that it is a highly unreliable measure of intelligence for individual students. The apparent reason for rather large discrepancies between its scores and those of the WISC and S-B is that the PPVT measures a much narrower spectrum of intelligence than either the WISC or S-B. The reading specialist should keep this in mind while working with it and in most cases merely interpret the score as a measure of vocabulary and experience and not as an overall measure of intelligence.

Cultural Influences

Although it is often difficult to diagnose cultural factors per se there are some cultural and/or socioeconomic factors that research has shown have a relation to, or contribute to, reading retardation. As a reading specialist you should be aware that these relationships exist.

The studies of M. Deutsh as reported by Edith Grotberg (1970) illustrate some of the problems that are often common to students who come from impoverished backgrounds. Deutsh found that impoverished children have inferior visual and auditory discrimination and inferior time and number concepts. No specific physical defects of the eyes, ears, or brain could be found in these children that would contribute to these problems. Grotberg suggested that impoverishment might create conditions of sensory deprivation, language restrictions, and low motivation for achievement and that all of these conditions acting together may then produce a child with the same characteristics as those referred to as learning disabilities.

Grotberg also emphasized certain differences along ethnic lines as reported from a study in which black, Indian, and Mexican-American children were asked to retell a story. Although there were no differences by age, sex, or socioeconomic background there were differences by ethnic group. The Indian children use fewer phrases and the black and Mexican-American children took longer to complete the story. Grotberg also indicates that children from lower socioeconomic levels have the same ability patterns and profiles as the cultural group to which they belong but they tend to score at a lower level. Apparently some ethnic groups tend to develop certain abilities in their children while they also neglect other abilities.

Further evidence of cultural influence was shown by William Philion and Charles Galloway (1969), who studied Indian children in relation to the reading program. One of their findings was that the Indian children made relatively poor gains in vocabulary and comprehension. They believed these children were only gaining in word-naming skill rather than in understanding of word meaning and concepts. They also noted a difference in the language of the Indian children. These children tended to use whole phrases or sounds that functioned as single huge words. For example, "What are you doing?" might sound like "Wh-ch-dn?"

Culture and socioeconomic level also tends to influence overall attitudes toward the school situation. James Stedman and Richard McKenzie (1971) found that middle-class Mexican-American attitudes were similar to those of Anglo middle-class Americans, but Mexican-Americans of lower-class backgrounds tended to place a lack of emphasis on formal education.

A multitude of cultural and/or socioeconomic factors apparently tend to work together to produce disabled versus normal readers. This is well illustrated in a study by Catherine Thurston, et al. (1969), who studied the differences between able and disabled black readers. The following differences were found:

1. The able readers came from families with more than one car.
2. More able than disabled readers liked to read poetry.
3. More able than disabled readers received money for working.
4. More able than disabled readers felt close to their friends.
5. More able than disabled readers had fathers who worked.
6. More able than disabled readers had mothers who worked away from home.
7. More able than disabled readers got a daily newspaper other than the local paper.
8. More able than disabled readers had a set of encyclopedias in their home.
9. More able than disabled readers had taken a bus trip on a bus other than a school bus.

10. More able than disabled readers had been to a county fair.
11. More able than disabled readers had ridden in an elevator.
12. More able than disabled readers had been hiking through the woods and hills.
13. More able than disabled readers played a musical instrument.
14. More able than disabled readers had been to more than one town to do their shopping.

Thurston and her group also studied a group of white able and disabled readers. In that group they found the following differences:

1. More disabled than able readers had only one car in the family.
2. More disabled readers had their own room. (This was a rather surprising finding.)
3. More able than disabled readers had parents who attended P.T.A. meetings.
4. More able than disabled readers had been to a music recital.
5. More able than disabled readers got a daily newspaper other than the local paper.
6. More able than disabled readers had taken a trip on a train.
7. More able than disabled readers had been in a building higher than eight stories.
8. More able than disabled readers had parents who visited their classrooms.
9. More able than disabled readers received the local newspaper.

It is evident from the foregoing information that various cultural and socioeconomic factors tend to influence students' reading ability as well as their academic functioning in general. However, it is also evident that seldom, if ever, could any one variable be identified as the primary cause of reading disability in a specific student. The reading specialist should be aware of the many variables that evidently contribute to reading retardation. And, at times, reading procedures will need to be modified to fit the special needs of students from impoverished backgrounds.

SOME IMPORTANT CAUTIONS FOR THE REMEDIAL READING TEACHER IN THE DIAGNOSIS AND REMEDIATION OF PSYCHOSOCIAL PROBLEMS

Studies such as those that show that children who have come from a low socioeconomic level tend to read more poorly than children who come from homes of a higher socioeconomic level should be interpreted with a great amount of care—so should such factors as those mentioned above. For example, the fact that more able readers had parents who had visited their classroom may mean that the parents took an active interest in their children and thus created an overall environment that was conducive to reading. On the other hand, the fact that more able than disabled readers had visited a building of eight stories or higher probably has very little practical value for the remedial reading teacher. Many disabled readers are simply lacking in the experience background that is necessary to learn to comprehend as well as those children who come from homes where they have been provided with richer backgrounds of experience. For example, taking this type of child to a building of eight stories or higher will not help his reading, but providing him with a rich background of experiences through films, filmstrips, field trips, discussion, etc., may in time develop his background of experiences to enable him to better comprehend what he reads.

PART B.   remediation

GENERAL TECHNIQUES

Most of the techniques generally suggested for working with disabled readers with psychosocial problems are simply good overall teaching procedures that would prove effective with any student. However, because of the high teacher-pupil ratio in many classrooms and because of the tendency of some teachers to become overly occupied with the subject matter being taught, some of these techniques are often overlooked.

It is important that the remedial program for each student be planned in conjunction with the student.   One of the important steps in a good counseling procedure is to encourage students to verbalize their educational problems and discuss the kinds of activities that would probably prove helpful in remediating those problems. The student who has had a hand in planning his remedial program is much more likely to see a need for each day's activities and become much more enthusiastic about them. For example, students often fail to see activities such as learning to divide words into syllables as having any relevance for them. If it is apparent that a student needs help in syllabication as a word attack skill, he can be shown some words he mispronounced in his oral reading. He can then be shown how learning to divide the words into syllables in conjunction with a knowledge of certain vowel rules would have helped him pronounce the words correctly. And at this point you may wish to cooperatively list syllabication as one of the planned activities for that student. In cooperative planning you should not leave the student with the impression that you are not sure what he should do. Be positive in expressing his diagnosed needs, but work with him to help him understand why certain activities are necessary.

Cooperative planning sessions with students can also do much to improve their self-concept. Many students come to view themselves negatively because they believe they are a part of an overall curriculum in which they have consistently failed. This, of course, leads them to believe they are not as intelligent as other members of their class. However, when a student sees the teacher is willing to take her time to talk with him about what he needs to learn and consequently sees that he can consistently be successful, his overall self-concept is likely to improve.

Students need to be constantly aware of their improvement. In a general classroom environment it is difficult for an individual student to really know whether he is learning or improving in various skills. In fact, a disabled reader is quite likely to believe he is getting worse since his faster achieving classmates constantly seem to be doing everything faster and better than he is. It is also difficult for disabled readers to achieve success because they have no measure with which to compare their progress. For example, most disabled readers are not aware of the scores they achieve on standardized tests, and even if they were, their progress as indicated by these scores would not be meaningful to them.

In remedial reading you can make students aware of their progress in many ways. For example, a basic sight word test administered to a student at the beginning of a remedial program can be used as the basis for cooperative program planning. This test can then be filed in the student's record folder. After a number of words have been learned the student can again be given the original test and shown the results of his progress. The same sort of thing can be done with phonic elements. Student progress can also be shown by tape recording a somewhat difficult reading passage at the beginning of a remedial period and then tape recording it a second time after the student's reading has improved. Students are often startled at hearing their improvement. Another method of showing improvement is to simply point out things the student has learned on a daily basis, e.g., making comments as, "Look, Sam, you knew the 'fl' sound today. Do you remember you didn't know it yesterday?" Or, "Did you notice you have learned the two hard words that you didn't know last week?" It is not only important to talk about these indicators of improvement but you should also get the student to verbalize the fact that he too notes this improvement.

The student needs to learn by methods that he enjoys. Many students in remedial reading come to view school, and especially reading, as drudgery. Most adults as well as children will not seek activities that they do not perceive as somewhat pleasurable, let alone those that they perceive as drudgery. One of the best methods of determining the type of activities a student enjoys is to simply ask him. Also provide several alternatives, if possible, and let students decide which alternative to choose. Many reading activities, for example, can be taught by games. Although at times games may be a less efficient method of learning than teacher directed activities, the change of attitudes that students experience in learning may more than make them worthwhile.

Avoid unfavorable comparisons with other students. These comparisons should be avoided whether it be on the basis of academic achievement, behavior, or other social or ethnic factors. Most experienced teachers have found that comparisons really never serve to improve the student being compared, but more than likely, make the student antagonistic. If comparisons are made they should be done on the basis of present behavior versus previous work or behavior. This gives the student no reason to become antagonistic.

Provide the student with as much success as possible. Although this may sound like an old cliché it is an important technique in working with disabled readers. As stated earlier a number of studies have shown that a large percentage of disabled readers possess a low self-concept. The reason for this low concept is in many cases due to repeated failures in reading and other reading related activities. For many students this then means that they must constantly experience success until they come to see themselves as successful. Other studies have shown that as a child grows older his self-concept becomes more stable and resistant to change. This, of course, means that the older student must receive large dosages of success over a long period of time if his self-concept is really going to change.

You can provide success for your students in a number of ways. One of these ways is to play reading games that depend on chance in which all students have an equal opportunity to succeed. Another important way to provide success in remedial reading is to apply the IRI criteria to books students choose to read so as to insure that they are at their free or independent reading level (see Chapter 11 for a thorough explanation of this procedure). You should also make sure that most seatwork lessons are comparatively short and well understood before students attempt to do them. One of the most successful methods of providing success for students is to let them read to students in the lower grades, or if their home situation permits, let them read to a pre-school age brother or sister. Students who are not disabled in a particular area of reading can also achieve a measure of success by helping other students who are disabled in that area. This also frees the teacher to do more individualized instruction.

Provide a friendly atmosphere in which students feel free to express their opinions. Many students perceive their teachers as authority figures with whom they are not free to discuss their likes and dislikes and opinions in general. You can easily let students know they are free to discuss their opinions without the necessity of receiving your stamp of approval or without being criticized for opinions that happen to be contrary to yours. As a remedial reading teacher you should also attempt to ignore antagonistic attitudes or at least not take them too seriously. Some disabled readers will be extremely antagonistic about reading and this antagonism will often appear to be directed toward you. However, most teachers find that as disabled readers begin to improve and perceive the teacher as being directly responsible for much of this improvement their antagonistic attitudes also improve.

Be consistent in your behavior toward students. Many students come from homes where they may receive verbal or physical punishment one day for behavior which would be accepted or tolerated on another day. You should attempt, as nearly as possible, to set up standards for behavior, and expectations for completion of assignments, in the beginning and then be consistent in these behaviors and expectations. Few things bother a student (regardless of age) more than not knowing what to expect from their behavior. When a student does not know what to expect he is also much more likely to experiment to try to determine what behavior on his part is likely to bring about a change of behavior on the part of his teacher. All students, and especially disabled readers, need the security of consistent behavior patterns from their teachers.

Attempt to improve each student's relationship with his peers. Studies such as that of Deon Stevens (1971) have shown that disabled readers are not as sociably accepted as their normal-achieving peers. To some extent this can be altered by arranging for disabled readers to demonstrate their strengths in other areas. If remedial activities are conducted outside of the student's classroom situation, the remedial reading teacher may need to work in conjunction with the student's homeroom teacher to arrange for this type of success experience. These experiences might include such things as the demonstration of hobbies or of reading material practiced in remedial reading.

Help students realize that unreasonable demands will not be made of them. Psychologists have known for years that some students become the class clown because it provides a justification for other students laughing at them. Students soon realize that in certain classes they are likely to be called upon to perform tasks such as working a difficult math problem or reading a difficult passage and that they are likely to be laughed at when and if they fail to do a good job. Students who feel assured that they will have no unreasonable demands made upon them are much less likely to feel a need to make others laugh to justify laughing should it occur. You can help assure students that unreasonable demands will not be made upon them by simply telling them that in most cases they will be asked if they would *like* to do most activities rather than be told to do them. You can also tell them and show them that you are aware of their abilities and inabilities and that you are not likely to call on them to perform tasks for which they are not ready.

COUNSELING DISABLED READERS

Most disabled readers can be expected to possess some degree of emotional maladjustment even though it is not always apparent. For this reason an integral part of the remedial reading program should be provision for counseling. Contrary to the beliefs of some people effective counseling can be done by the remedial reading teacher with brief training in a few specific techniques. This point has been emphasized by Lawrence and others who have carried on extremely effective counseling programs for disabled readers. The technique described by Lawrence was a nine-step procedure as follows:

1. The counselor introduced himself as a person who was interested in students and concerned about their happiness in school.
2. The counselor attempted to establish an atmosphere in which he was uncritical, friendly, and accepting of the student's personality.
3. The counselor attempted to provide a sounding board for the student's feelings. No attempt was made to interpret these feelings.

4. The interviews were student centered.

5. In most cases direct questioning was avoided. Any questions that were asked were done so in a general way.

6. In the beginning stages discussion was only possible through the use of drawings and pictures done by the student. In the later stages other pictures were used as a stimulus such as those of the *Children's Apperception Test.*

7. The student was asked for three main wishes and these wishes were discussed fully.

8. During the interviews the counselor attempted to find opportunities to praise the student's personality (not skills). In doing this the counselor attempted to build the student's self-image.

9. Various areas of the student's life were covered. These included the following: "relationship with parents; relationship with siblings; relationship with peers; relationship with other relatives; hobbies and interests; aspirations immediate and long-term; worries, fears, anxieties; attitude toward school, and attitude towards self." (p. 120)

A counseling technique that has been used effectively for some time in our Reading Center at the University of Texas at El Paso is one described by James Gardner and Grayce Ransom (1968). It is a rather comprehensive eight-step procedure that can rather easily be adapted to the needs of specific individuals. This procedure can easily be learned by teachers with only a minimum amount of study. Following is a description of this procedure:

1. *Provide the subject with an adequate rationale for his learning problem.* In this step the counselor (C) attempts to determine why the subject (S) believes he has failed to some degree in reading. As Gardner and Ransom point out many students manifest a strong underlying fear that they are mentally retarded or have serious brain dysfunction although the subject may mask this belief to some extent. The C then attempts to help the S realize that he does not fit the pattern of a mentally retarded or brain injured student. In doing this he can point out that the S is not in any of the special classes that exist for this type of student. The S is also made aware of his intelligent behaviors such as knowing the rules of complicated games such as Monopoly, baseball, and football and/or competencies that C and S may find to discuss. The S's background is then discussed in terms of possible reasons for failure. These might include such things as prolonged absence from school in the beginning years, lack of continuity of instruction because of family moves or because of perceptual immaturity. The C should fully explain to the S how these factors can impede learning progress so that the S can accept one or more of these reasons as an explanation or rationale for his learning problem.

2. *Provide social reinforcement for S's positive statements about school.* Whenever the S makes a positive statement about school, a teacher, or school related activity the C smiles and shows heightened or overall interest. The theory behind these actions on the part of the C is that changing the verbal responses of the S may lead to a corresponding change in behavior.

3. *Help the subject learn basic discriminations about his own behavior.* In doing this the C attempts to discover circumstances that lead to S's failure to complete assignments or the S's failure to act in a manner in keeping with a healthy academic orientation. This is done by asking the S to discuss the circumstances that lead to failure. After discovering these circumstances the S is helped to become aware of his undesirable behavior. This can be done by role playing in

which the S assumes his role of a student in the classroom and the C assumes the role of the teacher. Gardner and Ransom emphasize that the C must attempt to get an exact conception of precisely what the S does.

4. *Teach the subject the aversive consequences involved in the continued use of avoidance patterns.*   In this step the C attempts to show the S the immediate consequences, rather than delayed consequences of avoidance patterns. As Gardner and Ransom aptly point out we often tell students that they are likely to be unable to obtain a certain job or they will be unable to accomplish some other long-term goal. In most cases these long-term goals are unrealistic as far as children are concerned. In this step, however, the authors suggest showing short-term consequences such as those of the S who daydreams. The C might say,

> You look out of the window because you feel you are not a good reader. But now you are in a practice situation, with reading material that you know you can handle. But you have the *habit* of looking out the window. You must break that habit. It will cause nothing but trouble, for you look out the window and you miss the word. When you miss the word, you fall behind and lose your place. When this happens, you start foundering around, getting scared, thinking you are stupid, and getting mad at yourself and the teacher and the book. These are the things that happen when you start to look out the window. (p. 533)

5. *Help the subject to develop alternative modes of responding.*   In this process the C may help the S to develop alternative modes by assuming the role of the S and demonstrating S's avoidance behaviors. The S may then be asked to suggest alternative modes of responding or the C and S may both discuss alternative modes. Gardner and Ransom also emphasize the importance of maintaining communication with other teachers of the S so that they can be alerted to the types of behavior being developed. The responses can then be reinforced as other teachers note them.

6. *Help the subject label his feelings.*   As Gardner and Ransom point out most students are not able to discriminate among their moods or feelings. In this step the C should attempt to explain concepts such as avoidance and anger. In doing this the authors suggest stopping the student as he is reading something that appears to be difficult for him and asking him how he is feeling *right now*. Although, as the authors state, many S's will report feeling "funny" later discussion will often prove that the S is angry or disgusted at not being an able reader. Do not force the S to admit to feelings he does not possess; however, you may find that suggesting possibilities such as "afraid," "angry," "wanting to stop," "angry at the teacher," "angry with myself," or "tired" often helps the S to discover how he really feels.

7. *Maintain a positive attitude toward the personality and academic potentiality of the subject.*   This is often a quality that requires some reorientation on the part of the teacher doing the counseling. However, knowing that most studies show that all but about 2 percent of our school population *can* learn to read should help the C maintain a positive attitude. The C must show his belief in the worth of the S by everything he or she says and does.

8. *Maintain communication with the subject's teachers.*   Be sure that the S's other teachers know what goals you are attempting to achieve and what responses are currently being developed so that they can reinforce these responses when they occur.

This procedure can easily be adapted to the particular needs of each student. Some students, for example, may display considerably less avoidance behavior than others. When this is the case less time would naturally be spent in steps three, four, and five. You should be careful, however, not to overlook less apparent, yet important, avoidance behaviors.

Another important step in the counseling process with disabled readers is to make sure they understand and verbalize their diagnosed reading problems. Perhaps there is an appropriate analogy between remedial reading and Alcoholics Anonymous. Spokesmen for AA say that there is little hope in rehabilitating a person who does not first *admit* he is an alcoholic. Likewise, in remedial reading, it is important that students recognize and verbalize their problems. An initial interview with the student can readily reveal whether the student is aware of his problem. This can be done by asking such questions as, "What do you think about your reading?" or "Now that you have told me you do not read very well, can you tell me why you say that?" Students often respond to questions such as these with statements such as, "Well, I don't seem to understand what I read" or "I can't seem to figure out new words."

Some students with apparent problems will insist that they really have no difficulty in reading. For this type of student it is often helpful to tape record their oral reading and let them listen to it as it is replayed. While listening they can be asked to circle any words missed, repeated, or substituted. When doing this you should, of course, avoid argument with the student or appearing to be trying to "prove that he has a reading problem."

After the student recognizes his problem he should be encouraged to talk about it. You can then show him the kinds of things you plan to do to remediate the problem.

It is important to note that the procedures outlined here for counseling disabled readers are by no means meant to supplant the normal cognitive or academic aspects of the program. Rather, they should serve as a most important supplement to these activities.

COUNSELING PARENTS OF DISABLED READERS

Because of the close relationships that exist between inability to read and emotional problems connected with the home environment, parent counseling can be an important part of the remedial reading program. Although concrete research tends to be lacking on the effectiveness of large-scale or intensive programs there is some evidence to indicate that parent counseling can improve student achievement as well as parental attitudes. For example, Janice Studholms (1964) studied the results of group guidance with mothers of disabled readers. She found that the group guidance sessions not only improved the attitudes of the mothers, but that the attitudes of the students towards their lessons also became more positive. The students who developed the greatest positive change in attitudes also made greater achievement. Studholms noted, however, that the attitudes of the students tended to regress after the termination of the counseling sessions.

The type of counseling program instituted tends to vary a great deal depending upon the orientation of the counselor. It is not advisable for a remedial reading teacher who is not highly trained in counseling techniques to attempt to provide parents with anything more than a general orientation to the remedial reading program. This orientation might include the following types of activities:

1. A discussion of the basis for students' acceptance to the program with an emphasis on the fact that students in remedial reading are not mentally retarded but disabled readers who usually have considerably more potential than is being demonstrated.
2. Discussion of the fact that pressuring disabled readers to achieve usually results in more harm than good.
3. Coordinating activities of home and school.

If the parent counseling is to be done by an expert counselor experienced in group techniques, the sessions should include activities such as those mentioned above but might also include information such as that used in a counseling program described by Patricia Bricklin (1970):

1. Information to ". . . help parents understand their child's behavior as it refers to typical child development and to sort out those behaviors growing out of his learning disability. And . . . learn to recognize and accept their own feelings as well as those of the child." (p. 338)
2. ". . . help parents set more effective limits, accept and acknowledge feelings and develop appropriate independence in the child." (p. 338)
3. Help parents learn to cope with their own feelings about their child's problems.

IMPROVING THE DISABLED READER'S SELF-CONCEPT

During the past two decades many studies have been done to study the relationship between students' self-concepts and reading ability. Following are a few important generalizations that could be derived from these studies:

1. There is a fairly high correlation between the self-concept of beginning readers and their achievement in reading in the elementary grades.
2. The self-concept is learned and is amenable to change.
3. The self-concept of a first grader seems to be easier to change than the self-concept of upper elementary school or junior or senior high school students.
4. There is a fairly high degree of relationship between teachers' and parents' expectations and students' self-concepts.

These generalizations have some important implications for remedial reading teachers. One important implication is that the remedial reading program should have built-in provisions for the improvement of students' self-concepts as well as for the improvement of students' cognitive skills. This means that the remedial reading teacher should be constantly alert to capitalize on any opportunity to build the student's self-image. Some ways of doing this are as follows:

1. Accept the student as a worthy individual who is capable of learning.

2. Constantly look for things in which the student *is* successful and point these out to him.

3. If possible, arrange for older disabled readers to help beginning readers by reading to them or by helping them with other tasks.

4. Keep careful records of progress and share these with students.

5. Make sure disabled readers do not attempt to read materials at their frustration level. Before checking books out to them to take home to read for pleasure apply the IRI criteria as explained in Chapter 11. Or if you know the free or independent reading level of the student, make sure that any books he chooses to read for pleasure are not written above that level, as measured by one of the better known readability formulas.

6. Make certain that assignments are understood and can be done without a great deal of difficulty.

7. Encourage students to bring their hobbies to class and show materials relating to these hobbies to other members of the class.

8. Encourage students to think about and constantly imagine themselves as being excellent readers.

Another implication from the generalizations mentioned earlier is that students with mild reading disabilities should be located and corrective work should begin as soon as possible. Because of the inability of many classroom teachers to spot incipient reading problems some students' reading problems do not receive attention until they become severe enough to make them clearly noticeable. If a student does not receive remediation until his reading disability becomes clearly apparent, the remedial reading teacher is likely to have to deal with a student with a negative self-concept that will be much less amenable to change than it would have been during the student's earlier years in school.

IMPROVING TEACHER EXPECTATIONS

A number of studies done during the 1960s have shown that teacher expectation can have a strong influence on the achievement of students. There also seems to be a never-ending circular pattern between teacher expectation and students' self-concepts. For example, a teacher who has low expectations for a student is likely to relay her feelings to the student in one way or another without openly admitting it. The student sensing this feeling will tend to develop a poor self-concept and will consequently be likely to achieve less which, in turn, will verify the teacher's expectations for the student and make her even more likely to lower her expectations for him.

Through a series of studies Robert Rosenthal (1968) and other researchers have found that the teacher is able to communicate her expectations to a student, whether these expectations are high or low, without even being aware she is doing so. For example, Rosenthal found that when the interactions between experimenters and subjects were recorded on film and then reviewed it was discovered that only 12 percent of the examiners ever smiled at their male subjects while 70 percent smiled at their female subjects. In another study examiners were to examine subjects who were behind a screen out of their sight. The examiners were told that one group of subjects was brighter than another group. It was found that the examiners tended to obtain greater success from the so-called bright group even without being able to see them. Evidently verbal clues are relayed to the subject even when the examiner is not aware he is doing so.

Perhaps the most heartening thing about some of these experiments, however, is that some researchers have shown that many teachers are not influenced by information on students' achievement and IQs. The type of phenomenon mentioned earlier often need not happen if teachers are aware that their low expectations can influence students' self-concepts and achievement.

This type of information has a great deal of relevance for the remedial reading teacher. Some specific suggestions for dealing with the influence of teacher expectation are as follows:

1. Read the research of Robert Rosenthal (*Pygmalion In The Classroom*)[8] and others and become aware of the ways in which teacher expectations are relayed to students. Simply knowing of this phenomenon is much more likely to prevent you from forming and thus relaying low expectations to your students.

2. Realize that every student is a worthy human being and that nearly every student is capable of learning.

3. Look for the strengths that students possess and focus on these rather than dwelling on reasons for their inability to learn.

4. Do not be unduly influenced by IQ scores. Remember that many students with high IQ scores have reading problems and that many students with comparatively low IQ scores become excellent readers.

PSYCHOLOGICAL THEORY USEFUL TO THE REMEDIAL READING TEACHER

Any teacher dealing with disabled readers is likely to have had one or two introductory psychology courses and, in most cases, would be somewhat familiar with the most commonly used psychological terms as well as certain psychological theories or principles. There are, however, some terms and principles or theories that have a great deal of relevance for the remedial reading teacher. The purpose of this rather brief section is to recall some of this information and relate it specifically to remedial reading. Following are some important terms:

Reward.   Probably as a result of the work of Thorndike we tend to think of a reward as "anything received that is perceived as pleasant." It is important to note that perception enters into the picture at this point, i.e., what is perceived as pleasant to one person may not be perceived as pleasant to another. For example, little Cindy loves cherries but dislikes blueberries. A piece of pie for her might be a reward but could very well be perceived as something unpleasant. Likewise "two tickets to the opera" could be perceived as a reward, but on the other hand, they could also easily be perceived as something leading to an unpleasant evening.

[8]Rosenthal, Robert and Jacobson, Lenore. *Pygmalion In The Classroom*. New York: Holt, Rinehart and Winston, 1968.

Reinforcer.   Sometimes the terms reinforcer and reward are used interchangeably; however, some psychologists would contend that rewards tend to act as reinforcers and that a reinforcer is any event or substance following an act that tends to increase the probability of that act recurring. The differences are not as important as a general knowledge of the meaning of the terms.

Primary Reinforcer (or reward).   Things that are perceived as pleasant without learning them in conjunction with another reward are often called primary reinforcers or rewards. For example, a child may eat candy and simply like it without any other learning or occurance going on at the same time.

Secondary Reinforcer (or reward).   These are things that are perceived as pleasant because they are learned in conjunction with something already perceived as pleasant. For example, a child may perceive the words "good boy" or a smile as pleasant because he has learned that they often accompany primary reinforcers or rewards. Dogs usually perceive a pat on the head or being told they are a "good dog" as pleasant because these things have been accompanied by food earlier in their life.

In actual application it is sometimes difficult to distinguish primary and secondary reinforcers. For example, one might logically argue that a pat on the head is automatically perceived as pleasant for a dog and that it is not a learned pleasant response. On the other hand, certain reinforcers are definitely learned. For example, if you were to use a loud voice and scream, "You stupid fool" at your dog when you fed him he would soon perceive the screaming and being called a "stupid fool" as pleasant. On the other hand if you were to strike the dog with a paper and quietly whisper, "You're a good dog," he would soon perceive that as unpleasant. Again the important point is not that the remedial reading teacher become an authority on terms, but that she understand the major differences in the terms.

In applying psychological theories it is important to keep the terms just defined and their implications in mind. For example, some common secondary reinforcers commonly used by teachers may not be perceived as reinforcers by some students at all. A smile or a pat on the back may have little or no reinforcing effect on a student who comes from a large impoverished family who has not had enough experiences with either a smile or a pat on the back in conjunction with something already perceived as rewarding as candy or a favorite food. In a case such as this it would be up to the teacher to help the student learn to perceive smiles and other secondary reinforcers as something pleasant by accompanying them with some regularity, over a period of time, with primary reinforcers.

The research on the effect of primary reinforcers such as the effect of candy on the achievement of children from various socioeconomic levels tends to be rather contradictory, e.g., in some studies the use of material rewards has produced significantly higher achievement in students from low socioeconomic groups but this pattern has not held constant in all studies. However, the important point is that students do perceive some things as rewarding while other students will view the same things as having no value.

Following are some important theories and/or principles from the work of

B. F. Skinner and E. L. Thorndike that can quite readily be applied in remedial reading:

1. *Any behavior that persists is in some way being rewarded.* In applying this principle keep in mind that what one student perceives as a reward another may not. There are several possible rewards even for failure to do assigned work. For example, some students are likely to view staying after school and receiving considerable attention as rewarding. Some students who receive little or no attention from their father may even perceive a scolding as somewhat rewarding. Whenever a student continues a behavior that is undesirable consider the possible rewards he may be receiving and alternative methods of responding to his behavior. From a positive standpoint, note behaviors that are desirable and try to determine the reward students are receiving and continue them.

2. *Habits emerge when certain reinforcements are consistently being rewarded.* In applying this principle keep in mind that this applies to both good and bad habits or to desirable or undesirable behavior. If you see a new undesirable habit or behavior emerging, attempt to discover what reward the student may be receiving and cut off that reward. On the other hand try to consistently reward desired behavior until the behavior is established. Skinner and other psychologists believe that, once established, a habit is best maintained by only periodically rewarding it (approximately one reward for each ten occurrences).

3. *The quickest way to form a habit is to arrange for it to happen often and then reinforce it immediately.* This is, of course, the application of the number two principle. Many psychologists believe that immediate means no longer than three to five seconds following the occurrence of the act. However, some research shows that for human subjects, a slightly longer period of time may be just as effective (up to thirty seconds or more).

4. *Once established, the habit is best rewarded by only periodically rewarding it.* Psychologists have demonstrated that subjects, who are not rewarded for a habit or who are rewarded each time it occurs after it has been established, are likely to begin responding in alternative ways. Therefore, as mentioned previously, a reward of approximately one in ten occurrences may be best for maintaining a habit.

5. *The only effective way to stop a habit is to cease the reward.* Rewards vary from individual to individual. The problem in applying this principle is to determine what things are and are not rewarding for a particular individual.

6. *Punishment only lowers frequency and may even be rewarding.* In Thorndike's earlier experiments he believed that punishment was an effective means of breaking a habit. In his later work; however, he modified this concept. A better way of breaking a habit is to cease the reward and replace it with an alternative method of responding. Also note again, that some forms of punishment may be rewarding to a student.

It should be noted that the reinforcement pattern of the culturally deprived student may have differed somewhat from that of the non-deprived student. For example, Susan Gray and Rupert Klaus (1965) suggest that in culturally deprived homes the energy and time of the parents may have been spent in "coping" rather than "shaping." They also suggest that because of this and other factors the student from this type of home will have gotten less reinforcement from adult verbalizations and that reinforcement may have been received more in the form of deriving pleasure from gross motor activity such as racing about, or in riding a tricycle or bicycle. As Gray and Klaus put it, parents in culturally deprived homes will have used a restricted rather than an elaborated code. They also emphasized that reinforcement will have been given for those behaviors that tend to make coping easier, i.e., quiet, restricted, non-exploring behavior. This would, of course, tend to make the culturally deprived student less eager to explore and participate in open-ended activities.

SUMMARY

Psychological and sociological problems are often less visable in disabled readers. For this reason they are often likely to receive less attention in the overall remediation planned for disabled readers. Studies have shown, however, that remedial programs that incorporated counseling, along with teaching of the cognitive skills of reading, have been considerably more successful than those that omit these aspects of the overall remedial reading program.

Methods of diagnosing psychosocial problems are not as exacting as the methods used for diagnosing the cognitive skills of reading. However, certain observation procedures and informal assessment techniques can be useful in gaining insight into students' problems in these areas.

Counseling procedures have been developed which can quite easily be learned by the remedial reading teacher. There are also some important procedures developed from psychological theories that can rather easily be learned and applied by remedial reading teachers.

Chapter 7:   REFERENCES

Armstrong, Robert J., and Mooney, Robert F. "The Slosson Intelligence Test: Implications for Reading Specialists," *The Reading Teacher*. Vol. 24, (January, 1971), 336–340.

Bell, David Bruce. "The Motivational and Personality Factors in Reading Retardation Among Two Racial Groups of Adolescent Males," Doctoral dissertation, Texas Tech University, 1969.

Bricklin, Patricia M. "Counseling Parents of Children With Learning Disabilities," *The Reading Teacher*. Vol. 23, (January, 1970), 331–338.

Brunken, R. J., and Shen, F. "Personality Characteristics of Ineffective, Effective, and Efficient Readers," *Personnel and Guidance Journal*. Vol. 44, (April, 1966), 837–843.

Calloway, Byron, "Pupil and Family Characteristics Related to Reading Achievement," *Education*. Vol. 92, (February, 1972), 71–75.

Chronister, Glen M. "Personality and Reading Achievement," *The Elementary School Journal*. Vol. 64, (February, 1964), 253–260.

Gardner, James, and Ransom, Grayce. "Academic Reorientation: A Counseling Approach to Remedial Readers," *The Reading Teacher*. Vol. 21, (March, 1968), 529–536.

Gates, Arthur, "The Role of Personality Maladjustment and Remedial Reading," *Journal of Generic Psychology*. Vol. 59, (1941), 77–83.

Gray, Susan W., and Klaus, Rupert A. "An Experimental Preschool Program for Culturally Deprived Children," *Child Development*. Vol. 36, (December, 1965), 887–898.

Grotberg, Edith H. "Neurological Aspects of Learning Disabilities: A Case for the Disadvantaged," *Journal of Learning Disabilities*. Vol. 3, (June, 1970), 321–327.

Harootunian, Berj. "Intellectual Abilities and Reading Achievement," *The Elementary School Journal*. Vol. 66, (April, 1966), 386–392.

Krippner, Stanley. "Etiological Factors in Reading Disability of the Academically Talented in Comparison to Pupils of Average and Slow-Learning Ability," *The Journal of Educational Research*. Vol. 61, (February, 1968), 275–279.

Lamy, Mary, "Relationship of Self-Perception of Early Primary Children to Achievement in Reading," Doctoral dissertation, University of Florida, 1962.

Lawrence, D. "The Effects of Counseling on Retarded Readers," *Educational Research*. Vol. 13, (February, 1971), 119–124.

Neville, Donald, "A Comparison of the WISC Patterns of Male Retarded and Non-Retarded Readers," *Journal of Educational Research*. Vol. 54, (January, 1961), 195–197.

Philion, William L. E., and Galloway, Charles G. "Indian Children and the Reading Program," *Journal of Reading*. Vol. 12, (April, 1969), 553–560†.

Robinson, Helen. *Why Pupils Fail in Reading*. Chicago: University of Chicago Press, 1946.

Rosenthal, Robert. "Self-Fulfilling Prophecies in Behavioral Research and Everyday Life," Claremont Reading Conference. *Reading Conference Yearbook*, Vol. 32, (1968), 15–33.

Spache, George D. "Personality Problems of Retarded Readers." *The Journal of Educational Research*. Vol. 50, (February, 1957), 461–469.

Stedman, James M., and McKenzie, Richard E. "Family Factors Related to Competence in Young Disadvantaged Mexican-American Children," *Child Development*. Vol. 42, (November, 1971), 1602–1607.

Stevens, Deon O. "Reading Difficulty and Classroom Acceptance," *The Reading Teacher*. Vol. 25, (October, 1971), 52–55.

Strang, Ruth. *Diagnostic Teaching of Reading*. 2d ed., New York: McGraw-Hill, 1969.

Studholms, Janice MacDonald. "Group Guidance With Mothers of Retarded Readers," *The Reading Teacher*. Vol. 17, (April, 1964), 528–530.

Thurston, Catherine, et al. "Cultural Background Study in Relation to Reading Ability," *Reading and Realism*. Edited by J. Allen Figurel. Newark, Delaware: International Reading Association, 1969.

Wattenberg, William W., and Clare, Clifford. "Relation of Self-Concepts to Beginning Achievement in Reading," *Child Development*. Vol. 35, (June, 1964), 461–467.

DIAGNOSIS AND REMEDIATION OF PHYSICAL DISABILITIES

The first part of this chapter contains a review of those physical disabilities that research and experience have indicated tend to affect reading ability. Following this discussion methods are presented for diagnosing disabilities serious enough to require referral or remediation. The last part of this chapter contains specific suggestions for the remediation of those disabilities that fall within the realm of the school.

PART A. diagnosis

As indicated in Chapter 1 most of the physical disabilities with which we are concerned in reading could be classified under the headings of: problems of the eye, problems of the ear, problems with speech, neurologically impaired functions, and problems of general health. Because of the difficulties we encounter in dealing with problems of neurological disabilities, the information on this subject is omitted from this chapter and will be discussed in more detail in Chapter 9. As so often happens in the business of the remediation of reading disabilities we find that many of these areas tend to overlap so that it becomes difficult, if not impossible, to determine which factors are actively contributing to a student's reading disability and which factors, although not functioning normally, are merely concomitant.

In the diagnosis of educational problems we also face a number of problems that may not be of great concern to the medical doctor concerned with the problems of a student's physical health. For example, in dealing with problems of the ear, the physician may find that a student's ear appears healthy and that his auditory acuity is normal and thus discharge his duties in dealing with that aspect of the examination. From an educational standpoint, however, we could not assume that this same student would not experience problems in listening. Even though his auditory acuity is normal, his auditory discrimination may still not be adequate to learn without experiencing difficulties with certain phonemes. In addition to possible problems with auditory acuity and auditory discrimination the student may also experience difficulty with auditory memory. Problems with auditory memory will be discussed later; however, it should be remembered that only rarely would difficulties with anything but auditory acuity be discovered in a routine physical examination.

The diagnosis of reading difficulties as related to physical disabilities obviously requires much more than a report from the family physician. This chapter deals not only with those problems of the eye, ear, speech, and general health that are likely to become apparent in a physical examination, but also with some of the less visible problems that are likely to surface only through diagnostic teaching and careful observation. In addition to testing and diagnostic teaching you should also keep in mind that a parent interview can yield valuable information concerning possible physical disabilities that may have contributed, or are contributing, to the student's reading problem.

DIAGNOSIS OF PROBLEMS OF THE EYE

To properly understand a discussion of seeing as it relates to reading and learning it is important to understand the terms. It has become popular for many authors to create their own terms and definitions. This, of course, causes much confusion when trying to read material written by different authors. Terms here will be as common and as obvious as this complex subject will allow.

Seeing

This is a general and all-inclusive term.

Sight versus Vision

It is imperative that teachers and all others concerned with diagnosis of problems of the eye realize that, in reading, we are concerned with more than "sight." Although the exact terms may vary slightly, the term "sight" is often referred to as the ability to see, or the eye's responses to light, whereas "vision" refers to the student's ability to interpret information that comes to him through his eyes. Obviously then, a student without proper sight, unless corrected, can never have adequate vision. On the other hand, a student who has adequate "sight" may lack the "vision" or perceptual ability to correctly interpret various symbols.

Sight concerns the ability of the eye to resolve detail. This is a mechanical or physical process. The measurement of this ability to resolve detail is called *acuity*. Sight, then, is defined as the production of acuity. Sight can be likened to a snapshot camera and drugstore prints. Sight includes the snapping of the shutter; that is, the making of the optical image or picture in the back of the eye. This back part, called the *retina*, is like the film in the camera. Sight would include sending the image to the brain; that is, taking the film to be developed. Good sight means good acuity. The Snellen measure of acuity is 20/20 for good acuity. The larger the denominator and/or the smaller the fraction, the less the acuity. That is, the person with 20/80 acuity would need to be four times as close to an object as a person with 20/20 acuity to see it as well. Acuity has no relationship to how the student understands or perceives the detail or how efficiently he can read. Poor readers, in fact, often have good sight.

Vision is the processing of sight to give location, memory, and intersensory relationships. Vision is a mental process. It cannot be compared to the camera. Vision might be thought of as the work of a skilled darkroom artist; not just developing film but retouching the negative, deciding the portion of the negative to use, and getting the right shade of color to the picture.

Proper processing of sight should tell the student where the object is in space as well as its orientation. This processing should also give him memory of similar past experiences to compare and it should evaluate this with the other senses such as hearing and touch.

Perception is the end result of sight and vision. This is the output. Reading ability seems to be dependent not only on visual perception, but also on auditory perception and tactual perception. If the student cannot differentiate "b" from "d," the processing of sight for location is not good (visual-spacial perception). If he draws a triangle after he is shown a square, his processing to give memory is not adequate (visual memory). If the student cannot visualize the sequence of the letters "c-h-a-l-k" when he hears the word "chalk" spoken, or if he cannot relate visual stimulus to touch stimulus, he is deficient in intersensory processing.

The term vision is also often used as an all inclusive term to designate several aspects of the use of the eye. Stanley Krippner (1971) cites the writing of N. Flax as having developed a definition that should help clarify the definition for all professions. Flax refers to disorders of the peripheral nervous system (PNS) and the central nervous system (CNS). Krippner states,

> To Flax, PNS disorders refer to deficiencies of the end-organ system of vision (i.e., the eye); they include visual acuity, refractive error, fusion, convergence, and accommodation, all of which involve the eye mechanism and which are responsible for producing clear, single, binocular vision. CNS disorders involve deficiences in organizing and interpreting images received by the eyes and sent to the brain. In CNS disorders, a clear, single visual image may be present but the child cannot decode the printed word because of problems in organization and interpretation of what is seen. (p. 74)

In reading we usually refer to the CNS problems described here as visual perceptual problems.

The incidence of eye disorders often varies considerably depending on whether the research is discussing what Flax referred to as possessing problems of the PNS category, or both. These differences are often evidenced in the writings of ophthalmologists versus optometrists on the subject of vision.

The ophthalmologist (also called oculist) is a physician or medical doctor (M.D.) who has taken specialized medical training in the care of the eye after receiving an M.D. degree. He is licensed to prescribe glasses and other medication or to perform surgery to correct visual problems. The optometrist receives a

Doctor of Optometry degree (O.D.) in a college of optometry. He is a specialist in sight and vision. As Krippner points out, many optometrists also take more advanced study in developmental vision and become proficient in visual training which is concerned with the CNS aspects of vision. Because of the nature of their training there is a tendency for ophthalmologists to concern themselves more with the PNS aspects of the eyes and for optometrists to be more concerned with both the PNS and CNS aspects. This, of course, is a rather broad generalization, but it accounts, to a large extent, for the large differences often reported on visual problems as causative factors in reading disability.

Regardless of the type of doctor doing the testing it is generally agreed that certain types of disorders of the eye do contribute to, or may be causal factors in, cases of reading disability. The following are eye and sight skills and anomalies that are involved with seeing and reading.

ACCOMMODATION.   This is commonly called focusing. Like a camera, the eye must adjust the optics to make a clear picture. In the eye this adjusting of focus is called accommodation. The eye must accommodate for the printed words in a book at twelve inches or for the words on the chalkboard at fifteen feet. As the student's book gets closer he must increase the amount of accommodation. There is a neurological connection between this center and the center that causes the eyes to turn in. When the student increases accommodation, this other center causes the eyes to turn in. A student can have inaccurate accommodation, or he can have spasm (hypertonicity) of the muscles (ciliary muscles) controlling accommodation.

CONVERGENCE.   This is the turning in of the eyes. As a single point moves closer to the two eyes, they must converge to insure that the image in each eye is centered. Convergence is accomplished in two different ways. First, by the neurological connection with accommodation. The more stimulus to accommodate, the more stimulus is put into convergence. This convergence is called *accommodative convergence*. This can be thought of as automatic convergence as a result of increased accommodation. This accommodative convergence does not perfectly align the eyes on a point at the distance for which they are accommodated. Therefore, second manual convergence (manual convergence is turning the eyes in or out to complete the alignment after automatic or accommodative convergence) must be used to obtain perfect centering of the image in each eye. This centering is called *fusion*, and the manual convergence is fusional convergence. A student can have insufficient accommodative convergence, thus requiring more manual convergence. He can also have excessive accommodative convergence, thus requiring more manual convergence. He can also have excessive accommodative convergence, which means the student must manually diverge the eyes to get fusion. The student can also have a limited ability to manually converge the eyes for a very near point. This would mean that converging to the normal reading distance requires a high percent of the student's total ability to converge.

FUSION.   This refers to the aligning of each eye so that the image in each is centered. They center in identical places on the retinas (back of the eye) where each eye has maximum acuity. The point in the back of the eye with maximum acuity is called the macula. If the images are not properly centered, the student will see double.

HYPEROPIA.   This is commonly called far-sightedness. It is congenital and anatomical. Among the various refractive errors listed as causing reading disabilities this is perhaps listed most often. Hyperopia causes the student both excessive accommodation and convergence. Therefore, when it is present two of the occular motor skills function improperly. This will result in blurring, eye fatigue, headache, and loss of interest in close work.

MYOPIA.   The common name for this is near-sightedness. It is a refractive error and the symptoms are the reverse of hyperopia. There is a great deal of evidence that most myopia is developmental. Myopia does not interfere with reading; in fact, this is a common condition with good readers. Since the myopic eye is focused for a near point, this eye will require less accommodation. Uncorrected myopia will, however, cause the student to have problems with board work or other tasks requiring seeing at a distance.

ASTIGMATISM.   This condition, like hyperopia and myopia, is an optical or refractive one. Astigmatism can exist with hyperopia and with myopia. In fact, it is not usually a condition by itself and when it is, the eye is partly myopic and partly hyperopic. To understand astigmatism, consider the power of the optics of a narrow vertical section through the eye, and the power of a narrow horizontal section. If the power in the vertical is different than the power in the horizontal, the optical system has astigmatism.

Astigmatism causes the print to be blurred and causes eye fatigue. Since there are different focuses in the eye, the eye will do more changing focus trying to make the image clear. This can also cause headaches and interfere with reading efficiency.

Both hyperopia and astigmatism can cause suppression and strabismus. High amounts of hyperopia frequently cause crossed eyes due to the excessive accommodative convergence. If these children are properly fitted with lenses at an early age, the excessive convergence will usually be relieved and the eyes will straighten.

ANISEIKONIA.   This is a condition in which there is a different size and/or shape of the image of each eye. When there is no difference in refractive error of the two eyes, a difference in image size is due to a different physical size of the eye ball. A student with this condition would have difficulty fusing. Therefore, it would contribute to reading disability.

ANISOMATROPIA.   This is a condition in which there is a different refractive power in each eye. This is almost always accompanied by aniseikonia.

HETEROPHORIA.   This refers to the basic position of rest of the eyes as they relate to each other. The eyes assume this position of rest when one or both eyes are closed. This would remove any need to converge or align one eye with the other. There would be no stimulus to fusion. The eyes would be disassociated. When there is no stimulus to fusion and the eyes are outward from each other, the condition is *exophoria*. When there is no stimulus to fusion and the eyes deviate inward, it is known as *esophoria*. When disassociated (no stimulus to fusion) and one is turned above the other, it is termed hyperphoria (up) or *hypophoria* (down). Heterophoria means that any one of these conditions exist. The student can overcome heterophoria and obtain fusion without treatment. However, when the condition becomes severe it is known as heterotropia and cannot be overcome without treatment.

SUPPRESSION.   This is a neurological block of the picture stimulus from the macula so that the picture in that eye is not seen. This is done at the brain. Any time the student has difficulty with fusion, he may learn to suppress one eye. This relieves his need to fuse and he no longer has a fusion problem. Suppression works to block out the picture only in the central area. This is the point at which he is looking—the fixation target. The suppressor does not suppress the sight to the sides. If a student develops suppression at an early age, *amblyopia* almost always results.

AMBLYOPIA.   This is commonly called "lazy eye." It is lowered acuity in the suppressed eye. This is true even when the other eye (the good eye) cannot see. When suppression is not developed until school age, there is usually less loss of acuity.

HETEROTROPIA.   When a heterophoria (tendency of one eye to deviate in one or another direction) is great and cannot be overcome, the eyes will not be fused. One might say a heterotropia is a heterophoria that cannot be overcome. When the deviation is outward, it is *exotropia*, inward is *esotropia*, and vertical is hypertropia (or hypo). If the student is able to hold the eyes in alignment part of the time it is termed *intermittant tropia*. When one eye deviates at one time and the other eye deviates at other times, it is an *alternating tropia*. The student with a tropic condition either sees double or suppresses the deviating eye when the eyes are not fused (one deviated).

HYSTERIA.   This is a condition in which emotional upsets frequently cause lowered acuity, reduced sight to the sides, and difficulty in accommodation. There are usually no other signs of the hysteria.

FIXATION (ocular fixation).   This is the ability to precisely hold fusion on a given target.

PURSUIT.   This is the ability to maintain fixation on a moving target.

SACCADIC SKILLS.   This is the ability to fixate on a sequence of different targets. This may be back and forth on targets, to the left and to the right, several in a row left to right, or from far to near and back.

OCULAR MOTOR SKILLS.   This refers to the movement skills of the eyes. This would include heterophorias, convergence, accommodation, pursuit, fixation, and saccadics.

INSTRUMENTS FOR CHECKING VISION.   For years the most popular instrument for testing sight has been the Snellen Chart, which originated in 1862. The fact that it is used so widely is unfortunate since there is an overwhelming amount of evidence to indicate that it is inadequate as a screening device for testing vision in schools. One of the earlier studies criticizing its use was by George Spache (1939), who listed a number of reasons why it was inadequate for use in schools. Among the reasons listed by Spache were the following:

1.   It does not measure the efficiency of the eyes at reading distance.
2.   "Only 20-40 percent of all the children are identified who really need the help of an eye specialist." (p. 623)
3.   It does not measure the coordination of the eyes (phoria tests).
4.   It does not detect astigmatism.
5.   If it is used with a group of children some of the group who take the test last are likely to have memorized the letters. Spache also stated that some of the lines were especially difficult or easy to read because of the groupings of certain configurations of letters.

Somewhat later the Snellen type of instrument testing was criticized in a study by Malmquist (1965), who stated that the instruments of the Snellen type did not take into account vision defects at normal reading distance. Malmquist also mentioned that a number of other defects of vision were found to remain undetected when instruments of the Snellen type for measuring vision were used. On the other hand, the Keystone Telebinocular (another type of eye testing instrument) succeeded in identifying all the cases of visual difficulties, given the criteria of the visual examinations made by a group of medical eye specialists. A strong indictment of the use of the Snellen Chart also came from Gordon Bixel (1966), who stated that although it was a valid test in itself, its use was often detrimental. Bixel believed its use was detrimental because the results of its interpretation could ruin a child's future. Bixel points out that when children pass the Snellen test they are expected to perform tasks that many simply cannot see to do. They are then considered to be lazy or stupid. Bixel says, "No one would consider putting a thermometer in a child's mouth and, when the temperature registered normal, proclaim good health. But that is just what is being done visually. Letters are placed on the wall and if the child can read standard size letters, he is told he needs no glasses, his eyes are all right." (p. 181)

Other vision testers that have proven satisfactory for testing of disabled readers are the Bausch and Lomb Vision Tester (and School Vision Tester), and the Keystone Visual Survey Telebinocular. A description and illustration of each of these follow:

THE BAUSCH AND LOMB VISION TESTER AND THE BAUSCH AND LOMB SCHOOL VISION TESTER.   These are essentially the same instrument; however, a different set of slides are used for school vision testing. The School Vision Tester includes the following tests: Acuity Far (right eye), Acuity Far (left eye), Far Sightedness (right eye), Far Sightedness (left eye), Phoria Far, and Phoria Near. All tests can be completed in approximately two minutes. The Bausch and Lomb Vision

Tester is used more frequently in industry. In addition to the tests listed for the School Vision Tester it also includes tests for depth perception and color blindness.

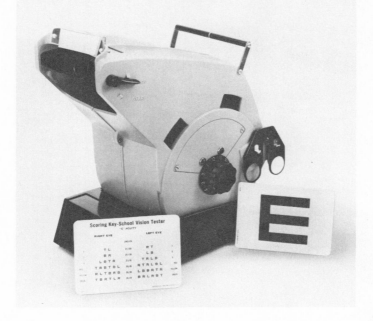

Figure 8–1. The Bausch and Lomb School Vision Tester[1]

THE KEYSTONE VISUAL SURVEY TELEBINOCULAR INSTRUMENT. This instrument is used for the following tests: Simultaneous Perception, Vertical Imbalance, Lateral Posture at Far Point, Fusion at Far Point, Usable Vision of Both Eyes at Far Point, Usable Vision of Right Eye at Far Point, Usable Vision of Left Eye at Far Point, Stereopsis, Color Blindness, Lateral Posture at Near Point, Fusion at Near Point, Visual Acuity of Both Eyes at Near Point, Visual Acuity of Right Eye at Near Point, and Visual Acuity of Left Eye at Near Point.

Although research information definitely indicates a need for near point vision testing it does present some problems for younger children. For example, Arthur Keeney (1969), an ophthalmologist, stated that visual screening at far-point is more reliable than visual screening at near-point or reading range and that near-point range is influenced by age, refractive error, light, accommodative effort, pupillary diameter, and convergence stability. He stated that the coefficient of reliability in near-point acuity is approximately .75 to .78 and the reliability coefficient for far-point acuity is approximately .95 to .97. He also emphasized that the plus lens screening procedure often used for farsightedness is somewhat unreliable. And that any screening instrument does not take the place of professional eye care, but should be thought of as an assisting device used to identify individuals needing care on the basis of a few salient points.

All students in remedial reading should be given a visual screening test as

[1]Reproduced by permission of Bausch & Lomb, Rochester, New York 14802.

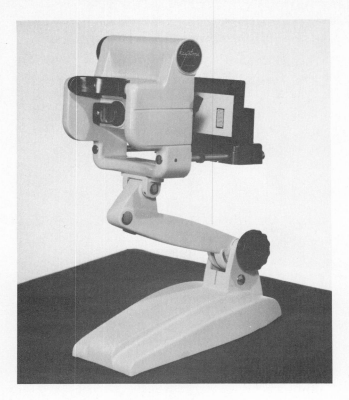

Figure 8–2. The Keystone Visual Survey Telebinocular[2]

part of their initial testing upon entering the program. But, as William Smith (1969), an optometrist, points out, "Even the most sophisticated and carefully performed tests are neither final nor absolutely conclusive. In doubtful cases, it is my practice to repeat tests on different instruments and at different times. It is not unusual to obtain variable findings when performed in such a manner. However, when results are repeatedly and relatively compatible, it is safe to draw conclusions as to probable complicity." (p. 148) In discussing a group of students with whom he had worked, Smith said, "Again using experience as the basis for evidence, I can add that many of the children in the group reported and in others (before and since), whose reading became markedly improved with orthoptic treatment, were, according to earlier reports, supposed to have had normally functioning, blameless visual systems." (p. 148)

During a four-year period in which accurate records were kept on the visual problems of students in our Reading Center at the University of Texas at El Paso we have found that approximately 50 percent of the students, who are disabled readers, had visual problems that had been undetected through normal school screening procedures. It is also interesting to note that our results in testing substantiate the

[2]Reproduced by permission of Keystone View Company, 2212 E. 12th St., Davenport, Iowa 52803.

EDUCATOR'S CHECKLIST [3]

OBSERVABLE CLUES TO CLASSROOM VISION PROBLEMS

Student's
Name _____ Date _____

1. APPEARANCE OF EYES:

One eye turns in or out at any time _____
Reddened eyes or lids _____
Eyes tear excessively _____
Encrusted eyelids _____
Frequent styes on lids _____

2. COMPLAINTS WHEN USING EYES AT DESK:

Headaches in forehead or temples _____
Burning or itching after reading or desk work _____
Nausea or dizziness _____
Print blurs after reading a short time _____

3. BEHAVIORAL SIGNS OF VISUAL PROBLEMS:

A. *Eye Movement Abilities (Ocular Motility)*

Head turns as reads across page _____
Losses place often during reading _____
Needs finger or marker to keep place _____
Displays short attention span in reading
    or copying _____
Too frequently omits words _____
Repeatedly omits "small" words _____
Writes up or down hill on paper _____
Rereads or skips lines unknowingly _____
Orients drawings poorly on page _____

B. *Eye Teaming Abilities (Binocularity)*

Complains of seeing double (diplopia) _____
Repeats letters within words _____
Omits letters, numbers or phrases _____
Misaligns digits in number columns _____
Squints, closes or covers one eye _____
Tilts head extremely while working at desk _____
Consistently shows gross postural deviations
    at all desk activities _____

C. *Eye-Hand Coordination Abilities*

Must feel of things to assist in any
    interpretation required _____
Eyes not used to "steer" hand movements
    (extreme lack of orientation, placement
    of words or drawings on page) _____
Writes crookedly, poorly spaced: cannot
    stay on ruled lines _____
Misaligns both horizontal and vertical series
    of numbers _____

Uses his hand or fingers to keep his place
on the page _____
Uses other hand as "spacer" to control
spacing and alignment on page _____
Repeatedly confuses left-right directions _____

D. *Visual Form Perception (Visual Comparison
Visual Imagery, Visualization)*

Mistakes words with same or similar
beginnings _____
Fails to recognize same word in next
sentence _____
Reverses letters and/or words in writing
and copying _____
Confuses likenesses and minor differences _____
Confuses same word in same sentence _____
Repeatedly confuses similar beginnings
and endings of words _____
Fails to visualize what is read either
silently or orally _____
Whispers to self for reinforcement
while reading silently _____
Returns to "drawing with fingers" to
decide likes and differences _____

E. *Refractive Status (Nearsightedness, Farsightedness
Focus Problems, etc.*

Comprehension reduces as reading continued;
loses interest too quickly _____
Mispronounces similar words as continues
reading _____
Blinks excessively at desk tasks and/or
reading; not elsewhere _____
Holds book too closely; face too close to
desk surface _____
Avoids all possible near-centered tasks _____
Complains of discomfort in tasks that
demand visual interpretation _____
Closes or covers one eye when reading or
doing desk work _____
Makes errors in copying from chalkboard to
paper on desk _____
Makes errors in copying from reference book
to notebook _____
Squints to see chalkboard, or requests to
move nearer _____
Rubs eyes during or after short periods of
visual activity _____
Fatigues easily; blinks to make chalkboard
clear up after desk task _____

OBSERVER'S SUGGESTIONS:

Signed _____

(Encircle): Teacher; Nurse; Remedial Teacher;
Psychologist; Vision Consultant; Other.

Address _____

_____

statement made by Smith that tests made at different times produce differing results. Referrals to eye doctors are only made after at least two visual screening tests in which *both* indicate that a referral is called for.

The problem encountered in obtaining differing results in visual screening lies not so much with the screening device, but with students themselves. For example, a student's eye muscles may be able to compensate for a slight muscle imbalance on one day, whereas, on another day the problem may appear somewhat more severe. Because of this problem it is imperative that the remedial reading teacher, as well as students' other teachers know something about the observable symptoms of visual difficulties. A checklist to guide your observations is shown on pages 203-204. In using such a device it should be emphasized that referrals should not usually be made on the basis of one symptom, but rather on the basis of the observation of the presence of a cluster of these symptoms.

Eye Movements and Reading Speed

Contrary to the belief of many people unfamiliar with the work of the eye in reading, the eye does not sweep smoothly across the page in reading. As we read, the eye stops and starts, making a series of short, quick movements. These are often referred to as saccadic movements. We do not see clearly as the eye moves, therefore, in order to see a word(s) our eyes must stop and fixate, move to the next word or small group of words, fixate again, etc.

The time it takes to fixate varies, according to our research studies, between one-fourth and one-sixth of a second with the average time for a good reader running between one-fifth and one-sixth of a second. Most researchers also agree that it takes from 1/25 to 1/30 of a second for the eye to move from one fixation to the next, and it also takes from 1/25 to 1/30 of a second for the eye to sweep from the end of one line of print to the beginning of the next. According to Albert Harris (1970) the average span of recognition of words or the average number of words it is possible to see clearly during each fixation runs from .45 for an average first grader to 1.11 for an average college student. We would naturally be able to see something to the right and left of each word or group of words as we fixate using our peripheral vision. However, most researchers agree that, even for the very best reader, it would be impossible to see an average of more than three words clearly enough to read them. In reading, then, we would have a pattern similar to the next illustration.

If we were to check the reading (or word seeing) speed of someone, assuming he had the widest span of recognition (three words), the fastest fixation time ($^1/_6$ second), the fastest sweep time from one fixation to another ($^1/_{30}$ second) and the fastest return sweep from one line to the next ($^1/_{30}$ second), the greatest number of words that could be read (or seen) per minute might be computed as follows:

6 fixations/second multiplied by 3 words/fixation
$6 \times 3 = 18$ words/second

18 words/second multiplied by 60 seconds
1080 words/minute

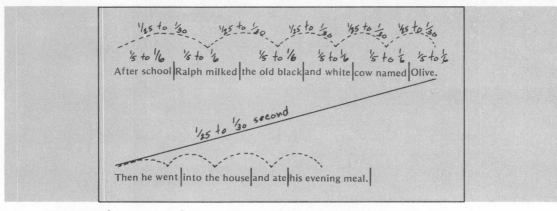

After school | Ralph milked | the old black | and white | cow named | Olive.

$\frac{1}{25}$ to $\frac{1}{30}$ second

Then he went | into the house | and ate | his evening meal. |

However, for every six fixations we would have five movements from one fixation to the next ($1/30 \times 5 = 5/30$ seconds.) If we assume that for every six fixations we also have one return sweep, that adds another $1/30$ of a second. Therefore, for every six fixations we have $5/30 + 1/30$ or $6/30 = 1/5$ second lost in sweep time. Roughly, then, we would have to subtract one-fifth of the 1080 words/minute we had previously calculated since that time would be lost to sweep time. Therefore, the total number of words this reader could read (or see) would be as follows:

$$1/5 \times 1080 = 217$$
$$1080 - 217 = 864$$

It would then appear that even under ideal conditions this reader could not *see* more than 864 words/minute.

Some writers have claimed that in reading we get enough clues through peripheral vision, even though all words are not seen clearly, to read as many as 3500 words/minute. It is my opinion that the evidence does not support this belief, but there is a possibility that a few people do have this capability. Note in my calculations I have differentiated between *reading* and *seeing* words. This is because there is a semantic difference between the two. If we consider *reading* to mean getting a general idea of what is contained in a passage, then it is often possible to read only the first few words or first sentence of each paragraph and still *read* the material. On the other hand, as stated earlier, it is probably not possible for even the best readers to *see* more than 800-900 words/minute.

The diagnosis of eye movements become somewhat commonplace during the decade of the 1960s. Although instruments for measuring eye movements had been available for doing this since the late 1800s, the influx of federal money through ESEA Title I Programs enabled many schools to buy devices for recording eye movements. One such device is the Reading Eye Camera[4] which makes a recording of students' eye movements as they read. The older models recorded eye movements on film which had to be developed after the student had completed his reading. A newer model records the student's eye movements directly on paper

[4]Manufactured and distributed by Educational Development Laboratories, Huntington, New York.

similar to a graph. These recordings can be analyzed to discover the number of fixations and regressions that a student makes as he reads.

Studies such as those of Miles Tinker (1958) have shown that undesirable eye movements are usually only symptomatic of various reading problems such as lack of word recognition. And when the word recognition problem is remediated, the student's eye movement pattern would become normal. Therefore, unless you wish to research these relationships it would appear to be a waste of time and money to bother to diagnose eye movement in terms of normal remedial procedures.

DIAGNOSIS OF PROBLEMS OF THE EAR

Classification of Auditory Problems

Auditory problems that are of concern to reading specialists could be classified under three categories. These categories are auditory discrimination, auditory acuity, and auditory memory. Studies of the auditory abilities of advanced and disabled readers such as that of Pauline Flynn and Margaret Byrne (1970) have sometimes shown that disabled readers, as a group, have inferior auditory abilities as compared with average or advanced readers. On the other hand, Guy Bond and Miles Tinker (1973) state that other studies report conflicting results to those of the Flynn and Byrne study. Tinker and Bond also state that the correlation between auditory disabilities and reading disabilities is also often low or insignificant. In other words there are likely to be a few severe cases of auditory disabilities within a group of disabled readers; however, the most disabled readers are not necessarily the same students with serious auditory disabilities.

AUDITORY DISCRIMINATION.   Auditory discrimination is the ability to discriminate between various combinations of sounds. In reading, of course, we are usually concerned with the ability to discriminate between or among similar sounding phonemes. We are also concerned with a student's ability to *mask*, which is the ability to hear a certain sound when interfering sounds or noises are present.

Auditory discrimination is obviously very important to the student learning to read, since he must hear the difference between similar sounds before he can accurately reproduce these sounds himself. It is also important that a student has the ability to mask other extraneous noises so that he can hear what the teacher or another student is saying. Therefore, any student who has difficulties with phonic word attack skills or who displays the symptoms (listed below) that are typical of difficulties with auditory discrimination should be given an auditory discrimination test.

The best known and most used test for this purpose is the *Auditory Discrimination Test*. [5] This is an individual test in which the examiner pronounces a

---

[5] Wepman, Joseph M. *Auditory Discrimination Test*. 950 E. 59th St., Chicago, Illinois. Copyright by the author.

number of pairs of words that are either alike, or alike except for one phoneme, e.g., lack-lack, and tub-tug. The student is to respond by telling whether the two words are the same or different.

When giving the *Auditory Discrimination Test* it is important that the student understand that "same" and "different" refer to the *sounds* of the words and not to the *meaning* of the words. If a student does poorly, it is also a good idea to wait several days and give the same test or an alternate form to insure that the results of the first administration were valid. If in giving the test you find that a great many students fail, you should consider having a sample of that group tested by another person to insure that your pronunciation is not at fault.

Although originally designed as an individual test, it may be given in a group situation. In this case give students a sheet numbered in correspondence with each pair of words on the test. As the words are pronounced, have students write a (+) for words that are the same and a (−) for words that are different. It also works well to record the test words on tape and give the test via the tape recorder. This will also insure more accurate results in most cases.

It is important to note that the *Auditory Discrimination Test* is only a test for "minimal pairs" and does not test other auditory discrimination skills such as the ability to mask sounds. If you suspect a student is having difficulty with masking, the best way to confirm your suspicions is to ask him to respond in writing to various questions in a normal classroom setting. For example, pronounce words and ask the student to write the initial consonant sounds, ending sounds or medial vowel sounds. When doing this, however, it is important that the student know the sound-symbol relationships involved.

Students with auditory discrimination problems may exhibit certain difficulties. Following is a list of some of these. It should, however, be stressed that any student may exhibit one or more of these symptoms from time to time and still not have problems with auditory discrimination. This list should serve only to alert you to the possibility that the problem might exist.

1. Phonics knowledge inadequate
2. Poor spelling
3. Frequent requests for a repeat of oral material presented by teacher
4. Difficulty in understanding what was said by the teacher or another student
5. Pronunciation of certain words unclear
6. Tendency to hold mouth open while listening
7. Tilting of head while listening

AUDITORY ACUITY.   This simply refers to the ability to hear sounds of varying pitch (frequencies or vibrations) heard at different degrees of loudness (measured in decibels). Normal speech frequency tends to run from 125 up to as high as 8000 cycles per second with more in the 130 to 4000 range. It has been noted that students with hearing loss in the higher frequency ranges (500 +) often tend to have difficulties in school because they are often taught by female teachers whose voices tend to be of higher frequency than male teachers. It is also important to note that certain consonant sounds such as *s, z,* and *t* are of higher frequencies than the vowel sounds. Students also experience hearing loss in terms of loudness. A loss of up to five decibels is considered near normal or would probably cause the student very little difficulty. A loss of six to ten decibels may cause slight difficulty and a loss above ten to fifteen decibels would normally cause difficulty, especially if the student was not seated near the front of the room or if he did not wear some corrective hearing device. Students with a hearing loss in any of two frequencies in one ear or the other at a decibel level (ANSI or ISO) are considered to have a problem serious enough to be referred for clinical evaluation.

Auditory acuity is measured by using an audiometer such as the MA-19 manufactured by Maico Hearing Instruments shown below.

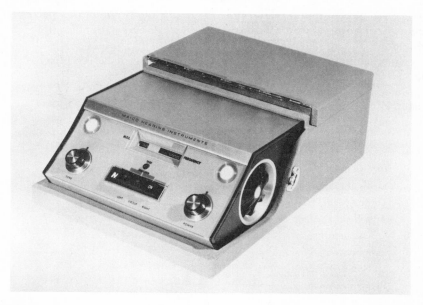

Figure 8–3. The Maico Model MA-19[6]

This portable instrument can be used for conducting tests for either individuals or groups.

Other manufacturers of audiometers are as follows:

Maico Hearing Instruments
7375 Bush Lake Road
Minneapolis, Minnesota 55435

Auditory Instrument Division
Zenith Radio Corporation
6501 W. Grand Ave.
Chicago, Illinois 60635

Precision Acoustics Corporation
55 W. 42 Street
New York, New York 10036

Royal Industries
Audiotone Division
P.O. Box 2905
Phoenix, Arizona 85036

Beltone Electronics Corporation
Hearing Test Instruments Division
4201 W. Victoria Street
Chicago, Illinois 60646

[6]Reproduced by permission of Maico Hearing Instruments, 7573 Bush Lake Road, Minneapolis, Minnesota 55435.

Many remedial reading teachers will not have an audiometer available for their use; however, in many cases audiometric testing is available through the school nurse. In some remedial reading programs audiometric testing is done as a matter of course for all students. Where a school nurse is available and willing to do this testing, the author recommends that it be done. On the other hand, routine audiometric testing is often not necessary unless it is indicated because of a student's failure on an auditory discrimination test or because of noted symptoms of hearing loss. It seems much more logical to do routine screening for auditory discrimination and then refer those students who fail the auditory discrimination test for auditory acuity testing. It can then be determined whether the problem of a particular student with discrimination is a matter of hearing loss or a matter of simply having not refined his perceptual senses. On the other hand, if a student does well on an auditory discrimination test it generally does not matter if he does have a slight hearing loss as shown by an auditory acuity test.

Since it will often be necessary to make referrals without the benefit of an audiometer, you should be aware of certain symptoms of hearing loss. These symptoms are as follows:

1. Cupping hand behind the ear
2. Complaints of buzzing or ringing noises in the ear
3. Gives the appearance of being lazy or of not paying attention
4. Drainage or discharge of ears
5. Tilts head at angle or turns head while listening
6. Opens mouth while listening
7. Frequent head colds
8. Does not respond well to oral directions
9. Reads in unnatural voice tones
10. Does not enunciate clearly
11. Stiff or strained posture while listening

Certain other informal tests—such as the "watch tick," "coin click," and "whisper" tests—have also been used by classroom teachers and reading specialists for many years. You should keep in mind, however, that testing a student's ability to hear a watch tick or two coins click is not the same as hearing the human voice in the classroom and are, therefore, likely to be very unreliable measures of a students hearing ability. The whisper test in which the tester whispers a word or phrase at various distances is somewhat more practical than either the "watch tick" or "coin click" tests, but is still a poor substitute for the *Auditory Discrimination Test*, auditory acuity testing with an audiometer, and careful observation in the normal classroom setting.

AUDITORY MEMORY.   This refers to the ability to listen to, and then remember or repeat, a series of words, digits, a sentence, nonsense symbols, etc. This ability is, of course, extremely important in learning to read. For example, in sounding a three-letter word the student must hold the first two sounds in memory to put them with the third letter in order to analyze the word. As word analysis becomes more difficult, e.g., in applying various syllabication principles, vowel rules, and individual grapheme sounds, the student is faced with a great deal of both visual and auditory memory. Comprehension of oral, and to some extent silent, reading also depends on the student's auditory memory.

Although auditory memory is an important skill for reading and the measurement of the skill is not difficult, there is some doubt about the importance of measuring it. The problem lies in the fact that few research studies have shown that training in the improvement of auditory memory skills results in an increase in reading ability, although auditory memory per se can be improved. Part of the problem in the past, however, may have been in training students in the memory of digits and nonsense or non-reading related sentences rather than in training them in materials directly related to reading. For example, research at our reading center has shown that students who cannot remember and repeat at least a five-word sentence benefit from auditory memory training that deals directly with listening to and repeating sentences. We should also remember that many exercises in phonics and structural analysis actually train students in auditory memory skills.

If you wanted a standardized test for auditory memory of digits, you could either administer the Digit Span subtest of the *WISC* or the *WAIS*. You should remember, however, that remembering a series of digits is not necessarily parallel to the auditory memory abilities required for reading. Memory for sentences can be assessed to some extent by using the "memory for sentence" items on either the *Stanford-Binet Intelligence Scale* or the *Slosson Intelligence Test*. It is also easy to develop your own test of sentence memory by simply writing several four-word sentences, several five-word sentences, etc., until you reach a point where few or no students can repeat the sentences. This can then be standardized by giving it to normal students at each grade level to determine the average sentence length remembered at each grade level.

From a practical standpoint, however, most remedial reading teachers can best diagnose auditory memory by careful diagnostic teaching, i.e., noting whether students can remember such things as a five-to eight-word sentence, a series of directions, or four to five letters in a word.

DIAGNOSIS OF SPEECH PROBLEMS

There is some disagreement concerning the relationships between various speech disorders and reading disability. Some studies have found the incidence of speech disorders among disabled readers to be no higher than among normal readers, while others have reported that 20 to 35 percent of groups of disabled readers had speech disorders. One of the major reasons for these discrepancies is probably the fact that in some studies reading ability was assessed with an oral reading test and in others it was assessed with silent reading tests. There is also considerable evidence that many speech disorders, even though present, cannot easily be recognized by a lay person. Also, when certain speech disorders are in evidence it is sometimes difficult to determine whether they are a hindering factor in reading.

There is often a relationship between problems of auditory acuity and/or auditory discrimination and speech disorders. If a student shows evidence of either of these auditory difficulties, you should note whether the student also shows evidence of a speech problem.

Most speech disorders, and especially those of an organic nature, should be diagnosed and treated by a speech specialist. The remedial reading teacher, however, should be aware of the symptoms of speech disorders and whenever a cluster of these symptoms appear, or when one or more appear to a serious degree, the student should be referred to a speech specialist. Some of these symptoms are as follows:

1. Inability to clearly produce the phonic elements shown on the test in Appendix A.
2. Inability to reproduce certain phonic elements after hearing them (closely related to auditory acuity and/or auditory discrimination).
3. Peculiar movements of the head and/or mouth on phonic elements or words mispronounced. Also watch for difficulty in forming lips to make certain sounds.
4. Too much or too little volume (closely related to auditory acuity).
5. Long pauses before certain phonemes or phonograms.
6. Refusal (or resistance) to talk.
7. Use of improper tonal quality (closely related to auditory difficulties).
8. Skipping or slurring certain words, phonemes, or phonograms.
9. Stuttering.

DIAGNOSIS OF GENERAL
HEALTH PROBLEMS

In most cases the educator is neither trained nor equipped to diagnose problems of general health. For this reason the remedial reading teacher will need to rely on information gained from the student's past health history and from careful observation. The parent interview can be an important source of information concerning general health. In interviewing the parents of disabled readers check into health background concerning any chronic illnesses or allergies, any medication taken for allergies or other illnesses, childhood injuries or diseases that kept the student out of school for extended periods of time, eating habits, general stamina as evidenced by outside activity, and sleep habits. Information from parents can be especially helpful, since they know the student and have, in most cases, had an opportunity to observe him longer than anyone else. I have found information gained from parents to be especially helpful where there are other children in the family with which they can compare a certain child. On the other hand, information coming from parents of an only child is often less objective, since they have no norm with which to compare that child.

Some health problems will not be apparent even with careful observation;

however, some health problems do manifest certain observable symptoms. Some of these symptoms that may have relevance to a reading disability are as follows:

1. Lack of energy, listlessness, or general fatigue (including falling asleep)
2. Poor eating habits
3. Susceptibility to colds
4. Labored breathing
5. Complaints of dizziness and/or headaches
6. Inability to concentrate for sustained periods of time
7. Irritability, especially after physical exercise or near end of the day
8. Evidence of much better work at the beginning of the day
9. Complaints of stomachache or nausea
10. Considerably overweight or underweight
11. Unsteadiness in writing or small motor activities
12. Chronic absenteeism

When a cluster of these symptoms appears, or when any one appears to a strong degree, the student should be referred to the school nurse; or the student's parents should be contacted concerning referral to a medical doctor.

PART B. *remediation*

REMEDIATION OF PROBLEMS OF THE EYE

In many situations the responsibilities of the teacher in eye treatment ceases once a referral has been made to an optometrist or ophthalmologist. The only problem with which the teacher is then concerned is that of the remediation of educational disabilities that may have been caused from eye problems. There are also many instances in which the teacher should work in cooperation with the eye doctor to carry out a total program adapted to the special needs of visually handicapped students. For this reason a clear channel of communication needs to exist between the teacher and the student's doctor. Generally teachers are not concerned with disorders of the eye involving the peripheral nervous system, i.e., visual acuity, refractive error, fusion, convergence, and accommodation after an eye doctor has examined the student and prescribed accordingly.

It should be noted that there is considerable disagreement among various optometrists and ophthalmologists as well as some disagreement among the members of each group concerning the value of orthoptic training and school-related visual perceptual training. For example, a rather typical statement concerning the beliefs of many ophthalmologists comes from Harold Martin (1971) in describing the beliefs of Dr. George Campian, a Clinical Professor of Ophthalmology. Martin says,

> He feels that if an orthoptic program aimed at muscle balance and convergence is associated with any improvement in reading, the reading improvement must result from the patient's increased concentration rather than from the exercises themselves. He also points out that refractive errors are of negligible importance in reading disorders. (p. 470)

The opposite viewpoint, perhaps more typical of the beliefs of many optometrists, is expressed by William Swanson (1972) in describing the results of his study of the effectiveness of optometric vision therapy. Swanson states,

> Study of 100 consecutive cases of learning disorders revealed that optometric vision therapy was successful in 93 percent of the cases. The accuracy of this figure was verified by a registered psychologist. The criterion for success was a definite indication of improvement in the person's learning ability, as verified by subsequent tests, by report of the parent, the patient, or the teacher. Fifty-seven parents reported improvement in their child. The teachers reported improvement in 48 percent, and retesting showed improvement in 82 percent. (p. 42)

Because of the apparent disagreement among various eye doctors it seems best to again recommend that a clear channel of communication be established between remedial teachers and optometrists or ophthalmologists and that suggestions for teacher work with specific students come directly from the examining doctor.

REMEDIATION OF PROBLEMS OF THE EAR

As stated in the section on diagnosis, problems of the ear could be divided into three categories in dealing with reading disabilities. These categories are auditory discrimination, auditory acuity, and auditory memory. Although all three areas are of importance to teachers who deal with students' auditory deficiencies, remediation of problems in auditory acuity is usually not within the realm of the remedial reading teacher.

Auditory discrimination. This can be improved in students deficient in this area, as demonstrated in a study by Nicholas Silvaroli and Warren Wheelock (1966). Silvaroli and Wheelock gave their students fifteen minutes per day of training in discriminating like and unlike pairs of words via tape recorded lessons. The training period lasted approximately five weeks. Students who received the training in auditory discrimination did significantly better, as measured by the Wepman *Auditory Discrimination Test,* than a similar control group that did not receive the auditory discrimination training. We have provided similar auditory discrimination training for disabled readers and, in most cases where their auditory acuity is not impaired, we find a rapid improvement in students' ability to discriminate among similar sounding phonemes within words (minimal pairs) with approximately the same overall time pattern as that described in the Silvaroli and Wheelock study.

Although practice in auditory discrimination, in general, may be somewhat beneficial, it is usually only necessary to provide remediation in those combinations with which the student has particular difficulty. These can, of course, easily be located by giving the *Auditory Discrimination Test*. For example, a student who cannot hear the difference between "vow" and "thou" will need practice in discriminating between the "v" and "th" phonemes. There are also certain combinations that cause difficulty for specific ethnic groups. For example, native Spanish speakers often have difficulty with the short "i" and short "e" sounds and with the "ch" and "sh" digraphs. You should be especially aware of these difficulties. It should be noted, however, that many children, as in the case of blacks from certain areas, can hear these differences in others' speech, and seem to be aware of them in reading, yet they do not pronounce them correctly in their own speech. In some black dialects, for example, the "s" is often omitted in speaking, yet many of these same students seem to have no difficulty in answering questions concerning comprehension of singular and plural concepts. Where these problems appear only in students' speech and do not appear to be detrimental to their reading, it is probably best to ignore them.

Remedial exercises for auditory discrimination may be done orally, but putting them on audio-tape will save much time in the long run. These can be categorized and retrieved when needed. (It should be stressed that teacher-made tapes should not be used unless the reproduction quality is very good.) Practice exercises for various pairs may be done as follows:

A. (Beginning level) Hearing likenesses and differences—*v* and *th*. (Try to avoid using the same combinations as those on the test so that it will not be repetitious for later use.)

Tape Script: "Listen to each pair of words I pronounce and decide whether they are the same or different. If they are the same, circle the word 'same' on your answer sheet. If they are different, circle the word 'different' on your answer sheet. Number one is 'van' and 'than.' Number two is 'then' and 'then,' etc."

The answer sheet would appear as follows:
1. Same–Different
2. Same–Different
3. etc.

The answer part of the script would be as follows:
"The first two words were different. They were 'van' and 'than.' Circle *different* if you did not do so before. The next words were the same. They were 'then' and 'then.' Circle *same* if you did not do so before, etc."

B. (Second level) Hearing beginning sounds—*v* and *th*. (This requires a knowledge of phonics.)

Tape Script: "Look at row one on your answer sheet. Circle the word that begins the same as 'very.' Now look at row two. Circle the word that begins the same as 'though.' "

The answer sheet would appear as follows:

1. th	v	b	c
2. v	b	th	f
3. etc.			

In making exercises of this nature it is important to also give the answers on the same script. This will teach and reinforce the concept and will also conserve the teacher's time. The correction part of the script for the examples would be as follows:

"Now we will check the answers. Number one was 'very,' the answer should have been 'v,' the second letter in the row. Circle it now if you did not get it right. Number two was 'th,' these letters are third in the row. Circle them now if you did not get them right, etc."

C. (Third level) Writing beginning sounds—*v* and *th*. (This also requires a knowledge of phonics.)

Tape Script: "Listen to the words I pronounce. They all begin with either 'v' or 'th.' After you hear each word I pronounce, write the beginning sound you hear in the blank by the number. Number one is 'van.' Number two is 'than,' etc."

The answer sheet would appear as follows:

1. _____
2. _____
3. etc.

The answer part of the script would be as follows: "The first word was 'van.' It begins with 'v.' You should have written a 'v' by number one. The second word was 'than.' It begins with 'th.' You should have written 'th' by number two, etc."

As you will note, this type of exercise takes the beginning reader from simple discrimination of similar sounds to the more difficult process of writing sounds when they are heard. When developing exercises of this nature you should also keep in mind that some students have difficulty with medial and ending sounds. Exercises for the remediation of these types of auditory discrimination problems can easily be devised with slight changes in the tape scripts.

Commercial materials are also available for the remediation of problems of auditory discrimination. These materials are listed in Appendix "C." You should remember, however, in using most commercial materials that it is usually very difficult to select lessons to remediate a specific problem without requiring the student to go through a considerable amount of other material that in many cases would be of little value to him.

Auditory acuity.   Auditory acuity difficulties should normally be treated by a medical doctor. However, in some cases the doctor is not likely to recommend or feel that the student's hearing is impaired enough to treat from a medical standpoint. He may recommend that allowance be made, within the school setting, for the student's auditory acuity problem. When such is the case you should, if possible, consult directly with the child's physician concerning suggested measures for dealing with the problem. In most cases recommendations would be somewhat as follows:

1. Place the student near the front of the room for any instruction in which the teacher or other students speak from the front of the room.
2. Try to remember to face the student when talking to him, and speak slowly and clearly.
3. If outside noises interfere through windows, seat the student as far away from these as possible.

4. Teach the student to use a visual mode of learning the spelling of words and word attack whenever possible.

5. To make sure he is receiving instructions and/or directions, have him write them from time to time. Also check immediately, once the student has begun work, to make sure he heard directions properly.

6. Use programmed materials if they are available for teaching certain concepts.

7. Try to use written directions along with oral directions.

8. Have the student use headphones when listening to recorded material.

Auditory memory. This is an important skill for reading; however, studies have tended to show that although certain memory factors can be improved, a corresponding increase in reading ability does not necessarily follow. Perhaps one of the major problems in the past has been in training areas not necessarily related to reading. For example, a student who cannot remember a series of digits forward or backward is also somewhat likely to experience reading problems in remembering a sequence of events. However, we know that remediation that focuses on practice in remembering a series of digits is not likely to result in a corresponding increase in remembering details or a series of events in reading.

Although research on the effectiveness of specific kinds of auditory memory training directly related to reading is lacking, a more logical approach would seem to be through exercises such as giving practice in having the student listen to and repeat sentences. Start with sentences using as many words as the student can remember and work up to sentences equivalent to those remembered by other students of the same age group. Another approach is to attempt to associate auditory sequences with visualization of the process. For example, have the student attempt to "see in his mind's eye" what he reads or hears. This, in my experience, aids in recall.

REMEDIATION OF SPEECH PROBLEMS *For oral reading.*

Students who have any speech defects should be referred to a speech therapist for an evaluation. Following the evaluation the remedial reading teacher should make it a point to personally consult with the speech therapist concerning any special treatment that should be afforded the student. In some cases the recommendations of the speech therapist may require that certain precautions be taken in teaching the student, e.g., teaching him only in a one-to-one situation without the necessity of performing before a group. In other cases the therapist may feel that exposure to group situations may be appropriate and even desirable. Because speech problems are so diverse and the problem of any one student may be entirely unique, general recommendations for the treatment of speech problems would be inappropriate.

In spite of the fact that general recommendations for the handling of students with speech problems are not practical, it should be stressed that the speech therapist should be informed about the nature of the remedial reading program. For example, the speech therapist should have a knowledge of such factors as the amount of time the student spends in remedial reading, the amount of individual versus group work, possible reasons for the student's reading disability, and the degree of reading disability. Armed with this information the speech therapist and remedial reading teacher can combine their efforts to plan a dual program of remediation.

REMEDIATION OF GENERAL HEALTH PROBLEMS

Once a student has been referred to a medical doctor for various problems of general health, there is usually little or nothing that can be done by the remedial reading teacher. However, the remedial reading teacher should attempt to stay alert to the symptoms mentioned under Diagnosis of General Health Problems and consult with the student's parents concerning any recommendations made by the student's physician for maximizing learning conditions. For example, some students may require more breaks for rest and relaxation, provision for mid-morning and/or mid-afternoon snacks, etc. The problem, however, as with dealing with other specialists, is to insure that channels of communication are always open.

SUMMARY

The physical problems with which the remedial reading teacher is usually concerned might be classified as problems of the eye, problems of the ear, problems with speech, neurologically impaired functions, and problems of general health. Because of the complexity of neurological problems they have not been discussed in this chapter, but they are thoroughly covered in Chapter 9. Problems of the eye are prevalent in a number of cases of students with reading disability. The remedial reading teacher should become familiar with instruments for vision screening and should learn to recognize symptoms of visual difficulties. The remedial reading teacher should also learn to administer tests for auditory discrimination and should learn to give auditory acuity tests or should refer to the school nurse or a hearing specialist those students who have inadequate auditory discrimination. Auditory memory is also an important skill required for reading. However, difinitive research is lacking which would clearly indicate that training in auditory memory will, in turn, improve students' ability to read.

There is some disagreement as to whether speech difficulties actually contribute to reading disability. In reality, a common factor such as inadequate hearing is probably more responsible for difficulties in speech as well as reading.

The remedial reading teacher should be familiar with symptoms of students who possess problems with their general health. When a cluster of these symptoms appear in a student, or when any one symptom appears to a strong degree, then that student should be referred to the school nurse or the parents should be contacted so that the student can receive attention from a medical doctor.

The remedial reading teacher is usually not concerned with the treatment of physical disabilities but should learn to recognize various symptoms when they occur so that a proper referral can be made. However, some types of exercises can be done to improve auditory discrimination.

Chapter 8: REFERENCES

Bixel, Gordon. "Vision—Key to Learning or Not Learning," *Education*. Vol. 87, (November, 1966), 180–184.

Bond, Guy L., and Tinker, Miles A. *Reading Difficulties—Their Diagnosis and Correction*. 3d ed., New York: Appleton-Century-Crofts, 1973.

Flynn, Pauline T., and Byrne, Margaret. "Relationship between Reading and Selected Auditory Abilities of Third-Grade Children," *Journal of Speech and Hearing Research*. Vol. 13, (December, 1970), 731–740.

Harris, Albert. *How to Increase Reading Ability*. 5th ed., New York: David McKay Co., 1970.

Keeney, Arthur H. "Vision and Learning Disabilities," A Paper Presented at the Annual Conference of the National Society for the Prevention of Blindness, Milwaukee, Wisconsin, 1969.

Krippner, Stanley. "On Research in Visual Training and Reading Disability," *Journal of Learning Disabilities*. Vol. 4, (February, 1971), 66–76.

Malmquist, Eve. "A Study of Vision Defects in Relation to Reading Disabilities and a Test of the Validity of Certain Vision Screening Programmes in Elementary School," *Slow Learning Child*. Vol. XII, (July, 1965), 38–48.

Martin, Harold. "Vision and Its Role in Reading Disability and Dyslexia," *The Journal of School Health*. Vol. XLI, (November, 1971), 468–472.

Robinson, Helen. *Why Pupils Fail in Reading*. Chicago: University of Chicago Press, 1946.

Silvaroli, Nicholas J., and Wheelock, Warren H. "An Investigation of Auditory Discrimination Training for Beginning Readers," *The Reading Teacher*. Vol. 20, (December, 1966), 247–251.

Smith, William. "The Visual System in Reading and Learning Disabilities," *Journal of School Health*. Vol. 39, (February, 1969), 144–150.

Spache, George. "Testing Vision," *Education*. Vol. 59, (June, 1939), 623–626.

Swanson, William. "Optometric Vision Therapy—How Successful Is It in the Treatment of Learning Disorders?" *Journal of Learning Disabilities*. Vol. 5, (May, 1972), 37–42.

Tinker, Miles. "Recent Studies of Eye Movements in Reading," *Psychological Bulletin*. Vol. 54, (July, 1958), 215–231.

DIAGNOSIS AND REMEDIATION
OF SEVERE READING DISABILITIES

The first part of this chapter presents a discussion of the dilemma of the reading specialist in dealing with the problem of severe reading disabilities. As you will note, even the terminology presents a problem. Information is then presented on the diagnostic aspects of severe reading disabilities, including typical symptoms and precautions to be observed. The last part of the chapter deals with prior theories and their success as well as present day theory and its implementation.

PART A.   *diagnosis*

THE DILEMMA OF SEVERE
READING DISABILITIES

Luckily, a large percentage of the disabled readers you are likely to encounter in your teaching career will present problems that are rather clear-cut or easily diagnosed. And, although a considerable amount of remediation may be involved, most of these students will show considerable improvement. The classroom teacher's as well as the remedial reading teacher's dilemma, however, is the student who simply does not appear to learn regardless of the amount of instruction he receives. To add to the dilemma this is often a student who has a normal or high IQ, who appears to be relatively free of emotional problems, presents adequate auditory acuity and discrimination, adequate vision, and generally appears to be in excellent health.

This type of student has often been referred to as a "learning disabilities" case. This term is perhaps used more in the case of teachers trained in special education. When the learning disability concerns reading, which it often does, there is often a tendency to say the student has "dyslexia." Although both terms tend to be somewhat unclear, at least some degree of agreement has been reached on their meaning. N. Dale Bryant (1972) points out that one definition emerged when the

Council for Exceptional Children met in St. Louis in April of 1967. Their definition is as follows:

> A child with learning disabilities is one with adequate mental abilities, sensory processes, and emotional stability, who has a limited number of specific deficits in perceptive, integrative, or expressive processes which severely impair learning efficiency. This includes children who have a central nervous system dysfunction, which is expressed primarily in impaired learning efficiency. (p. 51)

Bryant also noted that another definition emphasizing the basic nature of the language process was adopted by the National Advisory Committee on Handicapped Children in January of 1968. Bryant noted that this definition has been incorporated into federal legislation. This definition is as follows:

> Children with special learning disabilities exhibit a disorder in one or more of the basic psychological processes involved in understanding or in using spoken or written languages. These may be manifested in disorders of listening, thinking, talking, reading, writing, spelling, or arithmetic. They include conditions which have been referred to as perceptual handicaps, brain injury, minimal brain dysfunction, dyslexia, developmental aphasia, and so on. They do not include learning problems which are due primarily to visual, hearing, or motor handicaps, to mental retardation, emotional disturbance, environmental disadvantages. (p. 51)

Dyslexia and Learning Disabilities

A term often closely associated with learning disabilities concerned with reading is dyslexia. It should be stressed, however, that the term dyslexia seldom means the same thing to any two people. Therefore anyone using the term should be aware of the fact that simply using the term to describe a particular student may, in many instances, only add confusion to a diagnosis. In a rather long article Richard Adams (1969) makes the point that there is little agreement on the meaning of the term as defined in the dictionary, as used by educators, or as used by people in the medical profession. He also points out that the meaning of the term varies from dictionary to dictionary and among people who are working in the same profession. Helen Robinson (1970) has also noted that a great deal of confusion exists over the use of the term. She quotes Gilbert Schiffman who said, "While dyslexia no doubt exists, it is difficult to defend this concept which cannot be defined, attributed to any specific etiology, estimated as to its prevalency or frequency, identified with a particular syndrome, or remediated with a specific technique or school organization." (p. 138) Robinson, after reviewing the problem in considerable detail, states, "It would seem, therefore, that dyslexia is synonymous with reading disability and that it has little or no value as a label because it offers no help in teaching children to read." (p. 138) Harold Martin (1971), who is a medical doctor, would seem to agree with Robinson. He says,

> The use of the term dyslexia is disputed, its definition is unclear and continues to vary with different experts in the field, and it is of little or no use to the classroom teacher or

the child's physician. Inasmuch as its definition has been inexact and bastardized, the use of this term may be more harmful than helpful in trying to understand children who are reading poorly. (p. 469)

In summary then, it would seem that the remedial reading teacher should avoid the use of the term dyslexia simply because we do not know what the term means. On the other hand, you are quite likely to hear the term used in connection with a particular student. When you do, you might best think of it as meaning that the student has a "severe" reading disability and that in most cases there would be no well-defined causal factor or even no well-defined *set* of causal factors.

The Prevalence and Causes of Severe Reading Disability

Various authors and researchers have estimated the percentage of students with severe reading disabilities at from 2 up to 25 to 30 percent of the school population. This great discrepancy tends to exist because of the variation in descriptions of the severely disabled reader. Bryant, in discussing children with general learning disabilities, including reading, indicates that when the problem is limited to those who show evidence of specific neuropsychological dysfunction, the estimated proportion would be around 5 percent. He states, however, that the figures most often reported fall between 7 and 10 percent.

It should also be noted that the figures for various degrees of reading disability may reach from 2 to 3 percent in high socioeconomic levels in the suburbs to as high as 60 percent in the case of urban children from low-income families. Because of the great differences in these figures, it would seem unwise to classify severe reading or general learning disability cases as generally being of a neuropsychological nature. As Bruce Balow (1971) says,

> Obviously some few cases (perhaps that one to two percent found in suburbs) arise from an unusual neurological switchboard, scrambled circuitry, crossed wires or blown fuses, but the large mass of learning disabled are far more likely to derive from an innate or acquired vulnerability coupled with an environment in home and school that is inhospitable or downright hostile to learning in the basic skills. The operative agent is the educational environment, not the vulnerability, since it can be argued that nearly every pupil has some type of vulnerability by the time he enters school. (p. 518)

There is also evidence as reported by Edith Grotberg (1970) that a factor such as prematurity at birth is related to the presence of learning disabilities in low-income families. Grotberg reported studies indicating that premature infants from impoverished families do not overcome or compensate for the assault as do those infants from middle or high income families. Grotberg also reported research that indicated that learning disabilities may be produced through changes in body function which result from malnutrition. For example, after introducing food supplements to children who had low hemoglobin levels, the low hemoglobin level not only increased, but so did their IQs.

Characteristic Patterns of Severe Reading Disability

As mentioned previously, the causes of severe reading disability seem to be varied, which would almost certainly reflect considerable variability in the characteristic patterns of severely disabled readers. Elena Boder (1970) has, however, offered three classifications or sets of characteristics of students suffering severe reading disability that she terms "developmental dyslexia." Her reading-spelling patterns are described as follows:

> The reading-spelling pattern of children in the *dysphonic group* (Group I) reflects a primary deficit in letter-sound integration and in the ability to develop phonetic skills. They read *globally*, responding to whole words as configurations or gestalts. Lacking phonetic skills, they are unable to decipher words that are not in their sight vocabulary. Their numerous misspellings, being nonphonetic, are unintelligible. Their most striking errors are "semantic substitution errors," e.g., reading "funny" for "laugh," "chicken" for "duck," "answer" for "ask," "airplane" for "train."
>
> The reading-spelling pattern of children in the *dyseidetic group* (Group II) reflects primary deficit in the ability to perceive whole words as gestalts. They read *phonetically*, sounding out most words, familiar and unfamiliar, as if they were being encountered for the first time. Their misspellings, being *phonetic*, are intelligible. Examples are: "lisn" for "listen," "sos" for "sauce," "bisnis" for "business," "laf" for "laugh."
>
> Children who are *both dysphonic and dyseidetic* (Group III) are deficient in developing phonetic skills and in perceiving whole words as gestalts. Without remedial reading therapy they tend to remain *alexic* or *nonreaders*. (pp. 289–290)

Boder maintains that Group I is by far the largest of the three subtypes.

Another type of classification system for severely disabled readers-learners is given by Dale Johnson (1972), who also uses the term dyslexia. He refers to three subtypes called "visual dyslexia," "auditory dyslexia," and "dysgraphia." Johnson maintains that the most prevalent form of dyslexia is the visual type, which is the inability to translate printed language symbols into meaning. He also says that, although called visual dyslexia, the malady has little to do with vision itself, but rather a matter of misinterpretation of symbols. Auditory dyslexics, according to Johnson, have normal hearing according to audiometric tests; however, they are not able to identify small differences between sounds or are unable to associate phonemes with graphemes. The third type, mentioned by Johnson, is dysgraphia, which is a condition in which the student is unable to coordinate hand and arm muscles in order to write legibly.

As you can see, the classification systems suggested by these authors are somewhat different. This is, of course, illustrative of the problem that exists when dealing with severe reading disability. That is, even the "experts" do not agree on any one set of symptoms or on any one classification system. This should make us realize that, in most cases, we are not dealing with any one "type" of severe reading disability, but rather a complex problem which may be the result of a number of contributing factors interacting with one another to form a composite problem requiring intensive, long-term remedial procedures.

DIAGNOSTIC TECHNIQUES FOR SEVERE
READING DISABILITY

Specific Types of Tests for Severe
Reading Disability

THE WISC AND WAIS.   The WISC and WAIS have both been used a great deal in reading diagnosis. The author's doctoral dissertation was written on the use of WISC subtest patterns to attempt to diagnose reading disability. Although most studies have shown that any one group of disabled readers may have slightly different subtest patterns on the WISC from those of normal or good readers, I am of the opinion that it is of very little value in reading diagnosis for individual students. Its use as a diagnostic instrument can also be very inefficient. For example, you may find that a particular student does extremely poorly on the Digit Span subtest. This is some indication that he has poor auditory memory. However, it may or may not affect his reading ability. Auditory memory for reading might be tested more accurately by having the student repeat sentences of varying lengths.

I have seen hundreds of psychological reports containing information on the results of WISC subtests and subtest patterns. However, I have seen few of these that would be of substantial value to the classroom teacher or remedial reading teacher in terms of practical ideas for the modification of the student's reading program.

TESTS FOR HANDEDNESS, DOMINANCE, AND KNOWLEDGE OF LEFT AND RIGHT.   These have also been used and researched a great deal in the diagnosis of severe as well as mild reading disabilities. One such battery is the *Harris Tests of Lateral Dominance*.[1] It tests such factors as knowledge of left and right, hand preferences, eye dominance, and foot dominance. Many other researchers and diagnosticians have used somewhat similar but unpublished testing instruments.

It should be noted that at certain age-grade levels significantly more children who are severely disabled readers may, as Harris points out, (1958, p. 20) show more confusion in identifying left and right and mixed hand dominance or at other age-grade levels show strong left preferences. However, this does not mean that a student who exhibits these symptoms is likely to be mildly or severely disabled in reading, nor does this knowledge provide us with any information of significant value in planning a program of remediation for a severely disabled reader. In most cases, based on what is now known about severe reading disability, there is little to be gained from giving tests for handedness, dominance, or knowledge of left and right.

A number of other tests such as the *Bender-Visual Motor Gestalt* (BVMG)[2] and the *Developmental Test of Visual Perception* (DTVP)[3] have been used in the diagnosis of severely disabled readers. However, as in the case of dominance and handedness tests, the fact that a student does poorly on the BVMG test does not

[1]Harris, Albert J. *Harris Tests of Lateral Dominance*. New York: The Psychological Corporation, 1958.
[2]Bender, Lauretta. *Bender Visual-Motor Gestalt Test*. New York: The Psychological Corporation, 1938.
[3]Frostig, Marianne. *Developmental Test of Visual Perception*. Chicago: Follett, 1964.

mean that he is a severely disabled reader and, even if he is, the type of information derived from the test scores is of little use in prescribing meaningful remedial activities. The DTVP attempts to identify students who have problems in areas such as perception in space, and eye-motor coordination. However, many studies such as those reviewed by Donald Hammill, Libby Goodman, and J. Lee Wiederholt (1974) indicate that the types of activities prescribed for the remediation of weaknesses indicated on this test are of little or no value in the remediation of concomitant difficulties in reading.

THE ILLINOIS TEST OF PSYCHOLINGUISTIC ABILITIES (ITPA)[4] probably comes closer to measuring what we really need to know about the seriously disabled reader than most non-reading oriented tests. That is, it tends to indicate weaknesses in such areas as auditory decoding, visual decoding, and auditory association. However, the reliability and validity of the subtests have not been clearly established. Furthermore, it is somewhat difficult and time-consuming to administer. And, since no clear-cut information exists concerning the relationship of subtest weaknesses to reading disabilities, I would suggest that, at this time, the information derived from it in terms of program planning for remedial reading is not worth the time and effort required for its administration.

From this discussion it is apparent that most cases of severe reading disability are a complex phenomenon, the causes of which cannot easily be discovered by any of our most commonly used diagnostic tests. In an article on the study of psychoeducational assessment of learning disabilities David Sabatino, William Wickham, and Calvin Burnett (1968) indicated that global measures such as IQ are of very little value in assessing severe reading and/or learning disability. What they believe is needed is "specific information processing behaviors," i.e., information on how the student learns so that we may capitalize on his strong modes of learning and strengthen his weaker modes. They also point out the fact that gathering information on specific information processsing behaviors will enable us to modify the classroom environment to best work with this type of student. The information processing behaviors can, to some extent, be assessed by a psychologist or a diagnostician through the use of certain information derived from the tests discussed here and from other commonly used tests. It seems more likely, however, that the classroom teacher or the remedial reading teacher can, in most cases, gain a more thorough knowledge of a student's information processing behavior by careful observation and through diagnostic teaching. The diagnosis of information processing behaviors and the corresponding appropriate teaching techniques is covered in detail in Chapter 10.

Symptoms of Severe Reading Disability

Careful observation during the teaching-learning process is probably the best way to identify those students with severe reading disability. However, in order to make meaningful observations you must know what to look for. There are a

[4]Kirk, Samuel A.; McCarthy, J.J.; and Kirk, Winifred D. *The Illinois Test Of Psycholinguistic Abilities.* Rev. ed. Urbana, Illinois: University of Illinois Press, 1968.

number of symptoms that are typical of the severely disabled reader. You should realize, of course, that some of these symptoms are likely to be present in any student regardless of his reading ability. You should also realize that most severely disabled readers are likely to exhibit a number of symptoms, since one problem tends to interact with another to produce varying degrees of disability and thus varying symptoms. From the discussion on classification of various kinds of severe reading disability it should also be evident that any one student may exhibit some of the same symptoms as another, yet many of his symptoms may be quite different from those of another student. In summary, then, in the observation of symptoms of the severely disabled reader we are not looking for any one symptom or any one set of symptoms. What we would look for would be a cluster of any of the most common symptoms.

Following is a list of symptoms that often appear in cases of severe reading disability and are also often common to learning disability cases in general:

1. *Reversals of letters or words.* In the case of letters the student may reverse *b*'s and *d*'s, *p*'s and *q*'s, or *n*'s and *u*'s (less common) thus making "bad" read as "dab" or "baby" read as "dady." In the case of words, parts of the word may be reversed as in the case of "ant" for "nat," or entire words may be reversed as in "saw" for "was" or "on" for "no."

2. *Short or erratic memory for words.* Words that would be learned by a normal reader through using them in various teaching-learning situations may require many, many more exposures for the severely disabled reader. You may also find that he remembers and says a word correctly one time and the next time does not recognize it at all. This may even happen within a period of a few minutes in reading a paragraph.

3. *Oral rereading not improved after silent reading or after a first oral reading.*

4. *Inability to hold information in memory until needed.* This may show up as an inability to use context clues, i.e., the student cannot remember what has just been read so as to derive a new word from the context. It may also show up in using phonics or structural analysis in word attack. For example, in sounding a word with three phonemes the student may forget the first one or two by the time he gets to the third. In using structural analysis the student will often need to divide a word into syllables and then apply a specific vowel rule depending upon the position of the vowel in a syllable. Some severely disabled readers simply cannot hold enough information in memory to go through such a process.

5. *Difficulty in concentration.* Some students simply cannot keep their minds on a paragraph or story while it is being read or they cannot listen for periods beyond a half minute or more. Problems with concentration often become apparent when dealing with abstract relationships such as sound-symbol correspondence.

6. *Inability to see whole relationships or form a gestalt.* This often shows up in the overly phonetic speller who simply never seems to be able to form a mental image of a word. He may spell many words exactly like they sound, e.g., "liks" for "likes" or "hav" for "have."

7. *Emotional instability.* Most students tend to become irritated when they do not experience a certain amount of success. Some students with severe reading disability, however, have a tendency to become extremely irritated upon meeting a task with which they are not immediately successful. Their moods may also change very fast.

8. *Tendency toward impulsiveness.* This tendency shows up in the form of guessing at words rather than working them out using word attack skills. This is more prevalent where pictures are present on a page. For example, the student may say

"bunny" for "rabbit" where a rabbit is illustrated. It also shows up in the actions of the student in situations concerning behavior.

9. *Poor eye-motor coordination.* This tendency can be measured using tests such as the *Bender Visual-Motor Gestalt* test and the Eye-Motor Coordination subtest of the *Developmental Tests of Visual Perception.* It can also be noted quite easily by observing the student write. It can sometimes be observed in watching him do motor activities such as cutting with scissors or coloring. The tests mentioned above do, however, have the advantage of providing scoring criteria or norms from which the performance of a student can be judged against the performance of a normal student. On the other hand, most experienced teachers have a fairly good idea of how normal students write simply by watching normal learners.

10. *Difficulty in sequencing.* This may show up in poor spelling, but may be more common in remembering the specific order of words in a sentence or the order of events in a paragraph. The student who exhibits this symptom may not be able to repeat the days of the week or the months of the year in order at a time when they should normally be well known.

11. *Inability to work rapidly.* This shows up in reading assignments, but is equally common in written work. The student is always behind the pace set by other students. He often gets irritated if hurried. He simply does not seem to process information rapidly enough to keep up with other students. There is also a tendency to perseverate or dwell on a particular point for an extra long time.

12. *Omissions of words and phrases.* It should be emphasized that many students omit an occasional word, but some severely disabled readers consistently omit words, especially those not known. There is also a tendency for some severely disabled readers to skip whole phrases or lines and to constantly lose their place.

13. *Directional confusion.* This may show up, as mentioned before, in lack of knowledge of "b" and "d," etc., but it may go considerably beyond this in such areas as lack of knowledge of left and right, front and back, and before and after.

14. *Poor auditory discrimination.* This condition may be present even when the student's auditory acuity is excellent. Again many students have difficulty with auditory discrimination, but the severely disabled reader often has a great deal of trouble learning minute differences in words such as "pen" and "pin" or even "him" and "hen." They also tend to be erratic in their ability to discriminate sounds—being able to do so one time and not do so another time.

15. *Hyperactivity.* The student who is hyperactive may have a short attention span, but may always be seen constantly wiggling or squirming, tapping his fingers or a pencil on his desk, etc. These signs often become even more noticeable if the student is under any stress in doing an assignment.

16. *Poor syntax, stuttering, or speaking haltingly.* The student who exhibits these symptoms may seem to need to think ahead when talking, i.e., words do not flow normally or when they do they do not come out in a normal or logical order.

17. *Achievement in arithmetic considerably higher than in reading and spelling.* Perhaps there is a physiological explanation for this. Some people who have had strokes have been left unable to read but were still able to solve difficult math problems.

Some Cautions in the Diagnosis of Severe Reading Disability

One of the most important things to remember in the diagnosis of severe reading disability is that, regardless of the label attached to the student's condition, the student will still need to be taught to read. There has been a tendency over the years to use such labels as "dyslexia," and "minimal brain dysfunction" in describing students with severe reading disability. As yet no specific program of remediation has been shown as being superior with a specific condition; therefore, labelling beyond the term "severe" in terms of reading disability is not only unnecessary, but often damaging. For example, several years ago a professor's son was brought to our Reading Center for help with his reading. The professor and his wife said he had experienced a great deal of difficulty in learning to read because he was "dyslexic." When the boy himself was interviewed (age 14) he said, "You know, I can't read because I have dyslexia." The university student who was working with this boy and I both assured him that he was now at the age where most people automatically "get over" dyslexia (which is probably true to some extent). Within a period of six months this boy's grades in high school went from all D's and F's to all A's and B's and he no longer had any trouble in reading. A fairly normal or typical program of remediation was undertaken with this student which focused on his specific weaknesses in reading and especially in study skills. An important part of the remediation, however, was concerned with building this student's self-concept and getting him to realize that he was not saddled with some awesome disease from which he would never recover. The point of all of this is, of course, that the use of the label "dyslexia" was, in his case, probably highly damaging.

Another caution to be observed in reading diagnosis is to not place students in a non-reading oriented program on the basis of various types of perceptual tests. We have no evidence that perceptually oriented programs are of any value in the remediation of reading disabilities, and in fact they may waste valuable time that could be spent in activities more directly related to reading.

A third important caution is that we do not believe that a student with a severe reading disability cannot learn because of some congenital malfunction. In discussing students with severe reading disability John Nicholls (1969), who is a medical doctor, stated,

> There is accumulating evidence which indicates rather that this is a functional disturbance, and probably represents delayed maturation of a specific intellectual function. In my experience, demonstrable organic lesions are rare in these children. The vast majority of these children improve and reach normal reading levels for their age, given time, instruction suited to their needs, and care to see that emotional disturbances with consequent learning blocks do not supervene. (p. 358)

SUMMARY

If you are new to the field of reading, having read the foregoing discussion you may feel that I have said very little in terms of concrete procedures for identifying the severely disabled reader. This is quite true. The results of some of the most commonly used tests provide some help, but for all practical purposes the diagnosis of students with severe reading disability can best be done by the teacher through careful, guided observation and diagnostic teaching.

PART B. remediation

EARLY THEORIES AND LITTLE SUCCESS

Most of the early theories concerning the reasons for severe reading disability and their concomitant remedial techniques have met with little success. It is important, however, that the beginning remedial reading teacher be familiar with these to avoid the duplication of unfruitful efforts. Since reading tends to be a field in which new programs and materials constantly appear, it is also important for the remedial reading teacher to know what kind of programs have not been successful in the past.

Probably the best known of the early theories was one proposed by Samuel Orton (1928), a neuropathologist. Orton believed that the two halves of the brain were alike in size and design and reversed in pattern, i.e., the left hemisphere would bear the same relation to the right hemisphere that the left hand does to the right hand. Orton believed that it was, therefore, logical to conclude that records, or engrams as they were called, of one hemisphere would be mirrored copies of those of the other. He felt that if a student failed to establish a normal physiological habit of using exclusively those of one hemisphere, a confusion in orientation may result causing a student to be unable to recognize differences between pairs of words which could be spelled backwards such as "was" and "saw," "not" and "ton," and "on" and "no." Orton and his associates reported considerable success in the use of certain physical exercises, along with intensive remediation in reading, in overcoming the reading difficulties of a number of children. It is somewhat difficult now, however, to assess the significance of the physical therapy in relation to the direct remediation in reading. Orton was not given to making idle claims and his work has generally been considered of considerable value in helping us understand some of the possible causes of severe reading disability. In interpreting his work we must also keep in mind that even if his explanation of the causes of some reading retardation was correct, or partially correct, we should not automatically assume that a physical training program could correct damage already done.

Somewhat later, Carl Delacato, working on Orton's theory that severe reading disability was often caused from the failure of children to develop proper neurological organization, developed a program designed to overcome these difficulties. In his book entitled *The Treatment and Prevention of Reading Problems,*[5] Delacato suggested physical exercises and remedial procedures dealing with sleep patterns, tonality, handedness, visual control, etc. Delacato's program gained a great deal of notoriety and was well researched in a number of studies. Few of

[5]Delacato, Carl H. *The Treatment and Prevention of Reading Problems.* Springfield, Illinois: Charles C Thomas, 1959.

these studies, however, supported Delacato's theory. A number of medical organizations have also disclaimed the value of the type of treatment recommended by Delacato. Perhaps this is unfortunate and could be blamed, to some extent, on the users of the material as well as Delacato's own claims. It would seem logical from Orton's own writings that this type of treatment might be successful with only a very small percentage of the population, yet in many experiments very little care was taken to locate only students who would appear to benefit from this type of treatment. On the other hand, it might be said that Delacato's own writings would lead one to believe that a rather large percentage of disabled readers could be helped by his methods.

I am of the opinion that this type of training should not be dismissed for a small percentage of children. A great deal of benefit has come to many children through similar training in The Rehabilitation Center in Philadelphia directed by Glen Doman, as well as in other centers. However, these cases are carefully screened for possible benefit from these procedures. On the other hand, I would *not* recommend that the remedial reading teacher undertake the procedures, as listed by Delacato, in the classroom.

The use of various types of perceptual training programs at one time appeared to hold great promise for certain severely disabled readers. Our present evidence, however, indicates that this too is an area where little success has been indicated. It is true that many students who have a severe reading disability also have various kinds and various degrees of perceptual handicaps as measured by perceptual tests. In simple terms, however, it appears that for most students the remediation of perceptual handicaps does not result in an improvement in the ability to read or even in an improvement in the potential for reading. In a very thorough review of the literature on various perceptual training programs Donald Hammill, Libby Goodman, and J. Lee Wiederholt (1974) concluded, ". . . the results of attempts to implement the Frostig-Horne materials and Kephart-Getman techniques in the schools have for the most part been unrewarding." (p. 476) In an earlier review of the literature Bruce Balow (1971) states,

> . . . the case studies reported in the literature argue for the possibility that visual-motor programs *may* be a specific treatment for a very few unusual children. That, however, even if it were to be found true, is insufficient reason to argue the desirability of perceptual-motor activities for all pupils. While motor and perceptual skills weaknesses are frequently found in learning disabled pupils, there is great likelihood that these are most often simply concomitants without causal relevance; thus the argument cannot depend upon assumed etiologies for learning disabilities. (p. 523)

In spite of this type of statement, Balow suggests six reasons why one might consider the addition of these types of activities to the curriculum for all primary age pupils and as specific additions for other students who suffer serious deficiencies in school skills. Balow's six reasons are as follows:

1. The enjoyment and developmental appropriateness of motor activity, particularly for primary school boys for whom sitting still is so inappropriate developmentally.
2. The personal recognition of success that can attend motor-perceptual activities for pupils long used to failure in school.
3. The accompanying positive attention from significant adults, usually the classroom teacher but often others as well.

4. The fact of teaching, in direct drill form, a set of visual and motor skills that may be weak, or absent, and which relate to school demands but ordinarily are left to develop incidentally.
5. Teaching, via such visual and motor activities, habits and skills of attention, without which it is most difficult to succeed in school.
6. Teaching, via such visual and motor activities, habits and skills of following directions, without which it is most difficult to succeed in school. (p. 524)

Somewhat similar reasoning has been proposed by other authors who believe that such training will allow the student to concentrate better after they have had a chance to flex their muscles and that the development of motor skills may simply contribute to the good mental health of students. That is, a student with a low self-concept who is not well coordinated may begin to view himself differently when he sees a corresponding improvement in his own physical coordination.

I do not disagree with this general philosophy; however, it is my opinion that these same benefits can be derived from activities more directly related to reading. Furthermore, my own observation leads me to believe that teachers soon come to view such activities as an end in themselves. Perhaps most important, however, time spent in perceptual training is usurped from activities dealing more directly with reading disabilities.

SOME IMPORTANT CONSIDERATIONS IN THE REMEDIATION OF SEVERE READING DISABILITY

There are a few considerations which, although important for any reading program, are of special significance when dealing with severely disabled readers. One of these considerations is for an overall plan in dealing with these problems. An important first step is the early identification of children who, although normal in intelligence, seem to have a great deal of difficulty in reading and reading related activities. Another important step is to identify specific weaknesses and the methods by which the student learns best. This is discussed in more detail in Chapter 10. A third step is to formulate an educational plan based on the student's specific weaknesses and strongest learning mode. A fourth important step is to make sure that there is a continual assessment of the original plan in terms of weaknesses and strengths indicated through diagnostic teaching.

Another important consideration in dealing with severely disabled readers is that they are more likely to benefit from a long-term intensive type of program than from the less intensive type of program often found in the public schools. For example, Jules Abrams and Herman Belmont (1969) found that full-time specialized reading instruction was superior to that usually carried on in most remedial programs. John Heckerl and Russell Sansbury (1968) also studied severely disabled readers and concluded that the remedial therapy should be a daily occurrence. They also believed that an hour should be the minimum time for each session, except for younger students who could not tolerate such a long session. Heckerl and Sansbury also cautioned that you should expect a long-term program with little to be accomplished in six months or even in a year. They emphasized that provisions should be made for the severely disabled reader to receive intensive remediation for as long as he profits from it or until he becomes a functional reader.

An especially important point is to insure that the program remains flexible. Once a program has been devised, tried, and evaluated it should then be reevaluated in terms of its success. If little or no success is experienced by the student, then another plan and/or method of approach should be tried and again evaluated. This should be an ongoing process in any remedial reading program, but it is of special significance to the severely disabled reader.

SPECIFIC TECHNIQUES FOR WORKING WITH THE SEVERELY DISABLED READER

It should be emphasized at the beginning of this section that the techniques and materials recommended for the less severely disabled reader in the preceding chapters are often successful, as well as appropriate, for the severely disabled reader. It may be necessary at times, however, to modify those techniques for the severely disabled reader. For example, in learning basic sight words some of the methods suggested in Chapter 4 may often be successful, but they may simply need to be repeated more often and/or carried on over a longer period of time. It should also be emphasized that the methods suggested here are often appropriate for the less severely disabled reader. In most cases, however, the methods and materials suggested in this section are simply more time consuming and, in most cases, require an individualized teaching procedure.

THE FERNALD APPROACH

The Fernald approach is often referred to as the kinesthetic method. It was first described by Grace M. Fernald and Helen B. Keller in 1921. The following description of their approach, with minor changes, was taken from Fernald's[6] book published in 1943.

In the early stages of the Fernald approach no commercially prepared materials are used. The teacher asks the student what words he would like to learn. These are each taught until they are well known by the student. When the student has begun to build a storehouse of words he is then asked to compose a little story. The story is written by the teacher and any new words are taught that the student does not already know. After this the story is typed by the teacher so the student can read it on the following day. You will, of course, note that this is essentially the language-experience approach so often used today.

In teaching words four stages are identified. The stage used depends on the student's ability to learn. These stages are as follows:

[6]Fernald, Grace M. *Remedial Techniques in Basic School Subjects.* New York: McGraw-Hill, 1943. The Fernald approach is reproduced with minor changes by permission of McGraw-Hill Book Company.

Stage 1: *Tracing.*   In this stage the word is first written for the student. It may be written on the chalkboard or on a strip of paper or tagboard approximately 3″ × 9″ or 4″ × 10″. It may be written in either manuscript or cursive writing which, in most cases, would depend on the type of writing the student is doing in his normal classroom activities. The student then traces the word with his index finger or a combination of his index and middle fingers and says each part as it is being traced. This does not mean sounding the word letter-by-letter, but rather saying the part of the word being traced. This procedure is followed until the word can be traced from memory. The student then writes the word from memory, again saying each part as it is written. The word is later typed and read in typed form. New words are filed in a box in alphabetical order. In this stage certain points of technique are stressed: (1) It is important that the finger or fingers contact the paper. Writing in the air is less successful. (2) The student should never copy a word but always write it from memory. (3) The whole word should be learned at once or as a unit. (4) Each word part should be said aloud as he traces or writes it. (5) Whatever the student writes is typed for him and read by him before too long an interval has passed. This provides transfer from the written to printed form. (6) The student should not be allowed to write a word wrong. If it becomes evident that he cannot remember a word he should be stopped so that he can go back to the initial tracing practice.

Stage 2: *Writing Without Tracing.*   After some time, depending upon the student, the words will not need to be traced. At this stage the student looks at the word in script, says it to himself several times, and then writes it from memory. At this stage library cards are also substituted for the larger cards used initially. The words can be typed on one side of the card and written in manuscript or cursive writing on the other side. These cards are then filed alphabetically as in stage one.

Stage 3: *Recognition in Print.*   At this stage it becomes unnecessary to write each word in print for the student. He looks at the word and is told what it is. He then pronounces it once or twice and writes it from memory. At this time reading in books is usually started.

Stage 4: *Word Analysis.*   The student is encouraged to look at new words and try to identify word parts (families or phonograms) that he knows and apply them to new words. Phonic sounding is discouraged, but he is encouraged to develop the habit of looking for familiar parts of words.

In most cases the total nonreader would be started in Stage One and students with partial disabilities are often started in Stage Two. No special techniques are used to overcome word reversals, since the method teaches words in a left-to-right sequence.

Most research on the effectiveness of the Fernald approach versus more commonly used approaches has tended to show that there was very little difference in the effectiveness of either method. This is probably because students with very severe reading disabilities who are predisposed to learning by this method are simply not grouped together in the studies. It should be stressed, however, that this method should not be used with large groups of students, but is intended to be used with the student who fails to learn by more commonly used methods.

NON-VISUAL AKT

In an article by Harold and Harriet Blau (1968), the authors point out that many children seem to learn well using the kinesthetic method just described. However, they also point out that many students tend to learn in spite of the fact that there is some sort of short circuit between the eye and the brain. That is, something happens to the message the student sees before it reaches his brain so that most words come out scrambled. In an attempt to remedy this, the authors have described a method of teaching words somewhat similar to the Visual-Auditory-Kinesthetic-Tactile Method, but in using their approach the visual channel is bypassed. We have been using the Non-Visual AKT approach in our Reading Center for several years and have found it to be extremely successful with a few students who seem to exhibit the symptoms of a student who is not able to process information correctly when it comes through the visual channel. A description of this approach follows:

> Non-Visual AKT differs from VAKT in several ways, and variations of Non-V AKT are possible too. Primarily, however, the child is blindfolded or closes his eyes, and the word to be learned is traced on his back. As the teacher traces the word, she spells it aloud, letter by letter. Often, the second or third time around, the student can identify the letters being traced and he too spells out the word. Usually (until the student becomes too advanced for this), three-dimensional letters, arranged to spell out the word, are placed before the student and, still blindfolded, he traces these with his fingertips as he feels the letters being traced on his back. The letters are then scrambled, and still blindfolded, the student arranges the letters in the proper sequence. The blindfold is then removed, the student sees what he has done (often his first experience with coherent sequencing) and writes the word on paper, or at the board, and then on a file card for future review. (pp. 127–128)

We cannot be sure, of course, that the student's problem is in some malfunction of the visual channel. It may simply be that blindfolding him allows him to concentrate more attention on the auditory and kinesthetic aspects of the learning process.

GENERAL TEACHING PROCEDURES

Certain general teaching procedures seem to be successful with many severely disabled readers, although in most cases, these procedures are tedious and time consuming. For example, most severely-disabled readers require much repetition and drill to the point that is often referred to as overlearning. Overlearning, in most cases, merely refers to something that has been learned so well that it evokes an automatic response. It is this automatic response level that is often successful with the seriously disabled reader. Whether you are teaching word attack skills or sight words, the automatic response level must be reached. For example, in teaching the sight word "no," regardless of what approach is used it should be presented enough times so that the student automatically says "no" when he sees it written, without any hesitation whatsoever.

With most seriously disabled readers it is also helpful, if not absolutely necessary, to focus on one concept at a time. For example, in teaching the "d" sound do not try to teach it along with the "og" phonogram unless the "og" phonogram has been previously learned. For this reason a more modern or analytic system of teaching phonics is often not successful with the seriously disabled reader. He may simply need to learn the "d" sound in isolation until it evokes an automatic response. A modified analytic approach may, however, be used. For example, after teaching the "d" and "l" sounds to the automatic level, you could then teach the "og" phonogram by using the words "dog" and "log." Note, however, that no new concepts would be introduced until the first ones became automatic.

Many seriously disabled readers seem to be able to learn through the sense of touch or feeling (kinesthetic and tactile) regardless of the degree of impairment of their auditory and/or visual channels. There are a number of types of learning activities utilizing this approach which may be used. The type will depend, to some extent, upon the age-grade level of the student and the concept to be taught. Some examples of the use of this approach are listed below:

1. Use modeling clay to form letters and short words.
2. Use three-dimensional letters available commercially. (Some have magnetic backing to stick to a metal easel.)
3. Use salt or fine sand in a shallow box such as a shoe box lid in which the student can trace letters and words.
4. Place paper over a piece of screen wire (such as that used on screen doors) and have the student write on it with a crayon. This will leave a raised surface on the paper when it is removed so that each letter and/or word can be felt.

Although the use of immediate reinforcement for the accomplishment of goals should generally be practiced with all students, it can be especially helpful when working with the seriously disabled reader. This type of student needs reinforcement for short-term goals such as learning the "p" sound or the word "go" rather than longer-term goals such as "learning to read well enough so you can read this book." The importance of reinforcement was illustrated by Barbara Bateman (1974) in telling of a young cerebral palsied girl who learned to type at a rate of two to three letters per minute with the aid of a stylus held in both hands. Her performance was praised and visitors were often "treated" to her typing demonstration. However, when she was given the opportunity to earn playing time with a prized magnetic board contingent upon an increase in her rate, she soon began to type 25–30 words per minute.

Careful diagnostic teaching is probably the most important procedure to be followed in working with the severely disabled reader. Although this is not an easy procedure for the inexperienced teacher, it can be learned. For example, in working with a student on learning a new word be sure to note carefully any areas in which the student appears to experience difficulty. In teaching the word "man," carefully consider such questions as the following:

1. Were the "m" and "n" reversed?
2. Does the student seem to learn the word best as a gestalt (learning of the whole word picture), or does he seem to learn this and other words best by concentrating on the phoneme-grapheme relationships?

3. Was there anything that I did that made this word easier or more difficult to learn than others that I have tried to teach him?

4. Does having him write the word help him learn it faster than previous words taught?

5. Does he seem to learn this and other words faster when they are used in a sentence?

6. When working with the sounds, does he seem to be able to discriminate between the "m" and "n"?

7. What does *he* think helps him learn best?

8. Does he seem to learn faster when he says the word aloud or when he spells the word aloud?

9. Did he know all of the phoneme-grapheme relationships before we started, or do I need to go back and teach those if this is the preferred method? Did he even know the *names* of the letters?

10. After the student knew the names and letter sounds did he have trouble blending? Is blending a problem on other words as well?

Some commercial materials are available that are designed specifically for the severely disabled reader. For a brief description of these materials see Appendix C.

SPECIFIC TEACHING PROCEDURES AND CLASSROOM MODIFICATIONS

It would be futile to attempt to list a specific set of procedures that would be appropriate for all severely disabled readers, since the symptoms of each student tend to differ somewhat from those of other students. There are, however, some specific teaching procedures and classroom modifications that you may wish to consider depending on the particular diagnosed needs of any one student. Some of these specific procedures and modifications follow:

1. Review materials previously learned as often as possible until responses become automatic.

2. When teaching a new concept be sure, if possible, to illustrate the concept when giving a verbal explanation of it.

3. When giving either oral or written assignments do not give more directions than the student is able to cope with. For example, in a three-part assignment it would be better to divide it up into three parts and give directions for each part separately than to give all directions at once. As with all other suggestions in this section, this will depend on the capabilities of the student.

4. Provide a working environment in which the student is as free from distractions as possible. Use study carrels or free reading and study areas that are apart from other students.

5. When introducing new or distracting words use color cues such as a green letter at the beginning of the word and a red letter at the end of the word.

6. When asking the student to respond to oral questions, give him plenty of time to answer. One study showed that the average time a teacher allows for a student to answer is about two to three seconds. Allow at least five to ten seconds if needed. In some cases a half-minute may be more appropriate.

7. When the student is writing something new encourage him to verbalize the response at the same time.

8. In some cases it may be helpful to allow the student to use his finger, a pencil, an underliner (piece of paper or ruler), or a piece of paper with a window cut in it when reading.

9. Many authors suggest that students be allowed to give oral answers to tests in their regular classroom if they are unable to produce adequate written responses. In some cases this may be desirable. On the other hand, you should keep in mind that you are often reinforcing an undesirable habit in doing so. If at all possible, in my opinion, it is usually better to modify the time allowed for this type of student or provide questions that can be answered with short answers.

A FINAL NOTE ON TEACHING TECHNIQUES FOR THE SEVERELY DISABLED READER

Perhaps the problem of the severely disabled reader could be likened to the problem of finding a cure for cancer. Some medical researchers contend that there are so many different types of cancer that it is unrealistic to hope for "a" cure. We, no doubt, face the same problem in dealing with severely disabled readers. Most reading specialists now agree that the use of the term dyslexia, which is often used to label severely disabled readers, probably does more harm than good. That is, the use of that or any other "one" term to describe problems of so varying a nature is unrealistic and makes the problem appear to be less complicated than it actually is.

It would be less than honest to leave the impression that there are a number of almost magical techniques and/or procedures that are likely to work wonders for the severely disabled reader. As with the problem of cancer we know more about it today than we did twenty years ago, but progress has been slow and few, if any, miracle techniques have appeared. Luckily, however, most of our serious cases of reading disability, given intensive remediation for a long enough period of time, do learn to read. And, although we are not in a century of miracles, we are no longer living in the dark ages.

MEDICAL ASPECTS OF REMEDIATION FOR THE SEVERELY DISABLED READER

There is now a growing amount of evidence that some severely disabled readers, especially those diagnosed as hyperkinetic, can often be helped with either a change in diet and/or medication. For example, several well-known popular magazines have run feature articles in which it was stated that foods such as candy and drinks as well as certain preservatives sometimes added to milk have a tendency to cause some children to become overactive or unattentive. For this type of child a balanced diet that is high in protein and low in carbohydrates was recommended.

Samuel Nichamin and George Barahal (1968) reported considerable success using a combined treatment approach of a two dimensional program of methylphenidate (trade name Ritalin) and psychologic management with 100 children diagnosed as hyperkinetic (overactive) or hypokinetic (lethargic) with what they termed "faulty neurologic integration with perceptual disorders" (p. 1071). As the authors pointed out,

> In the psychologic and educational spheres, emphasis has been centered on motor re-learning with training exercises in coordination, remedial reading, and even cultist-type obtuse methods provided in special private schools and institutes, with results of questionable authenticity. Furthermore, these training procedures are prohibitively expensive and of prolonged duration. (p. 1071)

The authors reported that at least two-thirds or more of their patients showed dramatic results with their method. The authors stated, "With a purported incidence of 10 to 20 per cent of the school population having learning or perceptual disorders, the promulgation of such a practical, expeditious approach to therapy, within the milieu of private medical practice seems warranted." (p. 1072) Another important point made by the authors was that,

> Such early drug therapy, with its consequential beneficial effect, can forestall serious ego damage to the child. Untreated, such a child would develop a depreciated self-concept and patterns of desperation and defeat. Likewise, a chaotic family ego disorganization can be ameliorated before cumulative damage is perpetuated. Intensive psychotherapy and miscellaneous lengthy perceptual-training exercises can be avoided. (p. 1075)

The authors emphasized, however, that "Promiscuous use of this drug for a variety of school and behavior disorders, without a definitive diagnosis, would be shortsighted and inappropriate." (p. 1074)

One of the most serious problems, in the past, of making effective use of a combined educational and medical approach has been the almost total lack of communication between personnel in the two fields. Teachers, of course, cannot accurately diagnose which students may benefit from medicinal treatment. On the other hand, a student who literally "climbs the walls" in a normal classroom setting may act perfectly calm when visiting a medical doctor and thus appear perfectly normal. The result, of course, is that the medical doctor merely believes the teacher is overly concerned about a "few minor incidences in the student's behavior." The teacher, on the other hand, has no chance to describe the way the student reacts in the classroom setting and is told by the student's parents that the medical doctor believed nothing was wrong. The teacher should remember that only a medical doctor is in a position to prescribe medication for this type of student. But, on the other hand, the medical doctor should remember that the student's classroom teacher, or remedial reading teacher, having a chance to compare the student's behavior with that of many other students, is in a far better position to judge a student's behavior in relation to the behavior of other students.

Other drugs have been effective in stimulating the lethargic student to become a more active participant in school-type activities. Again, however, a combined approach with the teacher working closely with the physician to adjust dosages to an efficient level for maximum performance is often needed. As a remedial reading teacher, you should attempt to keep lines of communication open with the parents of students in your charge so that a three-way communication network may exist among the physician, parents, and teacher.

It is also important to remember that drugs presently used do not *teach* the student. When successfully used, they only make him more amenable to learning. Once a drug treatment is successfully under way the remedial reading teacher still needs to treat the student the same as any other disabled reader.

A LOOK TO THE FUTURE

The possibilities for a breakthrough in methods of treating or remediating the severely disabled reader seem almost as confusing as the problem itself. For example, in a seminar held at the Kettering Research Laboratory in Yellow Springs, Ohio, Professor Holger Hyden, a Swedish neurobiologist at the University of Goteborg, served as chairman. There were also a number of participants from the United States. During that conference Charles Silberman of Fortune magazine served as a reporter. In an article entitled ''Drugs May Be the Emerging Genie of Learning,''[7] Silberman detailed some of the highlights of the Seminar in relation to education. One interesting point was the information gained by David Krech of the University of California at Berkeley. Krech found that rats who were placed in an "enriched" environment after weaning, i.e., one which contained designs on the wall, ladders, hanging bells, platforms, etc., were smarter at solving problems such as learning to go through a maze than rats from a normal environment. He even found that this type of environment caused chemical and anatomical changes in the rats' brains that he believed were associated with greater intelligence.

James McGaugh of the University of California at Irvine injected strychnine and other drugs into rats just before, during, and after they were taught to run a maze. He found that learning and long-term memory appeared to be greatly enhanced if the drug was injected in a period running fifteen minutes before to fifteen minutes after the learning had occurred. McGaugh also reported that other drugs enhanced or suppressed short-term memory without affecting long-term memory. This, he believed, supported the view that these are quite different processes.

James V. McConnell of the University of Michigan and William L. Byrne of Duke University also discussed some of their experiments in "memory transfer." They prepared brain material from trained animals and injected it into untrained ones and suggested, although not proving conclusively, that learning can be transferred in this way.

Many participants believed that the day is close at hand (perhaps ten years) when we will be able to alter the intellectual capacity of children and perhaps adults through the use of drugs. They generally believed that chemical or pharmacological means of enhancing learning would be developed before we fully understand the biochemical processes of the brain. And, that ultimately, ''. . . there may be a whole arsenal of drugs each affecting a different part of the learning process, e.g., acquisition of information, short-term memory, long-term memory.'' (p. 30)

[7]Silberman, Charles E. "Drugs May Be the Emerging Genie of Learning," *The Texas Outlook*. Vol. 51, (September, 1967), 28–31.

The type of information presented here also seems logical in terms of information presented by Howard Gardner (1973). Gardner stated that there were cases where a person had known how to read an ideographic language such as Chinese and also knew how to read a sound-symbol language such as English. After experiencing a stroke some of these people would lose their ability to read English but retain their ability to read the ideographic language. Perhaps the damaging effects of the stroke or the damage that has evidently occurred in some children at birth, or somewhat later, may eventually be overcome through the use of chemotherapy. There also seems to be some implications here for teaching certain severely disabled readers, e.g., using concrete examples to illustrate ideas wherever possible.

A more pessimistic, yet perhaps realistic view, concerning the future for severely disabled readers was expressed by John Nicholls, a physician. After discussing the complexity of the problem, Nicholls stated,

> It is obvious then that in the matter of reading disabilities as a whole, one is dealing with an enormously complex phenomenon, with so many possible causative factors, having such varied expressivity, it is a great question whether we shall ever be able to deal with a child so afflicted in a highly scientific or formulated manner. Certainly our knowledge at present is so fragmentary that the day when such is possible is not close at hand. (p. 362)

This general attitude, although perhaps less pessimistic, is echoed by Balow, who said, "When some real answers are obtained, it is almost certain that they will be quite complex and will point to highly individualized programs of correction." (p. 513)

It would appear that, at present, we really know very little about students who exhibit various learning disabilities, including severe reading disability. For now, perhaps Martin was correct in his assessment when he said,

> At present, it seems most prudent to try to understand how the child can best learn rather than only focusing on the reasons he doesn't learn when taught by traditional methods. If educators and other professionals can recognize the factors and the environment in which the child will best learn—including motivation, perceptual strengths, style of learning—individualization of that child's teaching to capitalize on those strengths presently holds our most promising assistance to the handicapped child. (p. 471)

And, in summary, Balow's statement concerning learning disabilities seems especially relevant. He said, "Until experimentally proven otherwise, it may be that the simplest explanation of success obtained with any treatment for learning disabilities is the power and skill of the teacher who believes in it." (p. 519)

SUMMARY

Students with severe reading disabilities have presented a dilemma to reading specialists in the past and, in many cases, this dilemma is still present today. It is somewhat difficult to diagnose a specific group of students as those with severe reading disabilities, since each disabled reader usually presents a pattern of differing etiologies. There are, however, certain symptoms that are often associated with severe reading disability, although any one of these symptoms may or may not be present.

Programs that have been developed in the past for the remediation of severe reading disability have generally failed to prove their worth when thoroughly researched. There are, however, some procedures which appear to be highly effective in specific cases, but what appears to work well with one severely disabled reader often fails to bring results with another.

A number of severely disabled readers have received considerable benefit from the use of medication. And, at present, it would appear that if any major breakthrough is to be made in dealing with extremely disabled readers, it may come in this area.

Chapter 9:   REFERENCES

Abrams, Jules C., and Belmont, Herman S. "Different Approaches to the Remediation of Severe Reading Disability in Children," *Journal of Learning Disabilities*, Vol. 2, (March, 1969), 136–140.

Adams, Richard B. "Dyslexia: A Discussion of Its Definition," *Journal of Learning Disabilities*. Vol. 2, (December, 1969), 616–626.

Balow, Bruce. "Perceptual-motor Activities in the Treatment of Severe Reading Disability," *The Reading Teacher*. Vol. 24, (March, 1971), 513–525+.

Bateman, Barbara D. "Educational Implications of Minimal Brain Dysfunction," *The Reading Teacher*. Vol. 27, (April, 1974), 662–668.

Blau, Harold, and Blau, Harriet. "A Theory of Learning to Read," *The Reading Teacher*. Vol. 22, (November, 1968), 126–129+.

Boder, Elena. "Developmental Dyslexia—A New Diagnostic Approach Based on the Identification of Three Subtypes," *The Journal of School Health*. Vol. XL, (June, 1970), 289–290.

Bryant, N. Dale. "Learning Disabilities," *Instructor*. Vol. 81, (April, 1972), 49–56.

Gardner, Howard. "Developmental Dyslexia: The Forgotten Lesson of Monsieur C.," *Psychology Today*. Vol. 7, (August, 1973), 63–67.

Grotberg, Edith H. "Neurological Aspects of Learning Disabilities: A Case for the Disadvantaged," *Journal of Learning Disabilities*. Vol. 3, (June, 1970), 321–327.

Hammill, Donald; Goodman, Libby; and Wiederholt, J. Lee. "Visual-motor Processes: Can We Train Them?" *The Reading Teacher*. Vol. 27, (February, 1974), 469–478.

Harris, Albert J. *Harris Test of Lateral Dominance—Manual of Directions*. New York: The Psychological Corporation, 1958.

Heckerl, John, and Sansbury, Russell. "A Study of Severe Reading Retardation," *The Reading Teacher*. Vol. 21, (May, 1968), 724–729.

Johnson, Dale R. *Dyslexia in the Classroom*. Columbus, Ohio: Charles E. Merrill, 1972.

Martin, Harold P. "Vision and Its Role in Reading Disability and Dyslexia," *The Journal of School Health.* Vol. XLI, (November, 1971), 468–472.

Nichamin, Samuel J., and Barahal, George D. "Faulty Neurologic Integration with Perceptual Disorders in Children," *Michigan Medicine.* Vol. 67, (September, 1968), 1071–1075.

Nicholls, John U. V. "Reading Disabilities in the Young," *The Journal of School Health.* Vol. 39, (June, 1969), 357–363.

Orton, Samuel. "An Impediment to Learning to Read—A Neurological Explanation of the Reading Disability," *School and Society.* Vol. XXVIII, (September, 1928), 286–290.

Robinson, Helen M. "Significant Unsolved Problems in Reading," *Journal of Reading.* Vol. 14, (November, 1970), 77–82+.

Sabatino, David A., Wickham, William Jr., and Burnett, Calvin. "The Psychoeducational Assessment of Learning Disabilities," Catholic Education Review. Vol 66, (May, 1968), 327–341.

10

DIAGNOSING AND USING APPROPRIATE TEACHING TECHNIQUES FOR THE DISABLED READER

The first part of this chapter contains a discussion of the need for diagnosis beyond students' knowledge of skills. This is followed by a discussion of the theory of diagnosis for learning modalities. Information is also presented on how we learn, and the implications of this knowledge for the remedial reading teacher. The last part of the chapter contains information on diagnosing and teaching to specific learning modalities, cognitive styles, and learning rates.

DIAGNOSIS BEYOND KNOWLEDGE OF SKILLS

In teaching mildly disabled readers often little more is needed than a simple diagnosis of various skill deficiencies. And, with prescriptive teaching based on these skill deficiencies, success is often obtained in a matter of months. However, with the seriously disabled reader, as described in the previous chapter, it is not uncommon to work for one or two years with a student and still see very little progress. As Diane Sawyer (1974) points out, " . . . teaching to overcome specific skill deficiencies often results in teaching the same phonic generalizations or how to find the main idea over and over again." (p. 556) Sawyer also points out that with this type of student the only thing that is often different about his instruction from year-to-year is the teacher or the materials used. She further states that the research indicates a strong case for viewing the student as a problem solver or information processor, and as an individual who reacts with his environment rather than viewing him simply as someone who is deficient in his reading skills.

What we are implying, in reality, is that our view of the severely disabled reader is often much too simplistic. As a result of this simplistic view we then tend to use too simplistic a method of testing which results in inefficient teaching. Edward Wolpert (1971) stresses the point that various ambiguities arise when the modality concept is applied to the process of learning rather than to the act of reading. He states, as I have stated throughout the sections in this book on testing, that the tests often used do not test in a situation that is analogous to what a student actually does when he reads. For example, a student may be given certain subtests of the WISC, which in reality may have little relationship to reading, and on the basis of these subtests be classified as poor in visual perceptual skills. Although he may be poor in visual perceptual skills on the subtests of the WISC, this does not necessarily mean that he will not be a good visual learner in reading type tasks. Wolpert also points out that to even divide tasks as indicated on most tests as "auditory" or "visual" is probably a false dichotomy, since most tasks call for the use of a combination of both auditory and visual modalities even when the task is labeled as one or the other.

Perhaps a more realistic view of the learning task for a severely disabled reader is one described by Jean Piaget as related by John Blackie (1968). Piaget portrayed learning as being composed of two processes. These processes are assimilation and accommodation. Blackie says, "Assimilation is what is done to what has to be learned so that it can be learned, and accommodation is what the learner has to do within himself in order to learn." (p. 40) In the diagnosis beyond the level of skills it is these processes of assimilation and accommodation with which we should concern ourselves.

THE THEORY OF MODALITY DIAGNOSIS
AND ITS IMPLICATIONS

The most commonly recognized and diagnosed learning modalities are auditory, visual, kinesthetic, and a combination of all of these. When the various learning modes are referred to in the literature, however, they are usually listed as VAKT or visual, auditory, kinesthetic, and tactile. The term kinesthetic is an adjective derived from the noun kinesthesia derived from "kinema" or motion and "aisthesis" referring to perception. The term means sensation of position or movement through parts of the body such as nerve ends, tendons, muscles, and joints. The term tactile, of course, refers to the sense of touch. The term VAKT is also used, in some cases, to simply refer to a teaching method very similar to the Fernald Approach described in Chapter 9. Since it would be almost impossible to use a kinesthetic approach without using a tactile approach at the same time, the term "tactile" is often omitted when referring to the various testing and teaching modalities.

The Mills *Learning Methods Test*[1] has become one of the best known instruments for testing the various learning modalities. It is designed to determine whether a student learns words best by a "phonic or auditory," "visual," "kinesthetic," or "combination" method. The *Learning Methods Test* contains a series of words supposedly representing the primer, first, second, and third grade levels. Each word is on a card that has the word printed on one side and the same word and a picture representing the word on the other side of the card. The student to be tested is given the lists of words to pronounce until the lowest level is found in which he misses forty words. These forty words are then divided into groups of ten. Each day ten words are taught in strict accordance with the directions given in the manual for one of the four methods. The time for teaching the words is also controlled so that fifteen minutes is spent on each group of words. The *Learning Methods Test* can be used quite successfully by someone who is adept in its use. However, it has a

[1]Mills, Robert E. *Learning Methods Test*. Rev. ed. Fort Lauderdale, Florida: The Mills School, 1970.

number of drawbacks that make its use impractical in many situations. For example, after ten words are taught by one method the student is given an immediate recall test. He then comes in the next day and takes a delayed recall test on the words learned the first day. After taking the delayed recall test he is then taught ten words by another method and is then given another immediate recall test on the words just taught. He comes in on the third day and takes a delayed recall test on the words taught on the second day and learns ten more words by another method, etc. After the fifth day (it takes five days even though there are only four different methods, since one day must elapse before the student can be given the delayed recall test on the words taught on the fourth day by the fourth method), the clinician examines which method was most successful in getting the student to remember the most words on the delayed recall test, which is ultimately what one wants to accomplish. The fact that it takes five days or more where the student is not seen on a daily basis is a drawback for many clinicians, since they simply do not see the student on a daily basis or do not have a five-day period in which to complete their testing. It also presents a problem when the testing is not begun on a Monday, since it would then be necessary to complete the testing during the following week, which does not allow equal time periods to elapse between the testing for the delayed recall periods.

The methodology used in several of the approaches has also been criticized to some extent. For example, as a part of the visual approach the student is presented the ten words with the picture side up. He is told to look at the picture and then at the word. This practice is considered of dubious value in relation to actual reading. For example, S. Jay Samuels (1970) in a thorough review of the research on the use of pictures in reading quotes a number of studies that indicated that the use of pictures actually interfered with the reading act. However, perhaps the most serious problem is that as Samuels states, "Generally, concrete nouns and a limited number of adjectives and verbs can be illustrated. An additional shortcoming of pictures as cues is that they can not reliably elicit the same response from all children; for instance, when shown a picture of a plane, one child may say "plane," another, "airplane," and a third, "jet." (p. 401) It stands to reason that if one were to use the *Learning Methods Test* and determine that a student learned best by the visual approach in which pictures were presented, it would still not guarantee success for that student, since so many of the words he would be required to read in his normal activities would be words which could not be illustrated or would simply not be taught as they were presented in the test. In using the visual method Mills also suggests that a figure or outline of the shape or gestalt of each word be drawn on the board so that the student can match each word with this shape. This practice has also been questioned by a number of modern writers. The major problem, of course, is that many words have exactly the same shape, e.g.:

| one | now | new |

all have the same shape as do the following:

| this | then | than. |

Therefore, the shape is really of little value in helping a student distinguish between words. A third major criticism of the *Learning Methods Test* is that the directions are in some cases somewhat unclear. I have used it for some time in my Remedial Reading classes and have found that one student who reads the directions does not interpret the methodology the same as another student or group of students who have read the same directions.

In spite of what may appear to be rather severe criticisms of the *Learning Methods Test*, it is a good training instrument for students who are learning about the concept of testing the various learning modalities and I would recommend that it be used for this purpose, keeping the criticisms I have mentioned in mind. However, in a situation in which a reading clinician is unable to see a student for only a short period of time certain modifications need to be made in the Mills procedure. I would also suggest certain modifications even in a normal remedial situation because of the problems previously mentioned. These techniques will be discussed later in the chapter.

The concept of testing for strong and weak modalities seems to be supported by the research literature. For example, Harold McGrady, Jr. and Don Olson (1970) stress the fact that reading is a process that requires the integration of auditory and visual information. Since the English language is phonic in nature the letters represent sounds, and the written form (visual) of the language is symbolic and represents the spoken word (auditory). McGrady and Olson state, "Our clinical diagnostic studies of children with reading disabilities have revealed that many have problems with specific auditory or visual learning processes." (p. 582) These authors believe that these terms might best be termed psychosensory learning disorders. McGrady and Olson also state,

> Those who have psychosensory learning disorders cannot normally perceive and interpret sensation received through a particular sense channel. Similarly, they might not be able to relate sensory experience through a given sense modality to experience gained through another sense modality; for example, they might not be able to "auditorize" from what they see or "visualize" from what they hear. (p. 582)

In a review of the literature of modalities and reading, Bill Blanton (1971) indicates that it is virtually impossible to isolate any aspect of reading in which both the auditory and visual modalities are not involved to some degree. Blanton states,

> . . . there are a number of studies suggesting that mode of presentation does not determine the modality by which material is learned. Rather, the mental image is determined by the ideational type of the individual. In other words, the visual learner may still visualize material to be learned despite the fact that it is presented auditorially. (p. 211)

This kind of information would tend to lessen our faith in the use of modalities tests such as the Mills *Learning Methods Test*, but, on the other hand, it does reinforce the idea that certain students possess modality preferences and that the ultimate job of the teacher is to find an overall method that will be successful with each student.

There is also some indication that students' mode of learning may be cultural and experiential as well as constitutional. For example, Frank Riessmann (1962) indicated that culturally deprived students are often oriented toward physical and visual learning rather than aural learning. The fact that culturally deprived and/or economically deprived students are often poor in listening (aural) abilities has been demonstrated in a number of other studies. Typical of these studies was one by Ronald Linder and Henry Fillmer (1970), who studied the comparative effectiveness of auditory, visual, and a combination of auditory-visual presentations in second-grade, Southern, black male students who were disabled readers. Linder and Fillmer found the total auditory performance was significantly poorer than the total visual and the total auditory-visual for the tasks performed. However, there were no significant differences between students' performance on the total visual and the auditory-visual results. In concluding their study Linder and Fillmer stated,

> As in all studies, individual children in this study did demonstrate a preference for one modality over another. The results reported have been group performances rather than individual. But there are several cases in which the results of the group study were contradicted by individuals, making the listing of generalizations a hazardous undertaking. Once again research indicates that not all pupils may be expected to learn more effectively from one single type of presentation. (p. 22)

In addition to constitutional and experiential reasons for preferences in certain learning modalities, some authors have suggested that some techniques work well for other reasons. For example, William McCarthy and Joan Oliver (1965) suggest that the Fernald method may often be successful because of: "(a) concentration on the task at hand, (b) individual instruction, (c) novelty of approach and, (d) reinforcement in experiencing immediate success." (p. 419) They also point out that elements of these four points are part of all successful remedial reading programs. It should be emphasized, however, that the tactile-kinesthetic method of presentation of material is often inefficient and, for some students, does not produce results equivalent to other methods.

There is also some question as to whether it is better to teach students through their stronger modality or whether it is better to try to build upon their weaker modalities so learning can take place through any of their learning channels. The author is inclined to agree with the position that it is probably better to begin instruction in the stronger of the learning modalities, if it can be identified, while attempting to strengthen the weaker modalities at the same time.

HOW WE LEARN

An interesting study on how we learn in terms of later retention was done by the Socony Vacuum Oil Company,[2] which has some important implications for diagnosis and remediation. In this study the following results were obtained:

STUDENTS' POWER OF RETENTION

1. 10% of what they read
2. 20% of what they hear

[2]Ekwall, Eldon E., and Oswald, Lowell D. *Rx Reading Program — Teacher's Manual.* Glenview, Illinois: Psychotechnics, Inc., 1971, p. 1.

3. 30% of what they see
4. 50% of what they see and hear
5. 70% of what they say as they talk
6. 90% of what they say as they do a thing

It should be stressed that the information presented in this study is of a general nature and that the relative efficiency of one method of presentation over another often depends on several factors that will be discussed under the section entitled, "Research on Methods of Presentation." However, from this study it is evident that some of the teaching procedures most often used are of little value in getting students to retain what we teach them. For example, consider the value of simply "telling" students information (20 percent retention) versus getting them to say a thing as they do it (90 percent retention). From this it is also evident that even if we were able to cover twice as much information in a lecture it would be less efficient in the end than if only half as much information was covered, but if it was covered in one of the more efficient ways. Based on this type of information, in teaching we might then use more of the following types of procedures:

1. Whenever teaching a new concept we should at least illustrate it using the chalkboard or overhead projector so that students can hear and see the information at the same time. This procedure alone brings the retention percentage up to 50 percent versus 20 percent from an oral presentation alone.
2. Whenever possible we should also get students to voice a new principle, rule, word, etc., shortly after it has been taught (70 percent).
3. Whenever a new word, principle, rule, etc., is taught we should get students to "do" something with it. This might include such activities as writing or illustrating the rule, using a new word in a written sentence while they say the word and sentence, or getting them to act out action words as they say them. This can easily be done with some words such as "wash," "throw," "run," etc., but would, of course, be more difficult with others.

From the kind of information presented above, it is also evident why the kinesthetic-tactile or Fernald type of approach is often of considerable value for some students. The procedure automatically incorporates the most effective techniques discussed in this study.

RESEARCH ON METHODS OF PRESENTATION AND MODALITIES

Some important generalizations on the kind of presentations that are most effective for learning have been summarized by Sam Duker (1965). Some of these generalizations are as follows:

1. Combinations of visual and auditory presentations tend to be more efficient than presentations involving only auditory or visual presentations alone.

2. When the learner is familiar with the material he is likely to retain more from an auditory presentation. If the material is unfamiliar, he is likely to retain more from a visual presentation.

3. Students with higher intelligence seem to benefit more from a visual presentation.

4. Students who read better seem to learn better through a visual presentation.

5. As students grow older they tend to learn better through a visual presentation. At the age of six they learn better as a group through an aural presentation; however, by the time they reach sixteen years of age they learn better as a group through a visual presentation.

6. More difficult material seems to be learned better through a visual presentation while easier material is learned better through an auditory presentation.

7. Students' immediate comprehension of information seems to favor a visual presentation while their long-term comprehension seems to favor an auditory presentation.

8. The efficiency of a visual presentation seems to decrease as the interval of delayed recall increases.

9. One of the advantages of a visual presentation is the relative referability or opportunity for review of the material. When the material is of such a nature, or the teaching situation is of such a nature that less referability is possible, then the efficiency of a visual presentation is lessened.

10. Material that is well-organized or follows some type of sequence such as factual information or prose is better understood with an auditory presentation. Material that is more discrete and unrelated is better understood with a visual presentation.

11. One might consider two factors in considering a visual versus an oral presentation. These factors are ease of learning versus amount of retention. A visual presentation tends to favor ease of learning while retention seems to favor an oral presentation.

Some interesting and pertinent generalizations have also been given by Robert Mills (1965) from a study done using his *Learning Methods Test* to evaluate various techniques of word recognition. Mills stressed that the information presented pertained to the learning of words only and did not necessarily pertain to the teaching of phonics or other reading skills. Mills studied a group of male and female subjects in grades 2–4. His general conclusions were as follows:

1. The phonic method was least effective for the children with low intelligence (as a whole). The kinesthetic method was best for the same children with the greatest number of cases, but it was not statistically better than the visual or combinations methods.

2. For children with high intelligence the kinesthetic method was least effective.

3. The combination and visual methods were about equally good for children of average intelligence.

4. Children of high intelligence seemed to learn quite well by all methods; however, the visual method was superior to the kinesthetic method for this group.

5. For seven-year-olds the visual method appeared to be best and the same group did poorest on the kinesthetic method. The phonic and combination methods did not appear to be especially effective nor ineffective with this group.

6. The eight-year-olds did better with the kinesthetic method. Mills believed that the fact that this group was just becoming proficient with handwriting tended to make some difference in this case.

7. For nine-year-olds no method was outstandingly effective nor ineffective; however, the visual method did tend to be better than the kinesthetic method for this group.

8. Mills found that children who had higher intelligence tended to learn words faster than those with low intelligence; however, he found that there was no consistent relationship between age and a child's readiness to learn words.

In his conclusions Mills stated,

> Because different children learn to recognize words most efficiently by différent teaching methods, the classroom teacher must be aware of these individual differences when he applies group-instruction techniques. Our research indicates the need for the teacher to familiarize himself with all the various techniques and to be versatile in the use of these if he is to teach all the children.
>
> In individual cases of failure to make the expected growth in word-recognition skills, our research indicates the need for a diagnostic study of the child to determine the most appropriate method for the particular individual. (p. 225)

As can be noted from the information presented above there is little doubt at least some students do have a preferred mode of learning. No doubt many students become disabled readers because they are placed in a situation where they are exposed to teaching procedures which provide little opportunity for them to learn by a method that is best for them. To say that they do not learn because they are seldom or ever exposed to any portion of a certain method, however, would be an oversimplification since it is virtually impossible for any student to go through school without being exposed to a combination of the various methods discussed by Mills.

DIAGNOSTIC TECHNIQUES FOR DISCOVERING DOMINANT MODALITIES, COGNITIVE STYLES, AND LEARNING RATES

After a student has had an initial diagnosis and remediation is begun, three very important questions should arise in the mind of the teacher as she works with the student. These questions are: Is there a particular modality that seems most successful in getting the student to learn and retain information? Does the student seem to exhibit a particular cognitive style on which you can capitalize? How much instructional time is necessary or how much repetition is necessary in order to get the student to learn and retain information? This section contains information designed to help you develop the skills to answer these questions about each of the students with whom you are working.

DIAGNOSTIC TECHNIQUES FOR
DISCOVERING DOMINANT MODALITIES

Before offering specific suggestions on the diagnosis of dominant learning modalities I would again repeat that Mills' *Learning Methods Test* is an excellent instrument for learning about the techniques of modality testing. And, where time permits it can be used with considerable success. On the other hand there are certain features of Mills' test that make it difficult to use. Furthermore, it is my opinion that several of the techniques suggested by Mills have little or no value or practical application in the diagnostic-teaching process. What follows is a less formal technique for attempting to discover students' dominant modalities.

The Time Factor

Mills stresses, and I would agree, that when working with various modalities to discover which one seems best with a particular student it is important to control the amount of time spent on teaching by the use of each modality. Mills suggests a period of fifteen minutes for each modality with exactly ten words taught during this period of time. I would have had no argument with his time period nor the number of words that he suggests, except in many situations it is simply not practical to spend fifteen minutes per day on five successive days on each set of words. The essential point, however, is that approximately the same amount of time be spent in teaching using each modality. If your time is somewhat limited you may want to modify the time to five or ten minutes; however, the time period chosen should remain consistent for each modality tested.

Material To Be Taught

Students' preferences for certain modalities are likely to affect the way they learn many things; however, in reading it is usually diagnosed in their learning of words. This, in itself, presents some problems since some words can be illustrated with pictures while it is not practical to do so with others. Edward Wolpert (1972) studied the relation of word recognition to word length, word shape, and word imagery. Wolpert was concerned with the ease with which forty-two first-grade children learned words varying in imagery value, length, and configuration. He found that his subjects learned a significantly greater number of shorter (three letter) words than longer (five letter) words. His students also learned a significantly greater number of high imagery words (such as "nose") than low imagery words (such as "same"). On the other hand, word configuration did not seem to be as important as the other two factors. The important point, however, is that the results obtained in modality testing may to some extent, depend upon these extraneous factors which may not always be apparent. For this reason results obtained from modality testing should be reconfirmed several times through careful diagnostic teaching as the student's remediation progresses.

From the foregoing discussion it is also apparent that the words chosen to be taught should, if possible, be of somewhat near the same length and imagery value. Word length is quite easy to control, but imagery value, of course, presents a much more difficult problem. In our own reading center we simply try to pick words that do not appear to have high imagery value but which would generally be in the speaking-listening vocabulary of the student to whom the words are to be taught.

In using the Mills *Learning Methods Test* it is often difficult to find forty words at any level that older students do not know. However, in a less formal setting you can pick words from the basic sight word list given in Chapter 4, or another good source is <u>Fry's Instant Word List</u>[3] which contains 600 words from levels one through six.

One point that also needs to be emphasized is that although words on the author's list or Fry's list appear at pre-primer, primer, first, second grade levels, etc. it does not really mean that the pre-primer or primer words are easier to learn than the words on the second or third grade list. It only means that pre-primer words are pre-primer words because they have traditionally been pre-primer words. They may, and usually are, of higher utility (or appear more often in print) than words at a higher grade level. However, if the student does not know the words to begin with, there is very little difference in the difficulty of the words. On the other hand, after a student begins to read he is more likely to encounter the pre-primer or high utility words more often, and simply because of multiple exposure to these words he would be more likely to know them in a period of a month or two. But, for delayed recall of words (a day or two) the imagery value of the word and its length is of more importance in determining how well it will be learned than the grade level from which it was derived. Therefore, if the words are in an older student's speaking-listening vocabulary, or in other words if he can use them in a sentence, it really does not make any difference if words from several levels are mixed for modality testing purposes.

There may be some situations in which it is not practical to teach ten words by each of the modalities to be tested. If your time is limited you may wish to cut the number to five or six and teach two sets on any one day. The essential point is that the same number of words be chosen to be presented using each learning modality.

The Teaching Procedure for Each Modality

It is important to keep in mind that whatever learning modality, if any, is found to produce the best test results in terms of delayed recall (which is the ultimate goal) it must be of a nature that would make its everyday use possible in a practical teaching situation. For example, as stated earlier, many words cannot be illustrated by the use of pictures and, furthermore, many teachers are not artistic enough to illustrate them. For this reason it seems somewhat futile to concern yourself with whether a student can learn words when they are presented with a picture representing the word.

What follows then is a teaching procedure for four different modalities that

[3]Fry, Edward. *Reading Instruction for Classroom and Clinic.* New York: McGraw-Hill, 1972, pp. 58–63.

can be modified slightly for some students, yet should, in most cases, be practical for use on a daily basis.

K Poe

A. Phonic or Auditory Modality Approach

1. Print the words to be learned on cards (approximately 3½ in. × 8 in.) before attempting to teach them to the student.

2. Present the first card and pronounce it slowly while pointing to each phoneme. Do not try to pronounce it letter by letter if there are graphemes in the word that do not represent separate sounds. Do this a second time asking the student to pronounce each part after you.

3. Say the word rapidly and ask the student to say it rapidly after you.

4. Ask the student to use the word in a sentence. If he cannot, use it in a sentence for him. Then ask him to make up a sentence of his own.

(All students can do these first three initial steps and should be required to follow them as outlined. Whether the following steps are done will depend on the phonics ability of the student. A sequence is suggested, but if the student cannot do some parts do not waste time attempting them. Spend more time doing the parts with which he is successful. In other words this approach may be modified, to some extent, from this point forward to fit the learning style of any one particular student.)

5. Discuss the sounds in the word. If the student knows all of the sounds then simply go on to the next word. If he does not know the sounds then point to the first sound and ask him to think of other words that begin with that sound. Do this same procedure with middle and ending sounds. Do not have him look for little words in big words. If he notes a little word in a larger word and its sound remains the same in the larger word simply acknowledge that what he says is true, but do not encourage the practice. If the smaller word does not retain its sound in the larger word then explain that little words often change when they are a part of a longer word.

6. If time allows, you may wish to find and classify all words into piles that have the same beginning, middle, or ending sounds.

7. The time spent on discussion of other words that rhyme with the beginning sounds of words will vary with the time allowed for teaching and the number of words to be taught. Simply gauge your time accordingly. Be sure to allow time to review all words to be taught by this method during the last minute or so before stopping.

B. Sight or Visual Modality Approach

1. Print the words to be learned on cards (approximately 3½ in. × 8 in.) before attempting to teach them to the student.

2. Point to the first word or simply sweep across it and pronounce it, e.g., say, "This word is 'among.' "

3. Ask the student to use the word in a sentence. If he cannot, then use it in a sentence for him. Then ask him to make up a sentence of his own.

4. Ask the student to look at the word and see if he can see anything about it that will help him to rememer it, e.g., the double "e's" in "seen" or the length of the word. If the student does not respond well to this then repeat steps 1 through 3 with the next word and ask him to tell you how the two words differ.

5. After all words have been taught ask the student to make a sentence out of the words, adding any other words necessary to complete the sentence.

6. Have him separate the words into categories that seem significant to him,

e.g., all words with three letters and all words having no tall letters.

7. Allow time to review all words before stopping. This will again depend on the number of words to be taught and the time allowed to teach them.

C. Kinesthetic-Tactile Modality Approach

1. Begin this approach with nothing on the cards and with the specific words to be taught already selected which may appear on a small list beside you.

2. Print the first word on a card saying the part of the word as you write it. Then say the word and have the student repeat it.

3. Have him trace over the word several times using his middle and index fingers. Be sure both fingers are in contact with the part being traced. Be sure he says the word part as he traces it. Try to avoid emphasizing specific sounds.

4. As with the other methods have him use the word in a sentence. If he cannot do this, use it in a sentence for him and then have him use it in another sentence.

5. After he has traced it several times, give him a new card and have him attempt to write it from memory. If he begins to make a mistake simply stop him and repeat steps 1–4 again and have him attempt it again. *Do not let him write it wrong.*

6. Allow time to review all words before stopping. Again this will depend on the number of words to be taught and the time allowed to teach them.

D. Combination Modality Approach

1. Begin with the words printed on the cards.

2. Tell him the word and quickly trace over it pronouncing it as you do so. Then pronounce it quickly.

3. Have him trace over it, again using his middle and index fingers, saying the word parts as they are traced. Then have him say the whole word quickly.

4. Have him use the word in a sentence. As in the other approaches, if he cannot use it in a sentence then use it in a sentence for him and have him make up a sentence of his own.

5. Discuss any known sounds in the word and discuss the word length and any configuration that will help him remember it.

6. Have him classify words by stacking cards into piles with the same beginning, middle, or ending sounds and/or classify them by word length or specific configurations.

7. Allow time to review all words before stopping. As with the other approaches this will depend on the number of words to be taught and time allowed for teaching them.

In using the above modalities approaches, keep the following important points in mind:

1. Do not attempt to teach too many words in too short a period of time. It is better to learn fewer words and review them than to be so hurried on the last few words that they are not covered well.

2. It is delayed recall (at least a day or more) that really matters in terms of the best approach for a particular student. Keep this in mind even though immediate recall using a particular approach seems quite effective.

3. If certain parts of some modality approaches seem successful while others do not, do not hesitate to combine the approaches that seem to be most successful.

4. Remember that as a student learns, his modality strengths may change somewhat; therefore, do not become permanently wedded to any one approach but constantly diagnose as you teach to determine whether the original modality diagnosis was correct or whether slight changes from time-to-time may be in order.

DIAGNOSING AND TEACHING TO SPECIFIC COGNITIVE STYLES

For many years teachers have noted characteristics of certain disabled readers that relate to their learning style. For example, most of us are familiar with students who hurriedly guess at words even though we are relatively sure they possess adequate word attack skills. Other students continually make repetitions to correct omissions and/or insertions. And, some students, even though they can repeat numerous rules for word attack skills, will seldom attempt to read an unfamiliar word. This style of thinking and reacting about known information is often referred to as cognition, or we refer to student's methods of thinking and reacting as their cognitive style.

In addition to the general observations mentioned above, a number of studies have been done which indicate that disabled readers, as a whole, may often differ in cognitive style from normal readers, yet recent research is heartening in that it indicates that certain undesirable cognitive styles can be changed. For example, Sawyer reviewed considerable research on the relationship between cognitive style and reading disability. She noted studies by George Spache that indicated that disabled readers at the primary level " . . . exhibited less insight into the dynamics of a situation and exhibited less solution-seeking behavior." (p. 560) She also noted that Jules Abrams " . . . found that nonreaders were more impulsive and less able to respond appropriately to environmental stimuli than good readers." (p. 560)

Although there are many degrees and types of cognitive styles there has been a tendency recently to classify students as being either "impulsive" or "reflective." Although these terms probably oversimplify the situation they do, at least, help us to understand something about the nature of the problem. For example, Lester Butler (1974) did a psycholinguistic analysis of the oral reading behavior of second grade boys that he classified as either impulsive or reflective according to a test developed by Jerome Kagan (1965-1969). Butler found that the reflective subjects made more repetitions than the impulsive subjects. This was evidently because they corrected a greater number of their miscues through repetition. These results were in contrast to a study done by Kagan (1965-1966), who thought that reflective students tended to reflect more over their choices and would thus be likely to detect and correct more miscues than impulsive children. The difference evidently was in the fact that the errors that were made by Butler's group were corrected by repetitions rather than being noted before the error was made.

Alan Neal (1974) also did a study in which he studied reflectivity and impulsivity in fourth grade students. He concluded that the impulsive student's behavior could be modified through the use of verbal exhortation, a finding that should hold a great deal of hope for the teacher attempting to help the student who makes errors caused from what is often termed "carelessness."

In the studies by Butler and Neal mentioned above, impulsive and reflective students were categorized using a matching figures test devised by Kagan. Eldon Ekwall and Judy English Solis (1971) also found different reading frustration levels of third, fourth, and fifth grade students classified as "mixed cognitive style" versus "impulsive cognitive" style as measured by the polygraph. These students were classified on the basis of their scores on the *WISC*, *Bender-Visual Motor Gestalt*, *Rorschach*, and the *House-Tree-Person Test*. In all instances mentioned above, even though different instruments were used for the measurement of cognitive style, there is strong indication that various styles do exist and can be categorized.

Using Knowledge of Cognitive Style in the Classroom

From a practical standpoint, in dealing with cognitive styles, the remedial reading teacher can follow a diagnostic teaching procedure somewhat as follows:

1. Note whether the student systematically applies word attack skills to words. If he does not, teach the word attack skills necessary for attacking similar words. Once he has learned a few necessary rules note whether he seems to be able to "think through" and apply these rules. If he is able to learn rules for word attack and readily apply them, the more rule oriented route may be a correct path to follow. On the other hand if he can learn to give the rules verbally, but does not seem to apply them, give him some practice in the application of the rules. If after considerable practice he still does not seem to be able to apply the rules or generalizations, consider a more automatic or less rule oriented approach to word attack. For example, one popular supplementary phonics series, during the course of about three years (one hour per day), teaches about 120–130 phonic generalizations. Many students seem to do well with this program, but regardless of the time spent in the program some students simply never seem to apply these rules. For students who cannot apply rules in word attack the automatic type of approach may be called for. In teaching the automatic approach you may wish to teach automatic recall of most phonemes as shown in the test in Appendix A when students see the written forms (graphemes). They can then learn phonograms or word families of high utility or compile lists of these on their own. By learning the phonemes of high utility plus a number of word families or phonograms a student will almost automatically be able to attack a great many words. Although this method of word attack may never become as systematic as it is for students who know and apply rules and generalizations it will enable them to instantly attack a great many words without going through a long reasoning process of which many students seem almost incapable of doing.

2. Through oral diagnosis note whether the student reads very rapidly at the expense of errors that cause problems with comprehension. If he does, discuss the need for more careful observation of word configuration and/or phonetic or structural analysis.[4]

3. Keep in mind that some students seem to possess a sort of "sixth sense" or innate

[4]See Ekwall, Eldon E. *Locating and Correcting Reading Difficulties*. Columbus, Ohio: Charles E. Merrill, 1970, for a thorough analysis of the causes and remediation of specific types of errors.

psycholinguistic ability for learning the rules of the language. For this type of student an occasional error that does not change the meaning of a reading passage to any great extent or that does not generally hinder his word attack skills may not indicate the need for formal training in most word attack skills. His time might better be spent in free reading or other worthy endeavors.

DIAGNOSING RATE OF LEARNING

Most classroom teachers get to know their students well enough to know that some learn faster than others. We often hear statements such as, "Denise just can't seem to learn no matter how hard I try to teach her." or "We must have gone over that word twenty times in class and Syril still doesn't know it." The first statement is quite unlikely to be true, but the second one might very well be true and, in terms of research in learning, be nothing that should be considered extraordinary.

As stated in an earlier chapter most students require an average of at least twenty exposures to a word before it becomes a sight word for them. On the other hand it is not uncommon for slower students to require over one hundred exposures to a word before it is instantly known. Some may require as many as 200 exposures. Yet, many remedial reading teachers often feel that a student is almost incapable of learning if he has not thoroughly learned a word exposed four or five times a day in a period of three or four days. If the word was taught in some manner in which the disabled reader encountered it five times per day for three successive periods this would still be only fifteen exposures to the word or less than the minimum amount of exposures required for a rapid learner in a developmental situation.

Most of us as adults have simply forgotten how difficult it was to learn to read. Albert Einstein, for example, was reported to have said that learning to read was the most difficult task that man has ever devised for himself. What we must be cognizant of is just how difficult it is for some students to learn what we are teaching them so that we can develop an adequate perspective on how much time we must expect to spend with each student on learning a new word, a vowel sound, a vowel rule, a syllable principle, etc. When remedial reading teachers begin to do this on a somewhat scientific basis they are often pleasantly surprised to find that many of their disabled readers are, in reality, not slow learners at all.

From a practical standpoint learning rate can be judged by using some of the following techniques:

1. Make note of one or two sight words that you wish to teach to a particular student. Then note on your daily record form (See Daily Lesson Plan Form in Chapter 14), as accurately as you can, how many times the word was taught and reviewed. You may also wish to ask him to underline or count the number times he comes across the word in his reading. After it is evident he has mastered the word check, as nearly as possible, the number of exposures or the amount of teaching it has taken to teach the student the word so that it is a thoroughly learned sight word.

2. Use the same recording procedure after teaching other concepts such as a vowel rule and syllabication principle. Then note whether the student can merely state the rule or whether he applies it regularly. If he knows a rule or principle but does not apply it, note the number of worksheets or application lessons it has generally taken before the student was actually able to apply the rule. As mentioned previ-

ously some may seldom ever get to the point of actual application on a routine basis.

It would be unrealistic to do the sort of thing described above on a regular basis with nearly every word or concept taught. On the other hand, we find in our Reading Center that university students who are required to do this sort of exercise on a regular basis, with disabled readers who appear to learn very slowly, often change their entire perception, in a positive direction, of a student's ability to learn. This, of course, affects teacher expectation which, as previously stated, ultimately affects students' self-concepts.

SUMMARY

In teaching remedial reading it is often desirable, and in many cases necessary, to diagnose for more than students' knowledge of the various reading skills. Studies have shown that students learn through differing modalities. These modalities are usually classified as phonic or auditory, visual, kinesthetic, and combinations of the three. For some students there appears to be very little difference in the modality in which they learn best, yet for some students one modality may be superior to the others. Methods have been suggested for determining which modalities, if any, are best for a particular student. Factors which appear to influence modality preferences are age, intelligence, and prior experiences with learning.

There is also a growing body of research to indicate that students possess different cognitive styles of learning. It would appear feasible to note which cognitive style disabled readers possess so as to capitalize on a teaching method appropriate for each student's particular cognitive style.

The remedial reading teacher should also be aware of students' learning rates. Studies indicate that there is considerable variance in learning rates from individual-to-individual. By checking from time to time on the learning rates of individual students we are often pleasantly surprised to find that many disabled readers are, in reality, not slow learners. This can be beneficial in terms of teacher expectation which will, in many cases, influence student achievement.

Chapter 10: REFERENCES

Blackie, John. "How Children Learn," *NEA Journal.* Vol. 57, (February, 1968), 40–42.

Blanton, Bill. "Review of ERIC/CRIER Research on Modalities and Reading," *The Reading Teacher.* Vol. 25, (November, 1971), 210–211.

Butler, Lester G. "A Psycholinguistic Analysis of the Oral Reading Behavior Of Selected Impulsive and Reflective Second Grade Boys," A Paper Presented at the International Reading Convention, New Orleans, 1974.

Duker, Sam. "Listening and Reading," *Elementary School Journal*. Vol. 65, (March, 1965), 321–329.

Ekwall, Eldon E., and Solis, Judy English. "Use of the Polygraph to Determine Elementary School Students' Frustration Reading Level," Final U.S.O.E. Report, 1971.

Kagan, Jerome. *Matching Familiar Figures Test*. Unpublished test devised by Jerome Kagan. Harvard University, 1965–9.

Kagan, Jerome. "Reflection-Impulsivity and Reading Ability in Primary Grade Children," *Child Development*. Vol. 36, (September, 1965–6), 609–628.

Linder, Ronald, and Fillmer, Henry T. "Auditory and Visual Performance of Slow Readers," *The Reading Teacher*. Vol. 24, (October, 1970), 17–22.

McCarthy, William, and Oliver, Joan. "Some Tactile-Kinesthetic Procedures for Teaching Reading to Slow Learning Children," *Exceptional Children*. Vol. 31, (April, 1965), 419–421.

McGrady, Harold J., Jr., and Olson, Don A. "Visual and Auditory Learning Processes in Normal Children and Children with Specific Learning Disabilities," *Exceptional Children*. Vol. 36, (April 1970), 581–589.

Mills, Robert E. "An Evaluation of Techniques for Teaching Word Recognition," *Elementary School Journal*. Vol. 56, (January, 1965), 221–225.

Neal, Alan J. "Reflectivity-Impulsivity in Grade Four Students and the Apprehension of Meanings of Unfamiliar Words. A Study Which Relates Cognitive Study and Reading Behavior," Paper Presented at the International Reading Convention, New Orleans, 1974.

Riessman, Frank. *The Culturally Deprived Child*. New York: Harper & Brothers, 1962.

Samuels, S. Jay. "Effects of Pictures On Learning To Read, Comprehension and Attitudes," *Review of Educational Research*. Vol. 40, (June, 1970), 397–407.

Sawyer, Diane. "The Diagnostic Mystique—A Point of View," *The Reading Teacher*. Vol. 27, (March, 1974), 555–561.

Wolpert, Edward M. "Modality and Reading: A Perspective," *The Reading Teacher*. Vol. 24, (April, 1971), 640–643.

Wolpert, Edward M. "Length, Imagery Values and Word Recognition," *The Reading Teacher*. Vol. 26, (November, 1972), 180–186.

11

USING INFORMAL READING INVENTORIES, THE CLOZE PROCEDURE AND THE ANALYSIS OF ORAL READING ERRORS

The first part of this chapter deals with a general description of informal reading inventories and why we use them. Detailed descriptions are then given for their administration scoring and interpretation. Information on developing your own informal reading inventories is then provided as well as information on using the informal reading inventory criteria for matching students and instructional material. This is then followed by a section on the analysis of error patterns from oral reading errors. The cloze procedure is then explained along with information on developing, administering, and scoring cloze passages. Lastly, information is presented on techniques for using the cloze procedure to place students in graded materials, and on how to use the cloze procedure to select materials to meet the needs of students within a particular classroom.

THE INFORMAL READING INVENTORY

What Informal Reading Inventories Are and Why We Use Them

Informal reading inventories usually consist of a series of graded passages, usually from pre-primer to at least the seventh or eighth grade level. From the first grade level on there are usually two passages—one to be read orally and one to be read silently at each grade level. As the student reads orally his word recognition errors are recorded and from these a percentage of word recognition is computed. Following the reading of each passage (both silently and orally) the student is also asked a series of comprehension questions regarding the material. From these answers a percentage score is derived for reading comprehension. For older students the oral reading passages are sometimes omitted.

People who work with children on a day-to-day basis in reading often come to realize the inadequacy of many of our standard measures of reading achievement in terms of providing for the practical knowledge that is necessary for individualized instruction. Emmett Betts (1946) had this feeling when he described the criteria and idea of administering informal reading inventories (IRIs). Betts' feeling about the need for such an instrument has been demonstrated and written

[handwritten margin notes: IRI / graded passages / oral + silent / word recog. + comp.]

about many times since. For example, Frank Guzak (1970) refers to studies by P.A. Kilgallon and Robert McCracken pointing to the unreliable placement information received from standardized reading achievement tests. More recently Margaret Jones and Edna Pikulski (1974) have quoted various studies indicating that standardized reading achievement tests tend to overestimate children's instructional levels.

The fact that overestimation of reading levels is a serious factor in reading becomes extremely important when we hear statements such as one made by Edwa Steirnagle[1] that her experience and research lead her to believe that 60 percent of our reading failures are caused by the assignment of materials that are too difficult. Furthermore, Daniel Fader[2] claims that a survey by the Carnegie Foundation indicated that one-half the people with Bachelor's degrees never read another book as long as they lived! Fader attributes this partially to the fact that material is not provided that people generally like to read and *can* read.

The Purpose of Informal Reading Inventories

In terms of the information presented above it is obvious that one of the main purposes in using informal reading inventories is to accurately place students in available reading materials or to provide for a proper "fit" between the two. Another important purpose of informal reading inventories is to determine students' Free or Independent, Instructional, and Frustration reading levels. In determining these levels an assessment must be made of students' reading comprehension when reading either orally or silently and of their word recognition when reading orally. A third important purpose of IRIs is to analyze the amount and type of students' word recognition errors and to assess reading comprehension for diagnostic-remedial purposes.

The Informal Reading Inventory Criteria and Levels

Reading is essentially a process of recognizing and understanding words and recognizing and understanding ideas. Or, said another way, in order to read efficiently we must reach a certain level of "word recognition" as well as a certain level of "comprehension." In reading we normally designate these levels as follows:

FREE OR INDEPENDENT LEVEL
(CRITERIA TO BE WITHOUT AID
FROM EXAMINER)

Word recognition—99% or better
Comprehension—90% or better

[1]Steirnagle, Edwa. From an address delivered to the El Paso County Council of the International Reading Association, April, 1974.
[2]Fader, Daniel. From an address delivered to a group of publishers.

This is the level at which children should be reading when they are reading a library book or the level at which they should read their textbooks *after* the teacher has introduced them to the new vocabulary and built up a proper background of experiences for comprehending the concepts in the material. In general this is the level a student should be reading at when there is no one around to help him. Although placement is normally based on the criteria mentioned above we normally associate certain behavioral characteristics with this level of reading. These characteristics are described by Marjorie Johnson and Roy Kress (1965) as follows:

Rhythmetical, expressive oral reading

Accurate observation of punctuation

Acceptable reading posture

Silent reading more rapid than oral

Response to questions in language equivalent to author's

No evidence of lip movement, finger pointing, head movement, vocalization, sub-vocalization, or anxiety about performance (p. 6)

INSTRUCTIONAL LEVEL (CRITERIA TO BE MET WITHOUT EXAMINER AID)

Word recognition—95%

Comprehension—75%

This is the level at which children would normally be reading in their textbooks (social studies, science, basal reading) before the teacher has introduced them to the vocabulary and built up a background of experiences for comprehending the concepts in the material. Again, placement is usually based on the criteria mentioned above, but the related behaviorial characteristics while reading should be the same as for the "Free" or "Independent" reading level.

FRUSTRATION LEVEL

Word recognition—90% or less

Comprehension—50% or less

This is the level at which the material is too difficult for sustained reading and it is a level that we would hope to avoid. Placement is again normally based on the criteria mentioned above, but related behavioral characteristics are as follows:

Abnormally loud or soft voice

Arhythmical or word-by-word oral reading

Lack of expression in oral reading

Inaccurate observation of punctuation

Finger pointing (at margin or every word)

Lip movement, head movement, sub-vocalization

Frequent requests for examiner help

Non-interest in the selection
Yawning or obvious fatigue
Refusal to continue (p. 10)

HEARING COMPREHENSION
LEVEL (CRITERIA TO BE MET
WITHOUT EXAMINER AID)

Comprehension—75% (The responses to questions should generally be in language
equivalent to the author's.)

The criteria given for the various levels mentioned above are from Kress and
Johnson, cited earlier. Although other slightly different criteria for some reading
levels are sometimes given by other authors. It should be emphasized that these are
usually based on "hunches." My own research indicates that these criteria could
probably be considered as correct providing *all* repetitions are counted as errors.
(See Ekwall and English, 1971; Ekwall, et al., 1973.)

In order to determine the reading potential of a disabled reader we often
begin to read passages at levels that are progressively higher than their Frustration
level. Students listen as these are read to them and the material is considered to be
at their Hearing Comprehension level as long as they meet the above stated criteria,
i.e., that they can answer 75 percent of the comprehension questions. The highest
grade level at which they can do this is their Hearing Comprehension level. For
some disabled readers this may be one or more grade levels above their Frustration
level. It should be stressed, however, that using hearing comprehension as a guide
to reading potential is only a rough estimate of this potential since some students
may possess less innate ability for listening than others. It has also been demonstrated that students from low socioeconomic levels often have inferior listening
skills than students from middle or upper income levels. Therefore, misleading results can easily be obtained by putting too much faith in the accuracy of the Hearing
Comprehension level.

Administering Informal Reading Inventories

In administering an IRI the examiner normally sits across the table or preferably on
one side of a table while the student sits facing the examiner to the right or left side of
him. The student is given a booklet containing a series of graded passages. The
examiner usually has the student start at a level he believes will be rather easy for
the student or which might be equivalent to the student's Free or Independent
reading level. In order to determine the proper level to begin the IRI the examiner
often administers a graded word list so that a more accurate determination of the
Free or Independent level can readily be obtained. Several of the commercially
available inventories contain their own graded word lists for this purpose. (These
are discussed later in this chapter.) I have found the San Diego Quick Assessment
List, listed in Chapter 4, to be quick and quite valid for easily determining, the Free

Figure 11–1. A Good Position for the Teacher and Student When Administering an Informal Reading Inventory.

or Independent level at which to start and for estimating the Instructional and Frustration levels as well.

As the student is given the booklet of graded reading passages the examiner usually gives directions somewhat as follows: "Here are some passages or stories I would like you to read. Please read them clearly and accurately and try to remember everything you read so that you can answer some questions about them when you are done. If you come across a hard word try to read it as best as you can but I may help you if you cannot get it at all." In introducing each passage the examiner often makes some comment about the content of the passage. For example, in having a student read a passage about an airplane ride the examiner may wish to say something such as, "This is a story about a boy who went on an airplane ride. Have you ever ridden in an airplane?" When doing this, however, be sure to avoid answering any questions that will later be asked about the story. Handing the student the first passage say, "Here is the first passage, read it aloud. Again, try to remember everything you read so you can answer some questions about it when you are through; go ahead and begin."

As the student reads, the examiner should have a copy of what the student is reading so that any word recognition errors, hesitations, etc., can be recorded. It is better if the examiner's copy is double or triple spaced so that ample room is available for recording these errors. A code for marking oral reading errors is shown on page 265. Many people have learned another shorthand method of marking various kinds of word recognition errors. I have found that students learn this code rather easily, but the important point is that you are able to look at the recorded errors and accurately interpret them immediately following the reading or even six months or a year later. For this reason you should become thoroughly familiar with either this or a modified version of this code. Although, when giving an informal reading inventory, it is necessary for the teacher to mark oral reading errors as the student proceeds through the reading material, it is usually a good idea for the teacher to tape the student's oral reading. This will enable her to go back and check on the accuracy of her coding. This is especially important when major decisions are to be made about the placement of a student based on his performance on an informal reading inventory.

CODE FOR MARKING IN
ORAL DIAGNOSIS

TO BE SCORED AS ERRORS IN MARKING INFORMAL
READING INVENTORIES

1. Encircle omissions.
2. Insert with a caret (∧) all insertions.
3. Draw a line through words for which substitutions or mispronunciations were made and write the substitution or mispronunciation above the word. Determine later whether the word missed was a substitution or mispronunciation.
4. If the student reads too fast to write in all mispronunciations, draw a line through the word and write a "P" for partial mispronunciation or a "G" for gross mispronunciation.
5. Mark inversions the same as substitutions and determine later whether the mistake was really an inversion or a substitution. Examples of inversions are, "no" for "on," "ont" for "not," "saw" for "was," etc.
6. Use parentheses ( ) to enclose words for which aid was given.
7. Underline repetitions with a wavy line.

NOT TO BE SCORED AS ERRORS IN MARKING INFORMAL
READING INVENTORIES

8. Make a check (√) over words that were self-corrected.
9. Use an arced line to connect words where there was disregard for punctuation.
10. Make two vertical lines (ǁ) to indicate a pause before words.

EXAMPLE OF A CODED PASSAGE

Dwight ~~was~~ *saw* going to visit ∧ *with* his Aunt ~~Nadine.~~ He ~~packed~~ *P* his (suitcase). *G* Then (his)mother ✓

took him to the ~~airport.~~ *P* Before he left he gave his mother a big ~~hug.~~ *bug*

After the student has finished reading the passage the examiner should take it back from him (as casually as possible) and then ask the comprehension questions that have been prepared in advance. These questions should appear on the same sheet on which the student's word recognition errors were recorded and can be marked with a "+" (plus) for correct answers or a "−" (minus) for wrong answers. If the student does not give a complete enough answer to score it accurately, you should ask a neutral question to clarify the answer. Examples of neutral questions are, "Can you tell me a little more about that?" or "Can you explain that a little more?" On the other hand, try to avoid questions that give the student a 50–50 chance of getting it right. For example, in a question calling for specific details such as, "What color was the car?", you should not question further by saying something such as, "Was it blue or green?" There are also times when you may wish to record verbatim what the student says in order to take more time in scoring it later. On some answers half credit is sometimes given where even after neutral questioning the answer is still not clear-cut.

You are also likely to find some students who occasionally do not give any answer after a question has been asked. Remember that you should give ample time for the student to think about the question and try to answer it (usually 5–10 seconds at least). If, however, after a period of time the student does not answer, you may wish to say, "Do you think you know that?" If the student does not know the answer, he will usually say, "No." If he thinks he may know it, he will often say, "Let me think about it a little longer." The point in doing this, of course, is to avoid wasting a great deal of time in waiting for an answer from students who do not seem to take the initiative in simply saying, "I don't know."

After the student has read the first passage aloud give somewhat similar directions, in terms of remembering what he is to read, so he can answer some questions about them after he has finished reading the passage, and then hand him the set of graded passages again and have him silently read the alternate passage at the same grade level. After the student has finished again ask the comprehension questions. If, however, after the student reads the first passage, it is obvious that it is not easy for him (at his Free or Independent level), continue downward one or more grade levels, reading orally, until he is definitely reading at his Free or Independent level. Then continue upward again alternating from oral to silent at each level. Have him continue upward until his Frustration level is reached.

After the student's Frustration level is reached you may wish to begin reading to him in order to determine his Hearing Comprehension level. In doing this, however, you may wish to use another set of graded reading passages so as not to spoil the original set for an administration at a later date.

Scoring and Interpreting Informal Reading Inventories

In coding students' oral reading it often proves beneficial to code a passage exactly as a student reads it although as you will note only the first seven types of errors (see page 254) are counted in computing the percentage of word recognition errors. The coding symbols shown in eight through ten often provide information helpful in diagnosis of reading disability but are not used in computing the percentage of word recognition errors. One of the main reasons that hesitations and lack of regard for punctuation are not counted as errors is that one could simply not be objective in scoring them. For example, two scorers would seldom reach perfect agreement on the exact number of times a student disregarded punctuation or hesitated too long. Therefore, if these things were counted as errors we would often have a low interscorer reliability (two or more people would not end up with the same number of errors) and the informal reading inventory would lose considerable validity. The items listed in items one through seven, however, are mistakes about which objective judgments can be made and, therefore, high interscorer reliability can be achieved which can, in turn, make the IRI a valid instrument.

Most authorities have been in agreement (and I concur) that the types of errors shown in items one through eight should be counted as errors. There are some authors, however, who feel that repetitions should not be counted as errors in marking IRIs. There are still other authors who believe that only repetitions of more than one word should be counted as errors. These people sometimes argue as Guzak does in quoting Kenneth Goodman's research. Guzak states, "In his research on oral reading Goodman has found that the repetition or regression is frequently the student's means of reprocessing a selective bit of data necessary to the emerging story line." (p. 667) They, therefore, feel that since the repetition was only made to correct an error, it should not be counted as an error. Ekwall and English (1971), however, used the polygraph (lie detector) to measure students' Frustration reading level as they read progressively more difficult passages. Their findings were also reported by Ekwall, Solis and Solis (1973), and Ekwall (1974). These studies showed that when *all* repetitions are not counted as errors, students actually become physiologically frustrated before they reach the percentage of errors normally recognized as being at the students' Frustration level. That is, students become so concerned about their reading performance that their hearts beat faster, they begin to perspire, etc. just as one does when he is frightened or extremely nervous. With this sort of empirical research available it seems that there should be no doubt that, using the normally recognized criteria, *all* repetitions should be counted as errors.

It should also be kept in mind that although it may not seem "fair" to a student to count repetitions because he ends up with more errors, it is in reality, less fair not to count these errors. If the student appears to be a better reader than is actually the case, he will be given reading material that is too difficult. On the other hand, seldom do we have to worry about students' reading material that is too easy for them as a result of this scoring.

One of the major problems that teachers have encountered in the past is that they were not really able to understand how to interpret the scoring criteria as it was originally outlined by Betts and later explained by Johnson and Kress. Briefly summarized their scoring criteria is as follows:

READING LEVEL	WORD RECOGNITION	COMPREHENSION
Free or Independent	99% +	90% +
Instructional	95%	75%
Frustration	90% −	50% −

All of this seems easy enough until a teacher encounters several very confusing situations. First of all note that in word recognition and comprehension the percentages for the Free or Independent Reading levels are 99 percent and 90 percent "plus" respectively. On the other hand the Frustration Reading levels for word recognition and comprehension are 90 percent and 50 percent "minus" respectively. The criteria for the Instructional Reading level for word recognition and comprehension is 95 percent and 75 percent respectively and these are usually listed as "plus" which connotes that they are minimum levels. What we find then is a situation that might be graphically illustrated (using comprehension as an example) as follows in Figure 11–1.

It stands to reason then, that students scoring 90 percent or better are at their Free or Independent Reading level, those between 75 percent and 89 percent are at their Instructional Reading level, and those students scoring below 50 percent are at their Frustration Reading level. However, the problem in interpretation often comes

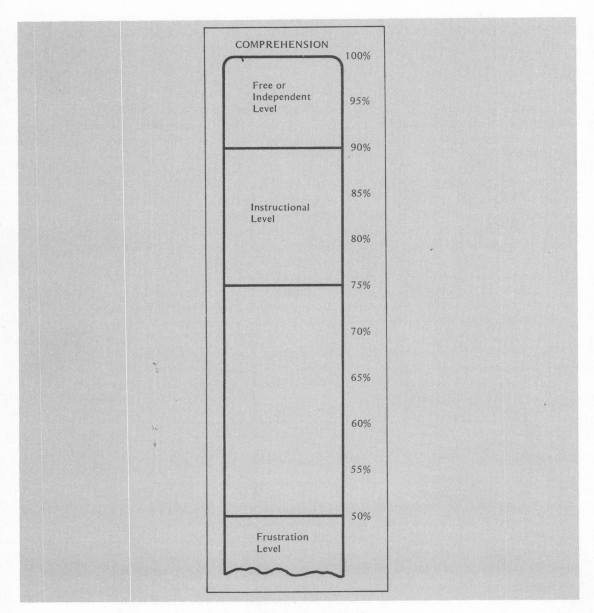

Figure 11–1. Illustration of various levels of comprehension

when the student scores above 50 percent or below 75 percent. We see then that by adding the "plus" and "minus" to our criteria we have created "four" categories while, in reality, we only have three levels. Although this is confusing to someone interpreting information derived from administering IRI's for the first few times it really allows the teacher to make some subjective judgment based on the student's overall performance. The unmarked area (between 50% and 75% on comprehension) might essentially be counted as Instructional Reading level *or* Frustration Reading level based on how well the student performed on word recognition. Or, if we are dealing with silent reading, the decision as to which level a student is in might be based on how interested the student appeared to be in the subject or how much difficulty he *appeared* to have with word recognition while reading the passage.

The same problem encountered with percentages of comprehension is also encountered with percentages of word recognition. In order to clarify how to make decisions for level placement based on both word recognition and comprehension we will look at some examples as shown in Figure 11–2.

In examining Figure 11–2 you will find the word recognition and comprehension levels of eight students (a through h). The exact percentages of word recognition and comprehension of each of these students on a particular reading passage is summarized below. Following this information an explanation is given of which overall reading level each student would normally be placed in when their word recognition and comprehension are both considered together.

STUDENT A: This student is above the minimum levels in both categories (comprehension and word recognition), therefore, he is reading at his Free or Independent reading level.

STUDENT B: This student is reading below the minimum levels in both categories, therefore, his overall reading is at his Frustration level.

STUDENT C: This student's word recognition score puts him in the high end of the questionable range where his overall reading could be considered as Instructional or Frustration level; however, since his comprehension is at the Frustration level, his overall reading level is also at the Frustration level. When either score (word recognition or comprehension) is in the Frustration level it would normally be impossible for the student to be at any other level regardless of how high his score was on the other factor involved.

STUDENT D: Again this student has a word recognition score that places him at Frustration level and, although his comprehension score was rather high (85 percent), he would still be considered at Frustration level.

STUDENT E: This student's score is in the Free or Independent level in word recognition and in the Instructional level in comprehension. The overall score would not normally be any higher than the lower of the two scores. Therefore, his overall score would be considered at Instructional level.

STUDENT F: This student's score is also in the Free or Independent level in word recognition but his score falls into the questionable range in the area of comprehension. Since his word recognition score is so high and his

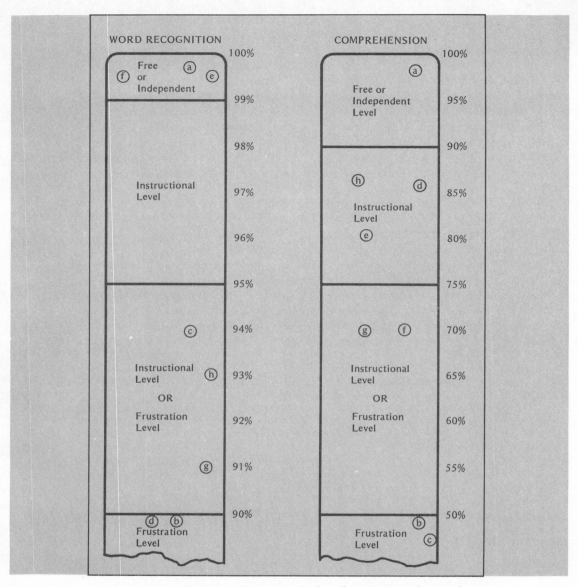

Figure 11–2. Illustration of various levels of word recognition and comprehension

comprehension score is in the high range of the questionable level (for either Instructional or Frustration) we would place him at the Instructional level.

STUDENT G: This student is in the low range of the questionable level for word recognition and in the high range of the questionable range for comprehension. We would not normally place a student in the Instructional level unless one of his two scores was above the questionable level. Therefore, his overall level would probably be considered to be at the Frustration level.

STUDENT H: This student scored in about the middle of the questionable level for

Using Informal Reading Inventories, the Cloze Procedure and the Analysis of Oral Reading Errors

word recognition. He scored fairly high in the Instructional range but not high enough to make us definitely feel that there is any reason to place him above his Frustration level. In this case, however, if the student was extremely interested in what he was reading or seemed to possess a great deal of perseverance, it would perhaps be proper for him to read at this level for a short period of time. As a general rule, however, students should not read material that would be this difficult for them.

As you can see it is somewhat difficult to make decisions about the overall reading level of certain students even when given a certain amount of guidance. On

STUDENT	WORD RECOGNITION PERCENTAGE	COMPREHENSION PERCENTAGE	PLACEMENT
a	99 or 100	100	Free or Independent
b	Less than 90	Less than 50	Frustration
c	94	Less than 50	Frustration
d	Less than 90	85	Frustration
e	99 or 100	80	Instructional
f	99 or 100	70	Instructional
g	91	70	Frustration
h	93	85	Probably Frustrational, but possibly Instructional.

the other hand you should keep in mind that it is really only the teacher who knows each student, their interests, their ability to persevere, etc. And, the fact that the informal reading inventory criteria is somewhat flexible is often beneficial.

Developing Your Own Informal Reading Inventories and Using the IRI Criteria

As stated previously, one of the purposes of using IRI's is to determine students' Free, Instructional, and Frustration reading levels. If this is your purpose, as it might be in an initial or final diagnosis done by a reading specialist or clinician, it would probably be much easier to simply use one of the commercially published reading inventories, discussed later in this chapter, such as Silvaroli's *Classroom Reading Inventory*[3] (which I prefer because of the ease of scoring) or McCracken's *Standard Reading Inventory*[4] which is a well-developed instrument but is more difficult to score.

It takes many hours or even days to develop a good inventory of this nature and there is little use in duplicating the efforts of experts such as Silvaroli and McCracken who have both devised good inventories for this purpose. On the other hand, simply applying the IRI criteria to materials within your own school to determine proper balance between students and materials is one of the most valuable uses of the IRI criteria.

[3]Silvaroli, Nicholas J. *Classroom Reading Inventory.* 2d ed., Dubuque, Iowa: William C. Brown, 1973.
[4]McCracken, Robert A. "*Standard Reading Inventory*," Klamath, Oregon: Klamath Printing Co., 1966.

Whether you wish to make your own complete informal reading inventory or whether you merely wish to select passages from existing materials to determine whether a student is in accord with those materials, you will need certain guidelines. For lower level passages (pre-primer through first grade) as few as twenty to forty words are often used. As the material increases in difficulty longer passages are usually selected (around 100-150 words at second or third grade level and up to 250-300 words at seventh or eighth grade level). Although research has shown that it is difficult to actually measure various comprehension skills, an attempt is usually made to devise comprehension questions over main ideas, important details, vocabulary, and inference. In order to insure a certain amount of validity at least seven or eight questions are usually asked concerning each passage. William Valmont (1972) has provided some excellent guidelines for constructing questions for informal reading inventories. These are as follows:

1. Questions should be in the approximate order in which the information upon which they are based is presented in the passage.
2. It is generally preferable to place a main idea question first.
3. Ask the most important questions possible.
4. Check the sequence of questions to insure that a later question is not answered by an earlier one.
5. Check questions to insure that two or more questions do not call for the same response, fact, or inference.
6. A question that is so broad that any answer is acceptable is a poor question. If special questions to test divergent thinking are created, insure that reasonable, logical responses may be made.
7. A question that can be answered by someone who has not read the passage (except for some vocabulary questions) is a poor question.
8. Avoid formulating questions whose answers call for knowledge based on something experienced by the pupil rather than from reading or application of information given in the story.
9. IRI questions are generally constructed to measure the student's comprehension of written matter. Therefore, insure that accompanying pictures do not aid the student in answering questions.
10. Keep your questions short and as simple as possible. Do not include irrelevant statements.
11. Generally, state questions so that they start with who, what, when, where, how, and why.
12. Do not let grammar or syntax unnecessarily complicate the questions.
13. Avoid stating questions in a negative manner.
14. Avoid overusing questions which require pupils to reconstruct lists, such as "list five ingredients" or "name four characters" or "tell six places." Anxiety or memory instead of comprehension may influence the pupil's performance.
15. Avoid writing questions with multiple answers which fail to establish specifications for the response.
    Poor: What happened after Susan heard the telephone?
    Better: What was the first thing that happened after Susan heard the telephone?
16. Do not mistake a question that calls for the reporting of several facts or details as an organization or sequence of question.

17. To learn about a pupil's grasp of the vocabulary, ask the pupil to define the word, not to recall a word from the story.

    Poor: What word told you about the age of the man?

    Better: What does *old* mean?

18. Avoid stating a question as if to call for an opinion when asking the pupil to relate a fact.

    Poor: How do you think Skip got to the store?

    Better: How did Skip get to the store?

19. If a question is asking for a judgement, phrase it as "Why do you or don't you believe . . . ." Do not reveal the information called for.

20. Avoid asking questions on which the child has a fifty-fifty chance of being correct: "yes/no" questions, or "either/or."[5] (pp. 511–512)

A Reading Level Guide To Calculate Reading Levels and To "Fit" Students and Materials

After working with beginning and practicing teachers for a number of years it was my feeling that few of these teachers really used reading inventories to advantage. For this reason I have created what I refer to as a "Reading Level Guide." There are several reasons why teachers have not used informal reading inventories or the criteria of the IRI for placing students in materials. These are as follows:

1. Most teachers have simply not had enough training in the field of reading to understand how to use the IRI criteria either for scoring informal reading inventories or for using the IRI criteria for placing students at the right reading level.

2. Those teachers who have studied the IRI criteria can usually interpret the results they obtain providing both comprehension and word recognition clearly fall into the "Free" or "Independent" reading level or the "Frustration" reading level. However, when either word recognition or comprehension differ considerably, the obtained results become much more difficult to interpret. The Reading Level Calculator eliminates the problems usually encountered in interpreting obtained data.

3. Teachers are often hesitant to take the time to calculate the percentage of words recognized as well as the percentage of questions that were correct. The use of Tables 11-1 and 11-2 eliminates the need for calculating any percentages.

THE PURPOSE OF THE READING LEVEL GUIDE. The purpose is to help beginning and practicing teachers, or the reading specialist, place students at the proper reading level. This information will enable you to quickly and effortlessly interpret information derived from informal reading inventories and, more importantly, it will help you match the reading levels of children and books by applying the criteria for interpreting informal reading inventories.

The use of the criteria for scoring informal reading inventories eliminates the need for teachers to work somewhat complicated and time consuming readability formulas on various classroom materials. It also eliminates the chore of attempting to assess the "reading level" of children. Furthermore there is considerable chance

[5]Valmont, William J. "Creating Questions for Informal Reading Inventories," *The Reading Teacher*. Vol. 25, (March, 1972), 509–512. (Reprinted with permission of the author and the International Reading Association.)

that a book based on a reading level obtained by a readability formula will not be in accord with a teacher's assessed reading level. This is true for several reasons which follow:

1. Readability formulas, at best, only produce a rough approximation of the level of difficulty of reading material.

2. Most tests only produce a rough approximation of a child's reading level. For example, a child whose reading level is based on a subject about which he is thoroughly familiar is likely to score quite high because of his knowledge of the vocabulary and his comprehension of the concepts. Because of this the child may be placed a grade level or more higher than he could normally read. On the other hand, material written on subjects in which the child is unfamiliar is likely to place him a grade level or more lower than he can actually function in most cases. The important question, of course, is how well does a *certain* child read a *certain* set of materials.

The problem then is that every book or every different set of reading materials presents somewhat different problems for different readers depending on their background of experiences. And, the only practical solution is to ask a child to read the materials that you wish to use in instructing him and see how well *that* child reads *those* materials. This applies whether you are a parent attempting to determine whether a certain library book is easy enough for your child to read or whether you are a teacher trying to find the right level of basal reader in which to place a student.

To determine whether a book or other reading material is at the proper reading level for a student use the procedure which follows:

1. Have the student orally read a passage from the material. For younger students in Grades 1 or 2 you will probably want to choose a passage of between 25 to 100 words. For students at Grade 3 or above you will probably want to use a passage between 100–200 words.

2. As the student reads, record the number of oral errors he makes using the *Code For Marking in Oral Diagnosis*. You may wish to have a copy of the material that the student is reading on which you can mark errors in word recognition. Or you may simply wish to make a fist and then hold up one finger (without the student noticing) each time an error is made in word recognition.

Coding the exact type of error will often enable you to locate certain reading difficulties that might not otherwise become apparent. If you are only interested in placement, you may wish to simply make a check for each oral error. If you do not mark each error, be sure that you jot down the total number of oral (Word recognition) errors.

3. Ask the student questions concerning the material he has just read. You should usually try to ask at least four or more questions. Questions should preferably be prepared in advance and should sample the following kinds of comprehension:
   a) Knowledge of the main ideas
   b) Knowledge of important details
   c) Knowledge of vocabulary
   d) Ability to infer from material read
   Note the total number of questions that were asked and the total number of questions missed.

4. In Table 11–1 you will find numbers representing the total number of words in various passages in the left-hand column. Find the number or range that corresponds to the number of words in the passage just read. Place your left hand on this row. Look at the row of numbers across the top that represents the number of oral or word recognition errors. Find the number of errors made by your student and place your right hand on this number. Now find the point at which the row that your left hand is pointing to intersects with the column at which your right hand is pointing. This number represents the percentage of word recognition (percentage correct).

5. Look in Table 11–2 and find the figure that corresponds to the number of questions asked and put your left hand on this figure. Then look across the top row of this table and find the figure that corresponds to the number of questions missed. Put your right hand on this figure. Find the point at which the row to which your left hand is pointing intersects with the column to which your right hand is pointing. This figure is the percent of comprehension questions that were correct.

6. Turn to the Reading Level Calculator and find the percentage of correct word recognition in one of the rows on the left-hand side and the percentage of correct comprehension in one of the columns on the top. Then find the point at which the row on the left intersects with the column on the top. If they intersect in one of the areas labeled *F*, the student is reading at his Frustration level. If they intersect in the area marked *Inst*, the student is reading at his Instructional level. And, if they intersect in the area marked *Free* then the student is reading at his Free or Independent Level.

When using either Table 11–1 or Table 11–2 you will find that some rows and columns intersect in an area marked *F*. Whenever this occurs it means that the child is reading at his Frustration level regardless of other scores. Therefore, there would be no need to use the Reading Level Calculator because his reading level would have already been determined.

In doing a quick check to determine whether certain materials are appropriate for a student you may often wish to omit the comprehension questions because of the time involved in both making up and asking these questions. Therefore, follow the same procedure previously described, but instead of asking questions simply consider the student's comprehension to be at the 100 percent level when using the Reading Level Calculator as described in Step 5 above.

To determine the grade level at which a student is reading use the procedure which follows. The procedure for using the Reading Level Guide for determining the grade level at which a student is reading is nearly the same as the previously described procedure with several exceptions. Before beginning this procedure you will need a series of reading passages of which the grade level of difficulty is already known. For example, you may have reading passages at the following levels:

> Pre Primer (PP)
> Primer (P)
> First Reader (F)
> Second Reader, Book One (2–1)
> Second Reader, Book Two (2–2)
> Third Reader, Book One (3–1)
> Third Reader, Book Two (3–2)
> Fourth Reader (4)

Table II-1. Guide for determining the correct percentage of word recognition

Number of words missed

Number of words in reading passage

	1	2	3	4	5	6	7	8	9	10	11	12	13	14	15	16	17	18	19	20
20-25	96	91	F	F	F	F	F	F	F	F	F	F	F	F	F	F	F	F	F	F
26-30	96	93	F	F	F	F	F	F	F	F	F	F	F	F	F	F	F	F	F	F
31-35	97	94	91	F	F	F	F	F	F	F	F	F	F	F	F	F	F	F	F	F
36-40	97	95	92	F	F	F	F	F	F	F	F	F	F	F	F	F	F	F	F	F
41-45	98	95	93	91	F	F	F	F	F	F	F	F	F	F	F	F	F	F	F	F
46-50	98	96	94	92	F	F	F	F	F	F	F	F	F	F	F	F	F	F	F	F
51-55	98	96	94	92	91	F	F	F	F	F	F	F	F	F	F	F	F	F	F	F
56-60	98	97	95	93	91	F	F	F	F	F	F	F	F	F	F	F	F	F	F	F
61-65	98	97	95	94	92	F	F	F	F	F	F	F	F	F	F	F	F	F	F	F
66-70	99	97	96	93	91	F	F	F	F	F	F	F	F	F	F	F	F	F	F	F
71-75	99	97	96	95	93	92	F	F	F	F	F	F	F	F	F	F	F	F	F	F
76-80	99	97	96	95	94	92	92	F	F	F	F	F	F	F	F	F	F	F	F	F
81-85	99	98	96	95	94	93	92	F	F	F	F	F	F	F	F	F	F	F	F	F
86-90	99	92	97	95	94	93	92	91	F	F	F	F	F	F	F	F	F	F	F	F
91-95	99	98	97	96	95	94	93	91	F	F	F	F	F	F	F	F	F	F	F	F
96-100	99	98	97	96	95	94	93	92	F	F	F	F	F	F	F	F	F	F	F	F
101-105	99	98	97	96	95	94	93	92	91	F	F	F	F	F	F	F	F	F	F	F
106-110	99	98	97	96	95	94	94	93	92	F	F	F	F	F	F	F	F	F	F	F
111-115	99	98	97	96	96	95	94	93	92	91	F	F	F	F	F	F	F	F	F	F
116-120	99	98	97	96	96	94	93	92	92	91	F	F	F	F	F	F	F	F	F	F
121-125	99	98	98	97	96	95	94	93	93	92	91	F	F	F	F	F	F	F	F	F
126-130	99	98	98	97	96	95	95	94	93	92	92	91	F	F	F	F	F	F	F	F
131-135	99	98	98	97	96	95	95	94	93	92	92	91	F	F	F	F	F	F	F	F
136-140	99	99	98	97	96	96	95	94	93	93	92	92	91	F	F	F	F	F	F	F
141-145	99	99	98	97	97	96	95	94	94	93	92	92	91	F	F	F	F	F	F	F
146-150	99	99	98	97	97	96	95	95	94	93	93	92	92	91	F	F	F	F	F	F
151-155	99	99	98	97	97	96	95	95	94	93	93	92	92	91	F	F	F	F	F	F
156-160	99	99	98	97	97	96	96	95	94	94	93	92	92	91	91	F	F	F	F	F
161-165	99	99	98	98	97	96	96	95	94	94	93	93	92	91	91	F	F	F	F	F
166-170	99	99	98	98	97	96	96	95	95	94	93	93	92	92	91	F	F	F	F	F
171-175	99	99	98	98	97	97	96	95	95	94	94	93	92	92	91	91	F	F	F	F
176-180	99	99	98	98	97	97	96	95	95	94	94	93	93	92	92	91	F	F	F	F
181-185	99	99	98	98	97	97	96	96	95	95	94	93	93	92	92	91	91	F	F	F
186-190	99	99	98	98	97	97	96	96	95	95	94	94	93	93	92	91	91	F	F	F
191-195	99	99	98	98	97	97	96	96	95	95	94	94	93	93	92	92	91	91	F	F
196-200	99	99	98	98	97	97	96	96	95	95	94	94	93	93	92	92	91	91	F	F

Fifth Reader (5)

Sixth Reader (6)

Seventh Reader (7)

Eighth Reader (8)

Have the student begin reading at a level that you think will be at his Free or Independent reading level and continue to read progressively harder passages. You may wish to determine this starting point by using the San Diego Quick Assessment List. Check the reading of each passage as described. In doing this, you should continue downward (if necessary) until the student's Free or Independent reading level is reached and then continue upward until his Instructional and finally his Frustration level is reached.

In giving informal reading inventories we would normally wish to determine a student's Free or Independent, Instructional, and Frustration levels for both silent and oral reading. To do this you would need two written passages at each of the levels of difficulty mentioned above. Proceed the same as described before; however, this time alternate from oral to silent on each grade level, e.g., at second grade level have the student read orally and then ask the comprehension questions. After doing this have the student read the other second grade level passage silently and again ask him questions to determine his percentage of comprehension. To determine the proper level for passages that are read silently simply find the percentage derived from Table 11–2 for comprehension, across the top of the Reading Level

Table II-2. Guide for determining the correct percentage of comprehension

Number of questions missed

	0	1	2	3	4	5	6	7	8	9	10
10	100	90	80	70	60	F	F	F	F	F	F
9	100	90	80	65	55	F	F	F	F	F	F
8	100	90	75	65	F	F	F	F	F	F	F
7	100	85	70	60	F	F	F	F	F	F	F
6	100	85	65	F	F	F	F	F	F	F	F
5	100	80	60	F	F	F	F	F	F	F	F
4	100	75	F	F	F	F	F	F	F	F	F
3	100	65	F	F	F	F	F	F	F	F	F

(left axis: Number of questions)

Calculator, and consider the student's word recognition to be at the 100 percent level. Then determine the point at which these two figures intersect. As explained in step 5, the coded intersection point represents the level at which the student is reading.

Briefly then, use the Reading Level Guide as follows:

1. Determine the number of oral (word recognition) errors.

2. Convert this to a percentage by using Table 11–1.

3. Determine the number of comprehension errors.

4. Convert this to a percentage by using Table 11–2.

5. Find the corresponding percentages derived on the Reading Level Calculator and determine the point at which these two percentages intersect. The coded intersection point represents the student's reading level.

Adapting Informal Reading Inventories For Use With Older Students

In most situations above grade six and even above the first and second grades a considerably larger amount of time is spent in having students read silently than orally. Some oral reading is done for practice in such areas as reading poetry and choral

READING LEVEL CALCULATOR

Percent of comprehension

Percent of word recognition	55[1]	60	65	70	75	80	85	90	95	100
100	Inst.	Inst.	Inst.	Inst.	Inst.	Inst.	Inst.	Free	Free	Free
99	F	Inst.	Inst.	Inst.	Inst.	Inst.	Inst.	Free	Free	Free
98	F	F	Inst.	Inst.	Inst.	Inst.	Inst.	Inst.	Inst.	Inst.
97	F	F	F	Inst.	Inst.	Inst.	Inst.	Inst.	Inst.	Inst.
96	F	F	F	F	Inst.	Inst.	Inst.	Inst.	Inst.	Inst.
95	F	F	F	F	F	Inst.	Inst.	Inst.	Inst.	Inst.
94	F	F	F	F	F	F	Inst.	Inst.	Inst.	Inst.
93	F	F	F	F	F	F	F	Inst.	Inst.	Inst.
92	F	F	F	F	F	F	F	F	Inst.	Inst.
91	F	F	F	F	F	F	F	F	F	Inst.

F = Frustration reading level

Inst. = Instructional reading level

Free = Free reading level

1 You will note in using this Reading Level Calculator that the student is not considered to be at his Frustration reading level below 75 percent if his word recognition skills are still fairly high. The polygraph research referred to in this chapter indicated that if word recognition remains high, most students do not actually become frustrated until their comprehension level drops below the 50 percent level.

reading. However, other than for these specific reasons it is difficult to justify oral reading for other than diagnostic purposes. For this reason in designing informal reading inventories to determine the grade level at which students are capable of functioning, or in applying the IRI criteria to match students and materials, there is often little need to have students read orally.

When a student obviously reads very poorly, further diagnosis including oral reading may be called for. However, a study by Robert Pehrsson (1974) indicated that students read better when they are not interrupted during the reading process. When Pehrsson's students were told to read for meaning, their comprehension and rate of reading improved.

For these reasons I would suggest that in working with older students you first consider what you want to know about them. If the answer to your own questions are those such as: Can Cindy read this social studies book at her Instructional level? Can Bill, who is in the ninth grade, read a particular trade book at his Free reading level? then you may wish to operate as described previously, but omit the oral reading, or word recognition errors, as a factor in making these decisions.

Commercially Developed Informal Reading Inventories

The *Classroom Reading Inventory* devised by Nicholas J. Silvaroli is probably the best known of the commercially developed informal reading inventories. The *Classroom Reading Inventory* is designed to be used by teachers in grades two through ten. It consists of three parts as follows:

Part I. Graded Words Lists
Parts II. Graded Oral Paragraphs
Part III. Graded Spelling Survey

Although the author states that the instrument is principally an oral inventory he does present three forms (A, B, and C) which make it readily adaptable as a combination oral and silent inventory or as a silent inventory for older students. Having equivalent forms is also an advantage for pre-testing versus post-testing or in using an alternate form for use in determining a student's Hearing comprehension level. The stories are well done and graded according to well known and accepted readability formulas.

The directions are well written and precise enough so that a beginning teacher can use it with little or no difficulty, yet it is sophisticated enough for use by reading clinicians or school psychologists. The *Classroom Reading Inventory* is also completely contained within one spiral bound booklet which makes it reasonably priced as well as facile to use. The publisher also grants teachers permission to duplicate the reading passages for oral coding and scoring which also makes it economical to use. However, it should be stressed that the passages in the *Classroom Reading Inventory* are very short and there are only a few questions following each passage. For this reason it tends to lose some validity that would be found in an inventory with longer passages.

The *Standard Reading Inventory* devised by Robert McCracken is also an adaption of an informal reading inventory designed for measuring reading achievement at pre-primer through seventh grade levels. The *Standard Reading Inventory* (SRI) contains two forms (A and B). Each form consists of eleven stories for oral reading and eight stories for silent reading. The SRI also contains word lists for assessing the starting point for the lower (Free or Independent) reading level. As stated by the author the Standard Reading Inventory measures reading achievement in four areas:

1. Recognition Vocabulary
   a. vocabulary in isolation
   b. vocabulary in context
2. Oral Errors
   a. word recognition errors in oral reading
   b. total errors in oral reading
3. Comprehension
   a. recall after oral reading
   b. recall after silent reading
   c. interpretation and word meaning in context after oral reading
   d. interpretation and word meaning in context after silent reading
4. Speed
   a. oral speed
   b. silent speed (p. 40, *Teacher's Manual*)

The SRI has some unique features not contained in the scoring of other informal measures of reading achievement. Based on our polygraph research quoted earlier, I cannot agree with the fact that the author does not count repetitions as a word recognition error. The author does, however, take repetitions into account in scoring.

McCracken presents some scholarly evidence of both content validity and reliability. On the other hand the complicated method of scoring the SRI would, in many cases, seem to defeat the purpose of administering an IRI in the first place. The SRI could perhaps best be used as a teaching instrument for reading specialists or by a well-trained reading specialist or reading clinician.

THE ANALYSIS OF ERROR PATTERNS FROM ORAL READING ERRORS

Although informal reading inventories can be a useful device for determining students' reading levels and for matching students' and reading materials one of their most important advantages is that they will allow you to diagnose specific reading difficulties from patterns of oral reading errors. A shorthand method of marking each specific type of error was described earlier in this chapter. Once you have become familiar with this marking system you will find that almost every student presents a pattern of errors that then becomes a blueprint for instruction. This section is designed to help you analyze these patterns so as to provide more accurate and effective remediation.

You will recall that in the shorthand system presented previously it was suggested that you learn to mark several types of characteristics of students' reading that are not counted as errors in computing the percentage of word recognition errors in informal reading inventories. Some of these characteristics, however, are important in the analysis of error patterns of disabled readers. In the section that follows a short description of each type of error, some possible reasons why students might make that particular type of error, and some remedial procedures for each error are presented.[6]

OMISSIONS. Students sometimes make omissions of parts of words (such as "s," "ed," or "ing" endings), whole words, phrases, or whole lines or sentences. Omissions are usually made either through carelessness, because a student lacks word recognition skills, or because he lacks word analysis skills. It should be emphasized, however, that the type of remediation would depend upon the cause.

Some students omit words simply because they are careless. If a student omits words at his free or instructional level as well as at his frustration level then it would be quite likely that his omissions were caused from carelessness. In such a case it should be called to his attention. This can be done by recording his reading and having him listen and underline or circle words that were previously omitted. In some cases it is also beneficial to have students bring their finger down and point to each word as it is read. This is more effective than having them slide their finger along a line of print since they are often inclined to read ahead of, or behind, where they are pointing. Another technique that is helpful in overcoming carelessness is to have the student choral read along with another good reader or to read along with a tape recorder.

If a student makes omissions at his frustration level but does not make them at his free or independent level then they are likely to be caused from difficulties in word recognition or word analysis. In such a case the omissions are only symptomatic of a larger problem. And, when the larger problem of word recognition or word analysis skills is remediated then the omission problem will in most cases disappear.

Methods of remediating difficulties in word recognition are given in Chapter 4; and methods of remediating difficulties in word analysis skills are given in Chapter 5.

INSERTIONS. Students sometimes make insertions of word endings or insertions of extra words. Insertions may be caused from lack of comprehension, from carelessness or when the student's oral language ability surpasses his reading ability. If the insertions that the student makes are correct within the context of the sentence, it can usually be assumed that the student is comprehending what he is reading. In this case it might be assumed that these mistakes are a sign of carelessness or the student's oral language ability may surpass his reading ability. When this is the case, you should call the student's attention to the mistakes. This may be done by simply telling him or by having him insert with a caret (⌃) all words on a reading passage that he has read previously into a tape recorder. It is also helpful to ask questions that call for exact answers that can only be answered correctly without the in-

[6]For a more thorough analysis of oral reading reading errors and their diagnosis and correction see: Eldon E. Ekwall, *Locating and Correcting Reading Difficulties*, Charles E. Merrill, 1970.

sertions. As in the case of omissions, it is also helpful to have the student point to each word as it is read or to have him choral read with one or more good readers or to read in conjunction with a tape recorder.

If the student's insertions do not make sense within the context of the sentence, the student is probably having difficulty with comprehension. In such a case the types of remedial exercises listed under the remediation section of Chapter 6 on comprehension development should prove helpful.

SUBSTITUTIONS AND/OR PARTIAL MISPRONUNCIATIONS. Substitutions usually differ from mispronunciations in that one complete (correct) word is substituted for another complete (correct) word such as "has" for "had." This might also be termed a mispronunciation, i.e., mispronunciation of the last part of the word ("s" for "d"). We often classify the use of one "basic" sight word for another as a substitution. And, the use of one adjective for another is also classified as a substitution. On the other hand, the substitution of incorrect word endings or "soft" "c's" and "g's" for "hard" "c's" and "g's" or the wrong pronunciation of a letter or group of letters within a word is usually referred to as a partial mispronunciation.

A student who substitutes one word for another may be a careless reader or may lack word recognition skills. The types of remediation for carelessness listed under omissions and insertions is also helpful in providing remediation for this problem. A student who mispronounces words because of poor word recognition skills may need help with word recognition as listed in Chapter 4. The student who makes partial mispronunciations will, in most cases, also profit from work in word analysis skills as listed in Chapter 5.

GROSS MISPRONUNCIATIONS. Gross mispronunciations refer to distorted pronunciation of words to the extent that the original pronunciation can hardly be recognized. Students who constantly make gross mispronunciations usually require help in any or all of the word analysis skills but especially in phonics and structural analysis. They may also need help in the use of context clues. The student who grossly mispronounces words should be given a phonics test such as the one listed in Appendix A of this text and should be checked for knowledge of vowel rules, syllabication principles, and context clues. For some students it is also helpful to check on their vocabulary knowledge since students with a rich oral vocabulary are often hesitant to say grossly mispronounced or what, to them, would be nonsense words.

INVERSIONS OR REVERSALS. Students sometimes make reversals of entire words ("was" for "saw" or "on" for "no"), partial reversals of words ("form" for "from"), or reversals or inversions of letters ("g" for "p," "b" for "d," "n" for "u"). Students make inversions or reversals for a number of reasons. For example, many younger students below the age of seven or eight tend to do so, but when they reach the age of seven and one-half to eight years, they almost magically seem to gain the perceptual maturity needed to overcome the problem. Some children simply never realize that English words are written from left-to-right and that English sentences are read the same way. Other more severely disabled readers seem to possess some sort of neurological dysfunction that causes the images of words and letters to reach the brain in a scrambled order.

Since it is difficult to determine why a certain student makes reversals or inversions of letters or words the teacher will in most cases find it unprofitable to worry about the etiology of the problem, but simply work on its remediation. Remedial procedures that have often proven helpful are as follows:

1. Letting the student type words on a typewriter and see them take shape as they are typed.
2. Using a green letter at the beginning of words and a red letter at the end. These colors should, of course, be removed as soon as the word presenting difficulty has been mastered.
3. Using the non-visual AKT approach as suggested in Chapter 9.
4. Using magnetic three-dimensional or felt or sandpaper letters and let the student trace these as he says them.
5. Using the Fernald Approach as described in Chapter 9.
6. Uncovering words from left-to-right and reading them immediately after they are uncovered.
7. Explaining to the student that English words and sentences are to be read from left to right.

AID. When a student lacks the ability to attack a strange word he will usually ask for aid or simply wait until aid is given. Students who do this usually lack word recognition and/or word analysis skills and often lack self-confidence in their ability to attack strange words. When this happens, you should begin by testing the student's word analysis skills as described in Chapter 5. In some cases you may find that the student is able to give various phonemes in isolation or may know certain rules but is unable to apply them in a practical situation. It would then be necessary to teach him to *use* his word attack skills.

REPETITIONS. Students may make repetitions because of poor word recognition skills, poor word analysis skills or because they have simply developed a bad habit. Before attempting to remediate the problem you should first determine the cause. This is, of course, necessary because the remediation given for repetitions caused from a bad habit would be considerably different from the remediation given for repetitions caused from poor word recognition or word analysis skills.

If a student makes a number of repetitions in material written at his own grade level (for example fifth grade level) you can usually determine the cause by having him read material written at a grade level several grades below the point at which he was making the repetitions. If the student continues to make as many repetitions in the material at a lower grade level, the problem is probably simply a bad habit. On the other hand, if the student makes considerably less repetitions in the easier material, then he probably has a problem with word recognition or word analysis skills.

Repetitions caused from a bad habit can be treated in much the same manner as described earlier for habitual omissions, i.e., having the student point to each word as it is read, having him cover the material with a small card as it is read, having him choral read with one or more good readers, or by having him read in conjunction with a tape recording. If it is determined that the problem of repetitions is not caused from a bad habit then it would be necessary to determine whether the student is lacking in sight vocabulary (poor word recognition skills) or whether he is poor in word analysis skills, or both. Procedures for making these decisions are described in Chapters 4 and 5.

It should be emphasized that many students make repetitions to correct errors which they discover as they continue to read. The errors are usually discovered from the context of the story line. Not all repetition errors are serious enough to interfere with comprehension or to seriously retard a student's reading ability. However, whether serious or not, they are usually indicative of some type of difficulty.

DISREGARD OF PUNCTUATION. Students may disregard punctuation because they are simply not familiar with the meanings of various punctuation marks, because they lack comprehension, or because the reading becomes so difficult for them that they simply fail to attend to punctuation. One of the first steps in determining the cause of the problem with a student who exhibits this problem is to give him material to read that is written at a lower level of difficulty. If he continues to disregard punctuation and appears to comprehend after being questioned concerning the material, he may simply need to work on the meaning of various punctuation marks. If he no longer disregards punctuation in the lower level passage then it can be assumed that the problem with punctuation is only symptomatic of a problem with comprehension or work recognition at higher levels. In this case it would be necessary to do further diagnosis to pinpoint the problem. However, punctuation per se could be ignored as a problem.

PAUSES BEFORE WORDS. A student who pauses longer than normal before words is usually either lacking in word recognition or word analysis skills or has formed a habit of word-by-word reading. If material written at a lower grade level can be located and given to a student who exhibits this problem, you can determine whether it is a habit of word-by-word reading or whether he has a problem with word recognition and/or word analysis. If the student continues to pause before words in material written at a lower grade level then you may wish to try putting some of the words that appear after the pauses on flash cards. If he seems to have almost instant recognition of the words on flash cards, you can feel fairly sure that he has simply not learned to phrase properly or has developed the habit of word-by-word reading. In this case activities such as drill with sight phrases with flash cards or with a tachistoscope would probably prove helpful. The student may also profit from choral readings with one or more good readers or by reading in conjunction with a tape recording of a good reader. Simply discussing the problem with him and letting him hear his reading via a tape recording versus that of a good reader will often call it to his attention.

If a student improves when he is given material at a lower level of difficulty, it can usually be assumed that he was having problems with word recognition or word analysis (or both) at the higher reading level. If the student pauses before words and then says them correctly, it can usually be assumed that he has good word analysis skills but poor word recognition skills or, in other words, he does not possess a sight vocabulary equal to his grade level. In this case activities such as those suggested in Chapter 4 would be appropriate. On the other hand, if he pauses before words and is still unable to say them without aid it can be assumed that he needs help with word analysis skills. In this case the type of remediation suggested in Chapter 5 would be helpful.

THE ANALYSIS OF A SPECIFIC PASSAGE.   The coded passage that follows is typical of the oral reading errors made by many disabled readers. Following the passage is a discussion of the types of errors and the kind of remediation that would appear to be appropriate for this student.

JOHN'S FIRST AIRPLANE RIDE

John's father and mother told him that he could go to//visit his grandmother and grandfather who\\lived on a farm. They told him that he could ride on an airplane to go to visit them if he wanted to. John was very\\thrilled and wanted to get started right away. When the time came to go John was very//excited. He packed his suitcase and got in the car long before his father was ready to take him to the airport.

When they got to the airport John saw many large airplanes waiting to leave and some that had just landed. When it came time to go John said goodbye to his father and mother. When he got on the airplane a lady told him to buckle his seatbelt. She told him that they would be leaving soon.

When the airplane started down the runway John was//afraid at first. But when they were in the air he was no longer afraid. The lady gave John something to drink and a sandwich to eat. John//enjoyed the airplane ride so much that he was sorry when it was over.

After studying the types of errors made by the student on the student's passage we are able to make certain assumptions about his reading. Some of these are as follows.

There were a number of words that were not in this student's sight vocabulary since he did not recognize them instantly as indicated by the pauses before these words (*visit, thrilled, seatbelt, afraid,* and *enjoyed*). However, it is evident that he does possess good word analysis skills since he was able to read the words (in most cases) after pausing briefly. He made repetitions a number of times before words at which he had paused. He may have been doing this to attempt to get partial clues from the context, but may have also done it simply to stall for time while he analyzed the word (knowing that the teacher would be likely to tell him if he did not get the word in a reasonable amount of time). He seemed to have difficulty with the word "when" which he constantly called "then." It should be noted, however, that when this word appeared in a context that required it be used instead of "then," he usually went back and corrected it, making a repetition to do so.

Knowing these things about this student's reading ability would provide us with some valuable information for instruction such as the following:

1. He needs to develop a larger sight vocabulary which could best be done through wide reading. We know that a word becomes a permanent "sight word," or in other words is instantly recognized, after the student has encountered it from at least twenty up to as many as 140 times. Since he is, in most cases, able to get

unknown words right because of his good use of word analysis skills, it would be safe to assume that he would be saying these unknown words correctly and thus improve his word recognition ability.

2. As just stated he makes good use of word analysis skills, including use of context; therefore, he would probably need very little more diagnosis or remediation in this area.

3. He should be given help with the word "when" so that he does not substitute it for "then."

4. Although he has made a number of repetitions, it is evident that he did so only to use the context on an unknown word or to correct a word that was miscalled (in this case, "then" for "when"). For this reason it would probably not be necessary to work on the repetitions as errors, i.e., they are only symptomatic of other problems. And, when the other problems were cured, he would probably stop making repetitions automatically.

5. Although he did not know the words "visit" and "afraid" the first time he read them, he did know them when they were encountered the second time. Although most students need many repetitions of a word before it becomes a permanent sight word, it is evident that he learns new words very easily and at least temporarily retains them.

6. After pausing before "thrilled" he then said it with the accent on the wrong part of the word. If "thrilled" was in his listening-speaking vocabulary he would have probably gotten it correct from having it in a usable context and by saying it correct except for improper accent. Therefore, he would need to be given help with the meaning of this word. This might also indicate a need, depending on his grade level, for more vocabulary (word meaning) development. A word meaning test or vocabulary test such as the Oral Vocabuary subtest of the Gates-McKillop Reading Diagnostic Test would be useful in helping the examiner decide whether his oral vocabulary was equal to his grade level.

THE CLOZE PROCEDURE

The cloze procedure is another technique that is useful for placing students in graded materials or for use in selecting materials to meet the needs of a particular group of students. The procedure consists of deleting every Nth word and replacing it with a blank line. Students are to then read the material and attempt to fill in the blanks using the correct word according to the proper context of the sentence. The percentage of correct answers are then calculated and from these percentages Free or Independent, Instructional and Frustration reading levels are derived.

John Bormuth (1967 and 1968) researched the use of the cloze procedure to derive the percentage of correct answers equivalent to the Free or Independent, Instructional and Frustration reading levels and to derive information on reliability. His studies were later duplicated and validated by Earl Rankin and Joseph Culhane (1969). Rankin and Culhane stated, "The results of this replication of two previous studies tend to corroborate the validity of the comparable cloze and multiple choice percentage scores found by Bormuth. . . ." (p. 197) Rankin and Culhane also studied the validity of the cloze procedure and compared its use to that of multiple choice tests.

These substantial correlations indicate that the cloze procedure is a highly valid measure of reading comprehension. The average validity coefficient was .68. Since the multiple-choice tests took several weeks to construct, the cloze tests are preferable for measuring comprehension or readability, and they are measuring substantially the same thing. (p. 196)

More recently Margaret Jones and Edna Pikulski (1974) studied the use of the cloze procedure with a group of sixth grade students. They pointed out the fact that their study concerned sixth graders only.

Given this limitation, the data suggested that the cloze test gave a considerably more accurate reading level placement than did the standardized test. If the cloze test can approximate reading levels on an informal reading inventory as much as 70 to 80 percent of the time, its relatively brief administration time recommends its use to the classroom teacher. Not only does cloze procedure appear to provide a reasonably valid determiner of instructional reading level, but its very ease of construction and administration makes it a practical tool for teachers who have had no special training in test administration. (p. 437)

Developing, Administering, and Scoring Cloze Passages

In constructing cloze passages you could omit every third, fifth, tenth, etc. word. However, most of the research that has been done is based on the deletion of every fifth word. Blank lines of equal length are then used to replace each word that has been deleted. It should also be stressed that the commonly used percentages for determining students' Free or Independent, Instructional and Frustration reading levels are based on the deletion of every fifth word. If every eighth or tenth word were deleted, these commonly used percentages would not apply.

Passages may vary in length depending on the grade level of the students; however, for students of age levels equivalent to third or fourth grade level, or above, passages of about 250 words are often used. The entire first and last sentence are usually left intact. If passages of 250 words plus an intact first and last sentence are used, and if every fifth word is omitted, there would be fifty blanks and every blank or answer would be equivalent to two percentage points.

Cloze passages may be administered in a group situation similar to the procedure with standardized reading tests. However, in administering cloze passages there are usually no specific time limits for completion of the work.

Using passages in which every fifth word has been deleted the percentages for the various reading levels are as follows:

Free or Independent Level	=	58 to 100 percent
Instructional Level	=	44 through 57 percent
Frustration Level	=	43 percent or below

In scoring the passages only the exact word omitted is usually counted as correct, i.e., correct synonyms are not counted as being correct. Bormuth's research has shown that the overall percentages change very little regardless of whether synonyms are counted as correct or incorrect. Furthermore, if words other than the exact word omitted were counted, it would make them much more difficult to score. That is, what one teacher might consider as an adequate answer another teacher may not. Thus we would tend to lose interscorer reliability. In scoring cloze passages, however, students are not usually penalized for incorrect spelling as long as there is little or no doubt about which word was meant to be used.

A plastic overlay such as an overhead projector transparency can be made of each cloze passage with the correct answers appearing on the plastic overlay. When this is superimposed on the student's copy you can readily check the number of right and wrong answers. These can, in turn, be converted to percentages.

Using the Cloze Procedure to Place Students in Graded Materials[7]

Often a teacher receives a new student and wishes to place him in one of several different books which vary in difficulty or grade level. As an example, look at the case of a fifth grade teacher. She teaches in a school where there are several sections of fifth graders but all are simply grouped heterogeneously so that each year she can expect to receive students reading from perhaps the first or second grade level through the sixth or seventh grade level. She has a number of basal textbooks available at various levels, but each time she receives a new student she is faced with the problem of which book to assign so that the student will be reading at his instructional level. The steps she could take to effectively use the cloze procedure to help her develop testing materials for the various levels of books and then place students accordingly would be as follows:

1. Select a number of passages from various parts of each book (from six to twelve passages depending on the size of the book.) Make sure each passage begins a new paragraph and is about 250 words in length.
2. Give the tests to a group of students (25–30) from classes in which the texts will commonly be used.
3. Determine the percentage of correct answers for each student on each passage. An example illustrating this follows. For illustrative purposes, however, only ten students have been shown as taking the cloze tests concerning each of eleven passages from a particular book. The mean score for each passage is then calculated and the mean of the mean scores is determined.

The mean of the means is determined by adding all of the means and dividing by the number of means or the number of passages (in this case eleven).

$$\frac{65.4 + 48.1 + 74.0 + 39.8 + 60.4 + 42.4 + 42.4 + 25.6 + 41.2 + 73.0 + 52.0}{11} = 51.3$$

4. Select the passage score which is closest to the mean of the means. In this case the teacher would select passage number eleven since its mean score is 52.0 and the mean of the means is 51.3. In other words this passage is most representative of the book as a whole.
5. The procedure described above would be followed for each textbook that the teacher is likely to use. These cloze passages (one from each text) would then be duplicated and compiled into booklets. When a new student or group of students enters the teacher's room, each would be given a test booklet containing the cloze

[7]The explanation given in this section is based on the following source: Bormuth, John R. "The Cloze Readability Procedure," *Readability—1968*. Prepared by a committee of the National Conference on Research in English, National Council of Teachers of English.

Percentage scores made on eleven passages from
a book by each of ten students

	1	2	3	4	5	6	7	8	9	10	11
Don	66	60	72	28	62	44	28	54	52	64	42
Dwight	72	52	76	32	38	62	48	26	38	72	52
Denise	56	38	64	42	42	38	52	14	30	64	74
Syril	42	20	86	46	74	28	38	22	28	88	44
Ed	74	42	84	42	56	22	42	18	50	78	50
Rick	76	48	72	48	72	74	54	14	52	86	62
Judy	72	62	64	38	58	64	46	26	36	56	58
Jack	58	73	58	52	64	28	38	28	34	72	34
Cindy	64	38	82	38	62	42	40	26	42	84	44
Dennis	74	48	82	32	76	22	38	28	50	66	60
Totals	654	481	740	398	604	424	424	256	412	730	520

Mean score for each passage
(Total ÷ 10)   65.4   48.1   74.0   39.8   60.4   42.4   42.4   25.6   41.2   73.0   52.0

passages. When a student's score falls between 44 to 57 percent on one of these passages it should be at his Instructional level. If it is above 57 percent it should be at his Free or Independent level and if it falls below 44 percent it would be at his Frustration level.

The reliability of the procedure described above would depend on the following three factors:

1. Test Length—Longer tests will be more reliable but will take longer to correct.

2. Number of Passages Used—If a larger number of passages are taken from each book, the one chosen is more likely to be representative of the book as a whole.

3. Variance in Difficulty From Page-To-Page—Some materials vary unevenly in difficulty as they proceed. This is especially true of many textbooks other than basal readers.

Using the Cloze Procedure to Select Materials to Meet the Needs of the Students

In many states a state textbook committee selects from approximately three to five basal textbooks from the many possible choices. These books may then be purchased using state funds. At this point, however, each school district often must select one textbook from the choice of three to five that best meets the needs of the students. In other instances a teacher may be given a choice of one or more of a number of books which best meet the needs of her students. Adequacy of teacher's manuals, supporting services and materials, and the format of the material itself are all important considerations in making such a choice. The most important factor, however, is whether the students with whom the material will be used can read the material. The following steps can be used to make this decision:

1. Select a number of random passages from each book or set of material. The same length of passages as described earlier can be used.

2. Select a random sample of the students with whom the book will be used.

3. Determine the mean of each passage from each set of materials or book.

4. Then determine the mean of the means from each set of materials or book as described earlier.

5. Any materials or books that fall within the range of 44 through 57 percent would be appropriate for use at the students' Instructional level. Materials at 58 percent or above would be appropriate for use at the students' Free or Independent level, and materials below 44 percent would be inappropriate since they would be likely to be at students' Frustration reading level.

In using the cloze procedure you should also exercise a certain amount of teacher judgment when making decisions concerning the difficulty of materials. For example, if a student is highly interested in a subject, or if he has the ability to persevere, it would be permissible to consider material just below the 57 percent level as appropriate for the student to read independently. This would be especially true if several of his errors were correct synonyms.

The analysis of errors on the cloze procedure can also provide the teacher with useful information on the reading ability of the student. Although no specific procedures have been developed at this time, an informal survey of a student's answers will give practical information concerning the student's ability to read and write. For example a great deal of information can be derived about the student's ability to spell and about his overall comprehension and knowledge of the vocabulary in the passages by noting whether substitutions for the original words are meaningful synonyms or whether they are completely out of context. You can also tell whether he has been able to remember details that were given earlier in the passage by noting whether he uses these to answer questions later in the passage.

The cloze procedure has also been studied to determine its effectiveness as a teaching device. An excellent review of the cloze procedure research in this area was done by Eugene Jongsma (1971). Jongsma indicates that most teachers who simply used the cloze procedure as a teaching device without any follow-up activities or discussion found it of little or no value in "teaching" comprehension. However, he did find several studies in which student's comprehension was improved when students discussed their answers on cloze passages, i.e., why one answer was chosen over another or in the process of filling in the blanks why one blank was chosen over another.

SUMMARY

Information concerning the reading level and reading disabilities of individual students cannot be accurately derived using most group tests. For this reason teachers should learn to administer, score, and interpret informal reading inventories. Informal reading inventories can be useful in helping teachers determine students' Free or Independent, Instructional, and Frustration reading levels. The criteria used in scoring informal reading inventories is also useful in helping teachers find the "proper fit" between students and reading materials. And, by coding a student's oral reading errors teachers can often gain considerable insight into that particular student's reading disability.

The use of the cloze procedure is rapidly becoming more popular among specialists. It is valuable in determining students' Free or Independent, Instructional, and Frustration reading levels. It is also valuable for use in selecting materials to meet the needs of a particular group of students or in placing a student at the proper level in a set of graded materials. The cloze procedure has been well researched and has an advantage over informal reading inventories in that it can be administered as a group test.

Chapter 11: REFERENCES

Betts, Emmett A. *Foundations of Reading Instruction*. New York: American Book Co., 1946.

Bormuth, John R. "Comparable Cloze and Multiple-Choice Comprehension Test Scores," *Journal of Reading*, Volume 10, (February, 1967), 291–299.

Bormuth, John R. "Cloze Test Reliability; Criterion Reference Scores," *Journal of Educational Measurement*, Vol. 5, (Fall, 1968), 189–196.

Ekwall, Eldon E. "Should Repetitions Be Counted As Errors," *The Reading Teacher*. Vol. 27, (January, 1974), 365–367.

Ekwall, Eldon E., and English, Judy. "Use of the Polygraph to Determine Elementary School Students' Frustration Reading Level," Final Report-United States Department of Health, Education, and Welfare, Project No. 0G078, 1971.

Ekwall, Eldon E.; English Solis, Judy K.; and Solis, Enrique, Jr. "Investigating Informal Reading Inventory Scoring Criteria," *Elementary English*. Vol. 50, (February, 1973), 271–274.

Guzak, Frank J. "Dilemmas in Informal Reading Assessments," *Elementary English*. Vol. 47, (May, 1970), 666–670.

Johnson, Marjorie S., and Kress, Roy A. *Informal Reading Inventories*. Newark, Delaware: International Reading Association, 1965.

Jones, Margaret B., and Pikulski, Edna C. "Cloze for the Classroom," *The Reading Teacher*. Vol. 17, (March, 1974), 432–438.

Jongsma, Eugene. *The Cloze Procedure As a Teaching Technique*. Newark, Delaware: ERIC/CRIER and the International Reading Association, 1971.

Pehrsson, Robert S.U. "How Much of a Helper Is Mr. Gelper," *The Reading Teacher*. Vol. 17, (May, 1974), 617–621.

Rankin, Earl F., and Culhane, Joseph W. "Comparable Cloze and Multiple Choice Comprehension Scores," *Journal of Reading*, Vol. 13, (December, 1969), 193–198.

Valmont, William J. "Creating Questions for Informal Reading Inventories," *The Reading Teacher*. Vol. 25, (March, 1972), 509–512.

12

DIAGNOSIS AND REMEDIATION THROUGH THE USE OF INTERVIEWS

The first part of this chapter contains a discussion of the interview as a source of information from parents and students. Specific techniques are then discussed, including the pros and cons of using a checklist to guide or structure the interview. A rather good parent interview and a rather good student interview is then illustrated and discussed in terms of technique and useful information derived. A rather poor student interview is then presented that illustrates some common errors to be avoided.

THE INTERVIEW AS A SOURCE OF INFORMATION

Interviews can be an important part of the diagnostic-remedial process in some cases, especially in a clinical setting or in cases where it is evident that more information needs to be obtained concerning the home environment. Some types of information can often be obtained from an interview that will seldom become available elsewhere. It should be emphasized, however, that interviews are often time-consuming and unless the remedial reading teacher or reading clinician believes that further useful information will be revealed through the use of the interview then, in many cases, this step in the diagnostic process should simply be eliminated.

In some cases, however, a remark by the student or information gained from an initial application form (see Chapter 14) will indicate that information can be gained from parents or a guardian that would be of considerable value in working with a student. Although you will not be likely to interview the parents of every student or hold a lengthy interview with each disabled reader, there is still need for the remedial reading teacher or reading clinician to develop the ability to skillfully conduct an interview. Some types of information that can be derived from an initial parental interview that may or may not be available elsewhere are described as follows.

Parental Views of Student's Problems

After having lived with a student for a number of years while he has been in school, parents are in a unique situation to have gathered a great deal of information about a student's problems. This is especially true if the parents have other children who are not disabled readers so that they are able to make accurate comparisons. Parents are often able to accurately describe a student's problems although they may not necessarily refer to them using the same terminology that the remedial reading teacher might use.

It is also important to determine whether parents understand the severity of the problem or whether they are overly concerned to the point of constantly badgering the student. On the other hand, they may lack the necessary understanding of the problem so that they may fail to provide a proper study environment, cooperation in library activities, motivation for improvement, etc.

I recently spent several hours one afternoon diagnosing the reading problems of a beginning second grade student. This student was so hyperactive that it was nearly impossible to do the testing in a one-to-one situation. His teacher had told his mother that he "jumped around a lot and would not sit still." The mother, however, had no other children with which to compare the child and consequently believed that the teacher was overstating the seriousness of the problem. The child was referred to a pediatrician who prescribed medication to calm him down. Following this the child's performance immediately improved. The important point, however, was that through the interview I could obtain the mother's views about the condition of the child and then provide immediate feedback in terms of suggestions for remediation of his problems.

Emotional Climate of the Home

A great deal of information can be gained from parents about the emotional climate of the home by a skilled interviewer. This might include information on parental discord or sibling discord or rivalry that may be harmful to the well-being of the student.

Health Factors

Although some information can be gained about a student's health from forms or applications, it is often desirable to elaborate on certain aspects of this information through the use of the interview. For example, we often find that in discussing eye examinations a parent is often led to believe that a student has had a thorough eye examination at his school when in reality all he may have had was a rough screening test for far point vision using the Snellen chart. Or, what may appear on a form to have been a minor ear infection during early childhood may, in fact, have been a chronic infection which has constantly contributed to a student's inability to use phonics because of inadequate auditory discrimination.

It is often difficult for a parent who is untrained in both health education and reading education to realize the important relationships that may exist between the two. For this reason a parent interview should usually cover various facets of a student's health in terms of those factors that contribute to reading retardation.

Reading Material Available at Home

Most homes contain some books, magazines, newspapers, etc. available for some members of the family to read. Many family libraries, in fact, contain fairly large quantities of books which parents may tend to perceive as good reading material for their children. In a few cases this may be true, but in most cases very little of the reading material available in the home library is of an appropriate nature for a disabled reader. Through the use of interviews, the remedial reading teacher can thoroughly discuss the kinds of materials available in terms of reading level and interest and can advise parents of materials that may be more appropriate for disabled readers.

Library Habits and Time Spent in Reading

Through the use of interviews, the remedial reading teacher can also obtain a much deeper insight into the actual amount of time a student spends reading, as well as his library habits. If a student is asked how much time he spends reading, his answer is quite likely to be somewhat meaningless since he has little basis for "a lot" or "a little" in terms of comparison with other students. Furthermore, until students reach the age of eleven or twelve, they tend to have little or no accurate perception of time. Parents can, however, provide much more accurate information on such matters. Parents can also provide accurate information on students' use of the school and city library. During the interview the teacher can also provide helpful information on how parents can select books to meet the reading levels of their children.

Study Habits and Study Environment

The interview also provides an excellent opportunity to derive information concerning study habits and the study environment of a student. For example, questions such as, "Is a specific *amount* of time set aside each evening for study?", "Is a specific *time* set aside each evening for study?", "Does the student have a room of his own or is it shared with another member of the family?" often reveal a great deal of useful information. Accurate information of this nature is difficult to derive from students because of their inadequate perception of time. It is also often difficult to derive from a parent through the use of forms or applications without further questioning.

Parental Expectation

Parental expectation, of course, varies a great deal depending upon such factors as the educational level of the parents, the socioeconomic level of the parents, and to some extent religious preference of the parents. Only through the use of the interview can the remedial reading teacher begin to determine whether the expectations a parent holds for a student is realistic in terms of that student's potential and achievement. The interview also provides an opportunity for the remedial reading teacher to counsel parents in terms of realistic expectations of the student in relationship to tests that have been administered for reading level and reading potential as indicated by IQ or, better yet, as measured by ability to learn reading related tasks.

Social Adjustment

It would be difficult to derive information on a student's social adjustment as easily as it can be obtained from parent interviews by using such questions as, "Tell me about Rick's friends." "Tell me about how he gets along with his friends." "Does he have a lot of friends or does he prefer to play with one or two friends or play alone?" "Does he make friends easily?" or "Do other students seem to notice that he has a reading problem?" Information of this nature can be especially helpful if the parents have other children with which to compare the social adjustment of a specific child.

Independence and Self-Concept

The parent interview is also excellent for deriving information about the independent work habits and self-concept of a student. Questions that often elicit such information are those such as, "Can Jim seem to do work on his own or does he need someone to constantly urge him on?" Or, an open-ended statement that may tend to draw out the same or more information might be, "Tell me about Jim's work habits." Information can also be derived about a student's self-concept that may be much more difficult to obtain from the student by asking questions such as, "How does Jim feel about his reading?" "How does Jim feel about himself?" or more specifically, "What do you think about Jim's self-concept?"

Duties at Home

Students who have certain duties to perform at home are often more likely to be inclined to independently carry out work on school assignments. These duties may include such things as emptying the garbage, mowing the lawn, and washing and/or drying the dishes. Through the parent interview, information can be derived on how many of these duties a student is expected to perform as well as how well he does those that are assigned to him. The parent interview is also a good opportunity to suggest the need for such duties to build independent work habits in the student.

Sleep Habits

A partial reason for the poor performance of many students is that they do not get the needed amount of sleep. Reading clinicians often find that information that appears on applications and forms filled out by parents is somewhat inaccurate. For example, a form to be filled out by parents may ask the question, "What time does the student normally go to bed?" Although a parent, in all honesty, may answer "9:00 PM," a careful interview will often reveal that this is, in reality, the time when parents would *like* the student to go to bed. In reality, the student may often be allowed to stay up much later to watch television programs, or the family may socialize a great deal keeping the student up much later than the "desired" bedtime.

Successful Practices With the Student

An interview with a student's parents is also often helpful in uncovering methods which the parents find successful in getting the best performance from the student. This might be a simple, "Please do this for me." to a small reward for successful completion of a task. A question that often elicits this information is to simply ask, "What do you find is successful in getting Dan to do things you want him to do?"

Previous Tutoring and Results

Many students who come to reading clinics or to a remedial reading classroom have previously been tutored. The parent interview presents an excellent opportunity for the remedial reading teacher to discover the length, and to some extent, the success of past tutoring. For example, many parents will have some knowledge of the types and success of activities carried out in the past. Others may have records or examples of what has been taught which, in some cases, may provide helpful information on the types of materials and activities to use or to avoid in future work with the student.

Information can also be gained through an initial interview with students that may be difficult to gain in other ways. Some examples of the kinds of useful information that may be derived from student interviews are as follows.

Self-Concept

Studies quoted in Chapter 7 have shown the importance of a positive self-concept for success in reading. And, although inventories are available for measuring the self-concept, a great deal can often be learned about how a student feels about himself, and about his ability to read, through an interview. Statements or questions that often elicit this type of information are those such as, "Tell me about yourself." or "How do you feel about yourself when you read?"

The Student's Perception of His Reading Problem

Since it is difficult to provide help for someone with a problem, who does not recognize that the problem exists, it is often beneficial to use questions such as, "How do you feel about your reading?" or "Tell me about your reading." or even, "Do you think you have a problem with reading?" Many disabled readers, of course, recognize their problems immediately; however, a rather large percent are either hesitant to admit to having a reading problem or simply do not recognize the fact that they are disabled readers. A student who does not admit to having a reading problem or who does not recognize his problem will often need to be diplomatically shown that, as compared to other students of his age-grade level, he does have a problem. This is an essential part of the eight-step counseling procedure described in Chapter 7.

Past Experiences in Reading

The interview also provides an opportunity to question students concerning their past experiences in reading. For example, students sometimes perceive themselves as having read a great deal when further questioning may reveal that, in reality, they have read almost nothing at all on their own. To the disabled reader simply looking at pictures in magazines or looking at comic books may actually be perceived as reading. When this is the case, inaccurate answers will be given on inventories dealing with such questions. During an interview, however, the interviewer can readily tell whether the student really reads by asking such questions as, "Do you remember the name of the last book you read?" "Tell me about it." or "Can you tell me the names of some books you have read this year?" One very common characteristic of the severely disabled reader is that they have often really never read a book on their own.

Attitudes About Reading

The initial student interview also provides an excellent opportunity for the remedial reading teacher to learn more about student attitudes about reading, i.e., Does he like to read? Has he had some extremely bad experiences with reading in the past? Questions that may be helpful in eliciting this type of information are those such as, "What do you think about reading?" "What are the good things you remember about reading?" "What are the bad or unpleasant things you remember about reading?" and "Would you like to become a better reader?"

Reading Interests

Since the initial interview with a student would normally come during the first time you had a chance to meet with him alone, it is a good time to derive information on his interests and hobbies. In this way you will be able to help him find materials to read that should be interesting to him. It should also be helpful in establishing initial rapport. The initial student interview can also provide information about interests in terms of future ambitions, vocational plans, etc., all of which can work to your advantage in establishing motivation for reading.

Reading Environment

It is a well-known fact that students tend to copy their peers' and parents' habits. The initial student interview usually provides an excellent opportunity for the remedial reading teacher to learn about the student's reading environment, i.e., Does he have a quiet place to read at home? Does he see various members of his family read a great deal? and Does he generally come from an environment where reading is encouraged and rewarded?

Instructional Techniques and Materials That Have Been Used

For most disabled readers who have experienced failure with a particular program or technique it is generally a good practice to change the technique as well as the materials. For example, we do not usually teach disabled readers using a hardbound basal reader since it might very well be negatively perceived by him. During the initial interview, the remedial reading teacher can often discover which materials have been previously used with the student. Although the student is not likely to remember the publisher of the materials, or in many cases the name of a particular book, he is likely to remember the names of various characters in basal reader series he has used. In our reading center we use a sheet that lists the names of many of the characters in the most commonly used basal reading series. The interviewer can then simply ask questions such as, "Did you ever use a book about a little black dog named Tag?" or "Did you use a book about Dot and Jim?" If the student answers yes to such a question, it is then easy to identify the type of program he has used in the past. In many cases the instructional program will also have generally utilized a particular technique. In order to make use of this type of information the teacher must be somewhat familiar with the most commonly used basal reading series.

If information on technique alone is desired, it can usually be obtained by using such questions as, "How did your teacher teach you words?" or "What did your tutor do to teach you to sound out words?" Although in some cases answers to such questions may be rather vague, further questioning will usually clarify techniques that have been somewhat successful and unsuccessful in the past.

As in the case of parent interviews, the student interview can also provide useful information on such things as the amount of television the student watches each week, his duties at home, the time he goes to bed, etc.

INTERVIEW TECHNIQUES

An interview can often be highly successful, or on the other hand, can be of little value depending on the skill of the interviewer. The skills needed for successful interviewing can quite easily be learned with a little experience and the mastery of a few important techniques. Some of the techniques that tend to help make interviews successful are as follows.

Make the Interviewee Comfortable

Whether it be an initial interview with a student or a parent, it is important to attempt to make the person being interviewed as comfortable as possible. Skilled counselors are usually masters at doing this from having had a great deal of practice.

In interviewing parents one of the best ways to make them feel comfortable is to get right down to business as soon as possible. They have usually come to the interview because they are concerned about their son's or daughter's reading disability. After an initial greeting and seating them in a comfortable chair, a statement such as, "Tell me about Don's reading" is often sufficient to break the ice and get them started talking.

In interviewing students the same situation exists. In this case, however, you may wish to simply say, "Tell me a little something about yourself." This leaves the student free to talk about anything he would like to. Sometimes, however, such a broad question is too open-ended for a student who may reply, "Like what?" In this case you may wish to prompt him further by saying something such as, "Well, tell me about some of your hobbies, your pets, or what you like to do."

It also works well to seat the student or parent to the side of your desk facing you rather than behind it so that the desk does not form a barrier between the two of you.

Use Open-ended Questions

Any experienced college professor or elementary or secondary school teacher knows that it is easy to set the tone of a class in the first few minutes. For example, if a professor begins the class with a lecture and then suddenly tries to hold an open discussion he is likely to get little or no response for the first few minutes after the lecture session. The same principle holds true for interviewing. When only questions are asked by the interviewer which call for one or two word answers, a tone or mood is often set which is difficult to change. On the other hand, when the interviewer begins the interview with open-ended questions he usually sets a tone or mood in which the interviewee does much of the talking. All that is often needed is a nod of the head, an occasional "Yes" or "I see" or perhaps another open-ended question to redirect a response that has gone off in an undesired direction.

Some good examples of open-ended questions or statements for parents are, "Tell me about Tim's reading," "Why do you think he developed the problem?" or "How does he feel about his ability to read?" Some good examples of open-ended questions or statements for students are, "Tell me about your reading," "Why do you think you have this problem?" or "Tell me about what you like to read about."

Give the Interviewee Time to Think

Since most of us are used to talking with various people on a daily basis, it may, at first, seem almost foolish to emphasize the fact that we often do not give the interviewee time to respond. For the untrained interviewer, however, there is often a tendency to feel the need for a constant or unbroken chain of verbal exchanges. You should remember, however, that in an interview the interviewee is often asked to recall information and/or to gather his or her thoughts and express opinions about matters of which he or she might not have been given much thought in the past.

In interviewing parents of disabled readers there is seldom any difficulty eliciting information since they have, in most cases, pondered many of the questions that you are likely to ask. On the other hand, in the initial interview with students it is often more difficult to get them to "open up" and begin talking. During this time inexperienced interviewers often feel ill-at-ease and feel compelled to keep a constant conversation going. It is often helpful to ask an open-ended question or to make an open-ended statement such as, "What do you think about your reading?" or "Tell me about a book you have read" and then give the interviewee ample time to speak, which in some cases may be as long as fifteen to thirty minutes.

Ruth Strang who was a world renowned authority in counseling and reading once interviewed a group of high school students in front of a class that I was taking. In the beginning she asked a few questions and there were several rather long periods of silence. A little later every one of the high school students began to open up and became extremely talkative. After the interview, Dr. Strang left and invited those of us in her graduate course to continue interviewing the high school students. One of the first questions asked of the students was why they suddenly became so talkative after being so quiet at first. They all agreed that Dr. Strang (whom they, of course, did not realize was an expert in interview technique) seemed so helpless in her quest for information that they all felt a compassionate need to help her out by talking! We can all learn a lot from Dr. Strang's technique when we find a rather shy student.

Refrain From Expressing Negative Judgment or Attitudes

Whether you are interviewing a parent or a student you are not likely to agree with everything they say. In the beginning stages of your work in counseling either students or parents, it is often wise to refrain from expressing negative judgment or attitudes about opinions which they may express. This is not to say that as an interviewer you should not be honest in your approach, but that you may need to temporarily hold back some rather strong convictions you may possess about certain subjects. For example, many parents berate comic books and tend to express the opinion that they would really prefer that their children did not read them. On the other hand, most reading specialists would probably tend to feel that if a student has not developed the reading habit, then even the reading of comic books would be a positive step in the process of improving his reading. During the initial interview, however, it is often wise to refrain from strongly disagreeing with the interviewee as they will soon begin to sense this disapproval and will, in turn, tend to attempt to terminate the interview. There will usually be ample time at a slightly later date to counsel either the student or parent about reading habits, etc. about which you believe a change in attitude is essential.

Avoid the Use of Technical Terms

Most of us have been in a situation where someone used a term that we were not familiar with when they spoke to us. We are then faced with the sometimes embarrassing situation of either having to ask what the term means, or of trying to "bluff" our way through the situation until the subject is changed. This sort of situation should be avoided when interviewing students and especially parents. Those of us who have been working in education for a number of years often find ourselves asking questions in which terms somewhat unfamiliar to parents are often used. For example, we might ask questions such as, "How does Rose-Marie get along with her siblings?" "Has she had any traumatic experiences during the past year?" or, "Do you perceive her as an introvert?" Some people may not know what "siblings," "traumatic," "perceive," and "introvert" mean. This would, of course, cause a great deal of embarrassment for the person being interviewed.

Promise Only What You Know You Can Accomplish

If you were told by a medical doctor that you had cancer, you would immediately ask such questions as, "What are my chances for recovery?" "How long will it take to recover if I do recover at all?" and "How much is it likely to cost?" Parents who have either known for some time or have recently discovered that their child has a reading problem are also naturally concerned about the remedial reading teacher's prognosis for success. This is quite natural. However, there is a natural tendency to tell parents that everything will probably be all right in a short amount of time. A number of research studies have demonstrated the effectiveness of remedial reading but most of these same studies have also demonstrated that for most disabled readers, and especially those that are severely disabled, regaining the ability to read at grade level is a long-term process.

Although parents should not be discouraged from seeking remediation for a disabled reader, they should be made to understand that most disabled readers need to learn what normal achieving students are learning in addition to making up for material they have already missed. And, in most cases, this is likely to be a rather long process. A fairly good rule of thumb, although with many exceptions, is that with good tutoring a student may take nearly as long to recover from a reading disability as he took to develop it.

It is easy to explain to a parent that their child made more rapid progress than you expected. On the other hand, it is much more difficult to explain to a parent, after a long period of tutoring, that their child has made little or no progress. For this reason parents should be reassured that progress from tutoring is usually forthcoming, but that the rate of achievement is likely to vary a great deal depending on such factors as potential for learning and the severity of the problem.

Do Not Undersell Your Own
Knowledge and Abilities

People, of course, vary a great deal in their self-concept as well as in their innate and acquired abilities. However, to some extent society demands that we display a certain amount of modesty in our dealings with other people. The display of a certain amount of modesty in some areas is only natural; however, the remedial reading teacher should not be so modest in her dealings with parents that the parents, in turn, tend to lose faith in the ability of the teacher. Most well-trained reading teachers realize that we really know very little about certain types of severe reading disability. When students appear to exhibit the symptoms of what is often termed "dyslexia" or severe reading disability, it is usually wise to tell parents that progress in remediation with this type of student is often very slow and that educators as well as people in other professions know very little about the exact type of remediation for these kinds of problems. However, if you are well-trained and realize these limitations exist, you should also convey to parents that you are as capable of dealing with the problem as any other "expert" in the field. You may also wish to convey to parents that if symptons appear that you are not qualified to deal with, you will recommend someone who is more qualified in a certain area.

The essential point, however, is that you do not sell yourself short. No one wants to think they are taking their car to a second-rate mechanic let alone placing their child with a second-rate remedial reading teacher.

Avoid the Use of Words that May Offend Older
Students

Every family appears to use various titles to be used in referring to members of the family. When dealing with students of any age, and especially older students it is usually a good practice to refer to parents as "Your mother and/or father" since these are terms that are not cold and yet do not appear childish to some students.

Avoid the Use of Overly Personal Questions

In interviewing parents you are likely to find a great deal of difference in their willingness to discuss certain factors that may affect the well-being of a child. It is usually a good idea to avoid the use of personal questions such as, "Do you have a happy marriage?" or "Is there a great deal of conflict in the home?" If a parent feels such matters are important, the same information can usually be elicited by open ended, less personal questions such as, "Can you tell me something about the emotional climate of your home?"

Refer to Yourself In the First Person

Most experienced interviewers and teachers of older students refer to themselves in the first person. However, there is a tendency for inexperienced interviewers and/or teachers of very young children to refer to themselves as "Mrs. Smith" or "your teacher." This is often quite offensive to middle grade and older students and should simply be avoided.

Ask Only One Question at a Time

A common mistake of inexperienced interviewers is asking several questions at one time. This reminds me of a presidential press conference where an overzealous reporter asks the President a whole series of questions to which the President may reply, "Now which question do you want me to answer?" or if he chooses to be less sarcastic he may attempt to answer the first one or two questions, but then finds himself asking, "Now what were the other questions?" Parents or students being even less adept at remembering a series of questions or in even remembering that more than one was asked usually answer the first question or the one they feel is most important anyway.

Remember That Children Usually Have an Inaccurate Perception of Time and Numbers

Teachers who are accustomed to working with older students (especially past the age of twelve), unless they have younger children of their own, often fail to realize that younger children have a very inaccurate perception of time and numbers. For example, in interviewing an eight or nine-year-old student about how much time he spends watching television there would be very little use in simply asking a question such as, "About how much television do you watch each week?" If you really wanted to get a much more meaningful answer to such a question, you should ask specific questions such as, "What programs did you watch last night?" or you can go through the *T.V. Guide* with them and have them tell you specifically which programs they have watched.

The same procedure should be used when dealing with numbers in asking questions such as, "About how many books have you read this year?" It would be much more meaningful to attempt to make a list of some of the titles that the student remembers.

THE USE OF INTERVIEW GUIDES AND/OR CHECKLISTS

The use of an interview guide or checklist may be advantageous or detrimental depending upon the skill with which they are used. The interviewer who uses a very detailed checklist has the advantage of being reminded to cover all of the information on the checklist. However, the use of a detailed checklist often has the disadvantage of structuring the interview to the point that it is likely to prevent the interviewer from carefully listening to the responses of the interviewee. When this happens, the interviewer may fail to capitalize on certain significant remarks made by the interviewee.

Personal experience indicates that the use of a broad outline of points to be covered in an interview is often helpful but that when the outline or checklist becomes too detailed the spontaneity of the conversation is too often lost. For this reason I would suggest that a broad outline similar to the following be used when interviewing students.

1. Interests
   1.1. Clubs-church
   1.2. Hobbies
   1.3. Friends
   1.4. How is spare time spent?
2. Student's Attitudes
   2.1. Toward his family
   2.2. Toward his school
      2.1.1. Favorite subjects and least liked subjects
   2.3. Teachers
   2.4. Friends
   2.5. His reading problem
      2.5.1 Is he aware of the problem?
      2.5.2 What does he think the problem is?
      2.5.3 How much trouble has he had?
      2.5.4 Why does he have this difficulty?
      2.5.5 What are his suggestions for solutions?
      2.5.6 Does he enjoy reading?
      2.5.7 What does he read?
      2.5.8 Does he go to the library or own books of his own?
   2.6 The student
      2.6.1 How does he feel about himself in relation to other students?

A similar broad outline may be developed for use in interviewing parents; however, in many situations parents will have filled out a form or application before meeting with the teacher. If such a form or application exists, it may, to some extent, serve as a guide to the interview, i.e., for clarifying information on the student's health history, the onset of his reading problem, etc. The outline used with parents will also vary depending on whether it is used in the public schools, a university clinical situation, etc. For these reasons you should develop an outline that is meaningful to you in your own particular setting.

EXAMPLES OF INTERVIEWS

The first interview is one that took place between a university student (I) who was meeting the mother (M) of a ten-year-old boy (Tim) for the first time. During this interview the boy was not present. After interviewing the mother, the university student asked the mother to wait in the Reading Center while he held a short interview with the boy (T).

As you read these two interviews, try to note any techniques used by the interviewer that seemed to work especially well. Secondly, note whether any information was gained that would have been helpful in working with the boy. Also note any techniques that could be improved upon.

INITIAL INTERVIEW WITH
TIM'S MOTHER

1. I: Who recommended Tim for the Reading Center?

2. M: Mrs. Jones had a friend who came here, so several of the teachers and I came up here last spring. She thought it would be good for Tim because they tried numerous things to pinpoint the problem.

3. I: It's difficult to pinpoint the problem, especially if you don't have the right tools. What seems to be his main problem?

4. M: I don't really know. I can't put my finger on it. He has difficulty, or maybe he doesn't even try to attack the words. I suppose he has the tools for them because he was tutored by the reading resource teacher.

5. I: Oh yes!

6. M: For a while she felt that he was not happy because there were too many other children and she was afraid that he felt he was being categorized as being not too bright. He has the tools for breaking the words down so let's take him out of the tutoring and see how he does. He comprehends well, and if you read the material to him, he gets it.

7. I: He understands what is read to him?

8. M: He doesn't. Usually I read the whole chapter for him but I don't do his reading for him because they do this at school but say he doesn't really want to read. He doesn't take books. We belong to one of the Weekly Reader Book Clubs because he wanted to, and those books just sit on the shelf. They are only third grade books, but he doesn't even try to read any of them. They are pretty long, and he really wants something quick so that he can read.

9. I: He wants something that's real quick to read?

10. M: He doesn't attempt words that he could sound out if he tried. He just guesses at them and it's frustrating for me because I think that he can do better. Sometimes I wonder if his memory needs training because he can look at those vowels and he can't tell you what they should say. I think by now he has had it every year.

11. I: You say he has a hard time with the vowel sounds, what about the consonant sounds?

12. M: Well when he first went to the second school, which was in the second grade, the teacher that tested him said that he had trouble with consonant blends and things like this but she could not find anything like dyslexia.

13. I: This is something that I will not categorize Tim with. Teachers are getting away from this kind of thing.

14. M: Well he can't read fast enough which makes all his achievement tests low because he doesn't get through with them. He does have a good attitude about school. I think the teachers say he does.

15. I: What kind of work does he do in his other subjects?

16. M: Well he doesn't. . . . I don't know. He doesn't knock himself out studying, but he does try.

17. I: He tries?

18. M: Yes, he really puts forth lots of effort in everything he tries to do. My helping him at home is not good because I get frustrated, and he is in tears. When he was in the second grade I really tried hard to work with him and it just made both of us nervous wrecks and so in the third grade my husband said just let him go. Either he makes it or doesn't. You're not doing him any good by yelling.

19. I: I see. When did you notice that he had a specific reading problem?

20. M: Well, after first grade and he came out with a "C" in reading, but he couldn't read.

21. I: He couldn't read at all?

22. M: Really! Like nothing could he read, and he was not happy.

23. I: I imagine that this upset him.

24. M: I think that he felt kids would make fun of him and that stuff. They did this usually coming home because he couldn't keep up in reading with the rest of them so we put him in another school and Mrs. Jones was his teacher. She would work with him on Saturdays. At the end of the year she realized how little he had to work with. She said that he had a poor foundation, or just had not retained what was given him. There was talk of holding him back but they said he had the ability to do the work and that he would be bored with doing the same things. She said he was just like being in a cage and couldn't get through to the material. So he doesn't mind school. He gets upset if he gets too much homework and stuff, but he is eager to learn. He was just beside himself to come here. Tim said that he could not wait until he could read better.

25. I: Yes. That's a good sign. I'm glad he wants to come to the Center. Now tell me, how does he get along with his peers?

26. M: He gets along with them all right, but since he goes to the new school, he doesn't know too many children in the immediate neighborhood. He goes

out and rides with them sometimes. I somehow think that he is a little immature because . . . I don't know. I used to think that he was.

27. I: He just turned ten?

28. M: Yes, just in August. I think maybe he depended on everybody because he is the third child and close to the others. The daughter just older than him took care of him. She did things for him. He didn't have to talk as early as everybody because we were always handing him things. Of course, he had the hearing problem also.

29. I: Yes.

30. M: So I thought maybe he couldn't hear all of these sounds or distinguish them when writing and spelling. But supposedly his hearing is in normal limits now. The loss that he does have would be with the female voice range which could have given him lots of trouble earlier in his schooling.

31. I: Yes, in the first grade when he was being taught to read. When did this problem get cleared up completely?

32. M: About two years ago. Whenever he gets a cold, his hearing level goes down. But he is not taking allergy shots now. We just give him an antihistamine when his nose starts running and this does all right. He hasn't had too many ear infections, but there is scarring in the ears. But anyway, the hearing tests indicate that his hearing is within the normal range.

33. I: I noticed this on the application. The previous hearing difficulties could have been a problem.

34. M: But in two years he should have been able to pick up all of the sounds.

35. I: He might have missed something important at the beginning that could be the cause of his reading problem. I hope to find out what it is. Do you read to Tim?

36. M: Well, we used to. My daughter used to read to him quite a bit. Nobody has read to him in the past year or so, and I'm sure he had less read to him than the older ones because I haven't had the time with the other children, you know. This isn't the right thing to do. Maybe there was too much television. So he didn't bother to read or listen.

37. I: Are his study habits good at home?

38. M: Oh no! I don't think they are particularly good. When I ask him what homework he has, he says none. They work individually at school, so most things he finishes there, unless he really goofs something up. Then he brings it home. Since he started this year, I haven't had to push him. I think he has kept up. Of course, he hasn't been in school very long. And he seems happy and content. Interested, at least. He comes home with tales on what has gone on. So I think he is enjoying school. The other night he said that he surely will be glad to read better, so he can read the instructions on model airplanes.

39.   I: That is interesting. Does he like most models?

40.   M: Yes, and he likes animals and stuff like that. He liked to read about them, but most of the books that have the information he wants are a little beyond him.

41.   I: Books that are more scientific?

42.   M: He just can't break down the words. They are just too much. He is unfamiliar with the words so they don't mean anything to him. His vocabulary is not very big. I am sure that is why he can't read very well. I feel his vocabulary is not as good as most children his age. He seems to understand anything we say . . . all of us talking. He doesn't act like he can't understand.

43.   I: That's good. Besides his ear problem, has he had any other serious illness?

44.   M: No. Just the normal things.

45.   I: Does Tim do much reading at home?

46.   M: Not much. He joined the book club, but this lasted only a year. He would never finish a book. I tried to encourage him to go to the shelf and read these books, but he wasn't too interested.

47.   I: Is he interested in the comics?

48.   M: Oh yes. Peanuts he always reads. Of course they don't have very much writing on them.

49.   I: But it is still reading!

50.   M: But he doesn't have much interest in books. If there's nothing good on television, he might sit down and read. He reads comic books like Archie once in a while. I think they're really trash.

51.   I: What are his favorite television programs?

52.   M: The cartoons of course. (laugh)

53.   I: Does he spend much time watching them?

54.   M: Yes.

55.   I: Does Tim like sports?

56.   M: He is not very well-coordinated. He can't catch a ball well or anything like that. I'm sure that's partly our fault. We're not very athletic. His older brother gets very put out with him because he can't catch any-thing. So he doesn't want to bother. I think Tim would like to except he doesn't do as well as the others and this discourages him. The kids always make comments you know.

57.   I: Kids are sometimes cruel to each other.

58.   M: Yes, they are. But Tim still tries. He goes to the "Y" three times a

week . . . he took a physical fitness test, but did not do very well. He clobbered himself on the chin ups and other things. He doesn't do them at home. He did not ride a bicycle as soon as most children do. There are a lot of hills . . . but he rode a lot this summer with a friend.

59. I: Does he make friends easily?

60. M: He doesn't go seeking new friends. Of course not going to the same school as the other kids in the neighborhood is probably bad. On the weekends he stays at home or tries to get a friend from his school to play with that lives near us. Or he plays with his younger sister.

61. I: I see. Well, would it be all right to get Tim's record from the school.

62. M: Yes. They said they would be glad to send the center anything that could be of help.

63. I: That is good. You've been very helpful. I appreciate the time you have given me very much. Thank you.

INITIAL INTERVIEW WITH TIM

1. I: Is there anything you want to start off telling me, Tim?

2. T: Well, I'm in the fifth grade and ten years old.

3. I: What do you like to do?

4. T: I like to draw and I like to do drama at school, and paint and do papier-mâche, and all kinds of art.

5. I: What kind of drawing do you like to do the best?

6. T: Of people.

7. I: Of people?

8. T: No, I don't really draw them. I just make them up.

9. I: So you just make them up. That's fine. What about your paintings?

10. T: On my paintings, I paint like pictures of the sun, or the grass or something like that.

11. I: I see. Getting back to people, what kind of people do you like to draw?

12. T: Well some of the time I draw them with glasses and big ears, and big chins and things like that . . .

13. I: Funny things? They call them caricatures.

14. T: Yes, that's right.

15. I: What about the drama? Do you like to act?

16. T: Yes.

17. I: In plays?

18. T: Well, in school the teacher would give us . . . well, like make up a pantomime for this week. So we would go home and practice and think of a pantomime, and practice it, and the next time we had drama we'd do it. And we'd talk about it and make criticisms about it. So the next time we could do better.

19. I: What do you like to pantomime?

20. T: Well, really it depends . . . like in a . . . like something sad, well not sad, but something unusual . . . that doesn't happen very often or . . .

21. I: Something out of the ordinary. Something that doesn't happen every day. What are some of the things you have done?

22. T: Well, today, I don't know if this is very unusual, but I took a chair, put a table in front of me, act like the chair was a car and the table was a car and it was in the middle of the road, and I tried to get it out of the way . . .

23. I: Did they guess what you were doing?

24. T: Yes.

25. I: What do you think about the way you read?

26. T: Well, I don't know. I guess I'm not too good?

27. I: What do you mean by that?

28. T: Like when I read, I don't know some of the words.

29. I: What do you do when you come to a word you don't know?

30. T: Sometimes I try to sound it out, but I can't do that most of the time.

31. I: Do you think we should try to help you with that?

32. T: Yeah, that would be alright.

33. I: Do you think you usually understand what you read?

34. T: Yeah, if I know all the words.

35. I: Well, tell me something, Tim. Do you like to read?

36. T: Yes.

37. I: What's your favorite story? Or books?

38. T: Well, there's not many books about monkeys, but I'd like to read about monkeys.

39. I: What about the other animals?

40. T: Well, I like them, too. Dogs, cats, yes I like them, too, and I like to read about them too—and Vikings.

41. I: And Vikings. You must like the seamen. What do you like about the Vikings?

42. T: Well, I'm not sure. They just seem brave and all this and they only liked to live in the cold and I also like things about the cold, like walruses, eskimos and things like this.

43. I: That's good. That's real good. That's interesting. I imagine you know a lot of things about these subjects.

44. T: Well, not a lot. But some.

45. I: You said you liked the Vikings. The Vikings were seamen. Do you like the sea?

46. T: Yes.

47. I: Have you ever seen the ocean?

48. T: Not in true life. In pictures and movies. But that's all.

49. I: That's good. Tim, how do you do your homework?

50. T: We don't have very much homework. We most of the time just do it at school.

51. I: What are you reading about in geography?

52. T: Well, we don't have geography. It's social science.

53. I: I see.
54. T: We talk about people and things. In the fifth chapter, they talk about prehistoric things. They told us in the first of it that this railroad company was digging . . . well, making a path and came across this great, big, old rock; tried to move it aside, and when they did, there were five skeletons there. And skulls. And this guy . . . I forget what they called them . . well, dug farther down and found their bodies . . . and this guy thinks they were prehistoric men.

55. I: That's kind of in line with your animals. You know they find a lot of prehistoric animals. Maybe we can find you some good books and stories about these.

56. T: Yes, that would be alright.

57. I: How much time, Tim, do you spend reading outside of school time?

58. T: Not much. Well, most of the time after school, I want to read but most of the books are too easy for me, or they're just . . . There's this one book that I was starting a long time ago. I stopped that one cause I was reading this other book, and another book, and finally I just read the same one to where I was before and quit.

59. I: And you quit at the same place?

60. T: Yes. That's all I read.

61. I: Well, maybe one of these days you can go back and finish it. Can you tell me the names of any of the books you have read this year?

62. T: Well, let's see. (pause) I guess I just can't remember any. There was this other book I told you about; but I guess I really don't read very much.

63. I: Do you think you would like to read if we could find something about monkeys or other animals?

64. T: Sure.

65. I: How much time do you spend watching television?

66. T: Well, let's see. On school days not much. Well, maybe a little, but most of the time I'm wrestling with my brother. Or I'm drawing pictures.

67. I: So you don't spend too much time watching television during the weekdays. How much do you watch during the weekends?

68. T: On Saturdays I watch quite a little bit. I like to watch Disney and things like that. I watch the cartoons.

69. I: Who do you watch them with?

70. T: If Sarah's awake, I take her down with me on Saturday. I put her by the door where all of the toys are. She plays and I watch her and the T.V. She's my baby sister.

71. I: Tim, how do you get along with your brothers and sisters?

72. T: O.K. most of the time.

73. I: Who do you play with most of the time?

74. T: My brother.

75. I: How old is he?

76. T: He's fourteen.

77. I: What are some of the things you do?

78. T: Sometimes we make up things. Like I made a model of this mummy and we decided like it was the year 2000 or something and I'd look at the mummy and say some mumble jumble, and say mummy, come alive. And really, most of the time we pretend that a lot of things are real. And my brother likes to read also.

79. I: Does your brother read to you?

80. I: Well, he used to. But now he doesn't.

81. I: Tim, I think that's about all for now. I want you to know that we're going to help you as much as possible during the coming weeks. You certainly have been helpful to me and I thank you.

In the preceding interviews you will note that each statement made by either the interviewer or interviewee is numbered. These numbers are used in the following discussion in directing your attention to specific techniques and/or information derived from the interviews.

INITIAL INTERVIEW WITH TIM'S MOTHER

Note the following techniques used by the interviewer:

3. Use of open-ended question to elicit what Tim's mother believed was his most important problem.

5. Use of simple statement, "Oh, yes!" to get her to continue talking.

7. Question to clarify whether the mother believed Tim had a problem with comprehension.

9. Repetition of enough of the mother's statement to clarify what she meant *and* to let her know he was listening very carefully.

11. Further questioning to clarify the problem.

13. The interviewer diplomatically tells the mother that we really don't know what dyslexia is and the term should probably not be used.

17. Very short repetition (in question format) to encourage the mother to continue.

21. Clarification of what the mother meant by "couldn't read."

23. Neutral statement that encouraged the mother to continue.

29. Again, the use of a simple "Yes" to get her to continue.

31. Clarifying question.

41. Again, simple statement that encourages her to continue.

49. Interviewer does not disagree but lets her know that reading comic books is still reading, which indicates his approval.

57. Encouraging, reassuring remark.

63. Expression of appreciation for mother's help.

Now note the following useful information derived from the interview:

4. Mother indicates that Tim probably has problems with word attack skills.

4. He has been tutored before.

6. Indication of a possible problem with low self-concept.

6, 8. There is some confusion about whether he comprehends well.

8. Tim does not read much, if any, on his own.

8. There is some indication that he might be encouraged to read if the interviewer could find something short that Tim could finish in a small amount of time.

10, 12. Indication of difficulty with consonants, consonant blends, and vowels.

14. Mother perceives Tim's reading speed as too slow.

14. Tim has evidently maintained a good attitude towards school.

18. As with many parents, mother cannot work well with her son on his reading problem.

20, 21. Indication of a problem from the very beginning of school.

24. More indication that Tim may have a low self-concept.

26. Mother believes he may be immature.

28. Some indication that he may lack initiative and/or self-confidence.

30, 32, 34. Possible explanation for Tim's poor start in school and a possible problem at the time he was interviewed. (Tests performed at the Reading Center indicated that he still had a severe hearing loss. When this was corrected he improved very rapidly.)

36, 38. Some indication of poor study habits.

38. An indication of Tim's desire to learn to read better.

38, 40. Information on what might motivate him to read.

42. His mother believes his vocabulary is low.

46. Indication that Tim does very little reading at home.

48. An indication that he does like comic books.

50. Mother has a negative attitude about comic books.

56. More indication of the possibility that Tim has a low self-concept.

60. Some indication that he does not have many friends his own age to play with at home.

INITIAL INTERVIEW WITH TIM

Note the following techniques used by the interviewer:

1. Use of open-ended question to let Tim talk about anything he wished to talk about.

3.   Another open-ended question to draw the student out.

5–23.   Interviewer indicated deep interest in Tim's interests and thus helped establish rapport.

25.   Open-ended question to uncover Tim's perception of his reading problem.

27.   Further pursuit of Tim's perception of his reading problem.

29.   Question to verify Tim's perception of his reading problem.

31.   Solicitation of Tim's commitment that he needs help.

33.   Diagnosis of Tim's perception of whether he has a comprehension problem.

35–47.   Eliciting of information on reading interests.

55.   Solicitation of Tim's commitment to read about things he is interested in.

57–61.   Questioning to find out whether Tim really reads on his own. Note that in (61) the interviewer "pins him down" so to speak and discovers that Tim really doesn't read any books at all.

81.   Assurance is offered that the interviewer will help him as much as possible, but no promises are made that cannot be kept.

Now note the following useful information derived from the interview:

4–24.   Considerable information is obtained about what Tim likes to do in his spare time.

26.   Information is obtained on Tim's perception of his ability to read.

28–34.   Information is obtained on Tim's perception of his reading problem.

34–48.   Information is obtained which should be helpful in locating materials that Tim should be interested in reading.

50.   Information is obtained on the amount of homework required by the teachers in the school he attends.

58–62.   Student does not read anything that is not required.

66–70.   Information on how free time is spent.

72–80.   Information on relationship with siblings.

Although psychologists often tell us that we should not teach by showing examples of what not to do, I have chosen to use one more example of an initial student interview that illustrates some of the problems beginning teachers encounter in learning proper interview techniques. As with the case of the two preceding interviews, it will be discussed more thoroughly at the end. However, as you read it, be sure to note the tremendous difference between this interview and the preceding student interview because this student did not practice the interview techniques discussed earlier in this chapter.

In this case the interviewer was also meeting this nine-year-old student, Danny, for the first time. An interview had already been conducted with his mother.

INITIAL INTERVIEW WITH DANNY

1. I: Hi, Danny. I'm Mrs. Stevens. How old are you?

2. D: Nine.

3. I: Nine years old, boy, that's getting up there, huh? What grade are you in?

4. D: Fourth.

5. I: Fourth grade. Did you have any trouble finding UTEP?

6. D: Ummm, yeah.

7. I: Did you help your Mother?

8. D: Nope.

9. I: You didn't.

10. D: Nope.

11. I: She didn't know the way and I told her you probably could help her. Is this your first time here?

12. D: Uh huh.

13. I: It's kind of big, huh?

14. D: Uh huh.

15. I: Think you'd like to come here someday?

16. D: Uh huh.

17. I: Go to school when you're all grown up and out of high school.

18. D: Uh huh.

19. I: Think you might, huh?

20. D: Uh, huh.

21. I: Well, where do you go to school?

22. D: Edwards.

23. I: Edwards, where is that—at Biggs Field?

24. D: Uh huh.

25.   I: Do you live on post?

26.   D: Nope.

27.   I: You don't? Where do you live?

28.   D: Biggs Field.

29.   I: Biggs Field. I know where that is. We used to live at Ft. Bliss. Do you know where Ft. Bliss is?

30.   D: Uh huh.

31.   I: Do you go there often?

32.   D: Uh huh.

33.   I: Just to the P.X., huh.

34.   D: Uh huh.

35.   I: That's a fun trip, huh? Do you participate in sports, play football, baseball?

36.   D: Used to.

37.   I: Which one—football or baseball?

38.   D: Football and baseball.

39.   I: You are not playing football this fall, huh?

40.   D: Uh huh.

41.   I: I understand your brother is playing and you wanted to go to the game to-night.

42.   D: Uh huh.

43.   I: That's just a practice one though, isn't it?

44.   D: Uh huh.

45.   I: So that's not too great, just to miss the practice one.

46.   D: I don't know.

47.   I: Do they play their games on Saturdays?

48.   D: Uh huh.

49.   I: Bet you won't miss many of them, huh? You won't miss any of them.

50.   D: Maybe, I got to go to catechism.

51.   I: Oh, you have to go to catechism on Saturdays. Well, what else do you do?

52.   D: Nothing.

53.   I: Nothing? Do you know why you came here?

54. D: Nope!

55. I: You don't know. Mother didn't tell you.

56. D: Nope!

57. I: Well, this is the Reading Center. Do you have any trouble with reading?

58. D: Uh huh.

59. I: Maybe you can tell me about it. What trouble do you have with it?

60. D: Hard words.

61. I: Hard words—when you say hard words, are they little words or big words?

62. D: Big words.

63. I: Big words, and why do they give you so much trouble?

64. D: (cannot be understood) They all have twenty letters.

65. I: They all have what?

66. D: Around twenty or fifteen letters in them.

67. I: They all have too many letters. Oh boy, you didn't learn how to break them down into syllables?

68. D: Yep.

69. I: Oh, you do know how.

70. D: Uh huh.

71. I: And they still give you trouble, huh?

72. D: Uh huh.

73. I: Anything else about them that causes trouble?

74. D: Nope!

75. I: Nothing else. How about little words, do you have any trouble with them?

76. D: Sometimes.

77. I: Sometimes. Do you know when?

78. D: Once in a while.

79. I: Once in a while, Umm. Can you tell me one little word that gives you trouble? (Long pause) Can't think of any?

80. D: Nope!

81. I: Maybe there aren't too many that's giving you trouble, huh, just a few.

82. D: Uh huh.

83. I: How long have you had trouble with reading? Do you know?

84. D: About a year.

85. I: About a year. Do you have trouble talking about what you've read?

86. D: Nope!

87. I: When you read, you can tell the teacher what you have read, what it was all about.

88. D: Uh huh.

89. I: O.K. Does your teacher give you any special help with your reading?

90. D: Nope!

91. I: Do you have any trouble when you are in the reading group?

92. D: Nope.

93. I: You don't. Do you have any special friends?

94. D: Yeah.

95. I: How many?

96. D: Five.

97. I: Boys or girls?

98. D: Boys.

99. I: All boys.

100. D: Uh huh.

101. I: Does the teacher help you with your reading if you have trouble?

102. D: Sometimes.

103. I: Sometimes. Well, what does she do when she doesn't help you? What do you do? Well, what does the teacher do?

104. D: She just sits around.

105. I: She just sits around.

106. D: Uh huh.

107. I: Does she let you figure the word out on your own or does she help you?

108. D: She helps me.

109. I: She helps you with it. What do you like to read, Tom? I'm sorry, I called you Tom. That's my little boy's name. Dan, what do you like to read?

110. D: Books.

111. I: Any special kind of books?

112. D: Nope!

113. I: No special kind?

114. D: Nope!

115. I: Do you like comic books?

116. D: Yep!

117. I: How about books on sports, football players?

118. D: Yeah! (Appears to be excited)

119. I: Can you tell me one that you have about a football player maybe.

120. I: (long pause) You don't know, huh?

121. D: I know one but I can't . . . I don't know his name.

122. I: Who is it about—Oh, you don't know the football player's name.

123. D: Uh huh.

124. I: Ummm, it wouldn't be Roger Staubach would it?

125. D: (Negative headshake)

126. I: No.

127. D: Nope.

128. I: Ah, is he an offensive player or a defensive player?

129. D: Defense.

130. I: Do you know which team?

131. D: Yep.

132. I: Dallas.

133. D: Nope!

134. I: Which one?

135. D: Minnesota.

136. I: Minnesota. Oh, boy I can't, I don't know many on the Minnesota team. O. K. Tom, I keep saying Tom. That's not great. O. K. Dan, can you tell me anything else about reading that bothers you?

137. D: Nope!

138. I: No! Can you tell me anything else that you like to do?

139. D: Nope!

140. I: Well, do you particularly like coming out here to the Reading Center?

141. D: Yeah.

142. I: Did you know I was a teacher?

143. D: Nope!

144. I: I am. Your Mother said she thought you knew. I teach first grade. What do you think about that? (Pause) They're all the little ones, huh?

145. D: Uh huh.

146. I: Is Mrs. James your friend?

147. D: I don't know. (very low)

148. I: Huh?

149. D: I don't know.

150. I: Did you like going to the special reading classes?

151. D: Uh, huh.

152. I: You did. Did they help you?

153. D: Yeah.

154. I: How about Mrs. Edwards? Is that her name?

155. D: Used to be.

156. I: What's her name now?

157. D: Her name is—(unfinished) She was it after school was out. Let's see, I'd go every Saturday.

158. I: You would go every Saturday to her.

159. D: Uh huh.

160. I: And she would help you with reading.

161. D: Yep.

162. I: At her house.

163. D: Yep!

164. I: Did you like that?

165. D: Yep!

166. I: What did she help you with? Do you remember? What did she have you do?

167. D: She'd write cards and write words on them and then I have to read it.

168. I: Read the word—she would write words on the card and you would have to read it.

169. D: Uh huh.

170. I: Did you ever read any stories?

171.   D: Nope!

172.   I: Did you ever learn any sounds? Did she just write letters and have you say the sounds?

173.   D: Uh huh.

174.   I: Were you pretty good at that?

175.   D: Yeah!

176.   I: How about ending sounds?

177.   D: Nope!

178.   I: You weren't good at those?

179.   D: Nope!

180.   I: Oh, well, we'll have to work on the ending sounds then, huh?

181.   D: Uh huh.

182.   I: Right! Can you think of anything else that we'll have to work with? Can you think of anything that Mrs. Edwards did with you that you didn't get too good at that maybe I can help you with?

183.   D: Nope!

184.   I: You can't? O.K. Do you think that maybe the next time we talk you'll be able to think of something else I can help you with other than ending sounds? O.K.?

185.   D: O.K.

186.   I: Can you think of anything else I need to know?

187.   D: Nope.

188.   I: O.K.

As you have, no doubt, realized this interviewer fell into the trap of dominating the conversation and failed, in most cases, to use open-ended questions. This resulted in a setting in which most of the student responses were one-word utterances such as "Uh-huh" or "Nope." Other problems encountered were as follows:

3.   Failure to use open-ended questions and allow student time to think.

17.   Interviewer talks down to student.

35.   More than one question at once.

45.   Argumentative statement that the student doesn't really believe.

55.   Interviewer again talks down to student as she might to a pre-school child.

59.   This is a good open-ended question, but when the student said "Hard words" the interviewer instead of saying, "Tell me more" actually took away the in-

centive of the student to give more thought and his own explanation of his problem.

67. The interviewer expresses an assumption that may or may not be valid.

81. The interviewer again puts words in the mouth of the student.

83. This statement should have been pursued in terms of the student's perception of why *he* thought he had had trouble with reading for just "one year."

103. Three questions at once!

109. The interviewer not only forgets the student's name but infers that he reminds her of her "little boy."

136. The interviewer again forgets the student's name.

144. Although there is nothing wrong with being a first grade teacher, it is not necessary, or probably wise, to emphasize this fact when working with a fifth grader who may tend to think that a first grade teacher can only teach "little boys and girls."

172. In this statement, as in a number of other instances, the interviewer practically tells the student how to respond.

188. The interview is ended very abruptly.

SUMMARY

Learning good techniques to use in interviewing students as well as parents is an important skill that should be practiced and developed by the remedial reading teacher. The interview cannot only supplement the use of applications and questionnaires but can, in many cases, bring out information that may not readily become apparent. There are a number of techniques, which if successfully applied, can help the interviewer obtain useful information by making the interviewee feel at ease, and thus enhance his or her responsiveness to the questions of the interviewer.

13

THE ADMINISTRATION OF THE REMEDIAL READING PROGRAM

This chapter begins with a discussion of the roles and responsibilities of various types of reading specialists and the importance of two-way communication in defining these roles. This is followed by a discussion of ways in which the remedial reading teacher, the administrator, and parents can extend their help in the remedial reading program. Suggestions are then given for selecting and scheduling students. Following this, suggestions are given for developing facilities for and evaluating the remedial reading program. And, in conclusion, the International Reading Association's recommendations are presented for a code of ethics and qualifications for reading specialists.

THE ROLE OF THE READING SPECIALIST

A number of titles exist for various types of reading specialists depending on the role they are expected to serve. The International Reading Association suggests four main roles as follows:[1]

A. *Special Teacher of Reading*
   A Special Teacher of Reading has major responsibility for remedial and corrective and/or developmental reading instruction.

B. *Reading Clinician*
   A Reading Clinician provides diagnosis, remediation, or the planning of remediation for the more complex and severe reading disability cases.

C. *Reading Consultant*
   A Reading Consultant works directly with teachers, administrators, and other professionals within a school to develop and implement the reading program under the direction of a supervisor with special training in reading.

D. *Reading Supervisor*
   A Reading Supervisor provides leadership in all phases of the reading program in a school system.

It should, of course, be remembered that in many schools and school systems

[1]Reproduced by permission of the International Reading Association from a brochure entitled, *Roles, Responsibilities, and Qualifications—Reading Specialists.* Professional Standards and Ethics Committee of the International Reading Association, Newark, Delaware.

any one reading specialist may take on a dual role and serve as both a special teacher of reading and as a reading consultant or as a combination of reading clinician and reading consultant, etc.

Need for Clarification of the Role of Reading Personnel

Problems sometimes arise, especially in the case of newly assigned reading personnel, when their roles are not clearly defined. The defining of roles should also be a two-way process. That is, the reading specialist and the administrators and teachers with whom she will be working should all perceive the reading specialist's job in the same way. As previously mentioned, however, problems are often created when there are diversified concepts of the role of reading personnel.

The problem of diversified concepts of the role of the reading consultant was illustrated by Richard Wylie (1969), who surveyed 100 classroom teachers and 100 reading consultants chosen randomly from four New England states. Wylie's questionnaire returns came from teachers in twenty-two communities and from consultants in sixty-three communities. Wylie asked several questions of consultants, but two which seem of importance in illustrating this problem were as follows:

> *Question 1.* "In what areas of reading instruction should the consultant give aid to the new teacher?" (p. 519)

The results of the teacher's and consultant's answers are shown in Table 13–1.

Table 13-1. Comparison of teacher versus consultant views on Question One

Teacher	Frequency	Percent	Consultant	Frequency	Percent
Materials	66	85	Materials	72	86
Demonstrations	63	81	Time allotments	68	81
Diagnostic and corrective procedures	63	81	Grouping	64	76
Grouping	58	74	Scope of total program	63	75
Interpretation of test results	57	73	Interpretation of test results	63	75

It is important to note that the teachers expected the consultant to come into their classroom or at least be invited to demonstrations on "how" to teach certain concepts or how to use new materials. On the other hand, the reading consultants did not even consider this as a part of their job. The teachers also expected help with diagnostic and corrective procedures, but again, the consultants did not perceive this as a part of their job. It is also important to note that the consultants were concerned with time allotments and the scope of the program, whereas the reading teachers did not consider these factors in evaluating this phase of the reading consultant's job.

Question 2. "How should the consultant extend this aid?" (p. 519)

The results of the teacher's and consultant's answers to this question are shown in Table 13–2.

Table 13-2. Comparison of teachers versus consultant views on Question Two

Teacher	Frequency	Percent	Consultant	Frequency	Percent
In-service education; small groups, grade level meetings	73	94	In-service education; grade level meetings	79	94
Demonstration teaching	70	90	Orientation program early in year	74	88
			Bulletins or letters to teachers	70	83
Free time to visit other classrooms— schools	67	86	Suggestions courses to take	61	73
Frequent meetings with reading specialists	62	79			
Workshops	44	56	Workshops	50	50

It should be noted that the teachers again believed that the consultant should do demonstration teaching and should free time to visit other classrooms within their school or other schools within the systems. Yet the consultants evidently believed that these two items were not a part of their role. It is interesting to note that the kinds of activities that the consultants believe they should perform would seldom take them out of their office and *never* take them into the classrooms to work with children.

The information presented by Wylie, as well as my own experience as a consultant and in working with other consultants, leads me to believe that before any new reading personnel begin their duties there should be a clear-cut understanding, in writing, of the role of various reading specialists. Further evidence of this problem was emphasized by Hesse, Smith, and Nettleton (1973), who studied content area teachers' view of the role of the secondary reading consultant. They stated,

> There are differences in perceptions regarding the role of secondary school reading consultants among administrators, content area teachers, and reading consultants.
>
> Perceptions differ within content area departments as well as among content area departments.
>
> Because these differing perceptions do exist, for the sake of harmony and staff

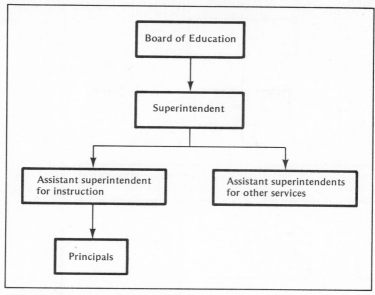

Figure 13–1. Administrative structure showing the position of the principal

> morale, it would probably be wise to assess the perceptions of all concerned personnel before the responsibilities of the consultant are decided. (p. 215)

Problems are also likely to arise in terms of the school administrative structure when dealing with various reading specialists. For example, the elementary school principal usually knows exactly how he fits into the administrative structure of most school programs. His position might be illustrated as in Figure 13–1. Likewise the remedial reading teacher, or even the person who serves a dual role of part-time teacher and part-time consultant within one school, usually falls into a common administrative structure as in Figure 13–1 because, they would simply extend below the principal as shown in Figure 13–2.

However, the problem sometimes becomes more complicated when we are dealing with full-time supervisors or consultants who work in several schools. In these cases the administrative structure may be more like that shown in Figure 13–3.

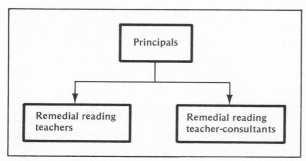

Figure 13–2. Administrative structure showing the position of the remedial reading teacher or teacher-consultant within any one school

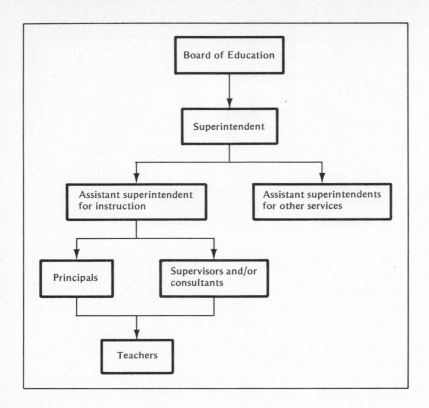

Figure 13–3. A school administrative structure in which there are supervisors and/or consultants

In a situation as shown, (Figure 13–3) problems are often encountered when teachers realize they really have more than one "boss." Further difficulties are often encountered in that there are no clear lines of authority between each school principal and various consultants and/or supervisors. Where the consultant and/or supervisor and principal are both congenial and diplomatic this may matter very little. However, when the consultant and/or supervisor possess beliefs considerably different from those of the principal, it is often difficult for both to work harmoniously together.

The point of this, of course, is that before any reading position is filled, a needs assessment in reading should be conducted in the school or school district. In conducting this assessment you should involve all school administrators who are likely to be involved in working with the program, some classroom teachers, and, if possible, a competent consultant from a college or university who is familiar with the training of various reading specialists, their duties, titles, etc.

The duties and title of the reading specialist will depend upon such factors as the size of the district, the number of schools with which the specialist will be expected to work, the competencies of teachers already within the school system, other reading specialists already employed and their duties and titles. However, in order to clarify the roles of various types of reading personnel and the duties they may be expected to perform, the guidelines which follow should be helpful.

Responsibilities of Each Reading Specialist[2]

A. **SPECIAL TEACHER OF READING**
- Should identify students needing diagnosis and/or remediation.
- Should plan a program of remediation from data gathered through diagnosis.
- Should implement such a program of remediation.
- Should evaluate student progress in remediation.
- Should interpret student needs and progress in remediation to the classroom-teacher and the parents.
- Should plan and implement a developmental or advanced program as necessary.

B. **READING CLINICIAN**
- Should demonstrate all the skills expected of the Special Teacher of Reading and, by virtue of additional training and experience, diagnose and treat the more complex and severe reading disability cases.
- Should demonstrate proficiency in providing internship training for prospective clinicians and/or Special Teachers of Reading.

C. **READING CONSULTANT**
- Should survey and evaluate the ongoing program and make suggestions for needed changes.
- Should translate the district philosophy of reading with the help of the principal of each school into a working program consistent with the needs of the students, the teachers, and the community.
- Should work with classroom teachers and others in improving the developmental and corrective aspects of the reading program.

D. **READING SUPERVISOR**
- Should develop a system-wide reading philosophy and curriculum, and interpret this to the school administration, staff, and public.
- Should exercise leadership with all personnel in carrying out good reading practices.
- Should evaluate reading personnel and personnel needs in all phases of a school-wide reading program.
- Should make recommendations to the administration regarding the reading budget.

The guidelines shown above are those suggested by the International Reading Association. As stated previously, however, many school districts do not differentiate among the four specific titles as clearly as suggested here. For example, in the Parkway School District in Chesterfield, Missouri, a great deal of the time of personnel working in reading is spent in teaching remedial reading. However, these reading specialists do not limit their time exclusively to the teaching of remedial

[2]Reproduced by permission of the International Reading Association.

reading. A description of the role of the reading specialist (1972) in the Parkway School District follows:[3]

ROLE OF THE READING SPECIALIST
PARKWAY SCHOOL DISTRICT (1972)

I. Remedial Reading
        The primary role of the reading specialist in the Parkway School District is the instruction of pupils possessing deficient reading skills in relation to their reading potential.

A. Instruction
    1. In the development of a caseload the following steps are taken:
        a. A reading survey test is administered to these pupils to determine present reading ability.
        b. The reading specialist, working with the staff, will obtain referrals of pupils considered to be disabled readers.
        c. Guidance counselors will assist the reading specialists in administering individual intelligence tests to these pupils.
        d. A "potential caseload" consisting of no less than 50 pupils is developed according to state guidelines. Normally, a total of 30 to 40 pupils will receive instruction at any given period of time, beginning with top priority pupils.
        e. Pupils may be phased out of the program when it is felt that further remedial instruction is no longer considered beneficial.
        f. The required state forms are to be submitted to the State Department by October 15.
    2. A course of study is prescribed for the pupils selected to receive remedial reading instruction in the following manner:
        a. A battery of diagnostic tests is administered to determine individual strengths and deficits.
        b. The reading specialist attempts to identify the pupil's preferred modality of learning.
        c. Awareness of pupil's attitudes and interests assists the specialist in motivating learners.
        d. Necessary data collected from the home, classroom, medical or other sources, as well as information used in the remedial process, will be placed in the folder required by the state for each child.
        e. A remedial reading program is planned for each student through the use of materials designed specifically to meet the needs of individual pupils.
        f. Cooperative planning by the reading specialist and the classroom teacher is necessary to provide methods and materials to be used in the classroom which correlate with the remedial reading program.
    3. Schedules will be developed with the following consideration:
        a. A schedule is established for remedial classes on the basis of common needs for groups no larger than six students.
        b. Time will be allotted for staffing with teachers, clinic personnel, and other non-teaching responsibilities.

[3]Reproduced by permission of the Parkway School District. Marti Sellinriek, Language Arts Coordinator.

4. Instruction is conducted according to the following procedures:
    a. Parents are informed of pupil's inclusion in the remedial reading program.
    b. Instruction is given to remedial pupils, individually or in small groups.
    c. Evaluation is a continual process and the individual instructional program may be changed when necessary.
    d. During the process of remedial teaching, feedback and recommendations to the staff concerning the students should also be continuous.
    e. Pupil's progress will be reported to parents through conferences or other means of communication.

5. Referrals
    a. Referrals to the Parkway Right to Read Reading Clinic will be made when deemed advisable by the reading specialist.
    b. A reading specialist may initiate referrals to Special School District or other outside agencies according to Parkway guidelines.

B. Advisory and In-Service Education
    The reading specialist serves as an advisor in the remedial area by working with administrators, teachers, guidance counselors, and the Parkway Right to Read Reading Clinic in the following ways:
    1. To interpret the role of the reading specialist and the remedial program.
    2. To help teachers administer diagnostic tests and interpret test results.
    3. To assist the administration in planning the budget in the area of reading.
    4. To help teachers understand materials used for remedial purposes.

C. Curriculum Development
    In the area of Remedial Curriculum Development, the reading specialist has the following responsibilities:
    1. To assist the district in development and/or location of materials for use by the disabled reader in the content areas.
    2. To assist the district in development of programs for the early identification of student's potential learning style as it relates to the teaching of reading.
    3. To provide orientation for new members of the reading specialist staff in the Parkway School system.
    4. To participate in providing programs designed to improve the skills of the total reading staff. This may be done in cooperation with the staff of the Parkway Right to Read Reading Clinic.
    The reading specialist will have a secondary role of assisting in the areas of corrective and developmental reading instruction.

II. Corrective Reading
    A. Instruction
        1. The reading specialist will introduce corrective materials for classroom instruction, upon teacher request.
        2. Emphasis will be placed on the use of alternative methods of instruction as a means of preventing reading disabilities.
        3. Follow up and evaluation of materials introduced shall be conducted.

    B. Advisory and In-Service
        The reading specialist will serve as a resource teacher in the following activities:
        1. Assists classroom teachers in initiating diagnosis of pupils and interpreting results of data collected.
        2. Assists the teacher with classroom organization for corrective instruction.

3. Observes disabled readers in a classroom situation, upon teacher request.
4. Evaluates pupil progress and performance in cooperation with the classroom teacher.
5. Assists in the evaluation and selection of appropriate materials utilized by the classroom teacher for corrective instruction.
6. Provides demonstration of new methods and materials.

   C. Curriculum Development
1. The reading specialist will evaluate programs presently in use for corrective instruction.
2. New programs will be evaluated to assess their appropriateness for use in corrective instruction in Parkway.
3. The reading specialist, in conjunction with the Parkway Right to Read Reading Clinic, will give assistance to teachers in developing corrective reading techniques.

III. Developmental Reading
   A. Instruction
      The role of the reading specialist is to become familiar with the developmental programs of each assigned school. This will allow the specialist to make suggestions for pupils' past reading experiences and present abilities.

   B. Advisory and In-Service
      In helping teachers, at their request, to initiate and develop reading programs in their class groups, assistance will be given in an advisory capacity toward a diagnostic approach to developmental reading instruction. This method would include the following activities:
1. Reviews current information available from individual pupils.
2. Obtains new information about the pupils.
3. Selects a teaching approach (personalized, basal, etc.).
4. Groups pupils for instruction.
5. Selects appropriate materials.
6. Plans periodic evaluation to assess the need for changes in materials or grouping.
7. Assists teachers in developing goals and planning budgets in the area of developmental reading.

   C. Curriculum Development
      The reading specialist:
1. Serves as a liaison between the classroom teacher and the language arts coordinator.
2. Assists teachers to become familiar with new methods and materials.
3. Plans and develops special reading projects.
4. Interacts with the director of Research and Planning in those areas involving reading.

Role of the Reading Specialist

Priority Chart:
1. Primary responsibility
2. Secondary responsibility
3. Advisory responsibility

	Instruction	Advisory and In-Service Education (within each school)	Curriculum Development
Remedial Reading	1	2	2
Corrective Reading	2	2	2
Developmental Reading	3	3	3

The position of reading specialist in the Parkway School District involves much more than simply being a teacher of reading. In that district the reading specialist might be considered as a "Special Teacher of Reading," "Reading Clinician" (since all teachers are highly trained in the clinical aspects of reading), "Reading Consultant," and in some ways these same people take on the duties of "Reading Supervisor" as outlined by the International Reading Association.

Evidence on the importance of task competencies that count among reading specialists was presented by V. V. Garry (1974). Garry developed an extensive list of various competencies using a research of the literature, interviews with reading authorities, interviews with advisors from the State Department of Education and from reading specialist training institutions. Garry's list of task competencies were then presented to randomly chosen reading personnel who were requested to assign a degree of importance to each task competency. Task competencies were rated on a scale of five through one. From a total of fifty competencies, twelve were rated in the highest quartile. These twelve were as follows:

1. "Helping teachers plan and provide corrective and remedial reading instruction and suggesting remedial techniques for disabled readers both in the classroom and special reading program."
2. "Teaching small groups of disabled readers."
3. "Assisting in interpretation of standardized and informal reading test results."
4. "Assisting classroom teachers in diagnosing and analyzing students' strengths and weaknesses in various skills areas."
5. "Diagnosing and recommending treatment for more complex and severe reading disability cases."
6. "Referring pupils with special problems to proper agencies such as guidance and psychological services."
7. "Providing guidance in determining extent of reading retardation by utilizing various procedures."
8. "Providing guidance in selecting and identifying candidates for remedial reading classes or a reading clinic."
9. "Providing guidelines and practical assistance for evaluating student progress in remediation."
10. "Suggesting and demonstrating use of instructional materials and procedures to teachers."
11. "Selecting and developing materials to promote higher level reading competency."
12. "Encouraging, helping, and stimulating teachers to use different strategies of teaching reading such as programmed reading language-experience, individualized reading." (pp. 609–612)

It is important to note that in the Parkway School District, as well as in the study just quoted, the reading specialist is not expected to perform any one very specific role such as "Remedial Reading Teacher" only. This is a healthy situation since it allows the reading specialist, whether referred to as a remedial reading teacher or not, to perform a role in which there is more communication between the classroom teacher and reading specialist. This communication, of course, provides an opportunity for the reading specialist to provide for more effective in-service education and inevitably to influence a school's reading program to a greater extent.

How Should The Remedial Reading Teacher Extend Her Help?

A traditional method in which the remedial reading teacher extended her help was to simply "set up shop" in a room and schedule students to come to her room for a specified period of time one or more days each week. Although this particular mode of operation often works quite well, it often does not lend itself to opening two-way channels of communication. For example, in this type of situation the remedial reading teacher often fails to visit the homeroom of many of the students in her class and thus misses the opportunity to coordinate the work of students with their homeroom teachers. In such a case there is also little opportunity for the teacher to provide the kind of information that classroom teachers need and want as indicated earlier in this chapter.

In a school system where reading specialists have specific titles, such as a Reading Supervisor who oversees or supervises the entire program, a Reading Consultant who provides in-classroom demonstrations and other kinds of help, it may be more practical to have special Remedial Reading Teachers who spend the greater proportion of their time in simply working with disabled readers. In such cases the Reading Consultant may take on many of the responsibilities for in-service education and, in some cases, may serve as a liaison person between the remedial reading teacher and the classroom teachers.

Some school systems have also found it quite feasible to use mobile reading laboratories which can be moved from school-to-school. These laboratories are usually trailer houses or campermobiles that have been converted to reading laboratories by removing much of the original equipment and replacing it with bookshelves, study carrels, small tables and chairs, provisions for audiovisual equipment and viewing areas, etc. Where a remedial reading teacher is expected to work in several schools on a rotating basis, the investment in a mobile laboratory often proves less costly on a long-term basis since there is not the necessity to duplicate rooms and equipment in several different schools.

In such a case the mobile laboratory is simply moved to a new school two to three times weekly and all facilities become immediately available after a main power cord for electricity has been attached. This also allows the remedial reading teacher to concentrate on providing only one attractive display of bulletin board materials and eliminates the upkeep and cleaning of two or more rooms. Most teachers working in such a situation also report a great deal of enthusiasm on the part of the students in being housed in this type of facility.

A more modern approach in which the remedial reading teacher can extend her help is to simply go into the classroom teachers' own rooms to work with disabled readers. It also enables the remedial reading teacher to observe the student in his own natural environment and allows the remedial reading teacher to work and coordinate assignments much more closely with the student's classroom teacher. It also allows the remedial reading teacher to demonstrate diagnostic procedures and remedial techniques within the classroom setting thus creating excellent rapport and providing in-service training for classroom teachers. Carroll Green (1973) studied the attitude of teachers toward children. She found that both the behavior and attitudes of teachers improved when the remedial reading teacher or reading consultant actually went into the classroom to work with children. She stated, "When teachers received help in improving their skill in working with the children in the classroom, three out of five demonstrated behavorial changes and four out of five improved their score on the attitude test." (p. 2) This type of operation, however, requires that the remedial reading teacher be very flexible in her approach to working with students and often requires the transporting of a considerable amount of materials from classroom to classroom.

Still another method that is proving worthwhile is to allow classroom teachers free time to work in the school's reading center or reading clinic either during a particular part of the day or for a semester or more of time. School districts providing such opportunities for classroom teachers usually hire a permanent substitute teacher to take over the duties of the classroom teacher while she is on extended leave in the reading clinic.

In a situation where the classroom teacher works in the reading clinic for one or more periods of the day it allows for a great deal of coordination of the remedial program of the classroom teacher and the reading clinician. And, whether the classroom teacher is released for only one or two periods, or for an entire semester or year, it provides an excellent opportunity for the classroom teacher to learn a great deal about materials and techniques that can be useful in corrective teaching in her own classroom.

The type of operation you choose will, of course, depend upon the size of your school system, and the amount of materials, funds, and facilities available. Perhaps more important, however, it will depend upon the present reading specialists and their willingness to work within a given situation.

THE ROLE OF THE PRINCIPAL AND OTHER ADMINISTRATIVE PERSONNEL

In an excellent article Sidney Rauch (1974) makes the point that the success of reading programs does not depend on any one special method, text, or type of organization within the classroom. Rauch lists basic characteristics of a successful administrator. These are as follows:

1. The administrator should be knowledgeable about the reading process. His own experience as a classroom teacher, his observation of extremely competent teachers, enrollment in graduate courses in reading, attendance at conferences, or extensive reading in the field may contribute to his knowledge.

2. He takes advantage of the training and expertise of reading specialists. He recognizes his own limitations in the reading area and knows that he and his staff can benefit from the knowledge and experience of specialists. Above all, there is a close relationship between the specialist and himself.

3. He consults with supervisory and teaching personnel before new programs are in-

stituted or changes are made. Before new programs are put into operation, he makes sure that the necessary in-service training is provided.

4. He realizes that teachers are severely handicapped if materials are lacking. Therefore, he makes certain that the budget includes the basic instructional materials, as well as the needed supplementary texts and other aids.

5. He encourages and supports experimentation and innovation. He is never satisfied with the status quo. At the same time, he doesn't abandon a successful program because of publicity given a "new" reading method, or because some school board member confuses exploratory research with a definitive study.

6. He has the support and respect of the community as a person and as an educational leader. (pp. 298–299)

In addition to those qualities listed above, other essential abilities or qualities that the administrator should possess are as follows:

1. He should be thoroughly familiar with his State Department of Education's recommendations and/or requirements as well as those suggested by the International Reading Association for the training and background of various types of reading specialists.

2. He should not only have the support and respect of the community for his reading program, as mentioned in number six above, but should consistently strive to make parents knowledgeable about the school's remedial reading program.

3. He should schedule adequate time for remedial reading teachers for conferences with students, parents, classroom teachers, and all other staff personnel directly related to the reading program.

4. He should encourage and provide for continual cooperative evaluation and take necessary steps to improve the program.

5. He should take the initiative in developing a professional library accessible to all teachers.

Rauch also lists a number of excellent suggestions for administrators. I have paraphrased some of these and added others as follows:

1. Study and learn all that is possible about reading. Observe reading specialists in action and observe the classroom reading instruction of master teachers. Rauch also lists the following books as being excellent reading material for the administrator:

Aukerman, Robert C. *Approaches To Beginning Reading.* New York: John Wiley and Sons, Inc., 1971.

Chall, Jeanne. *Learning to Read: The Great Debate.* New York: McGraw-Hill Book Company, 1967.

Newton, J. Roy. *Reading In Your School.* New York: McGraw-Hill Book Company, 1960.

Otto, Wayne, and Smith, Richard J. *Administering the School Reading Program.* Boston: Houghton-Mifflin Company, 1970.

Robinson, H. Alan, and Rauch, Sidney J. *Guiding the Reading Program.* Chicago: Science Research Associates, 1965. (p.299)

2. As mentioned previously, Rauch makes the point that there is a specific need to clarify the role of various reading specialists. The various reading specialists should know exactly what is expected of them and administrators and classroom teachers

should view their roles in the same way. Rauch suggests that a job description for each type of reading specialist be developed similar to that of the one shown previously for the Parkway School District.

3. Provide for continuous in-service training, not just in the form of lectures from "experts" or college professors but in the form of demonstrations. The most successful in-service programs have been those that actively involved the teachers in the day-to-day experiences given in in-service training sessions over an extended period of time.

4. Provide for effective use of audiovisual materials and other facilities and/or materials needed by both classroom and remedial reading teachers.

5. Recognize that reading is a complex process and that what works with one student may or may not work with another. Provide an open environment where some structure is maintained, yet where experimentation based on research is encouraged.

In conclusion, I would strongly agree with Rauch who states, "An administrator who knows about the reading process, who takes advantage of the training and expertise of reading personnel, and who recognizes the many factors that determine reading progress can mean the difference between the success or failure of a school reading program." (p. 300)

PARENTS' ROLE IN THE REMEDIAL READING PROGRAM

An area often neglected by the remedial reading teacher is in the active involvement of parents in the remedial reading program. Some ways in which parents can and should help their children are as follows:

1. By creating within the home a reading atmosphere in which a time and a place for home reading is provided. This might be a time when every member of the household agrees that there will be no radio, television, or, if possible, no visiting friends. This would also include the responsibility of making sure that adequate reading material was provided.

I have always required my own children to go to their room at least an hour before I thought they should be asleep. This has always been called "quiet time." They were encouraged to read, but not required to. However, during this quiet time nearly all of their time has always been spent in reading.

2. By helping the child develop habits of regularity in eating, sleeping, studying, and attending school.

3. By encouraging home responsibilities to develop feelings of satisfaction from successful accomplishments.

4. By exhibiting a genuine interest in the school and in the child.

5. By maintaining a relaxed, cooperative attitude toward the child's reading without the exertion of undue pressure.

6. By developing experiential background by taking and discussing excursions, such as trips to the zoo, planetariums, plays, parades, and sporting events, which will

assist in developing language facility and a background of experiences for comprehension.

7. By supporting students' interest in hobbies such as stamp collecting, model building, collecting matchbook covers, pamphlets, animal raising and care, etc. all of which require reading.

There seems to be a great deal of controversy as to whether parents should actually attempt to teach their children at home. There is also considerable disagreement on whether disabled readers should be asked to read to their parents. There are, in reality, no pat answers to such questions. For example, some parents are able to work with their children and maintain a completely relaxed manner. Yet other parents, including some who are teachers, simply cannot work with their own children without creating a great deal of tension. One of the best ways to decide whether to recommend whether parents should work with their child is to simply ask them whether they have the kind of working relationship that is conducive to good teaching. It is also a good practice to ask the student how he feels about having one or both of his parents tutor him.

There is also no pat answer as to whether a student should be asked to read to his parents. Again, however, if the student wishes to read to his parents, and the parents are willing to be patient and calm there is usually some benefit to this activity. Since many disabled readers have a low sight vocabulary caused from a lack of wide reading experience then multiple exposure to many words through oral reading is likely to be somewhat beneficial. Parents should generally be advised to simply tell children words they do not know, rather than to tell them to "sound it out." In most cases, if the student knew enough about word attack skills to analyze a new word he would do so without being told.

SELECTING STUDENTS FOR
REMEDIAL READING

Although the selection of students for participation in the remedial reading program may appear to be an easy matter, there are, in reality, a number of problems involved in the process. For example, in the selection process questions with which you are likely to be confronted are as follows: Who will make the initial recommendations and the final decision as to which students will actually be included in the program? Will number of years of reading achievement below grade level be used as a measurement of reading disability? Will reading potential or expectancy be considered? And, what types of tests will be used to determine the degree of reading impairment?

Problems in the Selection Process

One of the first steps in the initial selection process is to arrive at an acceptable definition of a disabled reader, or a reader who is a a candidate for remedial reading. One approach to this problem in the past has been to simply use a specified number of years of reading achievement below grade level (in many cases two) as the lone criterion for placement in the remedial reading program.

A number of authors such as Charles Ullmann (1969) have pointed out that "years below normal grade for age" is a vague measure and is likely to result in a somewhat misleading picture of the prevalence of reading disability. Ullman states,

> Whenever a fixed amount of grades or years below normal is set for defining reading disability, a progressively larger percentage of children, of each succeeding grade to which that standard amount is applied, will be defined as having a disability. This is due principally to deceleration in the average growth curve and the consequent reduction in the size of the steps from one grade to another. . . . It is no more appropriate to describe the gain between Grades 8 and 9 as equal to the gain between Grades 2 and 3, than it is to describe a 35-year-old man as 25 years taller than his 10-year-old son. (p. 557)

Another way of looking at this problem is on the basis of the percentage of knowledge lacking from normal, or 100 percent reading achievement. For example, a beginning third grader should have gained two years reading knowledge, i.e., one year in going from the beginning to end of the first grade and another year in going from the beginning to end of the second grade. If this student is two years retarded in reading he would have an achievement level of 1.0 (not really 0.0), or in other words, he would have 0 (zero) percent reading knowledge. But a student at the beginning sixth-grade level should have gained five years of knowledge. If he is retarded two years from his expected level he is still five minus two (5−2), or 3/5, or a 60 percent level of reading knowledge. Obviously then, the concept of a specified number of years of reading retardation is unfair and an inadequate measure.

Another method of measuring reading retardation is by use of some measure of a student's level of achievement versus some measure of potential. James Reed (1970) illustrates the great degree of variability in using such a method. For example, he quotes a study that indicated that an eighth-grade student with a measured IQ of 120 reading at a seventh-grade level would be judged to be two years, three years, or four and one-half years retarded in reading as judged by the Bond-Tinker, Tiegs and Clark, or Harris formulas respectively. As Reed aptly states, "Obviously, the amount of retardation is not an absolute but depends on the procedure used to measure it." (p. 347)) In a concluding statement concerning his study of the use of WISC IQs to measure students' reading potential Reed stated,

> Teachers and reading specialists should view with considerable skepticism any statement pertaining to the so-called intellectual, cognitive, or perceptual deficiencies of retarded readers. Many of the statements are interesting speculations, but nothing more. The particular pattern of deficits may represent only an artifact of the investigator's decision to use one measure of potential instead of another. A child's potential for reading is probably much more closely related to the materials and methods used for teaching than some arbitrary index of expectancy. (p. 352)

The problem of errors in measurement in identifying disabled readers was also studied by Robert Bruininks, Gertrude Glaman, and Charlotte Clark (1973), who compared the percent of disabled readers identified by use of five achievement expectancy formulas. They stated,

> Analysis revealed that the prevalence of third-grade children exhibiting reading difficulties varied widely because of survey techniques and type of IQ test (verbal or

nonverbal) used in the five achievement expectancy formulas. Using a nonverbal intelligence test score, the percentage of poor readers among third-grade children ranged from 16 percent with the Bond and Tinker formula to 54.6 percent for the formula using mental age alone. (p. 180)

These authors believed that rather than use an expectancy formula, it might be more realistic to use a criterion-referenced approach to test interpretation. In doing so one would measure a student's attainment of specific reading skills with a certain reading program rather than measure his achievement in relation to a group on a norm-referenced test. They also suggested that if reading retardation is measured according to the disparity between predicted and actual achievement, it should be done in relation to how long children have been exposed to systematic instruction (as in the Bond-Tinker Formula) and that they should have a larger disparity between predicted and actual achievement at higher grade levels.

The general philosophy of identifying students who are retarded in reading as soon as possible is strongly supported by research. For example, a PREP (Putting Research into Educational Practice) summary entitled *Treating Reading Disabilities* published by the Bureau of Research of the Office of Education stated, "Early diagnosis is important, and the rule is 'the earlier, the better.' A four-year survey of some ten thousand children showed that when pupils with reading problems were identified by the second grade, they had a ten times greater chance for successful remediation than did those who were not identified until the ninth grade." (p.5)

One of the major problems the remedial reading teacher has to deal with in working with older students is a low self-concept that is apparently much more difficult to change than a similar low self-concept of a younger student. This was illustrated by Erwin and Paul Pearlman (1970) who studied the effect of remedial reading training in a private clinic. They concluded that children in grades one through three made greater gains during remediation than children in grades four through six. Children in grades one through three also maintained their gains better than the older students. The authors believed that this was because the children in grades one through three had faced fewer defeats and had maintained a greater degree of self-confidence.

A Suggested Procedure For Selecting Students For Remedial Reading

The six-step procedure, explained as follows, for selecting the final case load is illustrated in Figure 13–4. You will note that some of the procedures vary somewhat from those used in many schools today. You should keep in mind however, that the procedures used in many schools today are simply based on precedent. The following procedure may, in many cases, not be the easiest way of developing the final case load, but if followed carefully it will usually result in a successful program.

STEP 1.   The first step concerns the initiation of a procedure for receiving recommendations from teachers for those students whom the teachers believe

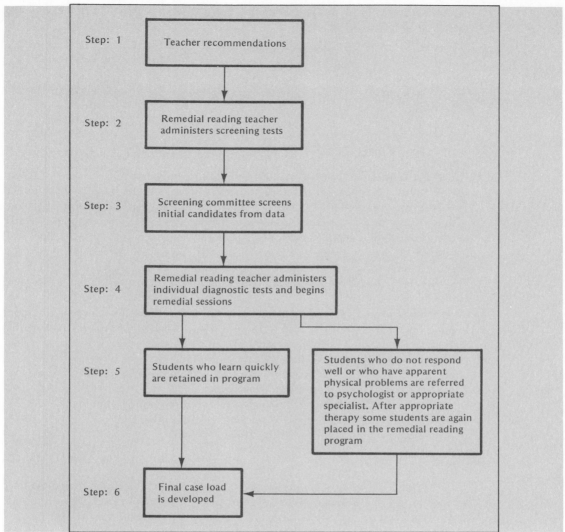

Figure 13–4. A suggested sequence for selection of the final case load

might benefit from the remedial reading program. The successful operation of this procedure will, to a large extent, depend upon the type and amount of orientation given to classroom teachers. Before attempting this step the remedial reading teacher, in conjunction with other reading and administrative personnel, must develop guidelines for the selection of students. The guidelines should include information on the degree of retardation considered minimal for selection, age-grade preferences, and methods of assessing retardation. These guidelines should then be communicated to all classroom teachers concerned with the program in an inservice meeting prior to their selection process.

As stated previously the degree of retardation should vary according to the age-grade level of the student. Some general guidelines for selection of students might be as follows:

Grade Level	Retardation for Recommendation
1	2—3 months
2	4—6 months
3	6—8 months
4	1 to 1½ years
5	1½ to 2 years
6+	2 years or more

However, most standardized reading tests will simply not measure the reading achievement level of individual students accurately enough for this type of referral. Two other approaches, either alone or in combination, seem more appropriate. One of these is to simply let teachers recommend those students whom they believe are reading considerably below grade level. The other approach is to have teachers use a graded reading passage (such as Silvaroli's Classroom Reading Inventory) appropriate for the grade level of the students in their class. Teachers can be taught how to code or at least count informal reading inventory errors. Then, based on each student's comprehension and word recognition, a decision can be made as to whether each student is reading materials at the instructional level for his age-grade level. If he is not he would, of course, be referred for further screening. In doing this all teachers need not be experts at administering informal reading inventories. The reading passages appropriate for each student's grade level can be given to teachers along with the number of word recognition and comprehension errors that are equivalent to the percentages required for placing students above or below their instructional reading level. By doing this the classroom teacher would not be required to administer a complete informal reading inventory, but merely about two (Oral and Silent) passages at the student's instructional level.

STEP 2.   The most common approach in this step is for the remedial reading teacher to administer one type of test to obtain a measure of reading achievement and another test to measure reading potential and then determine whether there is a rather large discrepancy between the two. Since, as stated previously, standardized reading achievement tests often do not measure individual student's reading achievement accurately enough to obtain a measure of achievement, this can be done more accurately with an informal reading inventory. A measurement of intelligence might then be derived by using the WISC, the Stanford-Binet, or the Slosson Intelligence Test. Reading potential is also sometimes measured by reading to the student and determining how much more a disabled reader can comprehend when listening than when reading the material himself. When using intelligence as a measure of reading achievement and reading potential, one of the more common reading expectancy formulas mentioned earlier in the chapter is used.

The remedial reading program of the El Paso public schools, which was selected as one of five outstanding Right-To-Read models in the country, uses a combination of an adapted Bond-Tinker formula and the El Paso Reading Formula. An explanation of their screening procedure follows:[4]

Pupil Selection: Refined Screening Procedures

Ranking of Potential Indices—After general screening has been completed, pupils should be ranked according to indices obtained by the use of two methods: The Adapted Bond-Tinker Formula and The El Paso Reading Formula. Their indices indicate an estimate of the ratio between a pupil's reading potential and his achievement, 100 per cent indicating his potential, and the index (expressed as a percentage) indicating his current achievement. By ranking the indices in numerical order, the teacher detects the pupils who are achieving the least in terms of their potential.

The difference between the two formulas is that The Adapted Bond-Tinker Index estimates the child's reading potential in relation to his I.Q. score, while The El Paso Reading Index estimates the child's reading potential in relation to his mathematics achievement. If the reading disability is extreme, or if a language disability exists, The El Paso Reading Index is considered the better estimate of a child's potential.

The Adapted Bond-Tinker Formula:[5]

$$\frac{R}{1Q\ (GP - 1.0) + 1.0} = B.T.I.$$

Subtract the whole number 1.0 from the grade placement (GP) of the child at the time the reading achievement test was administered. Multiply the result by the intelligence quotient (IQ) represented by a decimal figure. The resulting grade placement numeral is the pupil's estimated present potential in reading. Divide this numeral into the reading achievement score. The result is The Adapted Bond-Tinker Index which tells the degree to which the pupil's potential correlates with his achievement.

The El Paso Formula:

$$\frac{3R}{GP + 2\ (M)} = RI$$

Multiply the mathematics test score by two and add the child's grade placement which corresponds to the date on which the achievement tests were adminis-

---

[4]Reproduced by permission of the El Paso Independent School District. J. M. Whitaker, Superintendent.

[5]R = standardized reading achievement test score; IQ = highest recorded intelligence quotient; GP = grade placement at the time the achievement tests were administered (Grade placement for a grade five pupil whose test is administered in October is written 5.1 or one month into grade 5). M = standardized mathematics achievement test score; RI = The El Paso Reading Index (scores must be obtained from tests administered on similar dates).

tered. Divide the result into the reading score, which has been multiplied by three. The result is The El Paso Reading Index.

New pupils who have indices of lower than 80 percent from one or both formulas tend to produce the greatest reading gains in the reading laboratory; therefore, priority is given to these children.

Data and indices for three pupils are listed below and are followed by a tentative analysis of each child's potential.

	X	Y	Z
Reading	6.0	6.0	6.0
Grade Placement	8.0	8.0	8.0
Intelligence Quotient	.94	.85	1.05
Mathematics	8.2	6.4	5.4
Bond-Tinker Index	.79	.86	.71
El Paso Reading Index	.74	.87	.96

Note that all three pupils are in grade 8; all are reading two years below grade level; all scored as average or above average on intelligence tests. These facts basically qualify all three for remedial reading classes.

Because reading laboratory membership is limited, however, it may be necessary to eliminate one or two of the three candidates. This is accomplished by analyzing the BT and RI indices.

Pupil X should be given priority. His intelligence test score, although only 94, indicates a considerably higher reading expectancy. In addition, the fact that he has been motivated in one content area, mathematics, suggests the possibility that he can be motivated toward reading. He is working beyond grade level in mathematics; this suggests that at the time the test was given, he lacked reading skills, adequate facility with the English language, or adequate experiential background to obtain a realistic intelligence quotient score.

Pupil Y is not achieving at his estimated potential in either reading or mathematics. All indications predict that he will benefit from remediation but that only moderate progress can be expected.

Pupil Z, like pupil Y, is not achieving in either reading or mathematics. If a language disability or a reading problem existed at the time the intelligence test was administered, it may be that he is a gifted child. Whether he will profit from remedial reading depends on the ingenuity of the teacher. If this child can be motivated, he will gain more than either pupil X or Y. If the teacher fails to find the key to motivation, the pupil may not progress or may even regress in reading skills.

Another technique that seems promising is the difference score obtained between a normal administration of a standardized achievement test, and a later administration of the same test in which the teacher reads all testing material, including reading passages and answers to students. Crowley and Ellis (1971) used such a prodecure. They stated,

. . . Comparison of the two tests determined the potential for reading improvement. If both scores were the same, the child was considered to be, in all probability, achieving at his ability level. When the reading reinforced score was substantially higher, the opportunity for improvement was considered great. (p. 313)

The authors in this case suggested this as an initial screening procedure. They did, however, emphasize that information obtained should only supplement teacher recommendations.

STEP 3.   In this step the teacher works with other members of a screening committee to select those students, from the total number referred, who seem most likely to benefit from the remedial reading program. In many schools this screening is done by the remedial reading teacher without the aid of other school personnel. In some cases this works quite well, but the use of a committee for screening purposes can also be of great benefit to the remedial reading teacher. The use of a committee composed of the remedial reading teacher, the principal, at least one classroom teacher, and perhaps the guidance counselor can eliminate a number of problems that the remedial reading teacher is likely to encounter. For example, problems often arise when more pupils are taken from one teacher's room than from the room of another teacher. However, if a screening committee makes the decision there is less likelihood that any one teacher will feel that her students are not receiving equal consideration. The principal and guidance counselor can also add valuable input on such matters as scheduling and knowledge of students' home conditions.

STEPS 4 AND 5.   In these steps, after the initial candidates have been screened, the remedial reading teacher begins the administration of specific diagnostic tests and also begins remedial sessions with individuals or small groups. A part of the immediate battery of tests should include tests for auditory discrimination and for vision. Those students with problems in either area would be referred to a specialist for further testing. For example, the student with auditory discrimination difficulties would be referred to an audiologist to determine whether the student had a hearing loss or whether he simply needed training in discriminating sounds. And, the student who failed the vision screening tests would be sent to an optometrist or an ophthalmologist to determine whether vision correction was needed. During this period of time (perhaps two to four weeks) the remedial reading teacher would be working with a few more students than would be a normal case load for the entire year. This should be a period in which precise records are kept indicating exactly how fast each student learns. For example, a student who is weak in phonics would be given an individual phonics test during one of the first few sessions. After several weeks of work on specific phonemes missed, or on unknown rules, he would then be given another test for the purpose of determining exactly how much he had learned and retained. At this point several alternatives might be open. If the student had made considerable progress during this period of time, the remedial reading teacher would probably wish to continue the remediation along the same general lines as before. On the other hand if it was apparent that little or nothing had been learned or retained, the teacher would need to decide whether altering instructional strategy might be beneficial or whether referral to a psychologist or other specialists would be in order.

STEP 6.   Those students who seemed to learn rather quickly when taught would definitely be retained and made a part of the regular case load. Students who needed auditory or visual correction would also become a part of this final group. On the other hand those students who did not seem to benefit from instruction, as indicated in step five, would be referred to other specialists for help. For example, a child with severe emotional problems may need psychological help for an extended period of time. During this period the psychologist or psychiatrist may or may not recommend that the student come to remedial reading. However, many students would, sooner or later, again become a part of the final case load.

SCHEDULING CLASSES FOR REMEDIAL READING

One of the major problems faced by the remedial reading teacher and the principal is that of which classes to take students from for remedial reading training. I would suggest that, where it is possible, students be taken from either social studies or science classes to attend the remedial reading class. To begin with, much of the instruction in these classes is based on the reading of material from textbooks. Students who are candidates for remedial reading would, in most cases, not be able to benefit from that part of the instruction. Furthermore, we do not tend to have a national science or social studies curriculum much as we do in reading or mathematics. For this reason overall school achievement test results are not adversely affected to any great extent by having students miss a portion of these classes. In fact, most achievement tests only measure social studies and science vocabulary. And, my own studies tended to show that students who were encouraged to read books about social studies and science material in remedial reading gained as much, and in many cases more, in vocabulary knowledge as the students in regular classes.

If possible, students should not be taken from their regular reading classes or from physical education, art, or music classes. Much can be gained from their own reading classes if the teachers of these students understand their problems. And, in the case of classes such as physical education, art, and music the student is likely to miss a great opportunity to compete in a fun type of activity on an equal basis with other students.

THE NUMBER OF STUDENTS PER CLASS AND TOTAL CASE LOAD

The number of students in the remedial reading class will vary, to some extent, on the age-grade levels of the students and on the similarity of the problems of students who could be scheduled to work with the remedial reading teacher at the same time. A few students will need such intensive training that it will be imperative that they receive individual help, especially in the beginning stages of their remediation.

Many authorities in the field of reading and the research such as that of Edwa Steirnagle (1971) have indicated that classes ranging in size up to six can be beneficial without losing their effectiveness. In an evaluation of the El Paso Public Schools Title I Remedial Reading Program Steirnagle stated, "One surprising discovery was the fact that pupils who received one-to-one instruction from the teacher had not made the predicted progress. Classes consisting of five pupils who were instructed for a full hour, daily, produced the greatest gains." (p. 539) It should be pointed out, however, that later research by Steirnagle indicated that gains began to drop off rather sharply when the maximum number went beyond six to eight pupils.

Most reading authorities also agree that a teacher's total case load should not exceed forty pupils. In many cases, depending on the severity of the cases, and the amount of consulting the teacher is expected to do, the maximum case load might very well be thirty pupils. The length of the instructional period and the number of remedial sessions per week for each pupil will be discussed in the following section.

FREQUENCY AND LENGTH OF CLASS SESSIONS

Several research studies have been done in remedial and developmental reading classes to determine the effectiveness of differing lengths of class sessions as well as the effectiveness of the frequency of class sessions. As pointed out earlier in the chapter younger students have a much better chance of recovering from reading disabilities and of then maintaining these gains. For example, Cashden and Pumfrey (1969) studied thirty-six junior high school students. They were placed in three groups. One group was given remedial training in groups of four to six for thirty to sixty minutes twice weekly. Another group was taught in the same size group for thirty to sixty minutes once weekly. Another group served as a control group and was given no remedial training at all. Twenty-two months later there were no significant differences in the achievement or attitudes of the three groups. The authors concluded that students of this age group needed a far more intensive and integrated program than the "two term" project that was conducted.

Hicks, et al. (1968) studied the gains made by third- and fourth-grade students. Their subjects were assigned to one of three experimental conditions. These conditions were two, three, and four, half-hour remedial reading sessions per week. At no time were any classes longer than five. The experiment lasted for approximately one school year. The authors found that the third-grade group that was instructed three times per week made significantly greater gains than the group that was instructed only two times per week. They also found that the third graders that were instructed four times per week made significantly greater gains than the groups that were instructed only two or three times per week. On the other hand, their data revealed that the number of sessions per week did not produce any significant differences at the fourth grade level. These authors stated,

> The results of this study tend to indicate that time allotments are an important consideration in the development of a third-grade remedial reading curriculum, i.e., there is a direct and reliable relationship between the number of sessions and the amount of improvement in reading shown over the school year. No such relationship was demon-

strated for the fourth-grade pupils who served as S's in this study. Two sessions per week seem to be as beneficial as three or four. (pp. 439 and 744)

Hicks, et al. pointed out that their findings were consistent with those of Jarvis (1965) who found that lengthening the time per day for formal reading instruction over fifty minutes per day had no significant effect on the reading gain of fourth, fifth, and sixth graders in a developmental situation. Jarvis stated, "These data strongly suggest that we teach reading in the other curricular areas of the elementary school curriculum as well as in the formulized reading class." (p.204) It should be emphasized, however, that the findings of Jarvis may not have been applicable to children in grades one, two, and three.

In summary, it again appears that at third grade, and probably below, students will benefit from two or three sessions per week, but they will gain and retain even more if they are given four to five sessions per week. On the other hand, students at the fourth-grade level and above are simply not likely to gain and retain progress in a short-term program (one year or less) regardless of the number of sessions. There would, of course be many exceptions to this rule. For example, in our Reading Center we have seen one to two grade levels of improvement in students at the fourth-grade level and above in remedial sessions held once per week for a period of one semester. In general we might conclude that students in any grade can be helped, and the more frequently the sessions are held the greater the chance for success. However, for those students at fourth grade, or above, the remedial process is likely to take much longer.

The length of class sessions will, in many cases, depend upon the administrative structure of the school. However, if possible, a remedial period of 20–30 minutes for second and third graders and 40–50 minutes for fourth graders and above is usually adequate to teach a good lesson and yet keep them from becoming overly restless. If possible, these time periods should be broken up into several activities. Among these activities should be a time set aside for the selection of books for students to read on their own outside the classroom situation. Although students often require some assistance in book selection, this time period also allows time for record keeping by the teacher.

TERMINATION OF STUDENTS FROM THE REMEDIAL READING PROGRAM

Ideally students should be terminated from the remedial reading program when they are again reading up to grade level. A number of studies have shown, however, that it is often necessary to continue remediation on a less intensive basis to enable formerly disabled readers to maintain reading skills already learned as well as the keep up with their normally achieving peers. For example, Madeline Hardy (1968) studied the academic, vocational, and social adjustment of a group of young adults who had been disabled in reading and who had received clinical diagnosis and remedial treatment during their elementary school years. She concluded that it was possible to reduce reading retardation by a remedial reading program, but the amount of retardation tended to increase often at the end of the treatment. Gains made by the subjects were significant only during the periods of remedial work. Hardy also found that those students who displayed deficiencies in visual, perceptual, and motor skills at referral tended to retain these defects. She believed that because the disabled reader's problems tended to persist, remedial teachers should attempt to help the readers to understand, accept, and cope with their problems.

Balow (1965) also studied three samples of boys and girls from the Psycho-Educational Clinic at the University of Minnesota. All were fifth and sixth graders who, according to tests, were bright enough to be reading at grade level or above, but who were reading three, or more, years below their expectancy level. Balow's subjects were mostly from a middle-class or lower middle-class background. Prior to receiving remediation these students had been achieving at approximately one-half the rate of normal students. During their period of remediation, however, Samples I and II progressed at a rate of twelve and nine times their previous rates of achievement respectively. (There were no data available for Sample III.) Sample I did not receive any follow-up remedial assistance after being discharged from the clinic while the students in Samples II and III were given far less intensive but nonetheless some supportive help following their remedial period. The students in Sample I did not lose the reading skills they had acquired during their period of remediation, but they did not continue to develop on their own. However, those students in Samples II and III continued to gain in reading skills more rapidly than they had prior to entering the program, although they did not gain as rapidly as normally achieving readers.

Balow concluded:

> The unfortunate but highly instructive element of these findings is that severe reading disability is not corrected by short-term intensive courses of treatment, even though it is ameliorated by such help. Neither, it would appear, is the cure to be found in intensive treatment followed by maintenance sessions of an hour or so per week, although again such a program is far superior to no special help at all. The implication which follows naturally from these conclusions is that severe reading disability is probably best considered a relatively chronic illness needing long-term treatment rather than the short course typically organized in current programs. (p. 586)

Benjamin Willis (1971) studied the growth curves of third-year students in a remedial program. He found that the greatest growth in reading skills appeared to take place during the fourth month of instruction. Growth increased each month, but seemed to level off by the fifth month. Although the results obtained by Willis were probably to some extent, a function of the type of program provided and the age of the students involved, there seems to be definite evidence that if other factors are not hindering students' progress, they should show some definite improvement after four months of instruction.

In summary one might conclude the following:

1. The earlier disabled readers are identified (Grades 1–3) and placed in a remedial program, the more likely they are to gain the competence needed for achieving on

a level with their normal-reading peers. Even then, some type of follow-up program should probably be provided for these students.

2. Older students (Grade 4 and above) who are severely disabled in reading should be considered as chronic cases who will not only need long-term treatment, but should also receive some follow-up help after being discharged from the full-time, intensive remedial reading program.

3. Most students, and especially those at the third grade level or below, should be referred to other specialists if they have not shown considerable gain after four to five months of instruction.

FACILITIES FOR REMEDIAL READING

As stated earlier there are several ways in which the remedial reading teacher may wish to operate. That is, within the classroom of the teachers who have students in need of help, through the use of a mobile reading center, or in a more traditional setting of a classroom within the school in which students come to the remedial reading teacher. The importance of operating within a facility that is appealing to the eye cannot be overemphasized. Although students may not appear to mind coming to a room that is not brightly decorated and appealing, in reality most will probably be adversely affected by such an atmosphere. Although most students would not be likely to complain about their surroundings they do make a major difference. This difference was pointed out to me when I visited a federal penitentiary to discuss their reading program with officials of that institution. Prior to the time that I had visited the institution, the reading classroom they used was in a basement. In that facility there was little or no sunlight and there were a number of steam pipes running along the ceiling that tended to drip water from time to time. In general, it was a rather dreary atmosphere. The teacher of this class said that a day had seldom gone by that at least one physical fight did not break out between students in his classroom when the inmates were housed in this facility during the reading lessons. He stated, however, that after the reading class was moved into a sunny classroom that was brightly decorated there had never been one instance in which inmates had even come near the point of physical violence.

Most elementary or secondary students would, no doubt, be considerably more inhibited than the inmates of this prison. But, on the other hand, there is little doubt that they experience many of the same feelings caused by the influence of their surroundings as did the inmates of the federal penitentiary.

In addition to a pleasant classroom atmosphere there are a number of other facilities that are desirable. Some of these are as follows:

1. Office space for record keeping and conferencing parents and students.

2. Adequate storage facilities for equipment, paper, books, and other materials.

3. Facilities for duplicating materials. These facilities may be housed within the classroom or out of the classroom; however, the remedial reading teacher usually needs to duplicate a great many materials and for this reason should have easy access to duplicating facilities.

4. Chalkboard space and bulletin board space.

5. Sufficient electrical outlets for use with overhead projectors, tape recorders, filmstrip projectors, etc.
6. Tables and chairs suitable for individual or small group work
7. Individual study carrels with facilities for individual viewing of audiovisual materials and for individual study
8. Filing cabinets

In addition there should be adequate books, programs, and materials in general for the teaching of reading. These materials, as well as the criteria for their selection, are discussed more thoroughly in Chapter 15.

EVALUATING PROGRESS IN REMEDIAL READING AND MEASURING THE EFFECTIVENESS OF THE PROGRAM

Most remedial reading teachers are concerned with evaluating two aspects of the effectiveness of their program. One aspect is the effect of the program on individual students and the other aspect is the effectiveness of the program as a whole.

INDIVIDUAL EVALUATION. Individual evaluation can be carried out in a number of ways. One method of doing this is to simply keep very accurate records of pre-test and post-test performance on individual diagnostic tests. For example, in giving a phonics test, the teacher will note exactly which phonemes were missed. After a period of teaching, the same test can again be given so that the exact amount of learning in this area can easily be evaluated. The same type of measurement can be done with knowledge of basic sight words, contractions, vowel rule knowledge and/or application, etc. Many teachers are used to thinking about progress in terms of grade level scores such as 3.4, 4.2, etc. As pointed out in an earlier chapter, however, most standardized achievement tests do not measure achievement for individual students accurately enough to be of any real value for remedial work. Therefore, although grade level scores may give the appearance of being somewhat concrete measures, they are often misleading. And, in reality, criterion measures of gain in specific skills are much more meaningful in evaluating the effectiveness of a program for individual students.

Another useful method of measuring individual student gains is to use a checklist of the various characteristics and specific number of various types of errors when administering informal reading inventories. A checklist of this nature is shown in Chapter 2, page 36. In the first administration of the informal reading inventory each characteristic and specific number of each type of error (e.g., substitutions, insertions, etc.) can be noted. After a period of remediation the same passages can be given again. The second time, each characteristic and specific number of errors can again be noted. You can then figure the percentage of reduction in each type of error (hopefully) between the first and second administration of the test. If the overall grade level of the student has increased, however, it would be important that the percentages be computed only on the same passages that were given (up to frustration level) in the first administration of the test.

The informal reading inventory itself is also, of course, extremely useful as a measuring instrument for individual gains, i.e., in determining whether a student's overall free or independent, instructional and frustration levels have risen during the period of instruction.

Individual gains that may not always be apparent as the teacher works with students on a daily basis can often become very apparent when tape recordings are made of students' oral reading. The initial reading of several passages can be recorded and after a period of remediation the same passages can be recorded following the first, on the same tape. Allowing students to hear their own progress in fluency and reduction in errors is also often highly motivating.

GROUP EVALUATION.   Group evaluation of remedial reading programs can also be somewhat difficult in some situations. For example, one method that has been used in researching the effectiveness of special or compensatory programs is use of a control group. This method, while offering a number of advantages, also has some disadvantages. One disadvantage is that there must be a control group at all. In a small school one may not wish to deprive the control group of the benefit of a promising new program simply for the sake of measuring any possible significant differences in post-test results between the two groups. Or, on the other hand, if students in another school are used as a control group, there is no assurance that students in the two schools are of equal ability, therefore, a comparison of the two would yield inaccurate results.

The following is an explanation of a method of assessing gains which is relatively easy to interpret. This method deals with children's ratio-of-learning. Although the use of the concept of ratio-of-learning is not new, it is still unfamiliar to many people.[6]

The ratio-of-learning is a measurement of children's learning rate prior to entering a special program versus their learning rate while they are in the program. Because of the unreliability of group test scores for individual students, one should determine the ratio-of-learning for all students in a special program, rather than for individual students. The steps in using this method are as follows:

1.   Determine the average number of years that all children in the special program have been in school at the beginning of the program. Remember that second graders have only been in school for one year as of the beginning of grade 2, etc. Therefore, the number of years in school for most children equals their grade level minus one, unless they have failed a year. In that case the number of years in school would equal the grade level they should have been in, minus one.

   Example:
Sarah	–	Grade 3 (never failed)	$3 - 1 = 2$
Blanca	–	Grade 5 (never failed)	$5 - 1 = 4$
Elaine	–	Grade 4 (failed one year)	$5 - 1 = 4$
Bill	–	Grade 3 (failed two years)	$5 - 1 = 4$

[6]The explanation for ratio-of-learning is largely adapted from an article by the author entitled, "Measuring Gains in Remedial Reading," which appeared in the November 1972, *Reading Teacher*, Vol. 26, 138–141. Reproduced by permission of the International Reading Association.

Jennifer – Grade 2 (never failed) $2 - 1 = 1$

$$\frac{\text{Total number of years in school}}{\text{Number of students}} \qquad \frac{15}{5} = 3 \text{ years/student}$$

Therefore, this group has been in school for an average of 3 years per student.

2. Determine the average number of years of achievement of the group when they enter the program. Remember that achievement of 1.0 actually means no achievement at all, therefore, the number of years of achievement for each student is equal to his grade level score on an achievement test, minus one.
   Example:

Sarah	– Pre-test achievement test score	$1.5 - 1 = .5$
Blanca	– Pre-test achievement test score	$3.5 - 1 = 2.5$
Elaine	– Pre-test achievement test score	$2.5 - 1 = 1.5$
Bill	– Pre-test achievement test score	$2.5 - 1 = 1.5$
Jennifer	– Pre-test achievement test score	$1.0 - 1 = 0.0$

   Total years on achievement test 11.0

   $$\frac{\text{Total years of achievement}}{\text{Number of students}} \qquad \frac{6.0}{5.0} = 1.2$$

   Therefore, the average number of years of achievement for this group when they entered the program was 1.2 years.

3. Divide the average number of years of achievement by the average number of years that children have been in school. This will give you their average learning rate prior to entering the special program.
   Example:

   $$\frac{\text{Average number of years of achievement}}{\text{Average number of years in school}} \qquad \frac{1.2}{3.0} = .40$$

   The average learning rate for these children before entering the program was .40, or in other words, they had only learned four-tenths as much as they should have. Said another way, they were learning .40 month's knowledge, on the average for every month they had been in school.

4. Determine how long children were in the special program.
   Example:
   September 15th to May 15th = 8 months

5. Determine the average gain per pupil during the special program.
   Example:

Sarah	– Post-test achievement test score	2.8
Blanca	– Post-test achievement test score	4.8
Elaine	– Post-test achievement test score	5.2
Bill	– Post-test achievement test score	4.5
Jennifer	– Post-test achievement test score	2.3

   Total years on achievement test (post-test) 19.6
   Total years on achievement test (pre-test) 11.0

   $$\frac{\text{Total years gained during the special program}}{\text{Number of students}}$$
   (Difference between post-test and pre-test) $\frac{8.6}{5} = 1.72$ yrs/student

   The average amount of gain per pupil during the special program was 1.72 years per student. Note that it is not necessary to subtract one (1) from each student's score on the post-test and pre-test since you are only finding the overall differences in the two scores. However, subtracting one (1) from each post-test score and each pre-test score would give the same answer anyway.

6. Determine the average learning rate during the special program. The average learning rate during the special program is found by dividing the amount gained

during the program by the number of years (or months) the students were in the program.

Example:

Number of years gained during the program $\dfrac{1.72}{.8} = 2.15$

Years in the program

The average learning rate during this special program was 2.15.

7. Compare students' average learning rate before entering the special program with their average learning rate while participating in the special program. It was .40, or they had been gaining .40 month's achievement for every month they were in school. While they were enrolled in this special program, their average learning rate was 2.15, or they gained 2.15 month's achievement for every month they were in the special program.

As one can see, students were learning 5.4 times as rapidly as they had been (2.15 ÷ .4 = 5.4), or simply stated, they were now learning at a rate of more than two times that of the average student. There would certainly be no doubt that this program was effective. Any learning rate in this case that was greater than .4 (the students' rate of learning prior to the special program) would have indicated an improvement in this group's rate of learning.

QUALIFICATIONS OF READING SPECIALISTS

The International Reading Association has taken the lead in developing recommendations for the qualifications of various classifications of reading specialists. Many states have now developed their own standards for reading specialists based on these recommendations. The IRA recommendations are as follows:[7]

Qualifications:

A. General (Applicable to all Reading Specialists)
   - Demonstrate proficiency in evaluating and implementing research.
   - Demonstrate a willingness to make a meaningful contribution to professional organizations related to reading.
   - Demonstrate a willingness to assume leadership in improving the reading program.

B. Special Teacher of Reading
   - ✓ Complete a minimum of three years of successful classroom teaching in which the teaching of reading is an important responsibility of the position.
   - ✓ Complete a planned program for a Master's Degree from an accredited institution, to include:
     1. A minimum of 12 semester hours in graduate level reading courses with at least one course in each of the following:
        (a) Foundations or survey of reading.
            A basic course whose content is related exclusively to reading instruction or the psychology of reading. Such a course ordinarily would be first in a sequence of reading courses.
        (b) Diagnosis and correction of reading disabilities.
            The content of this course or courses includes the following: Causes of

[7]Reproduced by permission of the International Reading Association.

reading disabilities; observation and interview procedures; diagnostic instruments; standard and informal tests; report writing; materials and methods of instruction.

(c) Clinical or laboratory practicum in reading.

A clinical or laboratory experience which might be an integral part of a course or courses in the diagnosis and correction of reading disabilities. Students diagnose and treat reading disability cases under supervision.

2. Complete, at undergraduate or graduate level, study in each of the following areas:

(a) Measurement and/or evaluation.

(b) Child and/or adolescent psychology.

(c) Psychology, including such aspects as personality, cognition, and learning behaviors.

(d) Literature for children and/or adolescents.

3. Fulfill remaining portions of the program from related areas of study.

C. Reading Clinician

- Meet the qualifications as stipulated for the Special Teacher of Reading.
- Complete, in addition to the above, a sixth year of graduate work, including:
1. An advanced course or courses in the diagnosis and remediation of reading and learning problems.
2. A course or courses in individual testing.
3. An advanced clinical or laboratory practicum in the diagnosis and remediation of reading difficulties.
4. Field experiences under the direction of a qualified Reading Clinician.

D. Reading Consultant

- Meet the qualifications as stipulated for the Special Teacher of Reading.
- Complete, in addition to the above, a sixth year of graduate work including:
1. An advanced course in the remediation and diagnosis of reading and learning problems.
2. An advanced course in the developmental aspects of a reading program.
3. A course or courses in curriculum development and supervision.
4. A course and/or experience in public relations.
5. Field experiences under a qualified Reading Consultant or Supervisor in a school setting.

E. Reading Supervisor

- Meet the qualifications as stipulated for the Special Teacher of Reading
- Complete, in addition to the above, a sixth year of graduate work including:
1. Courses listed as 1, 2, 3, and 4 under Reading Consultant.
2. A course or courses in adminstrative procedures.
3. Field experiences under a qualified Reading Supervisor.

CODE OF ETHICS

All reading personnel as well as administrators, should be familiar with the International Reading Associations Code of Ethics which follows:

The members of the International Reading Association who are concerned with the teaching of reading form a group of professional persons, obligated to society and devoted to the service and welfare of indiviuals through teaching, clinical services, research, and publication. The members of this group are committed to values which are the foundation of a democratic society—freedom to teach, write, and study in an atmosphere conducive to the best interests of the profession. The welfare of the public, the profession, and the individuals concerned should be of primary consideration in recommending candidates for degrees, positions, advancements, the recognition of professional activity, and for certification in those areas where certification exists.

Ethical Standards in Professional Relationships:

1. It is the obligation of all members of the International Reading Association to observe the Code of Ethics of the organization and to act accordingly so as to advance the status and prestige of the Association and of the profession as a whole. Members should assist in establishing the highest professional standards for reading programs and services, and should enlist support for these through dissemination of pertinent information to the public.

2. It is the obligation of all members to maintain relationships with other professional persons, striving for harmony, avoiding personal controversy, encouraging cooperative effort, and making known the obligations and services rendered by the reading specialist.

3. It is the obligation of members to report results of research and other developments in reading.

4. Members should not claim nor advertise affiliation with the International Reading Association as evidence of their competence in reading.

Ethical Standards in Reading Services:

1. Reading specialists must possess suitable qualifications (see Roles, Responsibilities, and Qualifications of Reading Specialists) for engaging in consulting, clinical, or remedial work. Unqualified persons should not engage in such activities except under the direct supervision of one who is properly qualified. Professional intent and the welfare of the person seeking the services of the reading specialist should govern all consulting or clinical activities such as counseling, administering diagnostic tests, or providing remediation. It is the duty of the reading specialist to keep relationships with clients and interested persons on a professional level.

2. Information derived from consulting and/or clinical services should be regarded as confidential. Expressed consent of persons involved should be secured before releasing information to outside agencies.

3. Reading specialists should recognize the boundaries of their competence and should not offer services which fail to meet professional standards established by other disciplines. They should be free, however, to give assistance in other areas in which they are qualified.

4. Referral should be made to specialists in allied fields as needed. When such referral is made, pertinent information should be made available to consulting specialists.

5. Reading clinics and/or reading specialists offering professional services should refrain from guaranteeing easy solutions or favorable outcomes as a result of their work, and their advertising should be consistent with that of allied professions. They should not accept for remediation any persons who are unlikely to benefit from their instruction, and they should work to accomplish the greatest possible improvement in the shortest time. Fees, if charged, should be agreed on in ad-

vance and should be charged in accordance with an established set of rates commensurate with that of other professions.

Breaches of the Code of Ethics should be reported to IRA Headquarters for referral to the Committee on Professional Standards and Ethics for an impartial investigation.

SUMMARY

In initiating a remedial reading program it is especially important to develop a job description that the person or persons selected are expected to perform. There should be thorough communication among classroom teachers, administrative personnel, and reading personnel regarding both the title and duties that various reading specialists are expected to perform.

In each school, classroom teachers, administrators, reading specialists, and parents all have special talents, in relation to their roles, that they can contribute to the remedial reading program. It is important that each of these groups becomes familiar with the program and that each learns about the unique contributions of the others.

Another important aspect of the remedial reading program is the selection of the type of student who is most likely to benefit from remedial instruction. It is also important to obtain and/or develop materials that are appropriate for the specific difficulties of students with whom the reading specialist will be working. Still another important aspect of the program is the development of facilities conducive of learning.

It is also important to develop methods of measuring the effectiveness of the program. Traditional methods of measurement in remedial reading are often inadequate. The methods suggested within this chapter may be found to be more appropriate.

Lastly, it is important to select reading personnel that are highly qualified and who will perform their duties in a professional manner.

Chapter 13: REFERENCES

Balow, Bruce. "The Long-Term Effect of Remedial Reading Instruction," *The Reading Teacher*. Vol. 18, (April, 1965), 581–586.

Bruininks, Robert; Glaman, Gertrude; and Clark, Charlotte R. "Issues In Determining Prevalence of Reading Retardation," *The Reading Teacher*. Vol. 27, (November, 1973), 177–185.

Cashdan, Asher, and Pumfrey, P.D. "Some Effects of the Teaching of Remedial Reading," *Educational Research*. Vol. 11, (February, 1969), 138–142.

Crowley, Harry L., and Ellis, Bessie. "Cross Validation of a Method for Selecting Children Requiring Special Services, in Reading," *The Reading Teacher*. Vol. 24, (January, 1971), 312–319.

Garry, V.V. "Competencies That Count Among Reading Specialists," *Journal of Reading*. Volume 17, (May, 1974), 608–613.

Green, Carroll R. "Effects of Reading Supervisors on Teacher Attitudes Toward Children With Reading Problems." Abstract of Unpublished Doctoral Dissertation, St. Louis University, 1973.

Hardy, Madeline I. "Disabled Readers: What Happens to Them After Elementary School?" *Canadian Education and Research Digest*. Vol. 8, (December, 1968), 338–346.

Hesse, Karl D., Smith, Richard J, and Nettleton, Aileen. "Content Teachers Consider the Role of the Reading Consultant," *Journal of Reading*. Vol. 17, (December, 1973), 210–215.

Hicks, Robert A., *et al*. "Reading Gains and Instructional Sessions," *The Reading Teacher*. Vol. 21, (May, 1968), 738–739.

Jarvis, Oscar T. "Time Allotment Relationships to Pupil Achievement," *Elementary English*. Vol. 42, (February, 1965), 201–204.

Pearlman, Erwin, and Pearlman, Ralph. "The Effect of Remedial Reading Training in a Private Clinic," *Academic Therapy*. Vol. 5, (Summer, 1970), 298–304.

Rauch, Sidney J. "Administrator's Guidelines for More Effective Reading Programs," *Journal of Reading*. Vol. 17, (January, 1974, 297–300.

Reed, James C. "The Deficits of Retarded Readers—Fact or Artifact?" *The Reading Teacher*. Vol. 23, (January, 1970), 347–352.

Steirnagle, Edwa. "A Five-Year Summary of a Remedial Reading Program," *The Reading Teacher*. Vol. 24 (March, 1971), 537–542.

Ullmann, Charles A. "Prevalence of Reading Disability as a Function of the Measure Used," *Journal of Learning Disabilities*. Vol. 2, (November, 1969), 556–558.

Willis, Benjamin C. "Evaluation of the Reading Center's Remedial Program for the 1970–71 School Year." A paper presented at the Broward County School Board, Fort Lauderdale, Florida, December, 1971. Mimeographed.

Wylie, Richard. "Diversified Concepts of the Role of the Reading Consultant," *The Reading Teacher*. Vol. 22, (March, 1969), 519–522.

14

RELAYING INFORMATION, RECORD KEEPING, AND WRITING CASE REPORTS IN REMEDIAL READING

This chapter contains a discussion of the necessity for accurately relaying information to and from various individuals and agencies. A number of samples of forms for relaying this information are shown along with a short discussion of the use of each form. The latter part of the chapter contains a discussion of suggested techniques for writing case reports. This is then followed by an example of a final case report.

THE PURPOSE OF REPORTING AND RECORD KEEPING

There are a number of purposes for reporting and record keeping in remedial reading. One of the most important and obvious reasons is, of course, for the purpose of accurately transmitting information. Most people would not attempt to keep a record of a complex checking account in their head. Likewise, the information compiled on disabled readers becomes too complex for one person to remember. Furthermore, a number of people must often deal with the same student and it, of course, becomes necessary to accurately relay this complex set of information from person to person without taking the chance of misinterpretation or loss along the way.

A second similar reason for accurate record keeping is to provide proper guidance to the student. Most of us have a tendency to think we can remember more than we actually can. At a recent meeting of psychologists a questionnaire was circulated about one week after a speech to those psychologists who attended and heard the speaker's presentation. Only about 8 percent of the material the speaker presented was remembered at all, and 50 percent of the 8 percent (or 4 percent) was misinterpreted or inaccurately understood. As the remedial reading teacher works with each student, implications for further work and diagnosis constantly appear. If these implications are not written down they are usually soon forgotten.

Accurate record keeping and reporting also serves as a measure of progress of disabled readers. In working with a disabled reader on a daily basis it is often difficult to observe progress. This is analogous to the uncle or aunt who comes to visit and remarks how the children have grown. Yet, in being exposed to children on a day-to-day basis it is difficult to really observe any growth. For most disabled readers it is necessary to keep accurate records of progress to measure their growth in reading skills as well as to justify time spent in teaching them.

A third important purpose that reporting and record keeping serves is that of in-service education. As the remedial reading teacher does her diagnosis and reports her findings in written form and as she works with disabled readers and makes suggestions to classroom teachers for assignments, a great deal of reading education often takes place. When the classroom teacher sees positive results from the work of the remedial reading teacher and from work suggested by the remedial reading teacher, changes in the methods of the classroom teacher are likely to follow.

Legal requirements also make certain record keeping and reporting necessary. For example, many remedial reading programs are federally funded. This funding usually requires some sort of proof of the effectiveness or success of the program for which the funds were expended. Depending upon state and local district policies it is also sometimes necessary to obtain written permission from parents in order to enroll their children in remedial programs.

TYPES OF REPORTS AND RECORD KEEPING

The various communication lines necessary for a successful remedial reading program are illustrated below. In some cases the remedial reading teacher does all of her own diagnosis; however, in some cases at least part of the work is done by a diagnostician. Therefore, in illustrating these lines of communication I have referred, in some cases, to the teacher and/or diagnostician who may or may not be the same person.

1. Diagnostician or Remedial Reading Teacher ⟷ Classroom Teacher and Administrators
2. Diagnostician or Remedial Reading Teacher ⟷ Parents
3. Diagnostician or Remedial Reading Teacher ⟷ Other Educational Agencies

Reporting Information from the Classroom Teacher to the Diagnostician or Remedial Reading Teacher

The forms that follow are used by the classroom teacher to relay information concerning those students who she believes are good candidates for remedial reading. It should be emphasized, however, that before these forms are used it would, in most cases, be necessary for the remedial reading teacher to communicate information to the classroom teacher, which would provide guidance in selecting those students most in need of, and most likely to benefit from, remedial help. In most cases, the forms which follow would be distributed to the classroom teacher by the remedial reading teacher. If possible this should be done in an in-service meeting, at which time the use of the forms can be explained.

Form "A" which follows is easy for the classroom teacher to use and yet can serve as a device for helping teachers become more aware of students' reading problems. Before using such a form, many teachers with little or no formal training in reading will need help in interpreting and using this form. However, this can also be used to advantage when the form serves as the subject of an in-service meeting at which time the remedial reading teacher can explain the various categories of the reading skills and how to identify problems in each category.

(Form A)

Remedial Reading Referral

Teacher: _____   School: _____
Grade: _____   Date: _____

Nothing is so valuable in determining which students need remedial help as the opinion of the classroom teacher. If you have, or have had, students whom you feel need special help in reading would you please list them in the space provided.

Following is a partial list of common weaknesses. If you feel any of these apply to students you are referring, please list the corresponding numbers after their names. If there are other difficulties that you have noted, please explain these also.

1. POOR SIGHT VOCABULARY
2. INABILITY TO USE CONTEXT CLUES
3. POOR USE OF PHONIC ANALYSIS
4. POOR USE OF STRUCTURAL ANALYSIS
5. MAKES REVERSALS (saw for was, etc.)
6. CANNOT ADJUST SPEED TO DIFFICULTY OF MATERIAL
7. WORD-BY-WORD READS

8. MAKES INSERTIONS, OMISSIONS, ETC.
9. POOR WORK AND STUDY HABITS
10. POOR CONCENTRATION
11. LACKS CONFIDENCE
12. EXHIBITS POOR ATTITUDE
13. POOR COMPREHENSION
14. PHRASES POORLY
15. OTHER (please explain)

If you have additional information please enter it in the *remarks* blank. Please keep this form and it will be collected in the near future.

Student: _____
Remarks: _____
Student: _____
Remarks: _____
Student: _____
Remarks: _____
Student: _____
Remarks: _____
Student: _____
Remarks: _____

If you have additional students, please list their names on the back of this sheet.

Form "B" which follows is easy for most teachers to understand; however, it is more time-consuming for the classroom teacher. But, since the classroom teacher is often in a position to observe students over a long period of time, this type of form can often provide information that is of considerable value in working with disabled readers.

Teacher's Report for Remedial Reading Referral

Student's Name: _____ Teacher's Name: _____

1. What do you think is the student's main problem(s) in reading? _____
_____
_____

2. What is the student's reading level or what book is he presently using? _____
_____

3. How is this student grouped for reading? _____

4. How is this student grouped for other subjects and what is provided for any special reading problems that he/she may have? _____
_____

5. What are some other weak points that you have observed in this student? (Other than in reading.)
_____
_____

6. What are some of the student's strong points? _____
_____

6. What are the student's reactions to reading? (Interests, attitude, etc.) _____
_____

7. What is the attitude of the student?
   Emotionally calm _____
   Apathetic _____
   Excitable _____

8. How does the student react to authority?
   Resistant _____
   Accepting _____
   Overly dependent _____

9. Describe the student's relationships to other students. _____

10. Have you noted any unusual emotional behavior by this student? _____
_____

11. How does this student react to a difficult task?   Withdrawn: _____
                  Faces problem with little or no difficulty: _____
Acts impulsively: _____

12. How does the student act in the classroom?   Calm and quiet: (If withdrawn please explain.)
_____ Talkative: _____
                  Normal: _____
Other Information that you feel is important: _____
_____
_____

Reporting Information from the Diagnostician or
Remedial Reading Teacher to Classroom Teachers

Form "C" which follows is one type of report that can be used by the diagnostician or remedial reading teacher in reporting information derived in the initial diagnosis. A form such as this is often helpful in providing guidance in placement of students at

Individual Reading Diagnosis Report

Student:_____   Date Tested:_____
School:_____   Teacher:_____
Student's Age at Time of Testing:_____   Student's Grade at Time of Testing:_____

In accordance with your referral the above-named student was tested and in my opinion does _____
does not_____ need to be in the remedial reading program.

COMPREHENSION (Combination of the *Gray Oral Reading Test* and an *Informal Reading Inventory*.)

Percent of comprehension

```
100 |  +    +    +    +    +    +    +    +    +    +
 75 |  +    +    +    +    +    +    +    +    +    +
 50 |  +    +    +    +    +    +    +    +    +    +
 25 |  +    +    +    +    +    +    +    +    +    +
  x |_____
       1    2    3    4    5    6    7    8    9   10
```

Reading grade level
(comprehension)

1. FREE READING LEVEL Grade ____
2. INSTRUCTIONAL GRADE LEVEL Grade ____
3. FRUSTRATION READING LEVEL Grade ____

READING DIFFICULTIES:_____
_____

PHYSICAL OR OTHER DIFFICULTIES NOTED:_____
_____

TYPE OF HELP OR REMEDIATION RECOMMENDED:_____
_____
_____

1. FREE READING LEVEL: Reader level at which child can function adequately with no teacher help. Word recognition should be 99% accurate; comprehension of all types should average at least 90%.

2. INSTRUCTIONAL READING LEVEL: Reading level at which child can function adequately with teacher guidance and, at the same time, meet enough challenge to stimulate further growth. On a pretest at this level, word recognition should be 95% accurate and comprehension at least 75% accurate.

3. FRUSTRATION LEVEL: Reading level at which the child's abilities to function break down. Word recognition falls to 90% or below; comprehension, to 50% or below. May also be indicated by presence of symptoms of difficulty such as vocalization, tension movements, and so on. Serves as an indicator or rate of progress in that it shows how far above the instructional level learnings can currently extend.

the proper reading levels and in pinpointing specific weaknesses whether students appear to be proper candidates for remedial reading or not.

Forms "D" and "E" which follow are to be used by the remedial reading teacher in reporting information back to the classroom teacher once a student has been accepted as a candidate for remedial reading. As you will note, Form "D"

From: _____
To: _____

As you know _____ is receiving help in reading. This time amounts to approximately 35-45 minutes three times per week. That time is shared with from one to five other students. In order to make the most of that time, I hope we can work together with this student to his/her maximum benefit. I will try to give you a report from time-to-time on what I am working on with this particular student, and what I have asked the student to do between these sessions. If there is some question, please feel free to contact me or write a note at the bottom of this page and ask the student to return it to me.

Thank you.

Remedial reading teacher's diagnosis of the problem: _____
_____
_____

Work being carried on for correction of the above problem: _____
_____
_____
_____

Assignment for student: _____
_____

Comments from classroom teacher (To remedial reading teacher): _____
_____

(Form E)

ASSIGNMENT SHEET
Name: _____ Date Due: _____
Purpose of Assignment: _____
_____

The following work has been assigned to be completed before the next meeting with the student's remedial reading instructor:

1. _____
2. _____
3. _____
4. _____
5. _____

Remedial Reading Teacher _____

_____
(Signature of parent or teacher)

provides for continuous information on diagnostic information, work being carried on for correction of the student's problem, assignments for the student, and feedback from the classroom teacher. Form "E" is used for providing information on assignments either to the classroom teacher or to parents.

Reporting Information from the Diagnostician or Remedial Reading Teacher to Parents

As stated previously, in some districts it is required that teachers and/or administrators obtain permission from parents before enrolling students in programs such as remedial reading or special education. Form "F" which follows can be used for this purpose.

(Form F)

Parental Permission Form for Remedial Reading

To:_____

From:_____

Date:_____

    Your child,_____, has been given a series of reading and diagnostic tests and it is my opinion that _____ should be given the help that we can provide in the remedial reading program. This is a class for children of normal intelligence who have some type of difficulty in reading.

    I would like to extend the opportunity for you to visit with me concerning your child's reading problem and to visit the class in which we would like to enroll him/her. If you would like to visit this class, it meets on_____ from_____ to_____ in Room _____. Please feel free to visit at any time.

    You have my permission to enroll_____in the remedial reading program.

                                        _____

                                        (Signature of parent or guardian)

Note: Please ask your child to return this to me or send it to me at the following address:

_____

_____

_____

      Form "G" (page 366) can be used to report information from an initial diagnosis or from information derived from diagnostic teaching. As you will note, this form also provides a checklist of the types of activities that parents can do that are often beneficial to disabled readers.

Reporting Information from Parents to the Diagnostician and/or Remedial Reading Teacher

Teachers who work in university or public school reading clinics, as opposed to a regular remedial reading classroom, often come in contact with a greater percentage of seriously disabled readers. Although ample background information is desirable for any disabled reader, it is often especially helpful in order to properly diagnose the problems of seriously disabled readers. Some of this background information is usually available in the cumulative folders kept by the public schools or from the records of other educational agencies. Form "H" (page 367) may be adapted to your specific situation as a request form for obtaining students' records from these various educational agencies. Note that it contains space for a parent's signature. Many educational agencies require parental permission before they will release student records.

(Form G)

Progress Report to Parents

Date:_____

To:_____

From:_____ (Remedial Reading Teacher)

    As you know your child_____has been receiving help in our remedial reading program. We feel that his/her primary need is:_____
_____
_____

    In addition to the help that your child has been getting at school, it would also be beneficial if he/she could receive help from you in the following areas:

1. _____ Show interest in homework assignments that have been given and check to see that these are completed on the date that they are due.

2. _____ Take your child to the public library and help him/her to find books that he/she would like to read.

3. _____ Help your child by being a good listener when he/she reads to you. Do not be overly concerned with the teaching of specific skills. We will try to do this in the remedial reading program.

4. _____ Try to set aside a certain period of time each day for pleasure reading. This seems to work better if a *specific time* is set aside rather than a certain *amount* of time. In other words the amount of time is also important, for example, 30-40 minutes, but it is important that it be done at the same time each day if possible.

5. _____ Please comment in the "remarks" space below whether you believe your child has taken an increased interest in reading on his own.

6. _____ Other:_____
_____
_____

Remarks: _____
_____
_____

_____
(Remedial Reading Teacher-Signature)

    Form "I" which follows Form "H," is used at our Reading Center. As the title indicates, it is an application for admission of students to the Reading Center. Most of the information requested on this form is directly applicable to a thorough diagnosis of each student. However, a few items, such as information on handedness and birth history, are used for research information over a longer period of time.

Date:_____

To:_____

_____

_____

_____

The following student_____ who lives at _____ is receiving remediation at the Reading Center at _____. In order to facilitate his/her remediation, we would appreciate any test results or records that you might have concerning this child.

Thank you.

_____, Director

Reading Center,_____

You have my permission to release any records concerning my daughter ☐ son ☐

_____
(student's name)

_____
Parent

Sent to:

Application for Admission to Reading Center

(To be filled out by parents or guardians of student)

Name of Student: _____
                          (Last)   (First)   (Middle)

Address:_____ Telephone_____

_____
          (City)   (County)   (State)

Student's Birthdate:_____ Age:_____ Sex_____ Race:_____

School:_____ Grade Level: _____
          (If not in school, indicate occupation   (If not in school,
           of student)   last grade level
                                                                     reached)

Name of Parents or Guardians: _____

Address of Parents or Guardians:_____

Telephone Number of Parents or Guardians:_____

Occupations of Parents or Guardians: (A) Father_____
                                                            (Be specific)

Employed by: _____ (B) Mother: _____
                                                                  (Be specific)

_____ Employed by: _____

Fathers's Place of Birth:_____ Birthdate:_____ Age: _____

Mothers's Place of Birth:_____ Birthdate:_____ Age: _____

Father's Educational Level _____ Mother's Educational Level:_____

Is this student adopted?_____ If so, student's age when adopted: _____

Does student know he is adopted?_____ Father dead?_____ Mother dead?_____

Cause of death?_____ Are parents separated?_____ divorced? _____

Has either parent remarried?_____Has either parent been married before?_____
                                    (Which one)?

With whom does student live? _____

Religious Preference: Child_____ Father_____Mother_____

READING PROBLEM

1. Why is student being referred to the reading center?_____
_____
_____
_____
_____
_____
_____
_____

FAMILY HISTORY

1. List name, age, and sex of other children—oldest to youngest: _____
_____

2. Are the children all full brothers and/or sisters?   Yes_____ No _____
If the answer is no, then please explain. _____
_____

3. Which of the above children are presently living at home?_____
_____

4. Has anyone else ever lived in the home? _____
_____

5. Has your family ever lived with anyone else?_____
_____

6. What languages are spoken in the home?_____
_____

7. Do any other members of the family have a reading problem?_____
8. Have there ever been any physical deformities on either side of the family, in any generation?
_____
_____

9. Indicate general health of other members of the family:_____
_____

BIRTH HISTORY

1. Was child born premature?_____ (If so, how much)_____
2. Was birth completely normal? (If not, please explain)_____
_____
_____

DEVELOPMENTAL HISTORY

1. At what age did child say first words?_____
2. At what age did child first walk?_____
3. Did this child walk and speak first words at an earlier or later date than other members of the family? (Please explain.)
_____
_____

4. Has child ever had any serious illnesses?_____
_____
_____

5. Has child ever had any serious accidents? _____
_____

6. Does student presently, or has child ever, worn glasses?_____
If yes, who prescribed them?_____
7. When did student have last examination by an eye doctor? What were the results?_____
_____
_____

8. Has student ever had any ear infections?_____ If yes, please explain.
_____
_____

9. Has student's hearing ever been checked by a doctor?_____
_____

10. Do *you* think student hears well?_____

SOCIO-EDUCATIONAL

1. Any special schools attended?_____Name of school, type, where, when, and how long in attendance: _____
_____

2. Has student ever had an intelligence or other mental test?_____
If so: what test(s), by whom given, where and when, and results?
_____
_____

3. Has child ever failed in school?_____What grades? _____
4. Has the student ever missed school for any long periods of time? (If so, please explain.)
_____
_____

5. Usual scholastic rating: _____ 6. Best subjects?_____
7. Worst subjects?_____
8. How does student get along with siblings? _____
Other children?_____ Parents?_____

9. Disposition?   Happy?_____ Affectionate?_____ Dependable?_____
Concentration?_____ Temper?_____ Fears?_____
(Other comments)_____
10. Does student fatigue easily? _____ Symptoms observed:_____
11. How does student sleep?_____ At night?_____ Daytime nap?_____
12. Interests and abilities:_____
13. What does student like to do in spare time?_____
14. Does student like to compete with others? (Explain.)_____
_____

REFERRAL INFORMATION

   1. Who referred you to the reading center?
        Name:_____
        Address:_____
        _____
                (City)   (State)
   2. Full name and address of family physician or student's physician:
        Name:_____
        Address:_____
        _____
                (City)   (State)

CASE RECORD INFORMATION

Name of person who has completed this form:_____

_____
                   (Signature)   (Date)

Initial Case Analysis

Name: _____
Sex: _____
Grade: _____
School: _____
Teacher: _____

I. Test Results—Tests Administered at Clinic

   A. Reading Status

1. Informal Reading Inventory	Oral	Silent
Independent Level	_____	_____
Instructional Level	_____	_____
Frustration Level	_____	_____
Listening Comprehension Level	_____	

Types of Errors

(Indicate Number of Each Type)

First Trial		Second Trial	Percent of increase (+) or Decrease (−)
	Omissions		
	Insertions		
	Partial Mispronunciations		
	Gross Mispronunciations		
	Substitutions		
	Repetitions		
	Inversions		
	Aid		
	Self-corrected Errors		

Characteristics of the Reader

(Indicate with Check Mark (√)

First Trial		Second Trial
	Poor word-analysis skills	
	Head movement	
	Finger pointing	
	Disregard for punctuation	
	Loss of place	
	Overuse of phonics	
	Does not read in natural voice tones	
	Poor enunciation	
	Word-by-word reading	
	Poor phrasing	
	Lack of expression	
	Pauses	

B. Intelligence

    1. WISC   3. Stanford-Binet

        a. Verbal_____

        b. Performance_____   IQ_____

        c. Full scale_____

    2. Slosson Intelligence Test

        IQ_____

C. Other (Phonics, Basic Sight Words) Be specific, i.e., exact words not known, which areas of phonics are weak, etc.

D. Summary of Test Results from Student's School Records

II. Interpretation of Test Results

    A. Reading Tests

        1. Phonics

        2. Structural Analysis

        3. Comprehension

    B. Intelligence Tests

    C. Other

    D. Physical

        1. Vision

            a. Presently wears glasses   _____   _____

                                   yes   no

            b. Prescribed by whom_____

                 when_____

            c. Results of Visual Screening Test_____

        2. Hearing:

            a. Auditory discrimination test results

            b. History of hearing problems   _____   _____

                                    yes   no

                    (Explain)

3. Present general health (level of energy, activity, sleep, diet)

4. Health history (severe illnesses, operations, accidents, head and back injuries, allergies, etc.)

5. Other

E. Environmental and Personality Factors
   1. Home (parents, siblings, general environment)

   2. Home and Family Adjustment (security, dependence, independence, affection, warmth, etc.)

   3. Attitude Toward School (rebellious, submissive, indifferent, relations with teachers, etc...)

   4. Emotional Adjustment

III. Summary of results and possible and/or probable causes of reading difficulty

IV. Recommendations
   A. Place of treatment

   B. Materials and approach

   C. Prediction or conclusion in regard to the course and termination of the reading problem

   D. Instructional period with student
      Days: (circle) Monday - Tuesday - Wednesday - Thursday - Friday

      Hours: _____ to _____

Reading personnel working in reading clinics may wish to use an adaptation of this form or remedial reading teachers may wish to use a shortened version to obtain information considered pertinent for an immediate, thorough diagnosis.

Maintaining Student Records

As mentioned earlier in this chapter, one of the reasons for record keeping is to simply help the remedial reading teacher keep up-to-date on each student. When a remedial reading teacher acquires a case load of twenty-five or more students, the task of analyzing the diagnostic test results and progress is likely to become overwhelming without a certain amount of record keeping. It should be kept in mind, however, that the type of records kept will vary with such factors as the number of students with whom the remedial reading teacher is required to work, the degree of disability of the students, and the mode of operation of the teacher.

Form "K" which is used for the initial case analysis of each student who enters our Reading Center follows. Note that space is provided for the number of reading errors and characteristics of the reader on an informal reading inventory on the first trial as the student enters the program. The same passages are again read at

(Form K)

Meeting Number_____

Student_____

Date_____

Time_____

Relevant conditions (if any) of meeting_____

_____

Length of session_____

Summary of activities_____

_____

_____

_____

_____

Plan for next session_____

_____

_____

Diagnostic implications from today's activities_____

_____

_____

Teacher comments_____

_____

_____

_____

the end of the remedial period and the percentage of increase or decrease is computed. This type of information is often more valuable than a simple grade level designation which may or may not be accurate. The rest of the form is used to help the remedial reading teacher synthesize various test results and other information collected in the initial diagnosis.

Most remedial reading programs use one of two common types of operation. In one type of operation the remedial reading teacher works with each student or with only two to three students at a time. In doing so, information is often gained on planning the next session from diagnostic teaching during the day's activities. Teachers who are either required to, or prefer to, work with a larger number of students during any one period usually find this type of record keeping to be somewhat burdensome. For this type of operation a daily worksheet such as that shown in Form "L" may be preferable. When using Form "L" the teacher would often plan the activities of students a week or more in advance. This sheet may be posted or duplicated and put in individual student folders in which the student, with some guidance, checks his plan and works on his own. This is, of course, somewhat more like a conventional lesson plan for a class of developmental readers. It would also, in most cases, result in less individualization of instruction, which is highly important in remedial reading.

Reporting Information from Diagnostician or Remedial Reading Teacher to Other Educational Agencies

It is often necessary to send reports on students' progress to other educational agencies such as psychological evaluation centers, reading clinics and/or private and public schools. In many cases the diagnostician and/or remedial reading teacher may simply reproduce and send copies of tests that have been administered. Although various test results often provide valuable information, they seldom contain the kind of information that the teacher can provide after having worked with a student for a period of time. For example, an intelligence test may show that a certain student's IQ is 120, but if the student is unable to learn when he is taught, then the fact that his IQ is 120 has very little meaning. It is much more meaningful, for example, to know that he learns best by a specific procedure and/or that he responds well with a certain type of reward, or that he is interested in, and will read, books on a subject in which he is especially interested.

In order to provide this type of information, the remedial reading teacher often needs to write a final case report on students' progress. The final case report can summarize test information that the teacher believes would be of help to another person who might continue working with a student, but more importantly, it can provide information on how rapidly the student learns and what procedures and materials have been especially helpful.

Daily Worksheet

Date _____ to _____ Period _____ Grade _____

RFU - Reading for Understanding	RX - RX Reading Program
SRA - Reading lab	RFM - Reading for Meaning
LS - Literature Sampler	S - Story
PL - Pilot Library	O - Oral Reading
L - Listening	BBR - Be A Better Reader
T - Test	Mc - McCall Crabbs Tests
Ta - Tactics	PP - Programmed Phonics Books
SKS - Specific Skills Series	B - Boardwork or Overhead
SE - Self Expression	WS - Word Study

Name	Monday	Tuesday	Wednesday	Thursday	Friday

SUGGESTED PROCEDURES FOR
WRITING CASE REPORTS AND
RECORD KEEPING

The writing of case reports, although worthwhile, can be very time-consuming. For this reason the remedial reading teacher should attempt to improve her ability to include all pertinent information while learning to exclude information that would be of little or no value to someone reading the report. In the section that follows, a number of suggestions are given on procedures that should generally be followed when writing case reports or in keeping records. Following these procedures is an example of a final case report.

1. *Use a type of outline form that will make sections and subsections clearly visible.* For example, each important section might be underlined and each subsection might then be indented under the main heading. This will enable the reader to quickly scan and spot specific information.

2. *Include important information but exclude any information that would be of no value in working with the student.* This might be illustrated in the case of a student who came to the teacher knowing only a few basic sight words. In the final case report it would be important to mention the total number of basic sight words not known when the student entered the remedial reading program. However, if the student had learned nearly all of the basic sight words during the course of remediation then there would be little or no value in actually listing which words were not known at the beginning of the remedial period. On the other hand, it would be important to make a statement concerning how the student seemed to learn the words in the easiest manner. It would also be helpful to actually list basic sight words still not known at the end of the remedial period. This would, of course, eliminate the need for further testing by the person receiving the report.

3. *Where "impressions" are stated they should be identified as such.* This might be illustrated in the case of statements concerning a student's intelligence. For example, a statement such as, "Julie is highly intelligent because she seems to learn phonics rules rather quickly" would be inappropriate. It would be more appropriate to simple state, "Julie seems to possess the potential to learn phonics rules rather quickly." Some students seem to possess a high potential for learning some tasks; however, this would not necessarily mean that the student had a high intelligence quotient.

4. *List specific test scores and the source of each score.* It is important to state specific scores, but it is just as important to list the source of each score. For example, in discussing the reading level of a particular student as derived from several tests one might say, "Irma's instructional reading level would appear to be at the third-grade level as shown from her scores on the *San Diego Quick Assessment,* the *Classroom Reading Inventory* and the scores made this year on the *Iowa Test of Basic Skills.*"

5. *List specific skills needing remediation.* Some reports use vague statements such as, "Martha seems to need help with word attack skills." A statement such as this, however, is of little value since there are five main types of word attack skills and within each type there are a number of sub-categories. It would be much more helpful to be more specific in stating this student's needs, e.g., "Martha would

appear to benefit from instruction in the use of context clues. She also needs to learn all of the short vowel sounds and the following blends. . . ."

6. *Give a brief interpretation of the results of each test that may not be familiar to the person or persons reading the report.* An interpretation is especially necessary for some tests. For example, many people are not familiar with the norms of the *Wepman Auditory Discrimination Test.* To simply say "Jerry missed six items on this test" would not necessarily mean much to persons who were, or were not, familiar with the test unless they looked at the norms provided in the instructions for administering this test. In interpreting these test results a statement such as the following would be more appropriate. "Jerry made six errors on this test. For a child of his age it would indicate that he has difficulty discriminating among certain phonemes." It would also be helpful to list which phonemes the student could not discriminate between; however, that information would often be given in the "results" rather than in the interpretation.

7. *Keep sentence structure simple.* Make short, simple statements, as long complex sentences often become difficult to understand.

8. *Use third person when referring to yourself.* Rather than say "I think" or "It appears to me" it sounds more professional and perhaps less biased to say, "The clinician believes" or "The diagnostician would interpret this to mean. . . ."

9. *Make specific recommendations for the remediation of various difficulties noted.* As stated earlier, one of the purposes of writing case reports is that it serves as a vehicle for in-service education. For example, if it was noted that a student had a tendency to leave off or change endings such as "s," "ed," or "ing," it would be beneficial to most teachers to list specific workbooks and the pages on which you might find exercises for the remediation of problems such as these. It would also help to simply list exercises that would help, such as the following:
   a) Have the student fill in blanks in sentences from several choices as shown in this example:
   Pat _____ when she saw the snake.
   (jumps, jumping, jumped)
   b) Give the student a reading passage from a newspaper story and have him look for, pronounce, and circle all "ing," "ed," and "s" endings.

10. *Give exact dates of the administration of each test.* Since students are constantly learning and changing, the exact dates of the administration of each test may be significant.

11. *Show summary of significant strengths and weaknesses.* Some people who read reports are not directly involved in the remediation of the student's problem. In other cases it is simply a fact that some people are not likely to read an entire case report with extreme care. Where this is the case, it is helpful to include a summary of the student's significant strengths and weaknesses. Furthermore, for the remedial reading teacher, clinician, or classroom teacher who will be charged with further remediation of the student, the summary will prove helpful in digesting the entire report.

12. *Include possible causal factors for weaknesses of the student.* In many cases it cannot be determined what caused a student to become a disabled reader. In other cases possible causes may be so complex that it would be extremely difficult to isolate any one factor or small group of factors that were likely to have been causal factors in a student's reading disability. On the other hand, a teacher who has worked with a student for a period of time is likely to have gained a great deal of insight into the causal factors of a student's reading disability. When there are some definite signs that certain factors have contributed to a student's reading disability, these should be listed as "possible" factors. Knowing about such factors may prevent their reoccurrence.

THE FINAL CASE REPORT

The final case report that follows is somewhat longer than may be practical in many cases. It was chosen, however, because it illustrates most of the important points discussed in the previous section.

FINAL CASE REPORT

Name: Mark _____   Age: 9   Birthday: 11/12/__

School: _____   Grade: 4 (will be entering in September)

Examiner: _____

Period of Diagnosis and Remediation: September 5, 19__ to May 26, 19__

Date of Report: June 3, 19__

General Background of Student

HOME AND FAMILY ADJUSTMENT: Mark lives at home with his mother, stepfather, and five other children. Three of the children are his two sisters (10½ and 7) and a brother (9). The other two are half-brothers (6 and 4). After his mother's divorce from his father, Mark and his sisters and brother went to live with his grandmother. The four children lived with the grandmother approximately six years in Arizona. The parents feel that the adjustment of living with the grandmother to living with them was hard, but that he is fairly well adjusted now.

He reportedly gets along well with the other children in the family though he has an occasional fight with the older brother. He is generous and does not mind sharing. He has several close friends and bowls weekly in a league.

HEALTH HISTORY: His general health is reportedly fine and there is no record of his having any major illnesses. However, his mother stated that when he was quite small he used to run straight into things. His eyes were checked by a specialist in Arizona when he was about six years old, but no vision problem was apparent at that time. He was given a complete hearing examination at about the same time and was found to have no problem.

EDUCATION: Mark did not attend kindergarten. He attended school (first and second grade) in Arizona. The school was apparently an "Open Concept" type school. According to his parents, the school personnel were aware of his reading problem, but he has never attended any sort of special reading classes. During the past year, in the third grade, he has been in a self-contained classroom. This teacher has worked very closely with the examiner in carrying out various assignments and remedial activities.

RESULTS OF DIAGNOSTIC TESTS

WEPMAN AUDITORY DISCRIMINATION TEST: This test was administered on September 12, 19___. The student made only one error on this test. He was not able to discriminate between the letters "t" and "p" in the words "cap" and "cat."

INTERPRETATION

At the time the test was administered Mark was eight years old. A child of eight years old is not considered to have an auditory discrimination problem if he makes only one error on this test.

KEYSTONE VISUAL SURVEY TEST: This test was administered on September 12, 19 ___. Mark failed all of the subtests for near-point vision and the subtest for fusion at near point. He scored in the expected range on the remainder of the subtests. Mark was tested again on September 14, 19___ using the same test. The results were the same.

INTERPRETATION

Since the results of this tests indicated referral for further visual examination this was done. He was taken, by his mother, to an ophthalmologist on or about October 1, 19___. At that time he was given glasses to wear. He was told to wear them all of the time and has done so during the past school year.

SAN DIEGO QUICK ASSESSMENT: This test was administered on September 13, 19___ and again on May 24, 19___. This is a word pronunciation test to estimate a student's Free or Independent, Instructional, and Frustration levels. The results were as follows:

    Date: September 13, 19___
        Free or Independent Reading Level (Pre-Primer)
        Instructional Reading Level (Primer)
        Frustration Reading Level (First Grade)
    Date: May 24, 19___
        Free or Independent Reading Level (First Grade)
        Instructional Reading Level (Second and Third Grade)
        Frustration Reading Level (Fourth Grade)

INTERPRETATION

This is an indication that Mark's reading level (at least in terms of word knowledge) was no higher than First Grade Level at the time that he entered the remedial reading program. At the end of the program he had increased his word knowledge from two to three grade levels.

Diagnostic Reading Scales (Graded According to Informal Reading Inventory Criteria)

This test was administered on September 14, 19___ and again on May 25, 19___. Using the graded passages it enables one to obtain a student's Free or Independent,

Instructional, and Frustration reading levels as the student reads both orally and silently. The results were as follows:

Date: September 14, 19__

	Oral Reading	Silent Reading
Free or Independent Reading Level	None	None
Instructional Reading Level	None	None
Frustration Reading Level	First Grade	First Grade
Listening Comprehension Level	Fourth Grade	

Date: May 25, 19__

Free or Independent Reading Level	First Grade	Second Grade
Instructional Reading Level	Second Grade	Third Grade
Frustration Reading Level	Third Grade	Fourth Grade

INTERPRETATION

This is an indication that Mark's reading level increased from one to three grade levels during the period of time that he spent in remedial reading. It should be noted that his silent reading tended to be about one level higher than his oral reading. This is because he still has some problems with certain word attack skills; however, his ability to attack words has shown considerable improvement during the past year.

CRS BASIC SIGHT WORD INVENTORY: This test was administered on September 14, 19__ and again on May 24, 19__. It is a test of 299 basic sight words. These words are graded on at the Pre-Primer, Primer, First Grade, Second Grade (first half), Second Grade (second half), and Third Grade (first half) levels. The results were as follows:

Date: September 14, 19__

At this time Mark knew only eighteen of the words at the Pre-Primer level and twelve of the words at the Primer Level. Only seven words were known at the First Grade level. The test was stopped at the end of the First Grade level. Some examples of the errors made on this inventory are as follows:

WORD	ERROR	ANALYSIS OF ERROR(S)
big	bat	Medial vowel and ending consonant
him	his	Ending consonant
come	came	Medial vowel
three	their	Initial blend and ending sound
know	now	Vowel pair
your	yours	Insertion
play	pay	Substitution of initial consonant for blend

Date: May 24, 19__

At this time Mark knew all of the words on the CRS Basic Sight Word Inventory.

INTERPRETATION

Mark seemed to learn basic sight words quite rapidly with very little difficulty.

MILLS LEARNING TEST: (Adapted form in which pictures were not used.) This test was given between September 19 and 22, 19___. It is a test to determine by which (if any) method a student can best learn words.

INTERPRETATION

It was found that Mark learned best by using a combination approach. During the past school year nearly all sight words were taught by this method.

RX PHONICS SURVEY: This is a phonics survey that tests students' knowledge of the eighty most useful phonemes. It was administered on September 19, 19___ and again on May 26, 19___.
Date: September 19, 19___

At this time Mark knew only about twelve initial consonant sounds and about three initial consonant blends. He knew only one vowel sound.
Date: May 26, 19___

At this time he knew all of the initial consonant sounds, and all of the initial consonant blends and digraphs with the exception of the following:
"sw" and "scr"
He also knew all of the vowels (both long and short), vowel combinations, and special letter combinations with the exception of the following:
"ow" (as in cow), "ew" (as in flew), "oi" (as in soil), and "aw" (as in paw)

INTERPRETATION

At the beginning of the remedial period he knew very few phonic elements; however, he seemed to learn these quite rapidly. Much of the work in learning these was done using consonant substitution with known phonograms. The *Rx Reading Program* and *Webster Word Wheels* as well as the *Kenworthy Phonetic Drill Cards* were also very helpful in teaching phonics skills. Considerable teaching was also done using various commercial and homemade games.

No IQ tests were given since Mark seemed to learn nearly everything that was taught to him very rapidly.

GATES-MCKILLOP READING DIAGNOSTIC TESTS—ORAL VOCABULARY VIII–2: This test was administered on September 15, 19___. It is a test to determine the grade level of a student's oral vocabulary. The results were as follows:
Date: September 15, 19___
Grade Level 4.7

INTERPRETATION

At the time this was given it indicated that this student's oral vocabulary was considerably above both his oral and silent reading levels. It would indicate that any problems that he might have encountered in comprehension did not stem from a lack of oral vocabulary.

SUMMARY OF DIAGNOSIS

Significant Weaknesses:

1. At the beginning of the remedial period Mark had an extremely low basic sight word vocabulary and sight word vocabulary.
2. Mark had a tendency to ignore medial and terminal sounds.
3. He did not know but a few of the initial consonant sounds and almost no consonant blends, consonant digraphs, vowel pairs, and special letter combinations.
4. Mark had a tendency to repeat a number of words and phrases. However, this tendency seemed to disappear almost as soon as he began to develop a larger basic sight word and sight word vocabulary. For this reason the problem of repetitions was assumed to be caused from a lack of knowledge of words rather than from a bad habit.
5. A number of omissions were also noted at the beginning of the remedial period. This problem also seems to have been overcome with the learning of a number of sight words and an improvement in his word attack skills.
6. At the beginning of the remedial period Mark showed definite signs of discomfort during testing. This problem also seems to have been overcome since he has come to know the examiner better and since he also seems to have gained some self-confidence.

Significant Strengths:

1. Mark seems to learn almost any task rather quickly, especially when he receives tutoring in a rather small group or when he is tutored individually.
2. Although he seemed to have a rather low self-concept at the beginning of the re-mediation period, he now seems to have a rather good opinion of himself and believes that he can learn as well as anyone else.
3. He is rather large for his age and seems to excell in most sports. This seems to have been an important factor in building his self-confidence.
4. His ability to comprehend what he read was rather low in the beginning, but this was evidently caused from his lack of word knowledge. Now that he has enlarged his sight vocabulary he is able to comprehend quite well.
5. Mark seems to have an intensive interest in sports and is an avid reader of books on this subject.

Causal Factors in the Student's Reading Disability:

One of the causal factors in Mark's reading disability may have been the social adjustment of first going through the period in which his parents were divorced and then again having to go through social adjustment of moving in with his mother and stepfather after a period of about six years. Another cause of his reading disability may have been his eyesight. The tests conducted by the examiner, as well as those conducted by the ophthalmologist, indicated that he had a rather serious visual problem. A third possible cause of his problem was the fact that he had attended a new "Open-Concept" school that was in its initial stages of operation and he received no corrective help as his disability in reading began to develop.

SUMMARY OF
INSTRUCTIONAL PROGRAM

During the past year a lot of instruction was given on learning basic sight words and on increasing his sight vocabulary in general. This was accomplished through the following methods:

1. The use of drill with phrase cards.
2. The use of a programed textbook in phonics and structural analysis.
3. The use of the language experience approach.

   In the beginning stages the student dictated stories which the examiner wrote down. These were then compiled into booklets and were later read back to the examiner by the student on a daily basis. Later the student wrote his own stories and illustrated them. These were also compiled into booklets which he practiced reading over and over again. This material was also sent home once he had mastered it to some extent. The stories were also cut up into sentences (or words) and again assembled in order to recreate the original story or to make up a new one.

4. Whenever possible, the examiner gave a great deal of praise to the student for his accomplishments.
5. The student was taught the most useful vowel rules and syllabication principles.
6. A number of exercises were used in which sentences appeared with one word left blank. This word was usually one which the student had previously missed. Where-ever a blank appeared the student was given several choices of words to use in the blank. The word choices were normally those of similar configuration and would, in most cases, include the word that had been substituted by the student in place of the word missed.
7. Mark was encouraged to read a great deal on his own. At first he did very little of this, but after he had acquired a larger sight vocabulary he became an avid reader, especially of books concerning sports.

PROGNOSIS FOR SUCCESS AND
RECOMMENDATIONS FOR FURTHER
REMEDIATION

Prognosis:

During the past year Mark has steadily improved in his reading ability. He appears to learn rapidly and there seems to be no physical or emotional problems that are now hindering his learning progress. At this point, however, he still needs to learn to use his newly acquired skills in vowel rules and syllabication principles. It would appear that he could profit from at least one more semester of remedial reading at which time another evaluation should be made. He has learned rapidly during the time that he spent in remedial reading this year and if the present rate of gain is maintained he should be reading up to grade level in a year or less.

Recommendations for Further Remediation:

1. The student needs to do a great deal of free reading to increase his sight vocabulary through multiple exposure to many words.
2. Although he has become familiar with syllabication principles and vowel rules, he still needs more practice on using these skills.
3. Mark has been on a program of reading for approximately one hour per day during the past few months. His parents have set aside a certain time of day for him to read. This practice should be encouraged.
4. His parents should be encouraged to take him to the public library as often as possible.
5. It may be helpful to use some sort of reward system for a certain number of books read. He should, of course, be praised when he reads and should also be encouraged to try to find books that he would like to read on his own.
6. Mark still needs to learn the vowel pairs, "ow" (as in crow and cow), "ew", "oi", and "aw."
7. He seems to work best either by himself or in a small group. He seems to be highly distracted by large groups, especially when there is considerable noise in the room. Whenever possible, he should be taught either in a small group or individually.

SUMMARY

It is extremely important to develop a record-keeping system in teaching remedial reading to communicate important information derived from testing and teaching. The record-keeping system should be adequate but not burdensome, and should provide for communication among all the various people who are likely to come into professional contact with each disabled reader. Record keeping also serves the important purpose of measuring the progress of disabled readers and as a training technique, or as in-service education, for classroom teachers and parents. It is also extremely important that reading personnel familiarize themselves with techniques for the writing of case reports.

15

EVALUATION AND USE OF MATERIALS

The first part of this chapter deals with some important criteria to be considered in purchasing materials for teaching disabled readers. This is followed by a listing of some specific programs and books for use in remedial reading classes. The value and use of reading "machines" and/or mechanical devices is then discussed. The chapter ends with a discussion of the value and limitations of teacher-made materials and some specific ideas for creating these materials.

CRITERIA FOR EVALUATION

In purchasing materials for use in remedial reading there are certain criteria that these materials should meet that may not always be necessary when purchasing materials for developmental reading. Remedial reading deals with students who often possess weaknesses or gaps in learning in specific areas; whereas, in developmental reading the teacher is usually dealing with students who start from the beginning and need to learn the entire scope of reading skills. Following is a list of some of the important criteria that should be considered when purchasing materials for remedial reading.

Can Lessons Be Isolated For Teaching Specific Skills?

In most cases when teaching disabled readers it would not be necessary to have them go through an entire phonics program, learn *every* commonly taught vowel rule, learn all basic sight words, etc. For this reason materials and/or programs purchased for use in remedial reading should be of such a nature that various lessons can be pulled out for use in teaching specific skills without the necessity of the student going through the entire program. For example, if you were using a phonics program and knew the student was weak in only the "fl," "bl," and "gr" blends you should be able to locate and use the parts of the program designed to teach these blends without having a student waste his time in completing lessons that taught a number of other phonics skills that he already knew.

Some materials and/or programs are such that a certain "level" of placement within the program is desirable. Where this is the case, the materials and/or program should contain a placement test for that purpose.

386

Are Lessons Self-Correcting or Do They Require Considerable Teacher Direction?

Reading programs and/or materials vary a great deal in the amount of teacher time and direction that is required for their use. However, the teaching of remedial reading requires a great deal of individualized instruction. Because of this it is highly desirable that materials used in remedial reading be of such a nature that they require very little continuous teacher time or direction in their use. We are beginning to see more materials appearing on the market in which the teacher merely helps the student get started in a program and from that point on, the student, for the most part, can work on his own. This type of material and/or program is highly desirable for use in the remedial reading classroom.

Is The Cost Reasonable in Relation to the Lifetime of the Materials?

Some materials, such as workbooks, may appear to be relatively inexpensive when they are purchased. However, if they are quickly used up by students, the per pupil cost for their use may end up being considerably higher than nonexpendable materials that cost somewhat more. Therefore, when purchasing materials for use in remedial reading, consider the cost in relation to the total amount of usage available for each pupil.

Another important factor to consider is the amount of handling that materials are likely to receive. Materials that are likely to be handled a great deal should be of a heavy card stock and, if possible, should be laminated to protect them from heavy use. Cost, therefore, should also be considered in relation to the quality of the construction of reading materials.

How Many Students Can be Serviced by the Material at One Time?

Some materials are of such a nature that only one student may use them at any one time while others may be used by a number of students simultaneously. This is an extremely important factor to keep in mind when purchasing reading materials. For example, one new program requires the use of a rather expensive machine that will accommodate only one student at a time. Although each lesson is not high priced in relation to the total time it may last if handled carefully, the cost of the program then becomes extremely high priced in relation to the number of students that can be serviced during a specified period of time. On the other hand, many programs in kit form contain duplicate lessons on which several students can work at one time. Furthermore, since in many cases, students are not likely to be working on the same lesson, at the same time, a small kit type program may service a number of students at once.

Is the Cost Reasonable In Relation to the Spectrum of Skills Taught?

Some programs are extremely limited in relation to the number of reading skills taught while others may cover a much greater spectrum of skills. If the lessons within a program can be used without the aid of some expensive mechanical device then a program that covers a greater spectrum of skills is likely to be able to service more students. On the other hand, it is often desirable in remedial reading to cover certain concepts in depth. Where this is the case, a program with a number of lessons reviewing difficult skills may be desirable.

Can Lessons Be Replaced Without Purchasing a Completely New Program?

Any experienced teacher is likely to know that certain cards, tapes, sheets, etc. which are a part of a reading program are likely to be lost, especially where the material receives heavy usage. In purchasing a program you should consider the possibility that this may happen, and give preference to materials and/or programs in which various components can be replaced.

Another important factor to consider is the ease of access to replacement parts. For example, is a local dealer available who can repair or replace broken and/or missing items? Is the program one that has established a good reputation; and is it manufactured by a large reputable company that is not likely to discontinue the item?

Is the Teacher's Manual Adequate or Burdensome?

As the author of several programs for use by teachers in the public schools I know that teachers are not likely to read a teacher's manual that is extremely long or burdensome. I have also found that many of the sales representatives who make a large part of their living selling these products have also not read the manuals. Therefore, from a practical standpoint, in purchasing a new program you should examine the teacher's manual to see if it covers the program adequately and yet is not so burdensome that it is unlikely to be read in its entirety.

Is the Format of the Material Different From That in Which Students Have Previously Experienced Failure?

It is common knowledge among personnel working in a reading setting that certain types of reading materials, such as hardbound books, have a tendency to be associated with failure for those students who are disabled readers. For this reason materials purchased for use in remedial reading should be of such a nature that they do not closely resemble materials with which students might already have experienced failure. For example, materials that seem to be extremely popular with disabled readers are softbound books, kits that contain easy, short lessons, programs with audio tapes, etc. One way to select materials of this nature is to ask the sales people to allow you to use samples of kits, etc. for a short period of time and then simply ask students their reactions to these materials.

Are Materials Highly Motivating?

In visiting a reading center it soon becomes evident which programs and/or materials are popular with the students. For the teacher who is unfamiliar with various types of material it is advisable to visit other reading centers or remedial reading classrooms and simply ask other more experienced teachers which programs and/or materials are most popular with students of various ages. If possible, it is also advisable to obtain samples of materials and try them out with students before buying them in larger quantities.

Are Books and Other Materials Graded According to a Well-Known Readability Formula or Are They Based on Publishers' Estimates?

Materials purchased for remedial reading instruction should generally have a high interest level and yet contain a low vocabulary load. Numerous studies have shown that it is not uncommon for science and social studies textbooks for use by students at the seventh or eighth grade level to vary in difficulty from page-to-page from approximately the third or fourth grade level up to the eleventh or twelfth grade level. For example, many publishers advertise their trade books as having a certain interest level and as "being at an appropriate reading level for students from third through sixth grade." Any kind of books or material in which the readability level varies to such a large extent is inappropriate for use in remedial reading.

When possible you should attempt to purchase reading materials that have been written at specific grade levels on the basis of one of the better known readability formulas such as the Spache Formula for grades one through three or the Dale-Chall Formula for grades four upward.

SOME RECOMMENDED BOOKS FOR USE IN TEACHING REMEDIAL READING

Any given list of books for use in teaching remedial reading is likely to become outdated to some extent with the passage of time. This is true especially because publishers tend to drop certain books and series of books from the market. In the list of recommended books that follow, however, are a number that have stood the test of time and have been highly successful in remedial reading programs. For this reason they are likely to be available for some time. This list is by no means complete, but it is representative of the types of books that meet the criteria previously outlined. In Appendix C you will also find a rather lengthy list of materials that also meet many of the criteria of the list previously outlined.

1. **Benefic Press; 10300 W. Roosevelt Road; Westchester, Illinois 60153**

Cowboy Sam Series, by Edna Walker Chander. These exciting western-life adventures offer three levels of difficulty for each reading level. In each book, a section lists the reading skills covered.

TITLE	READING LEVEL	INTEREST LEVEL
Cowboy Sam and Big Bill	pp	pp—2
Cowboy Sam and Freckles	pp	pp—2
Cowboy Sam and Dandy	pp	pp—2
Cowboy Sam and Miss Lily	p	p—3
Cowboy Sam and Porky	p	p—3
Cowboy Sam	p	p—3
Cowboy Sam and Flop	1	1—4
Cowboy Sam and Shorty	1	1—4
Cowboy Sam and Freddy	1	1—4
Cowboy Sam and Sally	2	2—5
Cowboy Sam and the Fair	2	2—5
Cowboy Sam and the Rodeo	2	2—5
Cowboy Sam and the Airplane	3	3—6
Cowboy Sam and the Indians	3	3—6
Cowboy Sam and the Rustlers	3	3—6
Teacher's Manual for Series		

Button Family Adventure Series, by Edith McCall. This series offers enjoyable reading about a blue-collar family and the variety of situations they become involved in.

TITLE	READING LEVEL	INTEREST LEVEL
The Buttons at the Zoo	pp	pp—2
The Buttons See Things That Go	pp	pp—2
Bucky Button	pp	pp—2
The Buttons and the Whirlybird	p	p—2
The Buttons and the Pet Parade	p	p—2
The Buttons Take A Boat Ride	p	p—2
The Buttons and Mr. Pete	1	1—3
The Buttons at the Farm	1	1—3
The Buttons and the Boy Scouts	2	2—4
The Buttons Go Camping	2	2—4
The Buttons and the Little League	3	3—5
The Buttons and the Soap Box Derby	3	3—5
Teacher's Manual for Series		

Sailor Jack Series, by Selma Wassermann. Each of these books is about an adventure on an atomic submarine; all stress thinking skills.

TITLE	READING LEVEL	INTEREST LEVEL
Sailor Jack and Homer Pots	pp	pp—2
Sailor Jack and Eddy	pp	pp—2
Sailor Jack	pp	pp—2
Sailor Jack and Bluebell's Dive	p	p—3
Sailor Jack and Bluebell	p	p—3
Sailor Jack and the Jet Plane	p	p—3
Sailor Jack and the Ball Game	1	1—4
Sailor Jack's New Friend	1	1—4

TITLE		
Sailor Jack and the Target Ship	2	2—5
Sailor Jack Goes North	3	3—6
Teacher's Manual for Series		

Dan Frontier Series, by William J. Hurley. These adventure stories are about early frontier life in the Midwest. Dan, the main character, is a heroic frontiersman—not unlike Daniel Boone.

TITLE	READING LEVEL	INTEREST LEVEL
Dan Frontier	pp	pp—2
Dan Frontier and the New House	pp	pp—2
Dan Frontier and the Big Cat	p	p—3
Dan Frontier Goes Hunting	p	p—3
Dan Frontier, Trapper	1	1—4
Dan Frontier With the Indians	1	1—4
Dan Frontier and the Wagon Train	2	2—5
Dan Frontier Scouts With the Army	2	2—5
Dan Frontier, Sheriff	3	3—6
Dan Frontier Goes Exploring	3	3—6
Dan Frontier Goes to Congress	4	4—7
Teacher's Manual for Series		

Space Age Books, by Hazel W. Corson. Peter, the son of a space scientist, takes the reader on many adventures in space travel and exploration.

TITLE	READING LEVEL	INTEREST LEVEL
Peter and the Rocket Fishing Trip	1	1—4
Peter and the Rocket Sitter	1	1—4
Peter and the Rocket Team	2	2—5
Peter and the Unlucky Rocket	2	2—5
Peter and the Big Balloon	2	2—5
Peter and the Rocket Ship	3	3—6
Peter and the Two-Hour Moon	3	3—6
Peter and the Moon Trip	3	3—6

Tom Logan Series, by Edna Walker Chandler. Even slower readers are successful with the carefully controlled vocabulary in these stories about the Old West.

TITLE	READING LEVEL	INTEREST LEVEL
Pony Rider	pp	pp—2
Talking Wire	pp	pp—2
Track Boss	p	p—3
Cattle Drive	p	p—3
Secret Tunnel	1	1—4
Gold Train	1	1—4
Gold Nugget	2	2—5
Cattle Cars	2	2—5
Stage Coach Driver	3	3—6
Circus Train	3	3—6

Butternut Bill Series, by Edith McCall. These high-interest, low difficulty readers are about a boy named Butternut Bill and his life in the Ozark Mountain region.

TITLE	READING LEVEL	INTEREST LEVEL
Butternut Bill	pp	pp—2
Butternut Bill and the Bee Tree	pp	pp—2
Butternut Bill and the Big Catfish	pp	pp—2
Butternut Bill and the Bear	p	p—3
Butternut Bill and the Little River	p	p—3
Butternut Bill and the Big Pumpkin	p	p—3
Butternut Bill and His Friends	1	1—3
Butternut Bill and the Train	1	1—4

Animal Adventure Readers, by Gene Darby. These are scientifically-based, animal adventure stories for primary children.

TITLE	READING LEVEL	INTEREST LEVEL
Becky, The Rabbit	pp	1—3
Squeaky, The Squirrel	pp	1—3
Doc, The Dog	pp	1—3
Pat, The Parakeet	pp	1—3
Kate, The Cat	pp	1—3
Gomar, The Gosling	p	1—3
Skippy, The Skunk	p	1—3
Sandy, The Swallow	p	1—3
Sally, The Screech Owl	1	1—4
Pudgy, The Beaver	1	1—4
Hamilton, The Hamster	1	1—4
Horace, The Horse	1	1—4

Alley Alligator Series, by Athol B. Packer and Bill C. Cliett, Jr. These low-difficulty readers are about the adventures of three rangers and a baby alligator named Alley in the Florida Everglades.

TITLE	READING LEVEL
Alley Alligator	pp
Alley Alligator and The Fire	p
Alley Alligator and The Hurricane	1
Alley Alligator and The Airboat Race	2
Alley Alligator and The Hunters	3

Inner City Series, by Mike Neigoff. These stories deal with today's city life and how young people meet their problems with humor, imagination, and a determination to succeed.

TITLE	READING LEVEL	INTEREST LEVEL
Beat The Gang	2	2—5
Tough Guy	3	3—6
Runaway	3	3—6
New in School	4	4—7
No Drop Out	4	4—7

Racing Wheels Readers, by Anabel Dean. Readers of this series are taken on the racing adventures of Woody Woods and his friends. Particularly appropriate for below-average readers, the stories are mature and contemporary, but are written with a carefully controlled vocabulary.

TITLE	READING LEVEL	INTEREST LEVEL
Hot Rod	2	4—12
Drag Race	2	4—12
Destruction Derby	3	4—12
Stock Car Race	3	4—12
Road Race	4	4—12
Indy 500	4	4—12

Target Today Series, by Charles M. Brown, Dr. Helen Truher, and Dr. Phillip Weise. Each book in this series contains 100 short stories dealing with life today; the story characters are from many different ethnic and socioeconomic backgrounds.

TITLE	READING LEVEL	INTEREST LEVEL
Here It Is	2	4—12
Action Now	2—3	4—12
Move Ahead	3—4	5—12
Lead On	4—6	5—12

Sports Mystery Series, by Evelyn Lunemann. These readers would be very appropriate in remedial reading programs ranging from sixth to ninth grades. These are stories about teenagers, their problems and how they solve them, and the excitement they find in sports activities.

TITLE	READING LEVEL	INTEREST LEVEL
Ten Feet Tall	2	4—12
No Turning Back	2	4—12
Fairway Danger	3	4—12
Tip Off	3	4—12
Pitcher's Choice	3	4—12
Face Off	4	4—12
Swimmer's Mark	4	4—12
Tennis Champ	4	4—12

Mystery Adventure Series, by Henry A. Bamman. These mystery stories take teenage boys and girls into situations which test their determination, courage, and deductive reasoning. This series is for intermediate and junior high students who are reading below grade level.

TITLE	READING LEVEL	INTEREST LEVEL
Mystery Adventure:		
Of The Talking Statues	2	4—12
Of The Jeweled Bell	2	4—12
At Cave Four	3	4—12
Of The Indian Burial Ground	4	4—12
At Longcliff Inn	5	4—12
Of The Smuggled Treasure	6	4—12

2. **D.C. Heath and Company; 125 Spring Street; Lexington, Massachusetts 02173**

Teen-Age Tales, Second and Third Editions. By Ruth Strang, Ralph Roberts, Walter Barbe, Regina Heavey, Harriet Stewart, Amelia Meinik. These nine collections of stories are for teens with reading difficulties; the vocabulary is on the elementary level.

	READING LEVEL	INTEREST LEVEL
Book A, Second Edition	3	7—12
Book B, Second Edition	3	7—12
Book C, Second Edition	3	7—12
Book One, Third Edition	5,6	7—12
Book Two, Third Edition	5,6	7—12
Book Three, Second Edition	5,6	7—12
Book Four, Second Edition	5,6	7—12
Book Five, Second Edition	5,6	7—12
Book Six, Second Edition	5,6	7—12

3. **Field Educational Publications, Inc.; 2400 Hanover Street; Palo Alto, California 94304**

The Jim Forest Readers, Rambeau, Rambeau, and Gullett. This is an action-filled series about the life in a forest preserve; included in the stories are plenty of suspense, humor, and sound conservation concepts. The main characters are a young boy, Jim Forest, and his uncle, a forest ranger.

TITLE	READING LEVEL	INTEREST LEVEL
Jim Forest and Ranger Don	1.7	1—7
Jim Forest and The Trapper	1.7	1—7
Jim Forest and The Ghost Town	1.8	1—7
Jim Forest and The Bandits	1.9	1—7
Jim Forest and Lightning	1.9	1—7
Jim Forest and Phantom Crater	2.0	1—7
Jim Forest and The Mystery Hunter	2.2	1—7
Jim Forest and The Plane Crash	2.4	1—7
Jim Forest and Dead Man's Peak	2.6	1—7
Jim Forest and The Flood	2.8	1—7
Jim Forest and Lone Wolf Gulch	3.1	1—7
Jim Forest and Woodman's Ridge	3.2	1—7
Teacher's Manual for Series		

The Deep-Sea Adventure Series, by Coleman, Berres, Hewett & Briscoe. These twelve exciting novels for new readers are based on deep-sea adventures, such as: pearl diving, captured sharks and whales, a submarine rescue, frogmen, and smugglers.

TITLE	READING LEVEL	INTEREST LEVEL
The Sea Hunt	1.8	3—11
Storm Island	1.8	3—11
Treasure Under the Sea	2.1	3—11
Sea Gold	2.2	3—11
Submarine Rescue	2.4	3—11
Enemy Agents	2.5	3—11
Castaways	2.6	3—11

	READING LEVEL	INTEREST LEVEL
The Pearl Divers	2.8	3—11
Frogmen in Action	3.1	3—11
Danger Below	4.4	3—11
Whale Hunt	4.7	3—11
Rocket Divers	5.0	3—11
Teacher's Manual for Series		

The Morgan Bay Mysteries, by John and Nancy Rambeau. These controlled vocabulary books are fast-paced, suspenseful mystery stories—and in addition, they are humorous.

TITLE	READING LEVEL	INTEREST LEVEL
The Mystery of Morgan Castle	2.3	4—11
The Mystery of the Marble Angel	2.6	4—11
The Mystery of the Midnight Visitor	3.2	4—11
The Mystery of the Missing Marlin	3.5	4—11
The Mystery of the Musical Ghost	3.5	4—11
The Mystery of Monks' Island	3.7	4—11
The Mystery of the Marauder's Gold	3.9	4—11
The Mystery of the Myrmidon's Journey	4.1	4—11
Teacher's Manual for Series		

The Wildlife Adventure Series, by Leonard & Briscoe. These eight exciting stories deal with man and his relationships with nature's creatures.

TITLE	READING LEVEL	INTEREST LEVEL
Gatie the Alligator	2.6	3—9
Sleeky the Otter	2.8	3—9
Skipper the Dolphin	3.0	3—9
Tawny the Mountain Lion	3.2	3—9
Bounder the Jackrabbit	3.5	3—9
Thor the Moose	3.6	3—9
Ruff the Wolf	3.7	3—9
Arctos the Grizzly	4.4	3—9
Teacher's Manual for Series		

The Checkered Flag Series, by Henry A. Bamman and Robert J. Whitehead. Each of these eight stories deals with a different type of vehicle in various competitive situations.

TITLE	READING LEVEL	INTEREST LEVEL
Wheels	2.4	6—12
Riddler	2.5	6—12
Bearcat	2.5	6—12
Smashup	2.6	6—12
Scramble	3.0	6—12
Flea	3.5	6—12
Grand Prix	4.0	6—12
500	4.5	6—12
Teacher's Manual for Series		

4. **Follett Publishing Company; 1010 West Washington Blvd.; Chicago, Illinois 60607**

Beginning-To-Read Books. These low-level, high-interest books with their simple sentence structure are great for independent reading by primary children—as well as older children with difficulties in reading.

The reading level for each book is indicated on the spines and/or the jackets for easy reference; dots are used: one dot = end of Grade 1; two dots = middle of Grade 2; three dots = end of Grade 2 reading levels.

END OF GRADE 1 READING LEVELS:

The Animal Hat Shop
Big Bug, Little Bug
Big New School
Bing Bang Pig
The Curious Cow
The Elf in the Singing Tree
Follett Beginning-To-Read Picture Dictionary
Gertie The Duck
Grandfather Dear
Grandmother Dear
The Hill That Grew
In John's Back Yard
Jiffy, Miss Boo and Mr. Roo
Just Follow Me
Little Quack
Little Red Hen
Mr. Barney's Beard
My Own Little House
Nobody Listens to Andrew
Pearl Goes to School
The Roly Poly Cookie
Sad Mrs. Sam Sack
Something New at the Zoo
The Splendid Belt of Mr. Big
Too Many Dogs
The Wee Little Man

LEVEL TWO

The Four Friends
The Little Boy Who Wouldn't Say His Name
The Hole in the Wall
Mabel the Whale
Miss Hattie and the Monkey
Henry
Linda's Air Mail Letter
The O'Leary's and Friends
Who Will Milk My Cow?
Barefoot Boy
Shoes For Angela
The Dog Who Came to Dinner
Big Bad Bear
One Day Everything Went Wrong
The No-Bark Dog

LEVEL THREE

Benny and the Bear
Christopher Columbus
Peter's Policemen
Beginning-To-Read Poetry

A Day on Big O
Beginning-To-Read Riddles and Jokes
A Uniform for Harry
Sparky's Fireman
Ride, Willy, Ride
Kittens and More Kittens
Danny's Glider Ride

5.   Garrard Publishing Company; Champaign, Illinois 61820

The First Reading Books, by E.W. Dolch. Written with the very first sight words a reader learns; these books contain true and folklore tales about animals. These books are written on approximately a Grade 1 Reading Level; their interest level ranges from Grades 1—4.

In The Woods
Monkey Friends
On the Farm
Tommy's Pets
Zoo Is Home
Once There Was A Bear
Once There Was A Cat
Once There Was A Dog
Once There Was An Elephant
Once There Was A Monkey
Once There Was A Rabbit
Big, Bigger, Biggest
Dog Pals
Friendly Birds
I Like Cats
Some Are Small

The Basic Vocabulary Series, by E.W. Dolch. These true-life and folklore stories from all over the world are written almost entirely with the Dolch 220 Basic Sight Words and 95 most Common Nouns. Their reading level is Grade 2 and their interest level ranges from Grades 1—6.

Folk Stories	*Irish Stories*
Animal Stories	*Navaho Stories*
"Why" Stories	*Dog Stories*
Pueblo Stories	*More Dog Stories*
Tepee Stories	*Elephant Stories*
Wigwam Stories	*Bear Stories*
Lodge Stories	*Lion and Tiger Stories*
Horse Stories	*Circus Stories*

Pleasure Reading Books, by E.W. Dolch. These old classics have been rewritten with a simple vocabulary so that even slower readers can derive pleasure from them. The reading level of these books is Grade 4; the interest level ranges from Grade 3 and up.

Fairy Stories	*Old World Stories*
Andersen Stories	*Far East Stories*
Aesop's Stories	*Greek Stories*
Famous Stories	*Gospel Stories*
Robin Hood Stories	*Bible Stories*
Robinson Crusoe	*Gulliver's Stories*
Ivanhoe	

6. Houghton Mifflin Company; 6626 Oakbrook Blvd.; Dallas, Texas 75235; 110 Tremont Street; Boston, Mass. 02107 (Editorial and International Departments)

Read-By-Yourself Books. This series provides pupils with books they can read with ease and enjoyment. In addition, they are written by well-known authors of children's books.

TITLE	READING LEVEL
Tim and Terry	Primer level
I Want to Be a Bird	Primer level
The Cat In The Hat	First Reader level
The Cat in the Hat Comes Back	First Reader level
To Catch A Worm	First Reader level
Tiny Toosey's Birthday	First Reader level
Curious George Flies A Kite	First Reader level
David McCheever's 29 Dogs	End of First or Beginning Second Grade
Tiny's Big Umbrella	End of First or Beginning Second Grade
Herbie Changed His Mind	End of First or Beginning Second Grade
The Little Red Bus	End of First or Beginning Second Grade
The New Bed	End of First or Beginning Second Grade
No Hat	End of First or Beginning Second Grade
Plum Pie	End of First or Beginning Second Grade
Penny	End of First or Beginning Second Grade
What Is A Brother?	End of First or Beginning Second Grade
Tough Guy	Second Grade Level
Bill's Great Trick	Second Grade Level
You Can Fly—Why Can't I?	Second Grade Level
My Friend Mac	Second Grade Level
Spiders Are Spinners	Third Grade Level

The Piper Books. These are carefully graded books for the intermediate grades and are available in either cloth-bound or paperback editions. Some illustrative titles in the series are:

John Ponce de Leon: First in the Land
Sam Houston: Friend of the Indians
Horace Mann: Sower of Learning
Amelia Earhart: First Lady of the Air
Christopher Columbus: Sailor and Dreamer
Abigail Adams: The President's Lady
Henry Ford: Maker of the Model T

7. Penns Valley Publishers; 211 West Beaver Avenue; State College, Pennsylvania 16801

The Botel Interesting Reading Series, edited by Morton Botel. These books were developed for the numerous older students who have not learned to read beyond the third grade level; the reading level of this series ranges from third to fifth grade.

Buried Gold, by Leonard Eisner
Mystery of Broken Wheel Ranch, by Leonard Eisner
First Men in Space, by Sara Maynard Clark
Mary Elizabeth and Mr. Lincoln, by Margaret Melchoir Seylor
Great Moments in American History, by Gordon Parker

8. Random House; School Division; 201 E. 50th Street; New York, New York 10022

Beginner Books. These books are written by well-known authors of children's books; the readability level of each book is based on the Spache Readability Formula.

TITLE	READING LEVEL
The Cat in the Hat	2.1
The Cat in the Hat Comes Back	2.0
A Fly Went By	2.1
The Big Jump and Other Stories	2.4
A Big Ball of String	2.5
Sam and the Firefly	2.0
You Will Go to the Moon	1.8
Cowboy Andy	1.8
The Whales Go By	1.8
Stop That Ball!	1.9
Bennett Cerf's Book of Laughs	2.1
Ann Can Fly	2.0
One Fish, Two Fish, Red Fish, Blue Fish	1.7
The King's Wish and Other Stories	2.0
Bennett Cerf's Book of Riddles	2.2
Green Eggs and Ham	1.9
Put Me in the Zoo	1.5
Are You My Mother?	1.7
Ten Apples Up on Top!	1.5
Go, Dog, Go!	1.5
Little Black, A Pony	1.8
Look Out For Pirates!	2.1
A Fish Out of Water	1.8
More Riddles	2.3
Robert the Rose Horse	1.7
I Was Kissed by a Seal at the Zoo	2.1
Snow	1.7
The Big Honey Hunt	1.9
Hop on Pop	1.7
Dr. Seuss's ABC	
Do You Know What I'm Going to Do Next Saturday?	2.4
Summer	2.2
Little Black Goes to the Circus	1.8
The Bears' Christmas	2.4

9. Science Research Associates, Inc.; 259 East Erie Street; Chicago, Illinois 60611

Science Research Associates Pilot Libraries. Pilot Library selections are unaltered excerpts from selected juvenile books. Each Library contains 72 selections, from 16 to 32 pages in length, of graded levels of difficulty. For each of the Libraries, the teacher is provided with a handbook that provides a synopsis of each book and questions for discussion. A student record book provides exercise for testing the student's comprehension.

Pilot Library Ic, Third Grade
Pilot Library IIa, Fourth Grade
Pilot Library IIb, Fifth Grade
Pilot Library IIc, Sixth Grade and Seventh Grade
Pilot Library IIIb, Eighth Grade

10. Scott, Foresman and Company; 1900 East Lake Avenue; Glenview, Illinois 60025

Easy Reading Books. These modern stories, as well as classics, have been edited so that slower readers can read and enjoy them. 4—6 Reading Level.

ABOUT TEEN-AGERS

The Years Between
On the Threshold

COLLECTIONS OF STORIES, OLD AND NEW

Adventures with Animals
Eight Treasured Stories
Famous Mysteries
In Other Days
People to Remember
Six Great Stories

ADAPTED CLASSICS

Around the World in Eighty Days
The Call of the Wild
Captains Courageous
David Copperfield
Huckleberry Finn
Julius Caesar in Modern Prose
The Last of the Mohicans
Lorna Doone
Moby Dick
The Prince and the Pauper
Robinson Crusoe
Silas Marner
Tom Sawyer
Treasure Island
Twenty Thousand Leagues Under the Sea
When Washington Danced

MYSTERY STORIES BY GERTRUDE CHANDLER WARNER

Caboose Mystery
Houseboat Mystery
Mountain Top Mystery
Schoolhouse Mystery
Snowbound Mystery
Tree House Mystery

READING FOR PLEASURE ANTHOLOGIES

On Target
Top Flight
In Orbit

11. Webster/McGraw-Hill; 1221 Avenue of the Americas; New York, New York 10020

The Everyreader Series, adapted by Kottmeyer. These books provide high-interest reading for junior and senior high school students who are reading below their grade level. The interest level ranges from Grades 6—12, but the reading level does not exceed Grade 4.

Cases of Sherlock Holmes
The Trojan War
Robin Hood Series
Ivanhoe (by Scott)
A Tale of Two Cities
Simon Bolivar
Flamingo Feather
Men of Iron
Count of Monte Cristo
Juarez, Hero of Mexico
To Have and To Hold
Wild Animals I Have Known
Call of the Wild
Indian Paint
Bob, Son of Battle
On Jungle Trails
The Gold Bug and Other Stories
King Arthur and His Knights
Ben Hur
Greek and Roman Myths

Reading Incentive Series, by Edward G. Summers. This unique series, developed for students with reading difficulties, ranges in interest level from Grade 7 to Grade 12. The reading level increases from Grade 3 to Grade 7.

TITLE	READING LEVEL
Mystery in the Sky, Book 1	3
Swamp March, Book 2	4
Full Speed Ahead, Book 3	5
Venus Bound, Book 4	6
To Climb a Mountain, Book 5	7
Teacher's Manual for Series	

Reading Shelf I and II, adapted by Warren Halliburton. These 20 adaptations of stories by well-known authors range in reading level from Grades 4—6; the interest level ranges from Grades 7—12.

READING SHELF I

The Knife
Requiem for a Heavyweight
Marty/Printer's Measure
Call of the Wild
Ramblers, Gamblers, and Lovers: A Book of Poems
Stories by Jesse Stuart
The Year the Yankees Lost the Pennant
Ax
Stories by Edgar Allan Poe

READING SHELF II

Negro Doctor
The Off-Islanders
How to Win Friends and Influence People
Art Arfons, Fastest Man on Wheels
Dark Sea Running

Nigger
The Funny Bone
My Own Backyard
Follow the Free Wind
Look to the River

City Limits I and II, by John Durham, Halliburton, and Swinburne. These stories deal with inner-city living and the lives of young adults; they are written on a Grade 5—7 reading level. The interest level ranges from Grades 7—12.

CITY LIMITS I   CITY LIMITS II

The Long Haul and Other Stories   *Cutting Out*
Chico   *A Fist Against the Night*
Cry, Baby!   *Some Things That Glitter*
The Heist   *The Sniper*
Take the Short Way Home and Other Stories   *The Shark Bites Back*
Angelita Nobody   *A Birthday Present for Katheryn Kenyatta*

12. Wonder-Treasure Books, Division of Grosset and Dunlap; 51 Madison Avenue; New York, New York 10010

Easy Reader Series. These inexpensive books are available in supermarkets and dime stores; they are written with controlled vocabularies of 100 to 200 words.

Will You Come to My Party?
Hurry Up, Slowpoke
Miss Polly's Animal School
Billy Brown: The Baby Sitter
Laurie and the Yellow Curtains
Barney Beagle and the Cat
Barney Beagle Goes Camping
The Day Joe Went to the Supermarket
Let Papa Sleep!
The Secret Cat
The Duck on the Truck
Grandpa's Wonderful Glass

READING MACHINES — THEIR VALUES AND LIMITATIONS IN REMEDIAL READING

Many people untrained in the teaching of reading would consider various machines or mechanical devices as a necessary part of the remedial reading program. On the other hand, because they have read negative research information, remedial reading teachers often believe that most machines have little or no value in the teaching of reading. The truth about the value of the use of various machines and mechanical devices probably lies somewhere between these two opposing points of view.

Mechanical devices or machines most commonly used in teaching reading could generally be classified under one of two main categories. One category would be controlled reading or pacing devices and the other would be tachistoscopic devices. Controlled reading devices are generally used for increasing speed and tachistoscopic devices are used to present a timed exposure to a word, phrase, or group of numbers.

Since the remedial reading teacher is usually not concerned with increasing reading speed per se, the various devices for controlled reading have very little practical value in the remedial reading program. In developmental reading or in speed reading classes controlled reading devices have proven helpful in increasing reading speed. But on the other hand, numerous studies have shown that when students simply pace their reading with their hand their gain in reading speed is usually equal to, or excels, gains made while using a controlled reading device. The Controlled Reader[1] can be set to show an entire line at a time or can also be set to use a guided slot that moves from left to right thus preventing regressions and repetitions. It can be helpful for disabled readers who have developed the habit of making regressions or repetitions. It should be remembered, however, that regressions or repetitions are more often caused from lack of knowledge of sight words or difficulty with phonics or structural analysis or comprehension. When this is the case, the regressions or repetitions are only symptomatic of these causes and the use of a guided slot while reading would, in reality, be treating the symptom rather than the cause of the problem. Furthermore, a student can use a card to cover the line as he reads, or can point to words as they are read, and accomplish essentially the same purpose.

Tachistoscopic devices were originally designed for several purposes. One of these purposes was to attempt to broaden students' visual span and thus enable them to see more numbers, letters, or words with each fixation of the eye. Some studies have indicated that students' visual span can be increased slightly by a tachistoscopic exposure to a progressively longer series of numbers of letters or words. However, it is somewhat difficult to tell whether the students were really increasing their vision span or their visual memory as they wrote down what they saw. The important point, however, is that tachistoscopic training of this nature seems to make little or no difference in reading speed.

Tachistoscopic training can be helpful for the purpose of increasing students' attention to word endings, medial vowels, etc. for those students who need training in this area. The tachistoscope can also be used to present sight words and sight phrases to groups of students. When doing this students can call out each word or phrase as it appears. For most students this is an extremely enjoyable activity and appears to be an effective learning technique.

TEACHER-MADE MATERIALS: THEIR VALUES AND LIMITATIONS

Almost any experienced remedial reading teacher has probably constructed a considerable amount of the materials she uses in her classroom. These materials may include such things as flash cards, various types of games, and blending wheels. She may also have students with specialized types of problems with word endings or medial vowels that require her to construct specific types of exercises to meet the needs of these students. There is, therefore, little doubt that it is often necessary, as

[1]Controlled Reader, Educational Developmental Laboratories, Inc., McGraw Hill Book Co., Huntington, New York.

well as desirable, for the remedial reading teacher to construct her own material at times.

Before constructing materials for use in remedial reading you should, however, ask yourself such questions as: considering time limitations and my salary on a per hour basis, can I make materials as cheaply as I can purchase them? When considered in this light the answer is often, definitely, no. For example, consider the time required to prepare a set of flash or phrase cards using basic sight words. When the cost of materials is considered plus the amount of teacher time required for such a project, the cost of simply purchasing commercially prepared materials would, no doubt, be considerably cheaper. This would also be true of such things as blending wheels and many other types of materials. Another important factor to consider is whether the time and effort involved in the construction of materials might be spent more profitably in other activities such as professional reading, test analysis, program planning, etc.

In summary, the real value in the use of teacher-made materials is that specific needs of individual students can often be met using materials that may not be available elsewhere. Also time and/or budget limitations often do not allow the purchase of materials until a much later date.

EXAMPLES OF
TEACHER-MADE MATERIALS

Following is a listing of some specific types of things the remedial reading teacher can do to lengthen the lifetime of commercially-made materials, or materials that can be constructed that are not likely to be available elsewhere.

Laminating Materials for Longer Use

When materials are laminated they will last for a much longer period of time. Students can also write on laminated materials with an overhead projector pen or with a grease pencil used for overhead projector transparencies. The writing can readily be removed so that the materials can be used a number of times. For example, large flash cards can be laminated and students can write over words using a kinesthetic approach and the student's writing can then be readily erased using a damp cloth for overhead projector pens or a soft dry cloth for overhead projector grease pencils.

Another good use of the laminating process is to take workbook pages from a student workbook and place these back-to-back with the same pages from the teacher's edition for the same workbook and then laminate both sides. Students can do the exercises on the student edition side of the page and then turn it over and check the accuracy of their work using the teacher's edition which will have the correct answers on it.

There are three common ways to laminate materials. One way is to place laminating film over thin items that can easily be bent (such as a single sheet of paper). These are then run through a machine such as the 3M Brand Thermofax

Secretary Copier Transparency Maker shown in Figure 15-1. The machine then automatically seals the transparent film to the paper.

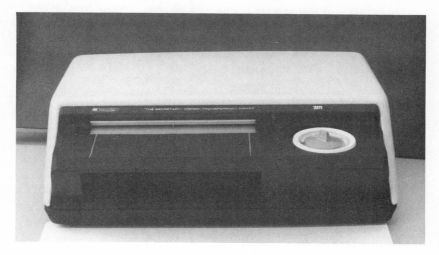

Figure 15–1. 3–M Brand Thermofax "Secretary" Copier/Transparency Maker.

Another method of laminating is the use of the dry mount press. The dry mount press is a machine which applies heat to a piece of laminating film as it is placed over a piece of material to be laminated. One advantage of using the dry mount press is that it can be used with thicker materials than can be run through a machine such as the 3–M Thermofax shown above. It is, however, more time-consuming to operate.

Perhaps one of the easiest and most economical methods of laminating materials now is to simply use laminate paper of the type that can be purchased in hardware stores. It comes in many colors, including woodgrain finishes, etc., however, it also comes in a clear plastic form. When the backing is peeled off of this material you simply press it onto the material to be laminated and it forms its own bond without the aid of any heat or machine.

Teacher-Made Materials for Using the Overhead Projector

The overhead projector has many uses in teaching remedial reading in ways that are commonly used by most teachers. However, it can readily be adapted as a tachistoscopic device. To do this you can simply take a piece of tagboard or cardboard and cut an opening in the center of it about the size of materials that you wish to present in a tachistoscopic manner. The tagboard or cardboard is then placed over the stage of the overhead projector where you would normally write so that light is emitted only through the cut out square in the tagboard. Transparencies can then be placed over the square and the transparency can be covered with an opaque object about the size of a package of cigarettes. When you wish to present a tachistoscopic exposure to a word or phrase you would simply uncover the hole in the cardboard momentarily so that the world or phrase is exposed for a very short period of time. This type of exercise is especially helpful in teaching students to attend to word middles and endings. If guides are placed above and below the cut out square, a strip of plastic can be cut to fit into the guides. This makes it easy to center the words or phrases over the cut out square when presenting words or phrases.

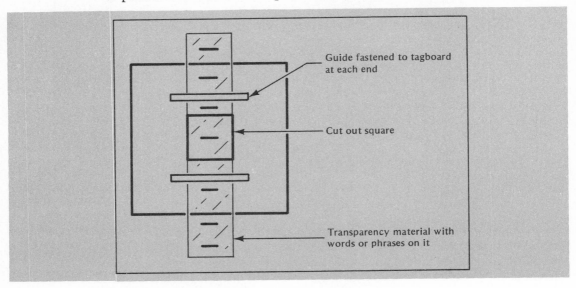

Making Your Own Slides for Use with a
35 mm Projector

The Kodak Carousel projector and several other brands of 35 mm projectors can be moved from slide to slide by simply pressing a button, or on some models you can provide for a timed exposure by setting a timing mechanism on the projector. Projectors such as these work well for providing for a tachistoscopic presentation of words and phrases. They can also be a helpful device for teaching phoneme-grapheme correspondence. You can easily make your own slides for use with a 35 mm projector by using overhead projector film. This is done by taking a common white piece of 8½ in. × 11 in. piece of paper and dividing it into squares 36 mm in diameter. When this is finished it will look like Figure 15–2.

In the upper left square the word "what" is printed with pencil, in the upper right the word "what" is typed with a typewriter, in the lower left a picture of a plate has been drawn or cut from a workbook and pasted on the paper and the "pl" has either been typed or written in pencil below this picture. In the lower right square the phrase "in the house" has been typed. These four illustrations simply show what can be done in each of the many squares that would appear on an 8½ in. × 11 in. sheet of paper. After placing whatever you wish to appear in each square, a xerox copy of the page can be made. This is in turn run through a machine such as the 3-M Thermofax copier and an overhead transparency is made that will have the same material on it as originally appeared on the completed 8½ in. × 11 in. sheet of paper. Each square is then cut along the lines so that you have squares approximately 35 mm in size. (The squares are drawn to approximately 36 mm initially because about one mm is lost in the cutting.) These 35 mm squares can then be mounted in slide mounts that can be purchased from photography stores or ordered

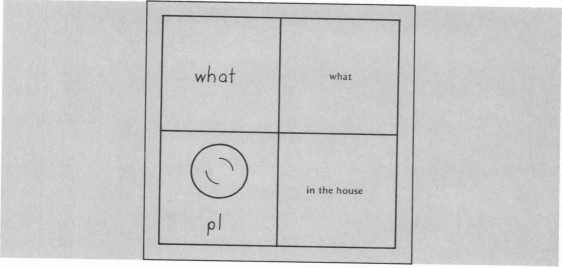

Figure 15–2.   Example of four 35 mm squares of an overhead projector transparency.

through photography magazines. Most of the slide mounts that are available are heat sealed. Once the slide made from the transparency is mounted, the edge can be sealed with a hot iron. Heaters for mounting these heat sealing slides are available, but unless you intend to do a great many of them a regular iron of the type used to iron clothing works quite well for sealing them. Slide mounts are also available that adhere once they are simply pressed together. These slides can be made for about one cent each plus the cost of the slide mounting, which if bought in larger quantities will run from one to two cents each.

Teacher-Made Materials for Use with the Tape Recorder

There are many ways in which the tape recorder can be used in teaching remedial and/or developmental reading. Some of these methods have been explained in previous chapters, but a few more ideas are listed below.

ADDING BACKGROUND MUSIC TO STORIES.   Students will find oral reading much more enjoyable if they have written the material and it is tape recorded and background music appropriate for the scene being described is dubbed in the tape recording. As students read, use an accompanying phonograph record with the proper sound effects to add music or sound effects. These sound effects records are available at some of the larger radio supply stores and are also available from the following source:

ITEM	Company & Address
	RECORDS
Sound Effects Records	Ziff-Davis Service Division
Volumes I, II, III, and IV	595 Broadway
	New York, N. Y. 10012

USING THE TAPE RECORDER AS A TIMING DEVICE.   There are a number of instances in which the tape recorder can be used as a timing device in teaching either developmental and/or remedial reading. For example, in any kind of timed reading you can simply say, "Begin the exercise." Then after say thirty seconds, say, "Thirty seconds have now passed" etc. When teaching a skill such as looking on a page of the dictionary to find a word that should appear between two guide words this procedure is also helpful. For example, the student can be given a list in which two guide words from the dictionary are shown at the top of the page. Following the guide words would appear a number of words. (The idea of using guide words, of course, is to be able to quickly decide whether a certain word would appear on the page between the two guide words shown at the top of the page.) The tape recorder would give directions such as the following: "At the top of the page are two guide words from a page in the dictionary. Following these words are a number of words that may or may not be on the page on which the two guide words appear. You will have five seconds to decide whether each of the words listed on this page would be found on the same page as the two guide words at the top of the page. When I say 'begin,' look at number one and mark a plus behind the word if it would be found on the same page as the two guide words at the top of the page. If it would not be found on that page then mark a minus after the word. We will now begin the exercise. Number one (wait five seconds), number two" (again wait five seconds), etc. After doing the exercise, the tape recorder can be used to check the accuracy of the student's work. In checking the work the tape recording would be as follows: "We will now check to see if you did each word correctly. I will say, 'number one' and then 'plus or minus' depending on which answer is correct. If your answer is correct then do not mark on your answer sheet. If your answer is not correct then circle the number by that word. Here are the answers: Number one, plus, number two, minus," etc. When the student has completed the work, you can instruct him to count the total number of correct answers and place that number at the top of the page.

USING THE TAPE RECORDER TO PRONOUNCE SPELLING WORDS.   The tape recorder can also save the teacher valuable time in doing such things as pronouncing spelling words and then correcting students' papers when they have finished. In doing an exercise such as this the recording would be as follows: "Before you begin this exercise number your paper from one to twenty-five. Turn the tape recorder off until you have done this. (Allow a four-second pause.) I will now pronounce each word and then use it in a sentence. When you hear each word write it by the number

I have just repeated. Number one is 'rather,' I would rather go than stay home. 'rather', Number two . . . ," etc. After pronouncing all of the words they can then be checked with the tape recorder which will also help the student learn words which were missed. In correcting this type of exercise the recording would be as follows: "Now we will check your paper. If you get a word correct then do not make any marks on your paper. If you do not get the word correct, write the word correctly behind the word that was not right. Here are the answers. Number one was 'rather'. It is spelled r-a-t-h-e-r. Remember to write it correctly behind the word if you did not get it correct the first time. Again the word is spelled r-a-t-h-e-r. Number two is . . . ," etc.

USING THE TAPE RECORDER AS A SELF-CHECK DEVICE.   Many of the exercises that are commonly checked by the remedial reading teacher can easily be checked using the tape recorder and letting the student check his own work. This not only saves valuable teacher time, but also gives immediate feedback to the student on the accuracy of his work and will enable him to learn more than he is likely to learn if a corrected paper is simply handed back to him.

USING THE TAPE RECORDER FOR BOOK REPORTING.   The tape recorder can also be used to enhance students' interest in reading. When a student has read a book let him go to the tape recorder and tell in his own words what he has read. These recordings can then be used by other students to decide if the book is one that they would like to read.

The teacher who is interested in furthering his knowledge of audiovisual techniques will find the following books to be helpful:

Drier, Harry N. *Career Development Resources: A Guide to Audiovisual and Printed Materials for Grades K–12*. Worthington, Ohio: C. A. Jones, 1973.

Hanley, John B. *Educational Media and the Teacher*. Dubuque, Iowa: William C. Brown Co., 1970.

Kinder, James S. *Using Instructional Media*. New York: Van Nostrand, 1973.

Murdock, Graham. *Mass Media and the Secondary School*. London: Macmillan, 1973.

Romiszowski, A. *The Selection and Use of Instructional Media*. New York: Wiley, 1974.

SUMMARY

Materials purchased for use in remedial reading should possess certain characteristics that may differ from those purchased for use in developmental reading. Remedial reading teachers and administrators should become familiar with these characteristics before they purchase these materials. The term "reading machines" has caused considerable confusion in and out of the field of reading. Reading specialists and administrators should also become familiar with various devices labeled "reading machines" and should also familiarize themselves with the research on the effectiveness of these devices.

There is now a wealth of materials available designed for both remedial and developmental reading. In spite of this, it is often necessary for the remedial reading teacher to create her own materials. Techniques for creating these materials should be learned. However, before the teacher spends considerable time in creating her own materials she should be sure to investigate the possibility that similar materials are not already available at a cost that would amount to less than the time and money spent on necessary raw materials.

16

INTERPRETING TEST AND RESEARCH
RESULTS IN READING

The first part of this chapter contains a discussion of the need for teachers to possess a basic understanding of some of the common terms needed in order to interpret and evaluate test and research results. The next part of the chapter contains an explanation of a number of terms necessary for interpretation of test evaluations and results. The final part of the chapter contains a discussion of the meaning of some common terms needed for the interpretation of research results in reading. This chapter was co-authored with Everett Davis.[1]

WHY TEACHERS NEED THE
ABILITY TO INTERPRET
TEST AND RESEARCH RESULTS

Under the present standards for certification, in some states, teachers are not required to take a course in tests and measurements; and in most states teachers can begin teaching with little or no knowledge of basic statistical terms. However, teachers should possess a knowledge of a number of terms commonly used in describing test results, as well as those used in describing how accurately a test measures what it is supposed to measure. Without this basic knowledge it would be very difficult for a teacher to evaluate test reviews such as those found in Buros' *Mental Measurements Yearbook*[2] or to even evaluate, in some cases, the descriptive information provided by the publisher.

As the remedial reading teacher begins to work in her field she is likely to find that knowledge gained in course work taken in college eventually becomes outdated and requires supplementation with material from professional books and periodicals. Much of the information found in these sources, and especially in professional periodicals, will present the results of research done by people working in the field of reading. In order to adequately understand much of this research at least some knowledge of statistical terms is needed.

The purpose of this chapter is only to provide the remedial reading teacher

[1]Dr. Davis is Associate Professor and Chairman of the Department of Educational Psychology and Guidance at the University of Texas at El Paso.

[2]Buros, Oscar K., ed. *Mental Measurements Yearbook*. Highland Park, New Jersey: Gryphon Press, 1972.

with knowledge of terms needed for interpreting test results and evaluations, and terms needed to interpret research results. It should be noted that an attempt is not made to provide teachers with a knowledge of how to do the problems involved in evaluating tests and test results or how to apply the statistical procedures discussed.

THE MEANING OF SOME
COMMON TERMS NEEDED
FOR TEST INTERPRETATION

Mean

The *mean* is simply the arithmetic average as illustrated by the set of reading test scores shown below.

Julie	68
Syril	49
Enrique	38
Dennis	67
Judy	68
Denise	52
Total	342

The total (342) divided by the number of scores is $\frac{342}{6} = 57$. The symbol often used for the mean is $\bar{x}$. A symbol used for each of the raw scores, i.e., 68, 49, is x, and n represents the total number of scores. The Greek letter *sigma* ($\sum$) is usually used to represent the total sum, which in this case was 342. Therefore the formula for the mean would be $\bar{x} = \frac{\sum x}{n}$.

Median

The *median* is the point (not always the score) at which one-half of the ranked scores are above and one-half are below a midpoint. This is shown in the scores below.

Julie	68
Judy	68
Dennis	67
Denise	52
Syril	49
Enrique	38

One half the scores are above a point one-half way between 67 and 52 and one-half of the scores are below this point. When there are an even number of ranked scores, as in this case, then the median is the midpoint of the two middle scores or $67 + 52 = 119 \div 2 = 59.5$. As stated above 59.5 is not a "score" but simply represents a midpoint.

If there are an uneven number of scores then the median is an exact score as in the example below.

Julie	68
Judy	43
Luis	41
Bob	40
Dolly	32

In this case 41 is the score at midpoint, or the median.

Mode

In a set of scores the *mode* is that score that appears most often. It is possible to have more than one mode if a set of scores contains two or more raw scores that appear the most often an equal number of times. In the example shown below, 54 is the mode.

Raw scores = 22, 28, 34, 38, 42, 48, 54, 54, 57, 62

In the example that follows there are two modes (32 and 53).

Raw scores = 28, 32, 32, 38, 43, 48, 53, 53, 58, 62

Range

The *range* is a measure of variability that simply indicates the range of distance between the smallest and largest score. It is calculated by subtracting the smallest score from the largest score as shown in the distribution of scores below.

18, 23, 26, 32, 33

If x_n = the highest score (33) and x_1 = the lowest score (18), the formula for finding the range is: Range = $x_n - x_1$ or in this case the Range = $33 - 18 = 15$.

The Normal Curve

Figure 16-1 illustrates a *normal curve*. When many types of educational measurements such as intelligence, or even physical measurements such as height are taken, the largest number of scores fall at the mean with slightly less above and slightly less below the mean. When the distribution is "normal," i.e., with more scores at the median or mean and a gradually decreasing number at the extreme left (below the mean) and right (above the mean) in equal proportions, we get a smooth bell-shaped curve as illustrated in Figure 16–1. It should also be noted that in a perfectly shaped bell or normal curve the mean, median, and mode would fall at the same point. This

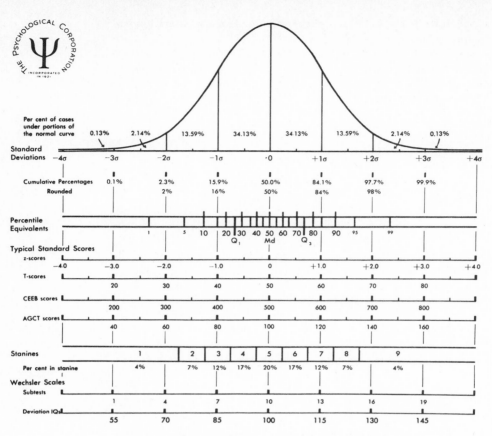

Figure 16–1. The Normal Curve, Percentiles and Standard Scores.

*Distributions of scores on many standardized educational and psychological tests approximate the form of the Normal Curve shown at the top of this chart. Below it are shown some of the systems that have been developed to facilitate the interpretation of scores by converting them into numbers which indicate the examinee's relative status in a group.

The zero (0) at the center of the baseline shows the location of the mean (average) raw score on a test, and the symbol σ (sigma) marks off the scale of raw scores in Standard Deviation units.

Cumulative percentages are the basis of the Percentile Equivalent scale.

Several systems are based on the standard deviation unit. Among these Standard Score scales, the *z-score*, the *T-score* and the *stanine* are general systems which have been applied to a variety of tests. The others are special variants used in connection with tests of the College Entrance Examination Board, the World War II Army General Classification test, and the Wechsler Intelligence Scales.

Tables of Norms, whether in percentile or standard score form, have meaning only with reference to a specified test applied to a specified population. The chart does not permit one to conclude, for instance, that a percentile rank of 84 on one test necessarily is equivalent to a *z-score* of +1.0 on another; this is true only when each test yields essentially a normal distribution of scores and when both scales are based on identical or very similar groups of people.[1]

---

[1]Courtesy of the Psychological Corporation. The scales on this chart are discussed in greater detail in *Test Service Bulletin No. 48.* The Psychological Corporation, New York, N.Y.

point is located at the center vertical line marked "0" at the bottom of the normal curve in Figure 16–1.[1] The tallest or highest point on a bell curve or normal curve represents the highest score, or scores, or measurements and the lowest point represents the lowest scores or measurements. It should also be stressed that you are not likely to obtain a smooth normal-shaped curve when measuring any characteristic unless you are dealing with large numbers of people from which that characteristic is measured.

Standard Deviation

Standard deviation (often designated by the Greek letter sigma "σ") is used to describe the variability of scores in relation to the mean. (The mean is a measure of central tendency.) One might think of standard deviation as a measure of the average distance of each of the scores, in a distribution, from the mean. Robert Koenker (1961) points out that *standard deviation, quantile deviation,* and range are the most commonly used measures of dispersion. He states,

> The purposes of measures of dispersion are as follows:
>
> 1. To find the spread or variability of a group of scores about the mean.
> 2. To compare the spread or variability of two or more groups.
> 3. To compare the spread or variability of one group on two different occasions. (p. 9)

The standard deviation would vary with the range in a set of scores. That is, the greater the range in scores, the larger the standard deviation. In a *normally* distributed set of scores, however, 34.13 percent of the scores would fall one standard deviation above the mean and 34.13 percent would fall one standard deviation below the mean as can be seen in Figure 16–1. Thus 68.26 (34.13 + 34.13) percent of the scores would fall within one standard deviation above or below the mean. It is fairly common to say that two-thirds (or 66²/₃ percent) of the scores in a normal distribution fall within plus or minus one standard deviation (sigma σ) above or below the mean. Likewise, as can be seen in Figure 16–1, 95.44 percent of the scores in a normal distribution would fall within plus or minus—two sigmas above or below the mean, etc.

Knowing the standard deviation of a set of scores can be useful in that it provides a standard index of measurement of any score from the mean. This can be useful to statisticians or to teachers in comparing individual scores on various types of data.

Percentiles or Centiles

When a teacher wishes to describe the relative standing of a particular individual in relation to other members of a group she often uses *percentiles*, or less often quartiles or deciles. A percentile score for an individual represents his score relative to the percentage of other individuals in a group falling below that score. Thus an individual falling at the 65th percentile would have done better on that particular test than 65 percent of the other people taking the test. It should be kept in mind, however, that the percentile score achieved by a student would be in relation to the group with which he was compared. For example, a student in a school district with poor achievement may score at the 86th percentile as computed from local school norms. However, the same student may only score at the 56th percentile if his score is based on national norms.

It should also be stressed that percentiles scores are not evenly spaced along a baseline as can be seen from Figure 16-1. Since more scores tend to cluster around the mean, the number of raw score points between, for example, the 40th to 45th percentile may be considerably less than the number of points at the extreme ends or, for example, from the 5th to 10th percentile.

One of the advantages of using percentiles is that they are usually readily understood by anyone who understands percentages. On the other hand they have one rather serious drawback. For example, in comparing students' percentile ratings near the center of a distribution we might see that John ranked in the 56th percentile and Mary ranked in the 50th percentile. Since it takes so few points to change percentile scores near the center of the distribution, a ranking of 50th versus a 56th percentile may make very little difference, or in other words, might easily have happened by chance.

It should be also pointed out that there is no 100th percentile since in reporting percentiles we are giving the percent of cases that ranked below the number given. Therefore, a percentile rating of 99 for a student means that 99 percent of the group ranked below that student. This, in turn, means that the student is in the top 1 percent.

Quartiles and Deciles

Quartiles and *deciles* also report an individual's relative standing in relation to other members of a group just as in the case of percentiles. The 25th percentile is sometimes referred to as the first quartile and the 75th percentile is then referred to as the third quartile. In the case of deciles, the 10th percentile would be referred to as the first decile, the 20th percentile would be the second decile, etc. It should be remembered that the first or third quartile or the first and second decile are *points* in the distribution of scores and do not represent proportions of the distribution. And percentiles of any kind are not equal units of measurement and, therefore, cannot be averaged or treated arithmetically.

Standard Scores

The use of standard scores enables one to interpret an individual's score in terms of the number of standard deviation units from the mean. Unlike percentiles, standard scores can be averaged and treated arithmetically. One of the most commonly used types of standard scores is the "z" score. In some statistics books the lower case "z" is used to indicate scores derived from the following formula:

$$z = \frac{x - \bar{x}}{s}$$

In this case "x" represents a student's raw score, "$\bar{x}$" represents the mean for that set of scores, and "s" represents the standard deviation of that set of scores. For example, if a student scored 120 on a test on which the mean was 112 and the standard deviation was 10, then we would have

$$z = \frac{x - \bar{x}}{s} \quad \text{or} \quad z = \frac{120 - 112}{10} = \frac{8}{10} = .8$$

This tells us that the student's score was $^8/_{10}$ or .8 standard deviation units above the mean.

In other books (and in Figure 16-1) "z" is transformed to a standard score in which the mean is 50 and the standard deviation is 10. These scores are referred to as "T" scores or "Z" scores. The advantage of using "T" scores is that they eliminate the use of decimals and negative numbers, as can be seen in Figure 16-1.

Some tests, such as the College Entrance Examination Board (CEEB), and the old Army General Classification Test (AGCT) shown in Figure 16–1, are reported in transformed standard score form. For example, the CEEB has a mean of 500 with a standard deviation of 100. This allows someone knowledgeable about statistics and test scores to easily assess the value of a particular score. If a student received a score of 700 on the CEEB it is easy to see that this puts him two standard deviation units above the mean. If one wished to interpret this score in terms of percentiles by following the vertical line in Figure 16–1 up to the cumulative percentages, we see that a score of 700 on the CEEB places the student at the 97.7, or approximately at the 98th percentile.

Stanines

The *stanine* is another form of standard score with a mean of five and a standard deviation of approximately two. The term is derived from the words "standard" and "nine" or "stanine." Figure 16-1 will also enable you to see the approximate percentage of scores that would fall within each stanine. Note, for example, that only 4 percent of the scores fall within the 1st stanine, but 20 percent fall within the 5th stanine.

The terms percentiles and stanines are sometimes confusing to people who have not worked with statistical terms. It should be noted that percentiles and stanines are not equivalent. For example, note in Figure 16-1 that the beginning of the 2nd stanine is approximately even with the 5th percentile and the beginning of the 3rd stanine is approximately even with the 12th and 13th percentile. The 90th percentile falls at approximately the beginning of the 8th stanine.

Standard Error

The term standard error is often used in describing tests. For example, a test author may report that the standard error for his test is five (5). The standard error may be thought of as an estimate of the reliability of this test score. The standard error is calculated by using both the test standard deviation and the test reliability coefficient. The use of the standard error enables us to estimate an interval of scores within which the individual's "true" score will fall. Thus, the test author who reports a standard error of five (5) is saying that there is a 68 percent chance that the so-called "true" score, whatever it may be, will be within the interval from five points below to five points above the obtained score. For example, if an obtained score for an individual was ninety (90) and the standard error was five (5), we would be saying that we estimate that his "true" score will be in the interval from 85 to 95, and we expect that our estimation will be confirmed sixty-eight (68) times out of a hundred—provided we could ever determine the so-called "true" score.

Wechsler Scales

The subtests of the Wechsler Intelligence Scale for Children and the Wechsler IQs are both forms of standard scores. The Wechsler Subtests have a mean of ten with a standard deviation of three. And the IQ Scale has a mean of 100 with a standard deviation of fifteen. The use of standard scores for both the subtest and IQ scales enables an experienced examiner to easily interpret the values of these scores. For example, if a student made a scaled score of seven on the Picture Completion Subtest, we would know it was one standard deviation below the mean. Likewise an overall Wechsler Full Scale IQ of 115 would be one standard deviation above the mean. Assuming all scores to be normalized (confirm to a standard normal curve) the student's Picture Completion Subtest score would place him at the 16th percentile and the overall Full Scale IQ score would place him at the 84th percentile.

Reliability

Reliability is a term used in relation to testing to refer to the consistency with which a test agrees with itself. In using the term "agrees with itself" we might think in terms of its producing the same scores on several occasions when given to the same individual during a short period of time. It should be stressed, however, that high reliability in a test does not guarantee that a test is worthwhile. However, for a test to be valid (which is discussed next) it must be reliable.

Some tests used in reading tend to have a high intra-scorer reliability but a poor inter-scorer reliability. That is, when the test is given by the same person, to the same students (intra), the same results are obtained. However, when the same students take the test from different examiners the results obtained are often different. This would probably mean that the examiners were scoring answers differently and thus the test could never be reliable when used by many different examiners.

Three methods of determining reliability are commonly used. One of these is to give the test and then repeat it at a later date (often called the *repeat* or *test-retest* method). If the students who performed high on it in the beginning perform high on it the second time and those who scored low on it the first time scored low on it the second time (or the students are generally in the same rank order on both administrations), the correlation will be high and it is considered to be reliable. Another method of measuring reliability is to take pupils' scores on the odd items and their scores on the even numbered items (often called the *split-half technique*) and again see if they are in the same rank order or if they have a high correlation. A third method of measuring reliability is to compare one form of a test against another form of the test. This is often referred to as the *equivalent form* technique or method.

Validity

A test's validity is a measure of whether it really measures what it is designed to measure. It is quite possible for a test to be reliable without being valid. That is, we may be able to design a test that will give consistent scores for a student or a group of students, but it may not really measure what it purports to measure.

A number of reading tests may appear to measure what they purport to measure (or be valid) when, in reality, they are not. For example, one well-known basic sight word text which requires the student to circle on the answer sheet one of four choices when the examiner says a word purports to measure students' knowledge of basic sight words. It should be remembered, however, that it is considerably easier to get a certain word correct when it is called by a tester and the student is to circle one of four choices than it is to simply see the word and pronounce it. Since word attack in reading is a matter of seeing words and pronouncing them, then a test which presents four choices is simply not valid. My own research[3] has shown that this method of testing basic sight words is not valid because students then miss many words in actually reading that would appear to be known on the test. The same situation often exists in the area of phonics. That is, we do not test in a situation that is analogous to what the student actually does when he reads; therefore, the test results do not coincide with the student's ability to actually use phonic word attack.

Several methods are used to determine the validity of a test. One method is to correlate the results of a test with the results of another well-known test, i.e., determine whether those who score high on the new test also score high on the well-known test and whether those who score low on the new test also score low on the well-known test or, in other words, if the students are generally in the same rank order on both tests. This method would be fine if we actually *knew* that the well-known test was valid to begin with; however, the fact that a test is well-known and even that it is widely used does not make it valid. Another problem with this method of establishing validity is that the number of items missed by students on both tests may tend to correlate (be in the same rank order), but the students may miss different items on each of the tests. For overall achievement tests this would make very

[3]Ekwall, Eldon E. *An Analysis of Children's Test Scores When Tested with Individually Administered Diagnostic Tests and When Tested with Group Administered Diagnostic Tests.* Final Research Report. University Research Institute, University of Texas at El Paso, El Paso, Texas, 1973.

little difference, but on a diagnostic test that purports to diagnose specific blends, digraphs, etc., it would be very misleading.

Another method of establishing vadility is to simply inspect the test or to send it to a group of specialists in the area for which it was designed. If the inspection or group consensus is that the test measures what it purports to measure, it is then considered to be valid. This is often called *content* or *face* validity.

A third method of measuring validity is to give a test to individuals (for example, a reading readiness test) and then measure their performance in reading at a later date. If the tests tend to correlate (the scores are generally in the same rank order) then we say the test has good *predictive* validity.

THE MEANING OF SOME COMMON NEEDED TERMS FOR INTERPRETING RESEARCH

Levels of Significance

In examining literature pertaining to research in reading as well as other fields, we often encounter the use of various levels of significance. Levels of significance are used in a number of statistical procedures to determine whether the results obtained would have been likely to have happened by chance. For example, in giving a reading test to each of two groups of fifth-grade students each of whom had been taught by different methods we might find that one group had a mean grade level achievement of 5.6 and the other group achieved a mean grade level of 5.9. With only this knowledge we would not really know if the group who had a mean achievement level of 5.9 merely happened by chance or whether the method of instruction used with them was so superior that these results could be expected nearly every year. In order to make meaningful comparisons between or among scores we make use of the various levels of significance or what are sometimes referred to as levels of confidence.

If the proper statistical procedure was applied to the scores of the two fifth-grade students, we could determine whether a mean grade level achievement of 5.9 was "significantly" better than the mean grade level achievement of 5.6. If we discovered that the 5.9 mean grade level of achievement was significantly better than the 5.6 at the .05 level of significance (or confidence), we could conclude that these differences were, in fact, great enough that we would have expected these differences to have occurred by chance only five times out of 100. If we had found that the 5.9 mean grade level of achievement was significantly better than the 5.6 at the .01 level of significance or confidence, we could conclude that these differences were great enough that they would have happened by chance only one time out of 100.

In reporting significance or confidence levels we often see the .05, .01, or .001 levels reported. These may be shown as follows:

$p < .05$ This would mean that the probability of that event occurring would be less than five in 100. A researcher usually selects a confidence level as being significant or not significant before the statistical procedure is completed. If the .05 level had been selected this p < .05 would be considered significant. This would, however, mean that there was a greater chance that the scores occurred by chance than if $p < .01$ or $p < .001$.

$p > .05$ This would mean that the probability of that event occurring would be more or greater than five in 100. Rather than show $p > .05$, researchers often simply label their results "NS" meaning "not significant" or, in other words, the chances of the event (that is, differences in test scores are greater than we decided to risk.)

$p < .01$ This would mean that the probability of that event occurring would be less than one in 100.

$p < .001$ This would mean that the probability of that event occurring would be less than one in 1000.

There is perhaps a growing tendency for researchers to simply report levels of significance as computed, e.g., the .02 level, and the .10 level. Some statisticians believe that when this is done, researchers are likely to claim that a level of say .10 or .15 is significant and, therefore, draw erroneous conclusions from their data.

Correlations

The term *correlation* is often used in a popular fashion to simply mean that there is some type of relationship or that two things have something in common. However, the term, when used in statistical research, usually refers to the coefficient of correlation (r) between two sets of variables. The most commonly used method of computing the coefficient of correlation is one devised by Pearson. It is often referred to as the Pearson Product Moment Correlation.

Correlations might be thought of as a measure of the rank order in distance from the mean or "going togetherness," of two sets of data or scores. Correlations may be highly positive or highly negative. A perfect positive correlation would be shown at 1.00 and a perfect negative correlation would be shown as -1.00. In order to compute a correlation coefficient (r) there must be two values or scores for each individual within a group. The correlation coefficient is then a measure of the rank order of scores on one test compared to the rank order of scores on the other test. The closer the rank order approaches 1.00, or a perfect positive correlation, the higher the chance that individuals who scored high on one test scored high on the other test and the individuals who scored low on one test scored low on the other test, or that all individuals within the group were in the same rank order on both tests. In negative correlation those individuals who tend to score high on the first test tend to score low on the second test, or, in other words, high scores on the first test are associated with low scores on the second test, and low scores on the first test tend to be associated with high scores on the second test.

Koenker (1961) states that there are a number of ways to interpret values in correlations. As an example he gives the following scale:

.84 to 1.00 highly dependable relationship
.60 to   .79 moderate to marked relationship
.40 to   .59 fair degree of relationship

.20 to .39 slight relationship

.00 to .19 negligible relationship (p. 52)

Koenker also points out that the same interpretation would apply to negative relationships. In that case, of course, the relationships between the scores would be in reverse.

It would be emphasized that the level of significance of a correlation should be reported in order to determine whether a high correlation between two variables might simply have happened by chance. For example, three students taking each of two tests could easily obtain the same rank order on the two tests simply by chance. However, 300 students taking each of the two tests would not be likely to obtain the same rank order simply by chance. In order to determine whether a given correlation is meaningful (highly significant), its level of significance is often reported.

It should also be pointed out that there is often a danger in drawing conclusions based on certain correlated data. For example, we might find that there was a high degree of relationship (or a high correlation) between reading ability in the first grade and the scores on a certain test for eye-motor coordination. This would not necessarily mean that training in exercises in eye-motor coordination would insure that students would improve in their ability to read. In fact, numerous research studies have shown that this does not occur. What evidently happens in cases such as this is that there is a common factor responsible, to some extent, for performance in both areas. However, that common factor, even though affecting both areas, may not be measured by either test.

t Tests and F Tests

In researching various problems in reading, it is often necessary to determine whether the test performance of one group is significantly better or higher than the test peformance of another group. In other cases it is necessary to determine whether the test performance of any one or more groups is significantly higher than the test performance of other groups. When researchers wish to make decisions of this nature the t test or F test is often used. Since the purpose of this chapter is only to acquaint the reader with enough information to understand research studies when they are read, the differences in these statistical procedures will not be discussed. What is important, however, is that the reader understand that with either the t or F tests we are concerned with whether measured differences between the means of two or more groups are significantly different. For example, assume a reading achievement test was given to each of two seventh-grade groups and the results showed an achievement level of 7.2 for one group and 7.4 for the other group. One would not really know whether these differences had occurred by chance or whether the differences were, in fact, great enough that we would not have expected them to have happened by chance more than five times in 100 (p $<$ .05), one time in 100 (p $<$ .01), etc. Whether these differences occurred by chance would depend on such factors as the number of students in each group and the standard deviation of the scores.

If the t or F test is used and the researcher reports significant differences between the means of the .05, .01, or .001 confidence levels we would usually conclude that whatever was done with the group that achieved the higher means was superior, or at least for those groups at that time, to what was done with the group who had the lower mean score.

Chi Square

The Chi Square Test (X^2) is used to test the distribution or ratio or frequency of a sample against another hypothetical or known distribution, ratio, or frequency. Or, as is often stated, it is used to test the difference between *expected* ratios, distributions, or frequencies and *observed* ratios, distributions, or frequencies.

An example of one use of the Chi Square Test in reading might be as follows: On a certain test, in previous research it was found that the expected distribution of mean scores for boys and girls was: Boys 75, Girls 75. However, in giving the test it is observed that the distribution or ratio of mean scores was: Boys 85, Girls 65. One would then tend to wonder if this observed distribution or ratio was different enough from the expected distribution to consider it significant. In order to determine the answer to that question, it would be necessary to use the Chi Square Test. After the Chi Square Test had been completed, we might find that this distribution or ratio was either not significant or significant at the .05, .01, or .001 level. If it was not significant we would, of course, conclude that it could easily have happened by chance. If it was significant at the .05 level of confidence, we would conclude that the observed distribution or ratio was different enough from the expected distribution or ratio that we would not have expected it to have happened by chance more than five times out of 100, etc.

THE BUROS MENTAL MEASUREMENT YEARBOOKS AND OTHER SOURCES OF TEST INFORMATION

Teachers and other personnel who find it necessary to use tests in their work should become acquainted with the Mental Measurement Yearbooks. The Mental Measurement Yearbooks are a series of books that have been published periodically (not yearly) since 1938. As stated by the editor, Oscar Buros (1968), the objectives of the test section of the Mental Measurement Yearbooks are as follows:

a) To provide comprehensive bibliographies of all standardized tests published in English-speaking countries.

b) To provide frankly critical evaluations of tests, written by competent specialists representing a variety of viewpoints, to assist test users to choose the tests which will best meet their needs.

c) To provide comprehensive bibliographies of articles, books, and theses dealing with the construction, validity, use, and limitations of specific tests.

d) To impel test authors and publishers to place fewer but better tests on the market and to provide test users with detailed information on the validity and limitations of their tests at the time the tests are first published.

e) To suggest to test users better methods of arriving at their own appraisals of both standardized and nonstandardized tests in light of their own particular values and needs.

f) To stimulate contributing reviewers to reconsider and think through more carefully their own beliefs and values relevant to testing.

g) To inculcate upon test users a keener awareness of both the values and dangers involved in the use and non-use of standardized tests.

h) To impress test users with the desirability of suspecting all standardized tests—even though prepared by well-known authorities—accompanied by detailed data on their construction, validity, uses, and limitations. (pp. xv-xvi)

There are now seven yearbooks plus two *Tests In Print.*[4] *Tests In Print* are a master index of the contents of the first seven yearbooks. They also contain a comprehensive bibliography of standard tests. These volumes indicate which of the first Mental Measurement Yearbooks (MMY) present the most recent information on various tests.

Of special interest to the reading specialist is an edition called *Reading Tests and Reviews*[5] which is a smaller volume dealing principally with information pertaining to reading. This volume contains the following information pertaining to reading:

1. A comprehensive bibliography of tests in print.
2. A reprinting of the corresponding test reviews from the first six MMYs.
3. A classified index to the tests and reviews in the first six MMYs.
4. A directory of publishers.
5. Title and name indexes.

Another source of information on tests of reading is Roger Farr's (1971)[6] annotated bibliography entitled *Measurement of Reading Achievement.* It contains information on the problems and procedures of assessing reading behavior.

Still another source of information on reading tests is a publication entitled, *Tests of Reading Readiness and Achievement: A Review and Evaluation.*[7] In this publication the authors present criteria for reviewing tests and information on various reading readiness tests and reading achievement tests.

SUMMARY

Remedial reading teachers are constantly faced with the task of reviewing descriptive information on new tests. They should also constantly review the

[4]Buros, Oscar K., ed. *Tests in Print: A Comprehensive Bibliography of Tests for Use in Educational Psychology and Industry.* Highland Park, New Jersey: Gryphon Press, 1961 (Vol. I), and 1974 (Vol. II).

[5]Buros, Oscar K., ed. Reading Tests and Reviews. Highland Park, New Jersey: Gryphon Press, 1968.

[6]Farr, Roger, ed. *Measurement of Reading Achievement.* Newark, Delaware: ERIC/CRIER+ IRA, 1971.

[7]Farr, Roger, and Anistasiow, Nicholas. *Tests of Reading Readiness and Achievement: A Review and Evaluation.* Newark, Delaware: International Reading Association, 1969.

professional literature in their field. Much of this literature is concerned with the results of research studies. In order to evaluate test reviews and research results at least some understanding of various statistical terms or procedures is required. The most commonly used of these terms or procedures are the "mean," "median," "mode," "range," "standard deviation," characteristics of the normal curve, "percentiles" or "centiles," "quartiles and deciles," "stanines," and various types of "standard scores." The teacher should understand the characteristics of the normal curve and understand when it might be appropriate to use tests of significance such as the "t" and "F" tests. Remedial reading teachers should also understand the meaning of, and be able to interpret, studies dealing with reliability and validity. It is also highly important that reading pesonnel be familiar with, and understand, the values and limitations of correlations. Reading specialists should also be familiar with some of the publications designed to help them evaluate tests.

Chapter 16: REFERENCE

Koenker, Robert H. *Simplified Statistics*. Bloomington, Illinois: McKnight & McKnight, 1961.

APPENDIXES

APPENDIX A. Ekwall Phonics Survey

DIRECTIONS

1. Before beginning the test make sure the student has instant recognition of the four stimulus words that appear in the box in the upper left hand corner of sheet A. These words should be known instantly by the student. If they are not, reschedule the test and give it at a later date after they have been taught and the student has learned them.

2. Give the student the Ekwall Phonics Survey Stimulus Sheet (A).

3. Point to the letter in the first column and have the student say the "name" of that letter (not the sound it represents). Then point to the word in the middle column and have the student pronounce it. Then point to the nonsense word in the third column and have the student pronounce it.

4. If the student can give the name of the letter, the word in the middle column and the nonsense word in the third column then mark the answer sheet (B) with a plus (+). If he cannot pronounce the nonsense word after giving the name of the letter and word in the middle column then mark the answer sheet with a minus (—) or you may wish to write the word phonetically as the student pronounced it.

5. If the student can tell you the name of the letter(s) and the small word in the middle column but cannot pronounce the nonsense word then you may wish to have him give the letter(s) sound in isolation. If he can give the sounds in isolation, he is unable to "blend" or it may mean that he does not know it well enough to give the sound and blend it simultaneously.

6. Whenever an asterisk (*) appears on the Answer Sheet (B) you may wish to refer to the "Special Directions Sheet" (C).

7. To the right of each answer blank on the Answer Sheet (B) you will note a grade level designation under the heading "PEK." This number represents the point at which most basal reading series would have already taught that sound. Therefore, at that point you should expect it to be known. The designation 1.9 means the ninth month of the first year, etc.

8. When the student comes to two or three letter consonant digraphs or blends as with "qu" in number 22, etc. he is to say "q—u" as with the single letters. Note: he never gives letter sounds in isolation.

9. When the student encounters the vowels (#60) he is to say "short 'a' " etc., and then the nonsense word in column two. If he does not know that the "breve" (ᴗ) over the vowels means short "a," "e," etc. then explain this. Do the same with the long vowels where the "macron" (—) appears.

10. All vowels, vowel teams, and special letter combinations are put with only one or two of the first eight consonants tested. Therefore, if the student does not know all of the first eight consonants these should be taught before you attempt to test for vowel knowledge.

11. You will note that a word appears to the right of some of the blanks on the answer sheet. These words illustrate the correct consonant or vowel sound that should be heard when the student responds to that item.

12. Only phonic elements have been included that have a high enough utility to make them worthwhile learning. For example, the vowel pair "ui" appears very seldom and when it does it may stand for short "i" as in "build," or long "oo" as in "fruit." Therefore, there is really no reason to teach it as a sound. However, some letters as "oe" may stand for several sounds but most often stand for one particular sound. In the case of "oe" the long "o" sound should be used. In cases such as this the most common sound is illustrated by a word to the right of the blank on the answer sheet. If the student gives another correct sound for the letter(s) say, "Yes, but what is another way that we could say this nonsense word?" The student must then say it as illustrated in the small word to the right of the blank on the answer sheet. Otherwise count it as wrong.

13. Stop the test after five consecutive misses or if the student appears frustrated from missing a number of items even though he has not missed five consecutive items.

EKWALL PHONICS SURVEY: ANSWER SHEET

Name: Sex: Date:
School: Examiner:

Mark Answers as Follows: (PEK) Point phonic
Pass +   element is expected
Fail − (or write word as pronounced)   to be known

		Initial Consonant Sounds						Ending Consonant "x"		
			Answers	PEK					Answers	PEK
1.	p	pate	_____	1.9		*23.	x	Lox	_____	1.9
2.	n	nate	_____	1.9						
*3.	s	sall	_____	1.9				Initial Consonant Clusters		
4.	t	tate	_____	1.9					Answers	PEK
5.	r	rin	_____	1.9		24.	pl	plin	_____	1.9
6.	m	mate	_____	1.9		25.	fr	frate	_____	1.9
7.	b	bate	_____	1.9		26.	fl	flin	_____	1.9
8.	d	dat	_____	1.9		27.	st	stat	_____	1.9
9.	w	wat	_____	1.9		28.	bl	blate	_____	1.9
10.	h	hin	_____	1.9		29.	tr	trate	_____	1.9
11.	f	fate	_____	1.9		30.	gr	grat	_____	1.9
12.	j	jat	_____	1.9		31.	br	brin	_____	1.9
13.	k	kall	_____	1.9		32.	sh	shin	_____	1.9
14.	l	lat	_____	1.9		*33.	th	thall	_____	1.9 (this or thing)
*15.	c	cate	_____	1.9						
*16.	g	gat	_____	1.9		*34.	th	thall	_____	1.9 (this or thing)
*17.	y	yate	_____	1.9						
18.	v	vin	_____	1.9		*35.	wh	whate	_____	1.9 (when)
19.	z	zat	_____	1.9		36.	ch	chall	_____	2.5 (church)
20.	c	cin	_____	2.5 (sin)		37.	dr	drin	_____	2.5
21.	g	gin	_____	2.9 (jin)		38.	pr	prate	_____	2.5
22.	qu	quat	_____	1.9		39.	sl	slin	_____	2.5

		Answers	PEK				Answers	PEK
40.	cl	clat	_____	2.5	68.	u	bume	_____	2.5
41.	gl	glate	_____	2.5	69.	o	tope	_____	2.5
42.	sm	smat	_____	2.5	*70.	oo	oop	_____	2.5 (moon or book)
43.	sk	skall	_____	2.5	*71.	oo	oot	_____	2.5 (moon or book)
44.	cr	crin	_____	2.5	*72.	ea	ean	_____	2.5 (bread or heat)
45.	tw	twate	_____	2.5	*73.	ea	ead	_____	2.5 (bread or heat)
46.	sn	snate	_____	2.5	74.	ai	aip	_____	2.5 (ape)
47.	sch	schat	_____	2.5	75.	ay	tay	_____	2.5 (hay)
48.	sp	spate	_____	2.9	76.	oe	poe	_____	2.5 (hoe)
49.	sc	scall	_____	2.9	77.	oa	oap	_____	2.5 (soap)
50.	str	strat	_____	2.9	78.	ee	eed	_____	2.5 (heed)
51.	thr	thrate	_____	2.9	*79.	ow	owd	_____	2.5 (cow or crow)
52.	shr	shrate	_____	2.9	*80.	ow	dow	_____	2.5 (cow or crow)
53.	squ	squin	_____	2.9	81.	or	orn	_____	2.5 (corn)
54.	sw	swate	_____	3.5	82.	ir	irp	_____	2.5 (hurt)
55.	spr	sprat	_____	3.5	83.	ur	urb	_____	2.5 (hurt)
56.	spl	splin	_____	3.5	84.	aw	awd	_____	2.9 (paw)
57.	wr	wrat	_____	4.5	85.	oi	poi	_____	2.9 (boy)
58.	dw	dwin	_____	4.5	86.	ou	dou	_____	2.9 (cow)
59.	scr	scrate	_____	4.5	87.	ar	arp	_____	2.9 (harp)
					88.	oy	poy	_____	2.9 (boy)
					89.	er	erd	_____	2.9 (her)
					90.	ew	bew	_____	2.9 (few)
					91.	au	tau	_____	2.9 (paw)

Vowels, Vowel Teams, and Special Letter Combinations

			Answers	PEK
60.	a	tam	_____	1.9
61.	i	mip	_____	1.9
62.	e	ped	_____	1.9
63.	o	nop	_____	1.9
64.	u	rup	_____	1.9
65.	i	rite	_____	2.5
66.	e	nete	_____	2.5
67.	a	mape	_____	2.5

EKWALL PHONICS SURVEY: STIMULUS SHEET

Test Words

at
in
all
ate

1. p ate pate

2. n ate nate

3. s all sall

4. t ate tate

5. r in rin

6. m ate mate

7. b ate bate

8. d at dat	27. st at stat
9. w at wat	28. bl ate blate
10. h in hin	29. tr ate trate
11. f ate fate	30. gr at grat
12. j at jat	31. br in brin
13. k all kall	32. sh in shin
14. L at Lat	33. th all thall
15. c ate cate	34. th all thall
16. g at gat	35. wh ate whate
17. y ate yate	36. ch all chall
18. v in vin	37. dr in drin
19. z at zat	38. pr ate prate
20. c in cin	39. sl in slin
21. g in gin	40. cl at clat
22. qu at quat	41. gl ate glate
23. L ox Lox	42. sm at smat
24. pl in plin	43. sk all skall
25. fr ate frate	44. cr in crin
26. fl in flin	45. tw ate twate

46.	sn ate	snate	65.	$\bar{\text{i}}$	rite
47.	sch at	schat	66.	$\bar{\text{e}}$	nete
48.	sp ate	spate	67.	$\bar{\text{a}}$	mape
49.	sc all	scall	68.	$\bar{\text{u}}$	bume
50.	str at	strat	69.	$\bar{\text{o}}$	tope
51.	thr ate	thrate	70.	oo	oop
52.	shr ate	shrate	71.	oo	oot
53.	squ in	squin	72.	ea	ean
54.	sw ate	swate	73.	ea	ead
55.	spr at	sprat	74.	ai	aip
56.	spl in	splin	75.	ay	tay
57.	wr at	wrat	76.	oe	poe
58.	dw in	dwin	77.	oa	oap
59.	scr ate	scrate	78.	ee	eed
60.	ă	tam	79.	ow	owd
61.	ĭ	mip	80.	ow	dow
62.	ĕ	ped	81.	or	orn
63.	ŏ	nop	82.	ir	irp
64.	ŭ	rup	83.	ur	urb

84.	aw	awd	88.	oy	poy
85.	oi	poi	89.	er	erd
86.	ou	dou	90.	ew	bew
87.	ar	arp	91.	au	tau

EKWALL PHONICS INVENTORY: SPECIAL DIRECTIONS SHEET

*3. If the student uses another "s" sound as in "sugar" (sh) in saying the nonsense word "sall" say, "What is another 's' sound?" The student must use the "s" as in "sack."

*15. If the student uses the soft "c" sound as in "cigar" in saying the nonsense word "cate" say, "What is another 'c' sound?" The student must use the hard "c" sound as in "coat."

*16. If the student uses the soft "g" sound as in "gentle" in saying the nonsense word "gat" say, "What is another 'g' sound?" The student must use the hard "g" sound as in "gate."

*17. Say, "What is the 'y' sound when it comes at the beginning of a word?"

*23. The student must use the "ks" sound of "x" and the word "lox" must rhyme with "box."

*33. The student may give either the "th" sound heard in "thing" or the "th" sound heard in "this" in saying the nonsense word "thall." Be sure to make note of which one is used.

*34. If the same "th" sound is given this time as was given in #33 then say, "Yes, that's right, but what is another way we could pronounce this nonsense word?" Whichever sound was *not* used in item #33 must be used here otherwise it is counted as incorrect.

*35. If the student uses the "hoo" sound of "wh" in saying the nonsense word "whate" say, "What is another 'wh' sound?" The student must use the "wh" sound as in "when."

*70. The student may give either the "oo" sound heard in "moon" or the "oo" sound heard in "book." Be sure to note which one is used.

*71. If the same "oo" sound is given this time as was given for #70 say, "Yes, that's right, but what is another way we could pronounce this nonsense word?" Whichever sound was *not* used in item #70 must be used here otherwise it is incorrect.

*72. The student may give either the "ea" sound heard in "bread" or the "ea" sound heard in "heat." Be sure to note which one is used.

*73. If the same "ea" sound is given this time as was given for #72 then say, "Yes, that's right but what is another way we could pronounce this nonsense word?" Whichever sound was *not* used in item #72 must be used here otherwise it is incorrect.

*79. The student may give either the "ow" sound heard in "cow" or the "ow" sound heard in "crow." Be sure to note which one is used.

*80. If the same "ow" sound is given this time as was given for #79 then say, "Yes, that's right but what is another way we could pronounce this nonsense word?" Whichever sound was *not* used in item #72 must be used here otherwise it is incorrect.

APPENDIX B. Reading and Reading Related Tests and Inventories*

READING TESTS

Name and Date of Test	Skills or Areas Measured						Time for Administration	Number of Forms	Grade Level	Group (G) or Individual (I)	Publisher[1]
	Vocabulary	Comprehension	Word-Attack	Speed	Listening	Other					
Botel Reading Inventory (1970)											Follett Publishing Co.[1]
Word Recognition						Estimates oral reading	10 min. (approx.)	2	pp–4	I	
Word Opposites		X					25 min. (approx.)	2	1–Sr. High	G	
Phonics Mastery			X				20 min. (approx.)	2	All	G & I	
Spelling						Spelling ability	10–20 min.	1	1–6	G	
California Reading Test (1963)	X	X					35–80 min. (depending on grade level)	4	4–14	G	CTB/Mcgraw-Hill

*These tests and inventories only represent a portion of the many tests that are available and those that have been discussed in the text.

[1] For addresses of companies see Appendix D.

Name and Date of Test	Vocabulary	Comprehension	Word-Attack	Speed	Listening		Time for Administration	Number of Forms	Grade Level	Group (G) or Individual (I)	Publisher
Classroom Reading Inventory (1974) (Second Edition)		x			x	Informal reading inventory for determining hearing capacity level and frustration, instructional and independent levels in oral reading—contains a spelling test	15–20 min.	3	2–10		William C. Brown
Cooperative Primary Tests (1965)					x	Subtests for: Listening	35 min.	2	1–3	G	Educational Testing Service
			x			Word-analysis	40 min.	2	1–3	G	
		x				Reading	35 min.	2	1–3	G	
						Writing skills	40 min.	2	1–3	G	
Corrective Reading System (1975)			x			Tests for nearly all of the reading skills except vocabulary and comprehension	Varies with each student	1	1–6 or older disabled readers	I	Psychotechnics, Inc.
Diagnostic Reading Scales (1972)			x								CTB/McGraw-Hill
Word Recognition Lists			x			Recognition vocabulary	5 min. (approx.)	1	1–6	I	
Reading Passages		x		x	x	Determine "independent," "instructional," and "potential" reading levels	10–30 min. (approx.)	2	1–8	I	
Phonics Tests			x			Auditory discrimination	Varies with each student	1	Any	I	

Skills or Areas Measured

Name and Date of Test	Vocabulary	Comprehension	Word-Attack	Speed	Listening	Other	Time for Administration	Number of Forms	Grade Level	Group (G) or Individual (I)	Publisher
Doren Diagnostic Reading Test (1973)	X		X			Spelling sight words	1–3 hrs.	1	1–6	G	American Guidance Service, Inc.
Durrell Analysis of Reading Difficulties	X	X	X	X	X	Handwriting	Varies with each student	1	1–6 or older disabled readers	G & I	Harcourt, Brace & Jovanovich, Inc.
Durrell Listening—Reading Series (1970)	X	X				Subtests for Vocabulary and Paragraph Reading and Listening	140–160 min. (depending on grade level)	2	1–9	G	Harcourt, Brace & Jovanovich, Inc.
Gates-MacGinitie Reading Tests (1964)											Teachers College Press
Primary—A	X	X						2	1	G	
Primary—B	X	X						2	2	G	
Primary—C	X	X						2	3	G	
Primary—CS				X		Accuracy		3	2–3	G	
Survey D	X	X		X		Accuracy		3	4–6	G	
Survey E	X	X		X		Accuracy		3	7–9	G	
Survey F	X	X		X		Accuracy		2	10–12	G	

Name and Date of Test	Vocabulary	Comprehension	Word-Attack	Speed	Listening	Other	Time for Administration	Number of Forms	Grade Level	Group (G) or Individual (I)	Publisher
Gates-McKillop Reading Diagnostic Tests (1962)	X	X	X			Oral vocabulary, spelling, auditory discrimination	45–90 min. (varies with each student)	2	1–7 or adult	I	Teachers College Press
Gilmore Oral Reading Test (1968)		X		X		Accuracy of material read	15–20 min.	2	1–8	I	Harcourt, Brace, & Jovanovich, Inc.
Iowa Tests of Basic Skills (1971)	X	X				Also: Work-study skills (map reading, reading graphs and tables, knowledge and use of reference materials) language skills (spelling, punctuation, usage)	67 min.	2	3–8	G	Houghton-Mifflin
Metropolitan Reading Tests (1970)	X	X					40–48 min. (depending on grade level)	4	2.5–9.5	G	Harcourt, Brace & Jovanovich, Inc.
New Gray Oral Reading Test (1967)				X		For obtaining overall oral reading grade level based on speed and number of oral errors (also gives an estimate of comprehension level)	10–20 min. (approx.)	4	1–16 and adults	I	Bobbs-Merrill Co., Inc.
Phonics Knowledge Survey (1964)			X			Phonics tests	10–30 min. (depending on student)	1	All	G	Teachers College Press

Skills or Areas Measured

Name and Date of Test	Vocabulary	Comprehension	Word-Attack	Speed	Listening	Other	Time for Administration	Number of Forms	Grade Level	Group (G) or Individual (I)	Publisher
Sequential Tests of Educational Development (1957)		X			X	Subtests for: Reading, writing, listening, mathematics, science, social studies	70 min. for each subtest	2	4–14	G	Educational Testing Service
Sequential Tests of Educational Progress—Series II (1969)	X	X				Subtests for: English expression, reading, mechanics of writing, and others	40 min. for each subtest	2	4–14	G	Educational Testing Service
Sipay Word-Analysis Tests (1974)			X			Tests word-analysis skills in detail	Varies with each student	1	All	I	Educators Publishing Service, Inc.
Standard Reading Inventory (1966)	X	X		X		Oral and silent reading level (recognition vocabulary)	40–50 min.	2	pp–7	I	Klamath Printing Co.
Stanford Diagnostic Reading Test (1969)	X	X	X	X		Auditory discrimination	91–137 min. depending on grade level	2	2.5–8.5	G	Harcourt, Brace & Jovanovich, Inc.
Stanford Reading Tests (1964)	X	X					30–83 min. (depending on grade level)	3	1.5 to 9.9	G	Harcourt, Brace & Jovanovich, Inc.
Tests of Academic Progress						Subtests for: Reading, literature, social studies, mathematics, science, and composition	45 min. for each student	2	9–12	G	Houghton-Mifflin

Name and Date of Test	Vocabulary	Comprehension	Word-Attack	Speed	Listening	Other	Time for Administration	Number of Forms	Grade Level	Group (G) or Individual (I)	Publisher
Wide Range Achievement Tests (1965)						Word pronunciation in oral reading, and spelling	15—30 min.	1	5—adult	I	Psychological Corp.
Woodcock Reading Mastery Tests (1974)	X	X	X			Sight vocabulary letter identification	20—30 min.	2	K—12	I	American Guidance Service, Inc.

441

READING READINESS

Name and Date of Test	Skills or Areas Measured					Other	Time for Administration	Number of Forms	Grade Level	Group (G) or Individual (I)	Publisher
	Vocabulary	Comprehension	Word-Attack	Speed	Listening						
Gates-MacGinitie Reading Tests: Readiness Skills (1968)					×	Listening comprehension, auditory discrimination, visual discrimination, following directions, letter recognition, visual-motor coordination, auditory bending, word recognition, and total			K–1	G	Teachers College Press
Lee-Clark Reading Readiness Test (1962)						A measure of reading readiness	20 min. (approx.)	1	K–1	G	CTB/McGraw-Hill
Maturity Level for School Entrance and Reading Readiness						Designed to determine whether children are mature enough to enter first grade and/or are ready to read	About 15 min.	1	K–1	G	American Guidance Service, Inc.
Metropolitan Readiness Tests (1964)					×	Measure readiness for reading and other first-grade instruction	30 min. + (depending on breaks between subtests)	2	1	G	Harcourt, Brace & Jovanovich, Inc.

TEST OF SOCIAL MATURITY

Name and Date of Test	Vocabulary	Comprehension	Word-Attack	Speed	Listening	Other	Time for Administration	Number of Forms	Grade Level	Group (G) or Individual (I)	Publisher
Vineland Social Maturity Scale (1965)						Designed to measure successive stages of social competence	20—30 min.	1	Infant to adult	I	American Guidance Service, Inc.

INTELLIGENCE OR SCHOLASTIC APTITUDE

Name and Date of Test	Vocabulary	Comprehension	Word-Attack	Speed	Listening	Other	Time for Administration	Number of Forms	Grade Level	Group (G) or Individual (I)	Publisher
California Test of Mental Maturity (1963)						For testing language and non-language intelligence	48–83 min. (depending on grade level)	1	K–adult	G	CTB/McGraw-Hill
Cognitive Abilities Test (1968)						A measure of cognitive abilities (successor to Lorge-Thorndike Intelligence Tests). Measures verbal, quantitative, and nonverbal skills	35 min. (each battery)	1	K–12	G	Houghton-Mifflin
Henmon-Nelson Tests of Mental Ability (1973)						A measure of academic aptitude	30 min. (no time limit on primary battery)	1	3–12	G	Houghton-Mifflin
Kuhlmann-Finch Scholastic Aptitude Tests (1957)						General mental development	30 min.	1	1–12	G	American Guidance Service, Inc.
Lorge-Thorndike Intelligence Tests (1966)						A measure of verbal and nonverbal intelligence	35 min. (verbal) 27 min. (nonverbal)	2	3–13	G	Houghton-Mifflin

Name and Date of Test	Vocabulary	Comprehension	Word-Attack	Speed	Listening	Other	Time for Administration	Number of Forms	Grade Level	Group (G) or Individual (I)	Publisher
McCarthy Scales of Children's Abilities						Numerical ability, perceptual performance, motor coordination, laterial dominance, and overall intellectual competence	45 min. for children 5 yrs. and younger and 1 hr. for older children	1	2½ to 8½ yrs.	I	Psychological Corp.
Peabody Picture Vocabulary Test (1959)						For testing verbal intelligence through the use of a series of pictures	15 min. (approx.)	2	Age 2.6 to adult	I	American Guidance Service, Inc.
School and College Ability Tests—Series II (1970)						For prediction of academic performance Subtests for: verbal, quantitative, and total	40 min.	2 3	4–14 12–14	G	Educational Testing Service
Stanford-Binet Intelligence Scale, Form LM (1972 Norms)	X	X				A measure of overall intelligence	45 min. to well over 90 min.	1	2–12 (older in some cases)	I	Psychological Corp.
Slosson Intelligence Test (1963)						A measure of intelligence	10–45 min.	1	1–adult	I	Slosson Educational Publications
Wechsler Adult Intelligence Scale (WAIS), (1955)	X	X				A measure of overall intelligence through a series of subtests	45–75 min.	1	16 to over 75	I	Psychological Corp.

445

Skills or Areas Measured

Name and Date of Test	Vocabulary	Comprehension	Word-Attack	Speed	Listening	Other	Time for Administration	Number of Forms	Grade Level	Group (G) or Individual (I)	
Wechsler Intelligence Test For children—R, (Revised Edition) (WISC), (1974)	X	X				A measure of overall intelligence through a series of subtests	45—75 min.	1	Ages 6–0 to 16—11	I	Psychological Corp.
Wechsler Preschool and Primary Scale (1967)	X	X				A measure of overall intelligence through a series of	50—70 min.	1	4 to 6½	I	Psychological Corp.
Wide-Range Vocabulary Tests (1945)						A measure of scholastic intelligence	10 min. (approx.)	2	3—adult	G or I	Psychological Corp.

PERSONALITY

Name and Date of Test	Vocabulary	Comprehension	Word-Attack	Speed	Listening	Other	Time for Administration	Number of Forms	Grade Level	Group (G) or Individual (I)	Publisher
California Test of Personality (1953)						For measurement of personality characteristics	40–50 min.	2	K–adult	I or G	CTB/McGraw-Hill
Edwards Personal Preference Schedule (1959)						For measurement of key needs or motives	about 45 min.	1	College and adult	G	Psychological Corp.
Inferred Self-Concept Scale (1974)						For evaluation of self-concept	15 min. (approx.)	1	1–6	I	Western Psychological Services
Minnesota Counseling Inventory (1957)						Family Relationships Social Relationships Emotional Relationships	About 50 min.	1	9–12	G	Psychological Corp.
Minnesota Multi-phasic Personality Inventory (1967)						For measurement of personality characteristics	40–90 min. for complete form 40–90 min. for shortened form	2	Older adolescents and adults	G or I	Psychological Corp.

PERCEPTUAL ABILITIES

Name and Date of Test	Skills or Areas Measured						Time for Administration	Number of Forms	Grade Level	Group (G) or Individual (I)	Publisher
	Vocabulary	Comprehension	Word-Attack	Speed	Listening	Other					
Developmental Test of Visual Perception (1964)						Subtests for eye-motor coordination, position in space, figure-ground, constancy of shape, and spatial relationships	30–50 min. (Individual) 40–60 min. (Groups)	1	Ages 4–8	G or I	Follett
Purdue Perceptual-Motor Survey Tests (1966)						Perceptual-motor skills	20 min.	1	Ages 6–10	I	Charles E. Merrill

ADDITIONAL TESTS

Name and Date of Test	Vocabulary	Comprehension	Word-Attack	Speed	Listening	Other	Time for Administration	Number of Forms	Grade Level	Group (G) or Individual (I)	Publisher
Survey of Study Habits and Attitudes (1967)						For counseling students about study habits	20–25 min.	1	7–13	G	Psychological Corp.
Wepman Auditory Discrimination Test (1958)						For counseling students about study habits	20–25 min.	1	7–13	G	Psychological Corp.

Commercial Materials for Teaching Reading Skills
in a Remedial Reading Center

Primary (1—3)
Intermediate (4—6)
Junior High (7—9)
Senior High (10—12)
Adult

Program	Reading Skills	Level of Difficulty

ADULT READERS
  Reader's Digest Services, Inc.
  Educational Division
  Pleasantville, New York 10570

Vocabulary Development
Word Analysis Skills
Comprehension Skills

Junior—Adult

This is a colorfully illustrated, high-interest set of material to reinforce basic reading skills. Each of the twelve readers offers mature-interest, low-vocabulary stories of courage, daring, self-reliance and adventure. It has easy-to-read-type and full-color illustrations with adult-appeal. There are short, practical exercises after each major story.

CATALOG FOR LIBRARY
RESOURCES
  Exemplary Center for Reading
    Instruction
  Salt Lake City and Granite
    School District
  2870 Connor Street
  Salt Lake City, Utah 84109

This catalog contains sections listing equipment, periodicals, professional books, reading games, films, records, kits, charts, research studies, filmstrips, tapes, discs, pictures, video tapes, tests, language arts texts, and 14,000 children's books graded by the Spache Readability Formula for Predicting Readability for grades 4 and up.

COMPREHENSION AUDIO LESSONS
  Reader's Digest Services, Inc.
  Educational Division
  Pleasantville, New York 10570

Oral Reading Skills
Comprehension Skills

Primary—Adult

Program	Reading Skills	Level of Difficulty

Each audio lesson helps to develop a specific reading skill—such as recognizing main ideas or noting sequence of events. Teachers can use this program with pupils on an individual, small group, or class basis. In each lesson a narrator first introduces the story, actors portray roles in the dramatization while music and other sound effects heighten pupil interest, reinforce reading skills, improve aural comprehension and oral reading, help diagnose a pupil's ability to comprehend ideas, and demonstrate correct pronunciation and intonation, especially for bilingual students.

CONTINENTAL PRESS MATERIALS
  The Continental Press, Inc.
  Elizabethtown, Pennsylvania 17022

Basic Sight Words
Vocabulary Development
Word Analysis Skills
Dictionary Skills
Comprehension Skills
Study Skills
Oral Reading Skills

Primary—Adult

Workbooks and liquid duplicating material to teach and emphasize fundamental and individualize instruction in reading skills.

DICTIONARY SKILLS AND USING
THE DIK*SHUH*NEHR*EE
  Xerox Education Publications
  Education Center
  Columbus, Ohio 43216

Dictionary Skills

Primary—Junior High

This program contains four books: book A is about a merry magician who teaches his tricks for alphabetizing; book B helps strengthen pronunciation and definition skills; book C works on root words, abbreviations, and parts of speech; book D reviews previous skills, stresses vowel and consonant sounds.

FIRST STEP TO READING AND
SECOND STEP TO READING
  Xerox Education Publications
  Education Center
  Columbus, Ohio 43216

Basic Sight Words
Vocabulary Development

Primary—Intermediate

First step teaches left-to-right progression by coloring, cutting, pasting,

painting. The pictures tell the youngsters which tools to use for each activity—such as pencil, crayon, scissors,
paste or paint. The second step contains three books for a reading readiness program. The books progress in
difficulty from "concrete" words to
more "abstract" words.

FLASH—X MATERIAL
　Educational Developmental
　　Laboratories, Inc.
　Huntington, New York
　Division of McGraw-Hill

Basic Sight Words	Intermediate—
Sight Vocabulary Development	Senior High

This is a set of training materials for
use with the EDL Flash—x apparatus
or the individual hand tachistoscope.
It is to be used for individual perceptual training, development of basic
sight words and sight vocabulary development. There is a set of three levels
of lessons 1-50.

GAMES
　Barnell-Loft, Ltd. and Dexter
　　and Westbrook, Ltd.
　958 Church Street
　Baldwin, New York 11510

　Garrard Publishing Co.
　Champaign, Illinois 61820

　Ideal School Supply Co.
　Oak Lawn, Illinois 60453

　Kenworthy Educational Service, Inc.
　138 Allen Street
　Buffalo, New York 14205

　Lyons and Carnahan
　Educational Publishers
　407 East 25th Street
　Chicago, Illinois 60616

　Science Research Associates, Inc.
　259 East Erie Street
　Chicago, Illinois 60611

Reading Skills:
Basic Sight Words
Vocabulary Development
　(Sight and Meaning)
Word Analysis Skills
Dictionary Skills
Comprehension Skills
Study Skills
Oral Reading Skills

Level of Difficulty:
Primary
Intermediate
Junior High
Senior High
Adult

These are addresses of companies that
have developed games (such as Riddle
Riddle Rhyme Time, Fun With Words,
Pronoun Parade, One Too Many, Time
for Sounds, Consonant Sounds, Vowel
Sounds, Phonic Drill Cards, Phonic

452

Program	Reading Skills	Level of Difficulty

Word Builders, Dolch Games, Phonic Word Blend Flip Charts, Phonics We Use) Learning Game Kits, SRA Reading Laboratory I: Word Games and others. These games are devised to help prepare children to read; teach children how to listen and follow directions, how to observe details, and how to express themselves by developing larger vocabularies. There are separate games to supplement phonics and reading instruction. Some games have directions for using the equipment to play additional games, and word building games that help students match their reading vocabulary to their listening vocabulary.

GOLDMAN—LYNCH SOUNDS AND
SYMBOLS DEVELOPMENT KIT

   American Guidance Service, Inc.   Word Analysis Skills   Primary
   Department RT-L   (specifically Phonetic Analysis)   Intermediate
   Circle Pines, Minnesota 55014   Junior High

There are sixty-four activities to stimulate production of the English speech sounds and recognition of their associated symbols. This kit contains puppet, tape cassettes, posters, picture cards, magnetic symbols and adventure story books.

GRAPHS AND SURVEYS

   Xerox Education Publications   Study Skills   Junior High—Adult
   Education Center
   Columbus, Ohio 43216

This program is an introduction to interpreting and preparing graphs and surveys; assembling information, evaluating it, organizing it, and translating it into graphic form.

GROW IN WORD POWER

   Reader's Digest Services, Inc.   Sight and Meaning   Junior High—Adult
   Educational Division   Vocabulary Development
   Pleasantville, New York 10570

Fun-to-do exercises that help students acquire a larger vocabulary and improve spelling skills. The word games and exercises include: Match words with meanings, juggling letters, double spellings, get the meaning from the context, chess game with words, word analogies, and geographical analogies.

Program	Reading Skills	Level of Difficulty
HAYES COMPANY MATERIALS Hayes School Publishing Co., Inc. 321 Pennwood Avenue Wilkinsburg, Pennsylvania 15221	Word Analysis Skills Dictionary Skills Vocabulary Development Study Skills Oral Reading Skills	Primary—Senior High

Workbooks and liquid duplicating material to teach and emphasize fundamental and individualize instruction in all reading skills.

Program	Reading Skills	Level of Difficulty
HELP YOURSELF TO IMPROVE YOUR READING Reader's Digest Services, Inc. Educational Division Pleasantville, New York 10570	Comprehension Skills	Junior High—Adult

Compelling "want-to-read" selections in a compact, do-it-yourself format emphasizing speeded comprehension. Each contains an essay, a narrative, a biographical sketch and a factual report. Each "self-help" reader features a word count for every selection, professional tips on previewing, adjusting reading speed and increasing comprehension. There is a comprehension quiz following each selection and self-help exercise.

Program	Reading Skills	Level of Difficulty
INDIVIDUALIZED READING FROM SCHOLASTIC Scholastic Magazines, Inc. 50 West 44th Street New York, New York 10036	Basic Sight Words Vocabulary Development Word Analysis Skills Dictionary Skills Comprehension Skills Study Skills Oral Reading Skills	Primary—Junior High

This material helps a student to develop his own reading program, by choosing what he wants to read from a wide range of children's literature in paperback. Students can progress at their own pace and sharpen important skills while becoming successful and independent readers. The titles of the program

454

Program	Reading Skills	Level of Difficulty

are: Reaching Out, Reaching Up, Reaching Higher, Reaching Forward, Reaching Ahead, and Reaching Beyond.

LANGUAGE MASTER
Bell and Howell Company
7100 McCormick Road
Chicago, Illinois 60645

Vocabulary Development
Word Analysis Skills
  (specifically Structural Analysis
  and Phonetic Analysis)

Primary—Adult

The language master is a card reader. The student inserts a card, watches and listens, records, and then immediately compares his responses to the information on the instructor track. The programs include a phonics program, alphabet mastery program, vocabulary builder program, word-picture program, and a language stimulation program. This program employs sight, speech, touch, and hearing in coordinated, effective instruction. The system includes a compact, portable unit which provides complete, self-contained dual track recording and playback capability. The unit is used with sets of cards containing visual material and a strip of magnetic recording tape.

LIBRARY SKILLS AND LEARNING TO USE THE LIBRARY
Xerox Education Publications
Education Center
Columbus, Ohio 43216

Study Skills

Primary—Senior High

This program contains four books: book A works with book parts, book B works with "cracking the code" of the Dewey Decimal system, book C works with learning how to use the Reader's Guide, and book D works with using different reference books, use of tools such as tapes, filmstrips, earphones, recordings, etc.

Program	Reading Skills	Level of Difficulty

LISTEN AND READ
  Educational Development
    Laboratories, Inc.
  Huntington, New York
  Division of McGraw-Hill

Comprehension Skills
Study Skills
Listening Skills

Junior High—Adult

This program consists of a set D for a fourth grade reading level; set GHI for levels seven, eight, nine; set JKL for levels ten, eleven, twelve; set MN for adult and college. There are thirty lessons with scripts of accompanying recordings, workbooks, and lesson books. Each lesson begins with an introductory sketch, dialogue, or sequence of sound effects in order to capture the student's interest and attention; the narrator introduces the students to the skill or concept being dealt with and then guides them through listening and workbook exercises in which they gain practice in various phases of the skill or concept.

MACMILLAN READING SPECTRUM
  The Macmillan Company
  866 Third Avenue
  New York, New York 10022

Basic Sight Words
Vocabulary Development
Word Analysis Skills
Dictionary Skills
Comprehension Skills
Study Skills
Oral Reading Skills

Intermediate—
Senior High

This program consists of the spectrum of skills which are word analysis level 1—6, vocabulary development level 1—6, comprehension level 1—6. The books are self-directing, self-correcting, and non-consumable. There are eighteen booklets providing sequential instruction in word analysis, vocabulary development, and reading comprehension. The spectrum of books offers two classroom sets of children's books that have been carefully selected, a set A for grades 2—6, and a set B for grades 3—8. Each set contains many books so that every child can choose what he wants to read. In every book there is a synopsis, a cast of characters, excerpts for "flavor," and comprehension and interpretation questions.

456

Program	Reading Skills	Level of Difficulty

MAP SKILLS FOR TODAY AND READINESS FOR MAP SKILLS
  Xerox Education Publications
  Education Center
  Columbus, Ohio 43216

Study Skills — Primary-Senior High

This program consists of five books that help the students use maps as learning tools by providing a thorough guide in map terminology, symbols, and other map skills.

MAP SKILLS FOR TODAY'S GEOGRAPHY
  Xerox Education Publications
  Education Center
  Columbus, Ohio 43216

Study Skills — Junior High-Senior High

This program is a review of basic map reading skills with grids, scales, map symbols and keys, and map projections. Students learn to apply these skills in grasping such concepts as the effects of prevailing winds, rainfall, and ocean currents on world climate patterns.

MERRILL READING SKILL TEXT SERIES
  Charles E. Merrill
  1300 Alum Creek Drive
  Columbus, Ohio 43216

Voculabulary Development
Word Analysis Skills
Comprehension Skills
Study Skills

Primary-Senior High

This program is a logically planned, developmental reading skills program designed to develop essential reading and learning skills through carefully devised sequential exercises. Some of the titles are Bibs; Nicky; Uncle Bunny; Ben, the Traveler; Tom, the Reporter; and Pat, the Pilot.

NEW ADVANCED READING SKILL BUILDER
  Reader's Digest Service, Inc.
  Educational Division
  Pleasantville, New York 10570

Comprehension Skills
Vocabulary Development
Study Skills

Intermediate-Adult

This is a set of books with audio lesson units, advanced reading tutors at levels 7-8-9, and supplementary readers. It can be used as a teacher's resource and audio aid. This program helps to develop specific reading skills, such as recognizing main ideas, noting sequence of events, etc. It is designed to spark the interest of both good and reluctant readers, reinforce reading skills, improve aural comprehension and oral reading, help diagnose a pupil's ability to comprehend ideas, demonstrate correct pronunciation and intonation, and serve as model for class dramatizations.

NEW MODERN READING SKILL
TEXT SERIES

Charles E. Merrill	Word Analysis Skills	Junior High-Adult
1300 Alum Creek Drive	Dictionary Skills	
Columbus, Ohio 43216	Study Skills	
	Comprehension Skills	

This program contains books 1, 2, 3 and a teacher's edition. It is used to improve the reading ability of older students. It provides a systematic development of important reading skills, teaches understanding words, knowing facts, extending ideas, organizing ideas and study word structure.

NEW PHONICS SKILL TEXT SERIES

Charles E. Merrill	Word Analysis Skills	Primary-Junior High
1300 Alum Creek Drive	(specifically Phonetic	
Columbus, Ohio 43216	Analysis Skills)	

This program contains books A-D and teacher's editions for A-D; is designed to teach accuracy and independence in word recognition and comprehension through recognition of the sound and structure of words. The series may be used independently or with any basal or individualized reading program.

NEW SERIES READING SKILL
BUILDERS

Reader's Digest Service, Inc.	Vocabulary Development	Primary-Adult
Educational Division	Comprehension Skills	
Pleasantville, New York 10570	Study Skills	
	Oral Reading Skills	

Each skill builder in the program helps to develop a specific reading skill such

458

as recognizing main ideas and noting sequence of events; comes with duplicating masters for each level and reading skill, It is used to spark the interest of both good and reluctant readers; reinforce reading skills; improve aural comprehension and oral reading; help diagnose a pupil's ability to comprehend ideas; demonstrate correct pronunciation and intonation. It may serve as a model for class dramatization.

ORIGINAL SERIES READING SKILL BUILDERS

Readers's Digest Service, Inc.
Educational Division
Pleasantville, New York 10570

Each skill builder in the program helps to develop a specific reading skill such as recognizing main ideas, noting sequence of events, etc. This program is designed to spark the interest of both good and reluctant readers, reinforce reading skills, improve aural comprehension and oral reading, help diagnose a pupil's ability to comprehend ideas, demonstrate correct pronunciation and intonation, and serve as models for class dramatizations.

Vocabulary Development
Comprehension Skills
Study Skills
Oral Reading Skills

Primary-Adult

PHONICS AND WORD POWER

Xerox Education Publications
Education Center
Columbus, Ohio 43216

This program consists of books 1-2-3; each book consists of three levels A-B-C which help children review, maintain, and build the skills to turn printed symbols into units of meaning. Program 2 is for recognizing words, developing vocabulary and phonetic and structural analysis skills, and program 3 is for multiple approach to word analysis skills.

Basic Sight Words
Vocabulary Development
Word Analysis Skills
    (specifically Phonetic
    Analysis)

Primary-Junior High

459

Program	Reading Skills	Level of Difficulty

PHONICS WE USE
  Lyons and Carnahan
  Educational Publishers
  407 East 25th Street
  Chicago, Illinois 60616

Vocabulary Development
Word Analysis Skills
  (specifically Phonetic
  Analysis Skills)
Dictionary Skills

Primary-Senior High

This program contains seven workbooks A-G with accompanying teacher's editions; each helps pupils associate written symbols with speech sounds; each book introduces new phonetic concepts and includes review and expansion of material taught in previous books.

PHONIVISUAL PHONICS PROGRAM
  Phonovisual Products, Inc.
  Box 5625
  Washington, D.C. 20016

Word Analysis Skills
  (specifically Phonetic
  Analysis Skills)

Primary-Junior High

This is a program for teaching phonics.

PICTO-CABULARY SERIES
  Barnell Loft, Ltd.
  958 Church Street
  Baldwin, New York 11510

Vocabulary Development
  (Sight and Meaning)

Intermediate-Senior High

This program consists of two sets which are used to stimulate pupil's interest in words and to enlarge their own vocabularies. Each set is of equal difficulty. Each is made up of two copies of each of six different titles for a total of twelve booklets. Worksheets and teacher's manual are included with each set.

PLAYS FOR ECHO READING
  Harcourt Brace and World, Inc.
  757 3rd Avenue
  New York, New York 10017

Vocabulary Development
Oral Reading Skills

Primary-Junior High

This is a self-directed program to improve reading at the primary level. It helps develop expressive reading, increase phrase perception, acquire more rapid and accurate word recognition, expand their reading vocabulary, and increase reading achievements. It contains twenty-eight plays, twelve paperbound pupil's books, eight long playing 331/3 RPM 12 inch records and a teacher's manual.

460

Program	Reading Skills	Level of Difficulty

PROGRAMMED READING AND PROGRAMMED READING FOR ADULTS (BUCHANAN AND SULLIVAN)
Webster Division
McGraw-Hill Book Company
Manchester Road
Manchester, Missouri 63011

This is a program that allows every child or adult to respond actively by using a linguistic approach to simplify reading for every pupil. It has programmed format which provides a "built-in tutor" allowing children to work independently.

Basic Sight Words
Vocabulary Development
Word Analysis Skills
Dictionary Skills
Comprehension Skills
Study Skills
Oral Reading Skills

Primary-Adult

PSYCHOTECHNICS RADIO READING
Psychotechnics, Inc.
1900 Pickwick Avenue
Glenview, Illinois 60025

This program contains thirty stories, fifteen tape cassettes, three hundred story booklets, teacher's edition, student booklets, two audio file cassette albums and steel file cabinet. It is designed to attract reluctant readers and encourages the formation of good reading and listening habits. The program is especially useful in remedial training and when working with the culturally deprived. It can be used for reading and listening skills.

Vocabulary Development
Word Analysis Skills
Comprehension Skills

Intermediate-Adult

READER'S DIGEST READINGS
Reader's Digest Services, Inc.
Educational Division
Pleasantville, New York 10570

Informative, high-interest selections for youth and adults. The first two books build on five hundred of the most commonly used words in English. The next two books build on one thousand words and the last two books build on two thousand words. Word selection was based on "The Teacher's Wordbook of 30,000 Words" by Thorndike and Lorge. This program is used to build basic sight words as an

Basic Sight Words
Vocabulary Development
Comprehension Skills

Junior High-Adult

461

Program	Reading Skills	Level of Difficulty

aid to vocabulary development. A comprehension quiz, plus a variety of word-study exercises, follow each selection. Quizzes measure the reader's ability to understand what he has read, grasp the sequence of events, note significant details, and interpret the content.

READER'S DIGEST READING SKILL PRACTICE PADS
Reader's Digest Services, Inc.
Educational Division
Pleasantville, New York 10570

	Vocabulary Development	Junior High—Adult
	Word Analysis Skills	
	Comprehension Skills	
	Study Skills	

These are high-utility workbooks that extend basic reading, writing, vocabulary, and word-study skills.

READING SKILL BUILDER KITS
Reader's Digest Services, Inc.
Educational Division
Pleasantville, New York 10570

Comprehension Skills — Primary—Adult

This is high-interest supplementary materials on a wide range of reading levels, conveniently boxed to meet the reading needs of every pupil in a classroom. The kits give every pupil a choice of three different readers at his own reading level and quizzes at the end of each story.

READING SKILLS LIBRARY
Reader's Digest Service, Inc.
Educational Division
Pleasantville, New York 10570

Comprehension Skills — Primary—Adult
Study Skills

This is a reading and listening resource unit that will aid in building critical reading skills. It offers material to meet the reading needs of all the pupils in a class or school through the use of books and cassettes.

READING SUCCESS SERIES
Xerox Education Publications
Education Center
Columbus, Ohio 43216

Vocabulary Development — Primary—Senior High
Word Analysis Skills
Dictionary Skills

This program uses a mature format, high-interest content and stimulating illustrations. This series plots a sequence of skills based on what discouraged youngsters do know. There are six different thirty-two page books numbered by skill steps, which are sequenced.

READING TUTORS

Reader's Digest Services, Inc. Educational Division Pleasantville, New York 10570	Comprehension Skills Study Skills	Primary—Adult

This program is a compact reading and listening comprehension unit that offers "private reading lessons" for pupils in a classroom. It offers self-contained learning materials. Pupils can learn at their own speed while the teacher moves from group to group or helps pupils with other activities.

READ-STUDY-THINK

Xerox Education Publications Education Center Columbus, Ohio 43216	Comprehension Skills	Primary—Senior High

This is a series of practice books designed to improve reading comprehension. These skills are reading for literal and concrete facts, interpreting meaning and drawing generalizations, and organizing information.

Rx READING PROGRAM

Psychotechnics, Inc. 1900 Pickwick Avenue Glenview, Illinois 60025	Basic Sight Words Vocabulary Development Word Analysis Skills	Primary—Adult

This program contains a reading and storage system with cards, check strips, and cassettes, a portable number board, a starter set, and a teacher's manual that contains all the information necessary to administer the program. The Rx is a diagnostic prescriptive approach to developing the basic reading skills of letter recognition, basic and sight word knowledge of common nouns, pictures, and phonetic word analysis.

SCHOLASTIC LITERATURE UNITS

Scholastic Book Service
904 Sylvan Avenue
Englewood Cliffs, New Jersey 07632

Vocabulary Development
Comprehension Skills
Study Skills

Junior High—
Senior High

This program contains titles such as Animals, High Adventure, Small World, Courage, Family, Frontiers, Moments of Decision, Mirrors, The Lighter Side, Survival, Success, and Personal Code. The students usually become interested when the subject matter of the course stems from his own most serious concerns. This program focuses on themes of vital interest, provides for individual differences, emphasizes major literary forms, integrates literature and reading skills, and develops good reading habits.

SPECIFIC SKILL SERIES

Barnell Loft, Ltd.
111 South Centre Avenue
Rockville Centre, New York

Basic Sight Words
Vocabulary Development
Word Analysis Skills
Dictionary Skills
Comprehension Skills
Study Skills

Primary—Adult

This program gives students specific and concentrated experiences in reading for different purposes. It provides practice material for pupils on a number of different reading levels. It is a structural reading program with all the advantages of programmed learning. Learners get additional drill in areas of need. Each booklet is concerned with the development of one reading skill on one reading level.

SPEECH-TO-PRINT PHONICS AND SPEECH-TO-PRINT PHONICS, 2nd Edition

Harcourt Brace Jovanovich, Inc.
School Department
757 Third Avenue
New York, New York 10017

Basic Sight Words
Vocabulary Development
Word Analysis Skills
  (specifically Phonetic Analysis)

Primary—Junior High

These programs contain two hundred and thirty-three applied phonics practice cards, thirty-four sets of pupil response cards, fifty-five lessons on phonemes, ten lessons on letter names and forms, cards that provide practice in using the newly learned phonics elements to solve new words, and letters, blends, yes-no and number cards to permit every pupil to respond to each learning situation.

SRA BASIC READING SERIES

Science Research Associates, Inc.
259 East Erie Street
Chicago, Illinois 60611

Basic Sight Words
Vocabulary Development
Word Analysis Skills
Comprehension Skills

Primary—Junior High

This program contains an alphabet book for the readiness level, readers from A—F, workbooks from A—F, teacher's manual, teacher's handbook, test from A—F, cumulative tests from A—F, and teacher's test guide. This program concentrates on developing children's decoding skills through controlled exposure to sequenced sound-spelling patterns in stories, poems, and teacher directed activities.

SRA READING LABORATORIES

Science Research Associates, Inc.
259 East Erie Street
Chicago, Illinois 60611

Basic Sight Words
Vocabulary Development
Word Analysis Skills
Dictionary Skills
Comprehension Skills
Study Skills

Primary—Adult

This program contains reading labs from 1a—c, 2a—c, 3a—b, and 4a, pupil booklets for labs, and is an individualized reading system based on the principle that learning is most effective if the student starts at his own level of reading, where he is assured success. It allows the student to proceed as fast as his learning rate permits.

SRA PILOT LIBRARIES

Science Research Associates, Inc.
259 East Erie Street
Chicago, Illinois 60611

Comprehension Skills

Primary—Junior High

This program contains five levels of reading from 1c, 2a—c, and 3b with student record books, teacher's handbook, and key booklet. This program

465

is designed to bridge the gap between reading training and independent reading with short excerpts, complete in themselves, from full-length books. Each pilot library kit contains seventy-two selections called pilot books to whet a young reader's appetite and lead him to the original work. The books are 16-32 pages long, are chosen for their interest, appeal, and reading level.

SRA READING FOR
UNDERSTANDING
  Science Research Associates, Inc.   Comprehension Skills   Intermediate—Adult
  259 East Erie Street
  Chicago, Illinois 60611

This program is a set of four hundred reading comprehension exercises designed to aid each student in improving his ability to get meaning from his reading.

SULLIVAN REMEDIAL READING
PROGRAM
  Behavioral Research Laboratories   Basic Sight Words   Primary—Adult
  Box 577   Vocabulary Development
  Palo Alto, California 94302   Word Analysis Skills
     Dictionary Skills
This is a programmed reading series.   Comprehension Skills
The material consists of textbooks,   Study Skills
workbooks, teacher's manuals, readers,   Oral Reading Skills
placement exams, and exams.

TABLE AND GRAPH SKILLS
  Xerox Education Publications   Study Skills   Primary—Junior High
  Education Center
  Columbus, Ohio 43216

This program contains four books in which book A teaches students to learn terms, symbols, and basic procedures that enable him to solve problems represented by tables and graphs. Book B introduces interpretive reading of tables and graphs. Books C and D introduce different kinds of graphs by pictures, box, bar, line, and circle and emphasize critical and creative reading.

Program	Reading Skills	Level of Difficulty

VOCABULARY AUDIO SKILLS LESSON
Reader's Digest Service, Inc.
Educational Division
Pleasantville, New York 10570

Vocabulary Development
Word Analysis Skills

Primary—Junior High

This program extends the audio program with dramatizations from thirty additional skill builder stories. There are six vocabulary lessons on three cassettes at each level from 1—6. The program concentrates on developing word study or word analysis skills such as mastering words by matching words and definitions, using key words correctly, identifying words with sensory appeal, identifying the correct word, using context clues to identify meanings and using context clues to identify special meaning.

Vx VOCABULARY PROGRAM
Psychotechnics, Inc.
1900 Pickwick Avenue
Glenview, Illinois 60025

Vocabulary Development
Word Analysis Skills

Primary—Adult

This program is a diagnostic vocabulary development program that develops the sight and meaning vocabulary of students through common nouns, pictures, service words and word analysis skills.

WEBSTER WORD WHEELS
Webster Division
McGraw-Hill Book Company
Manchester Road
Manchester, Missouri 63011

Word Analysis Skills
(specifically Structural
Analysis and Phonetic
Analysis)

Primary—Senior High

This program contains sixty-three wheels, seventeen beginning blends, twenty prefix wheels, eighteen suffix wheels, eight two-letter consonant wheels, and a file box. The purpose of this program is to teach students the basic phonetic and structural analysis skills needed for reading readiness, vocabulary development, and basic sight word development on an individualized reading basis.

Abingdom Press
201 Eighth Ave. S.
Nashville 2, Tn. 37202

Abrahams Magazine Service
56th E. 13th St.
New York, N.Y. 10003

Academic Achievement Centers, Inc.
3849 W. Devon Ave.
Chicago, Ill. 60645

Academic Paperbacks
The Academic Bldg.
Saw Mill Rd.
West Haven, Ct. 06516

Academic Therapy Publications
1539 Fourth St.
San Rafael, Calif. 94901

ACI Films
35 W. 45 St.
New York, N.Y. 10036

Acoustifone Corp.
8954 Comanche Ave.
Chatsworth, Calif. 91311

Adapt Press
104 E. 20th St.
Sioux Falls, S.D. 57105

Addison-Wesley Publishing Co., Inc.
Reading, Ma. 01867

Addisonian Press and Young Scott
   Books
Reading, Ma. 01867

Alexander Graham Bell Association For The
   Deaf
Volta Bureau
3417 Volta Place, N.W.
Washington, D.C. 20007

American Association For Higher Education
Dupont Circle Suite 780
Washington, D.C. 20036

American Book Co.
450 E. Huron St.
Chicago, Ill. 60611

American Education Publications
Education Center
Columbus, Oh. 43216

American Educational Film
132 Lasky Drive
Beverly Hills, Calif.

American Guidance Service, Inc.
Publisher's Bldg.
Circle Pines, Mn. 55014

The American Jewish Committee
Institute of Human Relations
165 E. 56 St.
New York, N.Y. 10022

American Library Association
Field Enterprises Education Corp.
Merchandise Mart Plaza
Chicago, Ill.

American Paperback Services
507 Jackson
Topeka, Ks. 66603

A.M.S. Press, Inc.
56 E. 13th St.
New York, N.Y. 10003

Ann Arbor Publishers, Inc.
616 Church St., Box 1446
Ann Arbor, Mi. 48104

Appleton-Century-Crofts, Inc.
Educational Division Meredith Corp.
440 Park Ave. S.
New York, N.Y. 10016

Armbrust Educational Publication
3163 Leavenworth
Omaha, Ne. 68105

Arno Press
330 Madison
New York, N.Y. 10017

Ashley Books Inc.
Box 768
Port Washington, N.Y. 11050

Associated Publishers
1538 9th St., N.W.
Washington, D.C. 20001

Association for Childhood Education
  International
3615 Wisconsin Ave., N.W.
Washington, D.C. 20016

Association for Supervision and Curriculum
  Development
Room 428, 1201 Sixteenth St., N.W.
Washington, D.C. 20036

Association Instructional Materials
600 Madison Ave.
New York, N.Y. 10022

Atheneum Publishers
122 E. 42nd St.
New York, N.Y. 10017

Audio Dynamic Research
1219 E. 11th St.
Pueblo, Co. 81001

Avon Books
959 Eighth Ave.
New York, N.Y. 10019

The Baker & Taylor Co.
Gladiola Av.
Momence, Ill. 60954

Baldridge Reading Instructional Material
14 Grigg St.
Greenwich, Conn. 06830

Bantam Books
666 Fifth Ave.
New York, N.Y. 10019

Barnell Loft, Ltd.
958 Church St.
Baldwin, N.Y. 11510

Barnes & Noble, Inc.
International Textbook Series
105 Fifth Ave.
New York, N.Y. 10003

Clarence L. Barnhart, Inc.
Box 250
Bronxville, N.Y. 10708

Beacon Enterprises
609 River St.
Box 1296
Santa Cruz, Calif. 95060

Beckly-Candy Co.
1900 N. Narragansett Ave.
Chicago, Ill. 60639

Behavioral Publication, Inc.
2852 Broadway-Morningside Heights
New York, N.Y. 10025

Behavioral Research Laboratories, Inc.
3250 Alpine Rd.
Box 577
Palo Alto, Calif. 94302

Bell & Howell Co.
Audio Visual Products Division
7100 McCormic Rd.
Chicago, Ill. 60645

Benefic Press
10300 W. Roosevelt Rd.
Westchester, Ill. 60153

Benzinger Bruce & Glencoe, Inc.
8701 Wilshire Blvd.
Beverly Hills, Calif. 90211

Biological Sciences Curriculum Study
P.O. Box 930
Boulder, Co. 80302

BIPAD (Bureau of Independent Publishers
  & Distributors)
122 E. 42nd St.
New York, N.Y. 10017

Bobbs-Merrill Co.
4300 W. 62nd St.
Indianapolis, Ind. 46268

Book-Lab, Inc.
1449 37th St.
Brooklyn, N.Y. 12218

Books On Exhibit
Mount Kisco, N.Y. 10549

Borg-Warner Educational Systems
7450 N. Natchez Ave.
Niles, Ill. 60648

R. R. Bowker Co.
1180 Ave. of the Americas
New York, N.Y. 10036

Bowmar Publishing Corp.
622 Rodier Dr.
Glendale, Calif. 91201

Bremer-Davis
161 Green Bay Rd.
Wilmette, Ill. 60091

Brigham Young University Press Pub. Sales
205 UPB
Provo, Ut. 84601

Burgess Publishing Co.
426 S. Sixth St.
Minneapolis, Mn. 55415

Burson Products
P.O. Box 9231
Austin, Tx. 78757

Cal Press Inc.
76 Madison Ave.
New York, N.Y. 10016

Calif. Assoc. for Neurologically Handicapped
  Children
Literature Distribution Center
P.O. Box 790
Lomita, Calif. 90717

California Test Bureau/McGraw-Hill
Del Monte Research Park
Monterey, Calif. 93940

Cambridge Book Co.
488 Madison Ave.
New York, N.Y. 10022

Cassetts Unlimited
Roanoke, Tx. 76262

Center for Applied Research in Education
521 5th Ave.
New York, N.Y. 10017

Century Consultants
6363 Broadway
Chicago, Ill. 60625

Charles E. Merrill Publishing Co.
1300 Alum Creek Dr.
Columbus, Oh. 43216

Child Study
Association of America
9 E. 89th St.
New York, N.Y. 10028

Children's Press
1224 W. Van Buren St.
Chicago, Ill. 60607

Citation Press
50 W. 44th St.
New York, N.Y. 10036

College Skills Center
101 W. 31st St.
New York, N.Y. 10001

Colonial Films, Inc.
752 Spring St., N.W.
Atlanta, Ga. 30308

The Combined Book Exhibit Inc.
Scarborough Park, Albany Post Rd.
Briarcliff Manor, N.Y. 10510

Commucad-The Dommunication Academy
Box 541
Wilton, Ct. 06897

F. E. Compton Co.
425 N. Michigan Ave.
Chicago, Illinois. 60611

Continental Press
520 E. Bainbridge St.
Elizabethtown, Pa. 17022

Cooperative Tests and Service
Educational Testing Service
Box 999
Princeton, N.J. 08540

Coronet Instructional Media
65 E. S. Water St.
Chicago, Ill. 60639

Coward-McMann, Inc.
200 Madison Ave.
New York, N.Y. 10016

Craig
921 W. Artesia Blvd.
Comption, Calif. 90220

Creative Visuals
Box 1911
Big Springs, Tx. 97920

Croft Educational Services, Inc.
100 Garfield Ave.
New London, Ct. 06320

Thomas Y. Crowell Co.
666 Fifth Ave.
New York, N.Y. 10019

Crown Publishers
419 Park Ave. S.
New York, N.Y. 10016

CTB/McGraw Hill
Del Monte Research Park
Monterey, Calif. 9340

Curriculum Associates
P.O. Box 56
Wellesley Hills, Ma. 02181

Curriculum of Texas Inc.
900 Old Koeing Lane
Suite 129
Austin, Tx. 78756

John Day Co.
257 Park Ave. S.
New York, N.Y. 10010

Dell Publishing Co., Inc.
750 Third Ave.
New York, N.Y. 10017

Denoyer Geppert Co.
5235 Ravenswood Ave.
Chicago, Ill. 60640

Dept. of Health Education and Welfare
U.S. Gov't Printing Office
Washington, D.C. 20402

Developmental Reading Distributors
1944 Sheridan Ave.
Laramie, Wy. 82070

Dexter & Westbook, Ltd.
111 So. Center Ave.
Rockville Center, N.Y. 11571

The Dial Press/Delacorte Press
750 3rd Ave.
New York, N.Y. 10017

A. B. Dick Co.
5700 W. Touchy Ave.
Chicago, Ill. 60645

Docent Corp.
24 Broadway
Peasantville, N.Y. 10570

Dodd, Mead & Co., Inc.
79 Madison Ave.
New York, N.Y. 10016

Doubleday and Co., Inc.
501 Franklin Ave.
Garden City, N.Y. 10017

Dreier Educational Systems
320 Raritan Ave.
Highland Park, N.J. 08904

Dutton, E. P. and Co.
201 Park Ave. So.
New York, N.Y. 10002

Early Years Magazine
P.O. Box 1223
Darien, Ct. 06820

The Economy Company
P.O. Box 25308
Oklahoma City, Ok. 73125

Edmark Associates
655 I. Orcas St.
Seattle, Wash. 98108

Educational Corporation of America
984 Livernois Road
Troy, Mich. 48084

Educational Activities Inc.
P.O. Box 392
Freeport, N.Y. 11510

Educational Aids
845 Wisteria Dr.
Fremont, Calif. 94538

Educational Book Division
Prentice Hall
Englewood Cliffs, N.J. 07632

Educational Development Corp.
Post Office Drawer 1007
Lakeland, Fl. 33802

Educational Developmental Laboratories, Inc.
A Division of McGraw Hill
Huntington, N.Y. 11743

Educational Games, Inc.
P.O. Box 3653
Grand Central Station
New York, N.Y. 10017

Educational Progress
Division of Educational Development Corp.
P.O. Box 45663
Tulsa, Ok. 74145

Educational Projections Corp.
3070 Lake Terrace
Glenview, Ill. 60025

Educational Publications
Dublin, N.H. 03444

Educational Records Bureau
21 Audublon Ave.
New York, N.Y. 10032

Educational Service, Inc.
P.O. Box 219
Stevensville, Mich. 49127

Educational Solutions Inc.
P.O. Box 190
Cooper Station
New York, N.Y. 10003

Educational Testing Service
1947 Center St.
Berkeley, Calif. 94704

Educators Publishing Service
75 Moulton St.
Cambridge, Mass. 02138

J. W. Edwards Publ. Inc.
2500 S. State St.
Ann Arbor, Mich. 48104

Electronics Futures Inc.
57 Dodge Ave.
North Haven, Conn. 06473

Encyclopaedia Britannica
Educational Corp.
425 N. Michigan Ave.
Chicago, Ill. 60611

E & R Development Co.
Vandalia Road
Jacksonville, Ill. 62650

Eric/Crier Clearinghouse
NCTE
1111 Kenyon Rd.
Urbana, Ill. 61801

Fawcett Publ. Inc.
1515 Broadway
New York, N.Y. 10036

Fearon Publishers, Inc.
6 Davis Dr.
Belmont, Calif. 94002

Fideler Co.
31 Ottowa Ave. N.W.
Grand Rapids, Mich. 49502

Follett Educ. Corp.
1010 W. Washington Blvd.
Chicago, Ill. 60607

Fonetik Books
19 Garfield
Palm Springs, Calif. 92262

Free Press
866 Third Ave.
New York, N.Y. 10023

Fun Learning Enterprises
Metchosin, British Columbia, Canada

Gage Educational Publications
164 Commander Blvd.
Agincourt, Ontario, Canada

Gamco Industries
Box 1911
Big Springs, Tx. 79720

Garrard Publishing Co.
2 Overhill Rd.
Scarsdale, N.Y. 10583

General Electric Co.
Corporate Research & Development #5-343
Schenectady, N.Y. 12345

General Learning Corp.
3 E. 54th St.
New York, N.Y. 10022

Gillingham-Slingerland
Reading Workshops
75 Moulton St.
Cambridge, Ma. 02138

Ginn and Company
9888 Monroe Dr.
Dallas, Tx. 75229

Globe Book Co., Inc.
175 Fifth Ave.
New York, N.Y. 10010

Goodyear Pub. Co.
15115 Sunset Blvd., Pacific
Palisades, Calif.

The Grade Teacher
Riverside, N.J. 08075

Grolier Educational Corp.
845 Third Ave.
New York, N.Y. 10022

Grossett and Dunlap
51 Madison Ave.
New York, N.Y. 10010

Grove Press
80 University Place
New York, N.Y. 10010

E.M. Hale & Co.
1201 S. Hastings Way
Eau Claire, Wi. 54701

Harcourt Brace Jovanovich
757 Third Ave.
New York, N.Y. 10017

Harper and Row Publishers
Library Dept.
10 E. 53 St.
New York, N.Y. 10022

Harper, Torchbooks
10 E. 53 St.
New York, N.Y. 10022

Harvard University Press
79 Garden St.
Cambridge, Ma. 02138

Harvey House, Inc.
Irvington-on-Hudson
New York, N.Y. 10533

Hawthorn Books
260 Madison Ave.
New York, N.Y. 10016

Hayden Book Co., Inc.
50 Essex St.
Rochelle Park, N.J. 07662

Hayes School Pub. Co.
321 Pennwood Ave.
Wilkinsburg, Pa. 15221

D. C. Heath and Co.
125 Spring St.
Lexington, Ma. 02173

Hertzberg New Method
Vandalia Rd.
Jacksonville, Ill. 62650

Highlights for Children
2300 Fifth Ave.
Columbus, Oh. 43216

Hoffman Information Systems
5623 Peck Rd.
Arcadia, Calif. 91006
or
4423 Arden Dr.
El Monte, Calif. 91734

Holiday House
18 E. 56th St.
New York, N.Y. 10022

Holt, Rinehard and Winston
383 Madison Ave.
New York, N.Y. 10017

Horn Book Co.
585 Boylston St.
Boston, Ma. 02116

Houghton Mifflin Co.
110 Tremont St.
Boston, Ma. 02107

Houghton-Mifflin Co.
One Beacon St.
Boston, Ma. 02107

(Test)
Hubbard Co.
Drawer 100
Defiance, Oh. 43512

Iansford Publishing Co.
P.O. Box 8711
San Jose, Calif. 95155

Ideal School Supply Co.
11000 S. Lavergne Ave.
Oak Lawn, Ill. 60453

Illinois Schools Journal
Chicago St. College
6800 S. Stewart Ave
Chicago, Ill.

Imperial International
Learning Corp.
Box 548
Kankakee, Illinois 60901

Incentive Publications
311 Lynwood Blvd.
Nashville, Tn. 37205

Independent Learning Systems, Inc.
18 Professional Center Parkway
San Rafael, Calif.

Individualized Instruction Inc.
P.O. Box 25308
Oklahoma City, Okla. 73125

Industrial Press Inc.
200 Madison Ave.
New York, N.Y. 10016

Initial Teaching Alphabet Foundation
52 Vanderbilt Ave.
New York, N.Y. 10017

Innovations for Individualizing Instruction
Box 4361
Washington, D.C.

Institute for Social Research
426 Thompson St.
Ann Arbor, Mich. 48106

Institute of Human Relations
165 E. 56 St.
New York, N.Y. 10022

Instructional Communications
Technology
Huntington, N.Y. 11743

Instructional Fair
Box 1650
Grand Rapids, Mich. 49501

Instructo Corp.
Cedar Hollow and Mathews Rds.
Paoli, Penn. 19301

Instructor Publications
Seven Bank St.
Dansville, N.Y. 14437

International Film Bureau
332 S. Michigan Ave.
Chicago, Ill. 60604

International Reading Association
800 Barksdale Rd.
Newark, De. 19711

International Teaching Tapes
Educational Development Corp. Bldg.
Drawer 865
Lakeland, Fl. 33803

International Universities Press
239 Park Ave. S.
New York, N.Y. 10003

Interstate Printers and Publishers
19-27 N. Jackson St.
Danville, Ill. 61832

I Red Inc.
205 Penn Lane
West Chester, Pa. 19380

Jamestown Publishers
P.O. Box 658
Portland, Maine 04101

Journal Films
909 W. Diversey Parkway
Chicago, Ill. 60614

Judy Company
210 N. School St.
Minneapolis, Minn. 554401

Ken-A-Vision Manufacturing Co.
5616 Rayton Rd.
Rayton, Mo. 64133

Kendall/Hunt Publishing Co.
2460 Kerper Blvd.
Dubuque, Iowa 52001

Kenworthy Education Service
Box 3031
138 Allen St.
Buffalo, N.Y. 14205

Keystone View Co.
Meadville, Da. 16335

Klamath Printing Co.
Klamath, Or.

Knowledge Aid Division of MJE Corp.
6633 W. Howard St.
Niles, Ill. 60648

Kraus-Thomson
Organization limited
Microform Division
Millwood, N.Y. 10546

Lansfor, Publishing Co.
2516 Lansford Ave.
San Jose, Calif.

Learn, Inc.
21 E. Euclid Ave.
Haddonfield, N.J. 08033

Lerner Publications Co.
241 First Ave. N.
Minneapolis, Minn.

Learning Corp. of America
711 Fifth Ave.
New York, N.Y. 10022

Learning, Education Today Center
530 University Ave.
Palo Alto, Calif. 94301

Learning Systems
4150 Chippewa St.
St. Louis, Mo. 63116

Leswing Press
750 Adrian Way
San Rafael, Calif. 94903

Let's Read
Box 250
Bronxville, N.Y. 10708

Library of Contemporary Education
Riverside, N.J. 08075

J. B. Lippincott Co.
E. Washington Square
Philadelphia, Penn. 19105

Lit Notes Corp.
218 Lafayette St.
New York, N.Y. 10012

Liveright Pub. Corp.
386 Park Ave. S.
New York 16, N.Y. 10016

Love Publishing Co.
6635 E. Villanova Pl.
Denver, Co. 80222

Lyons and Carnahan
407 E. 25th St.
Chicago, Ill. 60616

McCormick-Mathers Publishing Co.
450 W. 33 St.
New York, N.Y. 10001

McCutchan Publishing Corp.
2526 Grove St.
Berkeley, Calif. 94704

McDougal, Little and Co.
Box 1667
Evanston, Ill. 60204

David McKay Co., Inc.
750 Third Ave.
New York, N.Y. 10017

McQueen Publishing Co.
R.R. #1, Box 198
Tiskilwa, Ill. 61368

MacMillan Co.
866 Third Ave.
New York, N.Y. 10022

Macrae Smith Co.
225 S. 15 St.
Philadelphia, Pa. 19102

Majelix
4100 E. Walnut
Orange, Calif. 92669

Marfex
Marfex Associates, Inc. Pub.
111 Barron Ave.
Johnstown, Pa. 15906

Marie's Educational Materials
195 S. Murphy Ave.
Box 694
Sunnyvale, Calif. 94086

Marketing Services Division
The Lehigh Press, Inc.
7001 N. Park Dr.
Pennsauken, N.J. 08109

Mast/Keystone
2212 E. 12th St.
Davenport, Iowa 52803

MCM Corp.
P.O. Box 288
Old Greenwich, Conn. 06870

Media Materials
409 W. Cold Spring Lane
Baltimore, Maryland 21210

Mediax
21 Charles Street
Westport, Conn. 06880

Charles E. Merrill Publishing Co.
1300 Alum Creek Dr.
Columbus, Ohio 43216

Julian Messner
West 39th St.
New York, N.Y. 10018

Milliken Pub., Co.
Sound Photo Equip. Co.
Box 2953
Lubbock, Tex. 79408

Modern Curriculum Press
13900 Prospect Rd.
Cleveland, Ohio 44136

William Morrow and Co.
Lothrop, Lee and Shepard
105 Madison Ave.
New York, N.Y. 10016

Motivational Learning Programs
1301 Hamilton Ave.
Trenton, N.J. 08629

MultiMedia Education, Inc.
11 West 42nd St.
New York, N.Y. 10036

National Assessment of Educational Progress
201 A Huron Towers (Staff Office)
2222 Fuller Rd.
Ann Arbor, Mich. 48105

National Council of Teachers of Eng.
1111 Kenyon Rd.
Urbana, Ill. 61801

National Education Association
1201 16th St., N.W.
Washington, D.C. 20036

National Society for Programmed Instruction
Trinity University
715 Stadium Dr.
San Antonio, Tx.

National Textbook Co.
8259 Niles Center Rd.
Skokie, Ill. 60076

New American Library Inc.
1301 Ave. of the Americas
New York, N.Y. 10019

New Readers Press
Box 131
Syracuse, N.Y.

New Reading (The)
Garden City, N.Y. 11530

New York Public Library
Fifth Ave. and 42nd St.
New York, N.Y. 10018

Noble & Noble Publishers
750 Third Ave.
New York, N.Y. 10017

W.W. Norton & Co., Inc.
55 Fifth Ave.
New York, N.Y. 10003

Oddo Publishing
Storybook Acres
Beauregard Blvd.
Fayetteville, Ga. 30214

Ohio State University Press
2070 Neil Ave.
Columbus, Oh. 43210

Open Court Publishing Co.
Box 599
La Salle, Ill. 61301

Orthografik Reform
19 Garfield
Palm Springs, Calif. 92262

Oxford Book Co.
387 Park Ave. So.
New York, N.Y. 10016

Oxford University Press, Inc.
Business Office and Shipping Dept:
16-00 Pollitt Dr.
Fair Lawn, N.J. 07410

Pacifica Foundation
Pacifica Tape Library
Department E
5316 Venice Blvd.
Los Angeles, Calif. 90019

A. N. Palmer Co.
1720 W. Irving Park Rd.
Schaumburg, Ill. 60172

Parents' Magazine Press
8712 Twana Dr.
Garden Grove, Calif. 92641

Parker Publishing Co., Inc.
West Nyack, N.Y. 10994

F. E. Peacock Publishers, Inc.
401 W. Irving Park Road
Itasca, Ill. 60143

Penguin Books, Inc.
7110 Ambassador Rd.
Baltimore, Md. 21207

Penns Valley Publishers
307 W. Beaver Ave.
State College, Pa. 19801

Perceptual Development
Audio Dynamic Research
1219 E. 11th St.
Pueblo, Co. 81001

Pergamon Press, Inc.
College Dept. Maxwell House
Fairview Park
Elsford, N.Y. 10525

Perma-Bound
Vandalia Rd.
Jacksonville, Ill. 62650

Personnel Press
20 Nassau St.
Princeton, N.J. 08540

Phi Delta Kappan
8th St. & Union Ave.
Bloomington, Ind. 47401

Philosophical Library
15 E. 40th St.
New York, N.Y. 10016

Phonovisual Products, Inc.
12216 Parklawn Dr.
Rockville, Ma. 20852

Platt and Munk, Inc.
Division of Child Guidance Prod. Inc.
1055 Bronx River Ave.
Bronx, N.Y. 10472

Plays, Inc. Publishers
8 Arlington St.
Boston, Ma. 02116

Play 'N Talk "Phonics In Action"
Box 188804
Oklahoma City, Ok. 73118

Polaski Co.
Box 7466
Philadelphia, Pa. 19101

Popular Library Inc.
355 Lexington Ave.
New York, N.Y. 10017

Prentice-Hall
Educational Book Division
Englewood Cliffs, N.J. 07632

Professional Educators Publications, Inc.
P.O. Box 80728
Lincoln, Neb. 68501

Pruett Press
1428 Pearl St.
Box 1560
Boulder, Colo.

The Psychological Corp.
757 Third Ave.
New York, N.Y. 10017

Psychotechics Inc.
1900 Pickwick Ave.
Glenview, Ill. 60025

G. P. Putnam's Sons
Coward McCann Inc.
200 Madison Ave.
New York, N.Y. 10016

Pyramid Publications
919 Third Ave.
New York, N.Y. 10017

478

Rampo House
235 E. Fourth St.
New York, N.Y. 10017

Rand, McNally
P.O. Box 7600
Chicago, Ill. 60680

Random House, Inc.
457 Hahn Rd.
Westminster, Ma. 21157

Raymer Educational Films, Inc.
14118 Kiamesha Court
Houston, Tx. 77069

Reader's Choice
Division of Scholastic Magazines Inc.
904 Sylvan Ave.
Englewood Cliffs, N.J. 07632

Reader's Digest Services
Educational Division
Pleasantville, N.J. 10570

Reading Development Center
400 Westheimer, Suite 208
Houston, Tx. 77027

Reading Enrichment Program
A Keyboard Publication
1346 Chapel St.
New Haven, Conn. 06511

Reading Laboratory
55 Day St.
S. Norwalk, Conn. 06854

Reading Newsreport
11 W. 42nd St.
New York, N.Y. 10026

Responsive Environments Corp.
200 Sylvan Ave.
Englewood Cliffs, N.J. 07632

Revrac Pub.
1535 Red Oak Dr.
Silver Springs, Md. 20910

Right To Read
400 Maryland Ave. S.W.
Washington, D.C. 20202

Rinehart and Co.
232 Madison Ave.
New York, N.Y. 10016

Ronald Press Co.
79 Madison Ave.
New York, N.Y. 10016

Routledge and Kegon Paul
9 Park St.
Boston, Ma. 02108

W.H. Sadlier, Inc.
11 Park Pl.
New York, N.Y. 10017

Sage Pub., Inc.
275 S. Beverly Dr.
Beverly Hills, Calif. 90212

W.B. Saunders Co.
West Washington Square
Philadelphia, Penn. 19105

Schloat Productions
A Prentice-Hall Co.
150 White Plains Rd.
Tarrytown, N.Y. 10591

Scholastic Book Ser.
c/o Scholastic Magazine
904 Sylvan Ave.
Englewood Cliffs, N.J. 07632

Science Research Assoc., Inc.
259 E. Erie St.
Chicago, Ill. 60611

Charles Scribner's Sons
597 Fifth Ave.
New York, N.Y. 10017

Seabury Press
815 Second Ave.
New York, N.Y. 10017

Sigma Information. Inc.
240 Grand Ave.
Leonia, N.J. 07065

Silver Burdett Co.
Morristown, N.J. 07960

Simon and Schuster
630 Fifth Ave.
New York 20, N.Y. 10020

Ordering address 1W 39th St.
New York, N.Y. 10018

Singer Co./Graflex Division
3750 Monroe Ave.
Rochester, N.Y. 14603

Singer Education & Training Products
SVE-Society For Visual Education, Inc.
1345 Diversey Parkway
Chicago, Ill. 60614

Skill Development Equip. Co.
Division of Port-a-Pit, Inc.
1340 N. Jefferson
Anaheim, Calif. 92806

Slosson Educational Publications
140 Pine St.
East Aurora, N.Y. 14052

Society for Visual Education, Inc.
1345 Diversey Parkway
Chicago, Ill. 60614

Sonatone Corp.
Elmsford, N.Y. 10523

Sound Education, Inc.
P.O. Box 10245
Palo Alto, Calif. 94303

Stanford University Press
Stanford, Calif. 94305

Steck-Vaughn Co.
Box 2028
Austin, Tex. 78767

Sunburst
Pound Ridge
New York, N.Y. 10576

Superintendent of Documents
Gov't Printing Office
Washington, D.C. 20402

Syracuse University Press
Box 8, University Station
Syracuse, N.Y. 13210

Taylor Associates
Instructional/Communications
Technology, Inc.
Huntington, N.Y. 11743

Teacher
866 Third Ave.
New York, N.Y. 10022

Teachers College Press
1234 Amsterdam Ave.
New York, N.Y. 10027

Teachers Exchange of San Francisco
600 35 Ave. at Plaza
San Francisco, Calif. 94121

Teaching Resources Corporation
100 Boylston St.
Boston, Ma. 02116

Teaching Technology Corp.
Box 3278
North Hollywood, Calif. 91609

Technical Educational Services Inc.
P.O. Box 9231
Austin, Tex. 78766

Temple University
College of Liberal Arts
Philadelphia, Pa.

Texas Education Service Center
11th & Brazos Sts.
Austin, Tex. 78711

Texas State Teachers' Assoc.
316 W. 12th St.
Austin, Tex. 78701

Charles C Thomas
Publisher
301-327 E. Lawrence Ave.
Springfield, Ill. 62704

Thorndike Barnhart
by Scott Foresman & Co.
1900 E. Lake Ave.
Glenview, Ill. 60025

Time-Life Books
Time and Life Building
Rockefeller Center
New York, N.Y. 10020

Toronto Public Library
40th St. Clair Ave. E.
Toronto 290, Ontario

TRI
Educational Center
2797 S. 450 W.
Bountiful, Ut. 84010

True Sally
College of Education
University of S. Florida, Fla.

Twayne Publishers, Inc.
31 Union Square
New York, N.Y. 10003

United States Government Printing Office
Public Documents Distribution Center
Pueblo, Co. 81009

United States Government Publications
Public Documents, Dept.
Washington, D.C. 20402

United Transparencies
Box 688
Binghamton, N.Y. 13902

University of Alberta
Dept. of Elementary Education
Edmonton, Alberta, Canada

University Associates
P.O. Box 615
Iowa City, Ia. 52240

University of Chicago Press
5801 & South Ellis Ave.
Chicago, Ill. 60637

University of Michigan Press
615 E. University
Ann Arbor, Mi. 48101

University of Minnesota Press
2037 University Ave.
Minneapolis, Minn. 55455

University Park Press
Chamber of Commerce Building
Baltimore, Md. 21202

Viling Press
625 Madison Ave.
New York, N.Y. 10022

Villa Press
62-11 99 St.
Rego Park, N.Y. 11374

Visual Materials Inc.
Redwood City, Calif.

Wadsworth Publishing Co., Inc.
Ten Davis Dr.
Belmont, Calif. 94002

George Wahr Publishing Co.
316 S. State St.
Ann Arbor, Mi.

Walker Educational Book Corp.
720 Fifth Ave.
New York, N.Y. 10019

Franklin Watts, Inc.
845 Third Ave.
New York, N.Y. 10023

Webster Publishing Co.
1154 Reco Ave.
St. Louis, Miss.

Weekly Reader
American Education Publications
Education Center
Columbus, Oh. 43216

Publishers
Joseph M. Wepman
950 E. 59th St.
Chicago, Ill.

Western Psychological Services
12031 Wilshire Blvd.
Los Angeles, Calif. 90025

Western Publishing Co., Inc.
150 Parish Dr.
Wayne, N.J. 07470

Westinghouse Learning Corp.
2680 Hanover St.
P.O. Box 10680
Palo Alto, Calif. 94304

J. Weston Walch, Publishers
P.O. Box 6743
Providence, R.I. 02904

Albert Whitman and Company
560 W. Lake St.
Chicago, Ill. 60606

John Wiley & Sons, Inc.
605 Third Ave.
New York, N.Y. 10016

H.W. Wilson Co.
950 University Ave.
Bronx, N.Y. 10452

Winston Press
25 Groveland Terrace
Minneapolis, Minn. 55403

Wisconsin Council of Teachers of English
3700 N. 75th St.
Milwaukee, Wis.

Wisconsin Design For Reading Skill
c/o Interpretive Scoring Systems
4401 W. 76th St.
Minneapolis, Minn. 55435

Wisconsin Research and Development Center
  for Cognitive Learning
Madison, Wis. 53706

Word Games
P.O. Box 305
Healdburg, Calif. 95448

World Book
Division of Field Enterprises
510 Merchandise Mart Plaza
Chicago, Ill. 60654

World Publishing Co.
2231 W. 110th St.
Cleveland, Oh. 44102

World Traveler (The)
1537 Thirty-Fifth St. N.W.
Washington, D.C. 20007

Xerox Education Publications
1250 Fairwood Ave.
Columbus, Oh. 43216

Young Readers Press
Box 181
Northvale, N.J. 07646

Zaner-Bloser Co.
612 N. Park St.
Columbus, Oh. 43215

NAME INDEX

Abrams, Jules, 18, 20, 231, 241
Adams, Ernest L., 79, 85
Adams, Richard, 221, 241
Allen, Roach Van, 76
Allington, Richard L., 78, 85
Amble, Bruce, 150, 159
Ames, Louise, 11, 12, 20
Armstrong, Robert J., 177, 192
Aukerman, Robert C., 336

Balow, Bruce, 43, 48, 222, 230, 240, 241, 349, 357
Barahal, George, 237, 242
Barrett, Thomas, 54, 55, 63
Bateman, Barbara, 10, 20, 235, 241
Bell, David Bruce, 168, 192
Belmont, Herman S., 231, 241
Bender, Lauretta, 224
Betts, Emmett, 260, 267, 291
Bixel, Gordon, 200, 219
Blackie, John, 244, 258
Blanton, Bill, 246, 258
Blau, Harold, 234, 241
Blau, Harriet, 234, 241
Blumberg, Ellen L., 78, 85
Boder, Elena, 223, 241
Bond, Guy, 5, 7, 20, 207, 219
Bormuth, John, 133, 159, 286, 287, 291
Bortnick, Robert, 148, 159
Botel, Morton, 72, 89, 99
Bricklin, Patricia, 187, 192
Bruininks, Robert, 339, 340, 357
Brunken, R. J., 168, 192
Bryant, N. Dale, 220, 221, 241
Buck, John N., 165
Buerger, Theodore A., 43, 48
Burmeister, Lou Ella, 97, 124

Burnett, Calvin, 225, 242
Burnett, Richard W., 133
Buros, Oscar K., 411, 423
Butler, Lester, 255, 256, 258
Byrne, Margaret, 207, 219
Byrne, William L., 239

Calder, Clarence, 152, 159
Callaway, Byron, 161, 192
Capobianco, R. J., 8, 20
Carter, Dale L., 17, 20
Cashdan, Asher, 347, 357
Caskey, Helen, 143, 159
Cavanaugh, Lyman, 10, 20
Chall, Jeanne, 336
Cheatham, Richard, 41, 48
Chronister, Glen, 169, 193
Clare, Clifford, 170, 193
Clark, Charlotte R., 339, 357
Cohen, Alice, 7, 8, 9, 20
Cohen, S. Alan, 13, 20
Cohn, Marvin, 145, 159
Cohn, Maxine, 12, 20
Coleman, Howard, 4, 20
Cooper, Thelma, 13, 20
Cromer, Ward, 126, 127, 158, 159
Crowley, Harry L., 344, 345, 357
Culhane, Joseph, 133, 159, 286
Curtis, H. M., 66

Davis, Everett E., 166, 411
Delacato, Carl, 299, 230
Denner, Bruce, 17, 18, 20
Deutsch, Martin, 13, 17, 20, 21
Dolan, Keith G., 25, 48
Dolch, Edward W., 52, 63, 68
Downing, John, 150, 159
Duker, Sam, 248, 259

Dulin, Kenneth, 155, 159
Dunn, Lloyd M., 174
Durken, Dolores, 93
Durr, William K., 67, 85
Durrell, Donald D., 31, 65, 92, 130, 131

Eames, Thomas, 4, 5, 7, 20
Early, Margaret, 18, 20
Ekwall, Eldon E., 27, 52, 63, 65, 86, 90, 97, 166, 247, 256, 259, 263, 267
Ellis, Bessie, 344, 357

Fader, Daniel, 261
Farr, Roger, 424
Fernald, Grace, 11, 20, 83, 85, 232
Fillmer, Henry, 247, 259
Flynn, Pauline, 207, 219
Forness, Steven, 8, 20
Frostig, Marianne, 47, 224
Fry, Edward, 52, 63, 252

Gagon, Glen, 67, 85
Galloway, Charles, 178, 193
Gardner, Eric F., 95, 128
Gardner, Howard, 240, 241
Gardner, James, 41, 48, 184, 193
Garry, V. V., 333, 358
Gates, Arthur I., 11, 20, 92, 124, 135, 136, 162, 193
Gilmore, Eunice C., 130
Gilmore, John V., 130
Glaman, Gertrude, 339, 357
Glass, Gerald G., 7, 8, 9, 20
Goodman, Libby, 47, 49, 225, 230, 241

SUBJECT INDEX